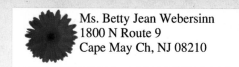
AND SO IT GOES

ALSO BY CHARLES J. SHIELDS

Mockingbird: A Portrait of Harper Lee

I Am Scout

AND SO IT GOES
KURT VONNEGUT: A LIFE

CHARLES J. SHIELDS

ST. MARTIN'S GRIFFIN ⚞ NEW YORK

www.stmartins.com

Design by Meryl Sussman Levavi

The Library of Congress has cataloged the Henry Holt edition as follows:

Shields, Charles J., 1951–
    And so it goes : Kurt Vonnegut, a life / Charles J. Shields.— 1st ed.
        p. cm.
    Includes bibliographical references.
    ISBN 978-0-8050-8693-5
    1. Vonnegut, Kurt. 2. Novelists, American—20th century—Biography.
I. Title.
    PS3572.O5Z855 2011
    813'.54—dc22
    [B]
                                                                2010045173

ISBN 978-1-250-01218-0 (trade paperback)

First St. Martin's Griffin Edition: October 2012

10 9 8 7 6 5 4 3 2 1

To my wife, Guadalupe

*Kurt will have the last word, if not the last laugh—and
we will miss that laugh! That ineffable, smoke-laden,
sardonically elated laughter that suffused and punctuated
his conversation. Laughter that at times seemed
inappropriate following the retelling of some of the most
ghastly events of the twentieth century. This laughter was a
mental bulwark against the madness of war he witnessed.*

SCOTT VONNEGUT, nephew,
Kurt Vonnegut's memorial service,
The Algonquin Hotel
New York, April 21, 2007

*I keep losing and regaining my equilibrium, which is the
basic plot of all popular fiction.
And I myself am a work of fiction.*

KURT VONNEGUT, *Wampeters,
Foma & Granfalloons* (1974)

Contents

AND SO IT GOES

Prologue:

Out of Print and Scared to Death

KURT VONNEGUT PLANNED to give this new teaching job at the University of Iowa his best shot. As he zoomed across the Midwest in early September 1965 in his son's new Volkswagen Beetle—his six-foot-three frame pressing his head against the roof liner—it was as if failure were clattering behind him like tin cans tied to the bumper. The ashtray was stuffed with the crushed butts of Pall Mall cigarettes and the windshield was tawny with nicotine from his chain-smoking. He had a lot to think about, and the twelve-hundred-mile cross-country drive between his home on Cape Cod and Iowa City, Iowa, gave him all the time he needed.

He was bored by his twenty-year marriage to his first love, the former Jane Cox, whom he'd married barely five months after his release from a prisoner-of-war camp at the end of World War II. This past summer, he had been trying to start an affair with a woman in New York twenty years his junior who, in turn, was waiting for the writer William Price Fox to divorce his wife so they could marry. If this writer-in-residence job in the respected Iowa Writers' Workshop didn't suit him, he was going to leave it and compensate himself for his trouble by coming on strong with Sarah.[1] On the other hand, he would remind her that he was an old boozehound, on the hunt for affection, and she was just a girl, and he was old enough to be her father. She needed him like a case of shingles.[2]

He did have a daughter almost her age, and five other children besides—three of his own with Jane and three from his sister and brother-in-law, who were dead. There was only enough money for him to come to Iowa City alone. He had not wanted to go, but everyone else seemed to think it was a good idea.[3] His buddy from the Cornell University *Daily Sun* campus newspaper, Miller Harris, had written him when he heard about the invitation, "For Christ's sake go, knowing that your classes will be peopled exclusively by meatheads. Some of them will be pretty girls, young and fresh looking and pretty, and will fall in love with you. But meatheads still. . . . Wothehell—you might get some funny material out of their bad papers."[4] Besides, as usual, he needed the money, especially since he had three children in college. So he had replied to the letter from John C. Gerber, the chair of Iowa's Department of English, saying he was humbled by the invitation and accepted.[5]

It was certain he needed the change of scene.[6] His temper was getting the better of him lately, rubbed raw by too much drinking and fears of being a permanent loser. About a month before he left for Iowa, his eldest daughter, fifteen-year-old Edie, had played a gypsy in a children's production of *Treasure Island* at the Cape Cod Playhouse. While she was signing autographs—including one for a star-struck seven-year-old Caroline Kennedy—some smart aleck standing beside him made a vulgar crack about her. He invited the guy out into the parking lot to say it again, and knocked him down between two cars. His opponent, dazed but still game, got to his feet, made another crack, and Vonnegut socked him again.[7] Things like that got around fast on Cape Cod.

Maybe it was only the remark that got to him, but he also hated the implication that he was a nobody. Obviously, the guy had no idea who he was—including that he was Edie's father. His neighbors hadn't read his novels, didn't care much about books, so he felt like he had no status at all.[8]

Not that the English Department in Iowa knew much about him, either. Actually, he knew more about their creative writing program than they knew about his work. An article about it had appeared in *Look* magazine just a few weeks before Dr. Gerber's invitation had arrived.[9] But he knew for a fact that the program's director, Paul Engle, "didn't know me, and I don't think he had ever heard of me. He didn't read that kind of crap. But somebody out here did, and assured him that I was indeed a writer, but dead broke with a lot of kids, and completely out of print and scared to death."[10] When the poet Robert Lowell backed out at the last minute, Engle had rescued him with a steady job.

The truth was, despite his four published novels and scads of short stories in magazines found in doctors' waiting rooms, Kurt Vonnegut's writing career had been a nonstarter for years. In college, he'd written satirical columns, news, and opinion pieces for the Cornell newspaper, but he dropped out after two years in 1943 because of bad grades and enlisted as a private in the army. After the war, he attended the University of Chicago on the GI Bill to earn a degree in anthropology but never completed his thesis. Now, in his forties, the only academic credential he had was a diploma from Shortridge High School in Indianapolis. Packed away in the Volkswagen, he had the notes for another thesis for Chicago—a casserole of ideas that conflated fiction and anthropology—which he dreamed he might be able to finish in Iowa City in maybe a month or so. He also wanted to work on a partially written screenplay for his most recent novel, *God Bless You, Mr. Rosewater*. Then there were the drafts of a wartime novel about his surviving the bombing of Dresden, a project he had been taking unsuccessful runs at ever since he got out of the service. Whether he could find time to work on all three would depend on his teaching schedule not being "murderously heavy."[11]

Ten miles outside of Iowa City, the Volkswagen began to thump and sway. He pulled off to the gravelly shoulder and got out, "surrounded by millions and millions of acres of topsoil" like the farmland outside Indianapolis, "as flat as pool tables and as rich as chocolate cake."[12] A tire had blown. It was quiet, except for the grasshoppers and cicadas hissing drily in the heat, and he looked around, weighing his choices.

1: You Were an Accident

1922–1940

THE WEDDING OF Kurt Vonnegut's parents, Edith Sophia Lieber and Kurt Vonnegut Sr. on November 22, 1913, in Indianapolis, Indiana, was spectacular.

Edith's father, Albert, owner of a giant brewery who reveled in his reputation as one of the richest men in the city, threw a gargantuan reception at the Claypool Hotel at the northwest corner of Washington and Illinois streets, reputed to be the finest hotel in the Midwest. There were six hundred guests, and those not chauffeured in automobiles arrived in horse-drawn carriages with jingling brass harnesses—an entire generation of rich Edwardians, silk-hatted or covered demurely by parasols, many of whom had been raised in Indianapolis's mansions on Meridian Street.[1] Albert Lieber knew what his guests expected and he did not disappoint. There was a sixty-foot bar, choice meats, champagne, and dancing to an orchestra in the ballroom lasting until six in the morning.

And to the satisfaction of some guests, there was plenty of gossip to go around, too. The bride had graduated from Miss Shipley's finishing school in Bryn Mawr outside Philadelphia in time to come out for the 1908 season in London. Her first serious suitor, Kenneth Doulton, whose family owned the world famous Royal Doulton Porcelain Works, had proposed. He said his father would buy them a house in Mayfair, hinting that they could live very well if her father would settle a good-sized dowry on her. But she suspected he was an upper-class idler who wanted a sinecure and not the responsibility of inheriting a giant brewery in Indianapolis. She broke off the engagement.

Then she had crossed the English Channel to live in her grandfather Peter Lieber's castle in Düsseldorf. There she caught the eyes of two German cavalry officers who competed for her affections. She had become engaged to the higher-ranking one, a captain—a Prussian, Otto Voigt, whose saber, boots, and brass buttons looked dashing. Unfortunately, like the English gentleman who had preceded him, he had no interest in the Lieber family brewery either. She ended that engagement too.

So she had retreated home to her father's estate, Vellamada, outside Indianapolis, where he built for her a cottage on a bluff overlooking the White River and furnished it according to her tastes, with a fireplace and a grand piano in the living room. Many days she spent hours strolling around the grounds alone.[2]

No one recalled exactly how the groom, Kurt Vonnegut Sr., came on the scene romantically, but he and Edith, four years his junior, had known each other since childhood. Both families belonged to Indianapolis's coterie of wealthy German Americans who gravitated to Das Deutsche Haus, the city's German cultural center. Money and the suitability of the young couple were on the minds of both families, naturally.

Kurt Sr., a promising, second-generation Indianapolis architect, already had the imprimatur of older successful men in the city who had invited him to join the exclusive University Club. He was a graduate of Massachusetts Institute of Technology (MIT) with a degree in architecture and had completed postgraduate work at Hannover Polytechnic in Germany, just like his father, Bernard. Two years after his father's death in 1908, Kurt Sr. had returned from abroad and joined his father's architectural firm, Vonnegut & Bohn, as a partner. He was short, blue-eyed, and fair with blond curly hair and long, thin fingers. His bride was a lovely woman with auburn hair, a fair complexion, and blue-green eyes. They had made a handsome couple at the altar of the First Unitarian Church, according to family members, the only ones invited to attend the actual ceremony. Apparently, the Unitarian Church had been chosen because the Vonneguts had been freethinkers for generations and the Liebers were Protestants—it was common ground.

The reception at the Claypool Hotel was the finishing touch to the combining of two elite families. Under the weight of millionaire Albert Lieber's inexhaustible largesse in the way of food and drink, all the propriety of Indianapolis's upper crust crumbled. "Never before or since have so many otherwise respectable and thoroughly conservative citizens of the dull community passed out in so short a time," said a family historian.[3] Dozens of guests were still recuperating in reserved rooms two days later.

Soon after their marriage, Kurt and his bride drove to the Indianapolis Speedway in a brand-new Oldsmobile and sped around and around the track in a delirium of happiness.[4] It was the beginning of their lives together. Conveniently, everything in Edith's trousseau was already monogrammed *L-V* from her engagement to the Prussian captain, Otto Voigt.[5]

THE WEDDING reception was fitting for wealthy young socialites starting out. While Kurt Sr. had been a bachelor, he had taught artistic lettering at the John Herron Art Institute and become friends with amateur artists. Edith had been a member of the Indianapolis Propylaeum, a selective literary and social club for women.

But after their marriage the Vonneguts were catapulted into realms generally open only to leading couples. The biggest coup was an invitation to join the Portfolio Club founded by the Hoosier Group artist Theodore Clement Steele and his late wife, Mary Elizabeth. The membership roster consisted exclusively of Midwestern artists, writers, or painters who supported the Arts and Crafts movement. There were monthly dinner discussions, and the group, said one onlooker, "considered itself to be the custodian of the aesthetic conscience of the community."[6] As the newest female member attending the club dinner in January 1917, Edith was chivalrously (and humorously) awarded the tail of the roast pig.[7]

The Vonneguts reciprocated by entertaining in their home at 1334 Central Avenue, located in one of the better neighborhoods. They sometimes had the director of the Indianapolis Symphony Orchestra to supper, or writers and painters, or architects who were colleagues of Kurt Sr.'s.[8] Edith's dinner parties were memorable just for their settings, three generations of inherited Lieber treasure on display: china, silver, linen, and crystal.

With such a heavy social calendar, the only way to keep the house in order was with a live-in servant, especially after the Vonnegut children began coming along.[9]

BERNARD VONNEGUT, named for his paternal grandfather, was born August 29, 1914. He was a serious-looking little boy, even in informal photographs. The earliest anecdote about him predicted a fascination with science and technology. One afternoon when he was a toddler, his parents left him in the care of a babysitter. They didn't return until late that evening, long after he was asleep. The next morning, they noticed he was "all excited and making unusual noises." The mystery was cleared up a few days later when a family friend mentioned seeing Bernard at Union Station in the arms of the babysitter. She had taken him down to the station—a half-hour walk—to meet her boyfriend on the platform. His "unusual noises" were the sounds of locomotives.[10] Many small children love trains, of course, but as soon as he was old enough, Bernard set up a laboratory in the basement to find out more about steam, power, and electricity.

The Vonneguts' only daughter came next, Alice, born November 18, 1917. In babyhood, she developed a serious case of pneumonia and nearly died from a high fever.[11] Kurt Jr. later believed it addled her a little.[12] She refused to tolerate anything that might upset her. She shunned books and preferred make-believe instead. The sight of a truck on the highway carrying chickens on their way to market sent her into hysterics, and only her parents' assurances that those chickens were on their way to a new farm could calm her down.[13] Perhaps having been lavished with her parents' concern when she was ill, she discovered a dependable way to keep their attention on her. And since Bernard was laying claim to being the brainy one, why shouldn't she be the one with overwrought feelings? Every child must carve out a niche for him- or herself in a family.

THE VONNEGUTS' youngest child, Kurt Jr. ("a beautiful boy with curly hair—an exceptionally beautiful child, really," said his father's sister, Aunt Irma), was born in Indianapolis on November 11, 1922, or Armistice Day as it was called before World War II.[14] As an adult, he was quite proud of being born on a day associated with peace.[15]

His parents were living by then in a new, larger house at 4401 North Illinois Street, located in a neighborhood of large brick and limestone residences on the city's north side near Butler University. It had been built with Edith's money, even though Prohibition in 1921 had caused a catastrophic downturn in her father's brewery fortune. But there was a building boom going on after World War I, and Kurt Sr. anticipated regular commissions to provide a comfortable financial bumper for his family.

Set back deep on a half-acre wooded lot, the house, which is still standing, is turned sideways, giving it a slightly unwelcoming look. The long flank of the three-story, six-bedroom house faces the street; the front door is toward the narrow side yard. The style is Arts and Crafts, and framed in a leaded, stained-glass window on the front door are the letters *K, E,* and *V* for Kurt and Edith Vonnegut. Underneath the window is an unusual door knocker, a woman with a Roman face, her head crowned with leaves, and two festoons of palm fronds beneath her ears, looping down to where they meet at a brooch, creating the handhold for rapping on the strike plate.

Throughout his life, Kurt Jr. insisted his father designed the house. Actually, it was done by the Indianapolis-born architect William Osler, some of whose other residences are still standing in Indianapolis and are similar in style to the Vonneguts'. There was very little input in the house from Kurt's father, and the fact that he engaged someone else to design his home is revealing about his talent or interests, for that matter.[16]

In his colleagues' estimation, Kurt Sr. was an architect with modest abilities.[17] His bread-and-butter income came from commercial projects such as Hook's Drugstores and Indiana Bell Telephone buildings. As his clients' buildings grew higher, wider, multipurposed, and blander, he relied on technical knowledge to bring in the fees, not style or character.

His father, Bernard, on the other hand, had enhanced the built environment of Indianapolis with dozens of distinctive structures, including the John Herron Art Institute, the Hotel Severin, and the enormous Das Deutsche Haus designed in German Renaissance Revival style with a beer garden and theater.[18] Bernard's design for the Pembroke Arcade in downtown Indianapolis, inspired by the architecture of the 1893 World's Columbian Exposition in Chicago, was a forerunner of the modern shopping mall. An Indianapolis historian and contemporary said of Bernard, "All of his work was carefully detailed and bore evidence of his scholarly tastes as an architect as well as of his superior technical ability."[19]

But no major projects from the hand of Kurt Sr. still exist, no "monuments to his genius," as his father's work was once described.[20] The apprentice lacked confidence in his artistic skills to exceed the master. He enjoyed experimenting in a dilettantish way with calligraphy, painting, and pottery, especially as he got older. And as an architect, he had a trained sense of style. Yet his youngest son, Kurt Jr., was never sure his "father wanted to be an architect, he was just the oldest son and he was told to become an architect."[21] He never heard his father mention anything about grandfather Bernard. He suspected it was because his father knew he was mediocre by comparison.[22]

Nevertheless, income from Kurt Sr.'s commissions and his wife's investments provided expensive garnishes to their lives. When they were flush with cash, they traveled and entertained. Typical was a trip aboard a ship from New York to Hamburg, Germany, in July 1924, to attend the wedding of Kurt Sr.'s sister, Irma, to a German, Kurt Lindener, who owned plantations in Honduras. Alice was seven years old by then and Bernard ten. Nineteen-month-old Kurt Jr. was left behind in the care of his paternal uncle Alex and his wife, Raye, who were childless. (Much later, when he was old enough to understand, he decided his mother had done it because he was an inconvenience.)[23] The family also took annual summer vacations to the seaside town of Chatham on the southeastern tip of Cape Cod, where the children could play tag with the waves.[24] If the Vonneguts needed money, they sold securities or borrowed it.[25]

A private education for the children went without saying. As soon as Kurt Jr. was of school age, his parents enrolled him in the Orchard School, a private progressive school with grades kindergarten through eighth on West Forty-second Street in Indianapolis, recently redesigned by Kurt Sr. and a colleague. Bernard had graduated from there and continued on to the Park School, a small private high school for boys. Alice was already an Orchard student in the middle grades when Kurt Jr. was enrolled as a kindergarten student in the fall of 1928.

The Orchard School operated on the educational theorist John Dewey's belief that the students should be a little community of doers. There were gardens, pottery making, music lessons, pretend bank accounts, shop class, pageants, outdoor biology, art, and folk dancing. Each child had a responsibility. An important influence on Vonnegut was a teacher who eventually became headmaster, Hillis Howie. Later in life, Vonnegut said, "The value system under which I try to operate relative to animals and plants and the earth and persons with cultures different from mine is one I learned from him. There are thousands of us who were lucky enough to come under his influence, and my guess is that we are more at home on this planet, and more respectful of it, than most of our neighbors are."[26]

This hothouse educational environment encouraged Kurt Jr.'s precociousness. One of his teachers commended him on how well he could read.[27] At home, he secretly pored over an unabridged dictionary from his parents' large library because he "suspected that there were dirty words hidden in there" and puzzled over illustrations of the "*trammel wheel*, the *arbalest*, and the *dugong*."[28] Later, when he was old enough, he dipped into his parents' complete works of Robert Louis Stevenson, Bernard Shaw, Arthur Conan Doyle, and a beautiful edition of *Lysistrata*, which he claimed to have read when he was eleven.[29]

Getting his teachers' attention was easy, he found, but his parents were another matter. His father, dignified and reserved, was said to take after his own father.[30] Toward his children, Kurt Sr. acted coolly. His conversations with his younger son tended to be "arch and distant."[31] Nor did he seem interested in teaching him how to become proficient at things, again according to Kurt Jr., who remained quite resentful about this; he never forgot it. "Nobody taught me anything—how to skate, or even ride a bike."[32]

His father could be witty, but in such a wry way that it was hard to tell whether he was joking. The sense of humor in the house was Schadenfreude—very Germanic—taking pleasure in the misfortunes of others. Listening one afternoon to act 4 of *Aida*, Kurt Sr. remarked in a bemused voice that the lovers sealed in a temple would last a lot longer if they didn't sing so much.[33]

The children's taste for Schadenfreude too expressed itself in a love of pratfalls. Alice, for instance, hearing a series of thuds, thought her younger brother had fallen down the stairs, and rushed to make fun of him. It was the gas meter man who had tumbled into the basement. She laughed even harder. Another time she caught sight of a woman falling out a bus door horizontally like an ironing board and doubled over with giggles.[34]

Likewise, Kurt Jr., for the rest of his life, had an odd (and sometimes disconcerting) habit of laughing suddenly in the middle of describing something unpleasant. It was hard to tell whether he was upset or tickled by absurdity. One of his favorite anecdotes in adulthood was about a fraternity brother who heard the news of Pearl Harbor while showering. When Vonnegut got to the punch line—the guy was so shocked he fell in the tub and killed himself!—he would try to suppress a wheezing, half-ashamed snigger.[35]

Edith Vonnegut behaved like a guest in her children's lives. To her way of thinking, parenting came under the general heading of household tasks, which, as a wealthy woman, she could pay others to do. "Mother," said Kurt Jr., "did not cook."[36] Nor did she sew on buttons, plant flowers outdoors—the yardman did that—or, as her son remembered it, speak to him very much.[37] She did enjoy dressing the children in fine clothes, however, which she selected from the best department store in town, L. S. Ayres (which had also been designed by her father-in-law), and lunching with her lady friends in the walnut-paneled Victorian tearoom. In the Vonneguts' home movies taken in the 1920s, she waves brightly to let us know she is present, but she never hugs the children to indicate that they are a joy to her.

The only sign of family affection—other than horseplay at the beach on Cape Cod, also seen in family films—occurs between Kurt Jr. and Alice, who guides her beaming, wide-eyed little brother past the camera tenderly by the hand. And in another scene, when they are seated beside each other in a toy wagon, he buries his face in her shoulder.

But a sister who is only five years older is not an adequate substitute for a mother. To find a "humane and wise" person to listen to his chatter, answer his questions, and read to him, he looked elsewhere.[38]

FORTUNATELY, THERE was such a person in the household, the Vonneguts' cook and housekeeper, Ida Young.

Mrs. Young was a middle-aged woman when she worked part-time for the Vonneguts. An African American born in Kentucky in 1883, she married her husband, Owen, a warehouse worker, at eighteen; the couple owned a home at 1940 Yandes Street, a good twenty-minute ride by trolley from the Vonneguts. She found employment with white families in 1926 because her husband had passed away and she was on her own. A few years later, one of her children moved in, bringing with him seven of her grandchildren. From then on, her life consisted mainly of work and caring for children. She cooked and cleaned for the Vonneguts five days a week, with Thursdays and Sundays off.[39]

Ida did not have the authority to take the Vonnegut children in hand the way she did her own.[40] Mostly, the Vonnegut parents disciplined passively "by showing discontent," as Kurt Jr. put it.[41] But he was very young, suggestible, and, most important, lonely. "She talked to me more than my mother ever did and spent more time with me than my mother ever did."[42] Ida often mentioned him to her grandchildren and was clearly very fond of him.[43] By responding to his eagerness for adult affection, she won his heart, making it receptive to what she had to say about kindness, honesty, and proper behavior.

She was a Methodist, and the Bible was her instruction manual for family life.[44] She "knew the Bible by heart and found plenty of comfort and wisdom in there," Kurt Jr. wrote later.[45] The Vonneguts attended services at the Unitarian Church only twice a year, on Christmas Eve and Easter, and the family said grace at meals, but in retrospect he termed it just a "theatrical event."[46]

Searching for something to read aloud to Kurt Jr., Ida found in the Vonneguts' library a popular anthology of stories, poems, verses, and essays called *More Heart Throbs*, the second volume in a series of books with inspiring passages. Many of the entries were anonymous verses, but there were also rhythmic, easy-to-read pieces by Ralph Waldo Emerson, Christina Rossetti, Emily Dickinson, Robert Louis Stevenson, and James Whitcomb Riley.[47] The frontispiece shows a woman in a long white dress reading as she walks in the spring. The caption says, "The little cares that fretted me, / I lost them yesterday / Out in the fields with God."

Years later, Vonnegut didn't recall any religious instruction from Ida, but said, "I'm sure she must have talked about God and I was interested to hear about it."[48] They pored over the book, and the effect of the experience, amplified by how a caring adult was taking an interest in him, affected him for the rest of his life. "There is an almost intolerable sentimentality in everything I write. British critics complain about it. And Robert Scholes, the American critic, once said that I put bitter coatings on sugar pills. It's too late to change now. At least I am aware of my origins—in a big, brick dream house designed by my architect father, where nobody was home for long periods of time, except for me and Ida Young."[49]

WHILE KURT Jr. was still a child in primary school feeling the effects of benign neglect at home, as he remembered it, Bernard, a high school student in the late 1920s, was earning a reputation in science that made his parents proud. His teachers at the prestigious Park School agreed with the assessment of Bernard's great-uncle Carl Barus, a founder of the American Physical Society, that he was "peculiarly gifted when honoring the scientific method with playful experiments involving ordinary materials close at hand."[50] Even when one of his experiments blew a bolt through the first floor of the Vonneguts' home, or his telegraph key blanked out every radio station in Indianapolis for three miles around, his parents were dazzled. Kurt Jr. later begrudged him his unassailable status in the family: "He was my parents' darling, as the firstborn should be, I suppose."[51]

To his teachers and parents, Bernard might be a young Edison, but how he lorded it over his brother and sister annoyed them. Kurt Jr. tried to play his older brother's assistant and helped when asked during experiments. But he began to feel resentful of the supposed superiority of that "hilarious baboon."[52] Science was all that mattered in his worldview. Litmus paper, slide rules, anemometers yielded real values; everything else was just opinion. Sometimes, in sheer childish frustration, Kurt Jr. flailed at his older brother while Bernard held him at arm's length, chuckling.[53] "He was a *boring bully*. Never hit me, but he would talk and talk about science until my sister and I were bored shitless."[54]

Enviously he watched one day while his father and brother performed what looked like alchemy in the backyard. Wearing thick rubber gloves, they dropped several dimes in a plastic bucket of nitric acid. A few more ingredients in the process and then there, glistening at the bottom of the bucket, lay grains of pure silver. Another experiment involved igniting black iron oxide and powdered aluminum at high temperatures to create molten aluminum oxide. Bernard used blobs of it to spot-weld nails into a spiny shape that could be separated only with a hacksaw. His power was astonishing![55]

By comparison, Kurt Jr. felt intense self-disgust. He kept a childish diary; even though "nothing ever happened to me . . . I wrote pages and pages."[56] No one was encouraging him, showing him experiments. His father was attuned to the intellect rather than emotional pleading. "Bernard was obviously gifted and it's like having a great chess player suddenly or a musician or whatever. He was something of a prodigy at least in terms of his enthusiasm for science. It was clear he was going to be a scientist from early on and when I tried it I obviously did not have the same gifts he had, so something genetic is going on there."[57]

Furthermore, Bernard's signs of genius gave him leverage in the family beyond the usual pride of place of an eldest child. In his world of facts and results, sensibility was gibberish. Alice demonstrated an ability to capture likenesses quickly in clay sculpture, but Bernard wasn't impressed. "Art," he was fond of saying, "is just ornamental." Visiting a local art museum in the company of his family, he jeered, "Look at those paintings! They just hang there!"[58] By implication, his father's vocation—architecture can be seen as extension of art, after all—was just as lowly.

By the time he was a teenager, Bernard began to look on his family as part of his laboratory and took a Skinnerian interest in what they did, how they behaved, and why. His curiosity about his parents' sexual relationship gave rise to an experiment when he was sixteen and Kurt Jr. was seven. Using the heat register in his parents' bedroom as a conduit, Bernard ran a wire for a microphone under his parents' bed and connected it to a tape recorder. Soon he had results about sex between adults that he was eager to share with his brother.[59]

They were riding together in the car when Bernard turned to him and said, "You were an accident." Kurt Jr. remembered feeling confused and fearful. "I didn't know what it meant to be an 'accident,' but I knew accidents weren't good.'"[60]

IN OCTOBER 1929, the Wall Street crash pushed the Vonneguts' upper-class life toward a financial precipice. They were overextended, house-poor, but in love with the amenities of the good life. Waves of bad economic tides lapped at Kurt Sr.'s profession, eroding his commissions.

Desperately, he and Edith leaped at a Ponzi scheme, buying into it with an inheritance left to them by grandmother Nannette Vonnegut, who passed away in December 1929.[61] Everything was lost. To keep going, they sold their securities and borrowed as much as they could.[62] It still wasn't enough. As a result, Edith Vonnegut, one of the richest women in town, slowly became, according to her son Kurt, "half-cracked."[63]

Fortunately, in 1930 an unusual project came Kurt Sr.'s way, the income from which kept the family afloat for a while. But more important, how expertly he handled the work involved implied that—as Kurt Jr. later suspected—his father had become an architect by default. His true ability was technological.

In downtown Indianapolis, the Indiana Bell Building housed all the telephone and telegraph equipment for central Indiana. The board of directors needed to add administrative offices at the site, but there was nowhere to build. After entertaining several unsatisfactory proposals about ways to expand, the directors were close to accepting that the eight-story, eleven-thousand-ton structure would have to be demolished.

But then Kurt Sr. proposed an extraordinary plan. The solution was to turn the whole building. This could be accomplished without damage to the building, and business on all floors could continue as usual during the move—no interruption to the tens of thousands of calls routed through the switchboards every day. The gas, light, and heat would stay on too, even the elevators would go up and down as the building advanced fifty-two feet forward off its foundation, then swung through a ninety-degree arc, and finally moved one hundred feet backward on rails. When at last it rested on its new foundation, the Indiana Bell Building would have been relocated, with all the employees inside, from its former address on Meridian Street to New York Street. In the rear would be plenty of room for expansion.

The board consented, either because Vonnegut was so persuasive or out of sheer curiosity to see whether such an incredible thing could be done.

Before the move, giant hoses were connected to utilities so that gas, water, and heat would continue as usual. Then underneath the bottom of the building, Vonnegut positioned eighteen jacks weighing one hundred tons apiece. On October 14, the turning around began. Engineers from all over the nation, as well as a few from abroad, came to observe what would happen. On a signal, each worker operating a jack gave the lever six complete up-and-down strokes. The building rose a fraction of an inch. Then the men rested. At the next signal, they gave the levers exactly six strokes and rested. This continued until the building was up a foot. Blocks and temporary jacks were knocked into place, and then the huge jacks repositioned to turn the building incrementally toward a set of rails. The rhythm of eighteen men working in syncopation continued.

Every workday, employees and customers arrived at the building's entrance via a curved walkway that was constantly being lengthened to keep up with the turning front door. Inside, telephones rang, operators put through calls, and meetings were held, but workers couldn't help glancing out the windows now and then to see how the view was changing. Site superintendents distributed squashed pennies from the rails to spectators as souvenirs of the historic event, including one for Kurt Jr., who was then eight years old. Finally, in mid-November 1930 the building came to rest on its new foundation.

It was the largest building of its time ever moved.

Throughout his life, Kurt Jr. mentioned his father's historic engineering achievement only in passing. National magazines carried the story, and requests for information about the technical side of the move continued to arrive at Indiana Bell forty-six years after the event.[64] Yet the son of the titan responsible for the deed preferred instead to let it be known that he was from a family of artists: "Here I am making a living in the arts, and it has not been a rebellion. It's as though I had taken over the family Esso station. My ancestors were all in the arts, so I'm simply making my living in the customary family way."[65] By insisting that the arts, and not technology, coursed through the Vonnegut bloodline, he made it clear that he was the true heir of his family's dreams, and not his older brother, Bernard.

DESPITE THE astounding success of the Indiana Bell Building move, the firm of Vonnegut, Bohn & Mueller, as it was then known, was forced to disband. Kurt Sr. set up a home office and accepted jobs, his son Kurt said later, that "would have been soporific to a high school drafting class."[66]

The big house on Illinois Street would have to be sold, it was clear, and in 1932 the Vonneguts put it on the market. But year after year there were no takers. A demi-mansion with servants' quarters was a white elephant in an era of hoboes, the Dust Bowl, and soup kitchens. Gradually, the Vonneguts were going under financially and began selling off ballast that had once anchored them in the upper class: china, jewelry, and artwork. The hired help was let go, including Ida Young, although the Vonneguts continued to give her clothes and items for her family.[67]

Edith kept reassuring her youngest child that the Vonneguts would rise to the top again, and he would resume his "proper place in society" when the bad times ended and "would swim with members of other leading families at the Indianapolis Athletic Club, would play tennis and golf with them at the Woodstock Golf and Country Club."[68] In the meantime, he would have to leave Orchard School and begin the fourth grade at a public school—"a wise use of resources," he thought bitterly as an adult.[69] Alice would finish at the private Tudor Hall School for Girls and Bernard at the Park School.

For Edith, the humiliation of her precipitous fall in society affected her mental health. Kurt Jr. likened it to withdrawal from a drug. "My mother was addicted to being rich, to servants and unlimited charge accounts, to giving lavish dinner parties, to taking frequent first-class trips to Europe."[70] With only a modest income, her husband was unable to provide the things that had formerly made her life as pleasant as a garden party.

Furiously, she turned on him, and Kurt Jr., only nine or ten, watched wide-eyed as his mother tore at his father.[71] "Late at night, and always in the privacy of our own home, and never with guests present, she expressed hatred for Father as corrosive as hydrofluoric acid."[72] Her insults were scattershot but always with the same target: he was a failure as a man. He was unfaithful, she said; his false teeth were cheap and disgusting; he couldn't make more money because he was afraid to try.[73]

Her doctor prescribed sodium amytal, a barbiturate with sedative-hypnotic properties, but it twisted her personality.[74] In the dead of night, she roamed the house, wrapped in a ghostly drug-induced mist, rattling doorknobs and dishes like a poltergeist. The family endeavored to keep her midnight-to-dawn craziness a secret.[75] Some of her behavior was histrionic—she would fall to the ground rather than have her picture taken—but according to Kurt Jr. "the hatred and contempt she sprayed on my father, as gentle and innocent a man as ever lived, was without limit and pure, untainted by ideas or information."[76]

To escape her assaults, Kurt Sr. retreated to an artist's studio he created on the top floor in the vacated bedroom formerly belonging to a servant. There he turned into, in his son Kurt's words, a "dreamy artist."[77] He painted portraits of friends and relatives, and many self-portraits, too. But there was something about his self-portraits that indicated he no longer recognized himself. On canvas after canvas he left sketches of his face unfinished, as if he couldn't decide on his own likeness or how he wanted to appear.[78]

Predictably, his parents' unhappiness put a strain on Kurt Jr. that surfaced in school. One day in the seventh grade, he was called into the office by the principal. "He asked me what was wrong, because I apparently was flunking everything and he said I might have to repeat the seventh grade and I didn't know what was wrong. I might have to repeat the seventh grade!"[79]

He didn't flunk middle school, as it turned out. He graduated eighth grade on time in June 1936 with the rest of his class. Part of the ceremony included each graduate receiving a diploma from the principal, then turning to the audience and announcing his or her career plans. When it was Kurt Jr.'s turn, he made an announcement guaranteed to please both his parents in the audience. "I said, I would cure cancer with chemicals while working for the Eli Lilly Company."[80]

In other words, he would try to grow up to be just like Bernard.

WHEN SUMMER came, everything was always better. There was a second home for the Vonneguts where the sunlight put a blush on everyone's face, and the water for swimming and bathing was pure as rainwater. The name of it, in the language of the Pottawatomie who once lived there, meant "clarity" or "transparent": Maxinkuckee. Lake Maxinkuckee was "an enchanted body of water to me," said Kurt Jr., remembering it many years later, "my Aegean Sea, perfect in every dimension."[81]

The basin of Lake Maxinkuckee was gouged into the sandy soil by the scraping heel of a glacier and is constantly refreshed by spring water. Two and half miles wide and a mile and a half long, the lake has a thirteen-mile shoreline of rocky beach ringed by forests of oak, beech, and maple. The small town of Culver sits on its northeastern side.

The Vonneguts and their relatives—the Schnulls and the Gloss-brenners, mainly—summered in five cedar-sided homes ("owned jointly and often acrimoniously" when it came to paying taxes) on the most desirable side of the lake, the sunny eastern shore. Another branch of the family owned Hollyhock Farm with a thirty-acre orchard of Jonathan, Grimes, and Wagener apple trees.[82] Taken as one holding, the property constituted a freshwater fiefdom owned by a German American family several generations deep.

The Vonneguts' exodus to Lake Maxinkuckee started soon after Memorial Day by driving down Meridian Street until it became a flat, two-lane road, Route 31. The trip was straight north for ninety miles through the Indiana countryside. Stopping for lunch, they arrived at their cottage at 782 East Shore Drive by early afternoon. Then came the ceremony of taking down the winter shutters, raising the windows, and letting sunlight and fresh air ventilate the rooms for the first time in many months. Last, the boathouse would be unlocked, freeing the canoes and the leaky rowboat that Kurt Jr. had christened the *Beralikur*—a combination of "Bernard, Alice, Kurt." That evening everyone would tuck into his or her first dinner at the lake, eating by the glow of a kerosene lamp.[83]

Evenings were spent reading—Tennyson, Poe, Dickens, Hawthorne, Stevenson, Emerson, and James Whitcomb Riley were favorites—or playing Old Maid, Pinochle, or Parcheesi. At sunset, Culver Military Academy fired a cannon. Hearing that martial sound, Kurt Jr. hoped never "to be yelled at and have to wear a uniform."[84] Before bedtime, he would run down the pier his father had built and fling himself off the end, clutching a bar of soap for his bath.

To BE German was celebrated at the lake. The older folks tended to converse in German to stay in practice.[85] Kurt Jr. resented it when his parents shut him out of the conversation that way.[86] His father, who was in better spirits on vacation, sometimes cupped his hands to his mouth and jokingly called out, "Epta-mayan-hoy?," which sounds Native American but is ersatz German for "Do abbots mow hay?" The proper response was for one of the children, sometimes as many as half a dozen during a single summer, to shout back, "Ya, epta-mayan-hoy!" ("Yes, abbots mow hay!")[87]

Later in life Kurt Jr. complained about how little he really knew about German culture. He likened his situation to the title of an opera by Richard Strauss. "*Die Frau ohne Schatten*—the woman without a shadow, I was a kid without a shadow, an ethnic shadow. My parents could have taught me German but they didn't. I had no ethnic awareness whatsoever."[88] He blamed his parents for this—another refrain of "Nobody taught me anything." But he also blamed anti-German sentiment during the First World War, which "so shamed and dismayed my parents that they resolved to raise me without acquainting me with the language or the literature or the music or the oral family histories which my ancestors loved. They volunteered to make me ignorant and rootless as proof of their patriotism."[89]

During World War I, fear of the Hun (and envy over German Americans' prominence in business) led the *Indianapolis Star* to print the names and addresses of eight hundred German immigrants who were not naturalized. Someone threw yellow paint on Das Deutsche Haus, the city's German cultural center, which the members voted to rename the Athenaeum.[90] One morning, Kurt Sr. reached into his mailbox to find an anonymous note: "Stop teaching your kids that Dutch"—slang for German.[91] Ironically, of course, neither Alice nor Bernard (Kurt Jr. wasn't born yet) had been taught to speak German. Kurt Sr.'s mother, Nannette, also suffered a scare. The chauffeur she hired, a well-educated gentleman, "turned out to be spying on us," said Kurt Sr.'s sister, Irma. "He was trying to find out whether we were disloyal or not."[92] Putting the lie to this kind of prejudice was the fact that eight Vonnegut men registered for the draft, including Kurt Sr.[93]

There were many reasons for German Americans in Indianapolis to feel affronted, angry, or defensive. But their behavior doesn't square with Kurt Jr.'s belief that his parents were ashamed. Regular junkets aboard ship to Germany by the family continued at an energetic pace throughout the 1920s and early 1930s. In fact, Kurt Sr. sailed to Hamburg aboard the brand-new luxury liner the *Deutschland* two months after the stock market crash.[94] The Vonneguts, the Liebers, and their relatives were proud of their heritage, but they thought of it in lyrical and cultural, not political, terms. Indianapolis was replete with the efforts of German Americans to improve the city: the German-English School Society, the Musikverein, the German American Veterans Society, the German Literary Club, the Freethinkers Society, and the soaring Indiana Soldiers' and Sailors' Monument, designed by a Berlin architect. Later, during World War II, there was a saying in the Vonnegut home that the only thing wrong with the Germans was that they were in Germany.[95]

Moreover, the intellectual tradition of German rationalism and liberalism ensured that families like the Vonneguts refused to be cowed by nativists and bigots. Said Kurt Jr. himself many years later, "To them this country did have religious documents: the Declaration of Independence and the Bill of Rights."[96] They endured the slings and arrows of zealots and moved on with their lives.

In any case, the greatest benefit from Kurt Jr.'s life at the lake wasn't cultural. It was the abundant affection he received from belonging to the saga of the Vonnegut clan at Lake Maxinkuckee. Just his being there—swimming, canoeing, lighting firecrackers on the Fourth of July—added to family lore that spanned three generations. The contentment he felt erased his feelings of loneliness and anxiety at home. He later came to believe that in a perfect world every child who is at odds with his parents—whether the adults were cold or too demanding—should have an understanding relative to go to.[97] That person would serve as a safety net in times of trouble or just lend a sympathetic ear. And in his family, there was such a relative—someone who was "responsive and amusing and generous with me . . . my ideal grown-up friend"—his uncle Alex Vonnegut.[98]

Uncle Alex was Kurt Sr.'s gregarious younger brother, Harvard educated, and a broker for the Provident Mutual Life Insurance Company. His favorite three words, he said, were *enclosed find check*.[99] Later in life he confessed to feeling disappointed that he hadn't lived up to his expectations.[100] Selling insurance was too easy, and he was bored. Still, "he was bubbling with good humor," said Kurt Jr.'s cousin Walt Vonnegut, and he loved children.[101] Alex once proclaimed humorously to a friend in a letter, "I am in the Prime of Senility."[102]

All of the nieces and nephews would claim him at Lake Maxinkuckee, pulling him by the hand out onto the porch of one of the cottages where they could fuss over him. They begged for an Edgar Allan

Poe story or requested his most popular trick, making a cat's cradle out of string, which was likely the inspiration for the title of one of Kurt Jr.'s novels years later.[103] He had been married since 1915, but he and his wife, Raye, had no children and never would. The reason—at least the one Alex gave to close relatives—was that he had contracted a venereal disease while making the Grand Tour of Europe after college and was incapable of fathering a child. Having missed this opportunity, he energetically acted the surrogate parent to his many nieces and nephews.

No doubt because Alex was partial to children, he put his finger on something troubling his nephew Kurt Jr. No one was listening to him. "When Kay was a child," Alex said later, calling him by his family nickname, "he complained about not being able to talk and that he was always being interrupted."[104]

THE TROUBLE was that he couldn't seem to say anything important enough to get the attention he craved at home. "My sister was five years older than I was, my brother was nine years older, and at the dinner table I was the lowest ranking thing there. I could not be interesting to these vivid grownups."[105] The give-and-take of conversation swirled around him, usually at the center of which was Bernard. "My brother was just full of baloney about wonderful things that were happening to him."[106]

And then, as he entered his teenage years, he stumbled on how to turn everyone's head in his direction. As he recalled it, the strategy was simple: "The only way the youngest kid, by far the youngest kid, can hold attention is by being surprising." After everyone else at the table volunteered, "Well, I had a pretty nice day today," he would add dramatically, "Oh, I didn't, not at all." The clatter of silverware stopped, and his siblings and parents waited to hear what had happened.[107]

At first, he was guilty of anticlimax, and his remarks failed to entertain and were generally met with a nod. He got the hook, so to speak, and the conversation moved on. But over time his stories and jokes became bolder, more imaginative, and better told, causing his brother and sister to stifle their outbursts of laughter.[108]

Learning how to amuse was a skill, he realized. And for being tutored in the art of creating situations, practicing timing, and delivering punch lines, the perfect tutor was the radio. One of his favorite programs was *Vic and Sade*, a couple in Bloomington, Illinois, with an adopted son, Rush.[109] Each episode took an ordinary event—a broken washing machine, an early morning errand—and spun it out with extremely droll dialogue, without a laugh track or live audience, as if the listener were eavesdropping on a family who didn't know they were funny. It was only fifteen minutes long. The listener had to be engaged, entertained, and satisfied in that brief space of time. Listening critically to the big radio in his parents' living room, he received his first fundamental lessons in writing. "It was beautifully timed and extremely clever. That was the Muzak of my life."[110]

And learning to be funny accomplished something he never thought possible: it changed the balance of power in his family. After he demonstrated to Alice that he could be a real card, delivering gags just like comedians, she moved closer to him. By comparison, Bernard, down in his basement laboratory or in his advanced classes, might be able to do wonders with electricity and chemicals and so on. But upstairs in the dining and living rooms, his brother was strengthening his alliance with their sister by becoming her partner in funny business. They became a duo performing favorite bits from Abbott and Costello, Burns and Allen, or Laurel and Hardy.[111]

The sweetness of this victory absorbed him all his life. Later, he often created characters in groups of three in his novels, two men and one woman.[112] The ability to control humor put him in control of "the family drama here: my sister, my brother, and myself."[113]

With a new weapon in his quiver, Kurt Jr. sallied forth to practice it in adolescence. Alice, eighteen, was about to leave home for a few semesters at art school, and Bernard had followed in his father's footsteps to the Massachusetts Institute of Technology. Where Kurt Jr. would attend high school, however, was dictated again by his parents' diminishing finances. Unable to afford the kind of private education they had provided for Alice and Bernard, they enrolled their youngest at the new powerhouse of public secondary education in the city, Shortridge High School.

Shortridge, at 3401 North Meridian Street, looks almost exactly as it did when Vonnegut enrolled as a freshman in 1936. The original building, where his parents attended high school, had closed in 1928, and the new Shortridge building was already bulging with more than the twenty-five hundred students it was intended for. The reason for the overcrowding was that jobless graduates were allowed to reenroll. "Hardly any of us had any money," said a classmate of Vonnegut's during the Great Depression. "But on thinking it over I decided that we *were* rich—we had the finest school filled with the best teachers—and indeed we did have everything."[114]

Shortridge has an air of monumentality: a three-story, brick rectangle building with a Corinthian facade featuring a front entrance with six columns. Panels above the doors illustrate scenes of a classical education: art, music, literature, commerce, philosophy, and ethics. The interior rooms and hallways are finished in golden oak, ceramic tile, and plaster. Kurt Jr. couldn't contain his excitement about this new chapter beginning in his life: "If your parents could get you there, you got to go there. God, I remember an ancient history course there, it was just a knockout. A real chemist headed the chemistry department, Frank Wade, who taught and worked as a chemist. So my brother, going to the Park School while maintaining his 'upper class status,' bicycled to Shortridge to study chemistry with Frank Wade."[115]

To choose his courses, he relied on what friends said about the best teachers.[116] But here Bernard stepped in, supplanting his parents' authority about his brother's choices. The first disagreement was over foreign language. Kurt Jr. wasn't interested in German, which Bernard recommended, despite his complaint later that he had been cut off from his heritage. He begged to be allowed to take Latin instead, so he could join the school's largest club, the Roman State. (Incredibly, twelve hundred students belonged—half the school.) "But I wasn't to study Latin, I was to study German, a technical language," because Bernard insisted it was more useful.[117] Two years of German, his parents decided, would be followed by two years of French because it was part of a liberal education. When it came to freshman science, he wanted to enroll in zoology because he liked animals, but Bernard pointed out "it wasn't physical science enough."[118] So zoology was out and chemistry was in.

Nevertheless, he did well his freshman year: all As and Bs in core courses such as English, algebra, and chemistry, which, considering that he later insisted he had no interest or talent for science, is worth noting.

The summer of 1937 he worked at the Vonnegut Hardware on East

Washington Street for his great-uncle Franklin Vonnegut. His job was running the freight elevator up and down between six floors, eight hours a day, a Sisyphean task that gave him a glimpse of life in hell, he later said.[119]

Franklin made a mistake, however. As the owner of the business, he assigned his nephew number two on the time clock, right under him, which was taken by the other workers as tiresome evidence of the unfairness of nepotism. Kurt was embarrassed.[120] Many of the men employed by Vonnegut Hardware were making the same salary he was—fourteen dollars a week. It was his first real-life lesson in social and economic disparity, illustrating what he had read in a book recently given to him by Uncle Alex: Thorstein Veblen's *Theory of the Leisure Class*. He reveled in its attacks on conspicuous consumption, "since it made low comedy of the empty graces and aggressively useless possessions which my parents, and especially my mother, meant to regain some day."[121] With the excitement of a youngster who has at last caught his parents red-handed, he realized he was being raised to become bourgeois.

SOPHOMORE YEAR, Kurt took up smoking—smart-looking Pall Mall cigarettes in the red package with a coat of arms and the Latin motto *In hoc signo vinces* (By this sign shall you conquer). He determined too that he would have a girlfriend. Girls liked him because he was polite and funny, and, for his part, he "fell in love with girls."[122] In fact, he had his eye on one in particular, Mary Jo Albright.

Christmas morning, he wrapped a present and left early for the short walk to her house on North Washington Street. Inside the gift box, he had a teddy bear. He hoped it would strike the right note between friendship and thoughtfulness.

Mary Jo's father answered the door and welcomed him in, calling for his daughter to come down and meet the young gentleman who had just arrived. From her expression, Kurt could tell she was surprised to see him. They sat on the couch and he presented his gift. Opening the wrapping, she fussed over the teddy bear and thanked him. But after a few moments, she explained they couldn't talk long—she was expecting her date, Bill Shirley. They had made plans to go skating together.

Kurt made the best of things and started making his exit, thanking her father and wishing them a Merry Christmas. It had been a sincere, if inelegant, expedition of the heart.[123]

In his bedroom he would stand at his window at night and watch a teenage girl, Nina Brown, undress in her lighted window through the backyard trees.[124] In his home life, the relationship between his parents illustrated almost nothing about tenderness and sexuality, and echoes of it can later be heard in his novels. His stories are rife with loneliness, bad relations between parents and children, unsuccessful attempts at romance, and a kind of chilliness of the heart that prevents the protagonist from feeling emotion.[125] In addition, the Vonneguts' twin belief systems going back several generations—unitarianism and freethinking—gave no guidance about sex and love.

His father tried to provide a passion that would unite them as men. He was an expert collector of guns, all kinds, but especially antique pistols and revolvers.[126] The rarest he owned was a one-hundred-year-old single-shot Belgian target pistol with blued barrel and carved stock inlaid with gold. It might have been used in a duel, when men would die rather than accept dishonor. He wanted his son to appreciate the whorls on a particular gun's etched barrel, the teardrop loop of its gold trigger guard, its dark walnut grip, fashioned when Napoleon was emperor.

The rites of initiation succeeded. Kurt Jr.'s cousin Walt paid him a visit and was hugely impressed by what he saw in Kurt Jr.'s bedroom. "Saw K's two automatic pistols," he noted in his diary. "He has 11 rifles & shotguns not including the one I borrowed, and 4 pistols. Of course, most of the guns really belong to Uncle Kurt, I believe, but K has them in his room."[127]

It was a kind of armory, a masculine citadel.

DURING THE summer between his sophomore and junior years, Kurt worked at Vonnegut Hardware again, this time on the sales floor, discovering that the customers stole regularly, and that working where there were no windows was not for him.[128] After ringing up a sale, he always added a complimentary gift to the customer's purchase: a twelve-inch wooden ruler that doubled as an "Indiana Legal Length Fish Gauge." Printed at the seven-inch mark was the prescient word *Trout*.[129] But he dreaded the fate of many male Vonneguts, which was to end up with a career in the venerable hardware store or, as he characterized it to a friend, "working in the nuts and bolts department."[130]

Finally, the big house on North Illinois Street sold in 1939, and his parents used the money to buy property in the Williams Creek subdivision of Indianapolis. In the meantime, until they could build a smaller house, they lived catch-as-catch-can, badgered by money problems and general unhappiness.

Edith took a fiction-writing course at the YWCA in the hope of selling short stories to women's magazines. She imagined that once her stories caught on, the family could vacation on Cape Cod again while she continued to write. Hearing her talk about editors, guidelines, and submissions, her son became intrigued with the idea of being an author. "It was my mother more than my father who stirred my interest in literature, except that whatever talent I have was his—his letters were exquisite."[131] But her stories were hopelessly out of date in tone and subject matter. They were country clubby and literary-sounding when readers wanted a bit of raciness and a few burning kisses to escape the dreariness of the Depression. "She never sold anything. I was aware of that."[132]

Meanwhile, his father, who had once spun around an eleven-thousand-ton building without anyone inside feeling a shudder, fussed over an invention that he hoped would bring in a dependable stream of money. It was a device for cleaning out pipe stems, a kind of piston in the stem. But it would require changing the design on every pipe made, and it would work only on straight stems. He took out a patent on it.[133] Predictably, no one expressed any interest.

JUNIOR YEAR in high school, Kurt Jr. took his first drink, a surreptitious one. One autumn afternoon, upon arriving home after school, "[I] discovered mother decorating the house, having a jug of sherry. There was a very pretty light coming through it. I took a slug from that and, man, it really felt nice."[134] Alcohol and cigarettes, two means of self-medicating his high and low mood swings, became addictions he would never be able to shake.

For another reason, a more salutary one, his junior year was important: Vonnegut began appearing in print regularly in the Shortridge High School *Echo*. About sixty students produced the *Echo*, although publishing it with an ever-rotating staff—a different one for each day of the week—was a scramble.[135] Every weekday morning, a new edition of the *Echo* appeared, providing the student body and faculty with the latest news about school activities, events, and sports.

The first article carrying Vonnegut's byline, "This Business of Whistle Purchasing," a lighthearted criticism of a school fund-raiser, was submitted at the urging of his sophomore English teacher. Then beginning in his junior year, he contributed a piece to the newspaper practically every week, sometimes as many as four—news, commentary, sports—which he sometimes signed, in place of his real name, "Ferdinand" or "Koort" or, his kookiest moniker, "Koort Snarfield Vawnyagoot II." Silly pen names aside, his work for the *Echo* launched him as a writer. His happiness from being in print stemmed from the realization that he had a gift when it came to putting words on paper. "Each person has something he can do easily and can't imagine why everybody else is having so much trouble doing it. In my case it was writing."[136] Looking back, he attributed basic elements of his fictional style to having an instant audience in high school: "I was writing for my peers and not for teachers, it was very important to me that they understand what I was saying." Also the journalistic style of short, punchy sentences, active verbs, and strong structure appealed to him. "Because I believed in the merits of this type of prose, I was quite 'teachable' and so I worked hard to achieve as pure a style as I could."[137]

An added benefit was that his articles were continual advertisements for himself on the social scene. Suddenly, the *Echo*'s gossip columnists began taking note of this new big-man-on-campus. "Tip to Kurt Vonnegut. Please look at the person to whom you are going to speak. It is rather disturbing to have you look the other way and then say 'hello.' Shortridge girls."[138] Another gossip columnist touted him as the best candidate to lead the junior talent show. "Plug for Kurt Vonnegut, who is planning on running for Junior Vaudeville chairman. Don't you think he would be a keen one, though? For if he applies a touch of that subtle Vonnegut wit to the Vaudeville, it should be really whizz-bang!"[139] He won the election.

He became known as something of a character. Humor and rudimentary charm were becoming his trademarks. At a dancing class, run by a Mrs. Gates, where Indianapolis's young ladies and gentlemen learned the waltz and foxtrot, he arrived one evening wearing the required blue serge suit and white gloves. As he glided over the floor, he quietly let a trail of marbles dribble through a hole in his trouser pocket, hoping couples would take indecorous pratfalls. "Everybody (except Mrs. Gates) loved him," said his partner that night.[140]

By midyear he was a member of the Student Council, the Junior Social Committee, the Press Club, the Drama League, the Fiction Club, and the Junior Pin and Ring Committee. The *Echo* noted his "intriguing personality," said he was an upperclassman "who is worshipped by freshmen femmes; thought of as 'wonderful' by Sally Evans, and 'intriguing' by Baba Kiger—Kurt Vonnegut remains oblivious to all. Universal opinion, Kurt—we need more people like you."[141]

He was Kurt Vonnegut Jr.—writer, wit, and mischief maker.

HIS SENIOR year, he turned his attention to life after high school, but in his mind, at least, the way seemed clear. His work on the school paper had led him to read H. L. Mencken, the acerbic critic of politics and American life: "I knew something about his life—that he had had a very exciting time as a newspaper reporter—and I guess later as a city editor. I read a couple of his autobiographical works, and as a result of this I wanted to be a newspaperman."[142] On his own, he found his way to the editorial offices of the *Indianapolis Star* and, in the course of asking some advice about how to get into journalism, was offered a job by the managing editor.

For a young man, it was a remarkable coup. And it would have been the first step toward independence, had Bernard not stepped in. His brother was by then in graduate school in physics at MIT. While Kurt Sr.'s star had sunk lower and lower as an architect and amateur artist until he was "completely demoralized," Bernard had proved by example that he had been right all along: the "arts were ornamental."[143] In the new world, the laurels would go to scientists, technicians, the practitioners of the practical arts—not daubers in art, like Alice, who had failed to complete art school, or, by extension, scribblers like the kind Kurt Jr. wanted to be. No one in the family had made good by chasing after the Muses. Humankind would be grateful to those who understood the natural and physical sciences.

Kurt Sr. could no longer speak with authority about what was worth spending your life on. His confidence had fled. The sum of his years spent drawing designs that he hoped would leave his imprint on Indianapolis, and his participation in societies devoted to discussing art, had come to nothing. His only advice to his namesake was "Be anything but an architect."[144]

It was decided that Kurt Jr. would attend Cornell, which his great-uncle Franklin Vonnegut, as well as a cousin, Richard C. Vonnegut, had attended. His major would be chemistry or perhaps biochemistry. But there must have been bad blood about it. When Kurt graduated from Shortridge High School in June 1940, neither of his parents was in the audience. He never forgave them for the snub. "Really low class." Later, they apologized.[145]

The summer between high school and college, Kurt and Bernard went hiking in New Hampshire's White Mountains. But in the back of his mind, Kurt was worried about his scores on the college boards and suggested they call Cornell to "just make sure everything's okay." To his humiliation, his admission as a chemistry major to Cornell was uncertain because, although he had received an A+ in high school physics, his math scores on the boards were low. Bernard drove him to Harvard, where he was accepted provisionally.

In the meantime, their father persuaded the principal of Shortridge to contact the admissions office at Cornell and vouch for his son. "And so yeah, I got admitted to Harvard, on a trial basis, or whatever. And to MIT, the same thing, but Bernie said I better go to Cornell, which was his idea of me, sort of third rate."[146]

Bernard had vetoed his dreams, which were to become a writer, and throughout his life he put the blame on his brother for interfering. "Bernie really fucked up my life. If it hadn't have been for him, all the shit that was about to happen to me wouldn't have happened. I enrolled in the sciences at Cornell only as a sop to him, no other reason. Later, I was in a real mess."[147]

2: One of the Biggest Fools on the Hill

1940–1943

VONNEGUT REGISTERED AT Cornell University in Ithaca, New York, in September 1940 to begin his freshman year. Standing atop the Hill, where most of the older academic buildings are located, he could see a panoramic view of Cayuga Lake's southern end with the forests on its western shore, so different from the grassy prairies of Indiana.

He was a science major, instructed by his father not to "waste time or money on 'frivolous' courses, but to give full attention to practical studies, principally physics and chemistry and math."[1] He had been pushed into college, counter to his desire to write for a newspaper in Indianapolis. Still, his father and brother had led him to campus, so to speak, but they couldn't make him study.

During fraternity and sorority rush week, he automatically received a bid from Delta Upsilon at 6 South Avenue, which was primarily a house of engineering students at Cornell, because it had been his father's fraternity at MIT.[2] He pledged, mentioning to the members, as if it were a watchword, that the arts were ornamental, parroting his brother, the success in the family.[3]

Freshmen weren't permitted to move into a fraternity or sorority house until the end of first semester, so in the meantime he roomed in a boardinghouse at 109 Williams Street with David Young, a freshman and fellow Delta Upsilon pledge from Philadelphia.

This was the first time Vonnegut had shared a room with anyone, and Young discovered his roommate was a cheerful slob. Vonnegut's dirty clothes landed on any flat surface—a desk, a dresser top, the bed. He liked nice clothes, but keeping them that way was a nuisance. Arriving at the home of Young's family in Philadelphia for a visit, he tossed his suitcase on the guest bed, announcing that the solution to clothes wrinkling in a suitcase was simple—pack them inside out, which is what he had done for this trip. That way the wrinkles would be less noticeable when the clothes were removed and turned right side out again. He lifted the suitcase lid as proof. The results were disappointing, until Young suggested that perhaps everything had gone in wrinkled.[4]

Young also noticed that his roommate and cigarette smoke were practically synonymous, although Kurt ignored the ashtrays in the room. Instead he took "great pleasure in antiquing desktops, chair arms, bookcases, windows sills, and any other horizontal surfaces with burn marks," said Young.[5] To relieve his frequent colds, he swore by dipping cigarettes into Vicks VapoRub to create "vaporettes," which precluded the need to stop smoking.

For the initiation banquet in the spring of 1941, Kurt delivered the toast for the initiates, under the gaze of his father, who attended the affair. After the formality of the dinner, "hell week" saw to it that all the new members were mildly hazed, but Kurt's task deeply embarrassed him. He was ordered to wear red flannel underwear that was a size too small. Rodney Gould, a fellow initiate, thought this was especially humiliating for Kurt because he was sensitive about being very tall and thin. Gould also thought Kurt was attuned to his place in the fraternity pecking order. He asked Gould what his father did for a living. Hearing that he was a sales engineer for Texaco, Vonnegut pressed further, wanting to know whether he was *the* top sales engineer, to which Gould replied no. It was Gould's impression that Vonnegut was wary of the "sons-of-the-affluent sameness of the house."[6]

Vonnegut and Young, who decided to room together again, set about making their quarters in the fraternity house distinctive right away. In the attic, they found a moth-eaten moose head, painted the antlers blue, and mounted it as the trophy of their residence, which they christened the "Blue Moose Lodge." Between the antlers they slung a bra. Bouncing a tennis ball off a wall and into the "pockets" became a fiercely competitive game of what Vonnegut called "Tit Polo."

"Gut," as his fraternity brothers dubbed him, was developing a reputation for his panache. After he passed out one night at a party, his fraternity brother laid him in the fireplace, wearing his full-length bearskin coat with his arms crossed, a lily held in one hand. To deflect attention from his inability to run far (or fast), he showed up for an all-house cross-country run dressed in mismatched pajamas and a knit cap, an ensemble that did not please his fraternity brothers. He was, as his roommate said, a "free spirit, a charming, humorous guy who craved attention."[7]

DESPITE BURSTS of silliness, he knew what was important to him, and in mid-October he made certain he was on time for an important evening meeting. In the news offices of the *Cornell Daily Sun*, located above Atwater's grocery store on State Street, he found a seat among the twenty-six other candidates competing for a handful of openings on the newspaper. The *Sun*, the oldest independent college daily in the United States, published every day except Sunday. The front page carried both national news from the wire services and campus news. Inside, the content was all student-written, and standards were high. Another "compete" vying for an entry-level spot was Parker Smith, who would later become news editor of the *New York Herald Tribune* and managing editor of *Newsday*.

The *Sun*'s editors distributed a sheet to the candidates on which were listed the raw facts of a newsworthy event. Each candidate was given half an hour to weave them into a news story. If he made the cut, Vonnegut would be heading in the direction of journalism, defying his father and brother. But his instincts told him that in this, at least, he could succeed. Bringing to bear his experience as biweekly editor of the Shortridge *Echo*, he handed in his submission and waited for the results.

Later that night, he was happily introducing himself to other staffers, along with Smith, as one of the new writers for the *Sun*.

VONNEGUT'S BYLINE began appearing regularly during his second semester. The editors started him out on "Innocents Abroad," a column of jokes featuring gags that were typical of comedians' patter on radio.

"Say, buddy, how about two dimes for a nickel? The change would do me good." He also covered sports, demonstrating a knack for that, too. "Holy smoke! Look at those guys run, and the first meet isn't until Feb. 28. Won't Yale, Syracuse, Colgate, and the big boys at the Intercollegiate be surprised—maybe."[8]

The managing editors, all upperclassmen, edited his submissions, showing him how to punch up his writing, although they noticed his copy was better than most beginners: "Always in on time and splendid," remembered one of them.[9] He took their advice to strive, as he said, for "clarity, economy, and so forth. The theory was that large, sprawling paragraphs tended to discourage readers and make the paper appear ugly. Their strategy was primarily visual—that is, short paragraphs, often one-sentence paragraphs."[10] Writing that was easy to scan would become one of the hallmarks of his fiction.

Humor was what he had written for the Shortridge *Echo*, and without a byline in the *Sun*, most of what he wrote was inseparable from all the other horseplay in the paper. His best writing, in which the barbs of satire can be seen, began appearing in a column rotated among several students called "Well All Right." The purpose of "Well All Right" gave him what he always needed to write well, which was "an ax to grind," he later said.[11]

Defending the Midwest against remarks made by another columnist, he dismissed his opponent with cheerful condescension. "In yesterday's column, Mr. Ted Eddy cut loose on the West with the vicious generalities and the wit of a blotter. . . . Little men with glasses and thin, trembling lips, stick close to your fireside, and take care what poison you so glibly spread."[12]

He tried his hand too at imitating the voice of popular humorists of the day such as S. J. Perelman, James Thurber, and especially Robert Benchley, whose trademark was joking at his own expense. In "Albino for a Day, or in the Pink," Vonnegut described a day in the campus infirmary recovering from a case of conjunctivitis: "We read, slept, and smoked. The most fun was to put out cigarettes with the nose spray—a close second was making Kleenex bonfires in the soap dish. They told us how contagious Pink Eye is, so we wrote several infected letters to our enemies, coast to coast."[13]

The *Sun*'s rival on campus was the *Cornell Widow*, the university's monthly humor magazine. Several times a year, the *Widow* lampooned national magazines, which would have been a natural venue for Vonnegut's writing, but he thought of himself as a journalist. He was friendly with writers for the *Widow*, however.

One was Knox Burger, a *Widow* editor whom he met during an event showcasing extracurriculars for newcomers to campus. Knox thought "Coffin Nail" Vonnegut, which is how Kurt listed himself on the roster for the annual baseball game between the *Widow* and the *Sun*, was likable, if "not especially studious."[14] But Vonnegut impressed him later for another reason.

As part of a rivalry that went back years, the *Widow* enjoyed needling the *Sun* with a cartoon series called "Sunman" about a knuckle-dragging caveman, impugning the intelligence of the *Sun* staffers, as well as their appearance. One day Kurt went to see Knox about it. The faces in the cartoons, he told Knox, struck him as anti-Semitic, and the *Sun* staff included a high percentage of Jewish students. He urged Burger to tone down the caricature.[15] Burger agreed that the cartoon did contain "mild but persuasive anti-Semitism."[16] The caveman changed his look.

ON ANOTHER issue he was more outspoken, publicly so, which eventually exposed him to accusations of being unpatriotic. Kurt was a cadet in Cornell's Reserve Officer Training Corps (ROTC)—a Cornell requirement. World War II was already consuming Europe and Asia. But he did not accept the premise that the United States should rush to arms. The reasonable response to Hitler, he believed, was isolationism, the position taken by his family, who were businesspeople and conservatives.

The Vonneguts were a clan of upper-class professionals who had become wealthy through entrepreneurship. They were by no means pro-Roosevelt or New Deal. "We were Republican people," said Kurt's cousin Emily Louise Diamond, whose grandfather Alfred M. Glossbrenner had run for mayor of Indianapolis on the Republican ticket in 1929 but lost because of the Wall Street crash.[17] At the Indianapolis Columbia Club, where Vonneguts had belonged since the turn of the century, members approvingly repeated the editorial stance of the *Indianapolis Star*, a reverently conservative newspaper that castigated Roosevelt as a traitor to his class and regarded his tinkerings with free enterprise as tantamount to communism. Kurt's uncle Alex and his wife, Raye, were "intellectual explorers" in regard to socialism, said Emily, but "I don't think they ever really committed to civic work along the lines of their beliefs."[18]

And when, beginning in the late 1930s, Roosevelt began calling for intervention in Europe's affairs as a moral imperative, the Vonneguts and others in their social class were appalled. For the United States to enter another continental war in Europe would be the second major conflict abroad in little more than twenty years at a time when hoboes were coming to the back door asking for something to eat. It was hypocritical to call for bailing out Europe.

The Vonneguts also had a personal reason for not wanting to risk a war with Germany. As Kurt said later, "I know my parents' feeling about the First World War, because they were sympathetic to Germans, because their ancestors were from Germany, and they really felt that Great Britain and France and Russia were as much to blame as Germany was in the First World War."[19]

Later in his life, he disingenuously claimed that he condemned war because his parents were pacifists: "I thought about it and decided they were right."[20] Pacifists of course don't register for the draft, which every man jack of the Vonneguts would after the attack on Pearl Harbor. But in the spring of 1941 while he was still a freshman at Cornell, he sided ardently with those who believed the United States must stay out of the war in Europe.

VONNEGUT'S FIRST volley against the interventionists accused the *Cornell Daily Sun* itself of censorship. An item had caught his attention about British parachutists triumphing over Nazi troops, written in grandiloquent language by a British reporter and given big play on the front page. "A story below black headlines looks vastly more important than one tucked away under a two-line light head," he pointed out. "Thus, while reports of the Egyptian and Ethiopian campaigns have commanded headlines, the story of severe native strikes and riots on the British Malaya rubber plantations has been so effectively hidden in recent papers as to be scarcely known at all. . . . We must know the shortcomings of the British—and of ourselves—as well as of the Germans if we would create any kind of lasting remedy, when dangers of the moment are averted."[21]

He also derided, in another column, the "my country right or wrong" of young hotheads who couldn't wait to fight. One day, riding a bus into Ithaca, he listened to his seatmate, an eighteen-year-old soldier, describe with gusto his lessons in bayonet practice: "Parry, stab, withdraw, smash, etc." Instead of expressing admiration, Vonnegut asked him what he thought his chances would be against a Nazi soldier who had been fighting since the invasion of Poland in 1939. "His eyes glistened, and he said that he just wished he had the chance." The young soldier informed Vonnegut he hated Germans, "all of 'em." Kurt was tempted to ask if Beethoven was typical of the Germans he hated but decided he "probably wouldn't get a very good answer."[22]

HE WAS gaining a reputation for his positions in print, and writing for the *Sun* was more gratifying than any of his other activities on campus, including courses he "wasn't doing shit about."[23] The tug of the newsroom was irresistible. Trudging up the Hill alone to his fraternity house from the editorial offices after midnight, he felt content knowing that everyone else—"university people, teachers and students alike"—was asleep. "They had been playing games all day long with what was known about real life. They had been repeating famous arguments and experiments, and asking one another the sorts of hard questions real life would be asking by and by. We on the *Sun* were already in the midst of real life. By God, if we weren't!"[24]

By the end of freshman year, his grade point average as a chemistry major was sagging near probationary status. To bolster it, he enrolled during summer vacation in 1941 at Butler University in Indianapolis, registering for two easy English classes, the credits from which he could transfer to Cornell.[25] Instead, after a few weeks he started goofing off, mocking the seriousness of the place: "Oh, noble halls from whose portals flow the nation's eager insurance salesmen," a remark not likely to please his uncle Alex if he found out about it, because he was quite a successful insurance salesman.[26] Unable to average better than Cs on papers and tests at Butler, he dropped out before the final exams.

This time the problem wasn't devoting too much time to extracurricular activities like fraternity socials, bar hopping, or writing for the *Sun*. He had fallen in love with a young woman. And he had made up his mind to marry her.

* * *

JANE MARIE Cox was one of Kurt's eight classmates in kindergarten at the Orchard School. They had been together every day, kindergarten through third grade, an experience he had always thought of as "bonding," until Kurt had left to attend public school.[27] She was a popular little blue-eyed girl with a small face and the nickname "Woofy." Her family was Anglo-Irish, moderately Quaker, and belonged to the same social set as the Vonneguts. Like Mrs. Vonnegut, her mother was convinced that belonging to the right clubs and bridge groups was vital. On membership lists of exclusive Indianapolis organizations for women, her name usually appears. Kurt's mother didn't think much of the Coxes, however, because Mrs. Cox had a reputation for emotional volatility.[28]

Mariah Cox, born Mariah Fagan but who preferred "Riah," was an itinerant scholar in Indianapolis. She had a master's degree in classical literature and in 1925 had coauthored the first textbook on principles of language learning. It became a standard in the field.[29] She taught at the Orchard School using her etymologist's training to teach students to notice four aspects of a word: its meaning, pronunciation, origin—from the Latin, Greek, French, Anglo-Saxon, Scandinavian, etc.—and its history in the development of English.

She was proud of her daughter, Jane, but touchy about what people might think about her younger child, Thomas Jr., nicknamed "Gussie." Although he was outgoing and friendly with his boyhood friends, Gussie was slightly disfigured as a result of an ear operation that had severed a facial nerve. A corner of his mouth hung in a perpetual frown. To Riah, her maimed son was an embarrassment.[30] A woman with stronger emotional resources might not care. But she was vulnerable. Her husband, Thomas Cox, an Indianapolis attorney, was an alcoholic, and Riah's composure cracked easily under stress.[31] Added to this, she suffered episodes of mania.[32]

Her fears of having more breakdowns made her appear to others at times like someone mimicking absolutely perfect, unimpeachable manners. A visitor to the house, cruelly poking through her pretense, wounded her by saying, "You know, Mrs. Cox, you just missed being charming."[33]

Jane compensated for the pall that hung over her family by being almost preternaturally upbeat about everything. Friends from her youth frequently described her as "sweet" and carefree. She was like Alice

Vonnegut in that respect. It's tempting to think that Kurt's infatuation with Jane transferred feelings for his older sister to someone very much like her.

When Kurt made up his mind that Jane was the young woman he wanted to marry, she was a freshman at Swarthmore College outside Philadelphia, an "extraordinarily cute, lovely young lady," in the words of one of her boyfriends.[34] In fact, one of Jane's roommates noticed she had a heavy social calendar and plenty of dates. A friend of Kurt's from high school, Vic Jose, escorted her to his fraternity formal and "got a lot of points" with his fraternity brothers for showing up with a pretty girl on his arm.[35] Jane's roommate had the impression Woofy was "always sort of going with Kurt," but she couldn't recall ever having seen him at Swarthmore.[36]

Nevertheless, before he returned to Cornell in the fall of 1941, he gave her a gift, an anthology of Emerson's essays and poems. On the endpaper he swore to love her forever.[37]

A month later, returning to campus, he penned a column for the *Sun* with the giddy headline RAMBLINGS OF ONE WHO IS WEAK IN THE EXCHEQUER, AND IN THE MIND. The whole campus needed to know about his happiness. "We wrote a letter to Jane, too. You haven't met Jane yet, but she'll be up here for Fall House Party. We're getting married in '45, you know."[38]

THEN IT was back to beating the tocsin in his columns about the dangers of the United States intervening in Europe's problems. Isolationism, he insisted, was the only honest choice. "Whether anyone else gives a hang or not about keeping out of World War II, we do, and from now on, readers may rest assured that material in this column has been carefully edited so as to exclude anything smacking in the slightest of propaganda."[39] He vociferously defended Charles A. Lindbergh, the hero of transatlantic aviation who toured the Third Reich and predicted that another fratricidal world war could destroy Western civilization. Lindbergh, wrote Vonnegut, "had the courage at least to present the conservative side of a titanic problem, grant him that. The United States is a democracy, that's what they say we'll be fighting for. What a prize monument to that ideal is a cry to smother Lindy. Weighing such inconsequential items as economic failure and simultaneous collapse of the flaunted American Standard of Living . . . and outrageous bloodshed of his countrymen, the young ones, is virtual treason to the Stars and Stripes—long may it wave. Lindy, you're a rat. We read that somewhere, so it must be so. They say you should be deported. In that event, leave room in the boat for us."[40]

The managing editor felt compelled to add a note in boldface at the end of Vonnegut's tirade: "The opinions above are those of the author and do not necessarily reflect the views of the *Sun*."[41]

SUNDAY AFTERNOON, December 7, 1941, Kurt was relaxing in a bathtub at Delta Upsilon when he heard that Japanese aircraft carriers had attacked the United States fleet anchored in Pearl Harbor, Hawaii. "I tore down to the office, and we laid out a new first and last page, keeping the stale insides of the previous [Saturday] issue. . . . We took whatever was coming off the AP machine, slapped it in, and were, I still believe, the first paper in the state to hit the streets with an extra."[42] He came up with the headline: JAPS START WAR ON U.S.

He was a night editor by then, responsible for ranking news and laying it out. The *Sun* had become the only meaningful part of his life at Cornell; the rest was just a "boozy dream."[43] Tests, papers, lectures, and final examinations were a lot of hooey, in his opinion. He came up with a prank to ridicule his classmates' angst over grades. Taking a seat for a final exam at midyear in a class he wasn't registered for, he waited until everyone was deep into the test. Then with a groan of disgust, he ripped the exam to shreds, stalked up the aisle, and tossed the pieces of paper into the astonished instructor's face, storming out the classroom door.[44] It started a fad among the student body that lasted a few semesters.

IN MAY 1942 of his sophomore year, a dean of academic advising summoned him to his office. He informed Vonnegut that unless there was a change in his grades he would not be continuing at Cornell. He would have one more semester, the fall, to improve. Stunned, Kurt scrambled to come up with a loophole of some kind, feeling like "one of the biggest fools on the Hill."[45]

Couldn't extracurricular activities count for something?

No, that wasn't possible.

He already knew, as everyone did, what flunking out would mean during wartime: military service under the draft. Formerly, he had been enrolled in ROTC, which would have earned him an officer's commission on graduating, but due to a "severe misunderstanding" (as he preferred to call it) he had been kicked out of the corps.[46]

The reason for his dismissal was a column of his, "We Impress *Life* Magazine with Our Efficient Role in National Defense," mocking the ROTC program. As a photographer from *Life* snapped pictures of him and his fellow cadets examining an artillery weapon, Vonnegut claimed they were fooling him with mumbo-jumbo like "Flathatcher! Biffle-block!" He predicted that when the feature in *Life* appeared, "Americans will rip into national defense with redoubled enthusiasm when they see that a deadly bunch of artillery men from Ithaca are working hand in hand with them."[47] That sarcasm, compounded with poor grades, had given the ROTC lieutenant the perfect excuse to return the insult by giving him the boot.

The dean left him with a bitter piece of advice: "Why not get a job and forget college entirely?" With no commission, his college degree hanging in the balance, no specialized training because he'd been taking only core courses so far, Vonnegut knew what might happen: "It was like stepping into a cold shower: we couldn't conceive of good old us being nothing but a private."[48] Although shaken, he wasn't expelled by the time he left the dean's office, after all, perhaps because he promised to straighten up come fall semester.

Explaining his humiliation in the *Sun*—"The Lost Battalion Undergoes a Severe Shelling"—earned no sympathy from some of his fellow writers on the paper, however. They had read his defense of Lindbergh's pleas to stay out of the war; his accusation that the *Sun* unknowingly ran propaganda; his send-up of training for defense. A few weeks later in a roundup of campus gossip, news about Vonnegut getting in trouble for another prank appeared under the subhead "Fifth Column"—a term used for a group in a country at war who are sympathetic to, or collaborating with, its enemies. "There's another story about this tall, gaunt fellow with the Nazi-like name . . . some sort of encounter with a certain dean by the name of Sibley—but perhaps this is better left untold."[49]

DURING THE summer of 1942, Kurt tried to put aside the cares of his failing college career by lending a hand baling hay on a farm outside

Indianapolis owned by his relatives the Glossbrenners. Civilian man-power was scarce due to the demands of the war. His uncle Dan Gloss-brenner, a World War I captain with the Rainbow Division, had reenlisted.[50] Kurt's cousin Walt was training at Fort Benjamin Harrison before being posted to the newly created Eighth Air Force as a navigator on B-17 Flying Fortresses. Another cousin, Franklin F. Vonnegut, was in the Army Air Corps as well.[51] In addition to putting up hay at the Gloss-brenners', Kurt labored for a pittance on a nine-hundred-acre stock farm. There were only seven workers handling the animals—"three under 15 years of age, two over 45, Mr. Bloomer, who had the IQ of a small dog, and myself."[52]

MEANWHILE, BERNARD'S career as a scientist had brought him rec-ognition and exemption from military service. He had discovered, in the laboratories of the Hartford-Empire Company in Newark, New Jersey, a better method for measuring the strength of certain kinds of surfactants used for cleaning up oil spills caused by German subma-rines torpedoing tankers on the eastern seaboard. After three years at Hartford-Empire, MIT had appointed him a research associate in the Chemical Warfare Service Department. On his own, he cracked the secret of why German gas mask filters were superior to the Allies'.[53] In contrast to his younger brother floundering at Cornell, he was doing important war-related work.

IN AUTUMN 1942, when Kurt returned to Cornell for his junior year, the *Sun*'s first headline welcomed MEMBERS OF THE CLASS OF '44 2/3, '45 1/4, OR WHATEVER. The gallows humor recognized that male under-graduates were on borrowed time. Some were postponing graduation and enrolling in accelerated officer training programs instead, an option not available to Vonnegut because of his grades. In his columns for the *Sun*, he also returned to his rather shopworn themes of isolationism and urging caution against invading Germany, despite the Third Reich sub-jugating most of Europe. "It will be a world-shaking tragedy, if [presi-dential candidate] Mr. Willkie . . . stirs[s] up the American and British people to make an undeniable demand for German blood on European soil before the proper time has come."[54] He would have been wiser to say "American blood" if he wanted to win over readers.

At Swarthmore Jane, unknown to him, had fallen in love with someone else. He was Kendall Landis, an eighteen-year-old freshman, a sandy-haired six-footer, and a diver on the swim team who found Jane a "ravishing junior" and a "delight and an amazing discovery."[55] His father was a banker, his mother a former public school teacher. He and Jane became lovers.[56]

That December, returning home to Indianapolis for the holiday break, Kurt developed pneumonia. Though serious, it was a kind of saving grace. He was failing both biochemistry and organic chemistry, and passing the semester exams in January would have been impossible. His career at the *Sun* had plateaued, as well. He was an associate editor and gunning for one of the top spots his senior year, but to a member of the editorial board who would vote on his application, "Kurt just seemed to be having too much fun to do the work. His talent was imaginative writing."[57]

In January 1943 he dropped out of Cornell and decided to enlist rather than wait to be drafted. It was the only sensible choice he had, having finally convinced himself that the conflict was, as he said later, "clearly a war that had to be fought and there are very few of those in history. It was worth fighting."[58]

His about-face might seem abrupt, but he was part of the flow of historical events overtaking the United States. After Pearl Harbor, the isolationist America First Committee dissolved. Lindbergh left the political stage entirely and pulled strings until he could get himself a seat in a fighter plane in the South Pacific, even though he was overage. The Allies were losing the war in both hemispheres, and the antiwar objections of the Right, the isolationists, and the libertarians faded away. Kurt went to a recruiting office in Indianapolis for a physical but came out on the street a few hours later, rejected as unfit for duty because of his pneumonia. The physician who examined him said he was underweight, too. In March, he tried again. This time he was sworn into the United States army.

Returning home with the big news, he announced, "I've just volunteered to join the army."

His father was disgusted. If his son had completed ROTC, he would have choices commensurate with his education and background. Now he would be a common foot soldier with a backpack and a rifle. As an indication of his scorn, he responded to Kurt's announcement with "Good, maybe they'll teach you to be neat."[59] His mother, on the other hand, reacted with anguish. Said a relative, "The prospect of losing her son in the impending holocaust made her cup of troubles overflow. She became despondent and morose."[60]

In March 1943, Kurt Vonnegut Jr., serial number 12102964—a "preposterously tall private," he thought—reported to Fort Bragg, North Carolina.[61]

3: To War in the Bridal Suite

1943–1945

IN HIS LUGGAGE for Fort Bragg, Kurt carried a typewriter, thinking he was beginning an adventure worthy of Hemingway and that "this was indeed first-rate literary material, of interest to a large readership."[1] The typewriter was too big to fit inside the locker under his bed, so he left it out, where it would indicate he was a rarefied foot soldier, if ever there was one. Returning to the barracks one afternoon, he discovered it had been stolen.

On the rifle range he was a natural, having practiced for years on handguns and weapons in his father's collection. "I had learned to fire a .45, I learned how to do that when I was a kid."[2] The M-1 Garand .30-caliber semiautomatic was a "wonderful rifle."[3] He taught himself how to take apart, reassemble, and fire a Browning Automatic Rifle because he admired its versatility as a light machine gun.[4] His assigned duty was assembling, firing, and maintaining the army's most powerful piece of field artillery, the 240-millimeter howitzer that threw a 360-pound shell more than fourteen miles. "We had all we could do to take care of that monster."[5] Yet despite thirteen weeks of training on tactics and weapons, Vonnegut later claimed he was unprepared to be an infantryman.[6]

Luckily, he qualified for the Army Specialized Training Program (ASTP) based on his aptitude test scores and IQ. If he completed the ASTP course of study, consisting of eighteen months spread over six three-month terms, he would graduate with a four-year degree in engineering from the University of Tennessee and an officer's commission.[7] At the beginning of the summer, he left for Carnegie Mellon University in Pittsburgh to study introductory mechanical engineering. In September he continued his coursework at the University of Tennessee in Knoxville.

His classes covered thermodynamics, mechanics, and machine tools. "I did badly again," he said years later. "I am very used to failure, to being at the bottom of every class."[8] But he didn't fail. He received a 68 in thermodynamics; an 85 in shop practice; a 68 in calculus; an 85 in statistics and dynamics; and an 86 in mechanical engineering drawing— a C+ average.[9] For friendship, Kurt preferred the company of "boisterous, prosperous" scientists from nearby Oak Ridge National Laboratory. Over a drink, the chemists, technologists, and physicists became loose-lipped about what they were working on. Most could only speculate about their mysterious work. A publicist for the lab, Richard Gehrman, confided to Vonnegut that his job was to keep the bibulous men of science guessing about how exactly they were contributing to top-secret projects.[10]

THOSE SIX months of studies at the University of Tennessee didn't lead to a promotion, as it turned out. In the spring of 1944 the army brass canceled the ASTP program because an additional fifty thousand men were needed to support the Allies' secret plans for D-day. Private Vonnegut was reassigned to the 106th "Golden Lion" Division, Second Battalion, 423rd Regiment and ordered to report to Camp Atterbury in Indiana to train as an intelligence and reconnaissance (I&R) scout. The forty-thousand-acre Camp Atterbury was close to Indianapolis, at least, and he could go home on weekend passes.[11]

Jane was in Indianapolis again as well, having graduated Phi Beta Kappa in English from Swarthmore. Kurt, thinking he was still in the lead for courting her, was writing her often and calling from the base pay phone. What he didn't know was that Kendall Landis was writing her just as assiduously. Landis had suspended his studies at Swarthmore at the end of his freshman year and enlisted as a cadet in the naval aviator program, which, if he didn't wash out, would lead to a commission. He loved Jane: "She was marvelous, and with her challenging intellect, she was constantly suggesting that I read books while I was in the Navy and I would report back to her on several of these books and we kept up a lively correspondence." To him, Jane was his girlfriend back at home.[12]

As a scout in a six-man squad, Vonnegut learned yet more battlefield skills at Camp Atterbury: patrolling, setting up observation posts, interpreting maps and aerial photos, and fighting hand-to-hand combat. His squad leader, Sergeant Bruce Boyle, instructed the men to choose a buddy.[13] Vonnegut paired up with a sardonic Irish-Catholic from Pennsylvania named Bernard V. O'Hare. For the duration, or until death, they were instructed to share food, ammunition, gear, clothing, and a blanket in freezing weather, if necessary.

O'Hare was a short man with a plain face—a big nose and high forehead—who smoked as much as Vonnegut, drank heavily, and talked laconically. His ambition was to practice law in his father's firm after the war. Vonnegut, in contrast to O'Hare's wry outlook, came off as a "tall, young, loudmouth guy. He was always talking and laughing and telling people what to do."[14]

In May, Kurt planned a surprise for his folks. For Mother's Day, he would arrive home on a three-day pass, unannounced, spit-and-polished in his uniform. Alice was visiting them too, married now to James Carmalt Adams, a University of Virginia graduate who had "majored in fun," said Jim's sister Donna, and was currently away on duty as a lieutenant flying spotter planes in the Army Air Corps.[15] Alice and Jim had known each other as children at Lake Maxinkuckee.

Edith and Kurt Sr. had been residing in their new Williams Creek home since Kurt Jr.'s freshman year at Cornell. Williams Creek, said the developer, in a classic piece of sales hyperbole, was the "Switzerland of Marion County," Indiana—four miles of curving streets through prairie hills. This time, Kurt Sr. had designed the two-story brick contemporary home himself. There was a large living room, a library, dining room, four bedrooms on the second floor, and a two-car garage. And in the basement, he built a workshop with a kiln for one of his hobbies, pottery making. Kurt Jr. found the house modest in size with a pleasant setting in the woods.[16] Their income was steady now because Kurt Sr. had been working as a technician in connection with the war effort, first at the Air Support Command Base in Columbus, Indiana, forty miles south of Indianapolis, and then as superintendent of materials control at Fall Creek Ordnance plant near his home.[17]

For Edith, however, the smaller house was a distressing step down. Few people outside her family knew, or would believe, that the plump, suburban Mrs. Vonnegut with the dyed dark hair and severe expression had once been a red-haired American heiress illuminating the social season in Edwardian London; that heel-clicking Prussian suitors right out of *The Merry Widow* had vied for her hand. Gone were the servants she had expected would always take care of the humdrum necessities of life. Under her window, no yardman raked up leaves on the lawn from beneath the elms, maples, and oaks. No maid straightened up her room, no cook made their meals. Even so, right before the Germans invaded France in 1940, she and Kurt Sr. had cashed the two remaining bonds left to them by his mother and spent three weeks in Paris. Said a relative, "It was going out with flair—all banners flying."[18] She adored that kind of melodrama and continued to infuse her short stories with it— stories typed by a secretary she couldn't afford—despite the fact that magazine editors kept returning her purple romances like bad checks.

After spending Friday and Saturday at home relaxing on leave, Kurt was awakened by Alice early Sunday morning, Mother's Day. Something was wrong with Mother, she said. Together, they went quietly into her bedroom, where Kurt bent over his mother. He left to get his father, who was sleeping in another room.[19] Edith Vonnegut, age fifty-six, was dead from an overdose of sleeping pills.

There was no note by the bedside.[20] There didn't need to be, although she might have left some words to assuage her family's grief. Edith Vonnegut's upper-class ideology had failed her. Faced with adversity, she couldn't adjust her hopes, her pretensions, not even her existence to the changes in her situation. Lying in bed for many days at a time, too unhappy to rise, she listened disconsolately to the radio and the laughter that might just as well have been directed at her. Later in his life, Vonnegut attributed his mother's death to a refined nature that wasn't strong enough to stand up to the times. "It was the war itself that wrecked my mother, and not war against Germany."[21] The simple truth was, Edith Vonnegut deigned not to go on living if she had to be like everybody else.[22]

The coroner ruled her death an accident, although Kurt Sr., according to his younger son, acknowledged to older relatives—not to his children—that his wife had killed herself.[23] He telephoned the local newspapers requesting that no news about her death or obituary appear. After his wife's funeral in Indianapolis's Crown Hill Cemetery, Kurt Jr. later wrote, his father became "a good man, in full retreat from life."[24]

To HER youngest child, Edith Vonnegut left a bedeviling "legacy," as he called it—"an air of defeat has always been a companion of mine."[25] Disquieting thoughts about self-destruction stung him throughout his life because of her deliberately timed death on Mother's Day. It jeered at his devotion. He inferred that she had not loved him, which created a self-hating syllogism: she did not love me; I didn't love her enough; therefore, I am a failure at love.

For the rest of his life, he directed people's attention to the manner of his mother's death as if it were something they should know about him. Meeting, for example, Donald M. Fiene, in 1972, then a PhD candidate in Slavic languages and literature at Indiana University, he brought it up almost immediately, Fiene recalled.[26] At a literary festival, fellow Indiana novelist James Alexander Thom remembered that Vonnegut "was warm, droll and charming as usual, but tended to steer the conversation toward suicide."[27]

Perhaps he talked about it often because he was never finished seeking a satisfactory explanation for why his mother would kill herself; on the other hand, he also may have sought ways to bring up the subject out of loyalty to her—a recognition of how she suffered—especially since his father didn't want his wife's death publicly acknowledged and refused to talk to his children about it. Another possibility is that Vonnegut felt guilty and wanted reassurance of some kind. What's certain is that his mother's suicide permanently erased some of life's luster for him. Later, when he began to write fiction, his obsession with self-destruction edges his fiction like a black border. As a character in one of his novels later says, "Sons of suicides find life lacking."[28] His fictional mothers too are always either morbid, crazy, or suicidal. One of them, formerly a beautiful woman in a Midwestern town as Edith Vonnegut was, swallows Drano and suffers a gruesome death. At least, says the narrator drily, "my mother ate sleeping pills, which wasn't nearly as horrible."[29]

Nothing could change that ghastly Mother's Day in Williams Creek, but Vonnegut knew what would have made his mother happier had she lived. She wanted to be a writer living on Cape Cod, where her family had spent halcyon weeks in the summer. As a retributive act, a gift to her spirit, he might try one day to do the same thing.[30]

LESS THAN a month after his mother's death, Vonnegut climbed into a jeep on June 15, 1944, and rode in a parade through Indianapolis's Monument Circle. The Normandy Invasion, D-day, had taken place just nine days earlier. Knowing he would be leaving soon, he decided he should propose to Jane.

His grief over his mother's death was reflected in his desperate attempt to force Jane to say yes. He tore open his shirt, exposing his chest. Dangling from a chain around his neck was a bloody molar, removed by his dentist. "This is how much I love you!" he pleaded, trying inarticulately to make a connection between sacrifice, pain, and love. Another version in the family lore describes him going down suddenly on one knee in her living room, as her astonished father looked on.[31] She did not say yes and gave no indication that she ever would.

Thus by late summer nothing between them had been resolved. Jane left for Washington, D.C., to begin a job as a clerk analyst in the counterintelligence branch of the Office of Strategic Services (OSS), the forerunner of the Central Intelligence Agency (CIA) located at Twenty-fifth Street and E Street NW. Meanwhile, Kurt's division, the 106th, spent all of September packing for overseas—a huge process for fifteen thousand soldiers and their equipment—to relieve the Second Division in Belgium at the front.

WAITING FOR the division when it reached New York was the RMS *Queen Elizabeth,* then the largest passenger ship ever built, painted in wartime colors of battleship gray. Its steel hull was a thousand feet long with a "great big wide entrance door, as big as a wall," said one of the men, awed, "and we went in there."[32]

Vonnegut discovered that he had been assigned, ironically, to the bridal suite on the top deck, airier and more spacious than the decks down below. On the morning of October 17 the *Queen* shoved off into the Hudson. Thousands of men on deck crowded against the railing and even climbed the rigging, cheering the Statue of Liberty. As protection against German submarines patrolling the eastern coast, a blimp followed them out to sea for two days, and then they were alone. The Grey Ghost, as it was called, moved the troops at an impressive thirty knots (thirty-five miles per hour).

In Cheltenham, England, where the 106th reassembled two weeks later, camp life was routinized and unexciting. Then orders in late November to attend information sessions about the enemy—their uniform insignias, light weaponry, and language—made things more interesting. Like travelers who were about to meet the locals, Vonnegut and the others sat in rows repeating German phrases, most of which Kurt remembered from two years of German at Shortridge High School. The only other man in his squad who understood as many words was Robert Kelton, drafted during his sophomore year at the University of Illinois, Urbana-Champaign. Finally, everyone received bundles of warmer clothes: long underwear, long wool socks, four-buckle overshoes, wool sweaters, and knit caps. Rumor had it the division was being sent to the Ardennes Forest, where it would be snowy and cold. The good news was that the Ardennes sector had been quiet for months.

When Vonnegut and the rest of the 423rd Regiment crossed the English Channel on December 6 and waded ashore at Le Havre at dawn, it began to rain. Some of the men laughed and made cracks about "Sunny France." Surrounding him in the town was the first evidence of combat he had seen: bomb craters, burned-out buildings, and German antiaircraft guns pointed skyward. In a field nearby lay the remains of a crashed Allied bomber.[33] Vonnegut hiked himself over the tailgate of a transport truck and found a spot on a bench inside. Studying the faces of the men as they climbed aboard, his rifle clutched upright between his knees, he felt proud. He had made a choice, one that showed commitment and responsibility. Bernard had once called him "an accident," which unfortunately his recent failures seemed to bear out. But what he was doing now was honorable. It testified to his value, and he felt "utterly beyond reproach."[34] The muddy trucks, loaded up at last with human cargo, growled into gear and joined the swaying convoy headed toward Dieppe.

At first the landscape resembled Indiana—flat and rural. The trees had lost their leaves and smoke curled from the chimneys of farmhouses. But over the course of a week, as the trucks rode higher and higher, through the mountains of eastern Belgium and Luxembourg, the road penetrated forests of snow-covered evergreens and the men could see their breath. Lining the ditches, like a traffic jam bulldozed out of the way, were hundreds of German tanks and trucks, strafed and burned-out.

The truck ride ended in the Belgium village of St. Vith, the final bivouac before moving up to the front. The 106th Division was there to replace the Second Division, man for man, gun for gun—every position on twenty-seven miles of the Siegfried Line that had been seized from the Germans the previous August. Jumping down off the tailgate, Vonnegut heard shouts of "You'll be sorry!" and "Good luck, assholes!" as old hands observed with glee the clean uniforms and shaven faces of their fresh, untried replacements. Then after two days of organizing, the 106th began a twelve-mile eastern march into a hilly portion of western Germany known as the Eifel, part of the Ardennes Forest lying across the continuous borders of France, Belgium, and Luxembourg. Vonnegut's regiment, the 423rd, together with the 422nd, took up positions atop fir-covered Schnee Eifel (Snow Mountain), the most exposed salient of the entire American front. Below was a valley, rimmed by mountains on the other side.

One night a bright moon came out, and beyond the eastern slope where the Germans were waiting, the snow-covered valley shone. From somewhere out there, the newly arrived Americans could hear the clink of mess kits and the squeaking of mechanized vehicles.

AT 5:30 AM on December 16, 1944, the sky flashed red, green, amber, and white as flights of German "Screaming Meemies" with ear-splitting shrieks tore over the treetops on their way to destroy St. Vith. Wire communications failed and radio frequencies were jammed. The ferocious impact of shells from fourteen-inch German railroad guns shook the earth as a coordinated artillery barrage fell on the line companies, unit command posts, road intersections, and artillery batteries—all the division's strong points.

It was the start of Operation Autumn Mist, Hitler's last gamble to dash to the sea 120 miles away. Two hundred thousand German troops—crack, battle-tested infantry—protected by six hundred carefully hoarded

Panther and Tiger tanks, were attempting to punch a hole in the American line of eighty thousand troops. And as Hitler's generals knew, the weakest point in the Americans' defense was the salient of the 423rd and 422nd regiments, because the 106th had replaced the Second without making a single strategic change. (Later, as the German offensive progressed east to west, it created a bulge: hence, the Battle of the Bulge.) At 9:00 AM, a second German artillery barrage, which a GI reported to be "unbelievable in its magnitude," began pounding the two regiments, trying to erase them from the forest floor.[35]

For the next three days, the German high command hammered at the 423rd and the 422nd, slowly encircling the two regiments by coming around the Schnee Eifel from the south through the Prüm Corridor, and linking up with units coming into Schönberg from the north along the Andler–Schönberg road, intending to snip the Americans off at the base and open a giant gap in the Allies' offensive.

On the nineteenth, Vonnegut's regimental commander, Colonel C. C. Cavender, ordered Sergeant Boyle's reconnaissance squad to report on the right flank. Boyle, Vonnegut, Bob Kelton, Richard Davis, Bernie O'Hare, and Bill Sieber set out and quickly encountered a few enemy columns closing in. Continuing on, they entered a thicket of firs that ended abruptly at the edge of a farmer's field. On all sides the snap and sputter of small arms fire sounded like rice falling on a tin pan. Sieber signaled that he would leave the safety of the tree line first. Venturing out a few yards, he glanced left, right, then a rifle cracked on a ridge and he fell over. He raised himself on one elbow, dazed. "I need a medic, I'm hit."

The squad weighed the idea of one of them running out, grabbing Sieber by the heels, and dragging him back while the others laid down fire. But suddenly a mortar round exploded within a dozen yards. Before the enemy could readjust, the men hightailed it back the way they'd come through the woods, kicking up the snow like surf.

When they reached headquarters, Kelton requested a medic. Colonel Cavender denied permission because the regiment was about to surrender, he said, and he didn't want the men spread out.[36] Vonnegut, hearing Sieber was going to be left behind, realized he was not a hero-scout doing something fine but a kind of flotsam floating on the surface of events. Years later, he remembered his rage at feeling powerless:

"We're so smart, we can go out where the real soldiers haven't been yet, and find out what's out there! And our whole purpose was to either step on mines or to draw fire. Nobody knows what's out there and we're so fucking smart we're going to find out!"[37]

He found a swale to lie down in and wait. A dozen or so other men collapsed in exhaustion beside him. They had only a few rounds each; someone suggested they fix bayonets to prepare for the worst. An odd feeling came over him, as if the pandemonium would be resolved now. Whatever happened, it was just about over. "It was nice there for a few minutes."[38]

From the forest surrounding them, a German-accented voice, amplified by a loudspeaker, echoed through the late afternoon gloom. "We can see you. Give up." When no one got to his feet, hands up, German half-tracks lowered their antiaircraft guns and fired into the branches above Vonnegut and the others, sending bursts of shrapnel in all directions. Wounded men screamed.

"Come out!" ordered the voice.

Vonnegut got to his feet and rapidly began breaking down his weapon, fumbling with his frozen fingers to remove the piston, the trigger mechanism, and the bolt, the pieces falling into the snow. Last, he grabbed the barrel and slung the rifle, end over end, as far as he could. It landed in a creek. O'Hare, paging haphazardly through his phrasebook, shouted, "Nein Scheissen!" to the advancing German troops, thinking he was pleading "Don't shoot!" They laughed, including one who looked to be about fifteen carrying a machine gun. What O'Hare had said was "Don't shit!"[39]

Vonnegut put his hands on top of his helmet and waited.

TENS OF thousands of American prisoners marched east, two and three abreast, in a dark green river flowing for miles over the snow, its course shaped by German guards. The sun had set almost precisely at the time of Vonnegut's capture, and as he trudged beside the members of his squad it grew dark. After a couple of hours, the guards indicated that everyone was to lie down in the open field they were crossing. Vonnegut slept belly-to-butt with the other scouts, turning over every half hour or so.[40] At dawn, the march continued.

For the next two days, he stumbled along as "the supermen marched us," he wrote later, until Thursday morning, December 21, when the column arrived at a railroad siding of freight cars at Geroldstein, Germany, east of Prüm and west of Koblenz.[41] The guards threw open the doors of boxcars and ordered them to get in.

Vonnegut got a whiff of fresh cow dung inside.[42] With their rifle butts, the Germans packed in about sixty captives before sliding the doors shut and locking them. There was room enough to stand or squat, but "we literally could not all find space to lie flat at one time," said one of the prisoners.[43] Except for cracks between the slats, the only air and daylight came from louvered openings in each of the four corners. It took almost two days to load several thousand men onto dozens of cars; the train didn't get under way until nightfall.

Eighteen hours later, on the morning of the twenty-third, the POWs could see the Rhine River through the boxcar slats at Koblenz. In late afternoon, they felt the train slow as it rumbled into a railway yard marked LIMBURG. Sounds of the locomotive being disconnected made them wonder if they'd reached a camp. Then the engine chugged away, leaving them behind.[44]

A few hours passed, then red flares began falling from the sky, accompanied by air raid sirens and the rumble of planes growing louder. Low-flying British de Havilland Mosquito bombers, assuming the train was carrying German supplies, swooped down for an easy kill. There were shouts of "Stay in the car! It's safer in the car!" but hundreds of men, freed by the guards, leaped off and tried to run away.[45] Those who headed straight out from the train entered a curtain of explosions and disappeared. Others took cover, or wobbled in the direction of a barbed-wire fence where there was a concrete shelter. Only one boxcar received a direct hit, killing sixty-three men inside. The bombers peeled off. Lying between the craters in the yard were dozens of dead GIs, some still clutching a piece of bread doled out earlier in the day. In Vonnegut's boxcar, the men could hear pleas from someone out there begging to be shot.[46]

The train didn't move on Christmas Eve day as rails were repaired and another locomotive was found. The men sang Christmas carols that night, and the interior of a few boxcars glowed with pale light from stubby candles, retrieved from the pockets of dirty field jackets. Sometime the day after Christmas the train started up again.

They traveled to a second destination, the POW camp at Bad Orb, but, like a plague ship, were refused because the camp was over capacity. The prisoners spent another day swaying in the boxcars until they arrived at Stalag IV-B in Mülhberg, where the guards ordered them off. Instead of leading them through the main gate, however, they herded everyone to a grove of pine trees and instructed them to lie down in the snow. During the night, some men froze to death.

The next day, Vonnegut stood near the western wire of the camp, stamping his feet to ward off frostbite, waiting in line for hours to be processed. At the main gate, an Australian attached to the Royal Air Force Bomber Command, Geoff Taylor, watched a "large part of an American infantry division—the 106th—stumble into captivity."

Never before have you seen men so near the end of their tether. Plagued with dysentery, twisted with frostbite, starving, dirty, unshaven, staggering on their feet from exhaustion, a long line of men stumbles endlessly into the camp.

Captured before they knew what hit them, marched hundreds of miles into Germany, stepping over the bodies of comrades who slumped to die in the snow, jolted for days in cattle-trucks and boxcars that were strafed and bombed by the Allied air-fighters, the Americans are macabre burlesques of men.

Sometimes a man staggers and bumps the man next to him and they snarl weakly at each other. They are too shocked and dazed to do otherwise. The frosted air is alive with the bark of men coughing. A lot of them won't live to walk again. This is the end of the road. Outside the wire, by the Kommandantur office, a mountain of GI battle helmets and liners grows visibly bigger, dwarfing the Germans who stand by it. Inside our barracks, confusion reaches fantastic heights.

It's just as well we organized the bunks and tin-bashed mugs and plates for the new arrivals. The shambles would have been unimaginable had we not. As it is, our carefully-balanced world of unwritten taboos, tribal laws and customs reels under the impact of thousands of men so shocked by their experiences that many are little more than animals stumbling erect.[47]

As the men came in through the main gate, tossing their helmets in a pile and receiving cast-off, frozen clothing with a distinctive red triangle to signify POW, a wagon passed, heaped with the bodies of Russians, dead from starvation and malnutrition. Hatred between the Russians and the Nazis ran deep, and the Russians were being allowed to starve, forced to feed themselves with the garbage and leftovers the British and Western European prisoners would not eat.[48]

On his third day in camp, Vonnegut was given a postcard as required by the Geneva Convention. He assured his family that he had come "through the whole God-awful slaughter without a scratch. . . . We prisoners will be the first sent home when peace is won, and then for a 90-day leave. This life is not bad at all. Contact the Red Cross for advice on parcels and dispatch them immediately." He asked for cigarettes "because they serve as money here and would make life considerably more lush."[49]

He wandered around the camp for a few days cadging smokes, attended a performance of *Cinderella* by the British in drag ("I should have left when midnight struck . . . lackaday, fucked my luck"), then a bit of news came his way.[50] With the stalag so overcrowded, a work detail was forming for the city of Dresden. During roll call one morning, the Germans came down the line and said, "You . . . you . . . you." Eventually 150 POWs from the 106th were selected, including Vonnegut, for Arbeitskommando 557, departing Stalag IV-B for Dresden on January 12, again by train.

Just days before, Kurt Sr. had received a telegram from the War Department saying his son was missing in action as of December 21, 1944. "That's that," Uncle Alex wrote sadly to Walt Vonnegut's wife, Helen.[51] Kurt's family would not receive his postcard from Stalag IV-B for months and didn't know whether he was alive or dead. Until then, except for a handful of men in the Arbeitskommando who knew him by name, he was just another prisoner living from moment to moment.

DRESDEN, ROYAL residence of dukes and kings of Saxony since the Middle Ages, whose Baroque skyline had inspired painters such as Canaletto, where Friedrich Schiller had written "Ode to Joy," and which Napoleon had seized for his imperial command, greeted the 150 POWs trudging into the city on January 12, 1945, with a billboard proclaiming TRINK COCA-COLA.[52]

Modernity had long since come to Germany's seventh largest city, resting snug in a bend of the Elbe River. But the first half of the twenti-eth century was just the patina on seven centuries of culture that had elevated Dresden to the title of "Florence on the Elbe." So deep and rich was Dresden's past that, after more than half a millennium as a center of art and technology, its museums preserved a continuous record of Western achievements in science and the humanities since the thir-teenth century. Everywhere the POWs looked, it seemed, war had not punctured the nimbus of this great city. The residents' belief that Dres-den was inviolable because of its treasures had given rise to a sense that they were on the sidelines of the war. Proof lay in the fact that there hadn't been a serious air attack, only occasional strikes.[53] The week before Christmas, the local defense commissioner, referring to the fighting in the Ardennes, declared, "This Christmas will be beautified for us by the fact that we can see our people back on the offensive."[54] To ring in the holidays, the renowned boys' choir of Dresden's oldest school had performed in concert under the towering dome of the mid-eighteenth-century Frauenkirche, where Johann Sebastian Bach had once given a recital. At the opera house, the city's Hitler Youth, stand-ing before a red curtain displaying a giant black swastika encircled in white, had sung patriotic and traditional songs of the season.[55]

The prisoners walked through the cobblestone streets under guard, largely ignored by Dresdeners. Work details of captives had become part of the city's traffic for several years now. Most mornings, small groups of them could be seen waiting at tram stops, accompanied by a guard who was either elderly, injured, or otherwise unfit for frontline duty. The city was under considerable stress, however, from the thou-sands of German refugees streaming into Dresden from the east, flee-ing the advance of Marshal Ivan Konev's Ukrainian army. The population had almost doubled, from six hundred thousand to a mil-lion. Six thousand refugees were living in a cavernous air raid shelter beneath the railroad station designed to hold only two thousand. Some of the strain on the overcrowding situation had been relieved by the clockwork deportation of Dresden Jews. Of the approximately six thou-sand at the beginning of the war, there were only a few hundred Jewish residents left, and they were slated for removal to the death camps later that spring.

The men of Arbeitskommando 557 finally arrived at their assigned quarters located in the oldest neighborhood in Dresden, the Altstadt, on the Grosses Ostragehege, a large area of common land. They were housed in a large rectangular slaughterhouse converted into a POW camp with the addition of an encircling wall topped by barbed wire. Despite the building's intended purpose—to prepare animals for slaughter—Vonnegut found nothing objectionable about this "nice new cement-block hog barn," outfitted with double-decker bunks, and tables and chairs, but only two small stoves for warmth.[56] The latrine was in the yards, and farther away was a tall warehouse beneath which were two levels of basements so deep they provided natural cold storage for hanging sides of meat.

The men assembled in the yard for instructions from an SS captain, a short middle-aged man with a small mustache like Hitler's.[57] The name of their compound, he said loudly, was Schlachthof-Fünf— Slaughterhouse-Five. It would be pointless to try to escape because the war was finished.[58] Even so, escaping POWs were still enemy soldiers and would be shot. Likewise, plundering was another offense punishable by firing squad.[59] And third, the guards were unlikely to know any English. Good daily relations necessitated an interpreter with enough knowledge of both languages to maintain lines of communication. The captain asked for volunteers who would admit to knowing enough German to serve as translator.[60] The interpreter would be exempt from some work assignments because he would have to supervise.

Vonnegut and three others volunteered, including Bob Kelton from the reconnaissance squad. Each was interviewed until the choice came down to two candidates: Vonnegut or Kelton. Vonnegut was chosen because he was more proficient in the language—a benefit of his two years of high school German.[61] From now on, he would serve as the foreman who would relay work orders to POWs and represent the prisoners if they had a complaint.

The following morning someone banging on a pan outside the slaughterhouse woke them up, yelling, "Get up, you lousy Chicago gangsters! Work, work, you lazy gangsters!"[62]

The men—most of whom had spent a good part of the night in the latrine with dysentery—assembled in the yard, exhausted. The noisemaker was a blond Hitler Youth about seventeen years old who lived on a mink farm, but relished coming into the city every day to play Nazi martinet.[63] He had been issued a rifle because his uncle was the former mayor of Dresden. Flanking him was a gray-haired sergeant, one eye covered by a black patch—"One Lamp Louie," the prisoners decided to call him. "You gangsters!" shouted the teenager. "We will show you how to work." He paced back and forth, rifle slung over his shoulder, one hand behind his back, looking tough.[64] The men derisively nicknamed him "Junior."

Their first assignment, One Lamp Louie patiently announced, would be clearing a side street blocked by rubble from an apartment building and grocery store destroyed during a minor bombing raid. In a double column they filed out the gate and were led by a handful of guards, including Junior, to the work site, where an avalanche of broken bricks and masonry had created a hillock in the middle of the street. Wagons stood nearby to haul the debris away. As the men worked, they uncovered bits of month-old food such as cookies from the grocery store—dirty and gritty but preserved by the cold and edible.[65] Looting was punishable by firing squad, but surreptitious bites of something now and then seemed reasonable.

The next day, and for several days afterward, women in the neighborhood left sandwiches for the prisoners wrapped in newspaper, perched on the rubble about half a block away. But one afternoon the guards ambushed them doing it and chased them off. The women didn't come back.[66]

RETURNING TO the barracks after a day's labor, the men received a bowl of watery soup and a half-inch-thick slice of black pumpernickel bread. Two times a week, bits of meat floated in the soup, and sometimes a piece of cheese accompanied the bread. The bread they were told to save until morning when the ersatz coffee arrived. Weekly Red Cross packages were supposed to be delivered, containing two pounds of tinned meat, one pound of powdered milk, sugar, prunes, raisins, M&M's, and dried biscuits that would puff up in water. But full packages arrived only once; then partial packages started to come infrequently with less and less food inside.[67] The men began to starve.

Food—just the word *food*—became sacred, an object of veneration and fascination. The prisoners described it, daydreamed about it, made menus of delicacies they were going to eat when they got home again.

A favorite subject was Thanksgiving dinner, and how bevies of mothers and grandmothers brought bountiful dishes to dining room tables of grateful, waiting relatives. Vonnegut obsessed about candy bars. He swore he was going to eat every kind ever made when he got home—Almond Joy, Milky Way, PayDay, Hershey's, Clark Bar—and loved to talk about what it would be like with his mouth stuffed. A fellow prisoner told him to shut up about it, and they got into an argument.[68]

White patches began appearing on Vonnegut's skin—impetigo from vitamin deficiency. His job as foreman required him to negotiate occasionally between the POWs and the guards, but hunger was making it hard for him to think. Some of their captors were fair, concerned about keeping the peace to avoid trouble with their superiors. One Lamp Louie, in particular, came across as avuncular and made small talk in broken English with the men. But others were sadistic.[69] Junior roamed everywhere like a ferret hunting for the weak.[70] One of his favorite tricks was to catch a man bending over and then hit him between the legs with the rifle butt.[71]

To dull the ache in his belly and sharpen his wits, Vonnegut, like everyone else, bartered smokes for food and vice versa. A good touch for food was Private Edward "Joe" Crone from Rochester, New York, because he would always swap his portions for smokes. Feeling a little guilty, the other prisoners took his bread, cheese, or soup in exchange for cigarettes, which he constantly craved.

In fact, there was something unworldly, and definitely unsoldierly, about Crone all around. Just a glance at his childlike face framed by big ears said he would never have a nickname like "Rocky" or "Brownie" the way two other guys in the Arbeitskommando did.[72] He told everyone he was going to be ordained an Episcopalian minister when he got home. Before the war, as proof of his seriousness about his ministerial calling, he had listed on his application to Hobart College the dates of five years of perfect attendance at St. Paul's Episcopal Sunday School in Rochester. His high school assistant principal, wondering how to praise a youngster who had a reputation for being physically awkward and shy, recommended Joe to the admissions office at Hobart as a young man "possessed of great moral courage."[73]

In his sophomore year at Hobart, he was drafted and Joe made an uncomplaining but terrible infantryman. On long marches, his assigned buddy in the 423rd regiment would get fed up having to "walk behind him and pick up all the utensils falling out of his backpack. He could never do it right."[74] He seemed unwilling to believe that his survival would largely depend on what he carried. Observing him, Vonnegut realized, "Joe didn't understand the war and of course there was nothing to understand. The world had gone completely mad."[75]

In this bewildered young man who kept expecting a rationale that would explain to his satisfaction the ultimate bedlam that is war, Vonnegut later found the protagonist, Billy Pilgrim, for his novel *Slaughterhouse-Five.*

SOME LUCK came Vonnegut's way when he was assigned to something better than clearing rubble—better because it would put him in the vicinity of food. He and a dozen other POWs were transferred to a malt factory, unloading bags of grain from boxcars and filling up burlap sacks with it before hauling them to a storage area.

In one part of the building, ovens roasted the ingredients of imitation coffee: wheat, sugar beet shavings, and chicory. In another section there was a kitchen where women were cooking and straining, in bubbling pots, malt and barley mash into high-carbohydrate syrup for pregnant women. He found excuses—everyone in the work detail did—to cut through the kitchen. As he passed the vats of malt stuff, he dawdled. Then, if the cooks were busy, he shoved a hot, dripping dollop of it into his mouth with a spoon. The women knew what he and the others were doing, but they "were sympathetic human beings," remembered one of the prisoners. They turned their backs just long enough so that ravenous young men—if they were quick and discreet—could gulp a dark golden blob of the wonderful syrup, which, said one, "warmed our stomachs and gave us additional energy and the desire to keep living."[76]

ONE DAY, when the men returned to the slaughterhouse, a stranger with an odd English-American accent hailed them. He was a representative of the Red Cross, he said, just arrived to check on their welfare. Were the fellas getting enough to eat? Were they okay? Naturally, the men showered him with complaints about the food, the threadbare uniforms, and the lack of wood for the stoves on cold nights. He listened with concern and recommended that they not wait for things to improve, because the war was turning against the Allies. The defeat in the Ardennes was just the beginning. It was true! In the meantime, the Germans were forming an elite unit of top-notch GIs to fight the Russians on the eastern front. Anybody who signed up would be guaranteed the works: warm uniforms, good food, and, most important, dignity. All they had to do was climb aboard.

No one spoke, so the stranger went through his spiel again, this time a little more urgently, until the POWs communicated by their throat clearing and loud spitting that they were getting annoyed. He shrugged, promised to report back to the Red Cross, and strolled away, seemingly unconcerned.[77] The following day, they found flyers left on their bunks awaiting their signature.

Vonnegut, thinking about the stranger's performance—weirdly scripted right down to using wooden American slang—decided he was a German actor hoping to euchre starving prisoners into fighting for the Reich if it meant food.[78]

THE BARRACKS had to be scrubbed down every day, and it fell to Vonnegut to tell the five prisoners on that detail what the guards wanted done, though after a month in the compound his supervision was hardly needed. Usually, his translations began, straight-faced, with "What these cocksuckers want us to do is . . ."[79] The men moved slowly, hobbled by lack of food as they swept the floor, cleaned out the potbellied stoves, wiped down the tables, and, last, emptied the brimming cans in the latrine. They went about the tasks, step by step, like tired automatons.

One morning Vonnegut watched with irritation as a new guard hassled a prisoner who was half lying on a table because he was sick, dragging a rag back and forth. The guard poked him with his rifle, prodding him to move faster. Clutching his stomach, the prisoner resumed wiping as best he could. But the guard, still not satisfied, raised his rifle and brought the butt down hard on the man's ribs.

"You fucking swine," Vonnegut said.

The guard struck him with the rifle, knocking Vonnegut out.[80]

His court-martial began the same day. The captain informed him that as translator he had insulted the honor of Germany and abused the privileges accorded him. Then he was beaten for insubordination. At the slaughterhouse, the men were taken aback at how he'd been worked over.[81] Not only had he been smashed in the face by the guard; his collar was dark with blood from a blow behind the ear that had split his scalp.[82] He would no longer be their foreman, he explained—another prisoner would be both interpreter and in charge of the rations. From now on he would be just a laborer.

HE FELL in for roll call the next morning, noticing Junior off to the side, just staring at him. The "pain in the ass," as he was ubiquitously known, had gotten up early and made sure to bring his rifle, but this time a sheathed bayonet was attached to it. A new game was about to begin, one that Junior had invented, and involving only two players: himself and Vonnegut.

"Each day, for weeks, as we reached our place of work," said another POW, "and the other ten or twelve guards scattered out among the one hundred fifty of us prisoners, the obnoxious kid whom we had nick-named Junior, would affix his bayonet to his rifle and then follow Kurt Vonnegut around, hour after hour." Whenever Vonnegut paused, slowed down, or stopped for a breath, Junior would jab him with the steel tip of the bayonet and snarl, "Vonnegut! You are lazy. You Americans are all lazy. You do not know the meaning of work. We Germans are strong!" The idea was to bait him into losing his cool. If he slapped away the bayonet, Junior could report that the prisoner had threatened him.[83]

The contest continued as the other prisoners watched the "trial of will between Junior and Kurt," said one, "wondering who would even-tually triumph."[84] Every night before lockup, Junior obviously relished ordering him to perform one last duty: emptying the latrine. "Vonne-gut, you must clean das shitters," forcing him to go barefoot in the snow at times.[85] But the tall American private wordlessly did that too and never gave his personal guard an excuse to have him killed.

THE WINTER weather in Dresden lifted abruptly on Shrove Tuesday, February 13, 1945, ushering in a hint of spring. On this last day before the beginning of Lent, small children begged to be allowed to wear their costumes early for the traditional Carnival Night, and teenage girls hurried to hem their dresses in time for visits to relatives' homes. North of the Elbe River, the Circus Sarrasani finished erecting its huge domed tent, expecting a full house because the skies promised to be clear.[86] The POWs were vaguely aware of the holiday, but everything seemed to be happening far away.

That night, air raid sirens sounded at 9:51 PM. Many of the Shrove Tuesday celebrants returning home barely hurried. Looking up, they saw no bands of blue-white searchlights crisscrossing the darkness overhead and no antiaircraft guns pounding at enemy planes, because there were no searchlights or antiaircraft guns remaining in the city at all. They had been dismantled and taken by trucks to protect the industrial areas of the Ruhr Valley.

Ten minutes after the air raid sirens began moaning, brilliant magnesium parachute flares fell from the sky—"Christmas trees," some romantic-minded Germans called them.[87] Dresden's buildings, fountains, statues, trees, rail lines, the zoo, the Circus Sarrasani—the Elbe River itself—were all illuminated for the last time, in a kind of flickering snapshot of seven hundred years of European civilization.

Looking down, RAF crews of eight hundred Avro Lancaster bombers saw their target crystallized by the flares and got ready to drop 1,400 tons of high-explosive bombs and 1,180 tons of incendiary bombs on the city. The first would devastate the railway yard, a meeting place of main lines to eastern and southern Germany, Berlin, Prague, and Vienna, and destroy Dresden's roads and telephone lines; the second would melt the rubber and lubricants on the machinery in factories, rendering them useless. Thirty-five miles away to the southwest, over Chemnitz, an equal number of bombers were pounding more railway yards and factories, and smaller groups were attacking Böhlen (a town south of Leipzig), Nuremberg, Bonn, and Dortmund.[88] With the infrastructure destroyed in key places, the Red Army would have an easier time advancing east. Regardless, the Russians would lose 405,000 troops in the last forty-two miles approaching Berlin, about the number of American army soldiers who died during all of World War II.[89]

At 10:05 PM, the target finder over Dresden in a howling Mosquito bomber dropped a red flare and called out into his headset, "Tally ho!" The first attack had begun.[90]

ONE LAMP Louie roused the POWs out of their bunks, hurried them across to the yard, and then sent them down the precipitous steps of the storage building toward the lower basement, sixty feet underground. A German corporal and three privates rushed behind, shutting the steel door after them.

There was room for everyone on the floor between the sides of beef hanging in rows from the ceiling on tenterhooks. Vonnegut listened, as "Giants stalked the earth above us. First came the soft murmur of their dancing on the outskirts, then the grumbling of their plodding towards us, and finally the ear-splitting crashes of their heels upon us."[91] Each convulsive blast overhead shook the rows of beef, making them dance, and white calcimine dust fell from the ceiling.

Even at eight thousand feet, it was hot work for the RAF bomber crews. Thousand-degree heat scorched the bellies of the planes, and smoke rose to fifteen thousand feet, making the aviators wet with perspiration. The intensity of the firestorm below created superhot tornadoes, mile-high vortexes ripping oxygen from the air to feed their roaring, thermal engines. The torquing effect on the atmosphere hurled people, animals, and furniture skyward, up from a city that was falling down underneath them.

The director of the Historical Museum and Weapon Gallery ran through the streets hoping to save a truck loaded with 154 paintings and irreplaceable items that had been due to leave the next day ahead of the Russian advance. The truck had left, but when he reached the museum, where forty-two large paintings still hung on the walls, too large to be moved, the building was in flames.

Below ground, thousands of Dresdeners became terrified at the thought of being buried alive. A seventeen-year-old girl cowering in her nightgown, "didn't even feel the cold, for the light went out, the children immediately began screaming again, then three of the women began to scream and rage like mad, while one old woman stood in a corner and prayed to God from the bottom of her heart."[92] In another basement, an eleven-year-old girl saw her father plant his feet and push with all his strength against a wall beginning to collapse.

Three hours after the first attack, the second wave of RAF bombers flew over as survivors, rescue squads, and firefighters scurried through the streets, lured above ground by a false notion that the bombing had ceased. Five hundred Lancasters released one thousand tons of explosives. At the Dresden train station, with its huge, vaulted roof, where thousands of people had crammed into the city's largest shelter during the first bombing wave, still more tried forcing their way in during the second raid, creating strata of corpses from the platforms to the bottom of the shelter.

AT DAWN on Wednesday morning the fourteenth, approximately eight hours after the first attack, Vonnegut and the others climbed the steps, Lazarus-like, to see what had happened. Overhead, P-51 Mustang fighters zoomed over streets and bridges, strafing anything that moved, adding fatalities like pebbles to the mountain of sixty thousand dead.

Blocking the top of the stairs was a side of beef, blown out from a locker and flash-cooked. The men rushed forward and tore off pieces, shoving them into their mouths and pockets. One Lamp Louie ordered them to stop, but they ignored him, grunting to get at the food. Shouting, he drew his Luger and fired several shots in air, getting them to back off, still chewing.[93] He instructed them to find a wagon and a tarpaulin to cover the meat. If they were seen stealing, there'd be trouble. They got a wagon, loaded it with meat, and then covered their treasure with blankets and pots.[94]

The guards ordered everyone to fall in. They had a predicament to solve: what to do with an enemy band of 150 men. The prisoners had practically no identity. They had emerged from the grave, so to speak, and if they were never seen again, it would be assumed that they had been turned to ash.

Vonnegut waited like the others, a skeletal survivor with ulcerated legs, swaying in the wind that was bleak and raw, or warm and shimmering, depending on whether it came over the river at his back or from a fire. There was no sound except the brush of freezing air against his filthy clothes and the susurration of buildings burning.

If he still had any feelings of being unique—the myth of invincibility typical of young people—despite the Battle of the Bulge, his capture, and incarceration, the dregs of those feelings must have drained off now, replaced by a profound loneliness and sense of almost cosmic isolation.[95] Hours passed, the morning of the fourteenth wore on, and the men were finally permitted to mill about, until word came down that all of Arbeitskommando 557 would be housed with the British South

African troops in the suburb of Gorbitz, four miles to the west. The prisoners spent the rest of the morning commandeering enough carts and wagons for the journey.

The first men exiting the gate of the compound gasped in surprise. There was a nude woman with a beautiful figure, lying on her back, arms upraised. It was a mannequin, they realized, the pattern of its torched dress tattooed on its plaster thighs.[96] All that morning, the effects from volcanic blasts of high explosives and the firestorms continued to present freakish tableaux as the POWS struggled through the streets pushing or dragging their carts. They passed the corpse of a boy with his burned dog at the end of a leash; bodies of children dressed in party clothes; blackened drivers slumped at the wheels of their cars; couples who had leaped into fountains for safety and plunged into boiling water instead. The Dresden zoo, blown open by direct hits, had released its ark of animals into the wild. The men spotted a llama mounting slopes of debris. Exotic birds, with no trees to sit in, preened themselves on twisted iron railings. A chimpanzee, once popular with children, sat alone without hands.[97]

The procession staggered on. The wheels of the wagons, iron-rimmed, banged over rubble and slid through sticky, melted asphalt. The hubs and axles became clotted with reeking pitch. Heaps of fallen bricks and burning vehicles sometimes rendered the way ahead impassable, and then the caravan would have to turn back and find another route. Behind them, they heard explosions as a third wave of bombers at midday, this time consisting of three hundred American Eighth Air Force B-17s, dropped eight hundred tons of high explosives on the railway yards.[98]

The last half mile of the trek was a Sisyphean push up a steep brick street. To keep the wagons from rolling backward, the wheels had to be chocked every few feet with rocks. At last they arrived, welcomed by the British South Africans who had spent three years in captivity and were eager for news. One Lamp Louie assigned the bunks, two men in each one. It was strictly the luck of the draw, and Vonnegut got a spot in the front row near two toughs from New York who made it clear nobody had better mess with them.[99]

With everyone settled, the old sergeant went home. One of the prisoners later heard One Lamp Louie had lost his parents in the bombing.[100]

*   *   *

THURSDAY MORNING, February 15, Arbeitskommando 557 was herded back into the city under guard to begin cleaning up Hell. Several times the column had to scramble behind heaps of rubble when a P-51 swung in and fired long bursts from its six .50-caliber machine guns, stitching the road with geysers of dirt. As they reached the outskirts of the city, gauntlets of incensed Dresdeners jeered and threw stones at them.[101]

They arrived at the slaughterhouse, where the SS captain with the Hitler mustache met them ready with new orders: the Arbeitskommando would be divided into work details of ten to fifteen. Some would clear rubble; some carry bodies; some retrieve what could be salvaged from the meat lockers. The punishment for looting was death by firing squad.

Eager for the work to get under way was Junior, bayonet affixed to his rifle, already rattling off his usual litany of invectives. To show he meant business, he punctuated his hectoring by jabbing a few of the men for good measure.[102] One of the prisoners, seeing the guards' backs were turned, suddenly wrenched the rifle out of Junior's hands and pushed him against a wall, the tip of the bayonet pressed to his heart.

"Get the *fuck* out of here!"

The teenager slid sideways along the wall until he reached the corner and then ran away. No one saw him after that.[103]

VONNEGUT'S JOB was finding the remains of residents smothered in basements by the firestorms. Superheated tornadoes had sucked out the oxygen and turned hiding places into tombs. Basements, he said, "looked like a streetcar full of people who'd simultaneously had heart failure. Just people sitting there in their chairs, all dead."[104]

Teams from the Arbeitskommando passed through a cordon of German soldiers to begin what Vonnegut called a "terribly elaborate Easter egg hunt."[105] Some Dresdeners couldn't contain their rage and grief as they watched the bodies of neighbors and family members, dragged by ropes around their ankles, disinterred from homes that had become their graves. A German officer grabbed one of the Americans, threw him against a wall, and put a pistol to his head, shouting, until the guards finally managed to calm him down.[106] In the streets, corpses were stacked high on wooden ricks, sprinkled with lime, and set afire.

To reach flooded basements accessible by narrow stairs, the guards formed the prisoners into relays, sending one captive down at a time. "Encouraged by cuffing and guttural abuse, wade in we did," wrote Vonnegut. "We did exactly that, for the floor was covered with an unsavoury broth from burst water mains and viscera."[107] Down there, the captives fought off hysteria when limbs of corpses snapped off or yanking a gas mask hose pulled off a head.

Weeks passed, and the funk everywhere indicated that the bodies burned on pyres represented a fraction of what still remained below. The captain assembled the Arbeitskommando for new instructions: they were to recover items of identification and valuables only.[108] Once the prisoners had resurfaced with everything they could find, German troops, some of them with experience in the death camps, stepped forward with flamethrowers. The ceremonies associated with respecting the dead had ended, and jets of ignited gasoline converted former sanctuaries for the living into catacombs.

BY GOING into cellars day after day, a POW named Michael Palaia saw what all the other prisoners did, too. There were subterranean pantries of pickled asparagus, pickled onions, apple butter, cherries, string beans, beets, carrots, jams, jellies, sausage, pie fillings, and berry syrup—groaning shelves of sealed jars that a starving man could steal if he were careful.[109]

Palaia was one of the older prisoners and unable to withstand the deprivations as well as the younger men. While he was in a basement on the last day of March, someone shouted down at him, "Hey, the SS troops are coming, you better get your ass out of there, if there's anybody in there!"[110] Selecting a jar of pickled string beans, he stashed it under his coat and walked back out into the street. The Arbeitskommando was about to begin the return four-mile march to Gorbitz, and he was looking forward to sitting on his bunk and eating the beans.

The SS officers who spotted him might have passed him by except he had made himself conspicuous through an earlier, fatal choice. From the frozen pile of overcoats inside the gate at Stalag IV-B, he had grabbed a heavy one that was different from most. On the back were the letters *CCCP*—the Russian abbreviation for Union of Soviet Socialist Republics. The SS ordered him to stop and unbutton his coat. There was nothing he could do—the contraband was a good-sized jar, and they plucked it out. Later that night, said Vonnegut, Palaia was court-martialed and ordered to sign a document he didn't understand, admitting he was guilty of looting.[111]

The next morning, April 1, Palm Sunday, guards issued shovels to Kurt and three other prisoners and took them to a rise within sight of the camp so the rest of the Arbeitskommando could see the example being set. The four men were ordered to dig graves while Palaia and a Polish soldier stood nearby.[112] When they had finished, an officer turned Palaia and the Polish soldier around by their shoulders, stepped back, and shouted an order. A firing squad shot the prisoners in the back; the Germans reloaded and shot them again. Vonnegut and the others were ordered to pick up the bodies and place them each in a grave. One of the Americans, knowing Palaia had been a Catholic like him, placed a rosary in his hands and said a prayer. Refilling the graves took a matter of minutes.[113]

Later, when telling his family how impassively the executions were carried out, Vonnegut burst into tears. "The sons of bitches! The sons of bitches!"[114] He would model a character in *Slaughterhouse-Five* on Palaia, Edgar Derby, the forty-four-year-old English teacher executed for stealing a teapot.

BY MID-APRIL 1945 there were signs that the war was ending. A furtive Dresdener in a dark suit passed the work gangs regularly and whispered the latest news while looking straight ahead: "The Allies are at Freiburg" (a day's march away) or "the Rhine."[115] The German authorities, thinking ahead to the Allies' arrival, gave the POWs an unprecedented two consecutive days off and arranged for their clothes to be washed while the men were deloused and stood around, naked beneath their greatcoats.

One of them, James Mills, yellow with jaundice, was transported to Reviere Hospital at Görlitz, fifty-five miles east of Dresden.[116] Lying on a cot across from him was Joe Crone, the Hobart College undergraduate who had wanted to be an Episcopalian minister. He had never given up trading his food for cigarettes, in a childish gesture of defiance. The cigarettes he had craved, but he was sure he wouldn't be allowed to starve. So he had held out, expecting the scales would be balanced out somehow through compassion, decency, or Christian charity. Now he was dying of the "thousand yard stare," Vonnegut heard later. "When one chooses the thousand yard stare, this is what happens: the person sits down on the floor with his back to the wall, will not talk, will not eat, and just stares into the space in front of him."[117]

He was nearly dead, but he only once asked Mills for help. "He was so skinny and weak and sick—he had to go to the bathroom during the night and all of us went over and tried to help him. We had to raise him up, get him at the angle, and somebody stick a can under him. He just absolutely couldn't do nothing and it took all of us to get him up so he would take a leak."[118]

The next morning he was dead.

Life no longer made any sense to Crone, Vonnegut said. "And he was right. It wasn't making any sense at all. So he didn't want to pretend he understood it anymore, which is more than the rest of us did. We pretended we understood it."[119]

The Germans buried him in a white paper suit because they had taken away his uniform while he was in the hospital. To Vonnegut, "he was beautiful," a kind of holy fool.[120]

ON FRIDAY, April 13, a passing tradesman whispered to some prisoners that President Roosevelt had died. That night, the guards informed Arbeitskommando 557 that the prisoners would be leaving the city in the morning. The guards seemed agitated, as if fearing that some tectonic shift was about to happen.

For the next two days, the column of hundreds of POWs, British and American, marched southeast along the Elbe River to the town of Pirna, and then up into the high mountains along the border separating Germany and Czechoslovakia to the village of Hellendorf, fifty miles in all. From the direction of the march, and the remoteness of the village, it was clear that the Germans wanted to lay low until they could be certain of surrendering to Allied forces and not Russian. For three weeks, the Dresden prisoners waited without enough to eat. They foraged in the fields for grass and dandelions.

The last straw for the guards came when Russian aircraft, roaring in low, machine-gunned anything on the ground, including cows grazing in fields. The Germans disappeared into the woods, leaving the British and American POWs to their fate.

Vonnegut, Bernie O'Hare, and four other men commandeered a horse and wagon, painted a white American army star on the sides, and plodded back in the direction of Dresden. Vonnegut couldn't remember why they headed back to the city, but once they arrived, he said, they were captured by Russian troops, taken in rickety Model A trucks to the Elbe at Halle, and traded one-for-one for Soviet prisoners in the custody of the Americans. Some of these, Vonnegut later heard, were Gypsies and collaborators. The Soviets shot or hanged hundreds of them.[121]

At Camp Lucky Strike in Le Havre, France, the POW repatriation center, Vonnegut stood in line, tossed his clothes into a pile, was deloused and issued a fresh uniform. He had lost forty pounds from a frame that was already thin; his legs were ulcerated; and a few of his teeth were loose from symptoms of scurvy. There were days of red tape and waiting. Getting out of Germany, he complained to O'Hare, was like walking in sand.[122]

During the trip home aboard a troopship, Vonnegut and O'Hare had time to talk. In Le Havre, O'Hare said, he had heard Mass and received communion for the first time in five months.[123] But it didn't take, he told Kurt.[124] Like Joe Crone, who saw with his thousand-yard stare a landscape where there was no God, O'Hare had lost his faith.

"I didn't like that," Vonnegut wrote later. "I thought that was too much to lose."[125]

4: Folk Society and the House of Magic

1945–1947

GETTING THROUGH MILITARY processing in the United States was as boring as killing time in Camp Lucky Strike had been in France. After arriving at Newport News, Virginia, in June, Kurt had said good-bye to his army buddy Bernie O'Hare. The rest of the month was spent waiting for the brass to finish the paperwork connected with Private Kurt Vonnegut Jr., who had been MIA for six months and still had part of his enlistment to complete. He was given a promotion to corporal, awarded a Purple Heart for frostbite, and assigned to report, following a furlough, to Fort Riley, Kansas, for easy duty: typing discharge orders for thousands of military men and women. His reaction was "Please, can't I go home? I've done everything I was supposed to do."[1] He spent part of the long unproductive days writing to Jane or calling her.[2]

"Well, the news about Kurt is that he hasn't gotten here yet," Jane wrote excitedly July 1, 1945, to her friend from Swarthmore, Isabella Horton Grant. "I'm as nervous as a cat."[3]

His letters were alternately funny, charming, or strangely downcast. In one he advertised himself as a vacuum cleaner, pointing out how he was all-purpose—always dependable, guaranteed, and hardworking. "Better buy Electrolux!"[4] In others, he was as romantic as a lovelorn soldier would be. He hadn't seen her since the summer of 1944 when he had proposed.

Then a letter arrived that left her feeling confused about where they stood. "I got the letter that said since he had a 60-day furlough and he might drop-in on me," Jane wrote Isabella, "in case I'm not married or some damn thing, signed 'As EVER, Your Chum'??? It took me a bit by surprise although I don't know exactly what I expected. . . . My chum indeed . . . the situation is nerve-wracking to say the least."[5]

But he was right not to assume too much. A year is a long time in the lives of young people, and Jane hadn't given him reason to hope. She still would not, until she had revisited a romantic avenue of her own, one more time. "Oh my, one of the main reasons I didn't write to my friend Isabella for so long was that I wanted to be able to say something really exceptionally dynamic, like a bombshell. . . . But then I guess dreams rarely come out just exactly as such—and as you can easily see, I had an alternative plan."[6] The alternative plan had been finding out whether Kendall Landis would propose before Jane's hometown boyfriend tried again. As leverage, she would use Kurt's year-old declarations of love.

Landis had returned to Swarthmore to resume his studies as a sophomore after serving two years as a pilot in the navy. It was only a three-hour drive from Swarthmore to Washington, where Jane was still employed by the OSS, and on a spring day in 1945 he and his "wartime girlfriend" met for a heart-to-heart. He was amused that she was still carrying around the government-issued .38 revolver in her purse. After catching up a bit, Landis remembered, "she told me that Kurt had proposed to her and she asked my advice as to whether or not she should accept that proposal."

He was twenty-two, only midway through college, and unable yet to take up a profession. Jane was slightly older, a college graduate with job experience, and in a position to settle down. He thought about her question, which was essentially whether he was going to let Kurt checkmate him. But he "couldn't, in any way, fancy becoming a partner in a marriage," he thought.

Should she marry Kurt then? she wanted to know.

He answered, "Why not?"[7]

It was the end of their relationship as lovers.

THE SECOND day of July, Vonnegut was allowed to leave Newport News for Camp Atterbury outside Indianapolis to officially start his furlough. But instead of taking the train directly home, he booked a route that would take him through Washington to see Jane. She went to meet him at Union Station, accompanied by her roommate, Marcia Gauger.

Amid the din of the hundreds of people on the platform crying out at the sight of loved ones, he stepped down from the train, hurried to give Jane a hug, and then made a deep bow.

"Aye, Lochinvar lovelies," he said in his best Scottish burr, "I will get the luggage!"[8] The two young women laughed.

Marcia noticed he looked very thin but "otherwise all right."[9] They asked him how he was feeling, and he replied pretty well, except for some problems with his skin. He hiked up a pant leg, revealing a polka-dot pattern of ulcers from vitamin deficiency, some of which had scarred over. Other than that, he insisted, he was fine—really.

He couldn't stay over in Washington for more than a day, but by coincidence, Jane was about to leave for Indianapolis because her mother was ill—one of her periodic breakdowns, unfortunately. So in a week's time, the erstwhile boyfriend and girlfriend would be back where they had first met as children in primary school. Kurt wasn't going to waste the home advantage. He intended to pop the question a second time.

KURT ARRIVED at Camp Atterbury on July 3. Replacing the air of suspense that had weighed so heavily the previous summer when his division was getting ready to ship overseas was peacetime, midsummer lethargy. Germany had surrendered two months earlier, and the war with Japan was winding down. Everywhere on the base, uniformed personnel were waiting with their duffel bags packed, or reading newspapers in the shade of the barracks, or listening to the Chicago Cubs disgrace the Boston Braves 24–2 on WLS radio. Kurt called home and Alice answered. He told her he would be outside the Officers' Club next day at three o'clock, ready to be picked up.

On the Fourth of July, Kurt Sr., Uncle Alex, and Alice drove through the front gate, Alex marveling at the thousands of GIs everywhere and work crews of German POWs keeping busy at odd jobs.[10] They parked as near as they could to the Officers' Club, but Kurt was nowhere in sight yet. Three o'clock came and went, but still no Kurt. And then, Alex wrote to relatives, "in the distance we saw a tall lad approaching, carrying a big heavy bag. Could it be Kay? Those long legs. It might be; it was!"

Alice ran to meet him, rushed into his arms, and kissed him. "Now, no emotions, please!" Kurt protested. Nevertheless, his father hugged him. Alex shook his nephew's hand warmly.

"I want to drive the car!" Kurt said, throwing his bag, inside of which was a Nazi ceremonial sword, in the trunk.[11] On the way home, he talked almost frantically to his family, building toward a catharsis. "I had never been really hungry before. I did not know what it means to be thirsty. To be really hungry is a strange sensation. You go nuts! But you mustn't give up—if you don't care, if you lie down and don't care, your kidneys go bad and you piss blood, and then you can't get up again and you just wilt away."

He tried to describe what had happened to Palaia for pilfering a jar of string beans, but he broke down. The cruelty of being shot in the back—he couldn't talk about it. "I want to get out. I've had enough of it. And I'm goddamned sick and tired of the whole damn fool bloody mess. I'm sick of it!"[12]

KURT WASTED no time in asking Jane to marry him, promising her "the future would be heavenly."[13] Where and when he proposed no one recalls, but by the end of July she had returned to Washington and was writing to friends that she was the fiancée of Kurt Vonnegut Jr.

In California, Isabella Horton Grant received news of the engagement from a mutual friend who had had lunch with Jane and gushed, "You should see her rock! It's so big that it practically covers her whole hand. It's an heirloom—his mother had a ring with two diamonds like that and then other diamonds around them and she had them made into two rings—one for Kurt and one for his brother."[14] Jane resigned from the Office of Strategic Services, giving as her reason, as so many Rosie the Riveters did in 1945, "to be married."[15]

The wedding of Jane Marie Cox and Kurt Vonnegut Jr. on September 14 took place on the terrace at the Coxes' home. Officiating the ceremony was a pastor from the Friends Church, a Quaker congregation. Ben Hitz, one of Kurt's boyhood friends, was best man; Jane had two bridesmaids: Alice Vonnegut Adams and a cousin, Mrs. Paul Fletcher. After the reception, the newlyweds left for a honeymoon at French Lick Springs resort on the edge of the Hoosier National Forest. From there they would come back up through Indianapolis and continue on to Lake Maxinkuckee. Kurt wanted his bride to see it with him.

Hitz, the best man, noticed something about his chum. Kurt "wasn't terribly happy. I think he was just back from the experience in the war and prison camps stuff that was still inside his head and it took a long time to come out."[16]

WHEN KURT and Jane arrived at Lake Maxinkuckee, the maple trees were showing signs of autumn. It was chilly in the morning but warm and sunny in the afternoon, an Indian summer. Kurt Sr. had sold their cottage at the end of the summer season, but the new owner graciously offered to wait a week before taking possession so that Kurt and Jane could have it to themselves.[17]

They went rowing, and Kurt explained proudly how, as a boy, he had swum the mile-and-a-half length of the lake with Bernard and Alice cheering him on from the *Beralikur*. Not much had changed since then. The Depression had put an entire decade under glass. Precisely at sunset, the cannon at Culver Military Academy boomed. And later, in the dark, a loon flipped to the surface and gave, as Kurt wrote, "its chilling, piercing, liquid cry of seeming lunacy."[18]

His friend Hitz was right about one thing having changed, however: Kurt was no longer the young fraternity man known for his campus high jinks. In fact, he had a rather humorless attitude toward marriage. He expected Jane to be a traditional wife who would blend her identity with his. Later he claimed it was just the tenor of the times: "Don't take any shit from a woman."[19] But his treatment of her had a sharp edge. Ever since high school, he had suffered, to his way of thinking, one aborted hope after another. Jane, by comparison, was a Phi Beta Kappa graduate of a highly selective university, and he was sensitive about that. To put her in her place, his favorite comeback to her suggestions was that she was "very ignorant."[20]

The truth was, she had a deep education in what he needed to know: literature. He wanted to return to writing and was already trying his hand at short stories, but his background was in the sciences, whereas she had aced courses at Swarthmore in American literature, eighteenth-century English literature, Shakespeare, Chaucer, Victorian poetry, modern literature, and the English novel. The "core of her dowry," as Kurt said, not unadmiringly, was a collection of twenty Modern Library editions of Russian authors from which she selected a novel for him to read during their honeymoon: Dostoyevsky's *The Brothers Karamazov*. It was the first Russian novel he had ever read.[21] Eventually, he worked his way through all her Russians. His favorite, not surprisingly in light of the direction his writing would take, was the satirist Nikolay Gogol.

Also during their honeymoon, Jane shared with him a gift from her favorite professor at Swarthmore, Henry Goddard, chair of the English Department. For every student, Goddard wrote a phrase from literature on a slip of paper, put it inside a walnut shell, and presented it at the end of the semester. For Jane, he had selected a sentence from Dostoyevsky: "One sacred memory from childhood is perhaps the best education."

Kurt referred to it for years as inspiration and solace.

DRESDEN TROUBLED his dreams.[22] It was part of a noisy concatenation of events that banged and jolted like boxcars coupled together. There was his mother's suicide; then being shipped overseas and landing on a beachhead marred by a titanic struggle; next, the humiliation of being cast into the largest defeat of American arms in history; and last, the conflagration of Dresden. Through naïveté, stupidity, or perhaps some truth that touched on his worth as a human being, he had arrived at twenty-three with much to explain.

For subject matter to write about, at least, the obvious choice was Dresden: it had the double potential of drama on a monstrous scale and originality because it was his story to tell. He had been there. He could find meaning in it. On the other hand, where was the suspense, the heroism? He had seen a beautiful city and then the ruins of that city. But during the bombing, he had been in a hole, deep underground, hiding. It was as if he had slept through the sacking of Troy and woke just as the Greeks were boarding their ships for home. The middle, act 2, was missing. In storytelling terms, he was mainly limited to the prologue and the denouement. Not interesting and too narrow in scope.

IN OCTOBER Kurt reported to Fort Riley and was assigned to the secretarial pool.[23] In his spare time, he continued to write stories and mail them to Jane, who was living with her parents in Indianapolis until Kurt's discharge.

One day she saw an advertisement in a magazine by an "author's counsel," Scammon Lockwood. His specialty, he claimed, was turning "Duds into Dollars" for frustrated writers; moreover, his office on East Twenty-second Street in Manhattan was just "Five Minutes from 1,000 Editors and Publishers." She sent for his free booklet and was pleased by his offer to review writing samples at no cost.

Eager to begin her role as wife to an aspiring author, she mailed Lockwood four of Kurt's short stories and a cover letter. "I personally am convinced that he is a potential Chekhov, and as soon as he's lived long enough to have something worth saying, he'll prove it. . . . I think that he considers what he has written so far pure drivel. It is—if you're looking for some tremendously significant subject matter. On the other hand, one of the stories has an idea that will make people stop and think (if it's printable; I doubt that it is), and the others have a warmth of expression and characterization that is appealing even if it isn't important."[24]

Fortunately, Lockwood knew his profession and the fiction market. A few of his short stories had been anthologized, and he had the satisfaction of seeing one of his mystery stories, "De Luxe Annie," adapted first into a play and then into a motion picture. His response to Jane's letter is that of an older man touched by a young woman's sincerity. But beyond that, his advice is as valuable as pearls to any beginning fiction writer hoping to sell his or her work.

You say you think that Kurt is a potential Chekhov. To this I fervently reply "Heaven Save Him!" This is a very revealing statement. I'm glad you made it. I hope the virus has not become so entrenched that it can't be driven out of his system. I recognize the symptoms of a widely prevailing ailment. . . . Read Chekhov and enjoy him, yes, and all of the other great and inspiring ones, but don't encourage Kurt, or anybody else, to try to write like them. If you want to sell in the current market you have got to write "current literature." I warmly applaud Kurt's desire to "say something" that will have some influence, however small, that will do something to help uplift humanity. Every writer worth a hoot has ambition. But don't think that it can't be done in terms of current fiction. . . . So then, what it adds up to or boils down to is this: you have got to master the current technique if you want acceptance for anything, good or drivel, in the current market. The "message to humanity" is a by-product: it always has been. . . . If you want to make a living writing you will first of all write to entertain, to divert, to amuse. And that in itself is a noble aim.[25]

Concerning Kurt's stories, Lockwood was encouraging, but he explained gently that they each needed heavy revising. He was impressed by "Suicide Note" but recommended Kurt "put it aside for a while."[26]

As it turned out, the young couple wasn't in a position to take advantage of Lockwood's services as consultant. Jane expected they wouldn't be able to because, as she had explained at the outset, her husband was about to be discharged and they were going to enroll at the University of Chicago. He intended to finish his undergraduate degree on the GI Bill, and she might enroll in a graduate program in Russian literature, provided she received a fellowship. "You can easily see that we won't have either $10, or $15, or $20 left over."[27]

Nevertheless, in the early years of his writing and submitting fiction to magazines, Vonnegut kept in mind Lockwood's caveat to avoid artiness. He pitched his fiction right to the heart of the popular, postwar market.

THEY APPLIED to the University of Chicago to enroll second semester. During the intake interview, Kurt sat while an admissions counselor read the personal background section of his application. He paused at Vonnegut's mention of being a POW in Dresden. "Well, we hated to do that," he said under his breath, explaining that he had been a crew member on the American bombing raid.[28]

They were accepted—Kurt as an undeclared major and Jane, to her joy, received a fellowship. By December 1945, the Vonneguts were in a brick apartment building at 3972½ Ellis Avenue in Chicago, south of the Loop and within sight of Lake Michigan, an "enormous presence there," he wrote.[29]

The GI Bill would pay for books and tuition, but Vonnegut didn't know what to study. Several relatives had attended the University of Chicago, but there was no journalism degree offered, and most of his credits from Cornell were in the sciences, so he reached out for advice. "I went to my faculty adviser, and I confessed that science did not charm me, that I longed for poetry instead. I was depressed."[30]

Fortunately for him, his adviser was good at helping floundering students and persuaded him to study for a degree in anthropology— cultural anthropology, "a science that was mostly poetry," as Kurt understood it, yet it was an opportunity to examine critically "every object and idea which has been shaped by men and women and children."[31] Anthropology would require heavy reading in history, psychology, and art, which would address some of the weaknesses in his liberal arts education. A drawback was that the endpoint of the program at Chicago was a master's degree, not a bachelor's, so when he chose it as a major he was signing on for the long haul—three years of coursework beyond the two transferred from Cornell. "That was okay with me, because it was a very exciting time in my life. I was ready."[32]

And Jane began her graduate studies as well, choosing from a buffet of courses in Russian and Soviet history, economics, political science, and anthropology in Chicago's prestigious Department of Slavic Languages and Literatures.

NOT SINCE high school had Vonnegut enjoyed his studies so much.[33] "The intellectual kick was great."[34] His instructors were impressed with his writing ability, too. "Excellent—good discussion of this complex problem," wrote a professor on one of his papers; "clear, well-written," complimented another.[35]

What was nourishing to Kurt about Chicago was that it allowed for latitude in thinking—nothing was too outré, provided it was reinforced with thorough research. The campus attracted skeptics, nonconformists, and left-wingers, completely different from the preppy atmosphere of Cornell. There were Progressives, Christian socialists, former Communists, and "pinkos" of every hue. To get into the spirit of things, he tried starting a fad of wearing blue denim work shirts to class. No one imitated him.[36]

By coincidence, his cousin Walt was also attending the University of Chicago, working toward a degree in philosophy. The two men decided to spend five days in June 1946 on Lake Maxinkuckee at Hollyhock

Farm, still owned by a branch of the family, just reminiscing and introducing their wives, who had never met.

It rained most of their stay at the lake, so the foursome spent the time talking and playing cards. Walt, who had found the teenage Kurt's high jinks a little tiresome at times, noticed that his twenty-four-year-old cousin was quite different now. "I was very impressed with him and I remember vividly that I liked him more than any other man I had ever known. His general knowledge of the world, current events, just his appreciation for other people's thoughts, positions, and ideas. There was a fumbling, eager intelligence, grasping at all sorts of things."[37]

Kurt was fascinated by how cultural anthropology examined people's values, symbols, and ideas. What he had believed about himself, his family, American society, he realized—all of Judeo-Christian civilization, for that matter—was contingent upon Western theories about time, knowledge, morals, law, and custom. "Culture is a gadget; it's something we inherit," he later wrote. "And you can fix it the way you can fix a broken oil burner."[38] His ironic distance as a novelist, sounding as detached as an entomologist observing insects, can be traced to his days as an anthropology student.[39] "I was confirmed as a cultural relativist, as the University of Chicago brought it home to me that my culture was not superior to anyone else's or even more complex."[40]

His insights are not unusual for a young man experiencing a rush of fresh, exciting ideas in a university setting. As yet, however, he was not far enough in his studies to understand how different peoples associate and create an identity.

Then he attended a series of lectures by the anthropologist Robert Redfield. Redfield was studying the modernizing process under way in many developing areas of the world, mainly in Mexico and Central America. His research had convinced him that there was a common denominator in how people came together—it was a stage, really, in human relations. He called it the "folk society" and wrote that the ideal folk society was small, homogeneous, respectful of sacred rituals, and held together by strong primary personal relations.[41] This is not to say, however, that primitive societies are Arcadias and big cities are automatically impersonal hells, Redfield cautioned. "In every isolated community there is civilization; in every city there is the folk society."[42]

To better understand how this duality could exist, Vonnegut made a copy of Redfield's journal article on the subject. The reason folk societies can exist under such different circumstances, Redfield explained, was that "the members of the folk society have a strong sense of belonging together."[43] In other words, people can make community wherever they are. Kurt underlined that explanation heavily.

In some ways the description of a folk society resembled the Vonneguts, Schnulls, and Glossbrenners huddled on the eastern shore of Lake Maxinkuckee, which was, as Vonnegut later wrote, a "closed loop." No matter in which direction he set off, he would always arrive at the same cluster of cottages pitched by the water's edge like tents "teeming with close relatives."[44] He concluded that extended family—or a folk society created out of any variety of beliefs, for that matter—could validate a person, give him or her a place to be in the world, and alleviate the pain of loneliness.

MEANWHILE, HE was trying to join the community of published writers. Since his discharge he had been submitting short stories to magazines, in addition to attending school full-time. He had so many rejection letters—from the *American Mercury, Collier's,* the *New Yorker, Glamour,* the *Atlantic Monthly, Harper's Magazine*—that he began using them for scratch paper. On the back of one from *Reader's Scope,* he made a grocery list for a picnic: corn, six wieners, Duff's Devil Food, Junket instant icing mix.

Optimistically, though, he sent a second submission to Charles Angoff, editor at the *American Mercury,* with a cover letter reminding him that he had submitted once to the magazine, and Angoff had encouraged him to try again. Enclosed was a story titled "Brighten Up!" based on his experiences as a POW in Dresden.[45]

Angoff rejected it.

IN SEPTEMBER 1946, after completing less than a year of her degree, Jane discovered she was pregnant. She dropped out of the University of Chicago and wept in front of her adviser about having to give up her fellowship.[46] She never resumed her coursework.

The Vonneguts' first child, Mark—named for Mark Twain—was born May 11, 1947. Jane worried about caring for a baby without help from family, most of whom lived in Indianapolis. "I can never get sick," she told Kurt. He realized that he "couldn't get sick, either. If there had been something seriously wrong with the kid we would have been in a hell of a lot of trouble."[47]

He wanted to complete graduate school and get his degree as quickly as possible. Thinking about a thesis topic that would impress his advisers, Kurt hit upon something contemporary. American anthropologists were mad for studies of Native Americans. (There was a joke at Chicago at the time that a Native American family consisted of a mother, a father, two children, and an anthropologist.) But he also wanted to inject something artier and edgier into a major undertaking, one that would make macroconnections between separate cultures, rather than microcomparisons among similar groups. He would need an adviser with interests along those lines, and fortunately there was a new faculty member in the department who might be sympathetic to his aims, Assistant Professor James Sydney Slotkin.

When it came to social anthropology, Slotkin was a big-picture person—no small scale for him. "At the outset, let us delimit the field to be studied and the approach to be used," he declared in the first sentence of his soon-to-be-published book, *Social Anthropology: The Science of Human Society and Culture*.[48] The fascinating thing to him was how commonalities between peoples leaped oceans and eons. Humans everywhere, it seemed to him, framed experience in similar ways. His approach was more typical of nineteenth-century anthropologists than his contemporaries, which may have been why, in the words of one of his colleagues, Slotkin "remained a marginal figure in the department" during his years at Chicago.[49]

But Vonnegut admired him; the young professor was a fountain of ideas, shooting (a little wildly) in different directions.[50] Slotkin told him it was important to know which school of art you're practicing in, and its tenets. It was necessary for a creative person to belong to a school of practitioners who shared the same principles and ideals, because no one could amount to anything in the arts unless he or she embraced an ideology.[51] Vonnegut took fire at this advice, he later said, thinking he was hearing a manifesto for becoming an artist, a writer.[52]

Inspired by Slotkin's broad-mindedness about social anthropology and creativity, he ambled off in a direction for his thesis that was, unfortunately, too challenging. In the outline of his forty-page thesis proposal, submitted to a department committee in spring 1947, he said he would argue that "similarities between the Cubist painters in Paris in 1907 and the leaders of Native American ... uprisings late in the nineteenth century could not be ignored."[53]

The committee unanimously turned it down with Slotkin abstaining. They recommended he not try to be so ambitious. The Indian Ghost Dance of the 1890s, for example, would be a more manageable topic, besides being more anthropological.[54]

The decision was reminiscent of being told by Bernard, with his father's acquiescence, where he should apply to college and what he should study. Another instance of know-it-alls telling him what was best for him. "I felt excluded by that bunch in the department, although they had admitted me."[55] Nevertheless, bearing down throughout the summer of 1947, he collected research for a different thesis, "Mythologies of North American Nativistic Movements." He intended to compare how new mythologies had been created by Native American groups to explain white conquest.[56]

It was straightforward, and his advisers, reading over his four-page outline, were encouraging. Some of what he proposed, in fact, was fresh ground for study. "Dear Mr. Vonnegut," wrote Professor Fred Eggan, who specialized in Pueblo peoples, "your M.A. thesis looks OK, but I think you might make it more useful by dealing with the relation between mythology and action—ritual or otherwise." He recommended a few titles. "Good luck."[57] Sol Tax, known for his studies of the Sauk Indians, wanted to meet and discuss the project. "Dear Mr. Vonnegut: I have your thesis topic proposal. It looks promising."[58]

The project would take a solid six months to a year, during which Kurt needed to complete more upper-level courses to be eligible for a degree. If he stayed on track, he would graduate in May or September 1949, provided he continued to pass three or four classes each quarter while working on his thesis.

He intended to keep writing fiction for the short story market, however, whatever the demands of his coursework. On the back of a page of research notes for his revised thesis, he sketched a few ideas for a story about a character named Plummer who dreams of a life in the arts as a director, producer, or playwright. He stops attending classes.[59]

And that's what Vonnegut did in August 1947.

* * *

THE COMBINATION of time wasted on a rejected thesis, expensive text-books, the demands of fatherhood, and the strain he had put on himself by trying to do too many things at once had finally discouraged him. At the end of summer quarter, with his second thesis only an outline, he dropped out of the university, "another of my failures."[60] By quitting in the fourth year of a five-year program, he still had no degree, only a high school diploma.

His cousin Walt was surprised when he heard the news. "He told me that he had passed all his courses with good grades and he had all the notes for the thesis, but he never wrote it. It struck me as rather odd though. I wondered, 'Gee, you are a writer, how come you didn't toss it off and get your MA?' He didn't seem to give a darn whether he got the MA or not, so he said."[61]

Since January, Kurt had been moonlighting at Chicago's City News Bureau, returning to an earlier love, journalism.[62] The purpose of City News was unique: feeding Chicago's four dailies—the *Daily News*, the *Defender*, the *Sun-Times*, and the *Tribune*—with all the downtown news the bureau's reporters could scrounge up on the streets, twenty-four hours a day.

City News reporters covered the courts, the jails, the precinct houses, and city hall, always digging for more stories that they would then dictate from phone booths to a rewrite man or woman who never seemed satisfied and pressed for more details. It was part of an initiation that included editors chewing out new reporters, heckling them, embarrassing them, belittling them to toughen them up and make them do their job right.[63] The bureau's motto was "If your mother tells you she loves you, check it out."[64] The final step in delivering a story to the dailies was putting it into a sealed canister and letting it fly via the vacuum-powered "news subway" through steel and brass pneumatic tubes snaking under the Loop directly into the newsrooms.

Vonnegut had been hired as copyboy at first because he was too green to be put on a beat.[65] But in August when he was available to go full-time, he was sent out on the streets hunting for stories.

He loved snooping around for dirt. When he was a boy, novels by the Chicagoan James T. Farrell about the lives of working-class Irish on the South Side had thrilled him. Now he was walking those same mean streets. "As a reporter, I'd go to police station after police station after police station, call on firehouses, and then I'd go and call the coast guard: 'Anything going on?' For eight hours I'd be on the South Side, the North Side, the West Side."[66] Stories about "floaters"—bodies in the Chicago River or Lake Michigan—always made for good copy. He covered a case in which a Mrs. Sosnowski sawed her husband, Tony, into two-foot lengths and dumped the pieces into the river. She had to make several trips to get him all in.[67]

MEANWHILE, BERNARD was becoming a highly regarded scientist and following a career track heading steeply upward. Married since 1943 to the former Lois Bowler, he had accepted an offer from General Electric in 1945 for a position at its research headquarters in Schenectady, New York.

The Schenectady Works was an ideal situation for a chemist, physicist, engineer, or mathematician who could adapt to working for a world leader in private industry. General Electric was the fourth largest publicly held company in the United States, and the third largest employer in the nation, with 136 factories in twenty-eight states. The company paid well for ideas, from practical ones to revolutionary. The products that poured from its factories—televisions and radios, refrigerators and washing machines, giant industrial devices such as steam turbines, military equipment, and ship motors—made General Electric synonymous with the "age of abundance" that swept the United States after the war.[68] With seemingly inexhaustible financial resources, the company would take on a crackerjack researcher like Bernard on the chance that he just might come up with something unique, useful, and, most important, profitable.

Bernard and Lois purchased a small home in Alplaus, a village within the town of Glenville, just across the Mohawk River and five miles northeast of the Schenectady Works, where many of General Electric's white-collar workers resided. Their son Peter, the first of five boys, was born in July 1945.

In his laboratory at work, Bernard chose an area of research that would confirm the company's faith in him: investigating methods of supercooling liquids in nature and seeking an answer to the tantalizing question: is it possible to make it rain? If so, the result would revolutionize climate control the world over.

Working with his colleague Vincent Schaefer, Bernard investigated methods of creating ice nuclei in the clouds that would cause instant condensation. On November 13, 1946, Schaefer rented a Fairchild light airplane and the services of a professional pilot. Over Mount Greylock in the Berkshires, thirty miles from the General Electric plant, Schaefer dropped three pounds of dry ice pellets into a target cold cloud as Bernard and his fellow scientists watched. "It seemed as though [the cloud] almost exploded," Schaefer wrote in his notebook, "the effect was so widespread and rapid."[69] Snow fell from a cloud layer along a three-mile path in western Massachusetts.

The next day, a headline in the *New York Times* heralded the OPENING VISTA OF MOISTURE CONTROL BY MAN. A *Boston Globe* headline announced, SNOWSTORM MANUFACTURED.[70] Capitalizing on General Electric's success, the company's new vice president for employee and community relations, Lemuel Ricketts Boulware, decided he would take a fresh approach to public perception about science and progress. He wanted employees, unions, stockholders, community neighbors, and the government to know that General Electric was trying "to do right voluntarily."[71] The first thing was to get some real journalists on board to hunt up stories at the Schenectady Works and keep a steady drumbeat of good news issuing from the plant.

Thus it happened that Kurt received a call in late August from George W. Griffin Jr., a General Electric public relations executive. Griffin explained that Bernard had recommended his younger brother as the kind of man they might be looking for: someone with a science background who was also a reporter. Would he be interested in interviewing for a job in Schenectady?

For the first time in their marriage, Kurt and Jane were in a position to be choosy. Since dropping out of the University of Chicago, he had been mailing out his résumé and was in an enviable spot for a young married man with a baby but only a modest education. While celebrating their second anniversary in September 1947 at a fancy restaurant on Michigan Avenue, the happy pair weighed their options.[72] In addition to the offer tendered by General Electric, Kurt had been offered an editorial position with Bobbs-Merrill publishing in Indianapolis, and the *Dayton Daily News* in Ohio said it would hire him as a reporter.

They went for the money and the change of scene. The pay at General Electric was triple what he would be making in Indianapolis or Dayton. There was just one hitch: he needed a college degree. So he told Griffin he had a master's in anthropology from the University of Chicago. His future boss never checked up.[73]

With the General Electric job offer in hand, he resigned from City News after nine months—most of it part-time work, though no one stayed there long, anyway. The hours had been awful, and the pay was peanuts, but Vonnegut later attributed his style to working in a newsroom on deadline. "I mean, a lot of critics think I'm stupid because my sentences are so simple and my method is so direct: they think these are defects. No. The point is to write as much as you know as quickly as possible."[74]

In late September, Jane stayed in Chicago to prepare for the move and he went ahead to upstate New York to find them a new home.

GENERAL ELECTRIC's Schenectady Works was nicknamed the "House of Magic." Inside the gates, thirty thousand employees worked in 240 buildings located on a six-hundred-acre campus, contributing to the development of engineering and technology on a scale that was unrivaled in the world. There was a softball diamond with grandstands and picnic benches, and a rifle range. On weekends, the athletic club was open for team bowling, tennis, basketball, or volleyball. A medical clinic was equipped to provide everything from aspirin to emergency treatment. A private police force guarded the grounds, and a nine-man fire department stood by for emergencies. At the company store, employees could purchase General Electric appliances and equipment at specially discounted prices. And after twenty-five years of service, employees received automatic membership in General Electric's Quarter Century Club. Forty-five hundred people belonged. The company picked up the tab for all kinds of entertainment: group outings to racetracks, boat trips down the Hudson River to New York City, sporting events, and fancy dress balls and dinners.

To add yet another level of esprit de corps, Vice President Boulware decided that, beginning in 1948, he would lead the first management training camp on Association Island in Henderson Harbor, New York. The idea was to combine a little rough-and-tumble horseplay (all of the executives were men) with leadership seminars. Participants would be divided into teams by colors—red, blue, and so on. He wanted a united front from management; otherwise, he believed, concessions to labor would lead, step by step, to a collectivist dystopia.[75]

JUST AROUND the corner from Bernard and his family in the hamlet of Alplaus, New York—five miles north of Schenectady—stood a two-bedroom house for sale at 17 Hill Street with a detached garage, fireplace, cedar shingles, and exterior windows trimmed in white. Kurt wired Jane that they could afford this gingerbready cottage, on a creek, with good heat and plumbing. All it needed was some decorating. He signed his telegram, "Love, Tarzan."[76] What he didn't know was that when the Mohawk River froze, the Alplaus Kill behind the house backed up and ice-cold water ran over the backyard, through the cellar, in one side, and out the other.[77] Nevertheless, the cottage shaded by forty-foot pines became their first home.

Alplaus was a hamlet of fewer than four hundred people, but bus service two times daily made it convenient for commuting to Schenectady. In the town center was Mrs. Ann Cheney's gas station and general store. Across the street stood the two-story brick volunteer fire department with two trucks. Kurt's new neighbors advised him to join, not only for civic reasons but because the firemen hosted dances, barbecues, and holiday events, too—it was the social hub. He volunteered and was assigned badge number 155. Next to the fire station was an old house with a dark, creaky post office on the first floor. Ida Dillman was the crabby postmistress, and Kurt decided he didn't like her.

The previous owners of the Vonneguts' home, the Grudgings, were a husband-and-wife pair of drunks, according to neighbors, and in the course of clearing out their debris, Kurt discovered a strange thing wedged in the rafters of the garage: a copper funeral urn. Jane called Mrs. Grudgings about it. Tearfully, the woman explained that the urn contained the ashes of her prized blue-ribbon collie.[78] Would Jane be a dear, she asked, and please save it as a memorial?

The Vonneguts, suspicious, called the Troy Crematorium and asked whether the previous owners had used the crematorium's services. The answer was yes, the ashes were those of the husband's former wife, Mrs. Helen C. Grudgings. When she became ill and lay dying, her husband had carried on with another woman—owner of the "prized blue-ribbon collie." They married as soon as Helen died and then decamped without the urn.

Jane and Kurt lost sleep wondering what to do. They called the local Catholic church because Helen Grudgings had been a Catholic, but it was too late for a proper burial because cremation was unacceptable. Word spread about the situation, and the neighbors, in good fun, referred to 17 Hill Street as the Vonnegut Mortuary. Finally, a Mrs. Larsen, a Norwegian who had known Mrs. Grudgings, said, "Helen loved her garden. She would have liked to have been buried under the lemon lilies."[79]

So on a nice day, Kurt, Jane, and Mrs. Larsen held a ceremony at the foot of a stump beside the lemon lilies in the front yard. They sang a hymn, Kurt said a prayer, and the ashes were laid to rest under a foot of soil.

"And that was the end of Helen Grudgings," Jane wrote to Gloria and Jack Ericson, who later purchased the house.[80]

VONNEGUT'S NEW job at General Electric offered a golden ladder. He had risen from a beat reporter to a white-collar job with one of the most respected companies in the world. General Electric hadn't hired him only because he was Bernard's brother and a competent writer, however. The Schenectady Works had plenty of writers. There was already a full-time publishing staff that created manuals, examinations, and visual aids for 250 instructors who trained a thousand new hires a year. No, what the company was after was a newspaperman who could pitch a story idea to a major outlet, interview employees, make photo assignments, and turn it all into a feature story. If nothing was happening, he was expected to find reasons for news releases, even if that meant just walking around the plant asking questions. The kind of work Bernard Vonnegut was doing in connection with cloud seeding, for instance, was exactly the kind of research they wanted a lot more press about.

At first, Kurt's desk was located in downtown Schenectady as part of General Electric's Advertising News Sales Promotion Group. But then it was decided that the department ought to be inside the plant, closer to the shops and laboratories. After that, every weekday morning, Kurt went through the main gate of the "House of Magic" wearing a business suit and fedora (company dress code) to the news office in Building 31 Communications and General Services, ready to track down glimpses of the future.

What he saw on his rounds made him proud to be associated with the company. Far from complaining later about being forced into science at Cornell, and his prophecies about technology dehumanizing the human race, he felt buoyant about General Electric's efforts to improve the fundamentals of modern life. "I think what we put on the market was good then . . . we were mostly making electricity, or keeping food from rotting, washing clothes or lighting up rooms."[81] And the corporate secrets he learned about convinced him that General Electric was indeed devoted to progress over politics. Two-thirds of the generators in the Tennessee Valley Authority dams, he found out, were General Electric generators, and to his way of thinking, "that was clearly socialism, public ownership of the utilities." He was amazed when engineers told him they had supervised the installation of General Electric turbines, waterwheels, and generators in Communist countries, "hauling these huge pieces of machinery with oxen and everything else and lowering them into place with very primitive leverage schemes and all that. And I wanted to tell this story and couldn't because you know, we'd helped the Communists, by God!"[82]

Before long, he was rattling away on his typewriter steadily, covering not only Bernard's work in atmospheric research, for which he wrote most of the publicity, but also the company's ongoing research in nuclear power generation with an inside view of the latest developments.[83] (A minor uproar resulted from a secretary retyping one of Kurt's news releases and changing "nuclear physics" to "unclear physics.")[84] In his new job, Vonnegut "learned to really love industry and I liked what the hell they were doing, the product was so good."[85] Within days of his arrival, he placed in the *New York Times* a piece about General Electric's new, safer sodium lights on bridges. George Griffin liked that kind of go-getter attitude and had responded by putting him in charge of promoting General Electric's sponsorship of the seven-car, red-white-and-blue Freedom Train when it arrived in Schenectady during its national tour on November 1, 1947. Inside were Library of Congress documents on which American liberties are founded. Again,

Vonnegut came through.[86] He was a good PR man with an instinctive knack for getting the public's attention.[87]

He liked the maleness of the office too, the camaraderie of men who tended to be young, married, and ex-GIs. One of them, he discovered, Ollie M. Lyon Jr., had been an infantry private aboard the *Queen Elizabeth* with him in transit to England; another, Bob Pace, had graduated two years ahead of him from Shortridge High School.[88] Given that so many of his officemates were ex-servicemen, Kurt had no difficulty persuading them to hand over a dollar apiece to support the United World Federalist organization, which was dedicated to creating a democratic world order to prevent future wars.

On slow news days, the guys had lunch at a favorite tavern, washing down pickled eggs with beer and joking about the "generous electric company." One night, in Bob Pace's basement, they watched porno movies on an eight-millimeter projector "borrowed" from the office, then rewound one of the reels and showed it backward, roaring as a bellboy bounced out of a woman's bed, hurriedly got dressed, and backed out of the hotel room carrying a tray full of drinks.[89]

Kurt believed he had a job for life, if he wanted it, womb to tomb, as the saying went in corporate life at the time—an extended family of professionals all engaged in furthering the company's work. But he was uneasy in his role as an organization man, as a foolish incident revealed. His misstep not only involved Bernard but, to make matters worse, deeply offended Uncle Alex.

ALEX HAD been following Bernard's career with eye-popping joy. Proudly he read in the *Indianapolis Star* about the career of his nephew—former science whiz kid, MIT graduate, now close associate of the Nobel laureate Irving Langmuir, the chief scientist at General Electric. Weather control was Promethean in its audacity, and to think that a Vonnegut was grappling with it! Finally, when a friend sent him a clipping of Bernard demonstrating his apparatus for cloud seeding, Alex wrote to the *Schenectady Gazette*, where the article had originally appeared, requesting a print of the photograph, explaining that he was a "wee bit proud" of his nephew. Thoughtfully, he included a dollar to cover the cost.

The *Gazette* forwarded Alex's request to General Electric, where it landed on Kurt's desk. Kurt, amused by the coincidence, pondered how to reply. He answered in a letter he thought was witty, but jealousy isn't hard to see between the lines.

Dear Mr. Vonnegut:

Mr. Edward Themak, city editor for the *Schenectady Gazette*, has referred your letter of November 26th to me.

The photograph of General Electric's Dr. Bernard Vonnegut originated from our office. However, we have no more prints in our files, and the negative is in the hands of the United States Signal Corps. Moreover, we have a lot more to do than piddle with penny-ante requests like yours.

We do have some other photographs of the poor man's Steinmetz, and I may send them to you in my own sweet time.[90] But do not rush me. "Wee bit proud," indeed! Ha! Vonnegut! Ha! *This office made your nephew, and we can break him in a minute—like an eggshell.* So don't get in an uproar if you don't get the pictures in a week or two.

Also—one dollar to the General Electric Company is as the proverbial fart in a windstorm. Here it is back. Don't blow it all in one place.

Very truly yours,
Guy Fawkes
Press Section
General News Bureau[91]

Alex, reading the letter, was crushed and angry. He contacted an attorney, inquiring whether there was some kind of legal redress for being treated with contempt, and threatened to write to the president of General Electric, informing him that he had an employee who didn't know his job or the value of a dollar. But before he did, someone explained who Guy Fawkes was—the seventeenth-century Catholic anarchist who conspired to blow up the Houses of Parliament—and reminded him that his other nephew, Kurt, worked in public relations. He cooled off, though it's hard to believe he accepted it as a "family joke," as Kurt later claimed.[92]

VONNEGUT'S EXPOSURE to technology at one of the preeminent research facilities in the world might have led to a career writing nonfiction books about science, transportation, space exploration—the world of a prosperous future, which tended to enthrall postwar Americans, but he was still determined to sell fiction. Before boarding the morning bus for Schenectady, he would make sure he had put in a couple of hours writing at a desk in the corner of the front hallway. He swiped a box of folders from the office and set up a file system to track the dates of stories submitted, responses from magazines, revisions, and resubmissions. Radio shows had taught him humor and timing; anthropology had given him insights into human nature; journalism had acted like a grindstone on his prose, shearing off pretension until plain English was left.[93] He could do this.

He told his coworker Ollie Lyon how he was going to reprioritize his time from now on, and Lyon wished him well but took a wait-and-see attitude. Other men in the office, when they found out, were skeptical. They too had dreamed of being the next Hemingway, they said, but responsibilities at home and the security of a good-paying job had made them quit daydreaming. An older gentleman reacted with sarcasm, telling him that hoping to get published was on a level with masturbation.[94] But Lyon, after a few months of asking him how the writing was coming along, realized Kurt "had a discipline that none of us had. . . . After a day at General Electric, he would go home and write, and also spend the weekends writing. Often, we did not want to bother them on weekends because we knew he would be writing."[95]

Even so, rejection letters landed in his mailbox again and again. "Not a striking plot—overdramatized—not on our level of interest," replied Arnold Gingrich, founder and editor of *Esquire*.[96] From *Collier's* magazine, a mysterious penciled note appeared at the bottom of a rejection letter. It sounded friendly, but he was suspicious. "This is a little sententious for us. You're not the Kurt Vonnegut who worked on the *Cornell Daily Sun* in 1942, are you?"[97] The signature was "Owen Buer, Orme Bruyes, or Dunk Bridges"—he couldn't make out the handwriting. In any case, some of his columns for the *Cornell Daily Sun* had backfired, and he wasn't eager to ruin his chances with *Collier's*, so he didn't reply.

The self-imposed regime of writing at home was tiring, but Kurt scored enough coups in public relations for the company to keep his boss, George Griffin, happy. Office politics being what they were, it was risky promising a feature story that flattered General Electric and then not delivering. He saw one of his coworkers inform the vice presidents in a widely circulated memo that he had just placed a big feature with *Life* magazine. Nothing materialized, and the man's career, Vonnegut said later, was over at General Electric.[98]

By studying the magazine market, Kurt developed his instincts about which General Electric stories would appeal to editors. There were projects that reinforced General Electric's Jove-like scientific powers. The transformer division, for example, produced bolts of deadly artificial lightning for research purposes, captured in midstrike by Alfred Eisenstaedt for *Life* magazine. And there were milder demonstrations that placed the company at the head of the American parade of progress. Kurt promoted a miniature town created to scale by company engineers that was powered, warmed, and illuminated by all sorts of Lilliputian General Electric products. It was a hit in newspapers and magazines, as if the corporate giant were stooping down to play.

"All is for the best in the best of all possible worlds," proclaims Dr. Pangloss in one of Vonnegut's favorite novels, Voltaire's *Candide*. It might just as well have been the company's slogan instead of "At General Electric, Progress Is Our Most Important Product." On the other hand, there were aspects of the "House of Magic" that portended dislocations in the American way of life.

One day Vonnegut watched a milling machine cut rotor blades for jet engines in Building 49. Normally, honing turbine blades was an expensive and painstakingly precise series of steps performed by a master machinist. But that day no machinist was involved at all. A computer-operated machine imitated every motion of a human being. The engineers told Vonnegut—a little guiltily, he thought—that the day was coming when "little boxes and punched cards" would run all sorts of machines.[99] It was as if they were aware of betraying their own kind.

Watching the computer-programmed lathe slide back and forth over the steel blades, honing them to within microns of perfection, was a seminal moment for Vonnegut. It was a small event but symbolic of much more. Craftsmanship was a mature talent, learned and passed through the generations. And here was a device operating tirelessly, doing what took a person a lifetime to learn. To have "a little clicking box make all the decisions wasn't a vicious thing to do," he understood. "But it was too bad for the human beings who got their dignity from their jobs."[100]

It was a strange paradox to consider inside a corporate compound where there was a restaurant, fire department, clinic, outings, and an athletic club—all the trappings of community, togetherness, and belonging. Two forces were vying—technology and humanity—and General Electric was at the center of the contest.

The conflict gave him an idea for what would become his first novel, one with overtones of science fiction. "There was no avoiding it," he said later, "since the General Electric Company *was* science fiction."[101]

5: Stop Being Such a Hardheaded Realist
1948–1951

A NOVEL, HOWEVER, NO matter how exciting the premise, would take months, maybe years, to finish, but in the meantime there was quick money to be made in the magazine short story market, if only he could break in. A piece of fiction in the *Saturday Evening Post* or *Harper's* might pay the equivalent of as much as six weeks of his salary. A windfall like that now and then, added to his paycheck from General Electric, would provide for extras that young couples dream about.

He spent nights after work and weekends in his hallway study at home in 1948, trying to pick the lock of the popular magazine market by studying dozens of issues. There were three categories of general interest magazines: middlebrow magazines (*Reader's Digest* and *Collier's*, for example); highbrow (*Harper's*, the *Atlantic Monthly*, and the *New Yorker*); and those aimed at women (*Ladies' Home Journal* and *Woman's Home Companion*). The hottest market for fiction writers, if they wrote fast and delivered what editors wanted, were the magazines for middlebrow readers and women because they purchased the most fiction. *Collier's* ran four to five original stories each week, in addition to a serialized novel.

The pages of *Collier's* or the *Saturday Evening Post* indicated that most popular magazine fiction was an extension of consumers' wish fulfillment. Attractive, smartly dressed young couples were perpetually entertaining or, in the case of male professionals, working at executive-level jobs. Big blocks of advertising, quarried from the same happy landscape, featured young men and women enjoying the good life—house, car, television, and home appliances. "The Golden Age of White People" was how Vonnegut later referred to the era.[1]

Consequently, nothing like the novel he was thinking about, that questioned postwar American life and the motives of manufacturers paying for advertisements, would enchant a magazine editor. The broad market for fiction was pretty much what Scammon Lockwood, author's consultant, had described to Jane. People wanted contemporary stories, and they wanted to be entertained, diverted, and amused.

He tried revising a story called "Mnemonics," for instance—a twist on O. Henry's "The Romance of a Busy Broker." In Vonnegut's story, a businessman takes a mnemonics course to learn to remember details. In love with his secretary, Ellen, he absentmindedly embraces her while visualizing beautiful starlets as memory hints. Surprised, she exclaims, "Well, praise be! You finally remembered *me*."[2] While Kurt was mulling over the awkwardness of this plot contrivance, he studied again the rejection letter from *Collier's*, looking for suggestions, and saw again the penciled note at the bottom: "You're not the Kurt Vonnegut who worked on the *Cornell Daily Sun* in 1942, are you?" He looked more closely at the signature, and this time he could make it out.[3]

It was "Knox Burger," his friend and editor of the humor magazine the *Cornell Widow*.

KNOX BRECKENRIDGE Burger was born in New York City on November 1, 1922, making him ten days older than Kurt, and raised, an only child, in Westchester County. His father, Carl Burger, was an illustrator of children's books, including *Old Yeller* and *The Incredible Journey*. In the spring of 1943, a few months after Kurt left Cornell, Knox enlisted in the army. By an uncanny coincidence, he too had seen the aftereffects of a cataclysmic firebombing, one worse than Dresden—perhaps the most destructive documented fire in history.

On the nights of March 9 and 10, 1945, American B-29s dropped a quarter of a million bombs on Tokyo, burning to the ground sixteen square miles of the city, an area two-thirds the size of Manhattan. Knox, a sergeant working for the Saipan bureau of *Yank*, the army's weekly newspaper, flew north to Tokyo after the Japanese surrender in August to interview survivors. His estimate of 100,000 killed has generally been accepted as accurate.[4] Next to the atomic bombing of Hiroshima, in which 130,000 Japanese perished, it was the single most lethal raid of the entire war.

After his hitch in the army, he transitioned from writing for *Yank* to freelancing. He and his first wife, Otis Kidwell, were down to their last one hundred dollars when, in 1948, he became, at twenty-six, *Collier's* fiction editor, quite possibly the youngest editor of a national magazine.[5]

He gave the impression of being a man's man: short, slim, an outdoorsman with dark hair and a Kirk Douglas jaw. He liked women, liquor, children (other people's), fly-fishing, and girlie magazines. A natural wit and pugnacious, he loved to dish it out. Receiving a submission accompanied by a fancy business card, he replied, "Your card is more suitable for a dealer in previously-owned kitchen appliances or a salesman of rubber goods than a novelist. We return the card herewith. Good luck with it."[6]

He wondered why Vonnegut hadn't replied to his personal note in connection with "Mnemonics," but he supposed he must have sounded patronizing and offended him.[7] So in June 1949, he was surprised to hear back. Yes, indeed, his correspondent was none other than Kurt Vonnegut, formerly of the *Cornell Daily Sun*. He asked if Knox was available for lunch in New York the following week.[8]

Knox replied immediately by telegram: PLEASE CALL ME AT MY OFFICE ON TUESDAY.[9]

ALTHOUGH IT had been only six years since they'd last seen each other, both men were much changed. Kurt was no longer the cut-up Knox remembered at Cornell; he seemed tenuous and preoccupied. Knox, when Kurt shook his hand, seemed like an utter stranger to him.[10] Nevertheless, Knox wanted to help, if he could. Besides, "Mnemonics" had piqued his interest. After reading it, he had sent an interoffice memo to his boss at *Collier's*, "It's a pretty nasty little thing, but 'different,' God knows, and it has some laughs."[11] The key thing in deciding whether to help Vonnegut was if he were a writer who would take instruction and revise. He was pleased to find then that his former college friend was "sensible about editorial advice."[12] There was just one thing that puzzled him: why had he used the absurdly quotidian pen name David Harris when his own was a lot catchier? Vonnegut explained that he wasn't in a position to jeopardize his job at General Electric. An entry-level publicist—especially one who was milking the company for story ideas—might get fired. That settled, Knox showed Kurt around the *Collier's* Park Avenue editorial offices.

Kurt later wrote to Miller Harris, a mutual friend from Cornell, that his meeting with Knox and editors in the New York publishing scene had gone just "smashingly."[13]

HE WAS so excited and encouraged that within a week of his trip to Manhattan he submitted more short stories to Knox. Each one arrived with a cover letter; Vonnegut justified a story titled "Robot Cop" by pointing out that he knew for a fact that General Electric engineers were designing robots, so the concept was feasible.[14]

Unfortunately, the problem didn't have anything to with feasibility. Science fiction, of which "Robot Cop" was one of several examples Vonnegut submitted, is a forgiving genre when it comes to pushing limits of credibility. The problem was that Vonnegut wrote like an amateur. Patiently, Knox edited his submissions, spending more time than he normally would, acting like a one-man writing workshop, trying to guide his friend toward something publishable. "There are some nice lines in this, but you have not arranged your final situation so that it falls into place with all the necessary reverberations," he explained about a short story called "The Case of the Phantom Roadhouse."[15] A quick revision of "Mnemonics" under a new pen name, Mark Harvey, still didn't make the cut, but Knox sent it back with a note: "I think we might be able to take this one if you do some more work on it."[16] Then, while Vonnegut worked on a third rewrite of "Mnemonics," Knox returned "Robot Cop." "The characterizations are not very deep and I think that readers would come away wondering what you are trying to prove."[17]

In the meantime, Burger had a weekly national magazine to publish. What Vonnegut needed was a professional to vet his stories before they reached an editor's desk. Burger called Kenneth Littauer, his former boss at *Collier's*, who had opened an agency in New York with Max Wilkinson, previously a story editor for Sam Goldwyn at MGM. Vonnegut, he told Littaeur, "might turn out to be a skillful and prolific writer."[18]

Kurt was overjoyed when he heard the news. He hardly dared hope that an agent would take him on. He put together a portfolio of his best work and sent it to the offices of Littauer & Wilkinson on Madison Avenue. Now he was getting somewhere!

THERE WERE fewer than thirty literary agents in New York in the late 1940s, and nearly all of them were men. Kenneth Littauer and Max Wilkinson were a pair of middle-aged, endearing gasbags who promised their clients, in the words of one of them, that "rainbow times, the silver ladies and the long green money lay just around another corner."[19]

Ken Littauer, known as the Colonel to friends, had been in the Lafayette Escadrille during World War I. He wore a bowler hat purchased from an exclusive men's store on St. James's Street in London and carried a black umbrella. Max Wilkinson addressed everyone as "my dear" and dressed in combinations of two dozen tailor-made suits, a dozen handmade shoes, and Borsalinos, homburgs, or straw skimmers. His distinction was that a drunken F. Scott Fitzgerald had punched him in the nose.[20] Wilkinson was also the master of the after-dinner toast at the Century Club, where he liked to take clients. One evening, feeling especially expansive, he insisted everyone raise his or her glass to the waiter. Said Vonnegut, Max was "a cultivated man who has been described as a love child of Robert E. Lee and Elizabeth Barrett Browning."[21]

When Burger recommended Vonnegut to Littauer & Wilkinson, the agency hadn't quite hit pay dirt yet, but another young, industrious writer had just joined its client list: John D. MacDonald, who would become one of the best postwar crime and suspense novelists of his generation. Another thing in Ken and Max's favor was that they could teach their clients how to become better writers. Vonnegut was cheered when Knox informed him that Littauer had looked over his submissions and liked them, in spite of, as Knox told Kurt drily, "your gift for anti-climax."[22]

Thrilled that he now had an agent in his corner, Vonnegut continued to spend mornings and weekends writing. Stories spat from his typewriter practically every week, which he then mailed to Littauer, who in turn edited them in the *Collier's* style, believing Vonnegut stood the best chance of being published in the pages of that magazine first.

But not even Ken's expertise could fix Vonnegut's story "Enterprise," judged by one of Burger's associates at *Collier's* as "lame and strained"; or "Mnemonics" after three revisions (turned down flat); or "City" (revised three times and still not good enough); or "Herr Dolmetscher" about an inept American translator during the war, which Knox suspected had been written with the *New Yorker* in mind. Knox found it slight and amusing, but again no. He was scornful too that Vonnegut insisted on using the pen names David Harris and Mark Harvey. "Why doesn't he use his real name on the story?" Knox queried Littauer. "Afraid GE will fire him for a Red?"[23]

And then, returning home from work one evening in late October 1949, Kurt found a sealed envelope from *Collier's* that Jane had propped on the piano's music stand for display. Inside was a $750 check—the equivalent of two months' salary—for "Report on the Barnhouse Effect," about Arthur Barnhouse, who develops the ability to affect physical objects and events through the force of his mind. When the military tries to turn him into a superweapon, Barnhouse decides that he is the first weapon with a conscience and goes into hiding. Kurt's first published story would appear in *Collier's* February 1950 issue, and under his own name. The money had come just in time, as their second child was due at the end of December.

Triumphantly, Kurt wrote his father: "I think I'm on my way. I've deposited my first check in a savings account and, if I sell more, will continue to do so until I have the equivalent of one year's pay at GE. Four more stories will do it nicely, with cash to spare (something we never had before). I will then quit this goddamn nightmare job, and never take another one so long as I live, so help me God."[24]

After reading his son's big news, Kurt Sr. glued the letter to a piece of masonite. On the back he penned a quote from *The Merchant of Venice*: "An oath, I have an oath in Heaven: Shall I lay perjury on my soul?"[25]

JANE AND Kurt celebrated the sale of "Report on the Barnhouse Effect" in a way that would become a tradition for them—by throwing a big party and spending the money. Then they would be "back to eating cereal until the next story," Jane told a neighbor gaily.[26]

As guests began arriving, Kurt sat grinning, sipping gin, and smoking, while Jane, noticed Ollie Lyon, "could hardly contain herself."[27] Ollie's wife, Lavinia, had a "happy little cry" for Kurt.[28] Friends were a little awed that they actually knew a successful writer. They studied this couple who seemed to have dropped down among them, a pair of bohemians, living in straitlaced Alplaus.

It was clear that housekeeping was not one of Jane's priorities. The number of books scattered everywhere bespoke the couple's interest in reading. Kurt had done a little handiwork here and there, such as paneling the wall around the fireplace with knotty pine. But beyond that, touches of eccentricity were everywhere. In the bathroom, guests noticed that the iron, claw-footed bathtub had toenails painted bright red and a pair of feminine eyes at one end. Opposite the toilet were sketches of the orchestra leader Paul Whiteman, the presidential candidate Thomas Dewey, and Ish Kabibble, a character on 1930s radio whose name was slang for "I should worry!"[29]

As the party picked up in tempo, Kurt sat down at the piano, decorated with cows and flowers, and began playing one of his favorite songs, "Back Home Again in Indiana." Two women scooted beside him, one of them pregnant. When they got to the part about the moonlight on the Wabash, the bench collapsed.[30]

Beneath the hilarity, though, several women got the impression that Jane, pregnant, already had two children on her hands: three-year-old Mark and her husband. "Being Mrs. Vonnegut," said one of her friends, "was not a nine-to-five-job because he was not inclined to do things for himself."[31] When attention strayed from Kurt, she tried to direct it back to him. He didn't seem like the typical father, either, at least to another dad at the party—rather distant, in fact. When Mark rode his tricycle into the room, Kurt said quietly, "Mark, that's gauche," and let it go at that.[32] Nevertheless, Jane whisked around at the party, floating on happiness.

Two months later, on December 29, their second child, Edith, was born.

STILL, VONNEGUT felt lonely, despite the recognition in Alplaus of having published and the surface bonhomie at the office. He wrote to his Cornell friend Miller Harris that he hadn't had a close friend since the war.[33] Loneliness seemed to be endemic to corporate life. He couldn't or wouldn't exhibit the fixed grin that was expected of him at the office. He was more of an observer, taking in what was said and going on, and thinking about it. On an anonymous performance evaluation by coworkers, the comment was made, "No personality."[34] Second, he was getting tired of hyping General Electric's achievements. He wanted to be a short story writer, and the work expected of him in public relations— writing news releases, wooing reporters—bored him. Ridiculing the slaphappy tone that was supposed to announce every technological advance, he sent a gag release to Miller Harris: "SCHENECTADY, NY, Feb. 16—General Electric engineers have developed a stupefying new electrical device which will make the second coming of Christ a matter of mere academic interest it was announced here today . . . etc."[35]

He began showing his discontent passively by the way he dressed. On Mondays, the meetings of the Publicity Department were casual—a sports jacket or just a sweater and chinos were acceptable. Instead, he began showing up in jeans and an open shirt, as if Sunday afternoon yard work had oozed into Monday and he was just not in the right frame of mind yet.

From his boss, he got the predictable result. Griffin had been a colonel in the Army Air Corps, and nothing rankled him like insubordination. He lit into Vonnegut every time, first about his appearance and then, when his reprimands didn't bring an improvement, about Vonnegut's output. "Picking on Vonnegut" became a ritual of the Monday morning meetings, and the other men grew restless listening to it.[36] Alplaus was a small town of junior executives, and it got around that General Electric didn't like Vonnegut any better than Vonnegut liked it.[37] Kurt realized he was turning into, he later told a friend, the "captive screwball. Every big firm has to have one. The captive screwball means you don't have friends, they just look at you as someone strange."[38]

To HASTEN the day when he could leave General Electric, he began, by his own admission, writing drivel, figuring he could raise the odds in his favor by putting more and more stories in the mail.[39] Miller Harris cautioned him about throwing over a steady salary on the strength of some extra cash in his pocket. (When a magazine publisher in Australia purchased reprint rights to "Report on the Barnhouse Effect" for twenty dollars, Kurt and Jane spent it on jelly beans.)[40] But Vonnegut was not dissuaded, even if his former classmate was now president of Eagle Shirt Company, one of the largest in the country, and knew something about business. Kurt had a plan: he would become known as a science fiction writer, even if it meant appearing exclusively in the slicks.[41] When in May 1950 Knox purchased "EPICAC" for *Collier's,* a story about a computer that falls in love and dies of a broken heart, Kurt couldn't resist gloating to Harris that he was making some real money now.[42]

Jane believed in him all the way. To a former boyfriend at Swarthmore, Fred S. Rosenau, who was now in marketing for Random House, she dropped a heavy hint about her husband, the budding writer. "Some smart publisher pretty soon ought to recognize genius dawning in this frostbitten little town and do something to ameliorate the awful conditions under which he has to work." When Rosenau advised caution about Kurt quitting, she shot back: "For the love of God and my husband's sanity, stop being such a hard-headed realist. All of this dismal talk—'it might be three years, it might be ten years . . .' Sure, it might, but I'll be damned if it will. We might drop dead tomorrow, too. You seem not to comprehend. K. has *got* to quit before any such gigantic length of time, because this idiotic job of his is such a drag on his spirit. It's making us both psychotic. And that isn't good for the children."[43]

At work, Kurt continued to refuse to be a team player, and he really didn't care if Griffin fired him because of it, either.[44]

Then a providential sign that it may indeed be time to resign came in a birthday greeting from his father. The old gentleman had put aside whatever disappointments he felt from his younger son's shaky start in life and was ready to give him his due.

Dear Sonny boy,

On the occasion of November 11, I heartily wish for your happiness, far beyond what is likely to be in store for most of us living in these stupid times. I am convinced that creative activity, such as your good talents make possible, can contribute the greatest contentment. I am extremely proud of you and want to believe that Mother is aware of our children's progress and shares my satisfaction.

Give a kiss to Janey and hugs to the children.

Affectionately,

Dad[45]

Kurt had one more major project to facilitate for General Electric, and then, he decided, he would give his two weeks' notice.

THE JOB was acting as company liaison with Columbia University, which, under the historian Allan Nevins's direction in 1948, began compiling oral histories. One of the topics was radio pioneers. In addition to interviewing industry leaders such as Fred W. Friendly, Columbia hoped to get General Electric's cooperation because several of its engineers and scientists had contributed importantly to the development of radio broadcasting.[46]

In his disobliging frame of mind, he wasn't eager to coordinate the schedules of a dozen scientists and researchers, including Irving Langmuir, some of whom worked in research facilities located outside Schenectady or were retired. Then a few weeks into the project, the Columbia interviewer said he was having difficulty finding biographical information about the engineers and scientists for Columbia's Special Collections Department, so researching those fell to Kurt as well. Finally, he would need to attend the interviews as the General Electric representative to see that things went smoothly.

He was skeptical about Columbia's "so-called 'Oral History Project,'" as he characterized it in interoffice memos. The concept of formalized oral history was as recent as the 1930s, when interviewers for the Federal Writers Project traveled around the nation recording personal narratives, and the ethnomusicologists John and Alan Lomax recorded interviews with folksingers and their songs. But once Vonnegut became involved, he changed his mind about its value. Listening to the interviews unfold, and writing biographies of the participants, gave him new insights into scientists.

One early autumn morning in 1950, Kurt arrived at Columbia University to help the retired scientist Albert W. Hull prepare for his interview. Hull, a reticent New Englander and the world's most prolific inventor of electron vacuum tubes, was convinced he could say all he had to say in fifteen minutes. Once the interview began, however, his passion for electronics, the personalities and intellectual challenges involved, resulted in two hours of recorded conversation. Hull had begun life as a farm boy, became a Greek scholar at Yale, and, incredibly, was a self-taught physicist, having taken only one undergraduate course in the subject.[47] His protean work in General Electric's laboratories had led to improvements in detecting noise from submarines, generating microwave power for radar, and protecting home appliances from conducting high-voltage surges created by lightning. His fifty-seven-year career resulted in ninety-four patents.

Judging from Vonnegut's report on the interview, he was awed.[48] His appreciation for great men and women of science, such as Hull—the forerunners, mentors, and colleagues of his brother—increased yet again when he started writing their biographies. They set aside time for him, flattered by his interest. They spoke happily about their careers, their families, and what they had hoped to accomplish. As he took notes, he grew unexpectedly sad, ashamed really. He realized he genuinely liked these men, and he wanted them to like him. Their success was deserved. They didn't grouse about the company; they were grateful. Hull recalled that when he was a young man at General Electric, his boss, W. R. Whitney, another of the radio pioneers, would visit the labs regularly, asking "Are you having any fun?"[49] Kurt, on the other hand, had become the resident malcontent in his department, while these men, whose talents and interests just happened to be scientific and technological, were "extremely interesting, admirable Americans."[50] Perhaps he had never really understood them because he had seen them as carbons of his brother.

His change of heart didn't stop him from proceeding with his decision to quit, however. In mid-December 1950, he submitted his resignation, effective January 1, leaving the oral history project without a point man. Not even his counterpart at Columbia University knew he had left.[51]

His replacement, Al Berry, reported for his first day in the Publicity Department a few weeks after Kurt's departure. Berry had been editor of his high school newspaper and had recently graduated from Stanford. He liked everything about sales, marketing, and advertising. After the obligatory tour of the plant, George Griffin took him to the desk vacated by Vonnegut and, pointing to it, said, "I hope you do a better job than the last guy who sat here."[52]

KURT ANNOUNCED to friends that he was going to write full-time and Jane backed him 100 percent. Knox Burger was shocked. "I never said he should give up his job and devote himself to fiction. I don't trust the freelancer's life, it's tough."[53] Vic Jose, his Shortridge classmate who had covered beats with him at City News in Chicago, was just as incredulous. "That's the dumbest thing I ever heard. Nobody ever made any money freelance writing."[54]

The first order of business was to get a place where he could write for hours, uninterrupted and undistracted by the children. The little study in the front hallway would no longer do. Writing was a job, and he would treat it as one. Alplaus had no office buildings, and he didn't have the use of a car—Jane needed theirs for errands—so he had to find a spot in town, a room of his own. He stopped at Cheney's general store to ask the owner, Ann, whether she knew of anyone in town who might have a room to let. He would need it only during the day as an office.

Mrs. Cheney liked Kurt and admired him for striking out on his own as a writer; she offered him her daughter's bedroom above the store. Her daughter, Mary Lou, was away at college, and he could have it rent-free. Kurt insisted he pay something—a few dollars every week, anyway. He wouldn't accept charity. She agreed rather than hurt his pride.[55]

Mary Lou's bedroom looked out on the main street, Alplaus Avenue. As the sun came up through the winter morning dark, he could even see his house on Hill Street behind the tall pines. During the workweek, commuters formed a queue in Cheney's parking lot, and if he raised his window a few inches, he could overhear their conversations before they boarded the bus bound for Schenectady. Around nine o'clock, Mrs. Cheney's early-bird customers arrived at the store to pick up a few things. An hour later, Ida Dillman unlocked the door of the post office and retreated inside again to sort mail in silence. Observing the rhythm of the day from daybreak until dusk was like being the narrator in Thornton Wilder's *Our Town*. Some of the people he saw every morning and a few of the remarks he overheard went into stories. In coming years, residents of Alplaus recognized themselves in the pages of *Ladies' Home Journal*, *Cosmopolitan*, and of course *Collier's*.[56]

At dinnertime, he walked home. One night a week, Thursday, Jane volunteered at the Ellis Hospital psychopathic ward in Schenectady, where she made coffee and assisted people coming in off the streets. Sometimes the Vonneguts went out on a date, and Mrs. Cheney's teenage son, Jim, babysat for them. He liked the extra money, but he had some difficulty getting Edith and Mark to behave. They seemed a little wild for small children, he thought.[57]

Now and then, Mary Lou returned home from college for a visit and to help with the store. She was persnickety about her rented-out bedroom and didn't like seeing the wastebasket stuffed with wadded sheets of Mr. Vonnegut's typing paper. Each time it happened, she burned them in her mother's incinerator. Years later, she regretted doing that.[58]

In February 1951, Vonnegut admitted to Harris, he hadn't made enough to buy a pack of baseball cards.[59] He was convinced Burger was being too picky, giving him the noblesse oblige treatment by reading his stories, but then sending then back with an apologetic note. Anyone would think he was selecting works for the Harvard Classics, Kurt complained.[60] Meanwhile, Jane was depending on him, and even though he wrote daily and fast, each story required one or two revisions, thus doubling or trebling the amount of time involved. Suddenly, the spell broke when Burger purchased "All the King's Horses," a Cold War fantasy about a game of chess with human beings as the pieces, and "The Euphio Question," about an invention called the "euphoriaphone," which creates instant contentment by whispering encouragement in the user's ear. The latter story was purchased for the largest amount yet—Burger increased Kurt's pay rate steadily. The two checks combined equaled almost eight months' salary at General Electric.

Jane and Kurt decided to spend part of the money renting a cottage that summer in Provincetown on Cape Cod, a community of artists, for an entire month to get a real taste of living and writing by the sea.

Cape Cod, Massachusetts, about seventy miles southeast of Boston, is shaped like the arm of someone flexing his biceps, and Provincetown is on the underside of the fist, turned inward toward Provincetown Bay.

Four-fifths of the Cape was forested then, and macadam roads and sandy paths connected the towns.

Since the 1920s, writers and artists had been drawn to the Cape by its remoteness and beauty. Fishing shacks, barns, and sail lofts could be converted to studios and galleries. Seasonal visitors created a demand for summer stock theater, and the Provincetown Players became famous for staging original dramas by Eugene O'Neill, Edna Ferber, Djuna Barnes, Theodore Dreiser, and many other playwrights. Musicians from New York followed, and cabarets featuring Ella Fitzgerald, Duke Ellington, or other jazz musicians put Provincetown's artistic scene on a par with Greenwich Village.

The Vonneguts rented a little shingled house on Commercial Street by the beach that ringed the bay. The vacation turned into a family reunion. Alice, her husband, Jim Adams, and their three boys under ten—Jim Jr., Steve, and Kurt—lived in a Boston suburb and made the trip easily. Bernard and Lois, six-year-old Peter, and the couple's one-year-old twins, Scott and Terry, arrived, for a total of six adults and eight children, counting four-year-old Mark and eight-month-old Edie. After the rest of the family departed, Kurt and Jane continued exploring what Provincetown had to offer. One afternoon, Jane looked up from reading Irwin Shaw's best seller *The Young Lions*. Kurt wanted her to meet the young man he'd just run into: Norman Mailer.[61]

Twenty-seven-year-old Mailer, big-eared, with curly black hair and blue-green eyes, was everything Kurt wanted to be. After graduating from Harvard in 1943, he had been drafted into the army and served in the Philippines as a cook. His experiences resulted in *The Naked and the Dead* (1948), a *New York Times* best seller for sixty-two weeks, and hailed by many as one of the best American novels to come out of the war.

Jane, over cocktails, thought Mailer was a "nice guy," but Kurt read much more into talking to him. "He was my age. He had been a college-educated infantry private like me, and he was already a world figure, because of his great war novel."[62] Two other novels by veterans seemed to be in everyone's hands that summer, too: James Jones's *From Here to Eternity* and Herman Wouk's *The Caine Mutiny*. Vonnegut thought he had a big book inside him, he knew it—he had been at the Bulge and lived through Dresden. But the alignment, some unity, hadn't snapped into place yet.

As the end of the lease on the cottage approached, Kurt and Jane reached a decision. Based on how happy they'd been in Provincetown, where the brio of the 1920s was still almost palpable, they would sell the house in Alplaus and move to the Cape. From now on, they would live for the arts. They would read the best and latest books, discuss them, make notes to each other in the margins, and give full rein to Kurt's career in a location that couldn't be more salubrious for creativity. They must do it—to be true to themselves.[63] And for Kurt it was the vicarious realization of his mother's dream to live and write on Cape Cod.[64]

As SOON as they returned home to Alplaus in late August, they put 17 Hill Street up for sale. They had no trouble finding a buyer immediately because of the postwar housing crunch, and the value of the house had increased by a third in just three years. As the new owners—an engineer at General Electric and his wife—walked up the drive with their attorney to complete signing the papers, Kurt greeted them by playing Chopin's "Funeral March" on the piano.[65]

The new owners, Gloria and Jack Ericson, were gardeners and got busy putting in bulbs for spring. One Saturday, as Jack was assiduously shoveling in the front yard under the lemon lilies, Mrs. Larsen, who had attended the burial of Mrs. Grudgings's ashes, stopped to watch him.

"Don't go down too far around that old stump," she cautioned, and continued on her way.[66]

6: The Dead Engineer

1951–1958

ONCE KURT AND Jane decided to move to the Cape permanently in the fall of 1951, they had to act quickly. Without taking time to house-hunt carefully, or investigate the villages on Cape Cod, "we acted on impulse again," wrote Jane to Walter and Helen Vonnegut, "and bought the second house we looked at, in a town we had never heard of before, each of us silently wondering if we had utterly lost our wits in the hecticness of the summer."[1]

They chose a brick ranch home in Osterville partly shaded by pine trees with a walled-in-backyard, a permanent grill, and a small in-ground pool. The beach was only a fifteen-minute walk away. Osterville's downtown was old-fashioned looking, if a little touristy, with antique shops in "every other house," Jane noticed.[2] Kurt liked that the Cape Cod Airport was nearby so he could fly to New York, anticipating that once his writing career took hold he would be needed in Manhattan now and then.

What they didn't realize was that the character of Osterville was different after Labor Day. The residents disliked tourists; they tolerated them only because the ice cream, funnel cake, and other summer "shoppes" relied on surges of vacation money June through August. Once the warm weather ended, charming Osterville reverted to being a button-down small town.[3]

Making the best of it, Jane shrugged off their hasty choice to Walter and Helen, who were homesteading on Guemes Island, a short ferry ride from Anacortes, Washington. Schenectady had been a "graveyard with lights," Jane wrote, but now they were pioneers too, only of the arts, "possessed of the romantic illusion of finding the 'ideal' place to write. There is, of course, no such place we now realize, on any map— 'ideal' being what you make of where you are."[4]

Kurt at least had a second-floor study, all to himself, with a balcony above the living room. It jutted out over the living room and he invented a new use for it. Occasionally, when he was bored or restless from writing, he would stride out on to the balcony and bellow, "The king is speaking!" Then Mark and Jane, with Edie in her arms, would hurry to assemble underneath him, palms upraised. Solemnly, Kurt would toss down handfuls of gumdrops or animal crackers, inspiring grateful cries of "Long live the king! Long live the king!" His benevolence over with, Kurt would return to the fastness of his study. It was "very ego-restoring for the King," Jane said.[5]

SHE AND Kurt had reason to feel playful, despite their slight disappointment with Osterville. In the summer of 1951, Ken Littauer had sold an option on Kurt's first novel, *Player Piano*—a contest between society and technology—to Charles Scribner's Sons, publishers of Edith Wharton, Ernest Hemingway, F. Scott Fitzgerald, and Robert Heinlein, among many others. The amount was small because Scribner's editor Harry Brague hadn't seen enough of the manuscript to offer a substantial advance.[6] Nevertheless, money for a novel was a sign that Kurt's career was on course, and he assured Ken that he could finish the manuscript by mid-November, the deadline for new books to appear in the Scribner's spring 1952 catalog. Littauer let Brague know that he could look forward to receiving a "first-rate social satire" from Vonnegut.[7]

Jane never doubted that leaving General Electric was the right thing for Kurt to do, but she tended to be rather Pollyannaish about the pressure on him to pay the bills. "Writing will always be an up-and-down thing to do," she wrote to Walt and Helen, "but we are adjusted to that now, and it has a magic quality that is priceless."[8] Kurt, on the other hand, began to appreciate that part of the "magic quality" about writing for a living was the lag time in getting paid. To pump some quick cash into their finances, he took a one-month job writing copy for an advertising firm in Boston. Also, he worked relentlessly on his novel, delivering a completed manuscript to Scribner's at the end of November.[9] Littauer was impressed: when his young client promised to finish his first novel in four months, the older, experienced agent had cautioned Brague, "I told him that he'd better hurry."[10]

Having produced a first draft, Vonnegut requested only two favors from Brague. His brother, he explained, was a scientist at General Electric. In no way should *Player Piano* be touted as a satire on one of the world's largest corporations or Dr. Vonnegut's career might suffer through guilt by association.[11] Second, he didn't want to lose, he said, a scene Brague wanted to cut.[12] A character in the novel, the shah of Bratpur, asks the supercomputer EPICAC XIV, "What are people for?"[13] Brague agreed.

As it turned out, the shah's query would become, over the next four decades, the riddle behind most of Vonnegut's novels.

WITH HIS first novel undergoing editing—although Brague's suggested changes were only moderate—Kurt returned to writing short stories aimed at national magazines. But he faced a problem he was reluctant to admit: top-tier magazines—those that paid the best, too—didn't want anything too close to the edge, which was exactly what he preferred to write about.[14] Americans were living in a Cold War "age of anxiety," and he wanted to address contemporary issues, the kind appearing in newspapers every day.[15] Why was it that editors tended to read his stories, he asked Knox, even comment on them, but so often return them? He admitted his approach tended to be out of the ordinary, but how could recondite subjects like nuclear fallout or immortality be dramatized with conventional storytelling?[16]

What he could not see was that by wanting it both ways—aiming at high-paying markets such as the *New Yorker* and *Redbook*, for example, but writing about social issues in ways better suited to *Astounding Science Fiction*—his fiction tended to be sui generis. In his bleaker moments, he complained sarcastically to Knox that his eager readership must be out there, wondering why there wasn't more from the pen of Kurt Vonnegut?[17] His agent, Ken Littauer, was unsympathetic: "Who asked you to be a writer in the first place?"[18]

For the sake of staying financially viable, he was forced to continue writing with mass-market magazines in mind. He could deliver what they wanted, although he wasn't happy about it. He claimed to love the act of authoring, he "loved every word" he typed, even if "a lot of it was miserable crap."[19] He sold "The Package" and "Poor Little Rich Town" to *Collier's* and "Souvenir" to *Argosy*—all three stories bulging with sentimentality. He asked Max Wilkinson, tongue in cheek, how to end a short story without killing off all the characters. Wilkinson replied airily, "Nothing could be simpler, dear boy: The hero mounts his horse and rides off into the sunset."[20]

He continued to clack away, pausing, when he was in a funk, to suspect that Littauer probably wasn't working as hard as he should be to put the really good stuff forward, the writing that would distinguish him.[21] He began to worry seriously about money. Jane asked him if maybe he had been blacklisted at *Collier's* for some reason.

The remark hurt because it implied he didn't know what he was doing, or maybe he wasn't talented enough. The "king" went into high dudgeon, after which he turned on Knox. In a hot letter, he informed his friend-the-editor that Littauer had a stockpile of his stories, so he should "demand" to see them. And room for a science fiction piece titled "Ice-9" could be found in the magazine, too—if Burger would bother to reexamine his editorial priorities. He might have spoiled the relationship for good when he sputtered that Knox was acting like a son of a bitch.[22] But Knox genuinely liked Kurt and put the letter aside, knowing he was doing everything he could to help his friend as it was.[23]

PLAYER PIANO, so titled to capture the idea of a device mimicking human ability, wasn't published in the spring of 1952 or even that summer. Scribner's, for reasons of its own, had decided to delay the novel's appearance until fall. To Kurt, the decision was a grave financial setback. He had a second novel under way (later rewritten as a play) with the working title *Grieve No More My Lord*. A second novel might mean another contract, and an advance, but with Scribner's waiting to gauge sales of the first novel, there would be no second advance anytime soon. He pleaded with Brague that delaying publication by six months would put him in a tight spot. He needed time to write, but he had to provide for his family, too. The sooner he had a reputation and the prospect of royalties, the better.[24] The best Brague could offer was a publication date at the end of August, with prepublication copies going out to book reviewers in June. Also, to create some buzz about the novel, Scribner's had already mailed copies to a long list of top engineers, scientists, and plant managers. It was a good promotional strategy.

Thinking he would go Scribner's one better, Kurt mailed a copy of *Player Piano* to Norbert Wiener, an MIT professor later credited with pioneering cybernetics—the science of communications and automatic control systems. For the twenty-nine-year-old, first-time novelist it showed a lot of gumption. And he was abashed by the response. When Wiener recognized his colleague mathematician John von Neumann portrayed in the novel by a character also named von Neumann, who leads an antitechnological conspiracy, Wiener wrote angrily to Brague warning him that his brash young author "cannot with impunity . . . play fast and loose with the names of living people."[25] In his view, the "new cult" of postwar science fiction was refusing to confront, as he was, the misuse of computers, opting instead to pen pointless fairy tales about the world of tomorrow.

Vonnegut was shaken. He thought he was on the same side as forward-thinking people like Wiener. Respectfully, he apologized in a letter to his first serious critic, but also maintained that *Player Piano* was, in his opinion, a fair "indictment of science as it is being run today."[26]

Having paid his obeisance to the great man and figuratively bowed out of the room, he and Jane fantasized about deadly, cutting things they'd like to say to him, Kurt told Brague. Vonnegut grumbled that Wiener knew as much about satire as he did about cybernetics.[27]

WHEN *PLAYER Piano* appeared in August 1952, the print run was 7,600 copies, a propitious number for a first-time novelist and reason for Kurt to be pleased. He dedicated it "To Jane—God bless her!"

From Indianapolis, Uncle Alex announced the big event on Provident Mutual Insurance stationery to dozens of Vonnegut relatives. At the top of each he wrote in large letters, "Act Now!" He recommended that the recipient purchase a copy of *Player Piano* as soon as possible and write to Kurt in Osterville to say that he or she had done so. In the left-hand margin Alex added, "If you do not do what I suggest you will break my heart!"[28]

Philip K. Dick, a young science fiction writer selling stories to the pulps, expressed what most writers in his genre probably thought: "Nobody knew who Vonnegut was."[29] But Dick was intrigued with the idea of a society in freefall because of its fascination with laborsaving devices. It was not the usual vision of a future in which humankind would be the master of machines. Instead, in Vonnegut's satire of the world to come, people are dispirited, largely useless, and the victims of planned obsolescence as if they were old appliances.

For the setting of *Player Piano*, Vonnegut doesn't stray far from General Electric. The fictional town is Ilium, New York, and the Schenectady Works is barely retouched as the Ilium Works. He departs hardly a jot, for instance, from General Electric's annual competitions for executives held on Association Island—Vice President Boulware's idea for team building—as hopeful wives waited on the mainland like so many Penelopes waiting for their Odysseus to return.

Vonnegut's techno-utopia is run by a management echelon dressed in gray flannel, one of whom is the novel's protagonist Dr. Paul Proteus, an engineer and a rising young man in the company. His wife, Anita, is almost pathologically ambitious. Proteus can foresee how human beings are hastening to bring about an end to their utility on the planet. Science and technology are not the villains; it's the failure to consider their impact on people's lives, under the excuse that progress is always good. Typical is the engineer who invents a machine that will render his own job superfluous. "'Thet's it,' said Bud with an eerie mixture of pride and remorse. 'Works. Does a fine job.' He smiled sheepishly. 'Does it a whole lot better than Ah did it.'"[30]

Proteus purchases a primitive farm as a sanctuary where he can retreat, think, and work with his hands. (Anita is horrified.)[31] But there's movement afoot to overthrow the masters of Ilium Works, and Proteus decides to join the instigators. Their plan is to blow up the machines and rebuild Ilium as a community of friends and relatives living "blamelessly, naturally, by hands and wits."[32] Vonnegut, thinking back no doubt on his boyhood at Lake Maxinkuckee and Robert Redfield's studies of folk societies, argues, through Proteus, that community is the answer to loss of purpose and loneliness. In the first of many such occurrences in Vonnegut's novels, Proteus turns against those who would demean life after he has spent time hiding with the conspirators underground, as Vonnegut did before witnessing Dresden's apocalypse.

In the end, however, Vonnegut hesitates over how to resolve the irrepressible human impulse to build, tinker, invent, and engineer. The rebellion in Ilium fizzles, and the workers who were thrown out of work by machines become interested in repairing ones they smashed. It's human nature—technology can be absorbing. As a humane solution to the continuing problem of men versus machines, Vonnegut implies that people should learn to collaborate, a nostrum that may leave some readers unsatisfied.[33]

PLAYER PIANO isn't adventurous science fiction because America *was* coming to rely increasingly on automation.[34] It's closer in spirit to sociology couched in fiction. In important ways, though, Vonnegut's first novel defines most of what will come from his typewriter over the next four decades. To start with, he demonstrates his love of debunking fixed ideas and institutions that are usually treated with reverence. Progress, for example, tends to be associated with positive change, but he isn't so sure.

Second, although *black humorist* is a term often applied to him, and *Player Piano* offered early evidence of that, Vonnegut isn't a "black humorist" and won't become one. A black humorist is a nihilist: existence is meaningless and chaotic. Characters are often grotesque and freakish; they respond to the absurdity of life by mocking it.[35] Vonnegut doesn't lampoon human beings or portray them as having no psychological depth.[36] They are people struggling to avoid corruption and traps laid for them by circumstance or the environment. He doesn't belittle them because imagination is often their only principal weapon against oppression. They are cunning, like Paul Proteus and his coconspirators, and conceive ways to destroy systems that would steal their dignity. They can be hapless at times, but they are striving to become better human beings. When Vonnegut's characters have at last achieved peace, it's usually because they have accepted their powerlessness over most things—not cynically but wisely. Considering how *Player Piano* and all of his subsequent novels are marked by humor, affection, and a desire to instruct, a better description for Vonnegut's mode is *comic-didactic.*[37]

But the most interesting aspect of *Player Piano* is its conservatism. This wouldn't seem to fit with Kurt Vonnegut of the 1960s, his face surrounded by a nimbus of curly, chestnut hair, underscored by a boomerang-shaped mustache. That man, a hero of hippies, would seem to be opposed to tradition almost on principle.

And yet there is much about tradition and free enterprise that is admirable to Vonnegut. He was proud to be descended from enterprising and civic-minded German American merchants and professionals. In addition to their workaday responsibilities, three generations of Vonneguts had served on boards and committees whose overlapping purpose was strengthening the network of business, social, and intellectual ties serving Indianapolis. He regretted the diaspora of his family from the city after World War II, convinced that families with generational roots in a region were emotionally invested in where they lived.[38] Within their own families, relatives in close proximity also filled the important function of caring for their members—not only taking in the old or dispossessed, but also helping children grow into healthy adults under the watchful eyes of elders.

In *Player Piano*, Vonnegut attacks the corporate bigwigs who have usurped the pride of place in families and parade about as self-appointed patriarchs. Big business and big government, he complained to Burger, were partners in foisting socialism on the country. How they sapped, in combination, Americans' spirit of individuality with guarantees that adults would be inured from failure was humiliating.[39] If it were up to him, the spunk of self-reliance shown in Indianapolis going back a hundred years would be the model for mid-twentieth-century society.

That mind-set is certainly not one most people would identify as belonging to a foe of free enterprise, whether he had long hair and a mustache or not.

REVIEWS OF *Player Piano* were cursory, and not many appeared. (Brague dismissed the *New Yorker's* "usual snotty little review.")[40] The Science Fiction Book Club ran a full-page ad in *Popular Science* listing it as a choice to its members. Years later, Vonnegut claimed he was bemused at being categorized a science fiction writer: "I was classified as a science-fiction writer because I'd include machinery, and all I'd done was write about Schenectady in 1948!"[41] But at the time, he told Miller Harris it was his goal to become one.[42]

Ultimately, *Player Piano* sold only 3,600 copies. Scribner's, as a favor to Vonnegut, went to the trouble of sending a sales representative on a special trip to Schenectady, but "it proved quite futile," reported the salesman.[43]

After that, Vonnegut tumbled into a twilight chasm as an author. Brague, on good faith, advanced him a small amount for a second novel (later published as *The Sirens of Titan*), but Kurt cautioned him that he was feeling too dejected to make much progress on it. It wasn't that he didn't have ideas, but when he went into New York he felt like a hick arriving in town on a Saturday night for a root beer and a picture show. In his current state of mind, he felt like he didn't belong in the company of publishers and authors.[44] Although he would place nearly three dozen stories with *Collier's*, the *Saturday Evening Post, Argosy*, the *Ladies' Home Journal, Esquire, Cosmopolitan*, and *Redbook* over the next decade, it would take almost twice that long—years of constant writing—until he was widely known.

MEANWHILE KNOX Burger had left *Collier's* to become an editor primarily of suspense novels for Dell paperbacks. Kurt continued to rely on him as a confidant about his work, his family, and even his marriage, sometimes writing him every other week. In the winter of 1953, Vonnegut reached out to him again, this time because he was tempted to be unfaithful to Jane.[45]

The snow was deep on Cape Cod. Mark and Edie, ages five and three, were confined in the house. Kurt was back in his study trying to make a buck at the typewriter. What he needed, he told Knox, was to give a woman a good tromboning; he had a candidate in mind, too: a friend of Jane's.[46]

The lady in question looked like trouble out of a Mickey Spillane novel: a bottle blonde who tottered around on spiked heels and flashed long, back-scratching red nails. Her husband, a well-built guy, smeared himself with hair oil and cologne, leaving an odiferous cloud behind him wherever he went. One day, half an hour after Jane had left for Indianapolis to take care of her mother (who had suffered another nervous collapse), the blonde stopped by to see Kurt. She suggested the timing was perfect for them to hit the sack.

Somehow he got out of it, but for the next week and half he walked around in a state of semi-tumescence waiting for Jane.[47] In the meantime, the oleaginous husband accused Vonnegut anyway of bedding his wife. Kurt assured Knox he hadn't, but he just might.[48] When Jane finally arrived home, she had a bad case of the flu.

Afraid that his resolve was deflating, he made an appointment to see a psychiatrist. The doctor, listening, reacted casually. It was normal to have urges, he said. He himself liked a good drink as much as the next man, but what did that mean? Nothing.[49] Kurt departed, feeling less like a satyr than just a normal, healthy husband tempted by a vamp.[50]

About a week later, the husband and wife came by. They had another proposition—a permanent wife swap: the kids would accompany their respective mothers to the new household, like furniture. The Vonneguts threw them out.[51]

THE WINTER of the oversexed blonde and her raunchy husband segued into a "very bad summer," and Kurt was no better.[52] Fortunately, offsetting his mental state, which he correctly self-diagnosed as a bout of serious depression, he and Jane joined two groups, a Great Books course and the Barnstable Comedy Club.

The Great Books course was his first systematic introduction to great themes of Western literature. In the course, he studied Aristotle's *Poetics* and discovered the fundamentals of theme, structure, climax, and characterization.[53] Covering all the works on the syllabus would take almost three years, but to a writer with a hybrid education—two years of science courses at Cornell and about two of anthropology at the University of Chicago—the readings and discussions of the group considerably strengthened his critical sense.

Then, through some accidental synergy, he also discovered drama, which amplified his readings in the Great Books course even further. The Barnstable Comedy Club, located four miles northeast of Osterville, was the Cape's oldest amateur theater group, founded in the 1920s. It had no playhouse of its own and staged its productions at the Barnstable's Woman Club or Barnstable High School. Anyone could participate; in fact, the club was always recruiting because of the time commitment—several nights a week during the spring, summer, and autumn seasons. As a result, many evenings Mark and Edie were put to bed by a babysitter when their parents had a Great Books class or play rehearsal.

Kurt's first appearance on a playbill was as a dinner party guest in the comedy *Dulcy*. Jane debuted as flighty little cousin Bella Hedley in *The Barretts of Wimpole Street*. After that, they could be counted on to work almost every show, either backstage (Kurt's preference) or by taking a role. Over the years, Kurt was seen in *The Curious Savage*, *A View from the Bridge*, *Cock-a-Doodle-Dandy* (sporting an Irish brogue), and *Tiger at the Gate*, during which he charged onstage dressed in a leopard skin and brandishing a spear. "He had a funny, wry sense of humor," one of his fellows actors remembered. "I adored Kurt. He had a tender side. He was shy by nature, but a good actor."[54] Jane was better, however. After major parts in *Harvey* and *Here Today*, she was the romantic lead in *Separate Tables*.[55]

The club also inspired one of Vonnegut's better-known short stories. First published in 1961 in the *Saturday Evening Post* as "My Name Is Everyone," it was later included as "Who Am I This Time?" in the 1968 collection *Welcome to the Monkey House*. A painfully introverted post office worker is an instinctive method actor who can handle practically any lead, including Stanley Kowalski in *Streetcar Named Desire*. Kurt only slightly fictionalized events at the comedy club, and the diffident hero of the story became a local celebrity.

HE WAS having a good run of freelancing in the early spring of 1954—two stories to the *Saturday Evening Post*, one to *Cosmo*, and one to *Esquire* ("but the good ones aren't selling")—so he rented half of an office at the top of some narrow, winding stairs above the Osterville Package Store at 11 Wianno Avenue.[56] Dividing the room in half was a paneled wall, still there, three-quarters high and finished off with lattice. Kurt's side faced the street; on the other side of the wall was Al Little, a self-employed certified public accountant in his thirties. It was like being in Alplaus and perched over Cheney's store again. He found his spirits rising.[57]

One day in May 1954, an enterprising door-to-door TV salesman found him writing in his rented office. The Vonneguts didn't own a television, and Kurt purchased one on the spot, having been promised same-day delivery. By late afternoon he was home watching the four networks—ABC, NBC, CBS, and DuMont—marveling at the quality of shows like *Rocky King, Inside Detective*, and *The Guiding Light*, but also feeling a sense of foreboding.[58]

The golden age of television broke over him—an era when hour-long plays by Paddy Chayefsky, Horton Foote, Tad Mosel, Rod Serling, and Gore Vidal, among others, brought acclaimed, live drama into the living rooms of millions of Americans. It was like having free tickets, every week, to theaters on and off Broadway. On a typical Thursday evening in 1954, Kurt and Jane had their choice between *Kraft Television Theatre, Four Star Playhouse, Ford Theatre*, and *Lux Video Theatre*. Young actors (such as James Dean, Warren Beatty, Paul Newman, and Suzanne Pleshette) and young directors (John Frankenheimer, Robert Altman, Sidney Lumet, and Sydney Pollack) illuminated the small gray screen with weekly portrayals of American life that were, by turns, serious, comic, or tragic.

Vonnegut saw immediately what this foretold: the decline of slick magazines as venues for fiction. When people could watch in their homes an evening of stories adapted for television, advertising would shift its money to the new medium, making "playing short story pinball for a living obsolete," he realized.[59] And he was right. The staticky television tube lured most would-be readers of magazine fiction. Within a few years, *Collier's* and other general interest magazines eliminated most of their short stories to save money.

To Kurt, it was just as well. He wasn't proud of two stories that had recently appeared in the *Saturday Evening Post*, "Ambitious Sophomore" and "Custom-Made Bride," because they were so ordinary, so pat.[60] Within weeks of purchasing a television, he declared to Knox that he was through courting the muse of fiction. From now on he would be a playwright.[61] With the same kind of impetuosity that made him throw over everything at General Electric, or decide on the spot that he and Jane needed to move to Cape Cod, he got busy cowriting a play, *Emory Beck*, with a friend, Robert B. Ruthman, a reporter for the *New Bedford Standard Times*.[62] They finished it in eight days and mailed the script to Littauer & Wilkinson.[63] Then they heard nothing and with good reason: the play was awful. Littauer already had a play dashed off by Kurt titled *Celeste*, and it had received the same treatment.[64]

Silence from his agent raised the specter of money worries again, and this time with more reason than usual. Somberly, he wrote Harry Brague at Scribner's that the strain on him would be increasing soon. Jane was pregnant with their third child.[65]

A NEW baby coming would mean a host of additional expenses. He was at the point of taking any writing assignment, if only he could snag one. Breaking from a jog into a run, he chased after more work. Brague had already optioned a second novel from him after *Player Piano* and, without having seen a word of it, advanced him a small amount of money as a gesture of support in late summer 1953.[66] But the second novel option called for half of the manuscript and a complete outline before any additional money would change hands. Almost a year passed, and Vonnegut had to admit to Brague that the story had stalled on him. However, in the spring of 1954, he submitted six chapters of a different novel: an expanded version of the short story "Ice-9" (which Knox had rejected for *Collier's*), retitled *Cat's Cradle*. He didn't expect a contract, much less any money, Vonnegut wrote solicitously to Brague. He only wanted a little encouragement.[67] Hearing nothing from Brague three weeks after sending the chapters minus an outline, Kurt complained to Knox that his editor was a real drip.[68]

Fortunately, a project that looked to be short and lucrative came his way through Jane's friend from Swarthmore Fred S. Rosenau at Random House. A heavily illustrated centennial history of Cornell University was in the planning stages, which Random House would then market to Cornell alumni. Rosenau passed along Kurt's name to the editors, saying his friend was the ideal candidate to write the text. The irony tickled Vonnegut. He had dropped out of Cornell, anticipating that he would be asked to leave anyway, and now the university was turning to him to write its history.[69] He estimated he would spend two weeks on campus in Ithaca researching, and would write the book during the rest of the summer, just in time for the baby's arrival in early October.

There was the problem, of course, of having accepted money from Scribner's to complete a second novel, and protocol required that an author work on books in order of precedence. But Max Wilkinson met with Brague and explained Kurt's situation: "The fee he will receive for this work will help immeasurably in keeping him as he goes on with fiction."[70] Brague graciously agreed to wait.

The Cornell book would pay a flat fee, just what he needed to carry him until he could return to the optioned second novel, and then do something about the orphaned six chapters of *Cat's Cradle*, provided Brague was interested in it. Timing was crucial, however—not just for Kurt financially, but also because Jane had been suffering for months from morning sickness, so badly that she needed regular antinausea shots. Soon, he wouldn't be able to leave her on her own for two weeks to go to Ithaca. He needed a contract and a payment schedule for the centennial book quickly. Promising Fred, who was a bachelor, a terrific time if he went with him on the trip, Kurt added pointedly, what was the holdup with finalizing the contract?[71]

But Random House and Cornell were on geologic time compared with his schedule. The proposed book was largely aimed at a niche readership, and there was no urgency about getting it finished. Spring became early summer while Kurt waited for word, but nothing definitive happened.

In the meantime, with Knox's help, he landed a short-term job writing for a special edition of *Sports Illustrated*. Leaving Jane with their Plymouth so that she could drive to the doctor's for her antinausea shots, he took a room at the private Cornell Club in the Hotel Barclay at 111 East Forty-eighth Street.[72] He had friends he could stay with in New York but he preferred hotels.[73]

The editors at *Sports Illustrated* put him on writing captions and short pieces. During his lunch hour, he moseyed over to Littauer & Wilkinson hoping for some good news, any reason to hope he wouldn't go broke. Noting Vonnegut's peripatetic entrances and exits, the office secretary, Carolyn Blakemore, came to refer to him as "the ectoplasmic Kurt." He would wander in, make small talk, and then suddenly he wasn't there any longer. "Maybe the problem was not that the agents didn't know what to do for him, but he didn't know what to do in the role of a writer."[74]

He wasn't sure what to do at *Sports Illustrated*, either, despite having covered sports at Cornell. Or maybe he was just so frustrated, or worried about Jane, that he couldn't think. In any case, one day, staring at a sheet of paper in his typewriter, he struggled with how to caption a photograph of a racehorse hurdling the track's fence. Finally he typed, "The horse jumped over the fucking fence."[75] He left the building without a word, packed his suitcase at the hotel, and went back to the Cape.

NANNETTE VONNEGUT was born October 4, 1954, and Kurt wrote to Knox that having the birth over with was "cathartic."[76] But this child being his third, having another baby wasn't cathartic; it was adding to the stress beginning to overwhelm him.

Player Piano had gone out of print in June, less than a year after its publication. His final royalty check from Scribner's had been a pittance sent by Harry Brague to Ken Littauer with the poignant note, unknown to Kurt, "I hope it helps the guy out, and I'm only sorry that it's not for a larger amount."[77] Bantam Books had purchased the reprint rights to *Player Piano*, and Kurt stood to make a significant amount of money from the sale, but so far he hadn't seen any of it.[78] Now, with the arrival of the new baby, he couldn't do the Cornell history project after all, either. He was embarrassed because he had hoped Random House would think of him as a writer to watch.[79]

At Cape Cod Hospital in Hyannis, Kurt glumly followed a nurse to Jane's room, where she was waiting with their infant daughter. After the nurse left them alone, he sat down heavily on the edge of his wife's bed, put his head in his hands, and began to sob.

He told her he almost drove off a bridge on his way to the hospital.[80] He couldn't stop crying.

OSTERVILLE WAS no longer the place for them, Kurt and Jane decided. A new beginning was called for. The town was too constraining, too stuffy, and, besides, their little brick ranch home was not suited for a growing family. Now was the time to relocate because Kurt had abruptly sold four stories in a row for a total of seven in 1954, making it his best year so far. At their Great Books group, a friend from Barnstable said he knew just the place for them: a big house in West Barnstable.[81]

West Barnstable is about halfway along the biceps of the Cape Cod arm. The house they looked at on Scudder's Lane was two hundred years old with six fireplaces and twelve rooms, surrounded by fields, marshes, and the Barnstable dunes. Also on the property was a small barn and a well house for a disused hand pump. From the house, a path rambled through waist-high sea broom to a beach of smooth stones.[82] The seller's asking price was a bargain because the house's charm was on the outside; inside, the rooms needed redecorating and the furnace was ancient.

Using the Osterville house as collateral, and the promise of the reprint money from Bantam, Kurt boasted to Knox that he was able to engage in some fancy financial footwork and purchase the big West Barnstable house.[83] Having rebounded from the birth of his third child just a few weeks earlier, he invited Knox down for some fishing after the Vonneguts took possession in the spring.[84]

Until then, they owned two homes. The combined mortgages would have strained the income of a salaried junior executive, let alone a writer who received fistfuls of cash now and then. But Jane assured Kurt that everything was going to be all right—"just grand." She "knew it in her bones," and he believed her.[85]

That settled, in November Kurt took Edie to see his father in Indiana for the old gentleman's seventieth birthday, leaving Jane on her own with six-week-old Nanny and seven-year-old Mark.

JANE WAS not as serene as she acted; she was seeing a psychiatrist for postpartum depression, but Kurt was confident that problem would clear up in a few sessions.[86] Her role in the marriage, after all, was to be the counterpoint to his anxieties about writing. He was unaware of how often she staggered emotionally under the load of what he demanded of her. Nothing except writing—constant, obsessive writing—was permitted to take priority in their lives, and when it wasn't going well he became defensive and drank too much. He worried about money, but he was careless with it, too—learned behavior no doubt from his parents, who gaily went through theirs with a sense of entitlement.

"I love him, I could never live with anyone else, this is true," Jane wrote to herself on a scrap of paper, "but he doesn't have the slightest idea how crazy he drives me. . . . All these goddamned ashes and ashtrays all over the place, but he will never see that and he will never change. . . . I have no business being here at all, and yet, I have to be, for him as well as for me and the children, too. He is a genius. . . . And it is wonderful. I love it, I hate it, it is awful, it will never be good. It will never be relaxed. We will never have piece of mind, but oh, lord, it is so wonderful."[87]

KURT SR. had purchased a cottage in Brown County near Nashville, Indiana, about twenty-five miles south of Indianapolis, having sold the house in Williams Creek a few months before Kurt and Edie's visit.[88] He had retired after ten years from the architectural firm of Vonnegut, Wright and Yeager and spent his days driving around the countryside, renowned for its rolling prairie, covered bridges, and autumnal colors. At home, he made ceramic pieces, read for hours, and smoked while listening to his favorite German Romantic composers on a crank-style Victrola phonograph player, a gift from his sister, Irma Vonnegut Lindener. In fact, his sister, during her long sojourns from Hamburg, "gave him the only sort of companionship which he would tolerate," said a relative.[89] He thought people talked too much.[90] Six-year-old Edie's impression of her grandfather was "a dignified man with a pipe. He was old wood—great old cuckoo clocks, and German clocks, and wood and alpines."[91] Inside the cottage, Kurt Sr. seemed to have stopped time to the era of his youth.

The visit was supposed to last a week, but father and son quarreled the first day. Kurt Sr. was "extremely proud" of his son the writer, as evidenced by the letter in 1950 lauding his talents, but Kurt Jr. felt a need to believe, as he did for the rest of his life, that "Father was so ashamed of me."[92] An insight into why he persisted in believing this, and why he would quarrel with his father, comes from the critic Leslie A. Fiedler: "The self-conscious artist of the new age feels himself at once of the middle class and estranged from it, the son of a bourgeois committed to oppose everything in which the bourgeoisie believes. By the very act of becoming a writer, he has (he cannot help feeling) betrayed his father, abandoned the male world of consciousness and action for a dark flirtation with the unconscious."[93] In other words, Vonnegut needed to feel at odds with his father and the values he represented (compounded by his father's delight in the Old World) to see himself as a social critic, artist, and imagineer.

After the argument, Kurt went pheasant hunting to relax with a local man who had hunting dogs. He shot at five birds and missed, without regret. Since the war, he didn't have much stomach for shooting things.

When he returned to his father's house, the air still hadn't cleared between them. At the end of the second day he left, taking Edie with him, and spent the rest of the time in Indianapolis visiting old friends. Returning to the Cape at the end of November, he wrote to Harry Brague that spending time with his father had made him appreciate the title of Thomas Wolfe's novel *You Can't Go Home Again*.[94]

Kurt Sr. felt bad about the visit going awry and sent a long letter to his son and Jane in early January. On Christmas Eve, he said, he had been home "with my tree and candles lighted, having a quiet time with my thoughts. They were cheerful, dominated by gratitude that I have three exceptional children and nine grandchildren of promise." He paid Jane the compliment of suggesting that, judging from her letters, she was contributing "much ghost writing for Kurt Vonnegut Jr." And then, because his rabbit stew was finished cooking on the stove, he ended by wishing them "a happy new year and God bless you!"[95]

KURT AND Jane's move into the house in West Barnstable in February 1955 coincided with Bantam reissuing *Player Piano*. But the auspiciousness of the occasion was marred by how Bantam ranked him as a writer. The reprint was retitled *Utopia 14* and graced with a lurid cover of writhing naked figures in a Dantesque landscape with machines. Instead of being distributed to bookstores, it wound up placed on rotating racks in drugstores and bus terminals beside other cheap paperbacks and comic books. When a reputable publisher resorted to tarting up his novel for readers who also might like *Conan the Conqueror*, it was a sign he was in the bowery of the book world.[96] He gave up his rented office in Osterville and assigned himself a room off the side of the house.

Needing money again and still convinced that the theater held more potential for him as a writer than fiction, he popped off plays like he was shooting clay pigeons—four in all, one after the other. To increase their chances of being produced, he intentionally created them as low-budget, off-Broadway pieces, or playlets for television.[97] He was done with hack work, he wrote Burger; the thrill was long gone of seeing his name on a short story.[98] Writing for television and the stage were his two new stratagems, and magazines could go to hell.[99]

Part of his bravado stemmed from getting into a quarrel with Jane about his career.[100] She was beginning to feel frantic; certain facts couldn't be glossed over with happy talk about how he was going to make it big: they were practically broke now and living in a huge house that needed repairs. They had two small children in school, who needed clothes, school supplies, and all the rest of it. And Nanny, the baby, had been sickly when she was born.[101] The pediatrician and other bills had to be paid. Maybe he couldn't survive—*they* couldn't survive—on his writing alone.[102]

The argument wound down to a sad admission by both of them that perhaps full-time writing wasn't working out.[103] He couldn't guarantee Jane that things would get any better soon, either. All he could do was try to put pressure on Littauer & Wilkinson to sell his work, especially the playlets aimed at television.[104] That was where the fast money was.

Jane retreated, as she often did at the end of their arguments. She disliked tension and tried to dispel it with a glad face, which she was good at mimicking even when she felt upset. "Cheerfulness in the face of adversity" was her standard response, she wrote later, but she couldn't expect the same from Kurt. "He preferred a kind of ironic desperation, blended with fits of manic mirth. Which is what kept him going. That and the agony." Increasingly, too, "he had discovered the flotative quality of alcohol."[105]

LIKE HIS mother, Kurt was not good at facing emotional adversity—physical, yes, as evidenced by how he survived the death march to Stalag IV-B, a starvation diet, and the fifty-mile march out of Dresden to Hellendorf, where he was forced to forage for grass and dandelions while waiting to be liberated. But emotional demands—particularly ones made on him by others—were harder for him to handle. He responded with humor, and to his male friends with a kind of teasing chumminess, but in general he distanced himself, especially from those who needed him most, rather than put his feelings at risk. A case in point is his behavior as a father.

The summer of 1955, Knox came up to go fishing for a weekend and have a look at Kurt's new home in West Barnstable. Burger, notorious for his grouchiness and sharp tongue, took the children on his lap, asked them about school and friends, and talked to them about their interests. "He was like more of that kind of a father to me than my father," Edie said. "And I love[d] Knox for that. So he was my idea of what a real father should be like. But I don't remember [my father] being that one-on-one as a little kid, not at all."[106]

Times when Kurt was affectionate stayed in Edie's memory because they were rare. "We would take picnics in a little motorboat across the harbor to a place called Sandy Neck for cookouts with their friends. And we'd always come home in the night, without running lights on the boats and it was really kind of coming back recklessly. But I remember being asleep and my father carrying me, but I'm not really asleep, I'm pretending to be asleep, and he's carrying me from the blanket where I fell asleep and to the boat through the stars and the sand dunes. I didn't have to be awake, I didn't have to get myself to the boat, and it's the only time I really remember being carried. And it was absolutely Sandy Neck and it was Dad."[107]

Glimpses of Vonnegut in the context of his family appear in a home movie shot by Ollie Lyon, his friend from General Electric who was vacationing on the Cape, also during the summer of 1955, with his wife, Lavinia. Kurt is wearing a gray sports jacket, white shirt, and chinos and lies on his side in the grass, his back to Jane and Lavinia, who are admiring Nanny, a blond infant blinking sleepily in the sunlight. Kurt fiddles with a wisp of straw, looking a little bored. Next, Ollie films him in the barn, painting a canvas (he made a gift of it to Lavinia). He glances over his shoulder to see whether the camera's running. Then the scene changes to Mark, Edie, and the Lyons' children, Mary and Philip, who are fishing with poles made of sticks, string, and safety pins at Coggins Pond near the house. Someone must be calling them, because they turn and trot back up a path. Mark tries to catch up with his father, who is walking up a slope toward the house. Apparently, Mark calls for him to wait, because Kurt, without turning, pauses. Once Mark is beside him, his father begins walking again, looking straight ahead.[108]

Money worries too, and anxieties about what he didn't have in comparison with other men his age, stirred up his defenses. The Vonneguts, for example, didn't attend Fred Rosenau's wedding to the former Ellen Miller earlier that year, but Kurt, during a trip to New York in July, accepted an invitation to have dinner with the newlyweds.[109]

Ellen was twelve years younger than Fred and had transferred from Vassar to Barnard College in Manhattan to be near her husband's work.[110]

Her father, vice president of sales for Random House, furnished the young couple's apartment as a wedding gift. Not long after Kurt arrived at their uptown address, the dinner became unpleasant.

"Kurt was so bitter," Ellen remembered. "He was probably broke and here's Fred all set up in a lovely apartment. Kurt was sort of snarling." Having come from a publishing family, Ellen suspected the tension had to do with Vonnegut, the creative personality, resenting Rosenau's prosperity. "It was very easy for the literary types to put down the people who were commercial successes." As the evening crept along, Kurt continued to drink heavily and the conversation became more poisonous, until finally he left. After the door shut behind him, Ellen made it clear to Fred that she didn't want him being treated that way again. Rosenau and Vonnegut were never friendly again.[111]

He knew he was acting terribly, he confessed to Knox at the end of the summer. He felt stuck in a ditch and unable to rock himself out no matter what he did. He wasn't happy with the way Littauer and Wilkinson were managing his career, and on top of that, he was feeling sexually frustrated. In a letter to Burger headed "Labor Day" in capital letters, he recounted his efforts to put Jane in a sexy mood.[112] He had been trying to get her to read Molly Bloom's amatory soliloquy in Joyce's *Ulysses*, but she wouldn't. Women, he was convinced, didn't really enjoy sex—only the power it gave them over men.[113] On a block of stone in the backyard, he chiseled Molly's words "yes I said yes I will Yes."[114]

His discontent expressed itself in his writing. A play, *Something Borrowed*, was about a man who loses an election and finds himself left with the quotidian responsibilities of being a father and a husband, stuck now in a kind of permanent hopelessness.[115] He was also writing a pulp novel, a noir plot about a man who murders his wife, and then goes looking for his son to explain why. The son is a teenager living a lusty, happy life with a beautiful, sensuous woman in a cottage on the Provincetown dunes.[116]

As far as his second novel for Scribner's was concerned, for which he had received a small advance, he wasn't doing anything about it. Months earlier, he had reiterated to his editor, Harry Brague, that he might as well forget about the project—there was too much pressure on him. Maybe if neither one of them pretended there had to be a second novel, he could think about it afresh.[117] Regarding the advance, he carefully didn't bring it up, knowing he couldn't repay it.

He had another idea for additional income, though—an original war game called GHQ. He pitched it to Saalfield Publishing Company, one of the largest makers of children's books, games, and toys in the world. The kids in the neighborhood were wild about it, he said. Included with his cover letter was a playing board, a set of instructions, and handmade pieces representing artillery, combat units, tanks, and ammo dumps.

Saalfield wasn't interested, not even remotely. Its representative replied that the game was too difficult to understand.[118]

HIS SISTER, Alice, was in practically the same situation he was—close to poverty stricken, only with more children, having married someone who, Vonnegut seemed not to realize, was a lot like him.[119]

Alice was middle-aged now, a woman with springy blond bangs and bright red lipstick who adored children and animals, and decorated the walls of her home with stencils of flowers and birds.[120] She and her husband, Jim, were without money to an absurd degree, and it was because his million-dollar ideas kept misfiring, one after the other. He was eager to become a self-made man, an entrepreneur. His father had been an early practitioner of Frederick Taylor's revolutionary time-and-motion scientific management in industry, and Jim was convinced he could be just as innovative because he had ideas too and a salesman's sunny disposition. After the war, the Adamses had moved to New Jersey within commuting distance of New York City because, in Kurt's words, Jim was a born wheeler-dealer and Indianapolis was too much of a Midwestern backwater for him.[121]

Jim's first product was "Putty Puss," a rubber ball with a face that could be molded or scrunched into just about any shape. Like Silly Putty, Putty Puss was simple and inexpensive to produce, but he didn't partner with a manufacturer soon enough before his seed money ran out. Next, his brother-in-law Bernard helped him cut the prototype of a brass door knocker that showed a man's face in profile thumbing his nose. When the knocker was lifted and dropped, the man's chin rapped the strike plate. But it too went the way of Putty Puss for lack of capital.

Jim's eccentricities weren't limited to his business ideas, however. Combined with Alice's flightiness, the Adams household was full-bore oddball by the mid-1950s. Inside the Adams residence, exotic birds flapped through the rooms above the heads of Jim Jr., eleven; Steve, nine; and the youngest, Kurt, six, who was nicknamed "Tiger" because of the way he cried lustily as a baby.[122] The children were permitted to treat the walls of the house as blank canvases and draw wherever they wished.

On weekends the family trooped to the New Jersey seaside to collect washed-up bricks because Dad was going to build a new house from them someday. One winter, because the furnace was either malfunctioning or broken, brick hunting was replaced by gathering driftwood to burn in the fireplace. Finally, it got so cold that Jim Sr. dragged a ten-foot piece of telephone pole inside the house and fed one end into the fireplace for days, a black cloud of burning creosote pouring from their suburban chimney. "We were not like the other families in town," Tiger remembered. "My father could have pulled it off and sort of fooled everyone into thinking he was like everyone else. He took the train into New York and he wore a suit and he looked the part. But I don't think my mother was ever the type to go to PTA meetings or help with our homework. I don't think she ever read the newspaper or followed politics or was engaged in the world in any substantial way."[123]

As a child, though, Tiger Adams saw nothing amiss because he was loved. His father "was a huggy kind of guy. You could sit on his lap and he was a warm father and easy-going. My mother lived an inner life with her kids and family."[124]

Then, in 1956, Alice became pregnant again.

KURT VONNEGUT Sr. died September 30 in his cottage in Brown County, Indiana. Diagnosed with lung cancer, he had refused to be hospitalized. Mornings he would get up, dress, eat a light meal, and then sit by the fire reading or listening to his record collection. He had no nurses, and no one came to check on him regularly, until near the end when he needed a trained nurse because he was bedridden.[125]

He was buried beside his wife in Crown Hill Cemetery in Indianapolis, where the Vonnegut family has many headstones. Always interested in the stock market, he had accumulated a significant amount of stock, which, during the bull market of the 1950s, had risen steeply in value. He left a substantial inheritance, equally divided among his children.[126] Alice's share funded her husband's continuing attempts at entrepreneurship.[127] Kurt Jr. also received his father's copy of *Webster's New International Dictionary of the English Language* and placed it, a "dear leviathan," on his shelf of reference works.[128]

For years, he kept "Jr." as part of his surname, in deference to his father.

SPRING 1957 found Kurt freelancing for a Boston advertising agency. One day in March, during the commute, he saw what he thought could be the solution to his financial problems. In front of him was a car carrier hauling half a dozen Saab automobiles—dinky Swedish cars shaped like an orange seed. He followed the truck until it arrived at a dealership. A salesman explained that the smart little import had front-wheel drive—a big help in slippery New England weather. Moreover, with just thirty horsepower and three cylinders, it was economical. Vonnegut folded himself into a brand-new model and went for a spin. He was sold; everyone on the Cape would want one, he decided, because it was chic and Swedish engineering couldn't be beat. (During the war, Saab had been an aircraft manufacturer.)[129]

Returning home, he talked Jane not only into buying one but also into opening the only Saab franchise on Cape Cod.[130] His idea was that a dealership would practically run itself. He could write, sell fiction, and infuse their checkbook now and then with income from selling a car. Because Saabs weren't given to dealerships on consignment, though, they would need to purchase six cars to get up and running, using his father's inheritance. She went for it.

The next step was to get someone to be in the showroom while he was at home writing. He persuaded a local artist, Arthur Bourbeau, to work in the sales office on commission. He could paint, too, while he waited for customers. If that weren't enough, he would also have a demonstrator to drive around as a way of advertising the dealership. Bourbeau was as excited as Kurt, and the new partners parked a spanking-new model outside their business on Main Street in West Barnstable. Kurt ordered letterhead stationery—"SAAB Cape Cod"—with his name in the left-hand corner as manager.

As a matter of company policy, Saab didn't advertise. Consequently Vonnegut had to place ads in local newspapers, proclaiming "SAAB— The Swedish Car with Aircraft Quality." After the costs of advertising and overhead were deducted, there was practically no profit. The "only way we could make a profit was to screw the customer on the radio and on the whitewalls," he later said. "People who have heard me say that before have just been shocked by this, this *moral rot*. It makes sense to me. . . . I'm not apologetic about it at all."[131] He hadn't worked summers in the Vonnegut Hardware store for nothing.

JANE'S MOTHER, Riah Cox, arrived from Indianapolis to see her three grandchildren during the summer of 1957 and pronounced the house in West Barnstable "charming but simply ancient."[132] Her description also hinted at the nature of life inside the house: the Vonnegut family was remarkably busy yet crazily disorganized.

Kurt and Jane did everything they wanted to do, and allowed the children to do whatever they wished, as well. Every Wednesday afternoon, Jane was "custodian" to twenty-four Brownies who arrived for games, projects, and treats.[133] She wondered why she was constantly behind or late, including for rehearsals at the Barnstable Comedy Club, until she noticed that all the clocks in the house showed different times. The phone rang constantly, usually for Mark or Edie, but if the call wasn't for them, they hung up or left the receiver off the hook. A neighbor telephoned one evening to remind Kurt that he had three people to contact for the Unitarian stewardship drive. But Jane couldn't find the information and "panicked." Edie, it turned out, had used the paper for coloring and covered the names assigned to her father.

Playdates depended on the children's whims. A lady named Margaret Stewart called to ask Jane whether Edie would like to come over and visit with her grandchildren. Edie wanted to know if the Stewarts were the ones from the South; on finding out they were, she decided she couldn't play with them because she was sick.[134] Meanwhile Kurt remained in the eye of the storm, writing and smoking in his study, where he was not to be disturbed.

Smothering beneath this pileup of Brownie meetings, rehearsals, and telephone calls was Nanny, two and a half. The pressure of having to compete for attention with two bright, assertive siblings, ages ten and seven, in a disorderly household caused her to act out with classic passive-aggression. Grandmother Cox, for instance, went to put clothes in the dryer and discovered Nanny trying to reach the "on" switch.

Crying inside the machine were the family's two cats, Ferdinand and Isabella.[135] A few weeks later, Kurt went into a rage when he caught her drawing in blue crayon on the new white wallpaper. Despite Jane's attempts to calm her down, her father's anger made her hysterical. Kurt shouted, "Leave her wounded!" and stalked off.[136]

That afternoon, Nanny developed a fever that rose to 103 degrees. Jane, rummaging through drawers looking for an aspirin, came across something strange. Her favorite instructor at Swarthmore, Harold Goddard, had given her the quotation "One good, sacred memory from childhood is perhaps the best education" and placed it inside a walnut shell as a memento. She had kept it for years exactly the way he had presented it to her. Opening the walnut for a sentimental peek, she discovered that the slip of paper had been torn in two.[137] It was disturbing, no matter who had done it.

COME DECEMBER, the Saab dealership went bust. The car's engine required a quart of oil in the gas tank because it was a two-stroke engine, and when the temperature fell below freezing the fuel coagulated, turning to taffy. Kurt started his fleet regularly to keep the engines warm, noticing how they belched "a smokescreen like a destroyer in a naval engagement."[138] Bourbeau's demonstrator kept breaking down in the snow, inadvertently advertising to everyone on the Cape that Saabs were imported duds, not automobiles with "Aircraft Quality."

From then on, Jane was aware that things were getting "sillier and sillier" and they would have to get out of the business.[139] Too late, Kurt became hard-nosed about money and insisted that Bourbeau buy the demonstrator. Arthur retorted that purchasing it had never been the understanding; anyway, he didn't want the car, didn't have the money. Kurt didn't want it either but was forced to take it back. Technically, Bourbeau hadn't bought it.

The argument over the demonstrator was the finale of the first Saab dealership on Cape Cod. Kurt lost his investment, and the former partners remained cordial but no longer friends.[140]

WITH THE car adventure ended, Kurt returned to full-time writing, "which is what he should have been doing the whole time," Jane wrote Walt and Helen Vonnegut, "if you can discount the fact that there is no money in that either, these days."[141] She was trying to be philosophical, but the truth was her fund of cheeriness, the antidote she used to inoculate herself and her family against bad luck, was just about spent.

She became ill in body and mind the winter of 1958, beginning with a case of the flu that was sweeping the Cape. Mark came down with it and couldn't serve his newspaper route, so Kurt and Jane took over his customers, driving up and down snow-packed Scudder's Lane in the predawn darkness. Then Jane got sick too, and Kurt continued alone as both driver and newspaper carrier.[142]

As the mother of three, it's not unexpected that she would catch a midwinter bug from one of them. But in her notes and letters at the time, there are signs of an unquiet mind, of mania. She seems preoccupied with perceiving glimpses of a deeper meaning in things, as if an unseen benevolent hand were ordering events. In a note to herself, she writes: "Maybe it's a non-stop adding machine. Continuous computer—everything adding up continually—smiles & frowns—and so on."[143] She wrote Uncle Alex a letter, which she never sent, in which she tries to explain the influence of Dr. Goddard on her, likening it to how she can see visions like the poet William Blake. She can "see new and wonderful connections between things and ideas, and people, and events—that adds an extra elusive dimension to life, makes it more exciting and meaningful, and poetry everywhere."[144]

Always a few hours before dawn, she had a recurring dream, one so frightening that she struggled to wake up before it could run its course. "The image in my mind's eye was of a huge red sun. It became clear that there was incredible life and energy in the enormous, fiery, red-golden sphere that filled my entire consciousness. The sphere was exploding, ever expanding, yet ever the same."[145] Waking up, she would go into the kitchen and take a sleeping pill with a glass of chocolate milk. She tried to describe the nightmare to Kurt, but "he wasn't particularly interested. I wasn't particularly surprised. He had other things on his mind and rightly so. I stopped trying to explain."[146]

WHAT WAS on his mind, hers too, was that the previous year, following the birth of the Adamses' fourth child, Peter, Alice had been diagnosed with breast cancer, which was considered a mortal disease. Jim Adams had been in sales and advertising steadily, but his attempts at entrepreneurship continued to burn through his wife's inheritance. They had very little of it left. The situation was distressing for a number of reasons, but Jane also understood the role her sister-in-law played in her husband's life and his writing.

Vonnegut more than loved Alice; he was unusual as an author because he wrote for an audience of one: his sister. Most writers imagine a large audience—readers "out there" who will appreciate the writer's efforts to be as entertaining as he or she can be. But Kurt had Alice in mind: "She was the person I had always written for. She was the secret of whatever artistic unity I had ever achieved. She was the secret of my technique."[147] He would pretend that his sister was leaning over his shoulder at the typewriter, laughing at his jokes, appreciating his storytelling. "'Alice would like this,' I say to myself. 'This would amuse Alice.'"[148] To lose her was too painful to think about, and he would do practically anything to prevent the events overtaking her.

THROUGHOUT 1958 Alice's health declined, and in September she was admitted to Monmouth Memorial Hospital in Long Branch, New Jersey. Later that month, on a warm, hazy morning, Jim missed his usual train to New York because he had to wait for Peter's sitter to arrive at their home in Rumson—his three other boys were at school. Next, he needed to do some grocery shopping and drop off the bags at home. Those errands finished, he looked forward to what promised to be a big day, a turnaround day.

In his briefcase he had the best idea he'd come up with yet: a new trade publication devoted exclusively to the adhesives industry. If this one caught on, it would be the first publication of its kind in the field.[149] He had an appointment with a backer to show him the mock-up, and if all went well he would have good news to tell Alice when he saw her that evening at the hospital.

They really needed this. Alice was so ill she was curled up like a child in her hospital bed.[150] He needed to bring home the bacon, big time, and deliver them all from this purgatory they were in. He parked their old beige station wagon at the Red Bank train station and called the advertising firm where he worked to say he'd be a little late. He would be taking the 9:14.[151]

Right on time, New Jersey Central Railroad train no. 3314, pulled by two diesel engines, arrived at the platform and Jim stepped aboard. Among the passengers was the retired Yankees all-star George "Snuffy" Stirnweiss; the mayor of Shrewsbury carrying $250,000 in negotiable bonds; an army secret courier with plans for a top-secret missile guidance device; and a four-month-old baby named Paul.[152] The next stop was Elizabethtown, and before pulling away the engineer, Lloyd Wilburn, who was sixty-three and close to retirement, waved to a friend in the control tower.

Sometime during the next few minutes, as the train picked up speed, Wilburn, who had high blood pressure, suffered a heart attack and died, his hand slipping from the throttle.[153] The fireman in the cab tried to regain control of the engine, but the huge diesels continued to accelerate, rumbling past three warning lights at forty miles per hour. Ahead was the mile-long Newark–Bayonne Bridge over Newark Bay. Passing beneath was a sand dredge, the *Sand Captain*, and a span of the one-hundred-fifty-foot wooden drawbridge was raised. Five hundred feet short of the bridge, the front engine hit an automatic derailing device, throwing the train off the rails, but its steel wheels crushed the wooden ties and the train kept straining toward the narrow passage between the trusses of the bridge beyond which there was only water below.[154] People began to scream and fight with the windows.

Watching from the deck of the ship, the crew of the *Sand Captain* saw the lead engine shoot off the end of the rails and dive nose-first into fifty feet of water, pulling the second engine and three cars after it like an iron serpent plunging to the bottom. The fourth car stopped short and teetered on the edge.

The water boiled, and Jim Adams's monogrammed briefcase popped to the surface amid other flotsam from the submerged train—hats, newspapers, and shoes.[155] He and forty-six other passengers, including the train fireman, drowned.

KURT AND Bernard agreed not to tell their sister what had happened until they could see her in the company of her doctor. But Alice, puzzled why Jim hadn't been to see her, called home the next morning. A neighbor answering the phone blurted out the news. Then Kurt, who had already flown from the Cape to Newark, got on the line. "I couldn't lie to her. She seemed to take it very well."[156]

She asked to speak to the boys. She told them they must stay together. Kurt got back on; she asked him to take the children because Bernard's wife, Lois, wasn't strong enough.[157] He said he would. Later that day, the brothers arrived at the hospital and saw her as planned with her doctor. By then, said Kurt later, "she seemed utterly bewildered and defeated by the thought of the insoluble problem of widowhood that faced her."[158] The last thing she said as they left was "Don't look back."[159] She died that night at midnight.

Kurt had made a deathbed promise and he was determined to keep it. But it was Jane who would have to open her heart, and her home, to four orphaned boys.

"The Vonnegut family," said Kurt Jr., "was built around what started as a general store on a mud street in Indianapolis." *(Indiana Historical Society)*

Kurt Vonnegut Sr., architect, in 1929; the Wall Street crash put an end to his family's upper-middle-class life. *(Courtesy Kurt Vonnegut, nephew)*

Edith Sophia Lieber, daughter of an Indianapolis beer baron and later Kurt Jr.'s mother, wearing her bridal gown in 1913. *(Courtesy Kurt Vonnegut, nephew)*

Vonnegut during his senior year at Shortridge High School, newspaper editor and runner-up for the most popular boy in the class. *(Indiana Historical Society)*

Jane Marie Cox during her senior year at Tudor Hall for Girls in Indianapolis, 1940. *(Courtesy Park Tudor School)*

Dresden, Germany, following three days of Allied air strikes in mid-February 1945. Vonnegut, a POW taken at the Battle of the Bulge, took shelter in a meat locker. *(Deutsche Fotothek)*

Basements in Dresden, Vonnegut said,
"looked like a streetcar full of people who'd
simultaneously had heart failure. Just people
sitting there in their chairs, all dead."
(Deutsche Fotothek)

Vonnegut, second from left, waiting with fellow
prisoners to be liberated. To his left, back slightly turned,
is Bernard V. O'Hare. *(Courtesy Greg Hansen)*

Kurt and Jane Vonnegut on
a visit to Lake Maxinkuckee
in 1946 while they were
enrolled at the University of
Chicago. *(Courtesy Walter
A. Vonnegut)*

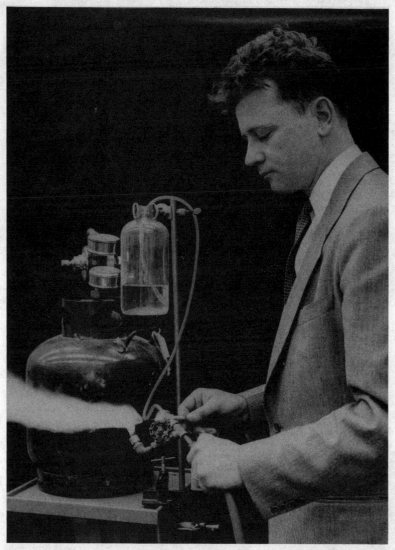

General Electric's publicists announced that
Bernard Vonnegut's co-invention of cloud seeding,
demonstrated by him here, was the start of a
"sensational vision of large-scale weather control."
Kurt later satirized the concept in *Cat's Cradle*.
(*Courtesy Schenectady Museum & Planetarium*)

Kurt (third from left), in public relations for General Electric takes notes during a visit of VIPs. "The General Electric Company *was* science fiction," he said later. At center, wearing a three-piece suit, is his fellow publicist Ollie M. Lyon Jr. *(Courtesy Mary Robinson)*

In a room above Cheney's store, Vonnegut began his full-time writing career after leaving General Electric. Jane is on the far right holding infant Edie; Mark is in front of Mrs. Ann Cheney, the owner. *(Courtesy Mary Herrick, far left)*

7: Cooped Up with All These Kids
1958–1965

KURT AND JANE had already decided they would take all four Adams boys before Kurt saw Alice in the hospital. On the way to the Barnstable airport the day of the wreck, "we agreed that if this situation was as bad as we feared, we would both want the boys to come here," Jane wrote to Uncle Alex and Aunt Raye in Indianapolis. But their reasons for wanting to do so were different. "I feel very much alive," Jane said, "and like a brand new mother."[1] For Kurt, rescuing Alice's children allowed him to be a pillar of the family for once. Bernard's wife, Lois, who cared for their three sons, was prone to nervous exhaustion. Raising a total of seven boys (three Vonneguts and four Adamses) aged two to fourteen was out of the question. But in the big twelve-room house in West Barnstable, there were two parents at home all day: Kurt grumbling in his study and Jane spinning around taking care of her husband and children. Combining the children under that ample sheltering roof was not ideal, but it was workable.

Jim Adams's sister, Donna Lewis, and her husband, Carl, had reservations about Kurt getting the Adams boys by default. But they were also unwilling to gainsay Kurt's pledge to Alice, or burden Lois Vonnegut with more than she could bear, or take the children themselves. So they assuaged their concerns to some extent by insisting that they must help out financially. Had they known how little money Kurt and

Jane actually had, they probably never would have consented to the arrangement.[2]

Privately, Donna didn't think much of Kurt. "He liked money, he wanted to make money, but he wasn't making any."[3] She came from the same conservative class of upper-middle-class Indianapolis merchants and businesspeople as he did, and her dislike of pretense was offended by how she caught him "posing for photographs as the great author."[4]

Since the Lewises' money was going to help support this blended household, they made it clear that they would come down from their home near Boston once a month to check on the boys' welfare. Second, they would expect to see how household money was being spent—not just whether the pantry was full, but to inspect an actual ledger and receipts. It wasn't that Aunt Donna and Uncle Carl mistrusted Kurt and Jane, but the boys would be the beneficiaries in a wrongful death suit filed against the Jersey Central Railroad. Sooner or later, the courts would want an accounting down to the last dollar because the Adamses were minors and wards of the state. It was best to be careful. Therefore Jane would have to keep two sets of books: one labeled "Vonnegut" and one labeled "Adams." Within the set of seven children, in other words, there would be two financial subsets.[5]

At the time, adoption was never seriously discussed because the Lewises wanted to keep the arrangement flexible. In later years, Kurt referred to his "adopted nephews," but that never happened. Aunt Donna, as the sister and sister-in-law of the deceased, had as much say about her nephews as Uncle Kurt, and she wasn't about to lose control over them. At bottom, said one of the Adams brothers later, it was a matter of "the practical people versus the artsy people."[6]

At the end of September, the four boys arrived in West Barnstable in two carloads. Kurt drove Alice and Jim's station wagon; Donna and Carl Lewis drove their car. The Adams/Vonnegut caravan wound past New York City and up the coast carrying Peter, two; Tiger, eight; Steve, eleven; and Jim Jr., fourteen. Riding with boxes of clothing, sports equipment, and toys were the Adamses' two dogs, Sandy and Yogi, also a cat and a bird named Bird. When finally the automobiles crunched up the gravel drive in West Barnstable, Jim Jr. tumbled out and lifted his aunt Jane off the ground. He was six foot three—as tall as his uncle Kurt.[7]

The other children Jane hardly knew. Peter, in diapers, stood out because the heat, noise, and strangers were making him cry. Steve, although only in seventh grade, was already six feet and wearing a Little League jacket. Tiger, keeping his emotions in check, waited politely. "You must be Aunt Jane," he said, extending his hand.[8]

But before they had a chance to unload the cars, Jane wanted everyone to come inside for fresh cookies, the first time in her marriage she had ever baked a batch, because "it seemed like such a motherly thing to do."[9] Off to the side, four-year-old Nanny stood watching the commotion, aware that her parents were "completely distracted and couldn't look" at her.[10]

NEWS OF the Adamses' arrival had preceded them. The human-interest angle was perfect for newspaper editors looking for a counterpoint to profiles of the dead and missing and garish nighttime photographs of the hulks of the passenger cars being hauled from the mud of Newark Bay. Papers from New York City to Boston carried the story of how the four sons of businessman James C. Adams, lost in the wreck, had been made parentless thirty-six hours later by the death of their mother, Alice. Headlines referred to them as "the orphans," and Kurt, as family spokesperson, gave interviews. "He is a tall, ruggedly constructed man, a very manly man," said the *New York Post*. "His eyes are red rimmed with grief and fatigue and his voice trembles. . . . 'They are courageous kids,' Vonnegut said, watching Peter, a laughing blond, playing at his feet."[11]

Jane collected clippings—some of them sent by friends and relatives—and put them inside a discarded manila envelope that Kurt had used for a story idea about Dresden, labeled "Armageddon in Retrospect." She placed it high on the shelf of a closet, thinking someday the Adams boys might want to know more about the accident and the deaths of their parents. It lay there untouched for twenty-three years.[12]

THE FIRST order of business in the Vonnegut household was figuring out who would sleep where. Jane designated the upstairs bedrooms as the children's quarters exclusively, doubling up siblings and cousins and redistributing the furniture, most of which was secondhand—broken, scratched, mended with glue. There were no curtains or rugs anywhere in the house. Kurt was handy and would need to enlarge the kitchen, patch holes in the bedroom ceilings, install new linoleum for the upstairs bathroom—the only one for nine people—and get the wheezing furnace fixed so it would heat the radiators upstairs.

These were just the logistics connected with accommodating a larger family, but the deeper effect of blending the children changed the birth order. Mark, the firstborn Vonnegut, was now second eldest child behind Jim Jr., who became, Mark later wrote, the "tormentor of my late childhood and adolescence, my replacement as eldest son."[13] Edie moved in with her sister Nanny and learned to "terrorize" her as a way of maintaining dominance as eldest daughter.[14] Edie lost the least ground in fact because she was still in the middle, only bracketed now by cousins, and handsome ones at that. With a middle child's sense of how to please, she took Tiger to school his first day and presented him to her class for show-and-tell.

As everyone tried to get settled, neighbor children came over to see the orphans and their pets. Jane ran out of lemonade, and Kurt went to the store for more. Discovering it was a neighbor child's birthday, Jane sent Kurt out again for a birthday cake.[15] From then on, it seemed, it was always someone's birthday.[16]

MARK, FOR his parents' sake, did his best to adjust, even though it was obvious he paled beside his cousins Steve and Tiger, who both had that indefinable flicker that makes a person likable right away. On meeting Tiger for the first time, Caleb Warren, a youngster who spent his summers in West Barnstable, decided on the spot that this new kid was going to be his best friend.[17] Mark had never inspired that kind of feeling. He was bookish, a chess player, mathematically talented, and nearsighted. His turn at bat usually meant a dose of public embarrassment because he couldn't see the ball whizzing past. Somehow, his parents hadn't realized he needed glasses.[18] Comparing himself to the Adams kids, he had to accept that they were silver and gold to his pewter. "They were blond, blue-eyed—all American kids." Nevertheless, rather than let his folks down, he kept reminding himself, "Gotta be nice to these orphans."[19]

Nanny, formerly the baby in family, had been bumped out of that position by Peter. She seethed with the kind of jealousy a four-year-old can't find the words to articulate. Suddenly, she was even expected to be the interloper's attendant. Jane showed the girls how to change the new baby's diapers, bathe him, and clean him up—a responsibility Edie enjoyed. To her, it was like fussing with a big doll. But Nanny's resentment tortured her. One day, she led Peter into the bathroom and took a bottle of toilet cleaner from under the sink. Tipping it over his head like she was dissolving a spot, she poured solvent slowly on his upturned face. He shut his eyes just in time.[20]

KURT AND Jane were aware of problems that would arise from having seven children scrambling through the house instead of three. Nevertheless, their hope was that the Adamses would feel welcome and loved. But it was difficult for the boys to wholeheartedly accept that love.

As children tend to do under such circumstances, they memorialized their parents by remaining emotionally loyal to them. With the exception of Peter, who was too young to understand (pathetically, he kept banging his forehead against the radiator for the first few days), the brothers couldn't, or subconsciously wouldn't, allow themselves to be other than nephews.[21] They explained matter-of-factly to new friends that, no, Uncle Kurt (or Kay) and Aunt Jane were not their parents, and Mark, Edie, and Nanny were not their siblings. "My uncle seemed to take pleasure in his kids up to a point, but he wasn't a really involved father," said Tiger. "So we always had the odd position of not being his natural-born kids, not that they made much of a distinction about that, but I don't think any one of my brothers would say that they felt Kurt became another father. He became an imposing figure in their lives, but he never replaced our own father."[22]

To keep their sadness at bay, the boys became utterly involved in their own affairs. Jane watched as Steve became "president of everything and captain of everything and everyone's best friend. . . . All his frenetic activity, his ceaseless socializing, was his defense against the terrible thing that had happened to him. He was the most susceptible of all the boys to the cruel machismo notion that brave little boys don't cry."[23] Tiger joined two other nine-year-old boys—the Terrible Trio they called themselves—who cornered the odd-job market in West Barnstable, pruning, mowing, clipping, raking, and weeding neighbors' properties from dawn until dark.[24]

The unhappiest was the eldest Adams, Jim Jr., who redirected his sorrow into swaggering anger. At the time of his father's death, he had been engaged in a primordial contest for the right to independence and young manhood. The last showdown between them had been over Jim Jr. combing his hair like Elvis Presley.[25] Minor though it had been, that skirmish was part of a larger battle that ended without a clear winner, leaving the eldest Adams boy feeling cheated. So instead he continued the contest with everyone else. "If [Jim] couldn't find trouble," Jane discovered, "he made it."[26]

His headquarters was the well house in the Vonneguts' side yard, from where he operated a laboratory-cum-house-of-horror. Small children were aghast when he threaded a piece of string up the back of his throat and pulled it out through his nose, or punctured his cheek clean through with a needle. The dogs Yogi and Sandy, fed hot dogs laced with Tabasco sauce, ran in agonized circles, yelping. For the delectation of younger boys, Jim shared a library of girlie magazines in the darkness of the well house too, replete with smiling "naked ladies."[27]

More serious problems were in the offing. The police began making visits to the Vonneguts because their nephew's name kept being mentioned in connection with broken windows, vandalism, and misbehavior at Barnstable High School.[28] Then, abruptly, Scudder's Lane became a demolition range. Propelled by M-80s, mailboxes leaped from their posts and landed on front lawns crushed and bent. Practically every property was targeted, but home owners were reluctant to press charges out of sympathy for the orphans and admiration for the Vonneguts.[29] Jim denied having anything to do with the explosions, and Uncle Kurt tolerated the excuses and lies as much as he could stand, but he was taking a real dislike to his sister's kid.[30] Moreover, he didn't appreciate being taken for a fool. Finally, with the tension in the house unendurable any longer, Kurt sat Jim down at the kitchen table and made him a proposal. "All right. We're prepared to believe you. We will believe you, and there will not be another word about this if . . . if you will give me your word of honor that you didn't do it."[31]

A few seconds passed. Jim averted his gaze then dropped his head. It was as good as an admission.

Jane confided to her neighbor, "What can I do about this boy?"[32]

ALICE AND Jim Adams had died intestate, and even with help from Donna and Carl Lewis, day-to-day cash for running the household was a problem.

The previous year, 1957, Kurt had sold two stories, and with 1958 coming to a close, he would sell only one to the moribund magazine market. There might have been hope for a financial lifeline from Scribner's, but Kurt's relationship with the publisher had turned sour because, to put it simply, he had left his editor, Harry Brague, in the lurch.

During the four years since 1953, when Scribner's had optioned a second novel after *Player Piano*, Vonnegut had delivered six chapters of a third novel, *Cat's Cradle*, but no outline. In the meantime, Brague had also received ideas for plays from him and sketches for novels, then a burst of seventy-five more pages for *Cat's Cradle*, but still no outline. Without that, or a complete manuscript, there would be no contract, no deadline, and author and editor were in limbo, year after year. In 1954, Brague, who was on the hook now for the second novel's advance, chided Vonnegut: "Is it still a prospect or have you laid it by for the time? I hope you haven't given the idea up in any event. If you think I am being a shad fly about this whole matter of novel writing, rest assured I am."[33] Two years later, in 1956, he was getting impatient: "As far as the new book is concerned, we are frankly a bit puzzled as to what to say. In fact, I don't think we can say anything until we have some further indication of what you propose doing with the book."[34] So he was stunned when, in October 1957, Vonnegut asked Brague to return his partial manuscript. In an injured tone, Kurt informed Harry that he needed support from a publisher and money, of course. Since Scribner's had been reluctant to provide him with either, it was time to see whether another publisher would.[35]

For most of the 1950s, Brague had been fielding anything Vonnegut kept hitting to him, while his author avoided the important game of writing, completing, and revising a second novel that had been partly paid for. Now Vonnegut was accusing him of bad faith. Carefully, Brague chose the tone and wording of his reply, but reminded Kurt about getting him an advance for the novel, sight unseen, which was a financial responsibility that could not be "sloughed off." If there wasn't going to be a book, the money would have to be repaid. Second, speaking for the Scribner's editorial staff (Brague was by then vice president and on the board of directors), "We also feel that the production has been very slow." And last he made the point that needed to be said, regardless of how Kurt's financial emergencies kept driving him from pillar to post: "We realize that you are stuck with being you, but we feel that that risk can turn into a very sound career for you if you would make a great effort to channel yourself in one direction and not spread yourself too thin."[36]

Offended, Kurt replied with two sentences, thanking Brague and assuring him he'd receive a copy of the novel if it ever came out.[37] To parry any attempt by Vonnegut to sell it elsewhere, Scribner's held on to the partly completed *Cat's Cradle* until it could get its money back. Jane, who could usually be depended on to be her husband's advocate in his quest to become a popular writer, blamed him for the sorry demise of the project. In a hot, hasty letter she wrote to Ken Littauer, but never mailed, she vented about having had to watch Kurt shilly-shally about a novel he should have delivered years before: "I have bawled my husband out for not making his position regarding whether or not to withdraw *Cat's Cradle* from Scribner's the least bit clear . . . [and] his feeling of hopelessness about getting actual writing of this damn book done. This feeling is so thick around here you could cut it with a knife. . . . Anyhow he says it is the work itself that has him down now. . . . [This] still is born mainly of despair at himself."[38]

WITH THE pressure on him to produce, Kurt labored in his study, emerging occasionally for a sandwich in the kitchen and to yell up the stairs, "What the *hell* are you kids doing up there? Shut the *hell* up!" To cut expenses, Jane took up knitting and gratefully received suggestions from Kurt's cousin Emily Louise Diamond of Lake Maxinkuckee days about how to save money by baking bread or buying potatoes by the hundred-pound sack.[39] She entered a contest sponsored by Robin Hood Flour by answering the question "What do you like about Robin Hood Flour?" The prizes were appliances and cash. Thinking she could combine themes of her duty as housewife and her husband's duty defending freedom, she wrote, "I like Robin Hood flour because its unfailing reliability gave me confidence in my task of feeding my husband, who was plenty hungry after six months in a German POW camp."[40] Her entry didn't win.

KURT ISOLATED himself in his study all day, working. The irony of moving to the Cape was that he thought he would be in the company of artists, but in West Barnstable no one else wrote fiction for a living. No one else strained to put the twenty-six letters of the alphabet into combinations that would pay the bills. He smoked constantly, cupping his hand around a match, taking a deep drag, and then snapping the match away impatiently, restless and annoyed. Days when he was jammed up creatively, he sat in his study, nursing a few beers and listening to his favorite jazz: Miles Davis, the Modern Jazz Quartet, Dave Brubeck, or, if he was feeling nostalgic, Bix Beiderbecke.

Some nights after getting blotto on martinis, he phoned his army buddy Bernard V. O'Hare, who was now a defense attorney with the family firm in Hellertown, Pennsylvania. O'Hare was a Pall Mall man too and liked his booze. For an hour or more, the two men would rumble through a dialogue not meant for anyone else to overhear, recalling the names of men they'd served with and half-remembered scenes, until at last, having exhausted himself in drunken conversation, Kurt went to bed.[41]

THEN SOMEHOW he learned that another writer—another *science fiction writer*—had just moved to the Cape. Theodore "Ted" Sturgeon, one of *Galaxy* magazine's most renowned fantasists, had moved from a backwoods home in Congers, New York, to Truro, Massachusetts, about an hour's drive from West Barnstable. It was serendipity. Sturgeon had won the Argosy Prize for science fiction magazine short stories in 1947, the International Fantasy Award in 1954 for a novel, *More Than Human*, and published two short story collections since then. Only four years older than Vonnegut, Sturgeon had been in print since appearing in *Astounding Science Fiction* in 1939 with "Ether Breather," a phenomenally prescient story about extraterrestrial creatures assuming holographic shapes as color television transmissions. When Ray Bradbury was a young man and trying to succeed in the same genre, he read Sturgeon "in an agony of jealousy," hating "his damned, efficient, witty guts."[42] Kurt asked Ted and his wife, Marion, to come over for dinner.

The first thing Vonnegut noticed about his guest was his long, intelligent face and whiskery Vandyke beard, which, added to his rawboned frame, made him resemble a carnival magician. Despite being one of the most widely anthologized American science fiction writers, Sturgeon was haggard looking. He had been writing nonstop for days. His readership for new novels was rather small, and despite his standing in the literary community of his peers, reviewers ignored him. What the conversation at dinner was like, Vonnegut couldn't recall later, but he never forgot what followed.

In high school, Sturgeon had been captain of his gymnastic team, and he announced that he would perform one of his best tricks. Clearing away some of the furniture in the living room, he stood with his feet together, back straight, arms outstretched, and suddenly whirled backward in a flip. But instead of landing upright, he hit the floor on his knees, shaking the whole house.

Struggling to his feet, "humiliated and laughing in agony," Kurt could tell, Sturgeon would become the model for one of Vonnegut's best-known characters: Kilgore Trout, the wise fool of science fiction, ignored, sold only in pornographic bookstores, and half-mad with frustration.[43] But Sturgeon wasn't a fictional character—his reversals and the blows to his pride were real. And Kurt was afraid he had just witnessed a glimpse of his own future, too. "Kilgore Trout is the lonesome and unappreciated writer I thought I might become."[44]

THE WINTER of 1958–59 came, and because it was the first one with seven children in the house, Kurt thought he would lose his mind. Kids were underfoot everywhere, he complained to Knox, and if he tried to go for a walk with the dogs, the snow was knee-deep.[45]

Knox was still at Dell Publishing. Under his direction, Dell had become the second house after Fawcett Publications to establish a line of trade paperback originals, underselling hardback publishers, who tended to be persnickety about the titles they would take because of the high production costs involved. Burger's generous offers brought professional, journalistic writers on the run who, like Vonnegut, were suffering from the vanishing magazine market. They had no illusions that Dell paperbacks would expect them to write literature, either. The destiny of their books was bus stations and drugstores, where passersby might spend a couple of quarters or less for a western, sex-and-crime mystery, joke book, or piece of nonfiction.[46]

At a cocktail party in New York, Knox asked Kurt if he had any ideas for a book. Actually, he didn't, but with the prospect of money hanging in the air, he began reeling off the story of a man who enters and exits time and space through a kind of tear in the fabric of the universe. As Knox listened, he suspected that the idea came off too glibly to be spur-of-the-moment. Perhaps his friend had already tried it on Scribner's (he had, it was the bare bones of the paid-for second novel).[47] Regardless, Burger was again in a position to lend a hand and signed him to write *The Sirens of Titan*.

Vonnegut, unblocked by the offer, made sparks fly from his typewriter and finished the novel in a few months. "Every mother's favorite child is the one that's delivered by natural childbirth. *Sirens of Titan* was that kind of book."[48] Then he gave it to Jane for revisions; she was pleased whenever Kurt turned to her for advice about writing because she considered them partners in his career.[49] To Knox, he expressed thanks for the opportunity: "You must know how grateful I am for your having given me the chance to do the book, and for your having showed it around to hard-cover people, and for all the rest of it."[50] Knox "got me started," Vonnegut wrote later, "and he kept me going until he could no longer help me."[51]

Thinking he was finally picking up momentum, Vonnegut wrote to Scribner's in April 1959 (the salutation was "Gentlemen," not "Dear Harry" as of old), hoping he could pry the half-finished *Cat's Cradle* from that publisher and sell it to Dell. "Would you kindly return the manuscript to me at the earliest possible convenience. I realize that you are in the position of trying to protect an investment of several hundred dollars. However, the best chance for you to recover that money, it seems to me, is to let me submit the novel elsewhere. You would share in the advance, if any."[52] Scribner's response, a month later, was just as cool. The manuscript had been returned to the offices of Littauer & Wilkinson "some time ago," the implication being that if his agent sold the book as a proposal to another publisher, Scribner's was certain to be paid back the "several hundred dollars." There was no signature, just "the Editorial Department." Thus ended the professional relationship between Vonnegut and the publisher of his first novel, *Player Piano*, and, unfortunately, the personal relationship between Kurt and his first book editor, Harry Brague.[53]

MEANWHILE, BURGER gave *The Sirens of Titan* a print run of 2,500, which would barely cover Dell's costs. The cover featured a juicy, tangerine-colored background dominated by a seminude woman in a paroxysm of passion as asteroids swirled around her. In the left-hand corner, a creature with a neck made of conduit extends its grasping tentacles toward her. "It was a ridiculous way to publish his work," Burger said. "He knew it and his agent knew it. But for a time, nobody else would publish his books."[54] Kurt dedicated his first novel in seven years to his uncle Alex, who was gratified by the acknowledgment, but on reading the novel he couldn't pretend to feel enthused. "I'm sure the young people will like it," he told Kurt mildly.[55]

THE SIRENS of Titan was more ambitious, less derivative than *Player Piano*. Ignoring the usual elements of novels (perhaps because of the pressure he was under), Vonnegut instead went for brief chapters, rapid characterizations, and a disarmingly simple style of telling an elaborate story. Everything was put in the service of the *effect* of reading the novel. He chose to be "aggressively unreal and make the reader accept an unreasonable premise and then keep going," to create something "grotesque" and not "directly about life."[56] The voice of the narrator, a future historian, is distant, as if relating a legend from long ago.[57] The setting is an era between "the Second World War and the Third Great Depression."[58]

Malachi Constant is one of the richest men on Earth, but otherwise he is a soulless, purposeless individual. Thinking he might learn something to his benefit, he arranges to meet Winston Niles Rumfoord. Rumfoord, a New England aristocrat, while traveling in his private spaceship with his dog, Kazak, encountered a temporal anomaly called a "chrono-synclastic infundibulum." This wrinkle in time allows him to travel both back to the past and forward to the future. Mostly, he and Kazak (a palindromic name) appear only as a wave spiral between the sun and Betelgeuse, materializing on Earth for a short while every fifty-nine days. He prophesizes that Constant will travel to Mars and father a child with Rumfoord's disdainful wife, Beatrice—certainly not the news Constant wishes to hear, but that is indeed what happens, no matter what else intervenes. There is no avoiding destiny. Likewise, a parallel, humorous subplot is that Earth's history has been manipulated by extraterrestrials from the planet Tralfamadore. They need a replacement part for a stranded spaceship, and all of human endeavor has been directed toward producing a rounded metal strip with two holes in it. The greatest of humankind's architectural and engineering achievements—Stonehenge, the Great Wall of China, and the Kremlin—are really only messages in the Tralfamadorian mathematical language, informing the spaceship's robot commander of how much longer he has to wait for the part. To underscore the universe's ultimate determinism, Constant returns to Earth and makes a remark that he thinks is profound and original—"I was a victim of a series of accidents, as are we all"—only to find that it has already been carved on a wooden scroll.[59]

The premise of a loopy "infundibulum" linking people through mysteriously meaningful coincidences was beguiling to Vonnegut.[60] And it was fresh in his imagination during the writing of *The Sirens of Titan* because of an experience that he and Jane shared the day Jim Adams died. "I have had one very flashy experience with telepathy or whatever, and my wife got the signals, too. They were evidently from my brother-in-law, who was being killed in a railroad train which had gone off an open drawbridge in New Jersey at the time. . . . I suddenly left my study that morning, went the length of the house to the phone in the kitchen, put in a long distance call to my brother-in-law. I had never telephoned him before, had no reason to call then. I telephoned him at his office, which he would never reach. There was a news flash over the radio about the railroad accident without any details. I knew my brother-in-law had been on the train, though he had never taken the train before."[61] After the disaster, Jane remembered how even "allowing for some fantastic Einsteinian time warp, that was close enough to simultaneous for me to think that something really weird had been going on here. I had not yet heard of Jung's word *synchronicity*."[62]

REVIEWERS OF *The Sirens of Titan*—the few that paid attention to it—tried comparing the novel to something identifiable. One likened it to an opera—Offenbach's *Tales of Hoffman*, only set in outer space—an expressionist subgenre of science fiction, maybe, but dosed with satire. Another speculated that it might just be a leg-pull, in which case the author was wasting the reader's time. A third dismissed it as "hokey."[63] No one raised the possibility that it might be literary fiction because Vonnegut was broadening the genre of science fiction to think about topics in an unusual way.[64]

He wasn't alone in breaking conventions of science fiction, but he was early on the scene and reviewers had a hard time recognizing what he was doing. Later, other experimentalists such William S. Burroughs, John Barth, and Thomas Pynchon would also use science fiction as a means to strain against the bonds of traditional narrative.[65]

There were advantages, too, as he saw them, in having characters dart around the universe and visit bizarre planets. Later, commenting on his work, Vonnegut said: "When I write, I don't want to write a story about a man, a love affair, or a trial. I want to write about the whole damned planet, the whole society. I try to discuss our whole planet in human terms. I'm not smart enough to do it, but I do try. An imaginary planet has a role like a clown in a Shakespeare play. Every so often an audience needs a breather, a fresh view. Other planets provide that. But every time I write about another planet it is deliberately so unrealistic that people can't really believe it. In a way it makes our own planet more important, more real."[66]

Even so, because *The Sirens of Titan* was one of the first postwar novels of its kind, and Dell wasn't a publisher of literary fiction, Vonnegut's second novel whirled around on racks of paperbacks in drugstores and bus stations, not chosen, a wallflower at the dance. Although it was nominated for the science fiction Hugo Award for Best Novel, *The Sirens of Titan* sold—not to Burger's surprise—miserably.[67]

THE SUMMER of 1959, Knox left Dell, frustrated by executives, instead of editors, exerting increasing control of acquisitions, as both the reprint and Dell First Editions lines continued to grow. He moved six blocks away to 67 West Forty-fourth as editor of Gold Medal imprints, where he was assured he would have more editorial control.

Gold Medal was also consummately a business, like Dell, primarily pumping out novels that were good reads for men—pulpy, action-packed stories of full-figured women in cocktail dresses, dusty gunslingers, and private detectives who got most of their tips in longshoreman's bars. The title of a novel hardly mattered: whatever would sell the best—the racier, the better (Wade Miller's *Kitten with a Whip*, for instance). On the top floor of the building was Vice President Roger Fawcett's penthouse, where guests were invited to get themselves a drink, dispensed from the penis of a Mediterranean god cast in gold.

* * *

THE SUMMER of his departure from Dell, Knox was recuperating from hip surgery, and suspense novelist John D. MacDonald invited him to come down to his home on Siesta Key, a barrier island off Sarasota on Florida's west coast. The agenda would be light: some fishing, beer drinking, and sightseeing. Crescent Beach, just down from MacDonald's place, had white sand like powdered sugar. Knox was mad about fishing and wanted to go, but he needed someone to drive because of his surgery. So he turned to Vonnegut, who was happy to act as his chauffeur in return for a vacation from seven children.[68]

Also, a trip to Florida would provide the perfect reason to be out of the house when something transpired that Kurt didn't want to face. Three-year-old Peter Adams was going to be taken away.

EVER SINCE the arrival of the Adams brothers, Aunt Donna Lewis had regularly phoned Kurt and Jane for updates on the boys. Once a month she had driven with her husband from their home in Boston to West Barnstable. But she wasn't pleased with what she saw going on in the big old house. Although she understood the desire to honor Alice's wishes, she told Jane, who was responsible for most of the care-taking, seven children were too many. Someone else, a married but childless cousin on the Adams side of the family, would consider it a privilege to raise Peter.

Jane wouldn't hear of it. Separating the boys after they had spent almost a year in West Barnstable was out of the question. She loved them and it would work, if Donna would only give it time.

Jane was shocked then, several days after Kurt had left for Florida, when Donna called and told her to expect her cousin Charles Nice from Birmingham, Alabama, the next morning. He would be arriving on the Boston express at the Barnstable train station, and he couldn't wait to meet Peter. Jane, going into one of the few shouting rages of her life, demanded by what right the Lewises thought they could do this. Donna, taken aback that Jane didn't know the details, explained that Kurt had called from New York, where he was picking up Knox for the drive to Florida, and had given his permission. Jane slammed down the phone and called Kurt, incredulous that, as she put it, "my supreme effort was being sabotaged."[69]

At MacDonald's house, things were just getting under way, aided by the arrival of a second crime writer, William Fuller, when the phone rang. Kurt took the call in another room. Knox heard "noises of shock," then Kurt returned, highly agitated. "I've got to get out of here and go home!" Within the hour he was at the airport and preparing to fly back to West Barnstable.[70]

Charles McKinley Nice held a law degree from the University of Alabama. When he was not yet forty in 1954, he ran for a seat in the house of the state legislature and won. Then two years later, he staked his political career on a matter of conscience over segregation.

Following the U.S. Supreme Court's ruling that segregated schools were unconstitutional in *Brown v. Board of Education of Topeka,* the Alabama legislature introduced a bill that would have the effect of sanctioning resegregation. Called the Freedom of Choice Bill, it ensured that no child would have to attend an integrated school. Governor James Folsom, a progressive in the South on issues involving civil rights and integration, indicated he would sign the measure as a compromise. Of the 105 elected representatives on the house side, only one spoke against the bill, a freshman, and cast the lone dissenting vote. For doing so, Charles Nice had been defeated for reelection in 1958.[71]

JANE MET Nice at the Barnstable train station, thinking she had no choice; besides, Kurt was in transit and wouldn't arrive until the following evening. On the drive to the Vonneguts' home, Nice explained that his wife, Clare, had a son from her previous marriage, Bill, thirteen years old, but Charles was unable to have children of his own. Being an Adams relative, it seemed only natural that he should meet Peter at least and see whether they could get along.

Jane and Kurt were in a vulnerable, almost untenable position because they hadn't adopted Peter. Furthermore, as an attorney, Nice was aware there were no legal impediments preventing Peter from going to Birmingham. What he did not intend to tell Jane was how much he wanted this chance at having a small child to love, and he would not leave without him.[72]

Jane led him into the living room to meet the children, who were arrayed in a semicircle on the opposite side. Two of Jane's friends, enlisted for moral support, were there as well. They had their minds made up: Peter was not going. The brothers were determined to abide by their mother's wish that they stay together; for their part, Edie and Mark Vonnegut were prepared to stand by their mother. Only Nanny, of course, wanted her rival gone. Nice nodded and smiled as Jane introduced everyone in turn. Then his eye fell on Peter, who was wearing a pair of fuzzy yellow footy pajamas.

Suddenly, the little boy rushed across the room and hugged Nice around the knees with such force that he tottered and laughed. The wall had been breached and Peter spent the rest of the day visiting and playing with Aunt Jane's visitor. By the time Kurt arrived near midnight the following day, exhausted after thirty-six hours of trying to make flight connections, it had been agreed that Charles Nice and Peter would leave together for Birmingham.[73]

For most her life, Jane blamed herself for splitting up the children. She internalized the promise Kurt made to Alice without thinking about the consequences of raising four more children. Letting Peter go was her failure, she thought, because she hadn't made the blended family work. And she assumed, when Peter left, that Kurt acted "almost as if this was something that was not happening" because he was so hurt.[74] In fact, his response was part of his desire to avoid unpleasantness. When it turned out that raising seven children was overwhelming, he arranged to be on a trip fifteen hundred miles away when Charles Nice arrived. In Jane's memoir, *Angels Without Wings: How Tragedy Created a Remarkable Family,* she avoids making the connection that Kurt left her to handle the situation alone.

By September, the Adamses had been with the Vonneguts for a year, and the division of labor between Kurt and Jane was clear. He was to be left alone so he could write; she was supposed to take care of everything else. As Tiger's friend Caleb Warren noticed, "Kurt was off in his study— Jane was busy being frantic about six kids she couldn't control."[75]

Allison Mitchell, Nanny's friend, spent whole days at the Vonneguts' "and I just loved Jane. Jane was this sweet woman. She had a sweet demeanor, and I think that she was very patient with Kurt, because she basically was the one who did everything, the bills, the shopping, the cooking, any cleaning she could possibly do and she did hold huge birthday parties for people." She was famous for stringing yarn through the house that led to clues for scavenger hunts. Her pièce de résistance more often than not was a large, crooked cake for the guest of honor. "She really was the glue that held the family together," Mitchell said.[76]

Kurt, on the other hand, could not be bothered with the tedium of day-to-day family matters, where being husband and father would demand his attention. His place was at the typewriter, doing what mattered to him. It paid the bills, after all.

Writing could be set aside, however, if another muse beckoned. "He used his artistic skills and sensibilities to decorate the house and patio and grounds in a charming way," remembered Tiger. "He also made beautiful furniture and painted pertinent quotes on various walls in the house. But vacuuming, no."[77]

In December 1959, he abruptly suspended work on his writing to construct an eighteen-foot sculpture of a comet for a restaurant at Boston's Logan International Airport. At one end of the piece was a ball of polished granite; behind it, a streaming tail of welded steel, brazed copper, and bronze strands.[78] Knox, when he heard about the project, was a bit nonplussed because he was busy showing *The Sirens of Titan* to people in the film industry. He assumed Kurt was hard at work writing.[79]

Kurt insisted that everything rotate around him, leading to outbursts occasionally that astonished youngsters who didn't expect to see tantrums in an adult. "He had a cruel side to him," said Tiger. "He had a nasty side and that's why it always struck me, the difference between the guy that you would imagine from his writing and the guy that is the real guy." His study was off limits, as jealously guarded as a teenager would his bedroom. Noise or fighting that penetrated his closed door goaded him from his lair like a furious dragon. Then he would deliver, Tiger said, "the most blistering lecture that would just peel your skin back, and it was scary, and you didn't want to get into trouble with him again."[80]

Children in the Vonnegut household and their friends often described Kurt as "scary." Allison Mitchell, Nanny's friend, thought Mr. Vonnegut was "intimidating. He was a very tall man with bushy eyebrows and sometimes he scared the living daylights out of me." Because children were always running through the kitchen anyway, one day Allison came through the backdoor looking for Nanny and instead discovered Kurt towering over her.

"Don't you ever knock?" he asked. "Where were you brought up, in a barn?"

She burst into tears and ran home.[81]

For a long time, Caleb was aware "there was this guy, someone named 'Kay,' that's what they called him. And we'd be in the kitchen and the kids were kind of afraid of him." When Kurt finally made an appearance while Caleb was there, Kay turned out to be a "daffy professor type. You'd hear ruffling from the far end of the house when Kurt was emerging from his study and coming into the kitchen and the kids would obviously tense up a little bit, like, what kind of mood was Kurt going to be in? Is he going to be distant, cynical, angry, or is he going to be just the most friendly adult you could ever imagine?"[82]

Sometimes he would be unexpectedly friendly, making a special effort to sit with the kids in the kitchen and find out what they were up to. He was the initiator of a game for catching houseflies, for instance. The Vonneguts' kitchen was so dirty that it was the only place Caleb wore his shoes in warm weather. On this particular day, Kurt offered to pay a nickel for every fly caught. He explained that flies had to drop before they could take off. Adding a few drops of dishwashing soap to a glass filled with water made a froth that reached the lip. Kurt stretched toward a fly on the ceiling to demonstrate. It dove into the bubbles and drowned. For the next couple of hours, fly catching from chairs and tabletops occupied everyone.[83]

And Kurt was the organizer of impromptu, twilight swimming trips to Dennis Pond, too. As the sun was going down, he loaded the boys and their friends into the Adamses's Rambler station wagon. Beside the pond, he leaned against the car, smoking as the boys splashed. One evening, Caleb spotted him "walking through the pond with his long pants on, and he went for his little swim with his long pants in the summer."[84] For the girls, there was "moonlight dipping," as he called it. Once a month, when the full moon was out, he chaperoned Nanny, Edie, and Allison on a private swim. "He would never watch us; he was very, very modest," Allison said. He would keep his back turned, silhouetted against the darkening sky, the ember of his cigarette bobbing up and down in the dusk.[85]

His best inspiration, however, at least from the neighborhood kids' point of view, was the annual "marsh tromp." When the weather turned warm enough, he would point to a distant landmark—a tree or telephone pole—beyond the warm, sticky salt marshes. The idea was to reach the goal through the ooze as fast as possible. The contestants fell, floundered, and slogged through the mush until they looked like life-size statues of wet potter's clay. With each passing year, the number of participants swelled, until it became a rite of summer in West Barnstable.

BUSINESS PICKED up for Vonnegut in spring 1960. Knox had seen portions of the new novel, *Evil, Anyone?* (the "Nazi book," Vonnegut called it) and liked what he read. He also spoke to a friend of his at Houghton-Mifflin, Sam Stewart, and was able to report that Stewart might be interested in bringing out *The Sirens of Titan* in hardback as a Gold Medal reprint. And Stewart indicated that once Vonnegut had completed *Cat's Cradle*, he would be interested in publishing it as a hardback reprint, too.[86]

On the strength of so much good news, and two stories sold in a row to *McCall's*, Jane and Kurt went to England for three weeks in May.[87] Just like when they were younger in Alplaus, they celebrated his victories expensively, knowing they would be "eating cereal" afterward. An older woman in the neighborhood was engaged to take care of the children, whom the combined forces of the Vonnegut and Adams children "drove insane," Edie remembered.[88]

Appearing in *McCall's* was bread and butter, but Kurt would have given anything to appear in the *New Yorker* instead.[89] As it happened, the day after he and Jane left for England, the *New Yorker* turned down a short story of his, "The Epiczootic," in which the United States is swept by an epidemic of people killing themselves for their life insurance.[90] Same old problem, probably—too outré. Stories in the slicks helped pay the bills, but he couldn't seem to rise above the status of a ham-and-egger as an author.

In August, however, the celebratory trip to England seemed justified. Sam Stewart informed Knox, "I had a solid and wet lunch today with Mr. Winston Niles Rumfoord of West Barnstable (alias Kurt Vonnegut)"; Houghton Mifflin had indeed decided to publish *Sirens* in hardback, slated for February.[91]

Knox, of his own accord, and without recompense, was doing better at getting his friend in print than Vonnegut's agent.

* * *

KURT'S TENDENCY to involve himself in creative projects other than writing—furniture building, decorating, intermittent painting and drawing—extended to experimenting with theater, too. He tried his hand at playwriting with a humorous retelling of Odysseus's return to Penelope called *Something Borrowed*. Local newspapers didn't review amateur productions out of courtesy, except to praise them. But the play must have been well received because in September 1960 it went into rehearsal again as *Penelope*, this time at the Orleans Arena Theater, up the Cape from Barnstable.

To a local reporter who interviewed him that summer, Vonnegut indicated he was drifting away from novel writing. "The theater seems closest to Kurt Vonnegut's inclinations and he is working on a third play in his spare time now. Although today writing is no longer the dilettante's luxury, still to bring up a large family, requires a certain budgeting of the direction the writer's efforts take."[92]

That was exactly the problem, however: budgeting time and energy. While he was preparing for the curtain to go up on *Penelope*, work practically stopped on *Evil, Anyone?* Knox, who was prepared to take the book for Gold Medal, tried a little reverse psychology: "Don't get yourself in such a sweat. If you can't do it, don't do it."[93] In mid-September, after *Penelope* had finished its run, he invited Mark and Steve to attend the World Series with him: the Pittsburgh Pirates versus the New York Yankees. Kurt was so pleased he said he would personally take the boys to New York and apologized for writing so slowly, promising to finish *Evil, Anyone?* as soon as he could.[94] He was fortunate to have not only a superlative editor in Knox, he had told him earlier that year, but an excellent friend, too.[95]

THE SIRENS of *Titan* debuted as a hardback in February 1961—the first Vonnegut novel to do so since *Player Piano* almost ten years earlier. But the occasion was marred a bit. Sam Stewart had moved from Houghton Mifflin to Holt, Rinehart and Winston and in January Holt had bid *Cat's Cradle* away from Gold Medal, intending to bring it out as a hardback first, not a reprint. Burger, justifiably, was miffed. As an editor, he didn't like having authors sold out from under him by the higher-ups at Gold Medal.

Kurt tried to assuage Knox as best he could, but in his excitement of having an original hardback scheduled for publication by a big publishing house he tended to patronize his friend by telling him not to be offended. He was an author, he reminded Burger, not an agent. If Holt expressed an interest in him and was willing to raise the ante on one of his books, what was he to do? Say no? Was he supposed to feel guilty? All he could offer was an apology.[96] Across the top of the letter, Burger wrote in large letters "No Reply."

BY EARLY summer, a solid draft of *Evil, Anyone?* was finished and Vonnegut returned to his interest in theater writing and directing.[97] His persuaded his fellow players at the Barnstable Comedy Club—"a far out club" he called it—to present Eugene Ionesco's *The Lesson*, an avant-garde postwar play, and "probably the greatest departure from the usual Comedy Club productions," commented the *Barnstable Patriot*."[98] It was a hit, earning the club second place in the 1961 summer drama competition sponsored by the New England Theater Conference.[99] A few weeks later, Kurt entered a script he had adapted from his short story "EPICAC" in the annual Cape Cod Arts Festival and won first place.[100] With his reputation rising in local theater, the Barnstable players elected him president to oversee purchasing the old village hall as the club's first permanent theater.

That summer, too, thanks to faithful Knox acting as go-between, Kurt received his first speaking fee. He appeared as a guest lecturer at Radcliffe College's summer writing program. His performance, he reported to Burger, was just so-so. But he was confident he would improve with practice because he knew something about public speaking from taking a class in it at Cornell.[101] Then, in August, more good news: Ken Littauer informed him that 20th Century Fox had optioned for television his short story "The Runaways," which the *Saturday Evening Post* had carried the previous April.[102] Vonnegut used the money to patch up the house because it leaked in rough weather from cracked timbers like a ship with dry rot.[103]

With so many auguries of good fortune as a novelist, short story writer, playwright, and play director, he purchased special letterhead stationery to advertise that he was something of a Renaissance man. Across the top it said, "Kurt Vonnegut/Cape Cod Talent Associates."

* * *

BURGER WAS editing *Evil, Anyone?* when he offered Vonnegut yet another opportunity. He would publish Kurt's first anthology. In October 1961, *Canary in a Cathouse* appeared, a collection of twelve of Vonnegut's short stories gleaned from magazines.[104] Knox promised a handsome book, and when it was published Kurt savored the heft of it and how the collection showcased his talents as a short story writer in one volume.[105] That month, too, the *Magazine of Fantasy and Science Fiction* carried what would become his best-known short story, "Harrison Bergeron," a tale of dystopian justice enforced for all. "The year was 2081, and everybody was finally equal. They weren't only equal before God and the law. They were equal every which way. Nobody was any smarter than anybody else. Nobody was better looking than anybody else. Nobody was stronger or quicker than anybody else."[106] But then Harrison Bergeron, a rebellious genius of exceptional strength, forces his way onto a television broadcast and defies the tyrannical government to stop him. He frees a ballerina from her disabling weights and chains and dances with her spectacularly until the "Handicapper General" shoots them both. The audience watching at home—too addled by drugs and ear-splitting shrieks over headphones to make sense of what they've seen—immediately forget what they've witnessed.[107]

On a roll now, Kurt hurried to finish correcting the galleys of *Evil, Anyone?* even though he suspected its subject was too grim, too strong, possibly even too offensive to ever make the leap from a Gold Medal paperback to hardback reprint.[108] Nevertheless, he was grateful that Fawcett was taking a chance on it. In light of what an unconventional story it was, Kurt had one more suggestion for Knox: how about on the cover, he suggested, a skeleton posing as a whore?[109]

THE TITLE *Evil, Anyone?* was replaced in favor of *Mother Night*—the personification of darkness in Goethe's *Faust*—because the latter did a better job of capturing the novel's paradox. Mephistopheles, the evil spirit in *Faust*, defends himself with fiendish logic: there can be no light, he points out, without Mother Night giving birth to it.

The protagonist is Howard W. Campbell Jr., an American imprisoned in Tel Aviv, accused of having aided the Nazis. Vonnegut imagined him as someone like William Joyce, the Irishman nicknamed

"Lord Haw Haw" who broadcast during the war from Berlin. Kurt had listened to him while stationed in England, wondering what could motivate a turncoat.[110] The other inspiration was the phony Red Cross worker in Dresden who tried to recruit POWs for combat on the Russian front by promising better food and clothing. Perhaps, Vonnegut imagined, he wasn't a German actor with an impeccable English accent, but an American engaged in a complicated double cross.[111]

Mother Night is Campbell's memoir, supposedly edited by Vonnegut. Over the years, Campbell explains, the state of Israel has pursued him as relentlessly as it has the monstrous Adolf Eichmann, who shares the same cellblock, suggesting that Campbell must be quite a prize. In fact, he has tried to avoid causes, politics, or even taking a stand on issues most of his life, his excuse being that he is an artist. If he is guilty of anything, he realizes, it is that he has been "a man who served evil too openly and good too secretly, the crime of his times."[112]

After World War I, Campbell immigrates to Germany when Berlin's cultural life attracted writers, singers, and other performers. As a foreign playwright who writes in German, he becomes well known. Then, with signs that a second European war is imminent, an American agent from the Office of Secret Services (OSS) contacts Campbell and appeals to his patriotism. He wants Campbell to pose as a Nazi propagandist, a mole in Joseph Goebbels's public relations apparatus. Campbell reluctantly agrees but is so convincing as a turncoat on radio, praising the Nazis' aims, that he is promoted to the top of the Third Reich's hierarchy, hobnobbing with Hitler himself, who turns out to be as insipid as Nazi ideology itself.

When the war ends, the Allies want to arrest and try Campbell for treason. He spends years as a fugitive because the OSS can't or won't clear his name. Finally, through a series of chesslike gambits, feints, and double crosses, Campbell is maneuvered into checkmate. In his cell, he commits suicide for "crimes against myself." Vonnegut, in a foreword added to a later edition of *Mother Night*, warns, "We are what we pretend to be, so we must be careful about what we pretend to be."[113]

The conflict in the novel was close to Vonnegut's heart. Raised in a family where admiration for Germany ran high, he submits that Western culture is also capable of veering into clownishness over destiny, greatness, and so on. Also, his ambivalence about fighting in World War II—he was an isolationist in college, then a warrior, and finally, chastened by his experiences in Dresden, a pacifist—is reflected in Howard Campbell's confusion. Campbell would prefer not to get involved, but he does take sides—more than one, in fact. A miasma of self-betrayal hangs over the novel. The historian Howard Zinn, himself a former bombardier aboard a B-17, said his friend Vonnegut "had the same ambivalence toward World War II that many of us who became very strong antiwar critics have. I know several other veterans of World War II who have become very fierce pacifists. And when they are looking back, they are torn, and in fact so am I."[114]

Overall, *Mother Night* is more convincing than *The Sirens of Titan* because Campbell's memoir is written in a real world where there is suffering, death, and punishment. No science fiction or fantastic devices—an "infundibulum," for instance—spares the reader from thinking about life's impenetrability. Campbell is whipsawed by currents of chance, "dumb luck," free will, destiny, or the "Hand of God." The pace of the narrative is again fast, breakneck, a stylistic trait of Vonnegut's becoming more prominent. In two hundred pages, there are forty-five chapters, some half a page, a page, or two pages; dialogue is punchy like a script.[115]

In the end, the most important riddle goes unanswered: what is real and what isn't? As Campbell discovers, today's virtues can be tomorrow's vices. One critic later said, the novel was a "triumph of ambiguity."[116]

Mother Night, just another thirty-five-cent paperback in autumn 1961, went unreviewed. To young readers, however, Vonnegut's deft presentation of moral relativism—good versus evil, right versus wrong—was, and continues to be, the reason for the novel's appeal. Still, it was a flop when it was published, and Vonnegut, convinced it would never be anything other than a paperback, fell into a period of temporary idleness and free-floating anxiety.[117] He read Harold Robbins's *The Carpetbaggers*, imagining, he joked to Knox, what it would be like to be riotously rich and have sex in a bathtub filled with champagne (he didn't specify a vintage).[118] But seriously, it mattered, he added, what people thought of his work. In fact, he sometimes thought that to feel real, to have a sense of personhood, depended on whether readers approved of him.[119]

SUMMER 1962 released children into the Vonneguts' home again like bees returning to a hive. Littauer & Wilkinson's secretary, Carolyn Blakemore, stayed for a weekend expecting a respite from the hurly-burly of New York. "You'd be sitting there quietly reading a book or talking to Jane and twelve large boys would come tromping in and drink about two quarts of soda and tromp out again. You didn't know where they lived or who they were. It was just sort of a madhouse, although the two girls, Nanny and Edie, were quiet and dainty." It was obvious to Blakemore the Vonneguts didn't have any money, but "Jane was very philosophical about it and she was crazy about Kurt."[120]

Jane's housekeeping trick was "gather as you go," but none of the older kids got the message.[121] She resorted to putting notes around the house: "Flush the toilet!" and "Put dirty clothes in the hamper." Instead of cooperation, she got sarcastic replies written beneath her instructions.[122] The floor was filthy; something in the refrigerator always stank; the dog Sandy had bloated ticks ringing its eyes and two Siamese cats yowled and ran underfoot.[123]

Jane wasn't worried about the house being dirty. She was overwhelmed with the demands of combining two families. Her days consisted of loading up the station wagon with bags of groceries, or making meals, or acting as mediator between the children. Since the days of Alplaus when her friends had noticed that Kurt demanded her attention, she had been trying to be devoted to him, but the needs of six children made that impossible. She tried to foresee problems that would annoy him, which had the effect of creating a feeling of suspense and edginess. Nanny sensed it as darkness hanging over them. "My memory as a kid was that it was very dark because my father set the tone in the house. My mother was always in his direction, always anticipating how to handle this force of nature. Her concern was always more for my father, and just trying to get through a day taking care of kids."[124]

Sometimes her efforts to douse small fires of contention before they became blazes failed, and then Kurt exploded. She would try to reason with him, groping to find out what was wrong. Particularly ugly fights drove her into the laundry room to cry alone.[125] Later she would emerge as if returning from an instant vacation, wearing sunglasses to hide her reddened eyes. Occasionally, when arguments reached a certain pitch, Kurt would slam out of the house, race the car's engine in the driveway, and make the gravel fly as he sped away to find a motel for the night. Once, pulling up to a motel office to register, he stepped out of the car wearing only his socks. Sheepishly, he drove home and put off running away until another day.[126] A sign that his anger had finally passed was when he would ask Jane, "Darling, are you okay?"[127]

AFTER THE nosedive of *Mother Night* he needed money again, and so he applied for a teaching job at Hopefields Riverview, a private school for developmentally delayed or behavior-disturbed boys on route 6A between Sandwich and Barnstable. Without a college degree, he was technically unqualified to teach, but Hopefield Riverview was private and the headmaster, after reviewing his application, offered to hire him on two conditions: he would have to dress neater (he was fond of tennis shoes and rumpled cardigans that he tended to button up wrong) and be clean-shaven.[128] He agreed.

As it turned out, he was a natural at teaching—relaxed, friendly, ready to talk to the boys about ideas, and encouraging. Since the curriculum was lax—the overriding goal was to teach the students to socialize well—Vonnegut chose literature that was interesting to him: science fiction. It was "catnip to the boys, any science fiction at all. They couldn't tell one story from another, thought they were all neat, keen. What appealed to them so, I think, aside from the novelty of the comic books without pictures, was the steady promise of a future which they, just as they were, could handle."[129]

"Just as they were" meant being on tranquilizers most of the time, dispensed by the nurse in little paper cups to boys who had been judged too wild or difficult for mainstream classrooms. Despite the students' semisoporific state, the headmaster—an angry, disembodied voice over the classroom loudspeaker—usually began the day's announcements by complaining about something they'd done. "I'm sick and tired!" was his morning mantra.[130]

After a day of teaching at the Hopefields Riverview School, Vonnegut was left with only nights and weekends to write, a repeat of what his life had been like working at General Electric. In essence, he was in the same circumstances—worse, in fact. More than a decade after quitting his "nightmare job" to write full-time, he had purchased two homes after leaving Alplaus, become father to a third child, and assumed responsibility for three nephews, but his writing career hadn't kept up with the pace of his life. Now he was back to writing part-time.

UNDAUNTED, IN early fall 1962, Kurt, using money from his teaching job, arranged to have the northwest wing of the house remodeled and turned into a studio. With his love of having just the right place to read, write, or listen to music, this latest configuration was his best setup yet. He let Knox in on all the details. Carpenters finished it off at twenty-two feet long, fifteen feet wide, with a beamed ceiling, a ridgepole at one end, and a blue, wood-burning stove to take off the chill: a workshop for turning out novels.[131]

Naturally, as soon as they could, the children sneaked in for a look at where he spent nights and weekends. The new studio smelled of cigarette smoke and the ashtrays were stuffed with butts. The corner beam near the desk had been carved with strange figures and designs. Under the bed, Allison Mitchell and Nanny found *Playboy* magazines.[132] Tiger, studying his uncle's nicotine-stained Smith-Corona typewriter, noticed the space bar had an indentation in the middle, grooved by Kurt's thumb striking it thousands of times over the years.[133]

Vonnegut buckled down to work on *Cat's Cradle* again because Holt had slated it for hardback publication the following year. For almost ten years he had been returning to it, until the story froze at around 250 typewritten pages. He rushed to complete it since two-thirds of a draft was already written after being in limbo for so long. There was no time left to waste any more energy fretting over it.[134]

CAT'S CRADLE appeared in 1963, after a long gestation, but the idea for it had occurred to Kurt as far back as his days at General Electric. A story often repeated at the Schenectady plant concerned H. G. Wells's visit in the 1930s. The head scientist, Irving Langmuir, had proposed an idea to Wells for a story about a form of water that solidified at room temperature. Wells, the most famous science fiction writer of the day, expressed interest, but his novels, at their core, were parables about humanity— a scientific conundrum didn't interest him.

Kurt, on the other hand, was intrigued by Langmuir's suggestion. Taking the concept a step further, he asked: what if water, the most common liquid on the planet, could be weaponized, the way that matter torn apart by nuclear fission had created the atomic bomb? At a party of mostly General Electric scientists and their wives one evening, Vonnegut described his idea to a crystallographer, explaining that humanity, in his story, would be threatened by water becoming stable like ice at room temperature. The scientist nodded and went over to a chair. He sat there, ignoring the talk and laughter, just thinking. Finally, as things were winding down, he returned and said, "No. There could be no such ice."[135]

Vonnegut might have put the idea aside except that his brother Bernard's cloud seeding experiments at General Electric convinced him that weather modification raised ethical issues more important than how water actually crystallizes. In 1952, the *Cape Cod Standard-Times* had interviewed Kurt about his next novel after *Player Piano*. "'Actually,' Mr. Vonnegut said in a worried tone, 'the atmosphere can be fouled up by anybody with an oil burner pointing at the right kind of cloud.' The situation is so explosive that he believes restrictive legislation is needed everywhere right now."[136]

Then the year he returned to *Cat's Cradle,* 1962, one of Bernard's experiments took on shades of a scientist trying to shock nature into doing his bidding. West of Champaign, Illinois, Bernard and his assistants strung thirty miles of piano wire over a sixty-square-mile area of farmland. On a signal, a 30,000-volt generator sent pulses of current through the wire, while Dr. Vonnegut and his team watched the skies for signs of rain.[137] Nothing happened, except that his brother, the science fiction novelist, saw how attempts to distort nature were a scenario ripe for satire.[138]

THE NARRATOR of *Cat's Cradle* introduces himself as John, although he invites the reader to call him "Jonah," foreshadowing disaster on a biblical scale. This is the first time Vonnegut has opted for the first person with no intervening voice. John explains, in the style of a memoirist, that he was a journalist researching a book titled *The Day the World Ended* about the destruction of Hiroshima on August 6, 1945. His research had taken him to Ilium (the setting of *Player Piano*) and

General Forge and Foundry Company, where Dr. Felix Hoenikker, "one of the so-called 'Fathers' of the first atomic bomb," was formerly the lead physicist.[139]

John is too late to meet the deceased Dr. Hoenikker, "a force of nature no mortal could control," but the scientist's son, Newton, tells John a revealing anecdote about the great man.[140] On the day the first atomic bomb was dropped, Hoenikker had been absentmindedly playing with a loop of string and making a cat's cradle with it. Newton adds that his father was more fascinated with toys, games, and turtles than with human beings.

The professional interests of Hoenikker directly overlapped Bernard Vonnegut's. Dr. Hoenikker's "last gift to mankind" was his creation of "ice-nine," a single grain of which "could make infinite expanses of muck, marsh, swamp, creeks, pools, quicksand and mire as solid" as iron.[141] This is the result of "playful" experimentation, of rearranging atoms, as Bernard had once explained the process of crystallization to Kurt. Crystals form in patterns depending on how the molecules set up. In other words, depending on how you stack cannonballs on a courthouse lawn, or oranges inside a crate, you get very different sorts of crystals. Sometimes you even get a crystalline arrangement in a fluid suddenly, which is why ketchup won't come out of the bottle. In the novel, ice-nine is capable of turning water into crystals instantly, and releasing a microscopic amount into water anywhere will turn the earth into a "blue-white pearl."

The three Hoenikker children, desiring love and approval their father failed to provide, have carelessly distributed ice-nine to powerful people. Those who live in terror of an ice-nine apocalypse have embraced Bokononism, a Caribbean religion "for the nitwits," as Vonnegut later called it, that preaches soothing lies and nostrums about reality. Central to the belief of Bokononism is that humanity is organized into groups that carry out God's will unknowingly. Just the sense of being in one of these groups—called a karass, but members never know who else belongs to theirs—is what gives them a sense of purpose in life.[142]

A consoling thought, but no spiritual guidance is enough to save the world from ice-nine. Due to a ridiculous accident, a terrible chain reaction releases the substance, turning all the world's seas, rivers, and groundwater to stone. Jonah and a beautiful woman named Mona escape to an underground shelter—reminiscent again of Vonnegut's taking shelter in Dresden—where Jonah tries to reaffirm life by making love to her. "I will not go into the sordid sex episode that followed. Suffice it to say that I was both repulsive and repulsed. The girl was not interested in reproduction—hated the idea. Before the tussle was over, I was given full credit by her, and by myself, too, for having invented the whole bizarre, grunting, sweating enterprise by which new human beings were made."[143]

This sex scene is part of a pattern in Vonnegut's works. In *Player Piano*, Paul has an unsatisfactory sex life with his wife, Anita; in *The Sirens of Titan*, frigid Beatrice can be ravished only when a man is desperate, and in a short story later published in 1968, "Welcome to the Monkey House," women must be raped to become sexually active. Not until *Slaughterhouse-Five* will a protagonist enjoy a sexual relationship with a woman that is mutually satisfying.

Other survivors in *Cat's Cradle* are sorry to be alive because Earth is ruined. And when Jonah finds the founder of Bokononism, he is writing a bitter conclusion to the religion's sacred texts: "If I were a younger man, I would write a history of human stupidity; and I would climb to the top of Mount McCabe and lie down on my back with my history for a pillow; and I would take from the ground some of the blue-white poison that makes statues of men; and I would make a statue of myself, lying on my back, grinning horribly, and thumbing my nose at You Know Who."[144]

IT WAS Vonnegut's best work so far, so inventive that he deserved to have been ranked as one of the better experimental American writers of the 1950s and 1960s, in the same company as John Barth, Donald Barthelme, John Hawkes, William S. Burroughs, and Robert Coover, for example. It was solidly part of the development that later came to be called postmodernism: stylistically playful, straddling the boundaries between high and low art, and outside the confines of the genre— science fiction, mystery, crime, romance, and so on—an "episodic collage" with 127 chapters (versus *The Sirens of Titan*'s twelve and *Mother Night*'s forty-five).

Yet *Cat's Cradle* is also in the tradition of the satiric, picaresque novel, in which a hero, usually naive, stumbles through a series of events that are often bizarre, random, and accidental. But no one along the way learns anything through experience. The same mistakes are made, the same things keep happening; the characters tend to be puppetlike because the author is using them for a moral purpose.[145] The moral statement in *Cat's Cradle* is fairly clear: no one has the right or the competence to hold the key to ending the world. Jonah speaks for Vonnegut on that point, heading toward doomsday, reporting live from the scene, as it were. It's important to keep in mind too the era in which *Cat's Cradle* was written. By the 1960s, death by man-made apocalypse inspired dread. The cleverness of ice-nine was that the concept was simple, original, and easily understood—subzero cold in contrast to hydrogen bomb's heat, but no less deadly. Vonnegut and other postmodernists recommend that we respond by celebrating nonsense as an emotional release, the way Edgar Allan Poe's "happy and dauntless and sagacious" Prince Prospero defies the approach of the Red Death by throwing a masquerade ball.

Readers often remark on how Vonnegut's humor contributes strongly to the sense of him being right there on the page. He creates this intimacy, for the first time in *Cat's Cradle*, by aligning himself with the reader through talking about something that's taboo.[146] He was a practitioner of what Freud called the "tendentious joke." This kind of humor, and Vonnegut will come to rely on it (some say too much), is obscene or hostile; it tends to be cynical, critical, and blasphemous, giving voice to a need to defy authority or air "bad thoughts."

The head of Bokononism in *Cat's Cradle*, for instance, suggests that the best response to God is to thumb your nose at him. Disrespect for the dead, another kind of profanation, comes into play when a physician in the novel takes his son outside to view a heap of corpses. Giggling, he lets his flashlight roam over the bodies. "Son, ... someday all this will be yours."[147] It's disrespectful, tasteless, but by inviting the reader to enter into the "joke" with Vonnegut, he creates an alliance, as much as when someone begins an inappropriate remark with "I know this isn't politically correct, but..." Later in his career, Vonnegut dispensed entirely with some words in the text and substituted a sketch, drawn with a felt-tip pen, of an anus (his, he said) or a vagina.

DESPITE ITS innovations, *Cat's Cradle* didn't outsell its initial printing of six thousand copies and received just a few reviews.[148] Terry

Southern, another but edgier satirist whose novel *Candy* was widely banned as pornography, came to Vonnegut's defense in a review for the *New York Times*: "Like the best of contemporary satire, [*Cat's Cradle*] is work of a far more engaging and meaningful order than the melodramatic tripe which most critics seem to consider 'serious.'"[149] The director Fred Wiseman optioned the novel for a film, but nothing came of it. Disgusted, Kurt wrote to Knox that maybe he should think about writing a book called *Clean Stories for Clean People in Drugstores and Bus Depots*.[150]

His standing in the world of publishing was near the bottom. In June 1963, at age forty, he found himself at a chicken-and-peas-type banquet at Indiana University, honored as one of six local authors because he had been born in Indianapolis. He and Jane might not have made the trip for the ceremony except that Kurt would be teaching at a weeklong writer's conference afterward, and Uncle Alex and Aunt Raye had flown out from their retirement home in California to see him receive his framed certificate. It was hard not to feel bitter. "I wasn't even getting reviewed. *Esquire* published a list of the American literary world back then and it guaranteed that every living author of the slightest merit was on there somewhere. I wasn't on there . . . [and] it made me feel subhuman."[151]

He began his fiction class on Indiana University's Bloomington campus, "a hell-hole, Gods knows," with a heavy heart.[152] At least the student union, designed by his grandfather Bernard, had four restaurants, a pool hall, a barbershop, a bowling alley, and a bookstore. The only other saving grace about the experience was that adults were allowed to drink in their rooms, which he did.

A YEAR passed, and he attended to his writing, pressed by the exigency to support his family. He preferred working early in the morning, from six to ten, because that's when he was "smartest."[153] When the writing went well, he had an unconscious habit of crossing his legs and wiggling his foot as he read over a page aloud, using different voices for characters, and gesturing with his hands. A page that was no good, he pulled from the typewriter, crumpled, and tossed in the direction of the wastebasket, starting all over again.[154]

His rumbling voice and the clack of the typewriter keys distracted him from noises coming from the main part of the house as everyone else woke up and began moving around. As the day wore on, the youngsters rarely saw an adult except Jane, trudging upstairs to collect dirty laundry. Kurt preferred not knowing what the adolescents were up to, in particular. Edie had a group of six or seven fourteen-year-old girlfriends nicknamed the Herd who smoked and made the Vonnegut house their headquarters.[155] Once, during an unannounced walk through the upstairs, Kurt nearly caught Jim Adams naked in the attic with a girl. "That was a time when sex and emotion were rampant and Kurt had difficulty with both," Adams said.[156] Nanny, nine years old, disdaining "the House of Sex," as she called it, tried to spend as much time as she could at her friend Allison's house down the lane where it was clean and quiet. Her mother baked and the little girls took long bubble baths.[157]

VONNEGUT WAS working on a promising story in 1964 that had practically fallen into his lap more than a decade earlier. It concerned Al Little, the self-employed certified public accountant who had shared an office with him over the store in Osterville.

Little, in addition to working on retainer for several businesses in town, offered a tax preparation service, but it was special. His clients tended to be desperate people who came to him because of his reputation for compassion. They were frightened that they might be in trouble with the government and unburdened themselves to him about family problems. Through the panel wall separating their offices, Vonnegut could hear people weeping, groaning, while Little murmured sotto voce, rumbling like an engine idling, "There, there, that's all right, oh, that's all right."[158] His clients were usually poor, and they unburdened themselves about family members with alcohol problems, relatives in jail without bail money, personal setbacks, and expensive mistakes they had made, while Little listened without interrupting. Often at the end of an emotional meeting, he would stand up and wrap his arms around the person in a back-patting bear hug.

One day, Vonnegut asked him about his clients.

"Well," he said, "when people finally get the courage to tell you how little they made last year, then they want to tell you everything."[159] Sometimes Vonnegut could overhear angry phone calls from Mrs. Little who scolded her husband for wasting time on people who couldn't afford him.

In Al Little—the businessman, humanitarian, and counselor— Vonnegut had a protagonist with three distinct facets. Just to add a little irregularity, however, he also gave him the gift of Midas, making it possible for him to help anyone to any extent he wished. But if he were wealthy, whom would he choose to help and why?[160] A year after the publication of *Cat's Cradle*, Vonnegut removed the final page of his latest novel from his typewriter, titled *God Bless You, Mr. Rosewater; or, Pearls Before Swine.*

ELIOT ROSEWATER—whose surname combines "Roosevelt" and Goldwater"—is the son of a Republican senator but behaves, as one reviewer later said, like the "crackpot Christ."[161] His conscience is tormented by a split-second miscalculation: during World War II he mistakenly shot noncombatant German volunteer firefighters. In partial atonement, as the president of the Rosewater Foundation in Rosewater County, Indiana, one of the largest family fortunes in the United States, he gives away money to less able people who have been failed by the American dream. In his simple office, he has two phones: one black for people needing help; one red for emergency calls from the fire department because he is a volunteer. He has no heirs, and one day everything will pass to Fred Rosewater, a distant relative. But until he either dies or is proven insane, the Rosewater Foundation fortune is his to do with as he pleases.

Enter a conniving young lawyer, Norman Mushari, who sees the opportunity for a commission from Fred if he can prove Eliot's insanity. The contest of wresting away control of the foundation causes Rosewater to have an apocalyptic vision. Approaching the outskirts of Indianapolis on a bus, he beholds the whole city being consumed by a firestorm like the one he had read about in a book about Dresden. Eliot temporarily loses his mind, and Mushari places him out of the way in a private psychiatric hospital.

But even then the contest has not ended. Rosewater is a typical Vonnegut hero—down but not beaten, accepting that he will be powerless against fate.[162] When he regains his sanity, Eliot declares that every child in Rosewater County will be his heir, each carrying the last name Rose-water, and instructs his lawyer to make his decision legally binding. "'And tell them,' he began again, 'to be fruithful and multiply.'"[163]

IF VONNEGUT'S readers recall only a few things about his work, most of them appear in *God Bless You, Mr. Rosewater.*

First, there's the virtue and efficacy of kindness. Eliot says the first thing newborns should be told is "God damn it, babies, you've got to be kind." Little can be done about the harm people have suffered in the past. But henceforward by extending decency, courtesy, and love to one another, humanity will heal gradually. Second, people have inherent dignity because they are human beings, which is separate from what they own or produce. Acknowledging another person's dignity is essential to compassion. And finally, as an antidote to loneliness or hopelessness, Vonnegut recommends the benefits of community once again. The reason Eliot stays in Rosewater County, a rather hangdog corner of Indiana, is because of his connections with others, symbolized by his joining the volunteer fire department. In a cameo appearance in the novel, the failed science fiction writer Kilgore Trout tells Rosewater that firemen are "almost the only examples of enthusiastic unselfishness to be seen in this land. They rush to the rescue of any human being and count not the cost. The most contemptible man in town . . . will see his enemies put the fire out."[164]

In fact, Vonnegut's characters often find substitute extended families in voluntary associations.[165] He was a believer in joining clubs and teams, because, as he later said, "you don't do that because you're crazy about bowling or about outboard motors or snowmobiles. You do it for the family, the artificial family."[166] He also recommended attending church as well, despite referring to himself as a "Christ worshipping agnostic." Later, when he became famous and readers would write to him about being lonely, he advised, "Get some people. What you need is people. You don't have enough people. But I tell them to go get a family. I don't tell them to swoon over Christ."[167]

A final aspect of *God Bless You, Mr. Rosewater* that recurs in Vonnegut's fiction is a difficult father-son relationship, in this case between Eliot and his father, Senator Rosewater. The senator is simultaneously outraged and despairing about how Eliot seems to be wasting his life and the family fortune on good-for-nothings. He's disappointed, reminiscent of how Kurt believed his father felt about him. On the other hand, practically everything we know about the relationship between Vonnegut Junior and Senior is one-sided and tends to reinforce Kurt's portrait of himself as misunderstood by, or at odds with, his father.

IN SEPTEMBER 1964, with *God Bless You, Mr. Rosewater* slated for publication the following spring, he returned to writing about the experience that had tantalized his imagination for almost twenty years: his through-the-keyhole view of the destruction of Dresden.[168] That perspective, however, was precisely the problem that had stymied him from the beginning. How to write about a tremendous event of war that he had been there for, and yet he had not been there for, because he was suspended underground?

Thinking he might be able to make a fresh and concerted start on the book, he went to New York for a week and checked into the Great Northern Hotel to be away from West Barnstable and its distractions. Going to New York also offered him the chance to socialize with other writers and friends in the publishing business, an antidote to the isolation he felt on the Cape.

A writer he had become friendly with through Knox Burger, for instance, was William Price Fox, raised in South Carolina, who had recently received favorable attention for a collection of short stories called *Southern Fried*. He was married, seeking a divorce, and had a girlfriend in the wings: Sarah Crawford. Sarah was in her twenties, a Barnard graduate with folksinger prettiness: long dark hair, dark eyes, and a wide, full mouth. She lived in Greenwich Village on Bleecker Street, and a photograph taken in Washington Square on a clear, cold day shows her bundled up in a wool coat, hood thrown back, and her arms wrapped around a black cocker spaniel. She was an editorial assistant for Knox, and one day, eager to consort with "madly entertaining people," she accompanied him to the Algonquin Club for lunch, where she met Kurt for the first time.

He asked her out. They took long walks together, and he was infatuated.[169] He felt happy with her because, as he wrote to her later, she responded to him with spunk and daring.[170] He was twenty years older than she, a middle-aged swain as awkward as an adolescent. But he wanted to pursue the relationship.

WHEN *GOD Bless You, Mr. Rosewater* appeared in the spring of 1965, it received more attention than any of Vonnegut's previous novels. While admiring his inventiveness, reviewers tended to be a little bemused by the novel, too. The *Washington Post* was certain Vonnegut's "new novel confirms his unique and outrageous talent."[171] The *New York Times* offered an unconventional review to suit an unconventional narrative: "Here is a book that is devoid of anything as square as a plot, its text broken up into short epiphanies, like poetic cantos, with typographical squiggles for segues. . . . Is this high camp? . . . Or maybe medium camp. . . . Well, no matter. Looking back at an earlier book by Mr. Vonnegut—*Cat's Cradle*, a work from the same unbroken mold—one sees that this is a writer with an excellent ear, a knack for arresting imagery, and a Message."[172]

In Indianapolis, where Kurt and Jane had gone to visit her parents, Kurt exulted in an after-dinner speech at a meeting of Theta Sigma Phi, the women's journalism society. "Good Taste will put you out of business," he said. "For some reason almost all good writers are dropouts" because students learn what is considered good taste at a stage "when they themselves aren't capable of doing very good work. So what they learn makes them hate what they write. And they stop before they ever get started."[173]

He needed to get back to his war book—at least he had a title he liked now, *Slaughterhouse-Five*. He decided to go see his army buddy and former fellow scout Bernard V. O'Hare.[174] The 1964–65 New York World's Fair was reputed to be dazzling, so he decided to combine two trips by taking Nanny and her best friend, Allison Mitchell, to the fair. On the way, they would spend the night with the O'Hares in Hellertown, Pennsylvania.

The trip was a wonderful adventure for the girls. Kurt later captured its spirit in the introduction to *Slaughterhouse-Five* by describing Nanny and Allison as wearing party outfits for the ride. Actually, they wore jeans and played in a nest of blankets in the backseat of the Adamses' old station wagon. Kurt smoked the whole way and periodically yelled "Shut up!" over his shoulder, which Allison remembered as "scary."[175]

In Hellertown, Mary O'Hare shooed the girls upstairs so the men could tell their war stories, and Kurt brought out a bottle of Irish whiskey. Even though Nanny was only eleven, she sensed the friendship was special. "There were a few times when I saw father as himself, and Bernard O'Hare was someone who understood him because of what they went through."[176]

The two men smoked, drank, laughed, and went over the details of their capture, the hardships, and their release—the same as they had countless times before—but Kurt was beginning to think he still didn't have much of a book because his perspective was no different from dozens of other novels about the war. Bothering him too was Mary, who kept banging the ice cube trays on the kitchen counter, closing doors loudly, and huffing. Bernard indicated that nothing was wrong but Kurt was getting uncomfortable.

> Then she turned to me, let me see how angry she was, and that the anger was for me. She had been talking to herself, so what she said was a fragment of a much larger conversation. "You were just *babies* then!" she said.
>
> "What?" I said.
>
> "You were just babies in the war—like the ones upstairs!"
>
> I nodded this was true. We *had* been foolish virgins in the war, right at the end of childhood.
>
> "But you're not going to write it that way, are you."
>
> That wasn't a question. It was an accusation.
>
> "I—I don't know," I said.
>
> "Well, *I* know," she said. "You'll pretend you were men instead of babies, and you'll be played in the movies by Frank Sinatra and John Wayne or some of those other glamorous, war-loving, dirty old men. And war will look just wonderful, so we'll have a lot more of them."[177]

He assured her that he wouldn't write a set piece for some Hollywood star to shout "Let's go, boys!" as the troops whistled their way into Berlin wearing laundered uniforms; he pledged that if he ever did write the novel, he would include the phrase "The Children's Crusade" in the title.[178]

Thus it took Mary O'Hare, who wasn't enamored of the ancient arms-and-the-man ethos about war, to push Vonnegut off dead center about his big book. The truth was that as a twenty-one-year-old private, he hadn't understood what was happening to him from the afternoon the 106th packed their gear at Camp Atterbury to the morning when he and the other POWs walked into Dresden at dawn. The intervening three months had consisted of long periods of boredom, followed by intense terror, and hunger, and then a weird sense of detachment, symbolized by Joe Crone's thousand-yard stare. There had been no Ajax, no Achilles in Vonnegut's anti-*Iliad*. The sacking of Dresden had been accomplished surgically, at night, from high above by men in machines who returned to their homes in a few hours, not years later like Ulysses. There were no classical heroes in twentieth-century total war, only victimizers and victims. It was the breakthrough he needed after two decades of false starts.

Even then, he might have preoccupied himself with projects that were easier, had not something come his way in the spring of 1965 that offered the ideal conditions for writing *Slaughterhouse-Five* straight through.

The University of Iowa offered one of only six creative writing programs on the graduate level in the country, the others being the University of Denver, Stanford, Michigan, Indiana, and Hollins in Virginia. For the 1965–66 academic year, the poet Robert Lowell had agreed to teach at the Iowa workshop but was forced to cancel. Time was short, and in June, John C. Gerber, chairman of the English Department, invited Vonnegut to join the faculty for the fall semester.[179]

He was humbled and not at all sensitive about being a last-minute choice. He knew where he stood in the ranks of published authors. Gerber's offer was prestige, a good salary, and entrée into a salon, so to speak, of fellow writers. He accepted, adding that he would be coming alone—almost as an implied condition, or a subconscious wish—because his family was too large to follow him.[180] He made noises at home like he was reluctant to go, but that just made Jane and the children urge him all the more.[181]

He couldn't leave, though, for a post on a university faculty without taking a Parthian shot at the critics who had ignored him, gloating in an essay for the book section of the *New York Times* at the literary snobs who had passed him by since *Player Piano*. "I have been a sore-headed occupant of a file-drawer labeled 'science-fiction' ever since, and I would like out since so many serious critics regularly mistake the drawer for a tall white fixture in a comfort station." His fault, apparently, was that he noticed technology, and "no one can simultaneously be a respectable writer and understand how a refrigerator works, just as no gentleman wears a brown suit in the city.... Mature relationships, even with machines, do not titillate the unwashed majority."[182]

Frederik Pohl, past master of science fiction, later admired Vonnegut's gumption: "He made the commercial decision to deny that he was a science fiction writer, because he didn't want his books in the science fiction section of the bookstore. He wanted them outside at the cash register, which was a very sensible decision, if he could make it happen."[183]

And so, rather huffily, he left for Iowa on September 10, 1965, driving Mark's Volkswagen, packed with a few belongings, his drafts of *Slaughterhouse-Five*, Sarah Crawford's address, and notes for a new master's thesis, hoping the University of Chicago might still accept one, almost twenty years late.

The seven years between 1958 and 1965 had been the most emotional, trying, and occasionally disappointing ones of his life. Constant pressure had been on him to produce for the sake of his family and his reputation, and he had barely managed to do so, but at forty-three he was still practically nowhere on the landscape of American letters.

8: A Community of Writers

1965–1967

W HEN VONNEGUT ARRIVED in Iowa City for the fall semester of 1965, all of his novels, except his most recent, *God Bless You, Mr. Rosewater*, were out of print. He hadn't sold a story to a well-paying magazine since 1963. *Slaughterhouse-Five* had approximately five beginnings, and the chapters were in various stages of revisions. Mary O'Hare's accusation that he was writing another book glamorizing war urged him to think differently about the novel. Until then, as Knox said, "he didn't know how to approach it."[1]

As he drove into town peering at street addresses for the apartment the university's English Department had found for him, he cut an earnest but amusing figure folded up inside Mark's VW crammed with boxes of his belongings. But no matter how this adventure turned out, he knew he had to get away from West Barnstable. The fighting between him and Jane was making everyone unhappy.[2] He was also tired of his loneliness on the Cape and frustrations caused by kid-related crises.[3] If nothing else, he would meet interesting people and be on his own for the first time in twenty years.

IOWA CITY, population 53,600 and home to the University of Iowa, seemed an improbable incubator for novelists and poets. Ponderous campus buildings slumbered in the lacy shade of hickories, elms, and maples. The downtown consisted of owner-run stores, second-floor law offices, taverns with pool tables in the back, and restaurants that served meat-and-potato meals. The Iowa River ran south through the center of town, looping around like the head of a safety pin—wide, flat, somnolent. The town existed mainly for the university, but Kurt liked the looks and feel of the place immediately.[4] It reminded him of Indiana.

The second-floor apartment reserved for him was in an old house—24 North Van Buren, a short walk from downtown. He unloaded the VW, carrying as much as he could upstairs. But when the door to his rooms swung open, he was crestfallen. Instead of a bed with a head- and footboard, there was a Hide-a-Bed too small for him.[5] The bathroom had a stand-up shower stall, no tub; there was a refrigerator with no ice cube trays, and no curtains or shades for the windows. The place was awful, he wrote Max Wilkinson. If it turned out he couldn't write in a dump like this, he was going to quit.[6]

He took the only framed picture of family he had brought, a self-portrait of Edie, a burgeoning artist, and propped it on a sideboard. Because the Hide-a-Bed blocked the window overlooking the street, he shoved a small table beside another window facing a grassy alley and put his typewriter on that.[7]

There was nothing to do, so he strolled over to the offices of Paul Engle, the workshop director, and swiped some office stationery while he waited for the director to arrive.[8] Growing bored, he left to find the campus gym, which was available free to faculty members. It had an Olympic-sized pool, which pleased him because swimming had been his forte since Lake Maxinkuckee days.[9]

Returning to his apartment, he wrote to Jane, saying he would reserve a room for a few days during Christmas at the Royalton Hotel in New York where they had spent a second honeymoon four years earlier.[10] Then he dropped a note to Sarah Crawford. She was right, he said, to scold him for going away from her. She liked to tease him by addressing him as "Mr. Vonnegut," accentuating the illicitness and impropriety of a single girl flirting with a much older, married man. He urged her to call him instead by his first name, and tutored her in pronouncing it correctly, the German way—"Koort."[11]

Later, he wrote Jane a second letter. Separated as they were by a great distance, he just wanted her to know that he loved her.[12] He wrote her nearly every day while waiting for classes to start, as if he were away at camp for the first time. He was homesick, friendless, he said.[13] He wanted her to come out as soon as possible: he would pick her up at the airport half an hour away in Cedar Rapids, because it was easier to fly into. After his phone was installed, he called her right away with his number.[14] He also made certain to keep Sarah on the hook by sending her a poem about how he was just a big, lumbering creature, sadly in love, although—he cautioned her—maybe a little less every day the longer they were apart.[15]

At a faculty get-acquainted cocktail party, he finally met Paul Engle and found him slender, a sporty dresser, and a tad pompous. Engle, gray-haired and in his early fifties, was the workshop's politician, power-broker, and fund-raiser. He believed in making no small plans and his vision of the workshop component of the English Department's master of fine arts program was "to run the future of American literature, and a great deal of European and Asian, through Iowa City."[16] He wanted no intimidating hurdles to discourage students from applying. The process was simple: submit an original story and complete an application for the graduate school. His sincerity was unquestionable, but his manner of speaking to people tended to be orotund and gran-diloquent. "We believe that you can only teach, where something in a mind is waiting to be taught. We do not pretend to grow blonde curls on an autumn pumpkin."[17] Engle's wife confided to Kurt that the president of the university avoided her husband because he pushed the workshop relentlessly.[18]

Also at the cocktail party, Vonnegut met some of his colleagues for the first time. Until now, his professional friendships had included mainly Grub Street writers: work-for-hire freelancers, copywriters, small-time journalists, scriptwriters for radio—no big names. But as a workshop faculty member, he would be teaching with Nelson Algren, Chilean nov-elist José Donoso, and poets Donald Justice, George Starbuck, and Mar-vin Bell. He was amazed.[19] He wanted to get to know his fellow instructors right away and talk shop, talk about craft. Iowa City might be an outpost of the literary life compared with New York, but he was going to make the most of it. He especially wanted to meet Algren, but he was still nowhere in sight as the first day of classes drew near and, in the meantime, Kurt hit it off with Vance Nye Bourjaily. Bourjaily was most recently the author of the autobiographical, realistic novel *Confessions of a Misspent Youth*. An infantry veteran like Kurt, he had left behind his life as a New York drama and literary critic to teach at the workshop.

In the august company he was going to be chumming around with, Kurt wished he had a degree. He didn't want to turn red-faced if a colleague or, worse, a student asked him about his alma mater. Short of his writing away to a diploma mill, though, the quickest thing he could do to get some alphabet soup after his name was to finish a thesis for the University of Chicago. A graduate degree in anthropology would be prestigious. He had the requisite courses, and as far as research and writing were concerned, he lived near university libraries. Mimicking the style of academic writing wouldn't be hard once he had studied it again.

The problem was he hadn't read anything about his unfinished topic, the effects of Western influence on American natives, in years. He did know about storytelling, on the other hand—its patterns, specifically— and, being the professional writer he was, he could quickly bang out a lengthy essay based on his experiences. He phoned the Anthropology Department at Chicago and asked if he could still have his degree after nearly twenty years. The answer was he could, if his thesis was "any good."[20]

He titled his paper, "Fluctuations Between Good and Ill Fortune in Simple Tales," the gist of which became a popular chalk talk he delivered to audiences over the years, and which later appeared in his collection of essays and speeches *A Man Without a Country*. He salted the introduction with terms he hoped would appeal to his degree-granting committee at Chicago, likening tales to arrowheads, with clues and traits that identified their origin or universality.[21] A "narrative" he defined as a chain of events that have happened, or not, and can entertain or educate an audience. Rather than slip into deep waters by discussing novels and prose poems, he said he would limit tales to those narratives that could be told in a half hour or less.[22]

As to his qualifications to write on the topic, he said he was a practitioner not a theorist, a bit of vanity that probably didn't help his case among professors, but he couldn't resist explaining that he was self-made. His bona fides, he said, were that he had been a professional writer of American fiction for fifteen years and was a literary critic for the *New York Times, Life,* and the *Nation,* which wasn't true. Presently, he was writer-in-residence at the University of Iowa.[23]

In the body of the thesis he took half a dozen classic tales, such as "Cinderella," and showed via graphics and accompanying text how they tended to conform to patterns. It took him two weeks to finish the project with the help of a typist.[24] At the same time, he worked on a screenplay for *God Bless You, Mr. Rosewater.*[25]

Members of the Anthropology Department at Chicago deliberated briefly about his submission and rejected it. The mentality of the department in the 1960s tended to be concerned with potsherds, bones, and sand paintings and the committee judged that "he had not done any work that qualified as 'anthropology' in some then current strict sense."[26]

Vonnegut wasn't just disappointed, he was incensed. At the time, he was too upset to recognize the benefit of organizing his thoughts about fiction. Until then he had been an instinctual writer—grateful to accept the instruction of helpful editors—but mainly relying on his sense of when something sounded and felt right. Compelled to explain, step by step, what experience had taught him, he would use "Fluctuations Between Good and Ill Fortune in Simple Tales" as his manual—twenty years' worth of writing and revising turned into a set of lesson plans.

And in the long run, the difficulty of doing it, mortifying as the end result was, couldn't have prepared him better for the challenge of teaching novice writers who wanted to know "What makes a good story?" But he couldn't see that. The eggheads didn't like his proposal, he was convinced, because "it was so simple and looked like too much fun. One must not be too playful. . . . The apathy of the University of Chicago is repulsive to me. They can take a flying fuck at the mooooooooooooooooon."[27]

THE COURSE schedule for the fall made it appear that Kurt had a light teaching load with just two classes—Form and Theory of Fiction and his section of the Fiction Workshop—but there would be hundreds of stories to evaluate and term papers to grade. In addition, the pay was low. Knox mentioned to Kurt that a former workshop instructor, R. V. Cassill, had offered to write potboiler paperbacks under a pen name for Gold Medal because his salary wasn't enough.[28]

It would have been some compensation for the chintzy wages if the classrooms were quaint—the University of Iowa had been founded before the Civil War—but they weren't. The writing workshop students and their instructors didn't meet in the English building but, like poor relations, in Quonset huts, which had been classrooms for troops during World War II, constructed of corrugated, galvanized iron, with cement-slab floors.[29] Small windows, halfway up the walls, cantilevered out, let in the warm, muddy smell of the Iowa River and the hardy farm flies. In winter, the students sat in class wearing heavy coats. "Our Quonset huts were cold, they were cozy, they were smoky, they were dirty, they were filthy," said Suzanne McConnell, a student in one of Kurt's classes. "And we were the writers. We didn't care about that stuff. We didn't need to be pampered, we wanted to get to the heart of stuff."[30] With satisfaction, the students noted their instructors' offices were furnished with sagging bookshelves and, facing each other, two overstuffed, dilapidated armchairs.

BEFORE THE first day of class, there was a preregistration orientation. The idea was that each instructor would talk a little about himself and the goals for his course. Then students would submit their first, second, and third choices for classes, based partly on their impressions of the instructor and what they had heard.

The sign-up orientation was held in the Chemistry Building lecture hall, the only room large enough to accommodate everyone. One hundred and fifty students faced the instructors on the dais below, backgrounded by a huge periodic chart of the elements. It looked like the start of a game show. Algren, who had arrived at the last possible moment, was winner of the National Book Award for *The Man with the Golden Arm*. Bourjaily was a playwright, journalist, and lecturer. José Donoso had received the William Faulkner Foundation Prize for his first novel, *Coronación*. Charles Wright, a poet, had recently returned as a Fulbright scholar from the University of Rome. Donald Justice, also a poet, was just completing a Ford Foundation Fellowship in theater. And George Starbuck, although only in his early thirties, was already the recipient of the Yale Series of Younger Poets Award, a John Simon Guggenheim Memorial Fellowship, an American Academy and Institute of Arts and Letters award in literature, and the Prix de Rome of the American Academy of Arts and Letters.

Vonnegut stood out as the tallest at six foot three. Clean-shaven with a crew cut, a little beefy with large dark eyes set wide apart, he was the least educated and accomplished of anyone on the faculty. If forced to summarize his résumé, he'd have to say he had nearly flunked out of Cornell his sophomore year; been discharged after World War II as an army corporal; dropped out of the University of Chicago without a degree; quit as publicist for General Electric company; and eked out a living as a freelance writer. It was true he had published novels and also short stories in magazines. But whether he could meet the expectations of the students, his younger competition, remained to be seen.

Actually, he needn't have worried. Most had no idea who he was.[31] And those who did had heard he was a hack science fiction writer. So the bar was set pretty low already.[32]

THE FIRST day of class was delayed two days because of the backlog of students registering. Kurt's class roster rose from forty to close to eighty. He blamed the crush on Engle accepting *"everybody."*[33]

As he feared, he bombed his first day, Friday, teaching the Form and Theory of Fiction section. The students were not fresh-faced undergraduates with the dew of high school still on them. There were military veterans sitting in the chairs, Peace Corps volunteers, and returning students with children.[34] Some had graduated from universities such as Vanderbilt, Harvard, and Yale and were accustomed to academic rigor.[35] A few were professionals in other fields. Vonnegut learned later that two of his best students were a lawyer and a registered nurse.[36] They were upset about the size of the class, which was as large as an undergraduate survey course—not the type of seminar environment they were expecting.[37]

Fortunately, he had an introductory announcement to make. His section would be divided into two, which mollified them somewhat. Next, as a way of inspiring a little discussion and camaraderie, he asked everyone to vote for the author they thought should win the Nobel Prize. When the votes were counted, Ayn Rand, John D. MacDonald, and Vance Bourjaily each received one vote apiece. Saul Bellow won by a landslide; the runner-up was Graham Greene.[38]

Then he took a piece of chalk from the tray, turned to the blackboard, and wrote "FUCK." Hesitantly, he began to teach. "If the magazine you want to write for doesn't embrace this word, don't use it."[39] He meant to stumble into some kind of lighthearted lesson about selling fiction and pitching to the popular marketplace. But it sounded like an inane remark to the students, practically all of whom had their sights set on rather outré small literary magazines such as the *Black Mountain Review*, and not *Ladies' Home Journal*.[40] The hour dragged painfully to its end. Already intimidated, he dropped the abstract word *theory* from the title of the course and changed it, he told Jane, to Form and Texture of Fiction.[41]

HE DID not look forward to facing his Monday class and began to wonder defensively if his students were just amateurs who were avoiding learning the craft of writing outside of college by trial and error.[42]

Tuesday, he had the whole day off and felt lonely. That evening he saw the film *The Umbrellas of Cherbourg*, a French musical about a shop girl in love with an auto mechanic. To Jane he wrote that the movie touched him, a middle-aged man who was long past the giddiness of having a first serious love.[43]

To Sarah he wrote approximately the same letter, word for word, but added that he wasn't going to pursue her any longer.[44] As lyrically as he could, he explained that there wasn't much hope for a long-distance, tenuous romance with a young woman half his age. They had never reached the stage of being lovers.[45] It was impossible to woo her at such a remove from New York and he had no plans to return there soon.

In a letter to Nanny, there's a suggestion that he didn't need to look in the direction of Greenwich Village for romance, anyway. He told her to mention to "Aunt Mother" that girls in the writing program—and there were few by comparison—were wan and fidgety, the way college students get when they spend most of their time sitting in classrooms or writing late into the night.[46] The subtext was that young women more available than Sarah were around, and he was noticing them.

AS THE days of his classes turned into weeks, part of his apprehension about teaching stemmed from his students' abilities, which they could hardly conceal during discussions. The program was an aggregation of remarkable talent, despite his complaint that Engle let anybody in. Facing him were future professors of literature such as Jonathan Penner,

Jon Lipsky, Mark Dintenfass, and John Goulet; the novelists James Crumley, Ian T. MacMillan, Joy Williams, John Casey, and John Irving; the novelist, screenwriter, and director Nicholas Meyer; the screenwriter Leonard Schrader; the young adult novelist and White House speechwriter Robert Lehrman; the television scriptwriter David Milch; the short story writer Philip Damon; and the playwright and novelist Barry Jay Kaplan.[47]

Most had sacrificed to be here: they had quit jobs, borrowed money, boxed up their belongings, and moved into apartments. John Irving's wife, Shyla, pregnant with their first child, taught kindergarten, while he shuttled between attending classes, working in the library stacks at night, writing his first novel, *Setting Free the Bears*, and selling pennants, seat cushions, and programs at Kinnick Stadium during Iowa home football games.[48]

Vonnegut would not be able to fool them about whether he had anything to teach them, nor did he want to. He wanted to deliver his best, although he doubted his qualifications. "They were engaged in a two-year graduate program which was to end, ideally, with the completion of a novel or a short story collection, or sometimes a play. They deserved help from their teachers, and there was time in which to give it to them."[49]

He fell back on what he knew. He was an authority only on the practical side of writing and selling stories: what worked with readers and what didn't. He was trying hard, he explained to L. Rust Hills, editor of *Esquire*, to get his students to think about three fundamentals: authorship, storytelling, and readers as an audience.[50]

In class one day, he read aloud "Harrison Bergeron," his story about a bizarre society in which everyone must be equal, regardless of their innate intelligence or abilities. He knew students suspected him of being "some science fiction writer," and he was hoping to show that he dealt with ideas and challenges to humankind, not ray guns and rockets.

Their response was mixed. "The absurdist extremity of it, the craziness, had an interesting effect," remembered Ian MacMillan. "About a third of the students loved it, myself included, and about two thirds were left skeptical, one I recall saying after class, 'this clown is going to teach us how to write?'" It wasn't snobbery, but rather a legitimate suspicion on the part of serious students about the mind-set of the instructor, who seemed too concerned about making a buck to be of much use to them.[51]

The "use" he could be to them was showing them how to get into print. They assumed that being published was a given because they were talented. Suzanne McConnell was struck by Vonnegut's singularly unromantic view of the writing trade. "You're in the entertainment business. Your first job is to hook the reader and keep him/her reading." He cited a story in which a character has something stuck in her tooth and, throughout, keeps tonguing it. "That," he said, "was compelling enough to keep the reader wondering, and therefore reading: is she going to get the damn thing out of her tooth, or not?"[52]

He encouraged them to use techniques for pulling the reader along: short sentences for action, versus longer ones for meditative moments. For sympathy, have characters trying to do something, wanting something, so the reader will hope right along with them.[53] Believable characters are hard to create, and Vonnegut's solution when all else failed was simple: "Steal from the best. If you can't think of a character for a story, think of Cary Grant and think of what Cary Grant would do. I mean, nobody's going to know it."[54]

Stories had a fundamental structure too, which he had figured out on his own, and to illustrate it he turned to the blackboard to summarize the point of his University of Chicago thesis, "Fluctuations Between Good and Ill Fortune in Simple Tales." At its core, he said, every story was essentially a man-in-the-hole situation. "Somebody gets into trouble, gets out of it again." He drew a horizontal line, above which the character slowly rises at first as his fortunes improve, but then events drive him below the line again. What decisions, what choices, what strokes of good luck will help the hero rise again?[55]

Watching him graph story structure as basically a "man in a hole," some students protested it was too reductive. "Where's the man in the hole in the *Odyssey*?" they wanted to know. His approach seemed too commercial, too formulaic to encompass all literature.[56]

Commercial, yes, he agreed, but putting food on the table came before art. They owed it to themselves, for practical reasons, to squeeze the last dollar out of a story. He explained his favorite method, using the analogy of an egg sorter: "It's like grading eggs. Do you know how it's done? There's a device with metal rims, one under the other. Each one has holes. The egg is dropped through the top rim with the largest holes. If it's too small, it drops down through smaller and smaller holes until it stops. When you send out a story, start at the top, the magazine that pays the most. Let it drop down until it sells for the highest price."[57]

Now and then their arrogance got the better of him. One afternoon, after listening to David Milch—who later created the television series *NYPD Blue* and *Deadwood*—mock businessmen, Vonnegut retorted, "Those men are my peers! They're respectable men."[58] During another class, hearing unpublished beginners referring to themselves yet again as "we writers," he almost shouted, "You're not writers!" meaning they had not served their apprenticeship.[59]

For readings and discussions, he chose carefully what he could handle, assigning excerpts from *Alice in Wonderland* or *Dubliners*, for instance. On the one hand, he didn't want to overemphasize his preference for satire.[60] On the other, he didn't want to wade into waters that were too deep for him, either. He was sensitive about his lack of grounding in a broad base of literature and criticism. References by students to Lionel Trilling, Edmund Wilson, the New Critics, and so on made him uneasy.[61] One day, his embarrassment caused a scene.

The story under discussion was E. M. Forster's short story "The Road from Colonus." Someone made a reference to Keats.

"Keats?" asked Vonnegut. "Who's Keats?"

The students laughed, thinking it was a setup for a joke. They were catching on to his droll sense of humor.[62] Then, suddenly, they realized he was serious.

"You know, Keats the poet . . . John Keats." Silence.

He sighed, threw his book against the wall, and strode out into the hall. It was a few minutes before he could regain his composure and return to the front of the class.[63]

THE WORKSHOP side of the program, when students discussed each other's fiction, was more difficult because it wasn't critiquing a story by an established (and often long-dead) author. Vonnegut was aghast sometimes at the lack of empathy or even simple courtesy.[64] Freewheeling discussions tended to become games of one-upmanship, where the goal was to be as mean and destructive as possible about someone else's effort.

The bearbaiting increased when his section was combined with two others in the Chemistry Building lecture hall for a total of about eighty students. One week, Vonnegut, Bourjaily, and Donoso might lead the discussion; the next time, another combination of instructors would take the dais. Submissions were supposed to be anonymous, but names would leak out and friends and foes of the writer arrived for the contest to attack or defend.[65]

Vonnegut disliked the format and began lobbying his colleagues to make changes. The sections should meet separately, he argued, with an instructor to guide the discussion. Second, anonymous submissions were a bad idea. A story didn't exist in a vacuum; a fellow student had written it, and civility was called for. And finally, the critiques were too subjective—opening the floor to potshots wasn't helpful. One that made him wince was a student's crack, "There are three things I don't like about your submission: the beginning, the middle, and the end." Discussions should be based on general criteria of what makes a successful story.[66] Eventually, all of his ideas were instituted.[67]

What he could not change was the behavior of a fellow instructor.

There was a nun in one of the sections, and one day, copies of her submission were distributed. It was more of a vignette, maybe a parable, than a full-fledged story. No one quite knew what to make of it, so she was asked to clarify what it meant. Cheerfully, she stood up to explain.

"Well, you see," she began, "a nun is speeding. And a big Irish cop pulls her over. But when he realizes that she's a nun, he feels guilty. So he tears up the ticket because she's a representative of the Holy Mother Church and the good she does far outweighs the small mistake of speeding." She sat down.

Algren stretched nonchalantly. "You know what would be perfect? What would be perfect is if the cop started masturbating in front of the nun. Now *that* would be perfect."

She never came to class again.[68]

THE NUN was an easy target, but most of the women in the program at one time or another experienced sexism. For one thing, they were in the minority. Vonnegut noticed an odd thing about enrollment in the English Department as soon as he arrived. Of the department's six hundred undergraduates, most were women. But in the graduate writing program, they numbered about one in four, he estimated.[69]

Condescension toward the women tended to be open and unapologetic. At one of the first workshop parties of the semester, Suzanne McConnell found herself talking to a male student who informed her that women shouldn't write; they belonged at home managing the "diapers and the dishes, those absorbing tasks that would allow her husband to write."[70]

Sometimes remarks were meant to be flirtatious, but the subtext was the same. McConnell recalled submitting a story to Vonnegut that he didn't care for: "So I told him I was writing another and he'd like it better. Whereupon he gave me a kindly twinkly smile and said, 'It's all right, Suzanne, you're a pretty girl. You will get married anyway.' I was struck dumb with my pretty jaw hanging and my pretty smile smiling."[71]

Nor were hints about sexual dalliance between female students and instructors considered inappropriate, either. As a late night party at Bourjaily's was ending and everyone was making for the door, a young woman turned to one of the instructors behind her and snapped, "Will you please stop pushing me?" to which he replied, "Oh, I'm not pushing you. I'm feeling you, my dear."[72]

As HIS teaching continued, Kurt discovered the rhythm of being a writer-in-residence had its advantages in terms of his work. He missed Jane, but the quiet couldn't have been better for spending long, uninterrupted hours writing. Up at 5:30 every morning, he wrote until eight, fixed breakfast in the apartment, returned to his writing for another two hours, then took a walk into town to run errands and swim at the gymnasium. After lunch, he read his mail and prepared for the afternoon's teaching. Nights in the apartment he cooked dinner, listened to jazz, or read, a glass of scotch at his side.[73] Knox complimented him on being "prolific as hell."[74]

Even so, he complained to Jane that sometimes he felt like he was going nuts from loneliness and maybe he should quit after the first semester.[75] She wouldn't hear of it; he'd have to finish out the year at least, because quitting would look bad. But she had an idea: Mark and Steve were in college—Mark at Swarthmore, Jane's alma mater. Tiger was at boarding school and Jim was considering the Peace Corps. There was no reason she and the girls couldn't join him in Iowa. His response to this solution, the gist of which he shared with Knox, was a shoulder shrug.[76] Having his wife and two daughters with him would be re-creating some of the dynamics of living in West Barnstable, which he was heartily tired of, creatively and personally. But it would put an end to his persistent loneliness, so he agreed.

He buttonholed Engle before he left for a trip abroad to recruit more foreign students, and the director quickly enlisted the department's help in finding the Vonnegut family a better apartment. Engle also, unasked, successfully made the case that Kurt deserved a raise from $8,500 to $12,500 because his classes had the highest enrollment. Vonnegut was bursting with pride, he told Jane, when he heard about the new salary.[77]

The new apartment was the entire first floor of a large brick Victorian house at 800 North Van Buren, perched on a hill. The seven-acre property included an orchard, a grape arbor, and a barn. Except for the graduate students living upstairs, his nearest neighbors in the workshop program were Andre Dubus II; his wife, Patricia, and their four children; and Ian MacMillan and his wife, Susan. Kurt had hoped for better amenities, but never a house with an entrance hall, parlor, dining room, back porch, large modern kitchen, bay window, piano, washing machine in the basement, and several beds. He drew a floor plan for Jane, labeling all the best features.[78] In a second letter the same day, he added playfully that he wanted to take her to bed as soon as possible, but she should keep in mind he wasn't as spry as he once was.[79]

With the new apartment ready to showcase, Kurt arranged to pick Jane up at the airport in Cedar Rapids the last weekend in October. By then, the first quarter of teaching would have ended, they could tour the campus and the town, and he would introduce her to his friends.

Then, abruptly, he urged her to reconsider coming. He knew she was looking forward to it, he wrote, but how could she really enjoy herself when problems at home would pile up and wait for her? Christmas was just a couple of months away—he would be home for all of winter break, and perhaps then they should celebrate being together again.[80] Instead of wanting to see her, and missing her, as he had written several times, he was counseling reasonableness about their separation and suggesting they make it longer.

THE REASON for this change was a second-year student in one of his classes, Lora Lee Wilson, a divorced mother of two in her midthirties.

Rick Boyer, one of her classmates and later author of the racy Doc Adams mystery series, described her in language appropriate for one of his femme fatales: "She was a willowy blonde woman with amazing eyes and a body that could stop a freight train."[81] "Loree" was the name she preferred to go by.

Bourjaily wasn't surprised the relationship developed quickly. "All the girls were attracted to Kurt. First of all, it was his wit. Kurt was about as dependably funny as anybody I ever knew. Second, he was a wild-looking guy. His clothes never really exactly fit him or sat on him right. So he was a disheveled man. But he was a very attractive disheveled man. And he was very tall."[82]

Kurt made the first move, inviting Loree to help pack food for voter registration drives in Mississippi and Alabama. Afterward, he suggested they have a beer together. The conversation drifted from the war in Vietnam to World War II. She listened, rapt by how his troubles began when he enlisted. His "voice lowered to almost a half-whisper," she said. "'My mother died before we even disembarked.' And then, more softly, 'She took pills.'" She reached across the table and took his hand. He asked whether her parents were still living, because his father had died eight years earlier; consequently, at forty-three, "I'm an orphan now."[83] Even his marriage had failed, he said. He was estranged from his wife.[84]

Thus with the decks cleared of having a spouse back home—that was Loree's understanding, anyway—their affair got under way. Kurt described what she looked like in the nude to Knox: a trifle oldish, in his opinion, with two kids and a scar from a Caesarean section, but always ready to laugh and have fun. She knew he was married—that's what he claimed—and that Jane would be out for second semester, but that was fine with her. She was a butterfly collector and there were only certain seasons when butterflies were available. He was amused by how easy it was to find pleasure in life by just getting away from West Barnstable for a while.[85]

Inconveniently, Jane couldn't be persuaded to wait for a reunion until Christmas and flew out at the end of October, as they had planned. For Kurt, it was a dicey weekend. They attended a faculty party and walked around campus. By sheer luck, no contretemps involving Loree occurred, and Jane returned to the Cape none the wiser.

Kurt need not have worried that someone would out him, however.

When Richard Yates was preparing to teach at Iowa the following year, a former faculty member reassured him that sexual extracurriculars were treated discreetly. "That is, everyone will know what you are up to, but no one will interfere."[86]

JANE HAD been so happy with the apartment, the campus, and Iowa City that she decided sixteen-year-old Edie should live with her father right away and not delay until second semester. She was in trouble at Barnstable High School for defying the dress code, and, as Edie put it, "I had like eight years of detention."[87] Kurt was sympathetic—especially because his daughter's grades were fine—and arranged to enroll her at University High School. But having her in Iowa City presented the problem, of course, of what he should do about Loree. He decided not to tell his paramour that Edie's arrival was a prelude to his wife and youngest daughter coming out after the semester.

Within two weeks of Jane's visit, Edie had flown alone to Cedar Rapids and moved into her father's apartment, where, she thought, they started "co-habiting nicely."[88] She knew her parents weren't getting along. Her mother was "wearing her sunglasses too much in the laundry room" for one thing, and the way her father spoke to her mother "was very sarcastic and mean."[89] But it was something the grown-ups would have to work out. She would just stay out of it, grateful to be attending university-level art classes for high school credit. While her father wrote in one room, she studied, drew, or painted quietly in another. "It was a stimulating, literary blast."[90]

For Kurt, the payoff of having Edie with him was that he expected to be taken care of. Returning to the apartment one day, he stormed at her, "'Why don't you do the dishes, or cook something, the house is a mess!" Instead of being taken aback, Edie thought, "He's treating me like I'm his wife! I remember him liking it too, because he was whining at me. We weren't in different worlds, we were in the same world, in a kitchen, trying to keep fresh milk in the refrigerator and that was fun. And it made me comfortable with him."[91]

FOR THE first time in his life, Vonnegut was in circumstances more conducive to getting his best writing done than he'd ever been in before. He was associating with writers, many of them famous. He was airing his ideas about fiction to an audience of discerning students. He was living in a comfortable home with one child, his favorite, instead of six. But the greatest of these, in terms of influence, was just lusty sex with a pert woman who was falling in love with him.

His affair with Loree would change the way he wrote about relationships in his novels. Until now, his novels had been rife with unsatisfactory or dishonest sexual relations between men and women. In *Player Piano*, for instance, Paul Proteus catches his wife in flagrante with another man, and no real sparks fly. Her defense is that she has been "no damn use" to Paul, anyway. "All you need is something stainless steel, shaped like a woman, covered with sponge rubber, and heated to body temperature."[92] In *Cat's Cradle*, Jonah feels abashed that beguiling, sensual Mona refuses to make love with him because, she says, now that the world has ended "that's the way little babies are made, in case you didn't know."[93] *Mother Night* features a sexual double cross. Howard Campbell discovers that the woman he thinks is his beloved, long-absent wife, Helga, is really her sister, Resi. After the ruse is revealed, Resi encourages Howard to write again so that she may star in his plays revealing the "quintessence of Resi," not Campbell.[94]

Even though Campbell recommends, "Make love when you can. It's good for you," for Vonnegut's protagonists, sex has never been redeeming or more than temporarily comforting. An air of defeatism surrounds the whole business, when it isn't being made into an outright joke. Sex, desire, procreation—all stumble onstage and off again, unconvincing, incompetent actors, whose purpose is to provide a few rueful snickers.

Slaughterhouse-Five lay in abortive drafts before him in Iowa City. But after he began his affair, there was a difference in his perspective. Vonnegut, so physically shy he would rather swim in his trousers than show his legs, now had a lover with whom he shared "sweet luxuries," as she described them.[95] She adored him as a man and a writer. He felt good about his body. Going for horseback rides at Bourjaily's farm, he felt graceful, marveling at how long it had been since the sensation of ease and coordination came to him.[96]

Years later, he would write to his Cornell friend Miller Harris that the Muses were female for a reason. Women knew how to renew men whose strength and imagination were flagging. After sleeping with his Muse in Iowa City, he found himself capable of writing again.[97]

One morning, Ian MacMillan stopped by and found Vonnegut meditatively drinking coffee over pages of *Slaughterhouse-Five* spread across a table.[98] For twenty years, he had been strangely confounded about the book, and intellectualizing its problems hadn't helped. At base, the antagonist was death, and life forces would have to sing a stronger, more convincing counterpoint in the novel. But now, because he was experiencing sex—the psyche's match for death—in ways that inspired him, he saw how to give the novel balance. He would introduce a fantasy lover with the titillating name Montana Wildhack, Loree's double, to rescue *Slaughterhouse-Five*'s protagonist, Billy Pilgrim, from the terror of existing in an empty, meaningless universe.

As FAR as his classes were concerned, however, Vonnegut continued to think he wasn't equal to his students' expectations. Many were competent writers already; he feared being found out.[99] He preferred the workshop sessions and the individual consultations in his office, because when he faced a class, he was afraid it was apparent that he really didn't know anything.[100]

Had he polled his students, they would have disagreed with his self-assessment. Without his realizing it, by second quarter, he was outstripping Algren, the English Department's big catch, because of the effort he put into teaching. As one student said, he was "so passionate and he was so forthcoming about his concern for everyone in the workshop." They found themselves becoming quite fond of him.[101]

Algren claimed that the students preferred him, but the truth was just the reverse.[102] Outside of class, Algren was derided as "disdainful" and a graduate of the "barroom school of writing."[103] He let it be known that Irving's novel-in-progress, *Setting Free the Bears*, was doomed because it was set in postwar Austria—much too ambitious for a beginner. He came to class without having read students' submissions beforehand. After skimming a story that had been painstakingly written, he tended to make remarks off the cuff about it or segue into long, time-killing disquisitions about things barely on the topic. Once, after noticing that Native Americans were mentioned in a story, he mused about the need for more stories about Native Americans.[104]

Word began to circulate that whatever Vonnegut lacked in academic preparation, it was refreshing to have an instructor who laughed, came to class prepared, doodled thoughtfully as he listened in class, and read from his own drafts. He tried out an excerpt from *Slaughterhouse-Five* in which God tears apart the heavens during Christ's crucifixion, warning that he will punish, from now on, anyone who torments a so-called bum with no connections. As Vonnegut tried to get through the piece, he broke down chuckling and wheezing.[105]

The lightness of his touch extended to class assignments too, which were exacting, but typically he couldn't help being tongue-in-cheek.[106] He assigned fifteen short stories from the class anthology, for instance, and instructed students to pretend they were editors of a superior literary magazine. Which three stories would they accept, and which would they reject? For each one, they were to supply a report written for the eyes of a skeptical, experienced editor. Vonnegut cautioned them not to gush, but not to be offhand, either. Keep in mind that their instructor was a man with a modest vocabulary, he concluded. He signed it "Polonius."[107]

Through his example he subverted the notion that literature was a sport strictly for the high-minded. And those students who liked how he debunked snobbery found themselves drawn to him as they would be to a wry uncle. Conferences with students in his office were leisurely, one-on-one consultations, as if he were a doctor listening to patients' complaints. He was convinced "you can't teach people to write well. Writing well is something God lets you do or declines to let you do."[108] But he could encourage them so they would continue writing. Students usually found him in his office dressed in his favorite comfortable clothes—slacks, a dress shirt, baggy cardigan, and Clarks desert boots—seated in a beat-up swivel chair, his big feet propped on the desk. A metal wastebasket, turned upside down, served as a pedestal for his typewriter.

Gail Godwin brought him a forty-page story titled "The Beautiful French Family," about the disastrous vacation in Majorca of a newly married English couple and the husband's difficult three-year-old son. In the margins, Vonnegut wrote phrases such as "sandbagging flashback!" or "lovely!" A few weeks later she asked him whether she should expand the story into a novel. He replied, "Oh, I think it's great as it is." At the next conference she announced she had definitely decided to make it into a novel. "Great idea!" he said.[109] He was so encouraging, "you wanted to bring him nice little fruits on a platter," she said.[110]

Some students had enrolled in the program, in his opinion, already "fully formed."[111] Barry Jay Kaplan was surprised to hear Vonnegut say, "Your stories make me very nervous." He paused, working a shred of tobacco off his tongue, and seemed slightly impatient. The silence continued. "I mean, I don't know what to say about them." He looked right at Kaplan then. "What I mean is . . . I just think you ought to keep writing them, don't you?"[112]

He also cheerfully acknowledged that his opinion was just one of many. When Robley Wilson arrived for his first meeting, Vonnegut was rummaging through some books on his shelf, until he realized Wilson was waiting. He turned around not saying anything.

Wilson asked, "I wondered what you thought of my story."

"The one about the girl and the apple?"

"Yes."

Kurt shook his head. "That's the worst goddamned story I ever read."

Wilson hadn't expected that sort of bluntness and replied defensively, "I have to tell you it was just accepted by the *Carleton Miscellany*."

"Really?" he said. "That's terrific."

"You mean because I got away with something?"

He grinned. "You sure as hell did."[113]

Vonnegut was getting a reputation as a character, to students and instructors both—not as an eccentric, just the opposite—someone with traits of an endearing adolescent. The fiction writers and the poets had equal contempt for each other, but Kurt bridged the divide by fostering friendships on both sides.[114]

One autumn evening, the poet Marvin Bell came out of a bar in downtown Iowa City and saw Kurt walking vigorously down the street, as if he were late for an appointment—backward.[115] On another occasion, during a croquet game in his huge yard, a ball bounced over the curb and sped downhill toward an intersection. Ian MacMillan, whose ball it was, sprinted after it. Behind him, he heard someone pounding along, panting. It was Kurt, holding a glass of wine upright without spilling a drop. "He didn't want to lose the ball down a sewer," MacMillan said. "After all, croquet sets were expensive."[116]

MIDWAY THROUGH first semester, the program's interim director, George Starbuck, asked Vonnegut to return for a second year, and he accepted.[117] Then a few days later, the *National Review*, a respected conservative magazine, reprinted Vonnegut's short story "Harrison Bergeron" as a morality tale about the dangers of hampering free enterprise.

The coincidence of the job offer and the appearance of "Harrison Bergeron" in a leading magazine for intellectuals illustrated how much had changed for Kurt in four years. "Harrison Bergeron" had been published in 1961 in the *Magazine of Fantasy and Science Fiction*, a paid-by-the-word, cultish monthly for hardcore admirers of literary science fiction. Back then, he was still studying the fiction markets like they were stock market reports, analyzing what was selling, trying to get the most money he could for a story by using the "egg sorter" method. Finally, he was tunneling out from under the walls of the science fiction ghetto. Reviews of *God Bless You, Mr. Rosewater* had indicated that some respect was being accorded his work. And financially, his university salary was equal to four Gold Medal paperbacks, provided he could write them in nine months, which was impossible. A major change was afoot.

Returning to the Cape at Christmas, he no longer saw his life in West Barnstable the same way. To Knox, he expressed a sense of unease, almost dread. He loved his family, but he hated the thought of returning permanently to the Cape.[118] Jane too felt a kind of free-floating anxiety that things were different. In a Christmas card to one of Kurt's cousins, her news concerned the children. There was practically nothing about her and Kurt. She added as an afterthought that they were living in "an almost empty house. Very interesting."[119]

For seven years, she had been the woman in the nursery rhyme who lived in a shoe with so many children she didn't know what to do. She had been unable to see past the time when it would end because the children were grown up. She enjoyed making enormous, lopsided birthday cakes, finding sitters so she and Kurt could rehearse at the Barnstable Comedy Club, and being the parent the children went to for warmth. Like so many women of her generation, she had been unable to imagine a future where she wasn't needed constantly. She considered teaching but just the thought, she said to Kurt's cousin, gave her "cold feet."[120]

KURT RESUMED his affair with Loree in January. He hardly ever mentioned Jane and only once spoke of "marital discord." He complained that his wife lived too much of her life through him and spun like a weathervane according to his moods, implying that she needed to get a life of her own.[121] An eventuality he preferred not to explain was that Jane and nine-year-old Nanny would be arriving in early March—the date had been set. In the meantime, Loree stopped in at his office, and he dropped by her apartment after her children were asleep. They went on a date to a Cedar Rapids club to hear a jazz combo and dance.[122] On Saturday evenings after dinner, Loree and her two children, Andre Dubus's three, and Kurt assembled at Dubus's house to watch *Batman*. Edie claimed she was unaware her father was having an affair, which would have made her the only one who didn't know.[123] The Dubuses certainly did—in fact, "everybody knew," Andre's wife, Patricia, told Nanny years later.[124]

As the beginning of March approached, Kurt brooded about how he would have to revert to "Kurt Vonnegut, married man." In a hopeless mood he wrote to Knox that Jane and Nanny would be on their way soon. Jane seemed like a stranger to him, though—like someone he knew by reputation. Not even their attempts at lovemaking inspired feelings of wanting her. With other women, he could be a man in bed, but not her. Instead of desiring her, he felt sorry for his wife. And he suspected that he was angry with her for letting the children come between them.[125]

A week before they were due in town, an attack of tightness in his chest was so painful he thought he was having heart problems.[126] The hour was drawing nigh when he would have to tell Loree the truth. While Jane and Nanny were en route to Iowa City by car, he broke the news over the phone instead of in person, avoiding an emotional confrontation. His wife and youngest child would be there the following day, he said flatly, and living with him, not visiting.

Loree, "totally taken aback," was speechless. "I simply could not comprehend why he hadn't told me this was a possibility, or at least given me more time to adjust or discuss it."[127] After Kurt hung up, she went for a drive in the country and sat on the banks of the Iowa River trying to understand how long she'd been fooled and how willingly.

Next day, as the Vonneguts reunited in the big house on Van Buren Street and filled the closets with belongings from home, Loree made an appointment to see a psychiatrist at the university hospital.[128]

To Kurt's students and colleagues, his wife was simply "Jane—whom we all were fond of," Ian MacMillan said. "She seemed to us like a bubbly teenager, although she was smart, very much with it, I suppose for some of us the image of the perfect writer's wife."[129] At some point she was introduced to Loree, who likened her years later to a "winged creature bouncing from flower to flower, in delight with life itself, but never quite sure of where she was landing in space and time."[130] Loree concealed the affair and her heartbreak, and the two women became friends.

Now that Mrs. Vonnegut was officially on campus, Kurt suggested she might wish to enroll in graduate courses in English or education—a faculty member's spouse could attend without paying tuition. But Jane acted "offended" by the idea of going back to school.[131] She was there to play. Pulling her salt-and-pepper hair into a ponytail, she took to wearing denim shirts and appointed herself hostess of Vonnegut parties. There was a head shop in town called Things and Things where she purchased candles, knickknacks, and batik fabric to decorate the house. Somewhere along the way too, Aunt Jane, according to Kurt, began smoking pot regularly.[132]

Her transformation from housewife to hippie mom was not surprising. Protests against the war in Vietnam disrupted the routine of going to classes and brought some students and faculty members together in a common cause. George Starbuck, for instance, organized teach-ins on campus about American foreign policy and submitted scathing poems about militarism to major magazines.

But Kurt was not as bold about voicing his opinions against the war. Perhaps as a new instructor he didn't feel he had the right to make trouble—and that's how college administrations regarded demonstrations on campuses. Some students, he realized, were in the workshop primarily to avoid being drafted, and not because of an overwhelming desire to write. Quietly, he let it be known that he didn't care whether the young men in his classes submitted anything; he wouldn't flunk them, which could result in losing their student deferment and making them eligible for the draft.[133] One evening at a party, he raised a glass and proposed a toast to General Lewis B. Hershey, the director of the Selective Service system: "To the man responsible for why many of you are here! Cheers!"[134]

THE END of his first year at Iowa, 1965–66, saw completion of a "murderously heavy" schedule of classes and paper grading.[135] Even so, he had been working steadily on *Slaughterhouse-Five* and anticipated that within a few months he would finish the novel, which would be about the size of the Bobbsey Twins, he wrote Knox. Its style was staccato, like a long telegram, he thought, but he felt that at last he had discharged a kind of duty to the past.[136]

In mid-June 1966, the Iowa contingent of the Vonnegut family—Kurt, Jane, Nanny, and Edie—returned to West Barnstable and found the house was a shambles from college parties hosted by Mark. During the weekend bacchanals, there had been "bodies lying everywhere," and furniture was broken.[137] Jane had a difficult time cleaning up, having fallen down some stairs in Iowa City. She was on crutches because of knee surgery. Kurt was back at work in his study, she wrote to José Donoso's wife, Maria, "and you know when *that* happens, we don't interrupt it."[138]

She was sorry to return to the old grind. When Kurt was in his study, "he was almost like a man possessed," Tiger said. "You'd almost think there was somebody else in the room with him, because while he was writing, he was mumbling, talking, he was going over the dialogue of whatever he was writing in his head and it was coming out his mouth, but in an unintelligible way." He emerged now and then to make a sandwich or a drink, without acknowledging other people's presence, and then "stomp right back. I mean he was intense."[139]

Jane wished they were still in Iowa City. There had been new friends, new things to talk about, and new experiences. She complained to Maria, "Things are conspiring to turn me back into a housewife, but I am fighting this turn of events with might and main."[140] Also in West Barnstable were all the old triggers that started fights with Kurt. His drinking increased when he was bored or frustrated. Annoyances occurred less frequently when he had been busy teaching, but embers of resentment smoldering inside him flared up when alcohol was poured on them. Swarthmore, for example, was still a subject that incited his sarcasm because she loved it so and had graduated Phi Beta Kappa. He hoped Mark would drop out of Swarthmore that summer and transfer to Iowa. He would take that as a gesture of allegiance to him.[141]

Jim Adams, Kurt's nephew, found "there was a definite disconnect between the kind of guy you would imagine Kurt must be from the tone of his books, the kind of guy who would say, 'God damn it, you got to be kind,' and the reality of his behavior on a daily basis. He was a complicated, difficult man. . . . I think he admired the idea of love, community, and family from a distance, but couldn't deal with the complicated emotional elements they included."[142]

Kurt, Jane, and the two girls returned to Iowa City in August 1966 for his second year of teaching in the workshop. Not to the house on Van Buren, which wasn't available, but another one—Vonnegut's third since he had arrived—located at 1191 Hotz Avenue.

He was aware that his career was gaining momentum now, as if breezes were lifting to carry him out of the doldrums where he'd been adrift.[143] Syracuse University offered to collect his papers. Its library was specializing in science fiction, among other fields, and invited him to add to a collection that included Hugo Gernsback, the magazine publisher who was often called the father of science fiction; the science fiction authors Damon Knight, Will F. Jenkins, and Frederik Pohl; and the surrealist filmmaker and playwright Jean Cocteau.[144] Vonnegut countered that he would like to come to Syracuse and bring his files with him.[145] In other words, he was fishing for a permanent position and would donate his papers if he were hired; otherwise, the papers were for sale.

The Guggenheim Foundation had contacted him, too—a surprise compliment—and he applied.[146] Once before, in the late 1950s, he had applied for a grant so he could continue writing, but he had been turned down. This time, he requested funds for a research trip to Dresden, a sign that *Slaughterhouse-Five* was not a few months away from completion as he had thought, but much further away.

Over the summer while he'd been at home in West Barnstable, the landscape of Iowa City, both personal and professional, had changed, too. Loree had completed her degree (her thesis was the first half of a novel titled *The Incomplete Puritan*) and relocated to Cedar Falls as an English instructor.[147] Cedar Falls was only ninety miles away, however, straight up Route 218. Under the excuse of delivering a guest lecture, he could visit her there, a strategem they used for the next thirty years.

Workshop classes were no longer meeting in the Quonset huts either, but on the fourth floor of the brand-new English-Philosophy Building. Air-conditioned with classrooms trimmed in blond wood, it resembled a dormitory, disappointing the romantically minded young writers in the program, including John Casey: "There are two ways of fishing. One is you get a wood pole, some string, and a bent safety pin. The other is you get the best equipment. But then you have to come up to that level. The Quonset hut is what we needed. When we moved in a better building, the extra gloss didn't help."[148]

And there was a new instructor on board: Richard Yates. Donald Justice had gone to Syracuse University. The schedule of classes was reshuffled, and room was made for Yates, the author of *Revolutionary Road*, a novel Vonnegut greatly admired.

Yates and Vonnegut were brothers-in-arms before they even met. Yates was a veteran of the Battle of the Bulge, during which he contracted pleurisy. Refusing medical attention, he continued to fight until he collapsed; the strain left his lungs in a weakened condition for the rest of his life.

Men generally liked him because he was a good drinking companion; women were attracted to his sincerity and vulnerability. Like Kurt, he had no patience for literary pretense. (Vonnegut wrote on one of Casey's stories about a Swiss boarding school, "perfume, perfume, perfume.")[149] Vonnegut said Yates reminded him of the depressed donkey Eeyore in *Winnie-the-Pooh*.[150] He had an unconscious habit of leaning his cheek against his fist and twisting his head back and forth as if saying, "No, no, oh no."[151] The critic Robert Towers wrote that Yates seemed to be "under some enchantment that compelled him to keep circling the same half-acre of pain."[152]

One day, Suzanne McConnell's sister arrived for a visit and wanted to sit in on the workshop. "I wanted to take her to Kurt's workshop, but he was gone," McConnell later recalled. "So we went to Yates. We were late. Our interruption made him angry. He was reading a story aloud. He would read a few sentences, then pause and go back over a line, and say, 'Listen to this woman! Listen to this line!' abandoning his involvement with it only long enough to glance at us, then back to the page." When the class ended, McConnell turned to her sister and said, "Well, we didn't make it to Vonnegut's section but you see what the workshop is about?"[153] Yates could go over the top too, quite often the result of having been on a binge. Reading aloud from Chekhov could cause him to begin weeping, "It's all so sad."[154]

But Kurt felt close to him. They both had traveled the hard-to-climb road of the self-made writer; neither had college degrees, and they both happened to be very tall, booze-loving, chain-smoking men. They set about campaigning to get William Price Fox, the former advertising man turned novelist, on the faculty for the following year so they could confound the academics by having even more instructors in the Writers' Workshop without college degrees.[155] As a result of Yates and Vonnegut's lobbying, Fox did eventually join the workshop faculty with his new wife, Sarah Crawford, the winsome editorial assistant Vonnegut had wooed briefly. But by then Kurt was gone.

THE FALL semester of 1966 had just begun when Kurt had some good news to trumpet to Knox: the *New York Times* had assigned him to review the new *Random House Unabridged Dictionary.*[156]

On the face of it, reviewing a dictionary was a pretty awful assignment. Some of the plum reviewing jobs that year had gone to writing about Arthur M. Schlesinger's exhaustive account of the Kennedy administration, *A Thousand Days*; Truman Capote's *In Cold Blood*; Cornelius Ryan's *The Last Battle*; Jacqueline Susann's *Valley of the Dolls*; and Bernard Malamud's *The Fixer*. A new edition of a reference book to review was a bone from the feast. But Vonnegut, never too proud to take advantage of an opportunity—any reasonable opportunity to advance his career—accepted the task gratefully.

Instead of dwelling on aspects of the dictionary that would have drawn a yawn from his readers—ease of use, etymology, and so on—Vonnegut's review was by turns funny, humble, and a little nonplussed. He had difficulty understanding distinctions about acceptable usage. "Prescriptive, as nearly as I could tell, was like an honest cop, and descriptive was like a boozed-up war buddy from Mobile, Ala."[157] And like a sixth grader, he hunted for dirty words as a litmus test of whether the dictionary was for ordinary users.

His verdict was mixed. Random House, like most dictionary publishers, hadn't "included enough of the words to allow a Pakistani to decode *Last Exit to Brooklyn*, or *Ulysses*, either—but they have made brave beginnings, dealing, wisely I think, with the alimentary canal. I found only one abrupt verb for sexually congressing a woman, and we surely have Edward Albee to thank for its currency, though he gets no credit for it. The verb is *hump*, as in 'hump the hostess.'"

He finished with a flourish. President Lyndon Johnson had used the phrase "cool it" in a speech. Asked by a reporter whether the chief executive should speak so informally, Random House's publisher, Bennett Cerf, had replied, "It's fine with me. Now's not the time for the President of the United States to worry about the King's English." The moral, Vonnegut concluded, was that "everybody associated with a new dictionary ain't necessarily a new Samuel Johnson."[158]

That zinger about Cerf, and Vonnegut's witty treatment of a reference book, caught the eye of one of Cerf's former vice presidents, an entrepreneurial-minded editor at Dell named Seymour Lawrence, known to his friends as Sam. He realized that anyone who could make a proverbial silk purse from a review of a five-pound dictionary must have talents as a novelist. If Lawrence also happened to read the *New Republic* three weeks earlier, he would have seen a piece by the critic C. D. B. Bryan, later author of *Friendly Fire*, arguing that Vonnegut's novels, taken as a whole, were the work of a serious but often misread author.[159]

In any case, Lawrence wrote to Vonnegut immediately. And when Vonnegut received this stranger's invitation to meet and talk, it turned out to be the most important development in both men's careers.

Vonnegut replied cautiously at first, not knowing what Lawrence had in mind, and recommended that perhaps he should contact his agent, if he had a proposal. Kurt's agent by then was Max Wilkinson, because Ken Littauer's health was failing and Max was handling most of the agency's business now. Vonnegut, thinking Lawrence wanted him to pitch a new book, confessed that his writing was going slowly. His teaching load was heavy and demanding. It was a peculiar letter, full of temporizing, but Kurt had become accustomed to being a sort of odd-jobber in his midforties who batted out books and articles on demand.

Despite the tone of Vonnegut's reply, Lawrence urged a meeting during Iowa's semester break. He had two offices: one at 90 Beacon Street in Boston and one at Dell in New York. As soon as Kurt was available, Sam would like to sit down with him. Boston, of course, would be more convenient for Kurt.

So it was that one day around the winter holidays in 1966, there was a knock on Lawrence's office door in Beacon Street and Vonnegut shambled in, not knowing what this well-dressed gentleman had in mind.[160]

* * *

SAM LAWRENCE had a specialty: nurturing authors who were down on their luck. He was not yet thirty when he became director of the Atlantic Monthly Press, an imprint in association with Little, Brown. The title director was well chosen because he was not an editor or a publisher. He was, as Vonnegut later called him, an impresario.[161] His philosophy was that turnarounds happened in writers' careers when talent met opportunity.

A typical example was his meeting with J. P. Donleavy, who was anathema to American publishers, agents, and "literary folk" after his first novel, *The Ginger Man*, had been banned for obscenity in Ireland and the United States. Lawrence arranged to meet Donleavy at a hotel in New York and, following some small talk, asked if he might take Donleavy's draft of a new novel, *A Singular Man*, to his room for the night. "And I dared to think," said Donleavy, "My God, this man actually thinks and verily believes I can write books."[162] The next morning Lawrence said without hesitation that he wanted to publish it.

That meeting was in 1961. Shortly thereafter, Lawrence struck out on his own with an independent imprint, and in 1965 he was able to parlay a special partnership with Dell—the publishing house where Knox Burger had been until 1959. The arrangement was unusual for the day but perfect for Lawrence's maverick style.

Dell had created a special hardback imprint, Delacorte (named for Dell Publishing founder George T. Delacorte Jr.), which offered multiple-book contracts to authors. As a canny racetrack bettor would, Delacorte's multiple-book contracts were a way of spreading the financial risk over an author's output. And sometimes a "horse" might win big as a paperback reprint, offsetting losses. The advantage to writers was financial security. Lawrence proposed to go Dell-Delacorte one better. Provided he could have his own imprint, Seymour Lawrence–Delacorte, he would serve as Dell's scout and find promising authors—literary ones—ahead of the competition.

Over the next two decades he delivered, assembling a remarkable list of authors, including Thomas Berger, Richard Brautigan, William Styron, Jim Harrison, Katherine Anne Porter, William Saroyan, Frank Conroy, and four winners of the Nobel Prize for Literature: Miguel

Angel Asturias, Camilo José Cela, Pablo Neruda, and George Seferis. "He chose his writers very carefully, and when he committed to our work, he committed for life, and beyond death," said Jayne Anne Phillips, who was also one of his finds.[163]

When Vonnegut arrived in Lawrence's office, his publishing history as an author looked, figuratively, like a house that had been ransacked. The rights to his novels—and their various iterations as paperbacks and hardbacks—were scattered among Holt, Rinehart & Winston, Fawcett, Scribner's, Dell, and there was an unexecuted contract with Harper & Row for a short story collection. Vonnegut explained that he was currently working on a new novel, *Slaughterhouse-Five*, but that none of his publishers had expressed interest in it because "my books don't sell."

Lawrence listened; he said he would take the new book and two as-yet-unwritten ones for $75,000.

Astonished, Vonnegut tried to talk some sense into him. "That's too much money—you'll never get it back."

"You worry about writing, I'll worry about money," Lawrence replied.[164]

On a handshake, they agreed to do business. After Vonnegut left, Lawrence set about prying loose the rights for all of his titles from publishers to create one corpus of his work under the Seymour Lawrence–Delacorte imprint.

Vonnegut misremembered some of the details of meeting Lawrence, but more than thirty years later his gratitude was undimmed: "When I was broke in 1965, and teaching at the Writers' Workshop at the University of Iowa all alone, completely out of print, having separated myself from my family on Cape Cod in order to support them, Sam bought rights to my books, for peanuts, from publishers, both hardcover and softcover, who had given up on me. Sam thrust my books back into the myopic public eye again. . . . Thus encouraged, this Lazarus wrote *Slaughterhouse-Five* for Sam. That made my reputation."[165]

Convinced that Lawrence had put wheels under his career at last, Vonnegut decided that two years at Iowa would be enough. His colleagues who stayed longer, he noticed, tended to wait to resign until their frustration got the better of them because not much time was left over for their own writing after paper grading, faculty meetings, student conferences, and preparing lessons.[166] Now that he had a three-book contract with Sam, not even a substantial raise would be an inducement to stay longer than he wanted to.

STILL, IT would be difficult to leave. "Vonnegut is the most popular writer-in-residence," wrote a feature writer for the *Chicago Tribune* who made the trek to see the workshop. "Tall and lean with close-cropped hair, he might be mistaken for a young executive on a perennial weekend."[167]

His homely analogies about egg sorters and so on, his emphasis on the practical side of writing and selling fiction—initially greeted with impatience by some students—had become his strength. Once rumored to be a science fiction hack, he was drawing students to his sections who wanted to be avant-garde like him.[168] "To open one of Vonnegut's novels," commented the *Chicago Tribune* reporter, "approaches the discovery of a new entertainment media."[169]

Maria and José Donoso remembered "the excitement, and the dose of envy with which we shared the news that the mail, cable and telephone brought him daily: a Boston editor offered him $75,000 for his next book, instead of the $3,000 that his publisher had advanced him for his next three books; a Hollywood motion picture company was interested in the rights to one or two of his books; the *New Yorker* wanted a short story; the *New York Review of Books* was dedicating two pages to him; the *Time* correspondent wanted an interview; foreign editors were interested in translating him. . . . The students, writers in blossom, were also partakers and the 'motors' of the excitement generated around Kurt's works that acquired more followers day by day."[170] As John Casey said, "We watched Kurt get famous before our eyes."[171]

SOME OF his fellow instructors might have been forced to set aside their writing while they taught, but Kurt stuck to his regime of rising early and writing for a few hours before attending to the day's tasks. Creatively, not only had he been liberated by his muse Loree, with whom he enjoyed a fulfilling sexual relationship, but he was also no longer

working in isolation. At Iowa he was experiencing the benefits, the fris-
son, of belonging to a community of writers. On the Cape, he had only
Jane to rely on as his first-draft editor, counselor, and critic. But here, in
this unlikely Midwestern town, he was part of a nucleus of professionals like himself, all of them vibrating sympathetically to the latest
changes in the environment of American literature.

During the course of talking about writing with fellow instructors,
he became intrigued with the ideas of a new faculty member in the fall
of 1966, Robert Coover. Coover was teaching courses in experimental
fiction and working on what would become his most highly praised
novel, *The Universal Baseball Association, Inc., J. Henry Waugh, Prop.*,
an early example of metafiction, as it came to be known.[172]

Metafiction is "fiction about fiction." The true subject is not the
characters or other conventions of realism—plot, setting, the suspen-
sion of disbelief—but the writer's self-consciousness. Through irony,
deliberate artifice, and digressions, the reader is reminded that the
story isn't real. Unrestrained by convention, many writers—students in
the workshop included—found they were free to insert themselves into
the narrative in ways that might be ironic, political, comical, meta-
physical, or polemical. Said one of Coover's students, "I learned to see
what I was doing in terms of traditions and possibilities more universal
than realism."[173]

Vonnegut's background in journalism had taught him the opposite:
that you must not become part of the story. But Dresden, on the other
hand, as he experienced it, was *his* story. And metafiction gave him
permission in a sense to tell it brokenly, hauntingly—the way it came to
him in dreams.

IN THE spring of 1967, he was in high spirits when he and Jane set off
for a St. Patrick's Day party at Gail Godwin's flat on Capitol Street. The
Guggenheim Foundation had notified him that he had been awarded a
fellowship for research in Germany. He arrived costumed as an Irishman in a green top hat and Jane as an Orangeman. Edie brought her
records and the crowd danced.[174]

Against a wall, looking on morosely, was Saul Bellow, there to
deliver a series of lectures. Kurt was curious about what had induced

the winner of the National Book Award for *The Adventures of Augie March* to come to Iowa. A break in the music gave him the chance to ask the famous author why.

"Loneliness," he said.[175]

DURING SPRING break an invitation arrived to speak to creative writing classes at Northern Iowa University, which would also give him an excuse to see Loree. But then Jane wanted to come along too and there was no reasonable way to deny her, so Loree offered them a bed for the night at her home near campus in Cedar Falls.[176] The turnout for his talk was small, about forty people, and so was his fee, which he donated to the pacifist American Friends Service Committee. All in all, the trip was not worth the effort, in more ways than one.

With his departure from the University of Iowa imminent, the English Department scrambled to get another instructor like him. The advantages of having someone on board who knew how to make a living as an author suddenly became as important as signing a big name in literature or a theorist in fiction. Kurt recommended Richard Gehman, whom he'd met while in army training at the University of Tennessee during the war. Since then, Gehman had become known as the "King of the Freelancers," selling hundreds of articles to magazines and publishing books, both fiction and nonfiction. Vonnegut's recommendation alone was good enough to land him the position.

He also offered Gehman some confidential advice. He would have too many students in class, but that didn't matter. The important work got done one-on-one during office hours. The new director, George Starbuck, was an excellent friend; Paul Engle acted as a consultant now, getting in the way, issuing papal bulls, as it were, and playing the pope of the plains. Vance Bourjaily was a terrific friend but a lousy teacher. Too lazy. Finally, the undergraduate women were tempting, but don't sleep with them. If their parents found out, there would be hell about it.[177]

The workshoppers threw a farewell party for Kurt and Jane at a farmhouse rented by John and Jane Casey and David Plimpton. The walls were decorated with Vonnegutisms such as THROW OUT THE FIRST TWO PAGES! and a banner that asked WHO'S KEATS?[178] Robert Lehrman asked him to autograph one of his novels. Vonnegut thought a moment. Then: "To Robert who, as a student of mine, would not change one fucking word of anything he wrote. He may have been right, but I doubt it. Anyway, love, Kurt Vonnegut, Jr."[179]

In June, they packed up for the trip home. It was difficult getting all their belongings into one car, including the dog, Sandy. The trunk was full, and Kurt was "always very sloppy about papers and things," said Nanny, so the passenger seats were partly taken up with bundles, too. At some point during the trip, Kurt pulled over beside a restaurant to get a pack of cigarettes. Jane scrounged through things between the seats for something she couldn't find.

When Kurt got back into the car he glanced at her. "You look like you've lost your best friend," he said.

She had found a love letter from Loree.[180]

ONCE HOME, Jane and Kurt tore at each other all summer while Nanny, thirteen, looked on. "My alliance happened with my mother then," Nanny recalled years later. "Nothing was ever the same. He was miserable, in love with Loree, and my mother would beg, 'Kurt, please!' Once, he took her head in his hands, she was tiny, and he yelled, 'You shut the fuck up!' Then he left. She's crying, I'm crying. The next morning Dad—it was so pathetic—he asked her, 'Are you okay?'"[181]

As the days wore on, Kurt resorted to a favorite refrain: "Well, if Bernie can put up with it, I can put up with it." His brother's wife, Lois, nicknamed "Bo," had never recovered from her bouts of nervous exhaustion and periodically needed to be treated.

"I am *not* Bo!" Jane retorted tearfully.[182]

At last, summer burned itself out, and Kurt hurried to get away to visit Dresden on his Guggenheim grant. Sales of his novels had been rising, and he had advised Sam Lawrence in June not to neglect reprinting *The Sirens of Titan* too, because fan mail from college students indicated that it was catching on.[183] Now, before setting out for Europe, he mailed Lawrence a package of stories for *Welcome to the Monkey House*, slated for publication in 1968, most of which had appeared in a previous collection called *Canary in a Cathouse*. To freshen up the contents, he added a few new stories. He also asked a favor. Edie, seventeen, would be starting school at the Boston Museum School of Fine Arts and living in a furnished room at 462 Beacon Street. Vonnegut asked Lawrence to please watch over her.[184]

To Knox he announced that he was at last ready to depart, in the company of Bernie O'Hare, now a district attorney in Pennsylvania, who was going along for old time's sake. For two guys their age to go on the bum in Europe alone, he said, they must have a real hankering to come down with the clap.[185]

And then, on October 10, he left.

9: The Big Ka-BOOM
1967–1969

T HE FRIENDSHIP BETWEEN Kurt Vonnegut and Bernie O'Hare
had begun in army boot camp and ripened into brotherhood during the Battle of the Bulge and their winter march into captivity as
POWs. But the event that melded their lives together was the firestorm
of Dresden. They talked about that experience in a private language,
usually late at night when both had had a few drinks, like a pair of
mediums conjuring voices and scenes from long ago. The trip they were
taking to Germany now, revisiting the ground they had walked over as
young men, was intended to verify that things they recalled had actually happened. Kurt needed O'Hare to help him resuscitate the dead for
the sake of his novel.

But whatever feelings of reverence or solemnity they may have
brought with them were forgotten as soon as they set foot in Germany.
The East Germans were anything but sentimental about a pair of
middle-aged American veterans looking for their youth and remnants
of the war.

Right off, Kurt discovered they had been flimflammed by a travel
agency behind the Iron Curtain.[1] Their itinerary was supposed to include
a six-day trip from Berlin to Warsaw to Leningrad, where Vonnegut
hoped to see the fiftieth anniversary celebrations of the Russian Revolution—he was still grateful to the Russian army for having liberated him.

But when they tried to board the train, a conductor informed them that their papers weren't in order. The train left without them.[2]

Stranded, they arranged to fly to Helsinki instead and catch a train there to Leningrad. In the Finnish capital, they spent a sleepless night languishing in a hotel waiting for morning. The street noise outside made Vonnegut think the city must be populated by dipsomaniacs who got sloshed every night about sunset.[3]

Two days behind schedule, they arrived in Leningrad, relieved to find the clerk at the Astoria Hotel still honored their reservation.[4] The six-story art nouveau and neoclassical Astoria Hotel, one of the handsomest buildings in Russia, is opposite St. Isaac's Basilica in the heart of the old imperial center. A bellhop carried their bags into spacious rooms, where members of Lenin's hierarchy had lived following the revolution.

Then, forty-eight hours later, they were asked to leave. Either the manager or the secret police had concluded that two middle-class American men traveling with no definite purpose must be homosexuals.[5] Disgusted by how red tape and suspicion were ruining their side trip, they decided to turn back toward Dresden. For the second time they landed in Berlin. At customs, a uniformed official examined their papers and informed them that they would not be allowed to enter East Germany.

Vonnegut blew up, remembering how they had been held prisoner for months.

"God*damn* it!" he said to O'Hare. "They wouldn't *fucking* let us out, now they won't *fucking* let us in!"[6]

But anger wouldn't work on the impassive East German studying them. Vonnegut explained that he was not a journalist—rightly suspecting that snoops were unwelcome in the German Democratic Republic— but a writer, actually more like a historian, who was there on a private grant. The Guggenheim program was internationally recognized; it was imperative that he and his friend be allowed to enter.

The functionary reconsidered, then stamped their passports and, with a bored wave, opened the road to the past.

DRESDEN IN 1967, Vonnegut said later, was as dull-looking as Cedar Rapids, Iowa, caught in the slough of the Great Depression.[7] But Cedar

Rapids, enfeebled by financial collapse, would have been an improvement over the gutted city that lay before him. Once one of the cultural capitals of Europe, Dresden seemed to be undergoing a grinding punishment under the Soviets for its pre-Marxist "excesses."

The din of ugly Trabant automobiles—two-stroke cars manufactured in East Germany—fouled the air with greasy exhaust and stained the facades of the buildings.[8] Above the streets, sagging networks of electrical cables gave the impression that Dresden ran on extension cords. Most of the residents lived in gray, slab-sided complexes of flats that were almost indistinguishable from one another. The British military historian Alexander McKee, who visited the city in 1958, said, "It was as though a woman reputedly the most beautiful in Europe turned out to be an old hag, wrapped in rags, with a cigarette dangling from her lips."[9]

The tourist trade was practically nonexistent, but Vonnegut and O'Hare found a friendly, English-speaking taxi driver named Gerhard Müller who offered to be their chauffeur and guide for as long as they needed him. Müller drove them down streets, some still pitted by the firestorm, in search of landmarks they would recognize. Historic edifices dating back centuries—the Dresden Castle, the Taschenberg Palais, Neumarkt Square—pulverized during the bombing in 1945, still lay in ruins, ignored by the Soviet planners. Nothing remained of the magnificent Frauenkirche (Church of Our Lady), completed in 1743, where Müller had been baptized as a boy.[10] Johann Sebastian Bach had played its famous organ, and the cathedral's acoustics were said to have inspired passages in Wagner's *Parsifal*. After the war, East German officials had dismantled the church's fire-blackened walls and dumped the stone blocks beside a fallen statue of Martin Luther.

The slaughterhouse compound that housed the POWs had stood near a bend in the Elbe, in an old pocket of the city, but as the taxi jounced and rocked over a broken, overgrown road they seemed to be heading into the countryside. O'Hare and Vonnegut said they wanted to stop and have a look.

Before the bombing, they could see rooftops and spires in all directions. There had been a hospital near the compound, they remembered, and a sports stadium within sight. But now they were surrounded by hundreds of acres of grass and weeds, strewn with broken masonry.[11] Rectangular outlines of cellar walls poked through the soil like family plots in a cemetery. In fact, the whole area had the feel of an abandoned necropolis with "tons of human bone meal in the ground," as Vonnegut later expressed it in *Slaughterhouse-Five*.[12] Carthage after the victorious Romans plowed it under couldn't have looked more desolate. There was nothing to see here. They asked Müller to turn around.

Lost in this city he barely recognized, Vonnegut turned to another source that might be able to aid his memory: his former guards. They would be men in their sixties and seventies now—with the exception of "Junior," the Hitler Youth whose real name he never did know. If he could locate a few, they might be able to help describe events he remembered. On the other hand, it had been twenty years since the fall of the Third Reich.

He reached for the Dresden telephone directory and put into play his training as a beat reporter in Chicago. O'Hare helped him recall last names of guards and officers, and they started calling from the hotel. More often than not they reached the wrong person, but every now and then an older man answered with a diffident "*Ja?*" Carefully, Vonnegut would explain he was an American writing a book about the POWs housed at the slaughterhouse in 1945. It was a novel, really, and he wondered if he might . . .

But no matter how he tried to ease into the conversation, he could sense his listener tensing on the other end. Older East Germans dreaded getting into trouble with the authorities. During the war they had lived in the long shadows of detention camps and the omnipotent SS. Because they lived on the mercy of the state now, they feared an even more nefarious enemy: their neighbors. Ten of thousands of private citizens in Dresden were in the employ of the secret police. An inquisitive stranger asking questions was a threat.

"*Nein!*" his former captors told Vonnegut in heightened voices, loud enough for anyone to overhear—about the past, they couldn't remember a thing.[13]

Writing about the Dresden massacre had always been a conundrum for Vonnegut. Perhaps he felt blocked for the same reason other people didn't want to talk about it: describing human slaughter smacks of more depravity. What was there to say?

He never said publicly what kept him going on *Slaughterhouse-Five*, especially when Dresden itself seemed to be seized with collective amnesia, except he thought it was his duty to write the novel. In letters to friends, editors, and authors, on the other hand, he talked about how, almost as a point of honor, it was important to see creative work through to the end.

The closest he came to a personal manifesto about the writer's challenge to keep working is in a response he wrote to a fellow author who was too discouraged to continue. By coincidence, he replied rapidly in longhand while he was in Helsinki about to travel to Dresden with O'Hare.

The letter he had received was from José Donoso, his former colleague at Iowa. For ten years, Donoso had been working on *The Obscene Bird of Night*, the novel he thought would be his masterpiece.[14] Now, he told Kurt, he was giving up. Everything seemed wrong with the book, the strain was overwhelming, and a decade of effort had ended in failure.

The Obscene Bird of Night had always been a dangerous novel for Donoso to write. The protagonist and narrator is Humberto Peñaloza, a poor writer who works as an assistant to an aristocratic Chilean family. When the family's only son, Boy, is born monstrously deformed, Peñaloza is instructed to protect him from knowledge of his mutation by isolating him in the family villa with other freaks as companions.

Peñaloza's goal—and by extension Donoso's—is to perpetuate a fantastic, many-layered fiction that deceives Boy and beguiles the reader. Several times, author fused with narrator, and Donoso experienced psychotic episodes. Suicidal thoughts plagued him when he felt unable to go on any longer, resulting from "sickness and pain. A feeling of impotence, of inferiority, of incapability, above all when confronted with writing."[15]

"I've scrapped *The Obscene Bird of Night*," Donoso wrote wearily to Vonnegut. "I've gone through some pretty bad nightmares about it— I've been working at it so long, that to go on writing and writing was just another way not to face the fact that the style and theme had died on me. So three days ago, I packed it and put it away . . . but to say goodbye to something which had gathered into something like 1000 pages, and which was working since 1960, well, it's not much fun. I'd like to talk to you about it."[16]

Vonnegut wouldn't hear of Donoso putting the book away. He realized this was not a time for consolation, but for rallying his friend. It was absurd, he wrote him, that this exhausted Donoso should abandon the Donoso of ten years ago. Clearly, he had lived too long with the book and needed the benefit of someone else reading the manuscript afresh. In most matters of life and friendship, his instincts served him well, but he was not qualified to judge his own work. At the very least, if Bourjaily had written a thousand pages, he would have divided them into four equal piles and rescued novelettes or short stories from them. Vonnegut adjured Donoso to hold tight and not let his big book slip into the grave.[17] His exhortations are all the more genuine because his own novel, which he had spent twenty years trying to write, was not finished, either.

BRAVE WORDS and good intentions alone are not enough to create inspiration, however. Visiting Dresden had turned out to be dispiriting, instead of spurring Vonnegut's imagination to finishing the book. So there must have been something else to come out of the trip that led him in a fresh direction after the postwar city rebuked him.

Two books he took to read on the trip impressed him deeply. One was the poet Theodore Roethke's collection *The Waking*; the other was Erika Ostrovsky's just published critical biography, *Céline and His Vision*.[18] If he had read them in Iowa City or West Barnstable, they might not have had the same impact. Yet suddenly, in light of his experiences in Dresden, he came to several realizations about the effect of time on making sense of experience. In Roethke's poem "The Waking," he found these lines:

> I wake to sleep, and take my waking slow.
> I feel my fate in what I cannot fear.
> I learn by going where I have to go.
>
> We think by feeling. What is there to know?[19]

As Vonnegut stared out at fields littered with broken masonry, or tried to place buildings in the context of twenty years ago, his landscape was an inner one. There would be no easy way to retrieve his submerged feelings, least of all by trying to gaff them with facts, interviews, and note taking like a reporter. In an unexpected way, it was a relief. He realized, "I need not show the bombing of Dresden," he said later. "I need not write this Cecil B. DeMille scene."[20] An artist's challenge, which in his case was to make use of the past, is to navigate by true feeling. He could not rely on historicity alone to tell his tale for him.

The second book in his luggage, Ostrovsky's *Céline and His Vision*, reminded him that he was "amazed and respectful of most of the writings of Louis-Ferdinand Céline," despite the French author being such an anti-Semite that "in one of his postwar books, there's an attack on Anne Frank, for God's sake. Talk about tasteless."[21]

Céline's bigotry aside, Vonnegut admired the power of the author's language. *Journey to the End of the Night* "penetrated my bones, anyway, if not my mind."[22] Céline spat words on the page, hurled images at the reader giving the sensation of events happening frantically, out of context. For the opening of *Guignol's Band*, a novel that Céline himself declared an "outrage" (to satirize his readers' reaction), he smashes language like a stained-glass window to capture how life appears to him: "A houseful of furniture rocks, spins from the casements, scatters in a rain of fire! . . . The proud bridge, twelve arches, staggers, topples smack into the mud. The slime of the river splatters! . . . mashes, splashes the mob yelling choking overflowing at the parapet! . . . It's pretty bad."[23]

In Céline's world, the hurtling arrow of time is responsible for this mess. The chaos of life, minute to minute, makes its meaning impossible to grasp. "Time obsessed him," Vonnegut realized. "Miss Ostrovsky reminded me of the amazing scene in *Death on the Installment Plan* where Céline wants to stop the bustling of a street crowd. He screams on paper, *Make them stop . . . don't let them move anymore at all. . . . There, make them freeze . . . once and for all! . . . So that they won't disappear anymore!*"[24]

Céline's characters, unable to control anything important in their lives, are paralyzed by feelings of nihilism and pessimism. *Stupid* is one of his favorite words to describe how people act dumbstruck in the face of events. With life being such a mélange of tragedy and howling absurdity, Céline wanted to know "where can a man escape to, when he hasn't enough madness left inside him? The truth is an endless death agony. The truth is death. You have to choose: death or lies."[25]

For Vonnegut to describe his feelings of shock and confusion as a young army private—feelings that later took shape as nightmares—the truth was useless: the number of Allied airplanes in the raids on Dresden, tonnage of explosives dropped, buildings destroyed, and residents killed. What he needed to communicate was the delirium created by his sense of chaos. And he could do it by playing havoc with time like Céline.

When he returned home at the end of October, he tried to explain to Sam Lawrence what he had seen. What he had recalled about Dresden was no longer there; fidelity to the past wasn't necessary. The ugliness of Soviet urban planning had been superimposed on the ruined German city, creating a place that he could make no sense of. This, however, freed him to create something new out of his imagination. *Slaughterhouse-Five* could take any turn, any theme he wished.[26]

Back in West Barnstable, he needed to attend to the upcoming publication of *Welcome to the Monkey House,* a collection of stories that had appeared in magazines. He wrote the flap copy himself, bringing to bear his skills as an ad man. It's interesting that he was aware of his increasing popularity on college campuses, and to see how he was working to reposition his books nearer the front of the store and the cash register, as Frederik Pohl put it. His popularity began, he wrote of himself, in college bookstores where the young generation embraced him as more than a science fiction writer. He tackles big questions, both comic and tragic, about man and machines. His reputation as a teller of tales is widespread and you might catch him on any of a number of college campuses, where he is in great demand.[27]

Jane suggested six different photographs of Kurt on the cover like a comic strip, again playing on the college-age appeal.[28] Kurt thought it was a great idea, but Sam Lawrence didn't agree. A photograph of Vonnegut, slipped into every reviewer's copy, explains the reason. He's clean-shaven, serious, and a little overweight. The man and the hip author described on the flap jacket seem mismatched.

NEVERTHELESS, FOR the first time since leaving General Electric and striking out on his own as a writer, Vonnegut was in such "rosy shape" that he could afford to tell Lawrence to withhold payments until further notice. Too much income would boost him into the next tax bracket.[29] Success gave him the benefit too of seeing in hindsight how his career had developed, and he felt easy, even a little proud of it. To Gail Godwin, seeking advice about publishing her fiction, he was not embarrassed to offer his career as an example: "Are you willing to pander to popular tastes in order to be published? If so, write about a love affair. It isn't so terrible to write for the women's magazines. That is how I supported myself more or less for about twelve years. I do not feel dishonored. . . . I don't know if you have it in you to be crude. I write with a big black crayon, you know, grasped in a grubby, kindergarten fist. You're more of an impressionist. If you want to kind of try what I do, take life seriously but none of the people in it."[30]

But it was not only the river of money heading in his direction, largely due to Sam Lawrence reprinting his works, that justified his dispensing advice to a young author. One of the hallmarks of having arrived as a fiction writer is an academic study of your work. At Iowa, he had become friendly with Robert E. Scholes in the English Department. In 1967, Scholes's book of literary criticism *The Fabulators* discussed Vonnegut's novels at length.

Fabulation, argued Scholes, originated with Aesop and later allegorists in the Middle Ages who used "controlled fantasy" to create narratives "more concerned with ideas and ideals, less concerned with things."[31] Storytellers of this type delight in design and form—stories within stories, digressions, and distractions—like visual artists intrigued with origami, Cubism, or symmetry. This characteristic distinguished fabulators from most novelists and satirists, Scholes said. Kurt Vonnegut, for example, created worlds to illustrate ideas, in the tradition of Voltaire and Swift. "Vonnegut's works exhibit an affection for this world and a desire to improve it—but not much hope for improvement."[32]

A few months before the publication of *The Fabulators*, C. D. B. Bryan in the *New Republic* had finger-wagged that Vonnegut had "not received the acceptance due him from the reading public" despite being "one of the most readable and amusing of the new humorists."[33]

At one time the appearance of a new novel by Kurt Vonnegut Jr. had been met with a shoulder shrug; now readers and critics were being scolded if they hadn't read him.

* * *

JANE WAS sailing into a new period of her life also, finding peace in Transcendental Meditation.

TM percolated into the Vonnegut household through Edie and her boyfriend Joe Clark, a rock musician and a close friend of Jim Adams.[34] Clark had been a wild teenager, but the teachings of the Maharishi Mahesh Yogi had turned him around, he said. Since then, he had felt contentment and peace for the first time. And he was, as anyone could see, a charismatic young man whose laughter could fill a room.[35]

Convinced by Joe's experience, Edie and Jane enrolled in introductory lectures and paid for their personal mantras, which they were instructed to repeat silently during meditation. Each mantra was said to be one-of-a-kind and a secret. Kurt participated too because "my wife and eighteen-year-old daughter are hooked. They've both been initiated. They meditate several times a day. Nothing pisses them off anymore. They glow like bass drums with lights inside."[36]

The Maharishi, by reputation, was a great man. His world tours attracted tens of thousands of adherents, including celebrities such as the Beatles, the Beach Boys, the pop singer Donovan, and the actress Mia Farrow. Recruiters for Transcendental Meditation fanned out through college campuses, airports, and city centers, distributing information about lectures, retreats, and classes. The Maharishi's message was nothing short of messianic: he would rid the world of all unhappiness and discontent.

Still, after practicing TM for a while, Kurt began to have doubts. For generations his family had made money in Indianapolis selling everything from hardware, to beer, to coffins, to Electrolux vacuum cleaners door-to-door. And his business antennae were up. When the Maharishi was scheduled to make an appearance in Cambridge, Kurt attended the press conference on assignment from *Esquire* magazine.

THE ROOM at the hotel was packed because so many reporters and writers had been invited. The Maharishi, a small, giggly man whose shoulder-length hair looked perpetually wet, was seated on a tall chair surrounded by flower arrangements. He explained the power of TM to improve people's lives, the work they do, and the global economy.

Then the attendees were guided through a sample meditation, after which "I opened my eyes," Kurt said, "and I took a hard look at Maharishi. He hadn't wafted me to India. He had sent me back to Schenectady, New York, where I used to be a public relations man—years and years ago. That was where I had heard other euphoric men talk of the human condition in terms of switches and radios and fairness of the marketplace. They, too, thought it was ridiculous for people to be unhappy, when there were so many simple things they could do to improve their lot . . . the Maharishi had come all the way from India to speak to the American people like a General Electric engineer."[37] He didn't accuse the Maharishi of being a fake, just another salesman for a product that doesn't quite live up to the advertisement. Furthermore, the rationalist tradition of freethinking in his family going back to his great-grandfather Clemens Vonnegut influenced his opinions about meditation. Freethinkers never saw a simplistic idea about ethics or morality—particularly when religion was involved—that didn't arouse their skepticism.

The benefits of meditation, he decided, were equal to ones he experienced while reading books. "When I read an absorbing book, my pulse and respiration rate slowed down perceptibly, just as though I were doing TM. . . . This form of meditation, an accident, as I say, may be the greatest treasure at the core of our civilization."[38] And so he delivered his article to *Esquire* that said, in effect, the Maharishi, a "darling man," was just pumping the handle of free enterprise as vigorously as the system allowed.

Unfortunately, his sentiments didn't stop there. He began deriding Jane's interest in TM. By joining the TM movement, Jane had pushed off in her own little boat to see what she might see. But Kurt, who from the earliest days of their marriage liked to remind his Phi Beta Kappa wife that she didn't know anything, objected to how she turned "more and more to making alliances with the supernatural in her need to increase her strength and understanding—and happiness and health. This was painful to me. She could not understand . . . why that should have been painful to me, or why it should be any of my business at all."[39]

Their disagreement mushroomed into quarrels over her delight in exploring things arcane and spiritual—not just meditation, but also Christianity, astrology, and the *I Ching*—all of which were faddishly popular again during the Age of Aquarius, as the late 1960s were characterized.[40] Kurt found none of these things offensive really. On the contrary, he wrote respectfully about Jesus and regarded astrology as a useful way to get to know someone, that is, "What's your sign?"[41]

What he bridled at was Jane's "failure to share my family belief" in unitarianism and freethinking, which would have scoffed at yogic flying, for instance.[42] To him, she was being stubborn, rebellious—call it insubordinate—by straying off on her own on paths that he decided were a waste of time.

VONNEGUT'S REPUTATION as a raconteur and speaker began at Notre Dame University's Literary Festival in the spring of 1968. For authors with a gift for public speaking, lecture tours and readings have provided a venue for selling books ever since Charles Dickens made American audience members faint in 1847–48 as he read scenes from *Oliver Twist* describing Nancy's murder. Mark Twain later plied the circuit with droll stories; Oscar Wilde called for more beauty; Edna St. Vincent Millay delivered her glimpses of it through readings of her poetry; and Truman Capote charmed audiences despite, said Shakesperean actor John Gielgud, that "ghastly little voice."[43]

On the podium with Vonnegut at Notre Dame was Joseph Heller, the author of *Catch-22*, whom he didn't know, but their meeting was the start of a lifelong friendship.[44]

Following some introductory remarks by a moderator, it "was Heller's turn to be screamingly funny," Vonnegut said, "and he got up there and he was just about to speak, no doubt with prepared material, and some sort of academic, a professor, came up over the footlights to the lectern and shouldered Joe aside politely and said, 'I just want to announce that Martin Luther King has been shot.'"[45]

Shock rippled through the auditorium, but Heller had no choice except to deliver his prepared speech while people half listened, despairing, murmuring, some of them weeping. Heller himself hardly listened to what he was saying, wishing that he could be home consoling his wife. Finally, he sat down.

Next it was Vonnegut's turn. His speech was written out, too—he never spoke without notes or a script. As he began, however, the audience seemed suddenly to be possessed by a fit of half-hysterical laughter, and "everything I said was funny. All I had to do was cough or clear my throat and the whole place would break up. . . . People were laughing because they were in agony, full of pain they couldn't do anything about."[46] His material was intended to be "mildly comic," but the audience's outsized response was an instance of comic relief intervening blessedly between fear and grief.[47] Without meaning to, he was illustrating perforce the use of laughter in the face of horror to provide relief for the soul—the quintessence of humor's purpose in his novels.[48] As was said of *Mother Night* and its cast of lackluster Nazi "masterminds," Vonnegut's extraordinary tone is that of humanity laughing instead of cowering, which can be "very funny without being crass or unfeeling."[49]

To Heller, the speech sounded extemporaneous. But when Kurt finished and resumed his seat, Heller shook his hand and "noticed he was drenched in sweat."[50] In the audience was the novelist and literary critic Granville Hicks, who thought Vonnegut's remarks were "as funny a lecture as I had ever listened to."[51]

The speech made Vonnegut a sought-after speaker, and in early June 1968 when he submitted his final draft of *Slaughterhouse-Five* to Sam Lawrence, he balked at Max Wilkinson's suggestion that they should start thinking about a ho-hum book tour. Vonnegut countered that he was getting more invitations to speak than he could accept, and nice fees for them too—why should he appear in places for nothing?[52]

For most of their marriage, Kurt and Jane shared so little interest in politics that it could fairly be said they were apolitical. Their sole statement of support for a national candidate had been to plant an Adlai Stevenson sign in their front yard during the Stevenson-Eisenhower race of 1952, marking them as eggheads and liberals on the otherwise conservative Cape.[53] But the assassination of Dr. Martin Luther King Jr. in April 1968 galvanized Jane to get involved in the presidential campaign.[54]

King and the Southern Christian Leadership Conference had been organizing a poor people's march in Washington, D.C., when he was killed in Memphis, Tennessee. The Poor People's Campaign, as it was later named, arrived in the capital on May 12. Nine long caravans of demonstrators from all over the nation prepared to demand passage of the Economic Bill of Rights. In Congress, Senators Robert Byrd of West Virginia and Russell Long of Louisiana predicted insurrection and mob rule and called for "shoot-to-kill" policies if the demonstrations turned violent.[55] Instead, three thousand marchers settled down in hundreds of tents, dubbed Resurrection City, in West Potomac Park adjacent to the Lincoln Memorial.

Jane got busy chartering buses for people from the Cape who wanted to join the demonstrations. "Whenever I hear the phrase 'soul power,' I think of Jane," said her West Barnstable neighbor Arnold Bossi. "She was the epitome of it. She was very conscientious of injustice and moral chicanery. And she did her work to stop it unassumingly."[56]

She attended mass meetings at the foot of the Lincoln Memorial; saw the flimsy sharecropper shacks erected in front of the Smithsonian Institution; listened to speeches by Black Panthers, migrant Chicanos, poor whites from Appalachia, American Natives, Marxists, and anti-war protesters. Too many agendas in fact hobbled the Poor People's Campaign, and two inches of rain saturated Resurrection City. In late June, Jane, Mark, and Edie returned home without seeing the Economic Bill of Rights passed, nor did it ever become law.[57]

But a week later when she happened to be in Boston, Jane dropped into Eugene McCarthy's campaign headquarters to pick up a bumper sticker. When she came out again, she not only had collected an armload of free materials but had agreed to become an organizer.[58]

"This is an act of war, you going off like this," Kurt warned her when he found out that as a result of a meeting held at their house she was cochairperson of the Mid-Cape Citizens for McCarthy.[59] Arnold Bossi would share the post, and Jane had already offered to put down four hundred dollars for two months' rent on a storefront campaign headquarters on Main Street in Hyannis.

Nanny, who had supported her mother ever since the Loree Wilson affair came to light, thought her father was being unreasonable. "My mother was so smart. And he was angry that their marriage didn't turn out to be a fairy tale. He had no understanding of what it was like to have babies, to have kids, to do the grind, day in and day out."[60]

His complaint was that all six Vonnegut and Adams children were going to be home that summer, and Jane's mother, Riah, who was in poor health, had arrived for a fresh air vacation by the sea. Even though

Slaughterhouse-Five was off his desk, he expected to continue working in his study undisturbed.[61]

Regardless, Jane was undertaking something important to her, and she could not be badgered into quitting. The tension in the house ratcheted up as the phone began to ring with calls from volunteers, and she had to leave the house regularly to get the Hyannis headquarters in order. Things reached the point where just mentioning "McCarthy" or "the election" could lead to a quarrel. She was forced to accept that the campaign was going to be "my bag for the summer" without his support.[62]

Privately, Kurt felt guilty. To Knox, he said that since completing his war book he had too much time on his hands. He was sick of writing and should probably consider signing up for volunteer work of some kind, instead of sitting around mooning while Jane campaigned round-the-clock for McCarthy.[63]

But he refused to help her.

WHEN JANE opened the doors of the Mid-Cape Citizens for McCarthy headquarters in July, she and Arnold Bossi found they were in charge of a kind of "children's crusade," the media's nickname for McCarthy's campaign because it had attracted so many young people, thousands of whom weren't even of voting age. At first, the cochairs thought the headquarters should keep a low profile because, in Jane's opinion, "this is such a conservative place. And, lots of people just stop talking to you if they think you're working against them." But the number of contributions and offers to help "was thrilling," and soon the headquarters was abuzz with volunteers on the phone—most of them college students home for the summer—and residents stopping in for posters, flyers, and stickers.[64]

Then too late she realized her inexperienced young staff was mishandling the get-out-the-vote drive. From a middle-aged friend she discovered that when adults called the office offering to help they were turned down. The heavy hint was that working with anyone over thirty would be a drag. Among disapproving Hyannis residents, the storefront headquarters was getting a reputation as a place where peaceniks, hippies, dopers, and draft dodgers hung out.

To undo the harm done and try to raise campaign donations, Jane and Arnold decided they should have an all-Cape event. A youngster on the staff promised that her father knew how to put on a clambake and would supply the clams, firewood, everything. Flyers were posted in windows of businesses advertising a come-one-come-all picnic, sponsored by the local McCarthy headquarters. Then the girl admitted her father wouldn't help after all. Panicked, the cochairs consulted a Time-Life cookbook for pictures of a clambake and figured out how to have one.[65] The day after the near-fiasco, a photo of Edie in a two-piece outfit on the beach, wearing a flower power McCarthy decal on her stomach, made the wire services.

Meanwhile, Kurt remained aloof in his study. "He only socialized in streaks," Bossi said. "I don't recall him working for the campaign."[66] He did climb aboard a bus chartered for an appearance by McCarthy at Fenway Park in Boston, but Jane suspected he went only because it was a "big event."[67]

On the night of the delegate vote at the Democratic national convention, the stalwarts of the Mid-Cape Citizens for McCarthy gathered in front of the television at the Vonneguts. On the screen, speeches from the convention floor played against scenes of violent fighting in Chicago streets between 10,000 demonstrators and 23,000 city police and Illinois National Guardsmen. When the balloting got under way, Hubert Humphrey took the nomination from McCarthy on the first round. "Clean Gene" lost by a margin of almost three-to-one, defeated by Humphrey's timely promises to restore law and order. While Mark played mournful jazz riffs on his saxophone, Jane and the others retired to the Vonneguts' barn for a victory party that had turned into a wake. "If I knew ahead of time how traumatic it would be, I probably wouldn't do it again," Jane told an interviewer for the McCarthy oral history project, "because, in personal terms, it was a really terrible, terrible summer."[68]

Asked whether her husband, as "spokesman of a generation," had lent a hand in the campaign, Jane replied, "Strangely, there was very little connection between the spokesman of the generation and that particular movement."[69]

ACTUALLY, KURT was preoccupied, but not with work. When he could get away from West Barnstable, he was romancing a woman in New York.

He had received a letter from Loree earlier in the year informing him that her "friendship" with an English professor at the University of Northern Iowa, Richard Rackstraw, "had transformed into marriage." He didn't reply and instead punished her with silence for a long time.[70] Unknown to him, however, she had admitted to Rackstraw she "couldn't deny any vague personal ambivalence" about her relationship with Kurt.[71]

Thinking his affair with Loree was at an end, Kurt pursued another woman, Jane Miller—everyone called her "Jimmy"—the widow of Warren Miller, a former student of Paul Engle's at the Iowa Writers' Workshop. Warren met Jimmy shortly after his separation from his first wife and asked her to pose for the jacket photo of the novel he was ghosting, *Love Me Little*, the American answer to the publishing sensation *Bonjour Tristesse* written by a French teenage girl. Miller used the pen name Amanda Vail, and the photo of Jimmy—a beautiful young woman with dark hair—completed the impression of the fictitious Miss Vail. The success of *Love Me Little* when it appeared in 1957 permitted Miller, a New York advertising executive, to begin a new career as an author.

Warren and Jimmy married the following year, but he was a heavy smoker and died at forty-four of lung cancer in 1966. Kurt never met Warren, but he admired his novel *The Way We Live Now*, an autobiographical story about a high-flying advertising executive who throws himself into a series of soulless love affairs.

When Kurt began dating Jimmy, she lived on Seventy-eighth Street between Broadway and Amsterdam Avenue, earning a living as a silver sculptor and jewelry maker. Her stepdaughter Eve described her as "dark, petite, very pretty, with a sculpted and chiseled kind of face." Emotionally, however, she reeled between depression and wild abandonment, a consequence of tranquilizers and barbiturates prescribed for her undiagnosed bipolar disorder. "After my father died she really went off the deep end, so when she met Kurt she was flipped out and getting wilder and wilder."[72]

Eve was only a child when Kurt was seeing her stepmother, but the tall, friendly man from out of town made an effort to pay attention to her. "I remember he gave me this really cool camera. For the day it was considered one of these very sleek, streamlined little snapshot cameras, and he thought I'd like it. I was thrilled to death."[73]

Vonnegut wanted the relationship to grow, but Jimmy couldn't see it happening. Despite being in her late thirties, she identified with hippies and smoked pot by the fistful. Kurt was an endearing man, but Jimmy thought of him as too old and more like an uncle: a member of the establishment who liked to go places in suits.[74]

Before they parted, he gave her a gift: an expensive Georges Braque lithograph signed by the artist. On a deep blue background, an awkward-looking bird in profile, wings folded, stands on nothing in midair, with a star above and a fish below.[75]

STILL ON the prowl, a few weeks later Vonnegut found another woman to bed, a former student at Iowa, Suzanne McConnell.

McConnell had never minded his penchant for flirting, even when his passes were strongly sexual. Once she had asked him to dance at a workshop party, but after a few moments he told her, "I can't dance with you anymore, Suzanne," the implication being that because he was drunk he might do something foolish.[76] Later as she was leaving, he said, "Come here and kiss me goodbye."[77] She did. He suspected she had slept with Vance Bourjaily and jealously asked her about it several times.[78]

He heard from her again in January 1969, a few months after the nonstarter with Jimmy Miller. He was at the University of Michigan in Ann Arbor as the writer-in-residence for the third quarter. She phoned him, inviting him to speak at Delta Community College, where she was teaching, about two and a half hours from Ann Arbor. He was pleased and accepted, although he dropped a clue about the nature of their reunion. He had been in Iowa recently, he told her, and made a pass at the wife of a mutual friend of theirs. She was "surprised and puzzled by that admission. Then I understood that he was alerting me to something about himself."[79]

The night before he was scheduled to speak, he called to cancel. "I can't speak there tomorrow, Suzanne," he told her. "Usually the people sponsoring the visit protect you, but they didn't [at the University of Michigan]. So I don't feel like speaking at your college. But I want to come up and see you."[80]

With *Slaughterhouse-Five* at his publisher, he was fed up with being lonely, with thinking too much, with being stuck in idle mode. In fact, he wanted out of his writer-in-residence commitment with Michigan after less than a month because, as he told the director of the program, "I've realized the only thing I hate more than listening to people is talking to them."[81]

The day of his canceled appearance, Suzanne was making her way across campus, shivering, when she spotted a big car with Massachusetts license plates crunching slowly over the snow in a campus parking lot, its flanks dirty with salt and frozen road slush.

"Kurt!" she yelled. She wasn't expecting him for hours.

He backed the car up and opened the passenger-side door. "I couldn't wait," he said. "Get in. Let's drive somewhere. We can take a drive north up along Lake Huron. I haven't been to this part of the country in a long time."[82]

THE NEXT morning at a motel, Kurt wrapped himself in the bedsheet to make the short walk to the bathroom, but not before saying over his shoulder, "It's the morning after." She offered to ask someone to cover her morning classes so they could have breakfast together.

"Are you sure you should do that?"

McConnell was taken aback by the apparent criticism in his voice. He asked her for a cigarette, although earlier he had said he'd quit. Then they went to breakfast after all, after which he dropped her off in the campus parking lot, where she had left her car. As he drove away, she wondered whether she should call after him to come back.

A week later she received a one-line letter from him: "I walk around and around and moon and moon."[83]

VONNEGUT FELT a good deal of trepidation about *Slaughterhouse-Five* as its March 1969 publication date drew near. Two decades' worth of false starts, slow-to-come realizations, and revisions had gone into it, and all the while the story—as well as he knew it—had resisted his efforts like granite.

One version opens with a forty-one-year-old Cape Cod architect introducing himself as the designer of forgettable houses, a shopping center, and a school.[84] Another draft anticipated the voice and character of Dwayne Hoover from *Breakfast of Champions*, which was still only in fragments. The narrator, named Billy Pilgrim, is a Pontiac dealer in the Midwest, a real stalwart when it comes to supporting his community. In a third iteration, Vonnegut begins to speak in his own voice, but it is autobiographical. He has been a novelist for so long, he explains, that he is unable to tell the difference between what has really happened in his life and what hasn't.[85]

Finally, he settled on a plaintive note: "All this happened, more or less. The war parts, anyway, are pretty much true," opening the door to the metafictional technique of the author entering the text.[86]

The type was set, the galley pages lying on his desk, but still he wasn't confident. He sent a typewritten copy of the manuscript to Bernard O'Hare, accompanied by an abject note asking if he and his wife would read it. If it was offensive or too goofy they should just say so.[87] They loved it.[88] He ceded the final decision about the book's jacket to Jane, his advocate and tutelary ever since he had started writing full-time above Cheney's gas station and store in Alplaus. When she approved of it, he was satisfied.[89]

Six months earlier, more of his 1950s work—a collection of his short stories aimed at magazine readers—had appeared as an anthology, *Welcome to the Monkey House*. One reviewer called it "old soup" that would fail to enhance his reputation.[90] Another noted the stories "were written to sell, as Vonnegut admits, and they carry along a burdensome weight of disguise. Some are simply extended gags. Some spoof the preoccupations of the magazines for which they were written."[91] It hardly mattered now, though. *Welcome to the Monkey House* was like an album of old photographs, acting as a foil for his new book about to be released, and throwing into high relief the changes in his style.

As for what kind of reception *Slaughterhouse-Five* would receive, whether it would be greeted with hosannas or hooted off the shelves, he couldn't be sure. Not even the estimable *God Bless You, Mr. Rosewater*, his most widely reviewed novel to date, had put him firmly over the top four years earlier. The most he could do to earn his latest novel maximum attention was to put his public relations background to good use.

To begin with, he cultivated the style of an author who was "in." Lawrence had done an excellent job of reviving his career by publishing his novels in uniform, hardback editions, giving them cachet as the collected works of Kurt Vonnegut. Moreover, sales of his novels were swooping upward, propelled by college students. As of March 1969, *Cat's Cradle* had sold over 150,000 copies and *Sirens of Titan* 200,000.[92] "What J. D. Salinger was to me in high school," enthused a twenty-year-old English major at UCLA, "Kurt Vonnegut is to me in college."[93] At Yale, *Doonesbury* creator Garry Trudeau "bought them two or three titles at a time, and loaned them to our friends, and, of course, never saw them again. Vonnegut books enjoyed a brisk currency, and any attempts to hoard them were doomed. They circulated until the glue turned brown and the pages fell out."[94]

To meet the expectations of his audience was key, especially because invitations to speak on college campuses were arriving more frequently. He lost weight, allowed his close-cropped hair to become curly and tousled, and grew a mustache—a big brown, upside-down chevron with points at the corners of his mouth à la George Harrison or Peter Max. He looked like an avant-garde artist and social critic now, not rumpled-Dad-in-a-cardigan as publicity shots in the early 1960s suggested.

He had learned a hard lesson too about pitching himself to a young audience the previous summer. The price was bafflement and embarrassment, but the timing for making an adjustment to his self-presentation couldn't have been better.

At the 1968 annual convention of the United States Student Press Association at Valparaiso University in Indiana, he was the keynoter. On the dais with him were two other speakers, the futurist Alvin Toffler and the black activist and presidential candidate Dick Gregory. In the audience were hundreds of young men and women, both college and high school students—sharp, informed, and many of the young men eligible for the draft.

But he misread what they were politically attuned to and expected to hear. In his day as a student journalist, he had covered after-school sock hops and the junior talent show for the *Echo*; but these young people were leaning into an era of advocacy journalism. Some of them were from Mississippi and Alabama and defying their school's administrations by covering civil rights demonstrations. Others had editorialized against the war in Vietnam and called for student strikes. During the conference, a bulletin came across the AP wire announcing that the Soviets had rolled into Prague, inspiring calls from some of the attendees for demonstrating in support of the Czechs.[95]

Kurt stepped up to the microphone for his keynote speech. "I said many screamingly funny things, but the applause was dismal at the end."[96] Startled, he sat down. Then Dick Gregory spoke. Eloquently, passionately, he attacked Lyndon Johnson, the Vietnam War, "capitalist exploitation," and the establishment. His final appeal brought the audience to their feet. He charged them, as the new generation, with changing the "sick ways of contemporary America."[97] When Toffler began to describe the challenges of "future shock," and how young people like them would experience a revolution in technology and information, they drank in the excitement of a new age, fraught with ethical questions.

Even then Vonnegut couldn't understand why he had been such a disappointment. That evening, he asked one of the conference hosts how he had "offended the audience." The reply was "they had hoped I would moralize. They had hired me as a moralist."[98]

Until then, he had seen himself as an author whose prognostications about the misuse of technology, about society's treatment of its weakest members, about an indifferent God were limited to the pages of his novels. The purpose of an artist, he believed, was to be a "canary in a coalmine," to warn of dangers "long before more robust types realize that any danger is there."[99]

True, but his audience had expected him to expound on his ideas, to moralize—not just entertain them like a Rotary lunchtime speaker. Though Vonnegut had read and admired Norman Mailer's polemical take on America, the aptly named *Advertisements for Myself*, he apparently failed to make the connection between the title and Mailer's bellicose persona.[100] There was both Mailer the bookish Harvard graduate who spent most of his day at the typewriter, and Mailer the two-fisted cultural critic who opined on the cult of the "good orgasm" in his essay "The White Negro." When audiences came to hear Mailer, they expected the intellectual brawler, not a timorous "canary in a coalmine."

Likewise, if Vonnegut, in an era ripped by social issues, was going to style himself after some of his favorite satirists and social critics—

Twain, H. L. Mencken, and Bernard Shaw—he would have to embody the role of an American castigator.

THUS, IN time for the publication of *Slaughterhouse-Five*, the new Vonnegut debuted. In an interview in *Newsweek*, he said, "I've got three kids [antiwar activist] Mark Rudd's age, and I share with them the sense that the system promotes to the top those who don't care about the planet."[101] Under his photo, the caption read, "Vonnegut: A Campus Orwell." He continued: "People are constantly demanding moralizing. There's going to be a lot of that this year—that's certainly what people want to hear when they ask me to lecture. Things like war crimes—that's what kids are thinking about these days."[102]

He came across as mature, empathetic, concerned. The fact that he was dressed for the interview in a Brooks Brothers suit and tie had the effect of playing against type. He was a critic of the establishment, but he was not Timothy Leary draped in love beads or Allen Ginsberg dancing to finger cymbals. He *was* the establishment, which added gravitas to his indictments of "the system."

On February 6, 1969, he let fly in a speech to a meeting of the American Association of Physics Teachers in New York, held in conjunction with a meeting of the American Physical Society. He titled his speech "The Virtuous Physicist." In the audience were physicists who were planning a one-day research stoppage to protest what they alleged was the misuse of science and technology. Some were wearing STOP ABM buttons to protest the development of antiballistic missiles for defense from a Chinese attack.

"Moralizing hasn't really been my style up to now," he said, but he assured the audience this time would be different. "What does a humanistic physicist do? Why, he watches people, listens to them, thinks about them, wishes them and their planet well. He wouldn't knowingly hurt people. He wouldn't knowingly help politicians or soldiers hurt people. If he comes across a technique that would obviously hurt people, he keeps it to himself. He knows that a scientist can be an accessory to murder most foul. That's simple enough, surely."[103]

The audience received his remarks warmly. During a news conference afterward, Vonnegut was asked what he meant by a virtuous physicist. "One," he said without hesitation, "who declines to work on weapons."[104]

*   *   *

THE SPEECH and his interview in *Newsweek* positioned him on the national scene as an author who would take stands on moral issues. His criticism of the status quo, however, created the impression that he must be a leftist. The country was so polarized politically that anyone who disparaged the war or the government sounded like he was on the side of hippies and antiwar protesters. In fact, Vonnegut was less a radical than a reactionary. He yearned for an old-fashioned America populated by Eliot Rosewaters and Uncle Alexes, for extended families, for a nation reluctant to go to war, for decency, and yes—even for businesses like General Electric at its enlightened best. But only a close reading of his works would reveal that.

The other reason he was associated with the Left at the instant he became nationally famous is that *Slaughterhouse-Five* was serialized before its official publication in the most widely read New Left magazine of its day, *Ramparts*.

Max Wilkinson, showing surprising acuity about placing the novel in front of exactly the right audience, sent galleys to the editor of *Ramparts*, Warren Hinckle.[105] With a circulation of three hundred thousand, *Ramparts*—expensively produced and graphically eye-catching—was the only magazine of its political stripe that could penetrate middle-class households. Essays and reportage by Noam Chomsky, César Chávez, Seymour Hersh, Tom Hayden, Angela Davis, and Jonathan Kozol put radical Left values on people's coffee tables in a way that underground newspapers couldn't.[106] Because *Ramparts* had come out early against the war, *Slaughterhouse-Five* jibed perfectly with the magazine's editorial values.

It was a publicity coup, his entire novel appearing in one of the leading intellectual magazines in the country, and guaranteed to generate seismic prepublication book buzz. Fifteen years earlier, his novels had been distributed along with westerns and teenage romances to drugstores and bus stations. Now his work was published in an au courant magazine where readers pored over Che Guevara's diaries, introduced by Fidel Castro, and the prison diaries of Eldridge Cleaver, later republished as *Soul on Ice*.

Suddenly, Vonnegut—who had been only mildly interested in politics most of his adult life—was perceived as a liberal firebrand, a prophesier about the wrongheaded direction America was going in, and a guru to young people on college campuses.

Two weeks before the arrival of *Slaughterhouse-Five* in bookstores in early March 1969, the North Vietnamese hit Saigon and more than one hundred South Vietnamese towns and military targets, killing approximately one hundred Americans in the first fifteen hours. During the first week of March, 453 Americans were killed, the highest American losses in nearly a year.[107] All ten thousand copies of the first edition of *Slaughterhouse-Five* sold out almost immediately, and the novel that Vonnegut had complained read like a telegram reached number one on the *New York Times* best seller list.

It was the beginning of, as Edie Vonnegut later said, the "big ka-BOOM!" in her family's and her father's lives.[108]

The full title was *Slaughterhouse-Five; or, The Children's Crusade, a Duty-Dance with Death*. The phrase "Children's Crusade" linked the World War II generation to the current one mired in the conflict in Southeast Asia. Vietnam made "our leadership and our motives so scruffy and essentially stupid," said Vonnegut, "that we could finally talk about something bad that we did to the worst people imaginable, the Nazis. And what I saw, what I had to report, made war look so ugly. You know the truth can be really powerful stuff."[109]

The novel is not, as it turns out, the story of the bombing of Dresden, which is how he would have approached it during his *Collier's* days, but his reaction to it.[110] "When I got home from the Second War twenty-three years ago, I thought it would be easy for me to write about the destruction of Dresden, since all I would have to do would be to report what I had seen."[111] But he had dispensed with trying to describe the attack in detail because, for one thing, he had seen very little of it—a narrative problem that had stymied him for years. And there was wisdom in hindsight in the poet Roethke's line "We think by feeling. What is there to know?"

Also, he was sensitive to Mary O'Hare's criticism that he would glorify war. Consequently, he took the everyman perspective of someone bewildered by events, in keeping with the theme that profound puzzlement is the only way to come to terms with death and mass killing.

It begins with an apology, the first of a number of times Vonnegut inserts himself into the narrative. "I would hate to tell you what this lousy little book cost me in money and anxiety and time." He recaps with disarming humor and self-deprecation the genesis of the novel, and sketches his current life as "an old fart with his memories and his Pall Malls." Then he hands control of the story over to a primary narrator.

"Listen:

"Billy Pilgrim has become unstuck in time."[112]

The story proceeds backward and forward in time, going from Pilgrim as a young man held by the Germans in Dresden, to Pilgrim as a senile widower imprisoned by extraterrestrials called Tralfamadorians, to Pilgrim in middle age at a convention of fellow optometrists. The form of the narrative, twisted like a paper loop into a figure eight, over which characters seem to be gliding away along the curves but keep meeting again at the point of self-intersection, is the culmination of Vonnegut's experiments with technique in the five preceding novels.[113] And nonlinearity is particularly well suited to the novel's design because memory is recursive.

Some critics scoffed at Vonnegut's strange narrative topology, and how recurrence becomes not just a device but also a theme.[114] Billy learns, for example, that "When a Tralfamadorian sees a corpse, all he thinks is that the dead person is in a bad condition in that particular moment, but that the same person is just fine in plenty of other moments."[115] The respected H. G. Wells, one of Vonnegut's favorite authors, would not have stated a space-time concept so baldly—and too often Vonnegut threw out a provocative idea and then failed to develop it. But the influence of his background in physics and chemistry, and his interest in contemporary science (he later discussed a curved versus a flat universe in his collection of essays *Wampeters, Foma & Granfalloons*), is rarely taken into account.[116]

He may or may not have known that the Greeks always associated time with circular movement and the "doctrine of eternal recurrence"—an idea taken from observations of the heavens.[117] But as a science undergraduate at Cornell, he certainly would have been familiar with relativity, which states that time does not flow at an even rate throughout the universe. Every moment of time is equivalent to every other; differences in time depend on the state of motion of the observer—his or her "proper time."[118]

ANOTHER MANIFESTATION of time that intrigued Vonnegut, just as it did Céline, was chaos. "Let others bring order to chaos," Vonnegut said in an interview. "I will bring chaos to order. If all writers would do that, then perhaps everyone will understand that there is no order in the world around us, that we must adapt ourselves to the requirements of chaos instead."[119]

Chaos increasing is how we perceive time passing. As Vonnegut would have known from his coursework in thermodynamics during his specialized army training, Newton's second law says that the future is the time direction in which disorder becomes greater.[120] Heat dissipates from objects, and gases disperse. He uses this phenomenon of irreversibility in nature to make the point that, much as we might like to, immoral acts cannot be undone. In one of the most memorable antiwar conceits in the novel, Billy watches a movie in reverse about American bombers in World War II.

> The formation flew backwards over a German city that was in flames. The bombers opened their bomb bay doors, exerted a miraculous magnetism which shrunk the fires, gathered them into cylindrical steel containers, and lifted the containers into the bellies of the planes. The containers were stored neatly in racks. The Germans had miraculous devices of their own, which were long steel tubes. They used them to suck more fragments from the crewmen and planes. But there were still a few wounded Americans, though, and some of the bombers were in bad repair. Over France, though, German fighters came up again, made everything and everybody as good as new.[121]

At the end of the film, the "dangerous contents" of the bombs are reduced to minerals again and shipped back to where they came from to be put "into the ground, to hide them cleverly, so they would never hurt anybody again."[122]

Unfortunately, of course, cities can never be "unbombed." The Tralfamadorians are intrigued with why their Earthling specimen, Billy, should worry about what might have been when the irreversibility of chaos is the signature characteristic of the universe. "'If I hadn't spent so much time studying Earthlings,' said the Tralfamadorian, 'I wouldn't have any idea what was meant by "free will." I've visited thirty-one inhabited planets in the universe, and I have studied reports on one hundred more. Only on Earth is there any talk of free will.'"[123]

The Tralfamadorians are determinists, they explain, because they see "all time as you might see a stretch of the Rocky Mountains. All time is all time. It does not change. It does not lend itself to warnings or explanations. It simply *is*."[124] The all-seeing extraterrestrials resemble the supreme being in the eighteenth-century mathematician Marquis de Laplace's theory that if "an intellect were vast enough" to know the positions of everything at any given moment, "the future just like the past would be present before its eyes."[125] When Napoleon asked Laplace where was God in his theory, he answered, "I have no need of that hypothesis."[126] It's a response that Vonnegut—a Unitarian, descendant of freethinkers, reluctant atheist, and student of classical physics—would have appreciated.

The Tralfamadorians may be "Laplace's demon," as his vast, supreme intellect was called, knowing all events simultaneously. But it doesn't matter. Billy must accept the redundancy of death, failure, and historical events as he rolls through the universe. "Take it moment by moment," a Tralfamadorian advises him, "and you will find that we all are, as I've said before, bugs in amber."[127]

Vonnegut's reply is famously "So it goes."

THERE'S ALSO a literary influence on Vonnegut's treatment of time in *Slaughterhouse-Five* that has been overlooked. It's become axiomatic that Vonnegut is Mark Twain's heir in style and outlook. Journalists and true-believing academics repeated the Vonnegut-and-Twain analogy so often that it's taken as self-evident. Actually, there is more under the hood of Vonnegut's fiction, particularly in *Slaughterhouse-Five*, borrowed from Ambrose Bierce, an almost forgotten American author, than from Mark Twain.

Vonnegut admired Bierce to the point of considering "anybody a Twerp who hasn't read the greatest American short story," Bierce's "An Occurrence at Owl Creek Bridge."[128] Bierce, a Civil War veteran, had seen too much wretchedness to believe that life had meaning or that humans were good. His description of desensitized, battle-weary men prefigures Vonnegut's fatalism. But there's more than just stoicism born of soldiering in Vonnegut and Bierce. The linchpin connecting these authors is how the experience of war influences their handling of time.

Most of Bierce's fabulist short fiction features drastic distortions of the past, present, and future.[129] In "An Occurrence at Owl Creek Bridge," the story Vonnegut loved best, the Confederate saboteur, Peyton Farquhar, moments away from hanging, hears the supernaturally loud ticking of his watch, but the seconds come farther and farther apart. As Vonnegut writes in *Slaughterhouse-Five*, thinking perhaps of Bierce, "The time would not pass. Somebody was playing with the clocks, and not only with the electric clocks, but the wind-up kind, too. The second hand on my watch would twitch once, and a year would pass, and then it would twitch again."[130] In Bierce's story, the prisoner Farquhar falls from a scaffold (a bridge), but in his imagination, he fantasizes a miraculous escape, filled with adventures, that lasts hours until the rope's noose suddenly snaps his neck.

Soldiers in terror of their lives, confused, hyperalert, often speak of time speeding up or slowing down—becoming weirdly elongated or even missing as they pit their rational senses against an avalanche of stimuli.[131] Perhaps the root of Vonnegut's and Bierce's time-disordered fables lies in a psychological condition not understood until later: posttraumatic stress disorder.

THERE IS a way out for Billy, however. Haunted by a sense of isolation, of purposeless, of stumbling along, he opts out of time and loses all sense of time's shape, similar to the sense of time of a schizoid person.[132] Episodes of trauma will snap him into the past again or propel him out to the planet Tralfamadore. "Billy has gone to sleep a senile widower and awakened on his wedding day. He has walked through a door in 1955 and come out another one in 1941."[133] It's Newton's third law now: for every action in nature there is an equal and opposite reaction. Only Vonnegut applies this principle to Billy's psyche, whipped back and forth by the force of widespread death in World War II.

He is redeemed at last from cycles in his mind, and from historical forces over which he has no control, by the simplest life-affirming act possible: sex.

On Tralfamadore, the extraterrestrials procure a mate for Billy: a twenty-year-old pornographic movie starlet named Montana Wild-hack.[134] She is sweet and trusting—a heterosexual male's fantasy. Billy's libido answers his fear of death and nothingness when he makes love to her, but only after Montana asks him to. They are hidden from sight by a canopy navy blue like the sky, and the narrator says of their coupling, "It was heavenly."[135]

This pretend Eden-like paradise on Tralfamadore where there is love, privacy for sex, and desire for it resolves Kurt's tie to his mother, too. The dead end of pleasing his histrionic mommy, the artiste manqué, by living and writing on the Cape has ended. Montana is to Billy what Loree was to Kurt when he was "adrift"; life energy restarts in both the author and his protagonist through the act of physical love, a strongly sexual relationship with a love who will never leave. When Montana gives birth to a child, the parallel with Kurt successfully taking up *Slaughterhouse-Five* again in Iowa is complete. Procreation and successful artistic creation are one.

"I felt after I finished *Slaughterhouse-Five* that I didn't have to write at all anymore if I didn't want to. It was the end of some sort of career."[136]

GRANVILLE HICKS, jotting down impressions as he read the novel, noted "Imaginative stuff—better than most sf [science fiction]."[137] Michael Crichton, in his first review for a major publication, the *New Republic*, praised Vonnegut's ability to load a weird structure with big ideas: "He writes about the most excruciatingly painful things. His novels have attacked our deepest fears of automation and the bomb, our deepest political guilts, our fiercest hatreds and loves. Nobody else writes books on these subjects; they are inaccessible to normal novelistic approaches."[138] Leslie Fiedler suggested that what was omitted from the novel gave beauty to it as a whole. *Slaughterhouse-Five* was "less about Dresden," he said, "than about Vonnegut's failure to come to terms with it—one of those beautifully frustrating works about their own impossibility, like Fellini's *8½*."[139]

Other critics saw *Slaughterhouse* in less flattering terms. Alfred

Kazin was turned off by what he termed Vonnegut's "impishly senti-
mental humor" about the absurdities of war. Vonnegut, according to
Kazin, "is at his best not in *Slaughterhouse-Five* (really a satire on the
Great American novel) but in spoofs of the American scene like *God
Bless You, Mr. Rosewater*."[140]

A former RAF pilot, writing to the *New York Times*, found the novel's depiction of the Dresden firestorm offensive: "May I record my
amusement at the present-day flood of crocodile tears over the 1945
bombing of Dresden? I refer particularly to recent reviews of Kurt Vonnegut Jr.'s novel, *Slaughterhouse-Five*. . . . Today in Dresden, tourist
visitors will find enlarged photographs that display the full effect of the
raids. Below this exhibit a placard refers to the 'terror bombing by the
Americans and British, a terrible accusation against those guilty of
mass murder.' Nowhere is it mentioned that Nazism brought on World
War II. Or that Dresden was bombed at the request of advancing Russian Army officials, who feared that Hitler was assembling his shattered
armies there."[141]

The unkindest blow was struck by Vonnegut's hometown newspaper. Just ten years earlier when he was a foreign-car salesman, an uncle
to three orphaned nephews, and a paid-by-the-book paperback writer,
he seemed like a good egg to his neighbors. But now he was a celebrity,
and the *Barnstable Patriot* caught the changing mood toward him
when it editorialized, "Kurt Vonnegut Jr., looking somewhat like the
crucified Christ, gazed out from the front page of the *New York Times*
Book Review section Easter morning."[142]

HE WAS a public figure now, and the bell jar of persona descended around
him. It was partly a result of the attention accorded *Slaughterhouse-
Five*, but it was also a consequence of including himself in the novel.
"I finally started talking about myself and said I actually had been in
the bombing of Dresden."[143] At various points in the story, he taps the
reader on the shoulder to say, "I was there. So was my old war buddy,
Bernard V. O'Hare," and "That was I. That was me. That was the author
of this book."[144] Seeing that the device was generally well received, he
went back and began writing personal introductions to all his earlier
novels, too.[145]

Creatively, it was amusing, and instead of canceling out Vonnegut's

individuality in the text, he allowed the reader to peep under the autho-
rial mask. By doing so, he increased the sense of intimacy between
himself and his fans, of which there were many now. On the other
hand, he wanted to portray someone who was a match—a "public
spokesperson," as the Vonnegut scholar Jerome Klinkowitz calls him—
with the bemused voice and humanistic values in the novels, too.

That's certainly what hippies expected to find when they began
making pilgrimages to West Barnstable to see "the man himself" beginning in 1969.

10: Goodbye and Goodbye and Goodbye

1969–1971

YOUNG ADMIRERS ARRIVED at the front door in West Barnstable hoping to meet "Mr. Vonnegut" almost daily. If he was home, he would usually invite them in, give them a few minutes of his time, and then try to shoo them on their way. Jane, on the other hand, tended to swoop down like Wendy playing mother to the Lost Boys in *Peter Pan*. Sometimes she called their parents; occasionally she insisted they spend the night or even stay for several days.[1] One morning Edie opened a big closet and discovered a few of her father's fans snoring in sleeping bags on the floor.[2]

Among the gaggle of hippies at the door one day were Steve Diamond, a young writer; his fellow freak Ray Mungo, cofounder of the Liberation News Service; and their friend Verandah Porche, "Queen of the Bay State Poets for Peace." All three lived at Total Loss Farm, a commune in Guilford, Vermont, as did most of the other pilgrims hovering in the background.

"What can I do for you people?" Vonnegut asked.

Steve Diamond spoke for the group: "We don't want you to do anything for us!"

Vonnegut indicated they should follow him around to the side of the house. Finding a sunny spot on the grass, they sat in a circle and chatted, though not comfortably.

"Actually there is a real reason we have come here," Diamond said finally. "We are forming an organization called 'The Old Farts.' To belong, you have to smoke a lot of Pall Malls, and you have to have a porch to sit on. We would like you to be President."[3] Vonnegut laughed. Eccentricity in youngsters appealed to him, and among his children's friends the oddest often had been regulars in the kitchen over the years.[4] So when these longhairs from Vermont urged him to attend their May Day celebration at Total Loss Farm, he accepted. Said Dan Wakefield, a friend of Kurt's and the author of *Going All the Way*, "Vonnegut didn't go looking for the kids, they adopted him."[5]

KURT WAS nearly fifty years old when a generation of young readers found him. "I certainly didn't go after the youth market or anything like that," he said. "I didn't have my fingers on any pulse; I was simply writing."[6] But he did have a theory about his appeal. It was because he addressed "sophomoric questions that full adults regard as settled": whether there is a God, for instance, what the good life consists of, whether we should expect a reward for moral behavior.[7] It didn't faze him that these and similar questions had already been addressed innumerable times by philosophers from Boethius to Camus. His purpose for draping ethical questions in humorous costumes was to "catch people before they become generals and senators and presidents, and you poison their minds with humanity. Encourage them to make a better world."[8] And who could disagree with the importance of practicing kindness, building community, and acting as stewards of the earth? It could be argued in fact that, as a friend wrote him sometime later, "your writing has the peculiar quality of only reflecting the reader's beliefs back on him."[9]

Idealism of this kind resonates strongly with young people, and his novels became part of the printed currency of the youth movement. They wanted to be as wise about human existence as the extraterrestrials in *Sirens of Titan* and *Slaughterhouse-Five*. They wanted Vonnegut to prepare them to meet what might turn out to be a dystopian future at the hands of fat cats like those in *Player Piano*. They had grown up expecting nuclear war, so the world's destruction by a hilarious accident in *Cat's Cradle* convinced them they were right to hate the Cold War and its players. In Vonnegut's easy-to-read parables, they were faced with their first exposure to existential despair.[10]

Offsetting his negativity, however, familiar characters in the novels reappeared like shoals of relatives arriving for Thanksgiving dinner: Fred T. Barry, an advertising man for Robo-Magic appliances; various members of the half-cracked Rumfoord clan; Kilgore Trout, the maligned science fiction writer; Bernard O'Hare (always in military uniform); the humanitarian Eliot Rosewater and his counterpart the rapacious lawyer Norman Mushari. These were some of the denizens of a zany Yoknapatawpha County for the Vonnegut faithful, replete with "in" references just for them.[11] To lighten the burden of hopelessness, there was community, laughter, and humanity.

Fans wrote to him as if he were an intimate friend. "Whenever I read anything by you," said one, "I always feel the emotion and intent come across as if we had privately discussed the matter and you'd personally explained each point to me. Your characters are all so very real and alive that they become, not bigger than life, but life itself with all its intricacies and absurd details."[12] A young man about to enter the air force confided, "I am 19 and not very emotional, and yet, I wept at the awesome beauty of your characters. Perhaps I should say at the beauty of your truths and ironies."[13]

HIS READERS assumed the voice they trusted in the novels was rooted in a combination of wisdom and sophistication, but the truth was different. Vonnegut was more like his readers than they could have guessed. His themes of community and extended family for persons who are naive or lonely had much to do with how he saw himself and idealized some of his boyhood. His summers at Lake Maxinkuckee had been his communal paradise lost—an upper-middle-class enclave of family cottages where everything was left to the elders. Being a child with few responsibilities in the palm of that environment had been the best period in his life, basking in love and affirmation like the Harmoniums in *The Sirens of Titan*, who live on Mercury and chatter back and forth: "Here I am, here I am, here I am" and "so glad you are, so glad you are, so glad you are."[14] When he returned home to Indianapolis, his life lacked the warmth and acceptance he found on the lake as a child in the company of affectionate relatives.

The upshot was he became a reluctant adult. Adulthood, as he saw it, was permanent expulsion from those halcyon days. Making a joke to Jane about how tallness tended to be equated with wisdom and leadership, he wrote that if the government assigned heights based on maturity, he would be much shorter. But that wouldn't bother him, he said. If he had his choice, he would be about twelve again, immersed in hobbies and leaving the nasty running of the world to grown-ups.[15]

His children drew the conclusion that he preferred being their contemporary. Mark likened it to a secret they shared. "As a child," he wrote to his father, "I always had the feeling that you were almost winking at me. . . . It was like you had to pretend to be an adult and I had to pretend to be a child."[16]

Edie, when she was twelve, felt "all confused about life and God" and asked her father for guidance. His response surprised her. He said, she remembered, that in "the grand scheme of things we were scarcely older than each other . . . we were both experiencing the same things at the same time for the first time. Like our dog dying was a first for both of us. That he had no more of a handle on things than I did. . . . Ever since then I've seen him as a sort of peer or buddy, and a plain ordinary person trying to sort things out in the dark, just like me."[17]

With the lines in the Vonnegut-Adams family blurred between the adults and the children—Jane could be seen going everywhere in a girl's kilt when she was middle-aged—the laid-back atmosphere seemed hip and exciting. One of Kurt's former students at Iowa, Barry Jay Kaplan, arrived for a visit and found the house "ideal, artistic and yet like an artist colony." His upbringing in a Jewish family in the Bronx had not been happy, but in West Barnstable he was invited to lend a hand with the ritual of carrying bags of groceries into the house after one of Jane's almost daily shopping trips into town. On the wall going up the staircase to the second floor, Edie and Nanny had painted a mural of the family, and Kaplan was impressed: "This is so great that the kids are not only allowed, but encouraged to express their artistic endeavors in the house." Kurt was out of sight most of the time, working in the studio on the side of the house. But Kaplan hardly noticed, basking "in the hilarity that was going on."[18]

There were plenty of adventures to hear about at the Vonneguts' kitchen table—some of them reckless—but not unsurprising in light of the permissiveness in the house. Jim and Tiger Adams had spent a couple of months exploring the Amazon and smuggled a kilo of marijuana through Mexican customs under the floorboard of their car. Edie and three friends were arrested for possession of pot near Acapulco. The federales confiscated their car, motorcycle, guitars, and drum set. While she waited in jail to be deported to Houston—without money, belongings, or even shoes—she saw a baby born in a cell and an elderly, disoriented man shot off a roof for trying to escape.[19] Peter Fonda, fresh off the premiere of the film *Easy Rider*, stayed the weekend in West Barnstable to discuss optioning *Cat's Cradle*. At one point, Kurt waved him into his study. He "inscribed a copy of *Cat's Cradle* and fished a joint out of his desk while asking me not to tell the children."[20]

Sometimes Kurt demanded that he be allowed to be a child, but it was mainly only his family who witnessed his outbursts. Mark tried not to defeat him too handily at chess; otherwise Dad might flip the board over. One afternoon, when Nanny was fifteen, she and a boyfriend were kissing in the barn on the Vonneguts' property. Suddenly, the door flew open. It was Kurt in a rage.

"You," he said, pointing at the boy, "get the *fuck* out of here!" Then it was his daughter's turn. "Where the hell were you, I almost called out the National Guard! How dare you do something like this!" He stomped off in the direction of the house.

Nanny, stumbling behind him, got down on her knees and clasped her hands together. "Dad, please stop, please, please, I'm so sorry." He turned around, dropped to his knees opposite her, and imitated her begging, in a high, singsong voice.

"Please, *please* stop. Oh, Nanny, can't I build you another rabbit hutch?" He gave her a contemptuous look, then got up and continued toward the house, while she remained kneeling in the grass.[21]

Few things ticked him off as thoroughly as being made to feel ridiculous. Consequently, the big bugaboos of his life—powerlessness, ineptitude, and inferiority—run throughout his work. His readers, eager to revenge themselves on teachers, parents, and the government, admired him for "telling it like it is."[22] But if he had been a fully mature adult, it's likely he would not have been able to frame young adults' worldview so well.

VONNEGUT'S POPULARITY was manifested in sales, of course, but another sign of it was how young, beginning writers paid homage to him. Twenty-year-old James Simon Kunen's first-person account of the 1968 student rebellion at Columbia University, *The Strawberry Statement: Notes of a College Revolutionary*, adopted the tone of the Vonnegut persona, resigned to the meaninglessness of life.[23] Vonnegut was Kunen's favorite author, and *Mother Night* was "him at his best. It very strongly stresses the blurriness of good and evil and the gratuitousness of how things come about."[24]

Just an approving nod from Vonnegut was gold in publishers' pockets. A favorable review by him and a blurb on the cover of *The Strawberry Statement* anointed Kunen as a national spokesperson for student unrest. Bantam Books, hoping to profit from Vonnegut's cachet with young people, sent him a collection of underground comics to comment on, but he decided the illustrators weren't as good as R. Crumb.[25] The eighteen-year-old journalist John Birmingham was astonished when he learned Vonnegut was going to provide an introduction to *Our Time Is Now: Notes from the High School Underground*. The resulting crush of attention was too much for him, and he retreated to Vancouver, British Columbia, where he could hang out and watch Laurel and Hardy films on acid.[26]

Offers to provide treatments or screenplays for films came his way, too. Al Brodax, producer of *Yellow Submarine*, the animated film about the Beatles, pitched him the idea of scripting a Peter Max version of *Alice in Wonderland*, but the money wasn't enough; Vonnegut wanted at least as much as Peter Max.[27] After all, critics of American culture such as Susan Sontag and Benjamin DeMott were discussing the Beatles and Motown as seriously as they would Baroque music, and Vonnegut was "perfectly tuned to the mind of the emergent generation," as DeMott himself pointed out.[28] Kurt expected his due.

DURING THE summer of 1969, Knox Burger and his wife, Kitty, spent a week with the Vonneguts. Kurt promised to take Knox out in his blue rowboat *Bob* to watch flights of seabirds in the marshes. When the moment was right, Knox broached an idea he wanted to share confidentially—a dream, really.

For ten years, he had been at Gold Medal paperbacks as the editor of forty-three mystery, crime, and detective novels by John D. MacDonald, and scads of others in the same categories by Philip Atlee, Lawrence Block, Alistair MacLean, and S. S. Van Dine. "He's the best in the business," said the editor in chief of a rival house. "Readers usually look for authors or titles, but there are thousands who go out looking for Gold Medal—for the trademark! No other publisher has that going for him."[29] With so many authors on his list, Knox thought he was perfectly placed, personally and professionally, to hang out his own shingle as a literary agent. Kurt would be welcome, he said, if he would be willing to jump ship from Littauer & Wilkinson along with "MacDonald and [William Price] Fox . . . and a dozen lame birds or writers [Wilkinson] hasn't known what to do with."[30] Having his old college and author friend as a client would ensure the viability of the enterprise, particularly in light of Kurt's sensational success with *Slaughterhouse-Five*.

Kurt responded without reservation, assuring Knox he could count on him. Moreover, after Burger returned to New York, Vonnegut followed up with a note again pledging fealty to his old friend.[31]

MEANWHILE, *SLAUGHTERHOUSE-FIVE* rode the best seller lists month after month, and Vonnegut found that moralizing made him a lightning rod, drawing thunderous publicity. The man, the author, and the teller of the tale were becoming indistinguishable. Like two intersecting lines, Vonnegut in fact and Billy Pilgrim in fiction had met. "I'm completely fatalistic about Dresden," Vonnegut told the theologian Robert L. Short. "Since it did happen, it must have had to happen."[32] Billy Pilgrim, paralyzed by humankind's proclivity for destruction, couldn't have explained what he had learned on Tralfamadore about free will more succinctly.

Thus Vonnegut the "public spokesperson" strode onstage in midsummer 1969 in a manner admirers of *Slaughterhouse-Five* would expect when the United States prepared to launch its first manned spacecraft to the moon. In keeping with his remarks before the American Association of Physics Teachers in winter 1969, which had garnered him press in the *New York Times* and *Newsweek,* he attacked what he saw as the space program's hubris. His sarcastic send-up of the big send-off appeared in the *New York Times* as a full-page essay, "Excelsior! We're Going to the Moon! Excelsior!"

"We have spent something like $33 billion on space so far. We should have spent it on cleaning up our filthy colonies here on earth. There is absolutely no urgency whatsoever about getting somewhere in space, much as Arthur C. Clarke wants to discover the source of those terrific radio signals coming from Jupiter. . . . It is the Houdini aspects of the space program which reward most earthlings—the dumb ones, the dropouts, the elevator operators and stenographers and so on." Astronauts in his opinion were "short-haired, white athletes" who go up in pressure cookers. Government grants had turned his brother, Bernard, into a "mendicant scientist" dependent on handouts. A colleague had spoken true when he said that for all the billions it consumes, NASA at least ought to discover God.[33]

The "Excelsior!" piece resulted in an invitation from CBS television to participate in a live panel moderated by Walter Cronkite the day of the moon landing, July 20. The other guests were Jerome Beatty Jr., author of children's books about space travel; Arthur C. Clarke; and Gloria Steinem—"a very unlikely group of people," Vonnegut thought.[34] With the imminent arrival of humankind on the moon just moments away, Kurt remarked that putting space exploration ahead of eradicating poverty was morally "untenable."[35] Steinem agreed. Even Beatty was lukewarm about the value to humanity of putting Americans on the moon. Cronkite pointed out that the moment was historic and the world was celebrating. He was mystified by their attitude—Steinem and Vonnegut in particular struck him as "bitter"—but he decided not to argue with them on the air.[36]

Then, live from the surface of the moon, the black-and-white images of Neil Armstrong bouncing down the ladder of the lunar module appeared on millions of television screens. Clarke, speaking by phone to Robert Heinlein, shouted, "It begins, it begins, it begins!" Seated near him, Beatty murmured, "It ends, it ends, it ends." "And what Beatty meant," Vonnegut recalled, "was there was nothing on the moon and there wasn't going to be much on anything else either."[37]

Over the next several days, CBS received thousands of angry, insulting letters complaining that Vonnegut and Steinem were un-American and had spoiled the event.[38] The irony, which pushed Vonnegut's reputation in the direction he wanted it to go, was that he had begun his career as a science fiction writer, been invited on the program in that spirit, but seized the moment to put himself squarely in the public eye as another activist with his dukes up, closer to Gloria Steinem than to Arthur C. Clarke.

* * *

RETURNING TO the Cape, Vonnegut found himself pilloried again a few weeks afterward in the local paper. Nationally, he was ascending on the horizon not only as a writer but also as a social observer and popular philosopher. But the *Barnstable Patriot* limned him as an egregious jerk: "During his years of residence in the northside village, the artist Vonnegut has become somewhat of a mystery man. Few local people read his books; of those who do, few like them. His style is not conventional, his approach is not delicate, his themes are not conservative. Barnstable Villagers are all of the above—conventional, conservative. . . . Kurt Vonnegut has achieved a significant degree of national recognition, especially among younger Establishment cynics. He has become, in fact, a minor hip hero with literate hippies on college campuses." Vonnegut owed his notoriety as a "pessimistic personality," in the newspaper's opinion, to the fact that "he is a man who has something bad to say about everything."[39]

It was the leading edge of a developing pattern. Shortly after the publication of *Slaughterhouse-Five*, Kurt had arrived in Indianapolis for an autographing session at the upscale department store L. S. Ayres. Over the entrance to the store was the landmark clock his grandfather had designed. As recently as the previous October, relatives reported to him that his collection of mainstream short stories *Welcome to the Monkey House* wasn't sold at Ayres department store.[40] He took a seat at a table in the book section. After three hours, he had signed and sold eleven copies, all of them to relatives.[41]

Some kind of split was happening in his life. Indianapolis, instead of welcoming him as the city's most famous author since Booth Tarkington, had yawned in his face. And yet at a peace march in Washington in November 1969, admirers recognized him in the street and shook his hand. Near the end of the year, he added his name to a letter of protest from PEN, the writers' organization, condemning the expulsion of Aleksandr I. Solzhenitsyn from the Soviet writers' union. Other signers included Arthur Miller, John Updike, John Cheever, Truman Capote, Harrison E. Salisbury, Yukio Mishima, Günter Grass, and Heinrich Böll. Because Vonnegut was a major American writer, his support was important.

The experience was a strange, preternatural sensation. "There was this ghost of me going around and so I didn't have to do anything. . . . I was simply present."[42] The author of enormously popular fiction waved to his former self on shore—Kurt Vonnegut, "hack," as he often referred to himself. He was working in public relations again, only now he was the product.

KURT DECIDED he needed an anchor, someone he could rely on before he got into trouble.

One evening the phone rang in Knox's home, and Vonnegut startled him by announcing he definitely, definitely, wanted to throw in with Knox's agency—still only a dream, of course. They both knew it would be a big setback for Littauer & Wilkinson now that he was a hot property, but Kurt had decided that this was the way to go. He wanted to do business exclusively with his old friend and onetime mentor.

Knox was surprised by the sudden urgency. "I really didn't know what to make of your call the other evening. . . . I haven't talked with Max for two or three weeks, and haven't yet gotten an answer to my request to look at his books." He would need to purchase the right to handle Vonnegut's works sold by Littauer & Wilkinson, and Knox knew for a fact that Max would want a great deal of money. But then, not wanting to sound like he wasn't equal to the challenge, he added, "There is no question in my mind but that you are riding the crest of a remarkably unique sort of wave right now, and ought to be making a great deal more money than you are."[43]

The problem was, the risk was all on Knox's side. Vonnegut could go wherever he wanted to, but Burger would be taking a major financial gamble by quitting Gold Medal. He estimated he would need to make $120,000 a year to stay afloat. And he would have to staff an office that was "responsive and efficient and effective."[44]

Whether to take the plunge would depend on the strength of Vonnegut's word.

IN DECEMBER 1969, neighbors driving by the Vonneguts' home on Christmas Eve would have noticed that things looked the way they always had during the holidays: cars in the driveway and lights in the windows. But the festiveness inside the house was strained. "Everyone got drunk the way they used to get drunk, everyone talked the way they used to talk. It was a sham," Mark said.[45]

Kurt was restless and bored. He was eager to continue the momentum started by *Slaughterhouse-Five*, but he couldn't make progress on his new book, *Breakfast of Champions*, forcing him to tell Sam Lawrence he'd better cancel Delacorte's plans for it.[46] He seemed to have wrung every drop he could from creative brainstorms on the Cape. There wasn't even anybody to talk to: his neighbors were a bunch of dullards. At night, listening to the stillness in the dark, he felt like he was on the moon.[47] His irritation manifested itself in drinking heavily and picking fights with Jane, usually about her fascination with New Age religion and meditation.[48]

She hated it when he baited her with the same tired complaints: that his home wasn't conducive to his work, and therefore she was no longer needed as partner, advocate, and advice giver. She had worries of her own. The children were grown, and she had given up a good part of her life to serve as "the expert handler of family tragedy, the picker-upper of all the crap."[49]

The carols playing on the radio sounded inanely saccharine to the Adams and Vonnegut children over the bickering in the background. The spirit of merriment was phony. Mark realized they all knew that it was "the last Christmas. The last Christmas we would all spend together. . . . Something was dying. It was more than Christmas. The magic that had filled the Barnstable house was dying. Our childhood was dying. What was killing it? Father getting famous? The changing times?"[50]

Early the next morning, all the "kids"—some in their twenties now—gathered at the top of the stairs. "Okay!" Kurt and Jane called, and everyone came running down to open their presents, laughing, giggling, and pretending they were children again.

DURING THE doldrums until New Year's, Vonnegut was killing time when he received a call from Vance Bourjaily in Paris. "Kurt, you want to go to Biafra?"

Bourjaily had been asked by the author Herbert Gold, who was completing a book about the Nigerian civil war, *Biafra Goodbye*, to visit the tiny country. Gold could arrange for a trip through a relief organization for Vance and another author, provided they would agree to write about the conditions there.

For Kurt, it was a chance to get out of the house and an opportunity to write an easy magazine article, probably for a major publication, because the desperate situation in Biafra had been in the headlines for months. He was on the phone in the kitchen where Jane and the rest of the family were seated around the big table, so he turned to them.

"It's Vance—he wants to know if I want to go to Biafra."

Bourjaily overheard their reaction. "They were all talking about something else. They just said, 'Go.' They wanted to get rid of him."[51]

WEARING A khaki outfit better suited to fly-fishing, Vonnegut arrived in Biafra with Vance on January 3 aboard a blacked-out DC-6 chartered by Caritas, a Catholic relief organization.

The Republic of Biafra, named for the Atlantic-side bay the Bight of Biafra, had seceded from Nigeria in May 1967. Fragmented by conflicts between Hausa and Fulani tribes in the north, Yoruba in the southwest, and Ibo in the southeast, Nigeria had dispatched its national army to annex the Ibo region of Biafra to regain its oil reserves, whittling down Biafra to one-tenth its original size. With bridges and roads blown up or blocked, the Ibo were dying from starvation.

As Vonnegut and Bourjaily stepped down from the plane, Ibo children surged forward crying "Hello, Father! Hello!" because Irish priests were the only white men who had stayed behind. The two men reared back because the children were grotesquely underweight and smelled bad. Most had huge rounded bellies, discolored hair, running sores, and everted rectums that swung like pink snouts between their legs. Vance, ashamed of his squeamishness, reminded Kurt that if Allen Ginsberg had been there, he would have hugged the children and gone down on his knees and played with them.[52] Vonnegut grasped little hands extended to him and, with a child clinging to every finger, he and Vance went to meet the on-site organizer of the trip, Miriam Reik, thirty-two, the daughter of the psychoanalyst Theodor Reik. She was tall, trim, and rather stern.

Reik was administering an exchange of Biafran and American writers and journalists, hoping to draw more humanitarian attention to the crisis.[53] She had hoped to escort Kurt and Vance to the front, from where Ibo villagers were fleeing, but that would mean going upstream against a flood of refugees. The best she could arrange was a trip by truck to a military training camp in the bush, not far from Owerri, the Biafran capital.

The road to the camp was a diorama of misery: more children with insectlike legs and arms, women too desiccated by hunger to nurse, and leathery people too weak to stand, staring at them as they sped past. Kurt tried to distract himself by making wisecracks and chuckling in a rusty, wheezing voice, a habit when he felt uneasy.

Miriam glared at him. "You won't open your mouth unless you can make a joke."[54]

They pulled into the base, its perimeter built from sandbags and empty oil drums. An Ibo officer saluted and led them over to a spot where a defensive drill was taking place. Three rows of men stood before dismounted .50-caliber antiaircraft machine guns lying on the ground, the type usually bolted to patrol boats. On a signal, each man in front lifted the staggeringly heavy weapon onto his shoulder. Two others leaned against him from behind, supporting his back with theirs and forming a human tripod. Then, because they had no ammunition, all three shouted, "Buppabuppabup! Buppabuppabup!"[55]

As if in answer, an incoming artillery shell crashed into the earth not far away. Vance remarked that the air-ripping roar and explosion were sounds he hadn't heard for twenty-five years, and *nostalgia* wasn't the word that came to mind.

Vonnegut began to get angry about the ludicrous preparations to meet the enemy. "Artillery fire is the worst way there is to die, Miriam. A round lands behind you, and then one in front, and then the next is behind again but closer. And a closer one in front. And there's this horrible, crushing noise rolling towards you, from both sides, closer and closer and building up, and there's nowhere to go, and you panic, and you can't contain your bowels or your bladder and you die in a state of awful, abject, craven, miserable fear in your own mess."[56]

At that moment, a shell landed about a quarter mile to the left and then a second one to the right. The methodical bracketing that would smash the camp in a vise was tightening on them. Vonnegut said nothing. Instead, he lit a fresh Pall Mall off the one he'd just finished. Tossing the butt on the ground, he crushed it with his heel thoughtfully.

"Okay, Miriam," he said. "You get over in the air-raid bunker, okay? Vance and I are going up on the roof and we're going to go, 'Buppabuppabup. Buppabuppabup.'"[57]

WHEN BIAFRA fell to Nigeria ten days later, they were among the last foreigners to reach the airport in time, driven pell-mell in a beat-up Mercedes. In the backseat, stretched out atop their baggage, an eight-year-old boy with nowhere to go lay sleeping.

Vonnegut wrote about his experiences for *McCall's* magazine and appeared on the Dick Cavett television show to describe what he witnessed, but there was practically nothing adequate he could say about the death of two million Biafrans by starvation, three-quarters of them small children.[58]

One night at home, at two in the morning, he sat up in bed and began sobbing in deep, dry gasps. It was utterly dark, and he said the sound from his throat was like a dog barking.[59]

IN FEBRUARY 1970, Kurt received a letter from Knox saying he had made up his mind to go solo as a literary agent. Vonnegut replied that he was behind him all the way and cheered him on. It was a million-dollar idea, he said, bound to succeed, and they would do business just as soon as Knox was ready.[60]

Because Vonnegut would be the cornerstone of the agency, Knox typed a list of his future client's "present involvements." There was the novel Kurt was writing, *Breakfast of Champions*, still in drafts, and another one he owed under the Littauer & Wilkinson contract with Seymour Lawrence–Delacorte. There were four novels in print, all with fresh covers in Delacorte paperback editions. Film companies had optioned *Player Piano*, *The Sirens of Titan*, *Mother Night*, *God Bless You, Mr. Rosewater*, and *Slaughterhouse-Five* for anywhere between $5,000 and $15,000 apiece. CBS had advanced $5,000 for an anthology of short stories scripted for television. And as of February 1970, *Slaughterhouse-Five* had sold fifty thousand copies in hardback.[61] Studying his rough balance sheet, and factoring in commitments from a few other authors, Knox was convinced he could make the leap from editor to agent. And so in April 1970, Knox established in partnership with his wife, the writer and sculptor Kitty Sprague, Knox Burger Associates, Ltd., in the basement of their apartment building at 39½ Washington Square South.[62]

And then Vonnegut backed out entirely.

HIS REASON, he said, was that on second thought he just couldn't hurt his longtime friend Max Wilkinson. Max's wife, Mary, was seriously ill, and the colorful old gentleman to whom everyone was "my dear" wasn't doing such a bad job, really; he was just getting up in years. Until Littauer & Wilkinson closed down or Max retired, Kurt couldn't leave until he could say goodbye with a handshake instead of a shot in the groin. But he hinted that Dan Wakefield might be in the mood to jump from his agent, as if to soften the blow.[63]

Knox was floored. Kitty was furious, but Knox composed a careful response that he hoped wouldn't ruin all possibility of Vonnegut ever coming in with him. "I suppose I should have known all along that you couldn't leave, though I wish you hadn't told me you would. The more you said you were, the more I doubted it. You want to be friends to all your friends, which is the height of nobility. It does get harder, though, as one's status grows. The fact is, though, I can stand a kick in the balls better than Max, which of course you recognize. . . . Remember, old friend, next time you get a little loaded or browned off at Max and ask me to represent you, I'll take you up on it."[64]

The dignity of the response (and perhaps Knox's reminder that Kurt had more than one "old friend") shamed Vonnegut into reversing himself. In a stiff reply, he informed Knox that he had thanked Max for his help through the years, but that from now on he wished to be represented by Knox Burger Associates, Ltd. Then he added a postscript denying he had hit him below the belt.[65]

Knox was delighted and relieved. But he wanted it understood that he hadn't meant to push Kurt into dropping Max precipitously. In any case, now they could work together, all was forgiven, and Burger adopted the tone of a go-getter agent on the prowl for his client. First, there was a scriptwriting opportunity for Kurt—Knox recommended asking for $50,000. Also a radio station in New York City requested permission to read "Harrison Bergeron" on the air: what were Kurt's wishes? And someone was interested in film rights to *Cat's Cradle*. They should move on that as soon as possible.[66]

At last, they were in business, and there was plenty to be done.

IN FACT, Kurt was already at work on a fresh project, a play, and making deals on the side.

In May, a month after Knox Burger Associates opened shop, he had been invited to dinner at the Long Island home of Donald C. Farber, a theatrical agent. Also at the table was Lester M. Goldsmith, a former vice president of Paramount who, just days earlier, had formed his own production company.[67] Goldsmith asked Kurt whether he'd ever written for the stage. Kurt replied jokingly that he had tossed the script for *Penelope*, performed locally on Cape Cod, into an empty beer carton in West Barnstable along with two other plays and forgot all about his theatrical aspirations.[68]

Before the evening was over, Goldsmith had optioned *Penelope* with Farber working out the terms.[69] Kurt would be chairman of a new production company created expressly for the play: Sourdough, Ltd. Vonnegut was dazzled and so excited about his suddenly resuscitated dramatic career that a few days later he sent Farber notes about his contract for *God Bless You, Mr. Rosewater*, thinking it might be suitable for the stage, too.[70]

Feverishly during the summer of 1970, he revised *Penelope*, renaming it *Happy Birthday, Wanda June*, and in August a call went out for auditions. The actor Kevin McCarthy landed the male lead, reading for the part in Farber's home with Kurt looking on.[71] Goldsmith reserved the Theatre de Lys on Christopher Street in Greenwich Village, by coincidence a few blocks from Knox Burger Associates, Ltd. In the meantime, Farber convinced Vonnegut that authors of his caliber needed professional representation on the speaking circuit and arranged for his engagements to be handled by Richard Fulton, Inc.[72] Fulton replied to Farber's request, "I shall be indeed delighted and honored to represent Mr. Kurt Vonnegut, Jr. for lecture and speaking engagements."[73]

When Knox finally learned of all the commotion swirling around his client, he was confused and looked to Kurt for instructions. He hadn't heard from Kurt for weeks. "I keep getting reprint and anthology enquiries. . . . And calls about film rights . . . should I tell them the rights are sold, or to get in touch with Farber, or what? . . . I really have no ground rules as to what to say."[74]

Who was Don Farber?

FARBER, AT forty-seven, was a year younger than Burger and Vonnegut. Raised in a family of three boys in Columbus, Nebraska, he had been an infantry sergeant during World War II. Afterward, like many veterans of his generation, he quickstepped back into civilian life, marrying Ann Eis in 1947. A year later, he received an undergraduate degree from the University of Nebraska, then ran as a Democratic delegate to the state convention for the 1948 national primary. In 1950, he completed law school.

Careful and rather diffident, he was drawn by polar forces to the excitement of theater and its personalities. When he discovered off-Broadway theater had few business or legal practices associated with it, he and Ann moved to New York. At first he commuted to Toronto to teach entertainment law, a specialty in the early 1950s, at York University. On his own, he created contracts for performers and production companies, while generating business as an agent in a niche market. One summer day in 1959, for example, he squired a flamboyant investor wearing a white suit and panama hat to a rehearsal on Sullivan Street in Greenwich Village. The visit was unannounced and the director disliked the intrusion, but the partnership that resulted led to *The Fantasticks*, the longest-running musical play in American theater history.[75]

Don was good at that sort of thing, and it was not by accident that Vonnegut happened to dine at his home with Goldsmith, who was hunting for hot properties to add to his new production company. By the time Knox realized his friend and client Kurt had "jumped off to a short lawyer," it was already too late.[76] In September, Kurt put Farber in charge of managing his future projects; Max Wilkinson would be left with a healthy backlist of Vonnegut novels as a continuing revenue stream. And as for Knox, he would just have to take it on his prominent chin.

Kitty never forgave her husband's "old buddy" for that.[77] Knox, however, didn't have the heart to drop Vonnegut despite what he had done.

LOOKING BACK on those months, Kurt realized that the autumn of 1970 was a time of "goodbye and goodbye and goodbye."[78]

Some of it was inevitable, the result of years passing and five of his six children becoming young adults. Mark, for example, after graduating from Swarthmore in 1969, had considered becoming a Unitarian minister until he decided he was too inexperienced to advise people about spiritual matters.[79] Eligible for the draft and possibly combat in Vietnam, he filed an application as a conscientious objector, including with it a letter of support written by his father. But it was denied, and he had been ordered to report for an Armed Services physical examination. When his official classification arrived in the mail, the draft board had designated him IV-F—ineligible for duty on the grounds of mental instability because he had pulled off, in his words, an "uncanny schizophrenic act."[80] Now he was in Vancouver, British Columbia, "reading the newspapers, smoking a fair amount of dope, doing odds and ends and occasionally driving around the country saying 'Ooh, ah, isn't that nice land.'"[81] His parents had given him a substantial amount of money for a down payment, and he envisioned living à la Walden Pond, hassle-free.[82]

Jim Adams was in Jamaica, operating a combination goat-and-dope farm; Edie lived there too in the seaside town of Lucea, camped out with a "charismatic drummer svengali bum" on the second floor of a rotting mansion with a tree growing through it.[83] Tiger piloted commercial aircraft for an airline in New England; his brother Steve taught English at Barnstable High School. Nanny was the only one left at home, living through the end of her parents' marriage, "witnessing the dregs of it."[84]

It was true: the terminus of Kurt and Jane's twenty-five-year marriage was approaching, as he later wrote, like a "terrible, unavoidable accident that we were ill-equipped to understand."[85] There were the obvious signs of unhappiness: their quarrels, Kurt's drinking and infidelities, his resentment of Jane's do-it-yourself religion. He would have been content if she were just a nominal Christian, preferably a Unitarian, but she was constantly drawn to new panaceas—astrology, astral projection, meditation, and Erhard Seminars Training (EST)—as if they were magic, healing ointments.[86] Most of them were just quack remedies, he insisted, which wouldn't have long-term, positive effects on her life. In fact, ever since the Kent State shootings in the spring of 1970, she had become *more* anxious, not less. "Now they're shooting our children . . . ," she wrote to Maria Donoso. "It could perfectly well have been Edie or Nanny or Tiger, or, or, or . . . Everyone is frantic and no one knows what to do. . . . Our President, everybody is realizing *really* this time, is insane. . . . Have to do survival type things now."[87] She thought their phone was tapped.[88]

And yet, hurrying to the next roadside shrine, the next emotional vortex, the next distraction had always been the pattern of her life. She had dropped out of graduate school at the University of Chicago when she became pregnant with Mark, and didn't reenroll, even though she had a fellowship; in Alplaus, she volunteered nights at the Ellis Hospital psychopathic ward in Schenectady, despite having two toddlers at home, Mark and Edie; she didn't say no when Kurt wanted to throw over a solid, middle-class job with General Electric, putting them all at financial risk; she waved the Adams boys into her home with nary a doubt that it would work, not wanting to think about the ramifications on her family or marriage; nor did having six children prevent her from taking lead roles with the Barnstable Comedy Club; later, when Kurt went to Iowa, she joined him there for the excitement, not because she wanted to complete a degree, leaving the house in the hands of college-age youngsters who trashed it; and as her marriage began running aground, damaged by Kurt's affair with Loree, she again found something else to do outside the home: she opened up the only campaign headquarters for Eugene McCarthy on Cape Cod.

Friends called her sweet, energetic, and youthful, but Kurt's take on her behavior was different. In the end, he came to believe something else was at work: a truth that was finally surfacing and couldn't be hidden beneath all the noise and pandemonium: she didn't love him, she had never loved him, he became convinced.[89] He was her second choice after Kendall Landis. He had always been the fallback suitor, plan B, who had to court her over and over until he finally wore her down. Jane Cox, the sweetheart of his youth, had been, he finally decided, a "good wife, a good friend, but not a romantic partner."[90] And the busyness, the fads, and the chaos over the years had been her way of not facing that terrible fact.

In the fall of 1970, he rented a place in Manhattan, a penthouse on Christopher Street in Greenwich Village belonging to a friend on Cape Cod. He needed to be in the city when *Happy Birthday, Wanda June* went into rehearsals. Writing to Bernard years later, he explained that he couldn't abide living in a house that rotated around what the children were up to, either. He wanted his work to be given right of way.[91] Harvard had offered him a position teaching creative writing too, which would entail a longer drive between New York and Boston two days a week than between Cape Cod and Boston, but how badly he wanted to teach at Harvard outweighed the inconvenience. There was a problem, however: the English Department required him to have a college degree, which, after almost twenty-five years, he still didn't have.

The University of Chicago was his best hope. His first thesis proposal had been turned down; the second one had been accepted—he didn't complete it; the third, fully written at Iowa, was turned down, as well. Yet he still might be remembered in the Anthropology Department, despite taking three swings for three strikes, especially in light of his sudden fame as an author and social critic. So he wrote to the department chair, Bernard S. Cohn, asking whether in lieu of a thesis one of his novels could be considered as fulfilling the requirements for a master's degree.

The request was put on the agenda at a faculty meeting, and a committee was appointed to read all of his published works, since most of the anthropology faculty were unfamiliar with them. The committee, on the basis of the imaginary island culture, religion, and customs in *Cat's Cradle*, recommended that the novel be accepted as commensurate with a thesis, and Vonnegut received his degree at last, just in time to accept Harvard's offer. To the Anthropology Department's chagrin, said Professor Emeritus George Stocking, Vonnegut later "skimmed over the fact that he had actually asked for the degree specifically so that he could become a certified teacher."[92] Among his fans, and scholars too, eventually it was taken as fact that Chicago had caved in to pressure and embarrassment at having refused to accept a thesis from Vonnegut. So much for the time and trouble the faculty took to read and evaluate his works. The escapade came to be referred to derisively in the department as the "Vonnegut affair."[93]

TWO HUNDRED and fifteen students submitted sample manuscripts for seats in the Harvard seminar; seven were full-length novels. Kurt spent one weekend "wading hysterically" through them, coming up with fifteen he liked. The rest "ranged from mediocre to worse."[94] Among the fifteen students chosen was the managing editor of the *Harvard Crim-*

son, a Nieman Fellow from *Newsday*, and a journalist who had written a chapter of the pornographic hoax *Naked Came the Stranger*. The best writer, in Vonnegut's opinion, was a South Korean chemistry major.[95]

It was hard for him to muster the energy to teach. At first, he came across as lemony and abrupt. He startled the students by saying creative writing classes were a terrible idea. He really didn't believe anyone could teach a person how to write if the ability wasn't there to begin with. Anyway, most creative writing courses he'd seen did more harm than good, because people tore into one another's best efforts in the meanest ways.[96] His role would be not telling them what he wanted them to be but "what they must become."[97]

Once he was through being defensive and crabby, he fell into a more pleasant mood and waxed about Shortridge High School, his experiences at General Electric, and his trials as a beginning writer. If he had learned anything that had carried over into his writing, it was that "people are not wholly bad. People are not wholly good, either. Try not to create characters in terms that are absolute—real people aren't like that."[98] His advice about plot, paraphrased by a journalist sitting in on the class was, "Life and death occur. There are no forms, there is only accident."[99] He rambled, he smoked, and he seemed preoccupied.

Some students, having run the gauntlet to be admitted to the seminar, were disappointed. "Nothing happens—he doesn't do that much," said one. "This is the first writing class I've had in which we don't sit around and discuss each other's work."[100] Personally, they liked him, though, and nicknamed themselves the "Nuggets," as in "Von*negut*." They thought he was kind, funny, and encouraging.[101]

Before they turned in their first piece to be workshopped, he asked that they not try to imitate him. But because most were too much in awe of him, they aped his style anyway, and having been exposed to metafiction in contemporary literature courses, perhaps too much, they tended to go overboard with weird plot scenarios.[102] One involved a man with broken legs trapped in a manhole; in another, the hero fell through a plate-glass window and the heroine froze to death in a block of ice.[103] There was no humanity, just goofiness in most of what they wrote, and hints of ridicule directed at people's helplessness. When the class ended, he was relieved.[104]

* * *

THE CAST of *Happy Birthday, Wanda June* served as a surrogate family and helped stave off the blues. He attended rehearsals as often as he could. To Dianne Wiest, who was Marsha Mason's understudy in the female lead of Penelope Ryan, he seemed delighted, and bewildered, and amazed by it all.[105] It was "an adventure" and "harrowing," he told Donoso.[106]

The idea for *Penelope*, which became *Happy Birthday, Wanda June*, occurred to him during the Great Books course on Cape Cod in the early 1950s. "We started rereading Homer, and Odysseus the hero coming home from the wars really got to me. The hero-warrior. He seemed so preposterous in modern terms."[107] In Kurt's updating of the epic, the time is 1970 and big game hunter Harold Ryan has returned home to the United States, having been presumed dead for several years. He finds that his wife, Penelope, has relationships with men who are not like him—a doctor and a vacuum cleaner salesman—because she's no longer attracted to fighters and he-men. They were about to mark Ryan's birthday in his absence with a cake that was supposed to have been for a golden-haired girl, Wanda June, who was hit by an ice cream truck before she could celebrate her birthday. From heaven, Wanda June and a Nazi named Siegfried von Konigswald talk to the audience about Harold below and how ably Jesus plays shuffleboard in the hereafter.

During rehearsals, cast members kept seeing a young, quite beautiful woman with black hair photographing Kurt. She was a freelance photojournalist who lately had made a specialty of photographing writers, and *Life* magazine had assigned her to photograph his writing seminar at Harvard for a feature story. When she learned he was also at the Theatre De Lys in New York, she showed up there, too.[108] Wiest didn't know who she was, but her determination to be near Vonnegut gave the young actress the impression that the woman was stalking Kurt and he was running away from her.[109] Jane's friend Lynn Meyer heard how he was being pursued "like a great elephant. There was not a feeling of spontaneity about her—she knew what she wanted."[110]

Finally, Jane came down to New York, ostensibly to drop in on rehearsals, but when she saw the woman, according to Edie, "the hair stood up on her arms—she sensed something about this woman who used the camera like a weapon."[111]

Her name was Jill Krementz. She was thirty years old and born in New York. Her mother, Virginia, a graduate of the Juilliard School of Music, had divorced Jill's father, Radford Bascome, a Broadway photographer of dance and ballet companies, not long after Jill was born, and married Walter M. Krementz, a wealthy jeweler. Eventually Jill became the eldest of four children.

Her upbringing was "very traditional, middle-class," she later said, but she attended exclusive private schools. First, the Peck School in Morristown, New Jersey, for children in kindergarten through eighth grade; then she boarded at the Masters School for girls at Dobbs Ferry, New York, a ninety-six-acre campus on the Hudson River. Her roommate senior year at the Masters School, Gay Talmey, remembered Jill as "dressed beautifully" with "beautiful skin and stellar eyes." She was "more mature than the rest of us—light-years ahead of where we were."[112]

Although the two girls shared the room, they weren't friends. "She would look at me like I was a piece of excrement. Her family was in the jewelry business. She knew a lot about nice jewelry." Their dormitory was First House, ironically not the one with the most status, but that didn't seem to concern Jill, who "believed she was a cut above the rest of us in intellect and looks and she couldn't be bothered with the great popularity chase."[113]

Her ambitions outstripped what most of the girls at the Masters School were thinking about. One day, walking in New York with her brother Tony after attending a theater performance, she said suddenly to him, "I so much want to be a part of this world."[114]

SHE ENROLLED at Drew University but left after a year to work as a secretary at *Harper's Bazaar*. In 1961, she accompanied a friend on a long ship voyage, snapping pictures with her first camera, a Kodak Brownie. Returning to the United States, she found a new job with *Show* magazine as a film and theater reporter.[115]

For her twenty-first birthday, she received a Nikon camera purchased in Japan, but the instructions were in Japanese. She took it to the art editor of *Show* magazine, who shook his head. "This is like having a Rolls Royce and not knowing how to drive."[116] He demonstrated how to load the camera and adjust the rings for exposure, depth of field, and so on. She brought him contact sheets from her rolls of film for his opinion.

On November 22, 1963—the day President John F. Kennedy was assassinated—Krementz roamed Manhattan photographing people's reactions. Some of her colleagues thought she was being callous because people were openly weeping in the street, but in an era when women journalists were consigned to the food and fashion sections of newspapers and magazines, she wasn't going to miss the opportunity to record a historic event.

When *Show* magazine folded in 1964, she joined the *Herald Tribune*, making her the newspaper's first woman photographer and, at twenty-four, its youngest as well. She covered race riots in Harlem, Malcolm X's funeral, the murder of the freedom fighters in Mississippi, Andy Warhol's parties, Churchill's funeral, and the Beatles at Shea Stadium; she also took portraits of such up-and-coming writers as Jimmy Breslin, Gail Sheehy, and Tom Wolfe.[117] Later, when Kurt's friend from Iowa Vance Bourjaily got to know Jill, he admired how she didn't depend on her striking looks to get the shot she wanted. "She used sharp elbows, same as any other good photojournalist."[118] A competitor, Bernard Gotfryd, remembered Krementz pushing her way to the front of an event, a petite woman loaded with heavy photographic gear, going mano a mano with her male counterparts to capture her subject.[119]

At a dinner party she met Henri Cartier-Bresson, the French photographer considered to be the originator of modern photojournalism. He suggested to her that the war in Vietnam was one of the most compelling photo stories of the day.[120] Traveling to Saigon, she checked into the Caravelle Hotel, the headquarters of journalists covering the war such as David Halberstam, Neil Sheehan, Morley Safer, and Peter Arnett.[121] Her specialty became what she called "peripheral" photography. Most news photographers concentrated on dramatic combat pictures, but she visited military camps, hospitals, and orphanages instead, examining the lives of soldiers and civilians. After a year in Vietnam, she published her first book, *The Face of South Vietnam*.[122]

Accustomed as she was to getting what she was after, she intended to capture Kurt, the famous writer, in his habitat, with her camera, even once following him into the men's bathroom.[123]

WANDA JUNE opened the first week of October 1970. Before the show, Vance Bourjaily, who happened to be in town, made reservations for dinner at one of Kurt's favorite restaurants, the 21 Club on West Fifty-second Street, to celebrate. Another reason to raise glasses high was that Sam Lawrence had succeeded in bringing out all six of Kurt's novels as a uniform body of work from Delacorte. While Bourjaily waited for Vonnegut to arrive, the maître d' asked, "Oh, you mean the gentleman with the hush puppies?"[124] But tonight the novelist-turned-playwright entered wearing a dark suit and a small pink rose in his lapel.

Arriving at the theater later, he was drunk, and he continued drinking right through the performance in a balcony where he could watch without being seen.[125] Below, sitting together like a tableau representing an earlier period of his life, were Jane, Edie, and Nanny. Trying to square things with Knox and Kitty, he had sent them a pair of tickets, too. At the cast party afterward, he stood with his back against a wall for support while leaning tipsily forward to smell the little pink rose in his lapel.[126]

Critics couldn't agree on what to make of the play. *Newsweek*'s Jack Kroll opined that American novelists tended to be better than "most of our thumb-tongued playwrights. . . . Vonnegut's dialogue is not only fast and funny, with a palpable taste and crackle, but it also means something." Stanley Kauffmann, on the other hand, writing in the *New Republic,* called it "a disaster, full of callow wit, rheumatic invention, and dormitory profundity." John Simon accused the playwright of "pandering to youth."[127]

Vonnegut took offense that he didn't have the wit to be funny around cosmopolitans. "The only theater we have is in New York, and it is a form of church with a fixed congregation. . . . If someone from Indianapolis is trying to put on Indianapolis jokes in New York, it doesn't work. My play *Happy Birthday, Wanda June* had Indianapolis jokes."[128] Privately, though, he thought the play was awkward and juvenile.[129]

WHILE *HAPPY Birthday, Wanda June* continued to run through the winter until March 1971 (it moved to the Edison Theatre after its first month), Kurt lived in the city, frequenting Sardi's, a famous haunt of show business celebrities in the theater district, and drinking in the taste of fame. Jill was on his arm quite a bit now, which shocked not only Jane but her friends too.[130] Some dismissed Krementz as another fling, like Loree in Iowa, but the humiliation was so public, said Carolyn Blakemore, Littauer & Wilkinson's former secretary, that it was painful to hear about.[131] "Jane had a lot of spine," said Marcia Gauger, her former roommate at Swarthmore.[132] Mrs. Vonnegut wished Loree would rescue her husband; she would even be willing to give up Kurt to her, a strange solution coming from a wife of twenty-five years.[133] But Loree was married and it was too late.

Midway through the play's run, Jill found Kurt a one-bedroom apartment at 349 East Fifty-fourth Street in Midtown, a few blocks from her walk-up on Second Avenue.[134] It had a small, enclosed garden in the back, and he could order meals from a stylish restaurant next door. One of his delights was taking a seat at the table on the patio at dinnertime. Then a liveried waiter would come through the back gate, spread a white cloth, napkin, place setting, and wineglass before him, and finally a silver serving dish. He felt like a millionaire.[135]

Jill was also a frequenter of parties attended by people in the arts and gave Kurt entrée to a society he had never known before. One of his former students from Iowa, Barry Jay Kaplan, observed the ascendance of Kurt Vonnegut, erstwhile writer of drugstore paperbacks, into the glitterati. "It was as if Kurt was just this sort of rube from the sticks and she was this smart city girl who was taking him in hand. Which, in a certain way, was what happened. I guess the worst thing you could say about Kurt was that he wanted to be a famous New York City writer and she helped him. And he did need help."[136]

Her influence, she told Kaplan, was simple: "I taught Kurt to play tennis and to make love."[137]

KURT WAS attracted to Jill for a number of reasons, not the least of which was her beauty, of course. But he was also amazed by her toughness.[138]

Jane, collapsing under a bombardment of Kurt's criticisms and rages, would barricade herself in the laundry room and then emerge wearing sunglasses as a sign of surrender. But Jill blunted his assaults completely. One way was to act strangely impervious to what he said. Words were sacred ammunition to him, but to her they were just that— words. "You can't hurt her!" Vonnegut told Bourjaily.[139] And he was intrigued by how she didn't need him. She was a master in her own field of photojournalism with a career stretching ahead more promising than his had been at her age. At thirty-one, he had been writing over a gas station in Alplaus, New York. Marrying him, she said, wasn't a goal, either; she had no plans for it, and she never wanted to have children (to his relief).[140] She would be ambitious for him, she would goad him, she would be his enthusiastic partner in bed, but he must be a man in his own right as she would be a woman in hers. Her intensity charmed him; there was nothing ironic in her.

AND THEN, like the embodiment of the family's collapse, Mark arrived unexpectedly in New York the month after *Wanda June* premiered, and he was clearly falling apart. He suffered uncontrollable, shame-faced bouts of crying like a little boy, even though he was twenty-two. He felt transparent, defenseless against fits of fear that seized him—usually dire intimations that something "twisted and evil" was going to happen to his father.[141]

His dream of starting a commune had been realized when he purchased a two-hundred-acre farm near the Powell River in British Columbia. It was reachable only by boat—twelve miles downriver from the end of Highway 101—and then another mile and a half on foot. He spent the days, shirtless in the sun, swinging mallets and axes, repairing the old house, chopping firewood, and planting a garden, not worrying that his "efforts were somehow subsidizing death and destruction."[142] But he had come back, primarily for a traffic court date, but also to check on his father.

Growing up, Mark had worried his father might leave by drinking himself to death or blowing his brains out. "He had hinted at it fairly broadly from time to time. Sometimes I thought the only thing holding him back was fear of how it would affect me."[143] Kurt had been in those days, after all, a harried small-time writer, a sometime high school teacher, and the owner of a foreign car dealership that failed spectacularly.

Now he was joshing and drinking with famous people—many of whom had never read any of his novels—while Mark, looking on, felt a desire to protect his father but was powerless to save him. "Automobiles careening. Drunks careening, junkies, pollution, misery ad infinitum, all careening."[144]

After a few days of following his father around Manhattan, he left, disappeared, driving across the continent, crossing the United States–Canada border north of Seattle, and sleeping in his worn Volkswagen until the first ferry could take him to Powell River, consoling himself with "I have the farm to go back to. None of this shit matters. Repeat. None of this shit matters."[145]

EDIE, ON the other hand, reacted differently from her siblings to her father's hegira to New York. Once before when he was living alone in Iowa and beginning a love affair, she had gone to live with him. Whether by instinct or because she knew her father would need an extra hand while he tacked in a new direction, she left Jamaica and moved into her father's tiny apartment on East Fifty-fourth Street. She found a job with Capezio Shoes as a designer and set up her drawing board in his living room.

Of the three Vonnegut children, she was the most in tune with him. "I got a little of Kurt in me. So I liked to punch up against him. I would know how to be with him, because I think I have a kernel of meanness in me, and my mother didn't."[146] When he was ready to take a break from writing, they would go for a walk together. "It may have been the most undemanding relationship either of us ever had."[147] He enjoyed the differences between how the women in his family treated him, and he encouraged rivalry by comparing one against the other. The payoff for him was holding their attention by making them vie for his approval. The sisters had been aware of the contest since they were small, but now, with their father separated from them, the competition became more earnest. Nanny learned that she was not welcome in New York where Jill was because "whenever he was around me, I was insecure, needy, apt to cry. He didn't like it, he hated that because it made him feel guilty."[148] The stakes were Dad's way or no way.

"This is getting very King Leary," Edie said to her.[149]

DESPITE THE quiet in his apartment, however, and Edie's salutary presence, he couldn't get anywhere on *Breakfast of Champions*. Many of the pages had been discarded from the manuscript of *Slaughterhouse-Five*, and he was trying to salvage them. Even so, Vonnegut thought his new novel was so asinine it embarrassed him.[150]

The problem was, as 1971 began, there was no reason to write well.

Creatively, he felt like "an animal in a wicker cage." He could put his name on practically anything and sell it. "For so long money motivated me and now there is nothing to move me off center. I don't know what to do."[151] Nor did he have the energy or patience to find out. With the exception of *The Sirens of Titan*, a novel took him years to write, and even then he made many false starts before he realized what it was about.[152] He was thinking that perhaps after *Wanda June* had finished its run, he should turn his hand exclusively to playwriting and forget about prose fiction.[153]

There was also his cryonic marriage worrying him. He and Jane were frozen as partners; nothing important had changed, despite the recurring flashes of pain. They hadn't discussed divorce, and Jane, unsure of what was happening, carried on as Kurt's wife, secretary, and general factotum. When Don Farber requested bank deposit slips, she replied cheerily, "So here are more than you will probably need, for a while, anyway. I wonder what we plan to do with the money? Crossing my fingers for *W. J.* these days—It's such a puzzle!"[154] When the professor of literature Jerome Klinkowitz inquired whether there was a bibliography of Vonnegut's work available, she went to the local library and compiled one herself, apologizing for the delay. "My husband is away, and things have piled up beyond my power to cope with them adequately."[155] With the money coming into their joint bank account, she fixed up the house and purchased new furniture. As far as Tiger Adams's best friend, Caleb Warren, could tell, "She was still the same person—the best person."[156]

It was hard for Kurt to know what to do in the face of her behavior. Her dignity had the effect, in the biblical phrase, of pouring coals of fire on his head.

11: Cultural Bureaucrat

1971–1974

IN FEBRUARY 1971, Mark Vonnegut went without food and water for twelve days at his farm on Powell River in British Columbia, after months of living on lentil stews and vegetables. The farm had turned into a commune, and he had become its mystic, staring into a candle flame—once for twelve hours—and starving himself, as the sweet odor of marijuana hung about the farmhouse like incense. With him was a chessboard formerly belonging to his grandfather Vonnegut, hand-made, on which the following lines were carved in Gothic lettering: "I do warn you well / It is no child's play." The admonition had great meaning to him now, as many things did, revealing to him from an invisible source that his girlfriend had died, his father had committed suicide, and the world was going to be rocked by natural cataclysms. At the end of a run of sleepless, manic nights, he collapsed, and friends put him in the bottom of a boat to ferry him to someplace safer.[1]

His father arrived looking "very worried, very nervous," and so out of place in a crummy apartment in Vancouver.[2] Mark's friends were standing watch over him in the apartment because earlier he had run outside naked and sprinted around the block. Trying to make sense of his father being there, Mark was bewildered at seeing him in the role of rescuer. "I could not relate to him as a physical presence. I wasn't really sure it was him."[3]

Kurt had come three thousand miles because one of his son's "flower children friends," he later said, "telephoned me to say he was in need of a father."[4] He helped Mark downstairs and into a hired car. They drove east to the town of New Westminster on the Fraser River where there was a mental health facility with the unlikely name of Hollywood Hospital.[5] Later, trying to portray his boy as a creative soul having some kind of apocalyptic experience, Kurt insisted that as they headed toward the "Canadian laughing academy," Mark was singing "vocal riffs worthy of his hero John Coltrane."[6]

The car reached Hollywood Hospital, and Mark stumbled into the lobby with Kurt holding him up. While they waited, Mark grabbed the cue ball from a pool table in the lobby and flung it through a window. He played with the ashes in a cigarette tray and when a male nurse arrived he drew streaks on the man's white lab coat. Following an intake interview, Kurt signed papers to have his son committed.[7]

A few days later, the phone rang at Walter Vonnegut's home in Anacortes, Washington. It was Kurt, his cousin from Lake Maxinkuckee days, apparently drunk, on the other end. He wanted to talk about Mark's hospitalization, and the purpose of the call, as far as Walt could surmise, was just to "get it off his chest."[8]

In the seclusion room where Mark was placed, there was a hole in the door large enough for a man to put his hand through. Kurt visited the hospital daily for a week and tried to talk to him through the portal, but Mark, weak from sedatives and underweight, kept falling asleep. Finally, needing to get down to Los Angeles—"the real Hollywood," as Mark put it—where filming of *Slaughterhouse-Five* was starting, Vonnegut pushed a rolled-up copy of Bruno Bettelheim's *Children of the Dream* through the portal.[9] He promised he would be back soon.

It was an oddly intellectual response to a dire emotional crisis. Bettelheim's book, a study of an Israeli kibbutz in the summer of 1964, concluded that children living there were altruistic, dedicated to the community, and to each other, but at the cost of their personality becoming flattened through loss of intimacy and individuality. Bettelheim's views dovetailed roughly with Vonnegut's opinion of communes. "For a community really to work," Vonnegut believed, "you shouldn't have to wonder what the person next to you is thinking. That is a primitive society. In the communities of strangers that are being hammered together now, as young people take over farms and try to live communally, the founders are sure to have hellish differences."[10]

But Mark was in no frame of mind to read about anthropology right now; he was too full of Thorazine to care.[11]

KURT HAD an office at Columbia Pictures for Sourdough, Ltd., the production company originally created for *Happy Birthday, Wanda June*, which was now a partner in the filming of *Slaughterhouse-Five*. The phone at Hollywood Hospital was usually busy and patients were not allowed to call out, but Kurt relayed updates to Jane to reassure her that Mark was doing better.

When he could, he visited the set of *Slaughterhouse-Five*. The film's director, George Roy Hill, cast him in a small part playing Professor Bertram Copeland Rumfoord, lying in a hospital bed next to Billy Pilgrim. Costumed in pajamas, a bathrobe, and a bald cap with gray tufts of hair at the temples, "Kurt was wonderful in the part—funny, acerbic, outrageous—all I could have asked for and more," Hill said. After the scene wrapped, Vonnegut flew back to Vancouver to check on Mark.

But while he was away, Hill saw the rushes and realized that Michael Sacks, the actor playing Billy Pilgrim, "looked terrible" in his makeup as a hospitalized middle-aged man. The scene would have to be reshot. He tried reaching Kurt, he said, but the shooting schedule demanded he cast another actor in the role of the bedridden Rumfoord. Later, he assured Kurt that the switch had nothing to do with his acting, but Hill was surprised when Vonnegut "fixed me with a cold eye and said, 'I understand—I just wish you wouldn't lie about it.'"[12]

MARK WAS released from Hollywood Hospital in March, but not before suffering a relapse and undergoing shock therapy.[13] Jane flew out twice to comfort him. He was still determined to return to the farm in the wilderness, however, and stopped by the post office on the edge of the Powell River to pick up his mail on his way back. There was a package waiting for him from his father, inside of which was a poster. Mark studied the "spaced-out, apocalyptic, mystic, back-to-the-earth quote. I don't remember that much of it or who said it. 'What we are doing is real . . . If we have to go to the headwaters of the Amazon to establish the enclaves of civilization . . . return to Caesar's grave . . . Not everyone should go ... artisans.'" Mark was puzzled, then crestfallen, wondering why his father didn't say something about the farm or about his breakdown. "But there was no enclosed letter or explanation of any sort, just the goddamned poster."[14]

The gesture of the poster was another indication of the split between the public and private Vonnegut. He could be "inspirational," said Caleb Warren; "he was a demigod, particularly when he got famous, and here was this clever, wise, witty person who could speak in front of an audience and be one of the most lovable people you could feel close to. But on an interpersonal level with those closest to him, it was a lot different."[15]

As far as Kurt was concerned, the episode involving his son's hospitalization was over. Mark's therapist hadn't been interested in who his father was, and Vonnegut was relieved to learn that family issues hadn't come up, either. "Ethically his cure took me off the hook."[16] To friends, Kurt explained that his son's crack-up was a "result of the Zeitgeist of the commune. People who went in for deeply dramatic behavior were admired by their peers."[17]

Settling back into his office at Sourdough, Ltd., he let Jane know he was aware of how he seemed to his family, but in Hollywood he would be indistinguishable from all the other bastards.[18]

ONE SPRING evening in 1971 not long after Mark returned to the commune, Edie attended a party at Elaine's restaurant given by George Plimpton and was introduced to Geraldo Rivera, then a twenty-eight-year-old television reporter. Hours later, they carried her belongings into his apartment on Avenue C in the East Village. "That's the way things moved in those days," Rivera said.[19] Kurt was unfazed by how precipitously his daughter exited, because he had told her she shouldn't be living with her father.[20] The couple had found an agent and dreamed of becoming movie stars.[21]

Despite being separated, Kurt and Jane continued to exchange news about the children—all of them, Vonneguts and Adamses—which didn't strike him as inconsistent.[22] He also still relied on her for advice about his writing, hoping that they might continue their partnership. He sent her a script, adapted from one of his short stories for amateur theater, and asked her to review it, improving it as she saw fit.[23] He confided in her too, long before he told anyone else, that he was going to resign from Sourdough, Ltd., because being a producer was not his métier. But the film version of *Slaughterhouse-Five* was better than anything he dared hope for.[24]

KURT HAD been away from West Barnstable for ten months and showed no inclination even to visit. One of his former neighbors, Betty Mitchell, had the impression that he was not welcome there.[25] But when Bernard's wife, Lois, died in May 1971, he joined the rest of the family at the graveside.

Lois had never been strong, and her constitution was undercut by decades of smoking two packs of Salem cigarettes a day.[26] In her final years, her family had grown accustomed to seeing her resting on the couch, coughing spasmodically from the effects of emphysema. She left behind five children: Peter, twenty-five; twins Terry and Scott, twenty; Kurt, eleven; and Alex, nine. The two youngest were still at home, and Bernard would have to juggle his responsibilities as a professor of atmospheric science at the University at Albany with raising two boys who were in elementary school. Kurt's side of the family doubted whether he was capable of handling both. Even teenage Nanny could see that her uncle "had his head in the clouds most of the time, literally."[27]

Bernard was exceedingly polite and droll, but highly cerebral: "Always generous and amiable, although somewhat absent-minded, no matter what was going on in the human sphere," Kurt said.[28] Exacting when it came to testing and quantifying the rules of nature, he preferred living the unexamined life, believing prosaically that, if left alone, "everything will turn out all right in the end."[29] While he chased tornadoes, lightning, and wind, trying to put genies from the sky into bottles, people would just have to take care of themselves. Relatives, looking on, understood that his two youngest boys, now that their mother was gone, would need all of his attention. But Bernard just wasn't grounded that way.

Another death in the family from cancer, like Alice's, and children deprived of parenting again, like the Adams boys. The funeral service was a reminder of all Kurt and Jane had endured as husband, wife, parents, uncle, and aunt. Kurt asked if his wife would consider being his date at an event two weeks away. The American Academy of Arts and

Letters had asked him to deliver the prestigious Blashfield Address at the academy's annual ceremony of new inductees—quite an honor. She accepted.

The Blashfield Address had a tradition of being a brainy affair. The year before, the novelist Muriel Spark had taken as her theme "The Desegregation of Art." Her point had been that "socially-conscious art" depicting suffering and victimization lulls viewers and readers into thinking they have fulfilled their moral duty by feeling pity alone.[30] For an audience of leaders in the arts, it had been a challenging and thought-provoking speech.

As Vonnegut waited on the stage seated between an elderly architect and the president of the academy, the statesman George F. Kennan, he felt "seasick with dread." To wash out in front of these people would be an unparalleled embarrassment. Thinking the architect beside him might have something heartening to say, Kurt confided that he was frightened. The gentleman said Kennan had read the speech and "detested" it. Kennan, overhearing, said that was so, "but don't worry about it."[31]

His heart in his throat, Vonnegut launched into "The Happiest Day in the Life of My Father," a string of anecdotal reminiscences of his father, then his grandfather Bernard Vonnegut, then his days studying under Robert Redfield at the University of Chicago, the nature of folk societies—a grab bag of observations, livened with asides about homo-sexuals, urinalysis, a wet dream, orgasms, and Billy Graham. His audience didn't know what to make of most of it. But it didn't matter to Jane; she beamed through the entire speech. To her it was a "happy and proud, welcoming delight of a day."[32]

They had dinner and afterward Jane checked into what had been their favorite hotel, the intimate, sixteen-floor Royalton, built in 1898 on West Forty-fourth Street, where Billy Pilgrim stays before going on television to "tell the world about the lessons of Tralfamadore."[33] From beginning to end, Kurt had planned the date around overtones of their long marriage, hitting notes of what had been best in their lives together.

Early the next morning, she went to the desk in the room and rapidly wrote an eight-page letter on hotel stationery. "I took courage in that and hope," she began, "knowing all along that I was taking enormous risks in being so candid about my profound dislike and distrust of Jill. . . . If she makes you happy, really happy, you should live with her. What I want in that case is for you to conduct the relationship in such a way as to spare me and the children as much humiliation, both public and private, as possible."[34]

Jill "will find ways to cut you off from your home," she warned, "your friends, and your own conscience—by working on your guilt and your fear (we all have them) and shame. . . . Of course you need relief from responsibilities and obligations. . . . And of course that's what girls like Jill are for, in the lives of men like you."[35] Perhaps the time had come to consider a separation agreement because neither of them wanted a divorce and "neither of us wants to remarry. Anyway, you told me you didn't." It should be a last resort, though, because "your children love you and need you, and in this whacked-out, insane way, so do I. . . . I don't want to be the one you see at funerals and hospitals, the one who stands discreetly back while she basks and slurps (there's a Fame river, too, as well as a Money river) when there is love and honor and glory and fun and excitement involved."[36]

She kept the letter to think it over, and the following day she added three postscripts: "Please don't come back to the Cape if it's only to tell me how much you hate it there"; and "Please don't come back to me if it's only to taunt me with how much happier you were with her." Finally, his "sexual insults" hurt her, "especially now when I am sexier than I have ever been and more frustrated, and am as much in need of love as you are."[37]

She didn't know how to reply to something he had said, however. He had asked her why she would want an unhappy husband.[38]

THEN SUDDENLY, in early June, he came back to West Barnstable. Jane was surprised but played it cool and allowed him to resume his place at the table. He went back to writing in the study and produced one of his best, most politically prescient essays, "Torture and Blubber," about the United States' misuse of force to "persuade" people.

> Simply: we are torturers. . . . Agony has never made a society quit fighting, as far as I know. . . . One wonders now where our leaders got the idea that mass torture would work to our advantage in Indo-

china. It never worked anywhere else. They got the idea from child-ish fiction, I think, and from a childish awe of torture. . . . But children believe that pain is an effective way of controlling people, which it isn't—except in a localized, short term sense. They believe that pain can change minds, which it can't.[39]

He continued his attempts at repairing things with Knox too, thank-ing him for selling a small article by Mark to *Earth Magazine*. When Edie's friend and the family's TM initiator Joe Clark stopped by the house to say that Mark's collapse resulted from not meditating regu-larly, Kurt told him to get the hell out.[40]

He was home again. Apparently, his fling with Jill was over. He felt confident enough about his state of mind to announce that he was going to New York, only to attend to some things, and then he would return. But Jane did not share his equanimity. "The confusion has reached new crescendos," she wrote to Knox, "reducing me to a state of paralysis, as far as being able to say how I am, or he is, or whether we are separated, or not. At the moment, he is back in New York, closing up the apartment 'til Wednesday. Maybe. The lady with the camera of course will be wait-ing, weapons unsheathed, so who knows what will happen next."[41]

A week passed, and then a letter arrived from Kurt. He and Jill were back together, and he would not be returning to West Barnstable after all.[42]

"Of course you are back with Jill," Jane replied bitterly. "It was pro-grammed that way. I think (at the moment) that you are crazy and a shithead and a bastard, and I think she's a manipulative bitch who feeds on the vulnerabilities of others. . . . Don't come home, unless you can get rid of her for real. You know you didn't mean it last time. I'm sick of games-playing. I still love you, though I can't imagine why, right now."[43]

He replied by asking her to donate a thousand dollars apiece to Swarthmore College, the University of Chicago, the Unitarians, Save the Children, and the National Council of Negro Women from the trust they had created. He also thanked her for calling him a crazy shithead bastard. He knew he deserved it.[44]

Then, three weeks later, he walked through the door again. By then Jane had taken off her wedding ring and Kurt contritely did the same.[45]

Nevertheless, he was big on traditions like the summer salt marsh tromp—his idea from years ago—and he intended to exercise the privilege, as the originator, of leading it as usual.[46] Edie and Geraldo arrived for the event; she was eager to integrate him into some of the goofier aspects of the family. About twenty neighbors ambled into the yard too, dressed in jeans and T-shirts, ready to slog through muck that was up to their shins. Jane, being a good sport, joined the group as another "tromper."

Kurt pointed to a distant landmark on the bay side of the Cape and reiterated the rules. The idea was to reach the goal by walking in a straight line, regardless of obstacles, touch it, and be the first one back to the house.[47] Hindering opponents by yanking on their belt loops, giving them a shoulder check, or splashing them was fair game. Any questions? The usual tittering remarks about quicksand, alligators, lions and tigers and bears rippled through the group, and then Kurt shouted, "Go!"

The newcomers tended to step lightly the instant the soupy water lapped over their shoes, but the more experienced scrambled ahead. Kurt flailed through the grass like a marionette, loose-jointed and jerky, dressed in khakis, a white T-shirt, and baseball cap, sending sprays of mud in the air with each heavy footfall.

Jane wanted to keep up. Her job was to have hot drinks ready when everyone got back from rinsing off in the waves on the beach, and being among the last to arrive wouldn't do.

He sensed that she was behind him and turned to grin. As she tried to get past, he gave her a shove that toppled her into the mud. Good-naturedly, she laughed and paddled some of the slop onto his trousers. He waited for her to struggle to her feet, then pushed her over again and towered above her, panting, hands on his hips. Then he was off again, his long legs going up and down like pistons.

She sat up and wiped her eyes with the edge of her sleeve. The marriage was truly over, she knew.[48]

THEY MARKED their twenty-sixth wedding anniversary in September quietly. Kurt was scheduled to leave for London with Lester Goldsmith the next day for an opening of *Happy Birthday, Wanda June*, and on the spur of the moment he invited Nanny to accompany them. At sixteen, Kurt's youngest child was a bit of a mystery to him. As often happens in families where heavy drinking is a factor, she was the lost child—harsh on herself, prone to overreact, and, in her case, heading toward anorexia to control her appearance. Earlier that summer, he had tried to explain to her the problems at home, attributing the unhappiness to too much fighting. Jill didn't abscond with him when he was vulnerable, he explained. He didn't believe anyone could be kidnapped into a relationship.[49]

In any event, father and younger daughter left for London to be footloose, far from West Barnstable, and far from, as Kurt admitted to her, the New York madness.[50] He was completely at her disposal, available to take her anywhere, to see anything—what did she want to do?

She just wanted him to take her to the zoo. Pandas were her favorite.[51]

Returning to the Cape, Kurt asked Jane whether she'd like to attend the Frankfurt Book Fair in mid-October 1971, the largest trade fair of books in the world at that time. The State Department was planning a book tour for him, too. But she couldn't go. She had just enrolled in the Simmons College master's program in social work, which would require commuting an hour and a half each way to Boston, three days a week for two years. None of the credits from the Slavic Languages and Literature program at the University of Chicago, earned during her fellowship so many years earlier, would transfer, so she had to complete all the requirements.

As she had done so many times before in their marriage, she found a reason to be good and busy. He decided it might not have been such a good idea inviting her to the Frankfurt Book Fair. Their conversations were often forced and crackling from a relationship that was short-circuiting, anyway.[52]

He turned his attention back to his work on *Breakfast of Champions*, feeling uneasy, though. Jill was on his mind and he was half tempted to just chuck the novel and the awful script of his marriage, a double move he had been secretly considering for months.[53] Nanny noticed he was snappish and as likely to end a conversation with "Shut up" as anything else. Jane's friend Lynn Meyer caught him "preening," as if he were studying himself the way an actor would his profile.[54]

One day, while Edie was in West Barnstable making plans for her marriage to Geraldo in December, she saw the page of a letter lying beside her father's typewriter, left there as if intentionally. It was from

Jill, describing in detail the parts of her body that missed his.[55] A few days later, he was gone again, back to his one-bedroom apartment in New York. He invited Jill to go to Frankfurt with him and she accepted.[56]

Word of Kurt's marital problems percolated back to Indianapolis. Uncle John Rauch, eighty-one years old, one of Kurt's distant relatives, was disgusted. Hearing from Alex Vonnegut about the trouble, and Kurt's peregrinations between New York and Cape Cod, he wrote to Jane: "Do you suppose he would come out here [Indianapolis] for a couple of days if I called him? Perhaps Alex and Irma could help me to discipline him. Of course it is quite apparent that Kay is suffering from a 'success syndrome' of symptoms. Being for most of his life starved for money, he is now surfeited, and struggling for years for recognition as a literary artist, he is now notorious, if not famous, as an author. As a result of his plays he has become involved in 'show business' and the fascinating world of the theater—with its overindulgence in drink and sex—maybe dope for all I know."[57]

Their marriage was in serious trouble, and Kurt and Jane's stress expressed itself psychologically. Jane began to have nightmares about drowning in ocean waves.[58] Kurt consulted a physician because he slept most of the afternoon; she prescribed Ritalin, which helped some.[59] His writing was a casualty, too. He was blocked creatively, rising to start work early as usual, but he sat for long stretches at his typewriter resting his fingers on the keys, waiting for words, but none would come. He was reluctant to see a therapist, afraid that unhappiness might be the true seed of his creativity and, without it, he would have nothing to write about. Mark "tried to reassure him that psychiatrists weren't nearly that good."[60]

Resigned to the idea that his mental health was suffering, he made an appointment to see Martha Friedman, who taught at New York Medical College. Friedman, he found, gathered "jumpy people together into little families which meet once a week."[61] Her specialty was treating clients who suffered from anxiety about success. In her 1980 book, *Overcoming the Fear of Success,* she attributed the source of this fear to parents who hold up one child as a model for the others. Kurt characterized her book as "a beautiful key to so many of the locks formed in childhood."[62] In December 1971, he fulfilled his role as father of the bride when Edie married Geraldo at the house in West Barnstable. It was a freezing day with snow outlining the mullions of the windows; tiny flames from candles in all the rooms reflected on the panes. Kurt took his place in the receiving line and accepted everyone's congratulations graciously, even though Edie sensed he was "very stiff," as if he were expecting to have to defend himself each time someone grasped his hand.[63]

THE MOST he could expect from Jane was civility now. She was going through stages of grief, and in early 1972 it transformed into rage. She had dinner with two of their friends, Justin Kaplan and his wife, Anne Bernays. As she talked about Kurt over drinks in the living room afterward, she began pounding her heels on the floor, growing angrier and angrier. Kaplan thought she was on the verge of a nervous breakdown.[64]

Part of her wrath stemmed from his expectation that she would continue to fill the role of life partner without the respect. Kurt asked her whether she would continue handling their finances, for instance, with the help of an accountant, of course. That would give him more time to write.[65]

She flat out refused. So instead, as if she were replaceable in that category too, he began turning over his bills to Don Farber, who created the Kurt Vonnegut Jr. Special Account and out of it paid his client's monthly rent, therapist, credit cards, lifetime health club membership, and a bill for a new rug.[66] He also regularly deposited checks made out to Jane in the Cape Cod Bank & Trust Company in Hyannis. Don handled fan mail too, answering the simple queries personally, and sometimes inviting young writers to stop by his office.

VONNEGUT WAS wealthy for the first time in his life and turned over the management of his and Jane's larger investments to Don as well, whom he authorized to make purchases and transfers. True to his roots as the descendant of generations of Indianapolis mercantilists, Kurt had dabbled in the stock market since the early 1950s.[67] In 1972, he opened an account with Merrill Lynch, Pierce, Fenner & Smith, and Farber regularly purchased stock for him and Jane from the Vonnegut special account. Despite demonizing big business in interviews and his novels—Kilgore Trout asks an old miner in *Breakfast of Champions* what it's like to "work for an industry whose business was to destroy the countryside"—he was an eclectic investor.[68]

He and Jane were stockholders, for example, in IBM and in Phelps Dodge, one of the richest mining concerns in the world.[69] It was also notorious for its antiunion views, resisting a union contract until 1946, and medical coverage for its employees until 1955.[70] Over the next several years, Kurt invested in Texas International Drilling Funds; Chicago Bridge; Dow Chemical, the sole maker of napalm during the Vietnam War; and Multivest Real Estate Fund, a development of apartment complexes and shopping centers in six cities.[71]

Vonnegut's choice of investments outwardly contradicts his public remarks about human beings' corrosive impact on the environment—"I think the earth's immune system is trying to get rid of us. . . . we are a disease on the face of this planet."[72] But his taking a seat at the high-stakes tables of capitalism as an investor isn't inconsistent at all. He believed in free enterprise. It had made his forebearers rich. And he recognized that many ideas of Western freedom are intrinsically tied to capitalism.

What he objected to was capitalist ideology, combined with Christian pieties, to justify the power of the rich over the poor. In *God Bless You, Mr. Rosewater*, for instance, an upstairs maid, raised in an orphanage, is made to say every week as a catechism, "I will be grateful to those who employ me, and will never complain about wages and hours, but will ask myself instead, 'What more can I do for my employer, my republic, and my God?' I understand that I have not been placed on Earth to be happy."[73] Senator Rosewater declaims in the Senate chamber that the historical linkage between the Roman Republic, free enterprise, and the founding fathers has created a natural carrot and stick to encourage success, except that a lot of do-gooders such as "labor crooks" have "buggered the logic of the system beyond all recognition."[74]

The system, Vonnegut would say, is not the problem; it's the tendency to blame the poor as a way of shifting responsibility away from the rich.[75] Eliot Rosewater marvels at what he is capable of doing as a wealthy man, which is the beginning of his conversion to philanthropy: "'Just think of the wild ways money is passed around on Earth!' he said. 'You don't have to go to the Planet Tralfamadore in Anti-Matter Galaxy 508 G to find weird creatures with unbelievable powers. Look at the powers of an Earthling millionaire. Look at me!'"[76]

Over the course of his lifetime, Vonnegut's satires on greed, consumerism, and people's addictions to goods opened him up to the lazy accusation that he was a socialist and a left-winger. It's true that his uncle Alex, a charitable man, had given him Veblen's *Theory of the Leisure Class* to read as a teenager, both giving him a perspective he never forgot about class differences and throwing into relief his parents as petit bourgeois. Nevertheless, he believed in capitalism as the best way to deliver money and personally invested heavily. His readers would have been shocked by his investments in a strip mining company, a shopping center development, and the manufacturer of napalm, but he agreed in economic theory, anyway, with the Yippie leader Jerry Rubin, who became a securities analyst in the 1970s. As Rubin said, "Let's make capitalism work for everybody."[77]

UNFORTUNATELY, MANY of his younger readers and fans misjudged him. They imagined a hirsute man of the people as the author who, despite enjoying sales of over four million books, turned a wry smile on the topic of money.[78] Sometimes their wrong impression created awkward, man-behind-the-curtain moments when at last they saw him in person. In the spring of 1972, for instance, he spent a morning at West Point visiting classes and in the afternoon delivered a lecture. At the end of the lecture, a cadet who had been looking forward to the event approached him. "And he said, 'I can't imagine you wrote those books,' and I had, I swear to God I had, but I was not the man he thought should have written those books."[79]

A few months later, at a fund-raising rally for Democratic presidential candidate George McGovern held in Constitution Hall in Washington, Vonnegut took the microphone to read an essay. As he left the dais, someone in the audience said loudly, "Who was that?" "Kurt Vonnegut!" came the answer. Louder applause. The next guest was Tom Paxton singing a song about pot smoking in Vietnam, followed by fourteen cast members of the musical *Hair*, invoking the Age of Aquarius.[80]

An even more farcical clash of cultures—tie-dye and bell-bottoms versus cuff links—occurred when Jefferson Airplane, pioneers of psychedelic rock, arranged a meeting with Kurt Vonnegut, hero of the counterculture, to brainstorm ideas for a new album. He arrived wearing a dark Brooks Brothers suit, black wingtips, and small-pattern tie. "The vibrations were just awful, I wanted out as fast as possible. They wrote me a letter about it and were apologizing for the bad vibrations. Why? They may have had funny ideas about who I am on the basis of my books, and I turned out not to be that way at all."[81]

Imploring, adoring drug-induced letters from fans and cranks arrived at Farber's office addressed to "Kurt baby" or some other attempt at familiarity.[82] And some midnight tokers didn't react kindly to businesslike replies from a law office. A young woman who had invited Vonnegut to have dinner with her and her husband later unloaded on Farber.

> I just got your "fill in the blanks" form letter. Since Mr. Vonnegut has so many "prior commitments" perhaps you can tell him for me that without his reading public he wouldn't have *any* commitments! And without us he wouldn't have the money to hire someone like you to send out form letters from him.
>
> Maybe I'm silly but I thought he'd be different. I thought he'd care just a little. How wrong I was. He's just a capitalist like everyone else. No time for someone truly interested, for someone who truly cares. From now on fuck you and fuck him! Who needs a 53-year-old capitalist around?[83]

Vonnegut resented fans' presumption that he was "valuable to them as a personality." He found this "disturbing in a way."[84] But he had created certain expectations by inserting himself so boldly in *Slaughterhouse-Five* and redoubling them by going back and adding folksy introductions to his earlier novels: "I want to be a character in all of my works."[85] It was easy for readers to extrapolate from Vonnegut's narrative voice the image of a writer who might resemble cowboy-booted Richard Brautigan or Lawrence Ferlinghetti in a denim work shirt. His style was so breezy, his jabs at society so on-target, his appeals for "common human decency" so praiseworthy. They took their hopes even a step farther and thought he might be like one of his characters— selfless Eliot Rosewater, say, or half-mad Kilgore Trout. Consequently, he felt chagrined by audiences' disappointment at what he looked like, how he talked.[86]

One solution he tried was identifying with an iconic American author to whom he was often compared: Mark Twain. Granville Hicks in his review of *Slaughterhouse-Five* pointed out that both were humorists and moralists. Kurt's gift for wryness and his sympathy with Twain's skepticism tended to reinforce that observation. "Pretend to be good always, and even God will be fooled" is the motto of the mental hospital in *God Bless You, Mr. Rosewater*. John Birmingham's *Our Time Is Now: Notes From the High School Underground* (1970) included this pronouncement from Vonnegut: "High school is closer to the core of the American experience than anything else I can think of."[87] And as to why Americans smoked heavily, Vonnegut speculated in *Welcome to the Monkey House* that it was because smoking was a "fairly sure, fairly honorable form of suicide."[88] Journalists, reaching for a way to convey an impression of him, a curly-haired and mustachioed Midwesterner who lacerated with aphorisms, found that the Twain parallel came easily to mind.

For Kurt, there were two important benefits to being likened to Twain. The first was that copying a famous and much-loved nineteenth-century author in public saved the reserves of his imagination. Writers fear they will tap out their aquifer of creativity, but having a literary avatar like Twain perform for audiences preserved the juices Vonnegut needed at his desk. Samuel Clemens also performed as Mark Twain, the folksy, cigar-puffing sage of the Mississippi. Stage engagements provided the financial means for him to pursue his abiding interests in science, technology, and investment.

Second, Vonnegut had been a practitioner of public relations early in his career and understood the profitability of any semblance between himself and Twain. Twain was a brand in American literature if ever there was one—the equivalent on bookshelves of an appliance made by General Electric. Some of Vonnegut's fellow authors sought to create trademark identities of their own that would show well in public, particularly on television. Hunter S. Thompson affected a cigarette holder, beachwear, and a bottle of liquor.[89] Tom Wolfe took to wearing white suits and a matching fedora, Gay Talese dandified his wardrobe, and Norman Mailer cultivated a pugnacious air. (Female and minority authors, such as Toni Morrison, James Baldwin, Rudolfo Anaya, didn't have the latitude among the reading public to resort to antics.) But Vonnegut had the good fortune to be styled by commentators as another Mark Twain primarily by virtue of his birthplace, hair, and sense of humor. It couldn't have been more serendipitous.

Sometimes advertising a kinship to Twain failed to impress, however. Kurt's Cornell fraternity brother Rod Gould (who also happened to have been in a B-17 over Dresden) attended a Vonnegut reading at Heinz Hall in Pittsburgh. He planned to escort his wife, Joanne, backstage and introduce her to his former classmate and friend, whom he hadn't seen since January 1943. But when the program began, it was "as if Hollywood casting had turned out the product. There was Samuel Clemens complete with the tousled hair-do and white suit. This artificiality sparked my disappointment. Then he began to respond to questions. That he was theatrical was not so bad. It was the conceit, downright know-it-all demeanor and flippancy that turned disappointment into alienation. By the end I concluded this was not the Kurt Vonnegut I had known. I could not bring myself to seek him back stage. We simply exited and returned home."[90]

At a PEN party in New York in the early 1970s, the novelist Hilary Masters encountered Vonnegut. "He was doing his Mark Twain imitation," he later recalled, "baggy white suit, bushy hair, and flowing mustache. He was standing a little apart, maybe aloof, like an icon of some kind. We all had been drinking a lot. . . . My attitude toward Vonnegut was that he was something of a poseur and that his impersonation of Twain was almost a theatrical device."[91]

The Vonnegut-as-Twain performances ended one evening during a speech at the Library of Congress, when a "circuit breaker" in Kurt's head, as he put it, snapped off. He had finished his "regular routine of Hoosier shit-kicking" when a man in the audience, apparently a recent immigrant from Eastern Europe, asked, "You are a leader of American young people," he said. "What right do you have to teach them to be so cynical and pessimistic?"

That question, ethically unanswerable, largely ended his pretending to be the "glib Philosopher of the Prairies. . . . I was not a leader of American young people. I was a writer who should have been home and writing, rather than seeking easy money and applause."[92]

His family, of course, had never bought the public persona—guru, sage, not even street-level activist. "He was sort of the darling of the hippie movement in the '60s and the '70s and he was like hipper than any of his kids," said Tiger Adams. "And he really wasn't, he just kind of had that image. And the image was created obviously from his writing.

People who saw his lectures had no idea of what he was like other than from his writing. So he sort of, I think, felt obligated to portray what he wrote about."[93]

He stopped exposing himself to the aggravation. From early 1972 through spring 1977 he declined speaking invitations, interviews, and requests to visit colleges, limiting his appearances to advocacy campaigns for causes he cared about or the rare commencement address. Unless he retreated, the persona, the "ghost" of him, as he called it, became like an itching, second skin he couldn't slough off. When a reporter asked him during dinner at a Manhattan restaurant "what New York was going to 'do' to him," his answer crackled with muted anger. "He responded quietly, yet with a sort of savagery that we ordinarily reserve for members of the family. He said, 'I'm not going to perform for you anymore.'"[94]

IT HAD been almost two years since he left Cape Cod, initially to attend rehearsals of *Happy Birthday, Wanda June*, but which had led to his marriage splintering beyond repair. Jill had been a wedge in fissures that were already evident, yet he had not fallen in love with her. He confided to Jane in May 1972 that he was without a companion, and as long as he was married to her, he wouldn't be able to find one.[95]

As he wrote to her, he mentioned that he was wearing an old suit jacket, purchased in Schenectady, a sentimental keepsake of the times when they were broke and had eaten cereal for dinner. Over the years they had coped with his drinking, tried to combine two families—with spectacular results, he added—and built a marriage that weathered all kinds of vicissitudes. He asked her whether they could move forward on a divorce now. They were good people, he had no doubt, and would continue to be; it was just that they were now only friends, not lovers or a couple.[96]

IN LATE August, Jill accompanied Kurt as photographer for their assignment from *Harper's* magazine to cover the Republican National Convention in Miami Beach. McGovern's democratic campaign looked to be a replay of McCarthy's quixotic bid, and Vonnegut was there to examine the conservative movement's response to it.

For the piece, he borrowed an ironic device from his fiction, which served him well in this instance as a commentator in Miami. "If I were a visitor from another planet," he began. He would observe the convention—its protocols, customs, claims to the truth, and high jinks by delegates—as if Republicans were a species of human beings and he were an extraterrestrial anthropologist.

The party stalwarts he encounters are an odd collection: the conservative columnist William F. Buckley Jr., the Quaker theologian D. Elton Trueblood, Birmingham mayor George G. Seibels, National Security Adviser Henry Kissinger, and the television daytime talk show host Art Linkletter. Strange too is the absence of the party's nominees for president and vice president, Richard M. Nixon and Spiro T. Agnew. Something substantive is missing.

What Vonnegut senses is that this convention is barely about party platform planks and position statements at all; this is not the Republican Party of Lincoln, Theodore Roosevelt, Dwight Eisenhower, or Barry Goldwater. Despite the heaviest bombing raids of the war in Vietnam occurring ten days earlier, and debates about equal rights for women, black unemployment, and urban poverty roiling through the electorate, the convention shies away from controversy. Instead, it celebrates the culture of the status quo and seeks to codify the values of the 1950s. Vonnegut suggests an axiom for the convention might be "Ignore agony."[97]

Few political commentators at the time perceived what Vonnegut did: the rise of the Religious Right within the Republican Party, the development of "theoconservatism."[98] Listening to a sermon by Dr. Trueblood, Vonnegut is astonished, "because I thought I heard him say that the sovereignty exercised by American politicians came directly from God. Some other reporters there got the same impression."[99]

As a counterpoint to the self-congratulatory rhetoric Vonnegut was hearing, he lets his eye fall on a group of Native Americans from different tribes, seated at a table, on which there is a mimeographed flyer for anyone to take. The flyer says, in part: "We come today in such a manner that must shame God himself. For a country which allows a complete body of people to exist in conditions which are at variance with the ideals of this country, conditions which daily commit injustices and inhumanity, must surely be filled with hate, greed, and unconcern."[100]

The *Harper's* issue containing his essay, "In a Manner that Must Shame God Himself," reached newsstands in November, just days before

Nixon achieved one of the greatest landslides in American political history. The article, derided by some as lacking in seriousness, nevertheless earned him a spot as a contributing editor to the magazine. He was quite proud of the piece, particularly of introducing a discussion of evil into national politics.[101]

THE FILM *Slaughterhouse-Five* had premiered in the United States more than a year earlier, in March 1971, and Kurt, fascinated by the director George Roy Hill's treatment of his novel, watched it twenty to thirty times, he said.[102] But reviews had been mild and box office sales mediocre. Not even the airing of a ninety-minute public television pastiche of Vonnegut's stories called *Between Time and Timbuktu; or, Prometheus-5* coinciding with *Slaughterhouse-Five's* release in theaters had added to the kind of momentum Universal Studios wished for the movie.[103]

There was still the European market, however, practically untouched in the fall of 1972. Hence, Kurt agreed to go on a promotional tour in London in mid-October, combined with a trip to Paris for him and Jill. He was also looking forward to meeting his Russian translator in Paris, Raisa Rait-Kovaleva, or, as she preferred to be called, Rita Rait (pronounced "right").

Vonnegut had known nothing of Rait translating his novels (or the royalties owed to him) because of the political filters between American authors and Soviet publishers during the Cold War. Then a Russian literature professor at the University of Louisville, Donald M. Fiene, brought her to his attention earlier that year. She was "frank and fearless," Fiene wrote Vonnegut, urging him to befriend her, because she wasn't a "Marxist but an international humanist and pacifist."[104] Kurt replied to Fiene with a telegram: IN ENGLAND BROWN'S HOTEL LONDON OCTOBER 21 TO 31. HAVE NOTIFIED RAIT. HAVE REQUESTED RENDEZVOUS ANYWHERE. YOU COME TOO.[105]

The afternoon Kurt and Jill came down from their rooms in the Mayfair section of London to meet Don and his wife, Judy, "Kurt was sporting an Afro that was as bushy as Angela Davis's," Fiene noted in his journal. "And I had a beard that came down to my belt buckle. We sort of giggled, then shook hands." The first topic of conversation over drinks was "brief comradely remarks on the suicides of our parents."[106]

After that unhappy subject had been exhausted, Fiene was eager to open Vonnegut's eyes to a readership he didn't know existed.

One reason for Kurt's popularity in the Soviet Union, Fiene explained, was that readers could identify with Vonnegut's victims of manipulative rulers and heartless, ubiquitous bureaucracies—and to feel the author was their spokesman.[107] Also, several Soviet critics had already remarked on some of the Russian, and even Dostoyevskian, features in Vonnegut's novels.[108] "He at once brightened, insisting that I tell him exactly what I saw."

Fiene hesitated, not expecting to have to produce literary criticism on the spot, but rallied with "You both have a strong chiliastic outlook." Kurt smiled appreciatively at the use of the word *chiliastic*—meaning belief in a future age of peace and justice.[109] But more than that, he was pleased to hear his work compared to Dostoyevsky's. The conversation lasted two and a half hours.

"I was much impressed by Vonnegut—a very sensitive guy, full of laughter, cigarette smoke and endless curiosity. Also rather vulnerable, it seemed. He also liked being rich and the center of attention."[110] Fiene also noticed that Vonnegut tended to praise Jill and her work as if he were trying to appease her for some reason. Apparently, the lady "had come to take Vonnegut's picture one day and just stayed."[111]

Rita Rait, when Kurt located her in Paris, turned out to be a tiny, white-haired woman in her seventies. The top of her head barely reached the middle of his chest. But her grandmotherly appearance belied a salty sense of humor, and she was a good teller of jokes learned from British and American sailors recuperating in Murmansk during the war. Jill photographed author and translator standing affectionately together, Kurt beaming as if he'd found a European relative. Then they spent the remainder of the day together, the three of them, touring the halls of Versailles and its gardens, which had inspired the Russian czar Peter the Great to build the Peterhof Palace west of St. Petersburg. Spreading her arms to encompass its magnificence, Rita said to Kurt, "I make you a present of this."[112]

RETURNING FROM abroad in October, Kurt sent Jane an affectionate letter, talking about how they were getting along better than most separated couples.[113] It had a wistful tone. He wrote José Donoso too, saying that he was back on a regime of taking antidepressants to combat what he supposed was a result of a chemical imbalance and the fact that his mother had committed suicide. Jane, sensing he was in a bad way, sent him a copy of Dag Hammarskjöld's spiritual meditations, *Markings*. But in his low state, he could find no comfort in the former Swedish diplomat and statesman's aphorisms, such as "On the bookshelf of life, God is a useful work of reference, always at hand but seldom consulted."[114] Perhaps such remarks reminded him of his quarrels with Jane over religion.[115]

In his present state of mind, he told Jane, he was not in the mood to read about destiny and living a meaningful life. His timeless end, he was convinced, would come in a ridiculous and humiliating manner, an ironic comment on his worth by creatures he had loved since boyhood. He believed that a dog would kill him.[116]

FOR KURT's fiftieth birthday in November 1972, Jill threw him a party. There was an additional reason to celebrate: he had finally completed *Breakfast of Champions*, a fiftieth birthday present to himself, he said. He felt as if he were "crossing the spine of a roof—having ascended the slope."[117]

Later that week, Jill and Kurt, a fixture at high-end events by now, attended a bash at Abercrombie & Fitch celebrating the life and era of Tallulah Bankhead, and Brendan Gill's just-released biography of her, *Tallulah*. Among the 425 guests were Joan Crawford, Otto Preminger, Mary Hemingway, Ethel Merman, Bobby Short, Joan Fontaine, and Hermione Gingold.

With such luminaries surrounding him, Kurt's friends and acquaintances saw him in a new light. "You could see Kurt's external circumstances had changed dramatically," said the former hippie Ray Mungo, in comparison to his days in West Barnstable. "He was no longer the nice paternal guy surrounded by all the kids in this big warm bosom of a family type of thing. He was going to restaurants, he was fully participating in the literary life. He was running what you might call a contemporary salon, and there were all kinds of interesting people always stopping by. Jill exploited the situation by taking photographs of all the famous writers that Kurt knew."[118] Mungo wasn't in that league; nevertheless Jill and Kurt were kind to him. He came to New York in the hope of making it as a writer, broke, and in his early twenties. They stood him a good meal, marveling at how he wolfed down all the bread. "Kurt arranged for me to get a five-hundred-dollar loan from the Authors' Guild, because at that time they had some kind of a fund for writers who were starving, and I was starving."[119]

FOR MONTHS, Kurt had been unable to bring about a satisfactory settlement with Jane and finally, as he dreaded, they had been forced to turn to lawyers. Trying to sound her out about supporting herself once she was single, he asked in December whether she was ever going to get a job, or was social work—volunteering and so on—just a hobby?[120]

His question stung. She shot back, "I can't tell you how successful I'll be at it any more than you could have told me how successful your books were going to be ahead of time. I'm the one who told you, remember?"[121] It was true that she had completed her first full year of social work classes. But in a note to Don Farber, she wondered rhetorically, "I wonder why I did it?"[122]

Her friend Lynn Meyer, observing how Jane didn't need to work any longer—Kurt's income saw to that—was convinced giving her money was the "best and worst thing" that could have happened to her in terms of getting on with her life. "Money insulated her from having to deal with the divorce. Also, she was going to Simmons for a degree in social work, but she didn't like the idea that they were making demands on her that conflicted with what *she* wanted to do," since there was no urgency about getting the degree. In Lynn's opinion, Jane was a typical postwar mother of the 1950s in outlook, a pre–*Feminine Mystique* wife, "very much on the cusp of 'self' and 'selflessness,' and money kept her from asking profound questions of herself."[123]

In an attempt to create a simple if inelegant solution to their differences about money, Kurt offered to give her everything—the house, savings, insurance policy benefits, and stock—and instead she send *him* an annual allowance of $10,000 a year.

That idea offended her. "I assumed that one of the few benefits of a divorce might be to afford each party the dignity of some degree of autonomy."[124]

* * *

JANUARY 1973 saw the most expensive presidential inauguration in history for two-termer Richard M. Nixon, the thirty-seventh president of the United States. Following his swearing-in, the National Guard kept close to one hundred thousand protesters away from the parade route, but rocks and bottles bounced off the presidential limousine anyway.

On Manhattan's Upper West Side, Kurt participated in a six-hour vigil of prayer, music, and readings at the Cathedral of St. John the Divine intended to focus on the "responsibility of Americans to heal the wounds of war."[125] Conservative pundits dismissed it as an exercise in radical chic, listing as proof Vonnegut's participation, along with Noam Chomsky, Dick Gregory, Black Panther minister of defense Huey Newton, Congressman Paul McCloskey, Black Panther Bobby Seale, Gloria Steinem, and Dwight Macdonald.

Even though he was not far left like Chomsky, and certainly not prepared to overthrow the system like the Panthers, he found that being in proximity to reformers provided venues for speaking to his readers. As he had said earlier in 1969, reflecting on the success of *Slaughterhouse-Five*: "I tell them not to take more than they need, not to be greedy. I tell them not to kill, even in self-defense. I tell them not to pollute water or the atmosphere. I tell them not to raid the public treasury. . . . These morals go over very well. They are, of course, echoes of what the young say to themselves."[126]

BREAKFAST OF Champions at last appeared in bookstores in March 1973, following a difficult birth, from a creative standpoint. In its first drafts, written sometime during the mid-1960s, it was titled *Goodbye, Blue Monday*, a prose poem of personal recollections about the Great Depression.[127] Then it was incised from *Slaughterhouse-Five* because it didn't fit with the rest of the narrative. When it was full-term, so to speak, his publisher, Delacorte, lost the manuscript and all of Vonnegut's marginal notes, fortunately after the galley proofs were printed.[128] Now, out of his hands at last, he was glad to be done with it, recognizing that it wasn't the equal of his earlier books, but he was tired of the effort it had demanded.[129]

An additional reason it had been difficult to finish was because it marked a departure. *Breakfast of Champions* is the beginning of his second major phase as a novelist. His earlier novels had largely examined issues of the present as seen in the rearview mirror of the future. "Everyone now knows how to find the meaning of life within himself," begins *The Sirens of Titan*. "But mankind wasn't always so lucky."[130] *Breakfast of Champions*, on the other hand, was rooted in the now, and Vonnegut roasted the present, the early 1970s, in the scornful voice of a latter-day H. L. Mencken. "As I approached my fiftieth birthday, I had become more and more enraged and mystified by the idiot decisions made by my countrymen. And then I had come suddenly to pity them, for I understood how innocent and natural it was for them to behave so abominably, and with such abominable results: They were doing their best to live like people invented in storybooks."[131]

In the first chapter of the novel, he laments the decay of common courtesy, the loss of rich cultural foundation in America, the absence of sacred beliefs, the lack of brotherhood, and the historical failures of capitalism.[132] Had anyone other than Vonnegut fulminated that when he was young life in America was better, he would have been called a reactionary.

The narrator of *Breakfast of Champions* is Philboyd Studge—a pen name for Vonnegut. We know this because Studge-Vonnegut mentions his mother's suicide, his birthday, and his preference for Pall Mall cigarettes.

Studge recounts the mental decline of Dwayne Hoover, a "fabulously well-to-do" Pontiac dealer who goes berserk after reading a novel by Kilgore Trout, Vonnegut's alter ego, the failed science fiction writer. Hoover becomes violent when he's convinced that everyone else in the world is a robot, and he is the only human being. Even God is a robot. Hoover's nervous breakdown is happening because America is cracking up due to racism, poverty, and what might come under the heading of general low-mindedness, which Vonnegut literally illustrates, with mixed satiric results, using his own felt-tip pen drawings. Text is interrupted by childlike pictures of an anus, an American flag, the date 1492, a vagina, little girls' underpants, guns, trucks, cows and the hamburgers made from them, chickens and the Kentucky Fried Chicken made from them, an electric chair, and the sunglasses that Vonnegut wears as he enters the story line. As one critic remarked, the novel carries "the metafictional impulse in Vonnegut's writing as far as it can go."[133]

He inveighs against the times he is living in, the things he sees and hears, which takes the novel in a direction his earlier novels have not gone before: it is strongly, even disquietingly personal. Near the center of the novel Dwayne Hoover cries out, echoing Dante in midlife, "I've lost my way. . . . I need somebody to take me by the hand and lead me out of the woods."[134]

Autobiography figured in Vonnegut's previous novels, of course, particularly in *Slaughterhouse-Five*. But the tone of *Breakfast of Champions* is abject and apologetic; Vonnegut ashamedly admits to thoughts of self-destruction: "'You're afraid you'll kill yourself the way your mother did,' I said."[135] He seems unable to muster reasons to live. As he explained to an interviewer, "Suicide is at the heart of the book. It's also the punctuation mark at the end of many artistic careers."[136]

Eerily, in the last few pages of the novel, he arranges a meeting between himself and Kilgore Trout, his alter ego, forever broke and struggling. Then, like someone who gives away his possessions before taking his own life, he tells Trout, "[I am] going to set at liberty all the literary characters who have served me so loyally during my career."[137] Trout, astonished, makes a last request of his creator: he begs for the chance to live his life over. "*Make me young, make me young, make me young!*"[138]

On the strength of Vonnegut's reputation, *Breakfast of Champions* spent a year on the best seller lists, proving that he could indeed publish anything and make money. But the novel disappointed most reviewers in general. Personally, he had never liked the book, calling it "asinine" at one point, but he took the criticism hard anyway because his innermost self and ideas were less fictionalized this time. He concluded that he was being taken to task for not being artful enough, for being too blunt. "I think I'm unjustly punished for my clarity."[139] It wounded him to think he was not being taken seriously when he was his most serious. And it made him think again about the private versus the public man, and which one of the two was becoming dominant. As far as he could see, his novels were "just out in the world on their own. They aren't me. Neither is my reputation."[140]

Jane met Adam Yarmolinsky, a Harvard law professor, at a party in Washington, D.C., in 1972. He was complaining of a stiff back, and she joshed him into lying on the floor so that she could walk up and down his spine in her stocking feet. When Adam's college-aged son, Ben, met Jane the first time, it was in September 1972. By the following spring, "they were pretty much, as far as I could see, a couple, an item." That summer, they vacationed in Aspen together.[141]

Adam was six days younger than Kurt and had just turned fifty. He had been a good soldier, literally and figuratively, his entire adult life. During World War II, he enlisted in the Army Air Corps, rising to the rank of sergeant. After the war, he married and then received a law degree from Yale University, later serving as a clerk to the Supreme Court justice Stanley E. Reed.[142] His parents, Babette Deutsch (a poet) and Avrahm Yarmolinsky (a scholar of Russian literature), had been Marxists and imprinted their values on him. After the war, Adam advocated, for example, building military bases only near desegregated communities.

In 1961, when President Kennedy called for the organization of the Peace Corps, Kennedy tapped his brother-in-law Robert Sargent Shriver Jr. to organize it. Yarmolinsky, Shriver remembered, was "among the first to show up for work in this new enterprise."[143] Three years later, during the Johnson administration, when Congress passed the Poverty Bill, Yarmolinsky received signals from the White House that he would become the deputy to Sargent Shriver in administering the program. And he wanted the post, not only because it would be a big step nearer to a cabinet position, but also because the legislation was historically progressive.

But southern Democrats wouldn't tolerate Yarmolinksy receiving the appointment. The *Washington Post* political columnist Mary McGrory listed the reasons why, starting with his efforts at integration. To southerners, he was also an "egghead, a New Yorker, and the son of liberal intellectual parents. Barely concealed anti-Semitism contributed to his downfall as well."[144] President Johnson, as the price for passing the bill, which he dearly wanted, jettisoned his nominee, and Adam saw the gold ring pass him by.

Shortly after accepting the law professorship at Harvard, a kind of sinecure in academia for a respected Cold Warrior and social reformer, he and his wife of twenty-five years, Harriet, divorced. When he met Jane, he was looking for a new start.

* * *

IT WAS important to him to get along with the Adamses and the Vonneguts because he had fallen in love with Jane.[145] It was a challenge, though, because being the epitome of rectitude and a compulsive fussbudget, he was not in his element in the disordered house in West Barnstable. One night, waiting for Jane to go into the kitchen, he got up from the table and quietly started scraping places where paint had dried on the windowpane, using a single-edge razor blade from his pocket. He objected to betting games at the kitchen table, even if the stakes were just pennies, but he resisted making an issue of it.[146]

His world was so different from that of Cape Cod that the young people regarded him as a curiosity and could hardly believe his naïveté. He phoned Edie, for instance, wanting the recipe for a sandwich she had made for lunch. "The one where the cheese melts," he said helpfully.

"You mean grilled cheese?"[147]

The Vonnegut and Adams offspring decided that if he were going to become a fixture in their lives, it was time to administer the acid test. Next to the main fireplace in the living room was a Dutch oven about four feet off the floor, used for two centuries to keep pies and bread warm. The iron door in front was approximately ten inches by sixteen. Inside, the brick interior, instead of being square, was shaped like a beehive. Growing up, if someone wanted to be a friend, he or she had to crawl all the way in. During one of Adam's visits, they threw down the gauntlet.

"Bet you five dollars you won't get in there far enough so we can close the door."

They waited.

Once, many years before when Yarmolinsky was in the Department of Defense, a colleague had tipped him off that the military personnel at the Pentagon would doubt he had the guts for the job until he made a parachute jump. On his own, he arranged for a plane and, with minimal training, made his first jump.[148]

With Jane's children looking on, he got up from the chair, took off his shoes, and squeezed inside the oven until the door clanked shut behind him.[149]

IN THE fall of 1973, Kurt did a "damn fool thing," he said, and succeeded the English novelist Anthony Burgess as Distinguished Professor of

English Prose at City University of New York.[150] Six weeks into the semester, he decided he would resign the one-year appointment at the end of the semester. "I can't get any writing done under these conditions."[151]

His decision had more to do with his becoming disenchanted with writing programs altogether than with time stolen from his work. His experiences at Iowa and Harvard had convinced him that a creative writing track didn't have to be in a university's English department. Some of his best writers in previous classes hadn't been English majors; they came from all fields of endeavor: premed, prelaw, engineering, and chemistry. And he doubted that students could be taught to become exceptionally good writers. It was disingenuous, in his opinion, how "most teachers of creative writing try to honor this impossible promise by welcoming everyone lovingly to the writing profession and by reserving especial praise for those who have managed to write anything at all, even a letter home."[152] Moreover, creative writing programs that lasted only a semester or even a year weren't long enough. Two years, like the Iowa workshop, ideally with the same instructor, should be the minimum. During that time, the instructor's responsibility was to watch for indications of what the student writer was meant to become—a short story writer, a novelist, an essayist, or just a competent writer—and help him or her in the process of becoming one.[153]

BEFORE LEAVING the position at City University of New York, Kurt went with Don Farber to look at a brownstone that was for sale in Manhattan at 228 East Forty-eighth Street. He had grown "used to the rootlessness" that went with his profession, but now that he had the money, becoming a permanent New Yorker seemed like the sensible thing to do.[154]

For one thing, it was better for one's writing muscles to strive against other heavyweights, he believed, and New York was the place to find them. When he was a boy, Indianapolis authors such as Booth Tarkington, George Ade, Kin Hubbard, and James Whitcomb Riley had made their reputations primarily as regional authors. Eventually, advances in communication put them in competition with other writers all over the world. In the end, "this withered them," Vonnegut believed.[155]

Second, New York was brusque, surly, and he liked that. When he had lived on Cape Cod, long walks by the seashore left him feeling peaceful, but that wasn't what he needed; he needed to feel indignant, to feel inspired to satirize, to find "something to be mad about."[156]

The brownstone he and Farber looked at was a beauty—nineteen feet wide by forty-six feet deep—located in the Turtle Bay neighborhood near the United Nations. Built in 1860–61 as one in a row of twenty such homes, it had an Italianate front with some Greek Revival detailing, heavy window moldings, and a high steep flight of stone front steps. Inside, a staircase curled along an interior wall, up the middle two floors to the third story, where there was a guest room and a little kitchen. David Halberstam lived across the street at E. B. White's former address.

There would be some sacrifices. The house had no garden in the back, just a sunken patio, and no restaurant next door to deliver him wonderful meals at all hours. But he liked the address, the architectural elements, and the layout a great deal, and so he purchased it. It was where he would live the rest of his life, the next thirty-four years.

Shortly after Kurt closed on the house, Jill rented its three-room suite at street level, which had a separate entrance, and ran her photography business from there.[157]

AN IMPORTANT sign that Vonnegut's work was no longer considered fringe reading, but representative of American literature, was that it began slipping into high school English classrooms in the 1970s. A trend toward elective, thematic, and media courses with titles like Man in Conflict, Folk-Rock Poetry, and The Ghastly Gothic gave teachers more latitude in choosing their literature selections.[158] The watchword was *relevancy* in teaching, and English anthologies sometimes known as *radical readers* included essays, articles, poems, short stories, songs, and other types of writing about issues such as the war in Vietnam, civil rights, and free speech.

Consequently, a teacher at Jefferson Davis High School in Montgomery, Alabama, was shocked in April 1970 when the school board met in emergency session and fired her for distributing a selection from *Welcome to the Monkey House* to her juniors. The board, perfectly illustrating an oxymoron, pronounced it "literary garbage." Writing to members of the American Civil Liberties Union, Vonnegut urged them to defeat "book-burners" and "self-styled censors."[159]

Several years later, school officials in Strongsville, Ohio, were considering adding *God Bless You, Mr. Rosewater* to the list of approved titles for the curriculum until a report submitted by an administrator called it "completely sick. One secretary read it for one half hour and handed it back to the reviewer with the written comment: 'Garbage.'"[160] Alarmed, the board voted not only to drop *God Bless You, Mr. Rosewater* from consideration, but also to remove *Cat's Cradle* and Joseph Heller's *Catch-22* from its approved list and all copies from the school library. The American Civil Liberties Union filed suit to reverse the decision, and Vonnegut appeared in district court, not to defend his novels but instead to raise issues about society's failures. "Maybe they think my books are why people smoke dope and get pregnant. I would like to hope that I have good morals. I consider writing an act of good citizenship."[161]

But an incident that infuriated him occurred in 1973 in Drake, North Dakota, a community of 650 mainly Catholic and Lutheran farmers. A sophomore complained that her English class was reading *Slaughterhouse-Five* and that it was profane. The school board went into special session and ordered the superintendent to burn all copies of the novel. On a freezing November day, three dozen were shoveled into the school furnace because, said the superintendent, "I gave them to the janitor as I would my wastepaper."[162]

Not satisfied that all copies had been destroyed, the principal inspected student lockers on the chance that some might have defied the board's order to turn in their books. Local ministers, appearing at a subsequent meeting of the board, decried any copies of *Slaughterhouse-Five* still in the hands of students as "tools of the devil." Then, without having read two additional works the teacher had also assigned, the five-member board destroyed all copies of James Dickey's *Deliverance* and an anthology containing short stories by Ernest Hemingway, William Faulkner, and John Steinbeck.[163] The issue split the student body, with some refusing to attend the teacher's classes. Others, one night after a board meeting, threw eggs, tomatoes, and garbage at the cars of the superintendent and the school board clerk.

Rolling Stone magazine wanted Kurt to spend a few days that winter in Drake, accompanied by a reporter, to chronicle what it was like when he moseyed into a town with four churches, three bars, three grain elevators, one police officer, and a restaurant to face his critics. But Vonnegut demurred; it was a setup that wouldn't accomplish anything except ratcheting up the public anger and increasing *Rolling Stone*'s circulation.

Instead, he vented in a private letter to the chairman of the Drake school board. The board had misunderstood his books from beginning to end, he said. He was not an advocate of wild, irresponsible, or antisocial behavior. Just the opposite. He militated for kindess and decency. By burning his books—books they hadn't even read, he suspected—the board had set a rotten example for the young people looking to them for wisdom and maturity.[164] In the spring, the Drake school board voted not to rehire the teacher who, in its view, had started the whole trouble. "I'm not sorry about the action the school board took," the superintendent said. "I don't regret it one bit, and we'd do it again. I'm just sorry about all the publicity that we got. People in Drake are sick and tired of all this publicity."[165]

LOREE'S HUSBAND, Richard Rackstraw, died January 8, 1974, but the cause of death, suicide, was omitted from the memo sent by the dean of the College of Humanities and Fine Arts to the faculty and staff of the University of Northern Iowa.

The evening before, Richard and Loree had dropped by to see their friends Robley Wilson and his first wife, Charlotte. As the two couples sat in the dining room drinking coffee, the conversation turned to marital difficulties. Seven years earlier, Robley and Charlotte had stood up for the Rackstraws at their wedding and were aware that the couple was going through a "rough patch." Recently, Richard had been in a psychiatric hospital in Waterloo. Robley, during a visit, thought his friend had acted "scarily subdued." Doctors recommended a new drug regimen to address Richard's depression, but Loree opposed it.

The marital advice Robley and his wife gave was general: "Hang in there; in the end things will resolve themselves." On the way out to their car, Richard asked Robley whether he would be home later that evening, saying, "I'd like to come back and talk." Robley waited up, thinking Richard wanted to get more off his chest, in private, but his friend never returned.[166]

In later years, Nanny Vonnegut believed Richard Rackstraw compared himself unfavorably to her father. The two men's point of intersection was Loree, but as Richard's marriage faltered, and his work suffered as a result of mental illness, Kurt rose to become a major American writer. Loree's interest in Vonnegut couldn't have been more consuming. It was both personal—they wrote and called often—and academic: six months before Richard's death, she interviewed Kurt at length, thinking she might write a series of essays about his work.[167] "I can't believe that her husband did not always, in the back of his mind, know how much in love she was with my father."[168]

IN APRIL, Delacorte published, in connection with Sam Lawrence, *Wampeters, Foma & Granfalloons*, a gallimaufry of Vonnegut's essays, reviews, short travel accounts, and human-interest stories written between 1966 and 1974.

A "wampeter," he explained to readers, "is an object around which the lives of many otherwise unrelated people may revolve" such as the Holy Grail. " 'Foma' are harmless untruths, intended to comfort simple souls. An example: 'Prosperity is just around the corner.' " And a " 'granfalloon' is a proud and meaningless association of human beings," such as Hoosiers, one of his favorite examples.

Commentary magazine, acknowledging that Vonnegut's readers numbered in the hundreds of thousands, pointed out that "only a writer with Vonnegut's power base could get a book of occasional writings published today, let alone get away with giving it such a title."[169]

The remark carried with it a hint of weariness over Vonnegut's indictments of "bad craziness," the phrase coined by Hunter S. Thompson in *Fear and Loathing in Las Vegas* to characterize Americans' screwy behavior. The nation was burned out after nearly a decade of student takeovers, urban riots, adjurations by rock 'n' rollers and acid-taking professors to "blow your mind," and a cops-and-robbers break-in involving the White House. Liberal trends had peaked, some halted altogether, and a few reversed direction. Perhaps it was cyclical; more likely it was just the result of political and social exhaustion.[170]

To allay the charge that he was always a pessimist, Vonnegut included in *Wampeters* a speech he had delivered to a graduating class at Bennington College in which he had urged the audience to "believe in the most ridiculous superstition of all: that humanity is at the center of the universe, the fulfiller or the frustrater of the grandest dreams of God Almighty."[171] It was a bouncy message, although at variance with practically everything he'd written in his novels about determinism, an indifferent God, and humanity dying from spiritual inanition. Many reviewers didn't buy it, or the importance of the collection, and a few began to question Vonnegut's tendency to throw one-liners like Koosh balls at suffering.

"When it doesn't work," wrote a critic for the *Chicago Tribune*, "which I think happens far too often, the laughter is a way of avoiding the pain . . . the real anguish that humor can't alleviate. . . . He comes close, but then he backs away, rarely facing it head-on. The wisecracks are a way of playing it safe."[172]

A few years earlier, the critic Benjamin DeMott had seemed pretty square when he summed up Vonnegut's views as "bull session simplisms."[173] Now, in the mid-1970s, following the United States' defeat in Vietnam and the first resignation of a president in history, the era had turned sour, and "foma" from anyone was regarded skeptically.

In October 1974, after returning from a memorial service at Town Hall on West Forty-third Street for the poet Anne Sexton, another suicide, Kurt wrote to Jane in a thoughtful mood. He was worried that his creativity was petering out, and that there were forces at work in America he could not understand or explain. Major, disturbing changes were afoot, though apparent only in clues here and there. It was mysterious. Whatever was happening, he wrote her, they should hang on and prepare to "wind up miles from here."[174]

12: Ripped Off

1975–1979

IN FEBRUARY 1975, Kurt suggested to Loree they get away for a long weekend in Key West. Jill would know nothing about it.[1] By giving her the slip, he would be "well out of reach of punishment," as he later described a character in his novel *Hocus Pocus* who hides in Key West.[2] Loree "hesitated only briefly," and they began, in her words, a "reunion filled with delight with no expectations of anything more."[3]

As Loree remembered it, she and Kurt strolled around like teenagers, holding hands. Kurt thought he knew where Truman Capote was staying, and they found him, purring like a cat in a hotel garden, appraising a photo of himself in the *New York Times*, taken by, of all people, Jill. "A nice likeness, don't you think?"[4] he asked innocently. But Capote, the consummate gossip, knew better than to ruin something juicy by inquiring about Jill in front of Loree. So instead he urged his visitors not to miss the sunset.

It was all pleasure, no business for Kurt during his time with Loree, except for a phone call from a B-grade science fiction writer who asked permission to write a novel under the pen name Kilgore Trout. He identified with Trout, he said.[5] Vonnegut, feeling expansive—after all, there was money flowing into his pockets from reprints, translations, and royalties—agreed.

At the end of their three days together, they drove to Key West International Airport a little early and pulled into Little Hamaca Park to wait at a picnic table in the shade. Kurt whittled their initials into the wood.[6] A few months earlier, his friend Don Fiene had asked him about the "perfectly beautiful trouble" he had gotten into at Iowa, mentioned in *Slaughterhouse-Five*. "Kurt seemed surprised that I couldn't guess at once he was referring to an affair he had. . . . And then he added, 'By the way, that was not just some ordinary affair. It was very beautiful, very tender.'"[7]

THE SCIENCE fiction writer who had called him during his weekend in Key West was Philip José Farmer. Farmer was approximately the same age as Vonnegut, born in Terre Haute, Indiana, and had looked like a real straight arrow when he began writing in the early 1950s: slight build, preference for short-sleeve shirts, open face, high forehead, and a buzz cut. But his novels were outer space sexual fantasies for male readers. On every other neutron star in Farmer's cosmos was a nymphet, unconstrained by Earth's mores. His first published short story, "The Lovers" (1952), featured sex between a human and an extraterrestrial. *Flesh* (1960) promised "the secret dream of every man . . . unlimited opportunity, inexhaustible ability." In *Dare* (1965) the she-alien "R'Li was incredibly beautiful—but she wasn't human." He also challenged tropes about futuristic, utopian worlds with satiric and caustic fables about greedy societies devolving into violence. In that sense, he was like the early Vonnegut, using science fiction for radical commentary.

Farmer had called Vonnegut in Key West not only because he identified with Kilgore Trout but because he had an idea in mind that seemed promising: What would it be like if Kilgore Trout—misunderstood as a writer of pornographic space fantasies—had a novel released by a mainstream publisher? How would it read, what would be the themes, given all the strange plots Vonnegut attributes to his alter ego over the years? As Farmer recalled the conversation, Kurt was fine with the concept.[8] Later, Vonnegut denied that was what had happened. "I never encouraged him in the project, which contained *nothing* but risks for me. Still, he kept after me, and I at last gave him my permission to borrow my readers and my inventions and my reputation—with no editorial or financial strings attached."[9]

In the Farmers' little house in Peoria, Illinois, Philip's wife, Bette, could hear him laughing downstairs in the basement as he wrote *Venus on the Half-Shell* by Kilgore Trout.[10] For the jacket photograph, Farmer disguised himself with a false beard and a Confederate hat. Then, because he always had a few writing projects going at once, he turned his attention to something else after he submitted the manuscript to his publisher.

The summer of 1975, *Venus on the Half-Shell* began selling thousands of copies every week, outstripping anything Farmer had published previously. (How soon it appeared after the call to Vonnegut in Key West suggests that he was already well into writing it.) The story line was slapdash but undeniably quirky and funny, lampooning pieties of science fiction as only a professional in the genre could. The greatest irony, however, was that Kilgore Trout was Vonnegut's creation—a hoax. But *Venus on the Half-Shell*, instead of paying homage to Vonnegut, was a spoof on *his* work, supposedly written by Trout.

The protagonist, Simon Wagstaff (double entendres tickled Farmer), is a musician and seeker of universal truth. Like a space-age Buddha, he sets out to explore the universe in search of the answer to suffering and death. With him are a female companion, a dog, and an owl. He visits a series of planets, one inhabited by car tires (their leader is a whitewall); a second with laws that are so strict everyone eventually ends up in jail; and a third on which a holy man eats the pilgrims who come to him to learn the truth. Centuries pass, and Wagstaff can find no answer to the meaning of life, except one: the universe is irrational, nihilistic.

What upset Vonnegut was that neither readers nor critics could tell the difference between a bona fide novel of his and Farmer's send-up. Most readers assumed he was the creator of Simon Wagstaff, another space wanderer in the mold of Winston Niles Rumfoord, and the humor of the novel, which tended to be salacious and offbeat, was passable Vonnegut. Leslie Fiedler, usually an admirer of Vonnegut's work, appeared on William F. Buckley's television program *Firing Line* and testified that the mocking tone of *Venus on the Half-Shell* indicated that Vonnegut had abandoned science fiction. Furiously, Kurt wrote to Fiedler, "Your slightly misinformed glee on the Buckley show was simply the first indication I had that nothing remotely pleasant was going to come from my giving Philip Farmer permission to write under the name of Kilgore Trout with no strings attached."[11]

Letters arrived at Don Farber's office addressed to Kurt, extolling

Farmer's knockoff. "I would like for you to extend my congratulations to Mr. Trout," enthused one reader. "I found his novel screamingly funny. . . . But be careful, I'm afraid he's stealing your style."[12] Another helpfully suggested that Vonnegut could learn a lot by going to school on Trout. "A friend of mine . . . gave me a present the other day. It was Kilgore Trout's *Venus on the Half-Shell*. Did you read that? You ought to—might give you some good ideas. Man—that guy's got some fantastic mind!"[13]

Kurt's professor friend Don Fiene wrote to say that the ruse seemed to have fooled everyone he spoke to about it: "I have not met one Vonnegut fan who isn't convinced that you are the author of this book. At least two of them have sharp literary insight. I'm amazed."[14]

Farmer, enjoying the controversy and the free publicity, coyly explained to interviewers that he had been motivated only by his admiration for Vonnegut. He was saddened that his fellow science fiction author would not hear of a sequel to *Venus on the Half-Shell*.[15] Vonnegut, more accustomed to dishing it out than taking it, hit back in a letter to the editor of *Science Fiction Review*.

Now then: Mr. Farmer has earned royalties on more than one hundred thousand books which most people at first thought were written by me. That is fine with me. I don't crab about that to anybody. I said from the first that the dough should all be his. I do wish, though, that he would not speak darkly of my being a multi-millionaire, which isn't true. And I don't think he should present himself by contrast as a man of the people, gamely up against something like Standard Oil. He got every penny of the swag in this case, an enormous boodle for only six weeks' work. Mr. Farmer has also been able to prove even to college professors, in a sort of blindfold test, that he can write my sort of stuff as well as I can any day. I am not surprised or mortified. That's life. All I have complained about so far is the abuse I have received in the mails and in reviews for having written such a book. . . . And this whole adventure has so muddied my reputation and depressed me that I have perfectly reasonably asked that my publishers not bring out any more books by Kilgore Trout. . . . I thank him [Farmer] for the honor he did me, and I congratulate him on writing a bestseller in only six weeks. It takes me years and years.[16]

He was rattled. The success of Farmer's parodic novel was a good horselaugh at his expense: a classic example of implying the emperor has no clothes.

Another sign of disrespect for his work that had reached his ears about the same time was the small industry of photocopying his short stories for classrooms—underground publishing by teachers, in his opinion.[17] Consequently, intellectual property rights were on his mind when he was asked by other writers to appear with them before a congressional subcommittee considering revising the copyright laws as *Venus on the Half-Shell* climbed to best-sellerdom.

Most of the authors attending the hearing, including Herman Wouk, Barbara Tuchman, Art Buchwald, Irving Stone, and others, read aloud statements comparing themselves to inventors with patents, or to visual artists who produced an original work of art. Some appealed to protecting the nation's cultural heritage from exploitation. Kurt listened while the science fiction novelist Frederik Pohl explained that copyright is a financial legacy to writers' families. "Sometimes all that's left is the books."[18]

Then it was Vonnegut's turn to speak. He rose and without notes began telling jokes—"a sort of shtick," Pohl recalled, as if he were performing a stand-up routine. It individualized him, brought into the room, indirectly, the matter of talent and style. People in the room, including members of the congressional committee, laughed appreciatively. And when he had finished, he broke into a tap dance that continued out of the hearing into the hallway. He didn't return. "He got a hand from everybody in the room," said Pohl. "He never really said anything relevant to the question of copyright, but he made everybody like him. He made the congressional people respond to him as a human being, and I think it worked pretty well."[19]

VONNEGUT OFTEN took a stand in defense of writers, encouraging them and befriending those in trouble. He appealed to PEN on behalf of Paul Engle to help fund the Iowa Writers' Workshop. Hearing that George Delacorte, the founder of Dell Publishing, was thinking about how he might help artists, Kurt recommended through Sam Lawrence that Delacorte consider donating $100,000 apiece to the Authors League Fund, the Artists' and Writers' Revolving Fund, and the PEN Fund for

Writers. As an officer of all three, he bolstered his case by providing exact figures from the organizations' reserves for artists' emergencies.[20] An upsetting visit to the novelist Jean Stafford, who was impoverished and breathing oxygen from a tank, resulted in Vonnegut insisting that Lawrence offer a contract for her three-hundred-page manuscript, "no matter what it is," and an advance that would cover her expenses for at least a year.[21]

So when he returned to New York from the congressional hearings on copyright, he was appalled by what he perceived as still another insult to his integrity. Without first obtaining permission, a University of Southern California film student, Dan L. Fendel, had already cast, filmed, edited, and screened a movie of Vonnegut's one-act play, "Fortitude," using sophisticated equipment borrowed from 20th Century Fox. "Fortitude," published in *Playboy* in 1968, satirizes to a grotesque extent the practice of keeping patients on machines. Airily, Fendel explained that his film was a fait accompli and that in two weeks prints would be sent to student film festivals everywhere. As to why he didn't seek permission first, the canny student filmmaker left that to the very end: "Frankly, I didn't want to be told no. I still don't, of course."[22]

Vonnegut's response was volcanic. He directed Farber to get from the University of Southern California the film's negative and all prints.[23] To Fendel, Vonnegut wrote a reply that combined a father's scolding tone with the indignation of a public figure who has been made a fool of. Youth was no excuse for larcenous behavior, he stormed at him. He might as well have broken into his garage and made off with his tools under the excuse that they weren't being used. He had behaved rudely and was no friend of writers who had been ripped off countless times, and in countless ways, though usually with less gall.[24] Vonnegut told Farber he hoped the letter would be enough to frighten the junior cineast into redressing the situation somehow.[25]

Instead, Fendel hired an attorney, saying he was only a college student who had made the mistake of taking a major American author at his word about humanity and compassion and love.[26]

The dickering by both sides dragged on for nearly three months, largely due to Fendel's attorney arguing that his client needed to complete the film—a "damn fine piece of work"—in order to graduate, and Farber insisting that "we couldn't care less whether it's a 'damn fine piece of work' . . . or a piece of garbage. . . . Our complaint is that he had no right to make either a good or bad film from the property."[27] Vonnegut temporized, not wanting Fendel to get expelled. A compromise was reached, allowing for a copy of the film to be kept in the offices of Fendel's attorney, which then could be loaned to him or members of the cast for job-hunting purposes only.

The dispute was never over money; it was Fendel's failure to seek permission. On the other hand, his excuse that he had only taken Vonnegut at his word about humanity and compassion and love was nevertheless an interesting parry and a palpable hit. Vonnegut was so closely identified with his works that the young filmmaker was throwing back at him the sentiments of millions of readers who believed that the author and Eliot Rosewater, for instance—"God damn it, you've got to be kind!"—were identical. Vonnegut had eliminated the narrative distance between himself and the reader by walking into his fiction, thereby erasing the line between art and reality. Unexpected consequences were beginning. As *Venus on the Half-Shell* demonstrated, his writing had a brand that could be parodied. And his public remarks and persona, always circling around humanistic themes, just like his books, created expectations about him.

Somehow he would need to stay fresh, surprise his readers and the critics, and not become predictable, which to an artist is death.

In July 1975, Kurt's uncle Alex Vonnegut died at the age of eighty-seven. The obituary in the *Indianapolis Star* described him as a retired insurance agent, Harvard educated, and the founder of the Indianapolis chapter of Alcoholics Anonymous, although he was not an alcoholic, the announcement hastened to add. This proviso Kurt called a "nice-Nellyism from the past" because Alex indeed did drink a lot of strong German beer at more than just family picnics, and at some point he quit drinking altogether.[28] But he had belonged to a generation when human weakness, physical or mental, was considered shameful, and the obituary, quietly protecting him from the public stain of alcoholism, reflected that.

Bernard made all the arrangements—flight, rental car, hotel—for himself and Kurt to attend the funeral, still playing the part of an older brother, Kurt noted.[29] During the flight, they reminisced about favorite dogs in their childhoods, and Bernard, like the teenager he had been in his basement laboratory, demonstrated a device that detected lightning flashes in thunderheads too far away to be seen by the naked eye. Between them was an empty seat, where Kurt thought Alice would have sat if things had turned out differently, completing the trio of Vonnegut siblings.[30]

The burial was at Crown Hill Cemetery on Boulevard Place. The hearse passed through the Gothic Revival limestone gate at the entrance and followed one of the narrow roads, first used for the funeral corteges of Union dead, until the mourners reached the family plot containing thirty-seven graves. Only a few years earlier, Kurt had visited his parents' headstone and wept. He had felt ashamed of crying, which he hadn't done in a long time, but he couldn't help wishing his parents had been happier.[31]

At his uncle's graveside, he listened for something comforting from the Unitarian minister, but there was no mention of God or an afterlife and he felt an absence of hope, spirituality, or redemption—anything that might consecrate the occasion beyond the performance of a necessary duty. Kurt was an agnostic, but his conservative nature took comfort in traditions marking the stages of life.[32]

HE WAS in his early fifties and thinking about growing old, sometimes mentioning his age and general health in letters to friends. In speeches and presentations, he began referring to himself more often as getting on. To the graduating class of 1976 at Connecticut College, he confessed to a peculiar feeling of having been born only a short while ago, and now, suddenly, he was fifty-four years old.[33] To his daughter Nanny, he tried to explain that this darkness falling on him wasn't Jane's fault; it wasn't Jill's fault—she had been very good to him—and it wasn't the fault of money and success. The whole nature of his life seemed to be cooling like igneous rock into unbearable heaviness.[34]

He tried to ignore thoughts of death. At one time he had considered suicide as a "perfectly reasonable way" to get out of the niggling demands of life once and for all—lectures, bills, cocktail parties, deadlines.[35] But he had decided his mother's death was a lesson. "The reason you mustn't consider suicide is because you leave that legacy to the next generation. You give them a reason to do it."[36]

* * *

HE MEANT it when he said Jill had been good to him. He credited her with saving him from killing himself with pills or the bottle.[37] He said he wouldn't marry her, though; she was a companion who fell into step by his side when he left West Barnstable for New York.[38] In his hundreds of letters written during the 1970s, he never says he loves her, although he had been living with her for several years. Meanwhile, month after month, he dillydallied over his divorce from Jane, maintaining a regular correspondence, calling, and sending her money without a settlement, which had the effect of keeping her on a string. With Loree added to the mix, he was tenuously connected to three women, lazily circling them. But Jill had pride of place, given that their friends in New York by this time thought of them as a couple. Apart from the obvious forces at work—her serving as guide into monied New York and offering herself as a much younger, highly desirable lover—what was holding him to her exactly and answering a need of some kind?

JILL WAS powerfully attractive and profoundly self-centered—"hardwired to the bowels of hell," Mark told Nanny.[39] Vonnegut's friends and family found it hard to converse with her, and even friendly relations seemed difficult. "In all my dealings with Jill," Nanny complained to her father, "I find myself feeling trapped and end up gnawing my own hand off trying to get out."[40]

But this woman was familiar to him, and he thought he knew how to placate her. His role was to humor her, to drop into a supplicating pose when necessary and win favor, in short, to act as consort to a narcissistic female who was much like the one who spurred his creativity in the first place—his icy mother. Creativity is often interpreted as a response to emotional pain. A domineering, cold mother or any kind of unhappy childhood, according to many schools of psychiatry, causes neurosis and anxiety, and neurosis can serve in some cases as a goad (a lash, some would say) to artistic pursuits.[41] "I cannot write unless I hurt myself some," Vonnegut confessed to a correspondent.[42] But to relive in his fifties what he had already experienced, to revisit boyhood guilt and uncertainty about his relationship with his mother, could risk his mental well-being.

In *Bluebeard*, a novel that Vonnegut had yet to write, Jill is the model for the aptly named Circe Berman.[43] Her first words to the narrator, the artist Rabo Karabekian, are "Tell me how your parents died." He notices she has "straight black hair and large brown eyes like my mother."[44]

THE RELEASE by Praeger Publishers of Mark Vonnegut's *The Eden Express: A Memoir of Insanity* in the fall of 1975 was surprising. Surprising first because his father refused to help him with it. One day, Dan Wakefield, answering a knock at his door on Revere Street on Boston's Beacon Hill, found Mark on the steps holding a clutch of typewritten pages. "Would you help me with this?" he asked. His father had told him, in effect, you're on your own—everybody has to learn to write the hard way. For the next several months, Wakefield edited and critiqued Mark's manuscript.[45] Next, for help with shepherding it through to publication, Dan directed Mark to his agent, Knox Burger, who found a publisher.

The Eden Express was also surprising because there was only one other memoir of mental illness, *Autobiography of a Schizophrenic Girl* (1951), written anonymously by "Renee" with interpretations added by her therapist, Marguerite Sechehaye.[46] But *The Eden Express* is Mark's own story, as he experienced it, without an analysis provided by a physician. With painful candor at times, he describes his failure to be an effective human being due to mental illness. He can't cope with his family; he isn't strong enough to take charge of the farm on the Powell River; he has sexually ambiguous feelings about his girlfriend, and she eventually leaves him. He's beset by auditory hallucinations, amplified in their intensity by mescaline, LSD, and marijuana. In the first edition of the book, he attributed his eventual cure to a regime of Thorazine, shock treatments, a high-protein diet, and vitamin therapy, although in an afterword for a revised edition he disavowed the efficacy of vitamins. Nevertheless, as Kurt noticed, his son depended on "embarrassing numbers" of bottles and pills and would continue to, he was given to understand, for the rest of his life.[47] When asked about his son, Vonnegut tended to equate madness with hypercreativity—a sort of curse of the gods vouchsafed to exceptional people. "He can see these great biblical visions coming with blood tests. [Doctors] can see these identifiable chemicals showing up in his blood stream and adjust his diet accordingly and his blood stream straightens out. Otherwise he'd see the Apocalypse, he'd see Revelations, and he doesn't want to."[48]

* * *

IT's A troubling book—a self-portrait of an immature man, overly concerned about pleasing others, highly self-critical, and possessed of the
counterculture code of conduct "If it feels good, do it." Mark puts
the blame on others—all of society, in fact—for manipulating him. The
more he rationalizes about the world being out of step with his lonely
march toward perfection, the deeper his psychosis becomes. His girlfriend should not leave (even when he acts tiresomely dependent); his
friends should always be faithful; and people should live in harmony
and peace with nature.

When Kurt arrives in *The Eden Express*, his outline is blurry. Mark
clearly loves his father but isn't sure what to make of him; Kurt, for his
part, doesn't seem to know what to do. He acts distant, embarrassed,
and unaccustomed to taking care of a child who needs him. Mark's
friends play as important a role as his father does in helping him. One
gets the impression of Good Samaritans, Kurt included, moving a drunk
from the sidewalk, where he might get hurt, into a doorway and then
stuffing a few bucks in his shirt pocket.

In any case, by the time *The Eden Express* was released, Mark had
recovered, married, and enrolled for his first year at Harvard Medical
School, studying medicine and orthomolecular psychiatry. On weekends he and his wife drove from their apartment on Boston's Beacon
Hill down to West Barnstable, where they kept a vegetable garden and
an eighteen-foot catboat barely big enough to sleep two.[49] After running
away when his parents' marriage was disintegrating, he was home again
for visits, but his father was gone.

THE WEEK of Ash Wednesday in February 1976, Kurt began receiving
mysterious sympathy cards, twenty or thirty a day—mysterious because
he hadn't suffered a loss. He and Jill put them on the mantelpiece like
Christmas cards, still puzzled about what was going on, until Kurt
recalled that Billy Pilgrim was killed on February 13, 1976, by an insane
ex-POW.[50] Readers, in the spirit of how metafiction straddles reality
and imagination, were acknowledging the death of his character.

It was a good omen for the novel he was about to deliver, *Slapstick; or,
Lonesome No More!* His public was solid, even though critics had disliked his previous novel, *Breakfast of Champions*.

The title *Slapstick; or, Lonesome No More!* was chosen for a couple of reasons. Sam Lawrence discouraged using just *Slapstick*, because it was too similar to *Ragtime,* published a year earlier by E. L. Doctorow.[51] Second, Vonnegut was rather proud of the phrase "Lonesome No More," which he had proposed as a campaign motto to Democratic vice presidential candidate Sargent Shriver during the 1972 election.[52]

To rest and celebrate before the inevitable book tour, he and Jill rented a beach house in East Hampton, eighty miles or so from New York City. He toyed with setting up an easel outside and painting, but he didn't really respect painting, or the rich people who would pay outsized amounts to decorate their walls.[53] About that time too he began adding six quick strokes of a felt-tip pen under his signature—an asshole, like the one that had appeared in *Breakfast of Champions.* He was an asshole, he explained to those who asked about it; however, "being human was an asshole condition," a conclusion bitterly apparent in his latest work.[54]

VONNEGUT DEDICATED his 1976 novel *Slapstick; or, Lonesome No More!* to the Depression-era comedians Laurel and Hardy, "two angels of my time." And as if by invoking their genius for blunders, the publisher made the mistake of leaving off "Jr." after his surname on the cover.

The novel begins with twenty pages of autobiography—"padding," some would later say—a feature that was becoming a permanent and increasingly larger feature of his writing. He mourns his sister, Alice, his uncle Alex, and the "village of summer homes" his family owned by Lake Maxinkuckee. Then abruptly we meet the fictional narrator, one-hundred-year-old pediatrician Wilbur Daffodil-11 Swain, a former president of the United States. Dr. Swain lives in the ruins of the Empire State Building in Manhattan, the Island of Death, with his pregnant granddaughter, Melody, and her lover, Isadore.

Wilbur Swain also has a twin, his sister, Eliza. When they were born, they were "neanderthaloids"—outrageously deformed babies "with massive brow-ridges, sloping foreheads, and steamshovel jaws."[55] Brother and sister are two halves of the same brain: Wilbur is the left side (logical, rational, able to communicate), while Eliza is the right (creative, emotional, but unable to communicate effectively). Subnormal in appearance, they are kept away from their parents until their fifteenth year, when they reveal their superior intelligence, filling their mother and father with remorse. Unfortunately, in an ill-advised attempt to encourage their individuality, they are separated and lose the power of their combined brilliance. Throughout the book, Wilbur claims that Eliza is the more intelligent of the two, but without his input she can't write.

As president of the United States, Swain goes on to create, among other things, a plan to end loneliness in America with immense extended families. All citizens are provided with distinctive compound middle names like Chickadee-1 or Oyster-19. Those with the same word in their middle name are cousins, and those with both the same word and the same number are siblings. Thus, family ties don't depend on kinship, just the luck of the draw, and everyone belongs to an artificial tribe. In the meantime, as Swain tinkers with fixing society, Western civilization is nearing collapse as its reserves of oil run dry. The Chinese, on the other hand, are making weird technological leaps by miniaturizing themselves and thinking collectively like ants.

Slapstick was an attack on what Vonnegut alleged was America's flagrant egocentricity and abdication of responsibility. Wilbur and Eliza cannot be complete as individuals; they are partial persons, developmentally hobbled by being palmed off to servants and day-care givers. The Green Death, an unspecified miasma that surrounds Manhattan, is a metaphor for viral materialism. The disintegration of community and the breakdown of families causes a typically Vonnegutian apocalypse.[56]

The novel was also a self-indictment. As he wrote, around his feet lay the detritus of his Barnstable family. Nanny in particular was suffering, plagued by an eating disorder and cravings for assurances that she was worthwhile. He felt guilty about the situation vis-à-vis Jane as well because their divorce, after five years of negotiating, was still unresolved. Like Wilbur and Eliza, they continued to act as halves of an identity they were loath to let go of. As the novel doggedly continues, one gets the feeling that he is writing to cheer himself up with wild scenarios, but then he returns to castigating the selfishness and behavior of people who should know better. The result is a relentless list of woes. When the last sentence finally arrives, "And so on," the reader is tempted to agree, "Whatever."

* * *

Reviews of *Slapstick* left him "wobbled" and "roundly embarrassed."[57] A year earlier, the *Newsweek* critic Peter S. Prescott had accused him of deliberately courting naive teenagers, an allegation Vonnegut then rejected as libelous. Prescott was a liar, he wrote to the managing editor; and *Newsweek*, by repeating Prescott's calumnies, was a liar, too.[58] Now, as scornful reviews of *Slapstick* made the same charges in different words, he felt like a bad citizen in the literary neighborhood.[59]

The novel was "flashy, clever, empty," and Vonnegut "an ideal writer for the semi-literate young."[60] It had "no center, and the antics become more and more frenetic as the material becomes less and less cohesive— until, at the end, there is the realization that we are dealing with an unsuccessful joke."[61] Some critics found Vonnegut too cavalier about serious issues. The repeated, interspersed uses of "Hi ho" and "And so on" after distasteful incidents particularly drew ire, as well as in-jokes from earlier works and the reappearance of certain characters. Some critics intimated that Vonnegut's best writing was behind him.

Two poorly received novels in a row raise the question of whether Sam Lawrence actually edited Vonnegut. "You didn't edit Kurt," said Arlene Donovan, Knox Burger's secretary when he was still at Dell.[62] His fiction after *Player Piano* was so stylized that not even Knox attempted to recast it. Judging from his correspondence, Kurt received notes attached to manuscript pages asking him to clarify or cut—the usual suggested emendations from editors—but his work didn't come back heavily revised. As for Lawrence, he was foremost a literary talent scout; he discovered writers, he didn't edit them. Kurt's prose, whether it soared or belly-flopped, was entirely his.

Defending *Slapstick*, he charged unfriendly critics with one of his favorite accusations: they were just snobs. It was true he hadn't made a systematic study of literature, and he had never made a secret of getting his start writing for the slicks. Because he wasn't of their ilk, didn't belong with the literati, they wanted him "squashed like a bug."[63]

He was so fed up he considered not writing anymore and sparing himself abuse. But the disappointment over *Slapstick* passed, and slowly, after recovering from being knocked down, he found himself "noodling around again at the typewriter" because "it's my trade and the only trade I know."[64]

* * *

STILL, IT was hard to shake off feelings that his reputation might be slipping after two poorly reviewed books in a row. Following up *Slaughterhouse-Five* with an encore of back-to-back losers raised the possibility the Dresden book might be his best, the core of his achievement in fiction. When he had turned fifty on the eve of publishing *Breakfast of Champions*, he had said he felt like he was crossing the spine of a roof and descending the other side.[65] It sounded prophetic now, an example of tempting fate.

Perhaps one difficulty was that he had dealt with Armageddon so many times in his fiction that he had inured himself to it. Perhaps *Slaughterhouse-Five* had exorcised its power over him for good.[66] On the other hand, *Slapstick* contained the greatest amount of autobiography of anything he'd written, and autobiography had been partly responsible for the appeal of *Slaughterhouse-Five*.

The long introduction to *Slapstick* was supposed to explain how life felt to him—grotesque, and full of pratfalls over love, growing old, and death, such as how his sister, Alice, terminally ill, had died hours after her husband dove off the end of a bridge on a commuter train.[67] Pushing himself further into the novel, he explained to the reader that the "terribly old man in the ruins of Manhattan" was really him experimenting "with old age, all that is left of my optimistic imagination, of my creativeness."[68] Don Fiene, reading *Slapstick*, was struck by how his friend yearned for Indianapolis of the 1930s, reminisced about Lake Maxinkuckee, even wished for "black men to carry the luggage and shine the shoes" in the city's Union Station again. "Kurt has quite given himself over to being a public person; that is—he has chosen to live in such a way that he has no fear of the world learning all his secrets."[69] By the time Vonnegut wrote *Das Ende* on the last page of *Slapstick*—a phrase remembered from his German American childhood—Kurt nevertheless believed the novel had a "feeling of wholeness to it."[70]

But there was no denying that the more autobiographical his work became, the less space he devoted to fiction. Defending his decision to do so, he retorted that standing before the world was a virtuous thing to do. "I don't mind invading my own privacy. That's Victorian thinking, you see, that you're not supposed to say anything that would embarrass the family. . . . I'm not vulnerable to that anymore."[71] He wanted to continue to appear as a character, which meant filling in more and more of his own backstory, voicing his cranky opinions, and elbowing aside the fiction if necessary. He was at a tipping point in the balance between fresh narrative and essayistic memoir.

He indicated in which direction he was leaning not long after *Slapstick* was published. An interviewer asked whether future novels would include more nonfiction. Readers, Vonnegut expected, would find "more to complain about. People will say it's not fiction any more, it's editorializing. And, you know, the stories are getting sketchier and sketchier and sketchier."[72] But the attention from poking his head through the scrim separating author and reader continued to be irresistible.

IN THE meantime, Jill's career as a photojournalist was following a steep, upward trajectory. Some of Kurt's friends suspected that Jill's ambition, always at full boil, was powered by a need to best him in the literary world. "Jill felt very competitive toward him," Vance Bourjaily was convinced. "It was important to her that she publish more books than he had."[73] Now, in addition to photographing writers, she had become an author of children's books. Her first was *Sweet Pea: A Black Girl Growing Up in the Rural South* (1969). It was a hit and led to a series of books featuring a child as a photographic subject. In *A Very Young Dancer*, published the same year as *Slapstick*, a ten-year-old ballet student describes her workouts and feelings at the School of American Ballet in New York as she prepares for her role in *The Nutcracker*. Next, Krementz turned to *A Very Young Rider* (1977) about a ten-year-old girl and her pony training for riding competitions. There would be nine "very young" books in all about children, for a total of twelve over the next fifteen years. Jill was in her late thirties, and the work, she said, "gave me a chance to almost have children of my own, to be involved with them on a very intimate level with enduring relationships."[74]

IN 1977, after an absence of almost five years, Vonnegut returned to regular public speaking. His reason for quitting had been that audiences expected him, as the author of edgy novels, to be less conventional than he really was. Now he needed to get back on the circuit after the fiasco of *Slapstick* to blow on the embers of his reputation.

And so, in late March he began a swing through college campuses, beginning in Iowa City, where he had taught at the Writers' Workshop twelve years earlier. He felt as if he were going home.[75] Fiction Week was the reason for his visit, featuring Kurt and one of his former colleagues in the workshop, Robert Coover; also William H. Gass, the short story writer and author of *Omensetter's Luck*; and Theodore Solotaroff, the founder in 1967 of the *New American Review*, which had become a showcase for a rising generation of writers. Relaxing in the student lounge between commitments, Vonnegut held a question-and-answer session with young writers during which, he recommended, among other things, they write blurbs for books they liked because "this doesn't cost you a cent and is great for public relations."[76]

His stop next was the University of Northern Iowa, where he stayed with Loree. Her small white house was simple inside, given to books, philodendrons, and art prints in a style that's ubiquitous in college towns and might be called "Academic Modern." His favorite spot to read and smoke was out beyond the back porch—"my patio," as he called it—beneath a one-hundred-year-old cottonwood.[77] The day of his lecture, the campus newspaper, the *Northern Iowan*, scheduled an interview. "I don't have a shtick for you," he explained about the event that evening. "The thing I'll do tonight is roughly what I did in Iowa City. It's not very carefully written or organized."[78]

That night, every seat was taken in the old auditorium for the hour-and-a-half presentation, which consisted primarily of a pretend interview conducted between Vonnegut and himself, using two distinct voices to ask and answer questions about his experiences as a prisoner in World War II.[79] He then read an excerpt from a novel-in-progress, *Unacceptable Air*, the forerunner of *Jailbird*.

He was in his old groove of speaking and writing again.

THE 1977 Frankfurt Book Fair that fall overlapped with Munich's Oktoberfest, and Kurt went with Sam Lawrence to attend both. Vonnegut's presence in the publishers' booths was large, with editions of his books in German, Finnish, French, Danish, Spanish, Swedish, and Italian. But outside in the streets of Munich, beer was the order of the day, not books, and Vonnegut was put off by the rowdiness.[80] There was too much jousting between young men looking for a fight, singing till all hours, and carousing for his taste. Then Jill arrived and, bidding

Sam adieu, she and Kurt left for a nine-day vacation in Vienna, Florence, and Milan. He felt in great spirits, no depression, and never better in his life.[81]

Meanwhile, Adam Yarmolinsky had accepted a post as counselor to the United States Arms Control and Disarmament Agency under the Carter administration.[82] He and Jane moved into a condominium at 3307 Highland Place NW in Washington, D.C.

Their relationship was the reverse of what Kurt and Jane's had been. "She turned into the Kurt to Adam," Edie noticed. "She was just so annoyed with him, and she'd snap at him." He was a well-meaning kibitzer and a fusspot, which at times drove free-spirited Jane crazy. "I think she was happy with him, but I think he was definitely a replacement—she would have liked to stay with Kurt, had that worked out, but Adam was very good to her."[83] No one had asked him to step in as surrogate father, either, but he saw an opportunity to be of use to Nanny if she would allow it. She was suffering from feelings of worthlessness and living on a self-abasing starvation diet. "He used to call and say, 'Nanny, you are all right.' And in the end, he loved me, and he was a father."[84]

The "acrimonious argle-bargle about divorce," as Kurt called it, had dragged on for almost eight years, and he was heartily tired of it. Jane too, weary of negotiating, agreed to let Don Farber, whom she trusted, draw up a separation agreement in September 1978 because she was "convinced that a separation agreement leading to a divorce is not only an entirely reasonable way to save money on taxes, but is also the most intelligent way to make more sense of our lives."[85] Farber would also file the divorce papers in court, eliminating the need for either party to appear before a judge.[86] Kurt insisted to Nanny that the divorce did not mean he intended to marry Jill, but it was unfair to ask her to continue to live with a married man.[87]

Farber finished his work, and the separation went into effect with Jane receiving title to the West Barnstable house, a portion of the stocks, bonds, and savings, and alimony of over $100,000 a year.

SUDDENLY, KURT's mood went into a deep downward swing at the end of 1978. The divorce was pending, plodding toward finality. Don Farber and his wife, Annie, had given him a chess-playing robot, Boris, for his fifty-sixth birthday, which cheered him up some. But he couldn't make it to Bernard Malamud's Christmas party, prevented by despair from leaving the house.[88]

A feeling of dread hung over him as he completed his latest novel, *Jailbird*. He had changed the working title from *Unacceptable Air* to *Mary Kathleen O'Looney*, after one of the novel's characters. But the Delacorte salespeople had trouble remembering it, so it ended up *Jailbird*, the first one-word title of his career.

His reservoir of ideas was tapped dry, he groused to Fiene.[89] He was sick of writing novels and wished for a kind of sinecure for novelists who had done their best and were finished.[90] Fiene, after poring over the galleys Vonnegut had sent him, tried giving his author friend a pep talk: "Probably you have the most fragile ego of any writer who has ever reached your level of success in this country. To me this has been apparent in your published writing from the beginning. It remains a total mystery to me that you have a sizeable number of vicious enemies (critics) in this country who regard you as some kind of charlatan with no sensitivity at all. . . . I guess some critics have a hard time dealing with your stuff, because there is nothing to compare it with; your near-unique genre does not lend itself to classification."[91]

Vonnegut felt a little better when early signs of *Jailbird*'s reception were favorable. The Book-of-the-Month Club scheduled it as featured alternate in September. Then the judges read the revised galleys and upgraded the novel to a main selection, along with Philip Roth's *The Ghost Writer*. It was the first time Vonnegut had been in that slot.[92] Lawrence, reading an advance copy, sent Kurt a telegram: WHAT A BOOK, THAT'S ALL I CAN SAY, WHAT A BOOK. I LOVED IT AND I LOVE YOU FOR WRITING IT.[93]

While he waited for the novel's official publication, and the reviews to come in—still months away—he kept busy by stoking the public side of his career. At a rally against nuclear power in Washington, D.C., in May 1979, he excoriated the industry's spin doctors as "filthy little monkeys": "I hate them. They may think they are cute. They are not cute. They stink. If we let them, they will kill everything on this lovely blue-green planet with their rebuttals to what we say today with their stinking, stupid lies."[94]

He also accepted the chairmanship of a committee making a list of 250 American books of "lasting value" published in the past five years to be on display in the American section of the Moscow Book Fair that summer. It was not an easy job. The list was expected to be broadly inclusive of American values and points of view. An unexpected bugaboo was the amount of obscenity in many of the works of fiction on the final list, and Kurt worried that the Soviets would take offense, but that couldn't be helped, he decided.[95]

THE DIVORCE between Kurt and Jane became final in late spring 1979 after thirty-four years of marriage, although they had been physically separated, on and off, for nine years, and legally separated for six months. It was, unsurprisingly, anticlimactic.

When Kurt had left West Barnstable for New York in fall 1970 to be near the production of *Happy Birthday, Wanda June*, none of the Adams or Vonnegut children had been married. Now several of them were, and they had children of their own. In nine years, Kurt and Jane had gone from being parents of teenagers and young adults to grandparents. During that time, they had continued to act mainly in concert over money and family matters, even after the marriage faltered for good in 1971. It was as if they had boarded separate ships, then spent a long time at the railings waving goodbye, reluctant to lose sight of each other, but when they did, the gradualness and inevitability of pulling apart erased some of the sadness.

Jane, almost as a concession to her new status as divorced woman, decided to attend a women's consciousness-raising group in Cambridge with her friend Lynn Meyer. There were eight other women in the group, and at first Jane refused to tell the others her last name. She wasn't using her maiden name—and never would—still referring to herself as Jane Vonnegut. Finally, at the fourth session, she explained who she was and felt surprised that the women were interested in her, not her famous husband. "It was fascinating for her," Lynn said. "[At fifty-six] she was the oldest woman in the group. What was fun was that we really served a role for the younger women. They were both happy and appalled that we had not solved all life's problems."[96]

KURT, DESPITE feeling blue at times, continued to attend celebrity events with Jill: a black-tie party at the Whitney Museum of Art following the premiere of Woody Allen's film *Manhattan* at the Ziegfeld Theatre, for example.

With friendships spanning all the neighborhoods of arts and letters, they decided it was high time they purchased a permanent home in the Hamptons, where other successful writers resided in the summer: E. L. Doctorow, Elia Kazan, Joseph Heller, Truman Capote, Willie Morris, John Knowles, Dwight Macdonald, and until recently James Jones, who had passed away in May 1977. Once, in the early 1950s, Jane and Kurt had taken a drive along the South Fork of Long Island and decided it was the loveliest vista of its kind they'd ever seen.[97] Now he could afford to live there.

About six miles from where Jill and Kurt used to rent during the summers in Sagaponack, they found a house for sale. The owner was the minimalist artist Frank Stella, who used part of the big potato barn on the property as a studio.[98] Built in 1740, the three-story, cedar-shingled house had cavernous fireplaces for logs five feet long, and a swimming pool too, although the ocean was only a half mile away. They decided to go in on the purchase together and split the cost.

It was a big step symbolically. Kurt owned the brownstone on East Forty-eighth Street, but this second home meant sharing property with Jill; she would have as much right to it as he did. There was also the connotation of serious commitment. For years he had been evasive about what exactly his lady friend meant to him. In letters to Nanny, Jill was someone who had come along at the right time, someone who saved him from self-destructive behavior. He was grateful. No passion, no expressions of love colored his descriptions. Now, he was splicing his life to hers in one of the most significant rites undertaken by couples: owning property jointly.

The day before closing on the house, he suffered spasms of chest pains so severe he thought he was having a heart attack. At South Hampton hospital, emergency room doctors rolled him on a gurney into intensive care. But electrocardiogram tests ruled out the worst; he had experienced a painful onset of angina pectoris. A physician recommended rest and giving up smoking.[99] To that, Jill added her own diagnosis: he drank too much.[100] Knowing he couldn't quit his Pall Malls, he compromised by cutting back on nightcaps, which would mean, he cracked, he wasn't quite the twinkle toes on the dance floor he'd once been.[101]

* * *

JAILBIRD WAS released in September 1979, and it was as if Vonnegut had thrown fantasy over his shoulder and sprinted to catch up with current American fiction, which was switching back in the direction of realism. Postmodernism was showing signs of becoming a recognized school—a sure sign of fossilization. Samuel Beckett, William S. Burroughs, and Jorge Luis Borges could be said to belong to it, for instance, by any graduate student in English, without fear of contradiction. Moreover, John Gardner, in a much-discussed book-length essay, "On Moral Fiction," administered an over-the-knee spanking to his fellow American authors, some of whom were postmodernists, saying none of them deserved to be considered major writers. He accused them of being more interested in showing off fake "newfangledness." The staple of fiction—sympathetic characters making moral choices—was absent, in his opinion, from Norman Mailer, Joseph Heller, John Updike, and Robert Coover, among others. Saul Bellow wasted his time in too much philosophizing in his own voice, like a rabbi rocking back and forth over the Torah, and Thomas Pynchon was full of "winking mugging despair." In short, the majority of popular postwar authors were tiresomely prominent in their own work, a charge that included Vonnegut also.[102]

JAILBIRD, VONNEGUT informed Don Fiene, would be a departure for him. No space travel, no metaphysics. It was about economics and the superficiality of American liberalism.[103] Even so, he could not resist a ten-page autobiographical prologue. In it, he returns to Indianapolis for lunch at Stegemeier's restaurant with his uncle Alex and Powers Hapgood, the wellborn socialist. Hapgood relates to the impressionable young Vonnegut how Sacco and Vanzetti were executed on spurious charges of murder because they were labor organizers. The protagonist of *Jailbird*, Walter Starbuck, will repeat Hapgood's tale as he confronts evil.

Starbuck is a government functionary, a bureaucrat who works in the basement of the White House—a location that once more shows Vonnegut's predilection for using hiding places and shelters as places of reckoning.[104] Starbuck entered public service believing in the economic ideals of the 1930s, and over the course of his long career he has witnessed the reactionary anticommunist hysteria of the 1950s, the upheaval in American values during the 1960s, and the final debacle in the Watergate scandal that drove Richard M. Nixon from office. Starbuck's role in the Watergate affair, although minor, resulted in a prison sentence. More awful to him, though, is the disgrace. He grieves over betraying his friend Leland Clewes; being inferior to his wife; having no expertise for the government work, just good intentions; and being a poor parent.[105] Now, he merely wishes to disappear and live quietly. Meanwhile, *Jailbird* ranges over the Whittaker Chambers trial, trade unionism, the Holocaust, and corporate greed. Against this diorama of history, hapless Kilgore Trout preaches the Sermon on the Mount but is tossed in jail for treason.

Then, as Starbuck tries to cope with guilt and loneliness, he stumbles upon a chance for redemption. On a New York street corner he encounters Mary Kathleen O'Looney, his erstwhile lover and comrade-in-arms for social reform, now apparently a bag lady. But in fact she is as rich as Croesus. In the manner of *God Bless You, Mr. Rosewater*, O'Looney redistributes her wealth to the nation's citizens just as she and Walter rediscover their love.

Vonnegut fits elements of economics and religion together like folding tabs into corresponding slots to create a society in which people belong. He concludes, "We are here for no purpose unless we can invent one. Of that I am sure," which answers the question posed twenty-seven years earlier in *Player Piano*, "What are people for?"[106]

IN LATE August, Kurt attended the funeral of James T. Farrell, an author he had admired as a young man, and who set his Chicago novels in Irish, working-class neighborhoods. During the service, Farrell's partner—the woman he had lived with for the past fifteen years but never married—was not acknowledged as his helpmate. How she was shunted aside struck Kurt as callous.[107]

It put him in a mind to think seriously about his relationship with Jill. She was nearly forty, and they had been living together for nine years. He had let the affair drift with no clear direction, a result of his grief over the demise of his marriage to Jane.[108] Besides, at the outset of their affair, Jill had made it clear she wasn't interested in marriage, wasn't interested in children, either. But shortly after the funeral for Farrell, Kurt decided they should marry, because it was the right thing to do.

He understood his children's divided loyalties but invited all of them to attend. He would have no best man.[109] To Nanny, he wrote that he and Jill were in love and going forward freely. He assured her that he had been monogamous during his marriage to Jane, and would be so with Jill.[110]

A few weeks before Kurt's marriage to Jill, Jane spent a day in Boston with Kendall Landis, now a vice president at Swarthmore. He remembered it as a "very romantic, totally impossible meeting." They had lunch and held hands walking through the Isabella Stewart Gardner Museum. They reminisced about things they had said and done thirty-five years ago as undergraduates. He was happily married now with three sons. "She was lonely and she was reliving a thing she'd had for me, I guess, and I for her. But she had all sorts of things to do yet, and I wasn't a part of that."[111]

Kurt and Jill's wedding ceremony, a small affair of about fifty guests, took place in the late afternoon of Saturday, November 24, 1979, in a Methodist church at Sixtieth Street and Park Avenue. Jill's father gave the bride away because it was her first marriage. She wore a custom bridal gown, created by designers for Henri Bendel; Kurt dressed in a black suit. There was a reception afterward a block north in a private room at the Regency Hotel. Included in the portrait photograph of the bride and groom was the couple's small, shaggy Lhasa apso, Pumpkin, at Kurt's feet.

13: Looking for Mr. Vonnegut
1980–1984

JILL WANTED TO have a baby. She deserved one and wouldn't feel complete until then.[1] Eight years earlier, when she had rented the lower floor of the town house on East Forty-eighth, she had made it clear that her priorities were her career and independence, not marriage, not children. She had been the very model of a feminist—liberated in all respects, including not wanting the domestic duties of motherhood. That fit well with Kurt's life plans because he adamantly did not want any more children.[2] Moreover, he had assured Nanny that nothing would change regarding an inheritance because he had three children and three nephews.[3] But now, at forty, Jill wanted a chance at motherhood.

Kurt hadn't been a new father for twenty-five years. In fact, he had two grandchildren: Mark's sons, Zachary and Eli. On the other hand, he didn't feel it was his place to argue because it was a woman's decision, particularly since she would have to raise the child.[4] When she learned she was pregnant in late October 1980, it happened to coincide with Kurt's finishing *Palm Sunday: An Autobiographical Collage*, so they celebrated the last week of December by going to Haiti for a vacation.[5]

No sooner had they returned to New York, however, than Jill miscarried at three months.[6] Sam Lawrence, among many other friends, wrote to Kurt saying he and his wife were "saddened by the news about Jill. Our feelings go out to both of you."[7] She wanted to keep trying, though, and Kurt agreed they would.[8]

PALM SUNDAY was an easy book for Vonnegut to assemble during the first year of his marriage. A collection of essays, family history, reminiscences, and speeches, it was strung together by personal "connective tissue": three hundred pages of prologue, in a sense, without a novel.[9] His rationale for creating his second complete work of nonfiction was that he was nearly sixty, and his reading public had a "yearning" to "know who did this and what is he like?"[10] The tone was nostalgic, reflective, and even apologetic in places. Without the veil of fiction, he comes across as a pretty cheerless soul, who wrote matter-of-factly about himself, his family, and his relatives—nothing like the foxy persona promulgated by his novels. He quotes long passages from his uncle John Rauch's rather dry family history of the Vonneguts, eschewing chances to add personal anecdotes or even humor.

A possible explanation for the air of wistfulness in *Palm Sunday* might have to do with a piece of advice he had shared with students at the Iowa Writers' Workshop years before: "Think of writing as writing a letter to someone." One of them, Suzanne McConnell, got the impression as she read *Palm Sunday* that it was a letter to Jane, his wife of thirty-four years.[11]

When Jane received a copy in spring 1981, she bored into it, taking notes as she went and not turning the last page until 3:00 a.m. She looked for references right away to herself and the children, bristling at how he described his West Barnstable years in ways "just enough right not to be libelous, but also just wrong enough to be hurtful," she jotted down privately to herself. "Kurt doesn't mind being hurtful, really, although he talks a good game to make you think the opposite. He's fooled most of his public now, for a long time. You see, he doesn't really know what he's doing. He's really very innocent."[12]

He summarized his move to New York in 1970 as if he were a forty-seven-year-old Horatio Alger trying his luck. "I left the house and all its furnishings and the car and the bank accounts behind, and taking only my clothing with me, I departed for New York City, the capital of the

World, on a heavier-than-air flying machine. I started all over again."[13] Yet Jane knew that her files of correspondence and documents—some going back ten years—and hundreds of billable hours for legal advice told a different story. In spite of how his family came apart, he assured the reader that "there are many affectionate reunions a year in the big old house on Cape Cod," omitting to mention that he was not usually invited.[14]

Jane also examined his writing carefully, like the unpaid editor she had been throughout their marriage, noting it went "down like candy." His penchant for repeating phrases, however, seemed mannered to her, a crutch, she suspected because "the author/artist is bored, bored, bored out of his skull."[15] His theme, as she interpreted it, was "You're *supposed* to feel depressed—can't you understand? Life is just a crock of shit." She laughed in some places, yawned in others, tired of being reminded by her former husband of how bored he was; "(poor thing: someone is not being entertaining enough). Either that [boredom] or blow your brains out, a pretty threat."[16] In fact, he refers to death thirty-five times, about once every ten pages on average. His novels, in retrospect, Vonnegut graded A+ for *Cat's Cradle* and *Slaughterhouse-Five*, C for *Breakfast of Champions,* and even D for *Slapstick*. Jane's verdict on *Palm Sunday* was that she hated it.[17]

His tone of ennui interested her, however. She felt the opposite— excited and invigorated. She wished she had seen a therapist years before, as José and Maria Donoso had recommended, because now that she was in counseling regularly, a spigot inside her was gushing.[18] The therapist, a woman, identified turning points in Jane's life she had missed by always being in constant, heedless motion. Why hadn't she questioned her ability to deal with so many children when her nephews came to live in West Barnstable, for instance? Where were her own decision-making powers as an adult?[19] Answering those questions honestly meant a new beginning, a new understanding of how she had acted as Mrs. Kurt Vonnegut.

Therapy had also freed a desire to write, something she had promised herself she would do since she and Kurt had moved to Provincetown with children in their arms. She was doing it now, writing a memoir, and it was coming easily. She felt an urgency to write, and she had finally found a subject she really cared about: her life as mother in the blended Vonnegut-Adams family.[20] It was part retrospective, part celebration, part *introspection*.

KURT DID feel bored and anxious; Jane had been absolutely right in spotting that in *Palm Sunday*. He still rose at dawn to write, but he had trouble accomplishing much, except perhaps dashing off a letter, usually a dependable means of warming up his fingers at the keys. One morning, John Irving, who lived around the corner from him in East Hampton, discovered Vonnegut on his front porch at dawn. Irving invited his former instructor to come in for a breakfast cup of coffee, at the end of which Kurt said, "Well, I better let you get back to work." Later, Irving's children announced they had counted six cigarette butts on the ground left behind by Mr. Vonnegut—he must have been out there a long time.[21]

He spent time brooding about the decade just completed. When an invitation arrived to attend a performance at the University of Southern Maine of his 1970 play *Wanda June*, he turned it down, thinking he couldn't stand to sit through that damn play and its unpleasant associations for him.[22] During the ten years that followed *Wanda June*, he had published three novels, two of them poorly received and then at last *Jailbird*, considered one of his best yet. The critic John Leonard defended him in a review of *Jailbird* from academics' charges that he was simplistic and "insufficiently obscure; he is not loud enough about ambiguities." In fact, said Leonard, "the simple—courtesy and decency—is hardest" to write about.[23]

But there were those who refused to take him seriously under any circumstances. They were snobs, Vonnegut intimated in *Palm Sunday*: "Any idea which can be grasped immediately is for them, by definition, something they knew all the time."[24] Furthermore, if an author was an experimenter, but the workings inside his narrative ran beautifully like the hidden, tiny gears in a watch, then the experimenter must be a hack because none of the effort showed.[25]

These same naysayers would even deny him popularity as a measure of success, attributing his sales to the revolution in paperback mass marketing of the 1970s. From a publishing standpoint, *Cat's Cradle*, *Mother Night*, and so on were the equivalent of bodice-rippers for middlebrows, the argument went—inexpensive to reprint in paperback, widely read, but of questionable literary value.[26] Novels by Richard Brautigan, Thomas Pynchon, and Frank Herbert were beneficiaries of the same dynamics of the marketplace. The critic Anatole Broyard, writing in the *New York Times*, predicted that with *Palm Sunday* the Vonnegut fad had crested: "Watching various reviewers trying to avoid saying anything unkind about Kurt Vonnegut's new book, *Palm Sunday*, one realizes that, contrary to public opinion, a literary reputation is the hardest thing in the world to lose."[27] Vonnegut was so angered that he took the unusual step of responding to Broyard directly. He apologized for having the bad taste to continue writing and publishing when it was clear his career deserved a headstone, not a review. But he had this problem: all of his books continued to be in print, and thousands of readers clamored for more. What was he to do? Embalm himself? It was a puzzlement. In the meantime, he and a lot of other miserable scribblers would continue to kowtow when they happened to encounter real talent in the flesh: the august Anatole Broyard.[28]

"I'm finally sick of this," he complained to an interviewer about the label of cult author, pandering to youth. "It's a lazy way for critics to say that something is wrong with me without having to describe it in detail. So they say that I'm just the kind of person that immature readers enjoy."[29]

To DISTRACT himself, he devoted more attention to his on-again, off-again hobbies of drawing and painting. His abstract doodles, as Don Farber called them, were usually pen-and-inks of heads, still lifes, and nudes.[30] Still, he was disquieted. Although *Palm Sunday* had been a kind of summing-up—a rounding off of his career after the success of *Jailbird*—circumstances at home indicated there would be no rest for him personally, no sailing into a quiet harbor at last after navigating through a rough decade. In July 1982, Jill and Don Farber became coexecutors of his newly executed will, which included additional language about heirs beyond his Adams and Vonnegut children.[31] Jill was still determined to have a child, and he was nearly sixty.

Thoughts of wish fulfillment sometimes seep onto a writer's pages. The new novel he was working on, *Katmandu*—later to become *Deadeye Dick*—harkened back to when he had been an adolescent gun fancier in Indianapolis. In those days, he had been reckless at times with firearms. Once, he squeezed off a shot in the general direction of some sheep, and another time discharged a gun in the house, putting a bullet through a wing chair in the living room.[32] In the new novel, a teenager fires a rifle up in the air on Mother's Day. Far away, a pregnant woman is vacuuming. The bullet hits her right between the eyes.

As Vonnegut was devoting time to recasting his will and thinking again about the responsibilities of fatherhood—a road already once traveled in his life—a stone from long ago bruised his heel. Knox Burger wrote to him in July 1982 to say he did not appreciate receiving calls from people "requesting information about this or that aspect" of Kurt's past.[33]

Vonnegut had dealt Knox a blow by going back on his word about becoming a client when Knox started his own agency twelve years earlier. Despite that, Knox Burger Associates had flourished, done brilliantly, as a matter of fact. He had sold Martin Cruz Smith's *Gorky Park* to Random House for a handsome one million dollars and watched it run *Palm Sunday* off the road in terms of sales. Knox wasn't Vonnegut's patsy any longer. He wished to remain cordial, but for strangers to call about a "tribute or whatever" for Kurt—and Knox pointedly mentioned that apparently he would not be invited to contribute—was too much. Moreover, Vonnegut's out-of-date reference to him in a 1977 *Paris Review* interview continued to send "loonies left over from the '60s" to his doorstep and their crummy manuscripts over his transom. It was an embarrassment.[34]

Kurt, stung by the righteous tone of Knox's letter, exploded. Painful feelings he had tried to rinse himself of with the help of time and therapy were suddenly welling up again. He shot back a note saying Burger was losing his marbles. He wasn't aware of any "testimonial." Furthermore, he didn't have ESP and couldn't warn him when some clown might call. Up until now, he had avoided telling his "old friend" what he really thought of him. Maybe it was about time—he'd think about it. In the meantime, if Knox didn't want to be bothered, he should get an unlisted phone number.[35]

But Burger refused to take Vonnegut's backhanded slap this time. He reminded his erstwhile friend that he had supported him for almost fifteen years when no one in the publishing community believed in

him. And he resented an "Orwellian revision" of Kurt's rise to popularity that omitted his role in it. "Figuring out what you really think about
me" was really based on "guilt, as you were candid enough to confide to
me some years back."[36]

Having landed a few solid blows on each other, they backed off
finally, neither one clear about the "tribute or whatever" that had started
the quarrel in the first place. (It was a sixtieth birthday present Jill was
preparing.)

BY REMINDING Kurt about the support he had received in the old
days, Burger inadvertently hit him where he was vulnerable—his conscience. Knox didn't know that recently Jane, Kurt's in-house critic,
sounding board, and advocate from his earliest years as a writer, had
been diagnosed with ovarian cancer.

For weeks she had been receiving platinum treatments, making her
intolerably nauseous. As it was, her hair was falling out. But ever optimistic and believing in the power of positive thinking, she was still
merry. To look nice for Nanny's marriage to the realist painter Scott
Prior in October, she was debating whether to wear a wig or just a lovely
scarf.[37] Mark, a physician now, told his father he expected that the cancer would be unstoppable, a prognosis Kurt disgustedly derided as
"informed pessimism."[38] As an antidote against thoughts of death, Kurt
told Nanny he would pay for everything connected with the wedding,
and that she should go for broke, hold back on nothing.[39]

It was not a pleasant thought that his life was turning ironic. Irony as
an element of fiction, a plot device, was an important tool in the kit of
any writer. But when he had shoved off into the money river after the
success of *Slaughterhouse-Five*, he couldn't have imagined the strength
of its strong, midstream current. He felt rudderless; there was no steer-
ing, just observing his "progress," if it could be called that. Having likened himself to Mark Twain, he was more like Huck on the raft, shooting
past the point of return and traveling deeper into unsafe territory.

An outdoor birthday party he and Jill attended in September for
Craig Claiborne, food editor of the *New York Times*, stands as a good
example of the disconnect between the values he espoused and the life
he was living. At the "Binge for the Beautiful People," as the *Washington Post* called it, thirty-six chefs arrived in East Hampton, in addition

to cookbook authors and food luminaries from as far away as France, Mexico, and San Francisco. Two hundred guests were invited, but 450 crowded into the tent to feast on, among the dozens of entrées, a three-foot-square Hungarian meat pie, filled with layers of stuffed peppers, boned squab, cabbage, sausage, and duck liver dumplings under a golden crust carved with Claiborne's initials. For dessert there were baked cakes and tarts. A woman in a summery pink dress was seen surreptitiously stuffing a shopping bag with wrapped cookies. Asked by a reporter what he thought of the affair, Kurt characterized it as a "bit of conspicuous consumption," using the phrase coined by Thorstein Veblen in *The Theory of the Leisure Class*.[40]

Veblen's indictment of the parasitical rich had been given to him by his uncle Alex when Kurt was still a teenager. Reading it, he learned about socialism and the underbelly of fat cats. Also about that time, Alex had invited his nephew to meet Powers Hapgood, the Indianapolis-born social reformer. Over the years, Vonnegut insisted that what he learned about equity among humankind during his impressionable, idealistic youth had never left him. Not long before the exclusive gorge-fest in East Hampton for the hungry rich, he had spoken to the Eugene V. Debs Foundation in Terre Haute, Indiana, warning the audience of labor union members that "modern attitudes are sickening us," adding that we discuss the degradation of people "as if we were discussing bauxite or some other mineral substance." It was a pity how the "bit players in real life" are degraded, he said.[41] To appreciative nods in the audience, he quoted Debs, a four-time presidential candidate of the Socialist Party of America, who said at his sentencing for sedition, "While there is a lower class, I am in it, and while there is a criminal element I am of it, and while there is a soul in prison, I am not free."

"How many of us can echo those words and mean them?" he asked.[42]

He had made choices, consciously or unconsciously, that had created multiple and even contradictory identities. He was a counterculture hero, a guru, and a leftist to his fans; a wealthy investor to his broker; a champion of family and community and yet a distant father; a man who had left his "child-centered" home to save his sanity, but then married a younger woman who was leading him into fatherhood again; a satirist of American life but feeding at the trough of celebrity up to his ears.

* * *

DEADEYE DICK, renamed from *Katmandu*, appeared in October 1982. On the surface, it's a piece of realistic social commentary, continuing the approach in *Jailbird* about how unintentional acts can lead to despair. Both novels are first-person accounts by despondent older men who committed an act that cast a pall over their lives. The tone of *Deadeye Dick* is darker, however, taking its lowest notes from Vonnegut's references in *Palm Sunday* to his loneliness, depression, and sense of having outlived his usefulness. As the narrator of *Deadeye Dick* says resignedly, "We all see our lives as stories. . . . If a person survives an ordinary span of sixty years or more, there is every chance that his or her life as a shapely story has ended, and all that remains to be experienced is epilogue. Life is not over, but the story is."[43]

Following a short autobiographical introduction, Vonnegut switches to the voice of middle-aged Rudy Waltz, nicknamed "Deadeye Dick." At age twelve, while fooling with his father's rifle, Rudy fired a shot over the rooftops of Midland City, Ohio (also the setting of *Breakfast of Champions*), and accidentally killed a pregnant woman. This is an infinitesimally smaller tragedy than the one caused unknowingly by Rudy's father, however, who once befriended and gave hope to a young artist named Adolf Hitler. On the micro and the macro scale in Vonnegut's universe, cause and effect collide like free radicals.

But all of that is spoken of in the past tense. Rudy lives in Haiti now, co-owning a restaurant with his brother because a neutron bomb detonated in Midland City, either by accident or through the government's secret, experimental intention, killing everyone but leaving the machines and buildings intact.

Mass destruction had become a bit of a Vonnegut trope by now. He was genuinely concerned about the arms race with the Soviets, which was heating up during the Reagan administration. In a speech delivered at the Cathedral of St. John the Divine, he warned, "Humankind is running out of time."[44] Following a similar theme, *Deadeye Dick* contends that scientists who place nuclear weapons in the hands of politicians are just as irresponsible as the scientist father in the novel who gives Rudy the key to the gun closet, leading to a deadly accident.

But novels deeply rooted in concerns of an era—especially political issues—don't usually wear well, and *Deadeye Dick* tends to demonstrate that rule of thumb. Absent strong characters, the novel is idea-heavy and didactic. More interesting is to gloss what Vonnegut was thinking about as he wrote.

Rudy's father, Otto, is a stand-in for Kurt Sr.—German, a gun collector, and incapable of showing much warmth to his sons because of a setback in midlife. Rudy's mother (Edith Vonnegut) "never had any work to do. Her servants had raised the children. She was purely ornamental."[45] Their coolness toward him implies that Rudy doesn't inspire their love. By killing an innocent person through sheer misadventure, Rudy becomes an outright pariah, as if confirming that he has always been a mistake, an anomaly—Vonnegut's specter from childhood that he was "an accident," as Bernard flatly informed him. Pain in connection with love has left Rudy "neutered"—numb to emotional experience. "I wasn't to touch anything on this planet, man, woman, child, artifact, animal, vegetable, or mineral, since it was likely to be connected to a push-pull detonator and an explosive charge."[46]

Like Rudy, Vonnegut had used up his emotional reserves. Six years earlier, in *Slapstick*, he had confessed to weariness with life, requesting just "common decency" in his relationships with others. "I cannot distinguish between the love I have for people and the love I have for dogs."[47] The lament continues in *Palm Sunday*—a backward glance, heavy with regret, a sign that he wishes he could refashion the previous decade, starting with his play *Wanda June* and all the heartbreak that followed. In *Deadeye Dick*, Rudy wins a prize for his play *Katmandu*, which entitles it to be produced in New York. But as a piece of drama, it's just as pretentious and cockamamie as *Wanda June*, and rightfully judged a catastrophe. Rudy Waltz, ersatz playwright, retreats into the emotional safety of feeling small and numb again. Extrapolating this onto Vonnegut's life, the message is that quitting after *Slaughterhouse-Five* might have been the best direction he could have taken. But the persona he created continues to pull him into the public eye as if he were a ventriloquist's dummy taken out of a trunk for another performance. As Rudy says, "Voices began to describe me and my surroundings. Nothing they said could be appealed."[48]

Not long after *Deadeye Dick* had been released and reviewed,

Vonnegut had lunch with Martin Amis, then a young author who admired him. In a crowded trattoria on Second Avenue, Amis asked Vonnegut above the din, "How would you grade *Deadeye Dick*?"

"I guess it's sort of a B-minus," he answered after some thought. "I have to keep reminding myself that *I* wrote those early books. *I* wrote that. *I* wrote that. The only way I can regain credit for my early work is—to die."[49]

In mid-November, Jill threw a surprise sixtieth birthday party for Kurt at Michael's Pub on East Fifty-fifth Street. In a cocktail dress by Oscar de la Renta, she welcomed the 110 guests on the invitation list she had drawn up herself: Norman Mailer, George Plimpton, John Irving, Bernard O'Hare, Loree Rackstraw, Marsha Mason, Shana Alexander, and John Updike, for example, as well as Vonnegut and Adams relatives and their spouses. The tables were numbered, and guests found their name on a card beside the place where Jill had specially arranged for them to sit. (Loree moved hers, annoying the hostess.)[50]

The highlight of the evening was Jill's gift to her husband: a Festschrift—a volume of tributes by friends, relatives, and colleagues recalling anecdotes about Kurt, from those who had known him as a child in Indianapolis to the current day. The 164-page, red cloth hardback with photographs, in a limited edition of five hundred, had been assembled and edited by Jill, with help from Morgan Entrekin, at Delacorte. Inside, the dedication from Jill read, "Dearest Kurt: This book is a present for your 60th birthday. It's also a thank you, of sorts, for making our lives on this planet so much the better. You're the nicest person I know and I love you dearly, Jillio."[51] As a way of thanking his birthday guests, Kurt sang a vaudeville song. He also announced that Jill's newest book for young readers, *How It Feels to Be Adopted*, had just been published. They were holding a party the following week for the sixteen children she had interviewed.

Missing from the pages of the Festschrift was a salute from Knox. Kurt, still smarting that Burger had complained about the unwelcome phone calls regarding his former client, couldn't resist giving him a dig later, saying he had been excluded from the Festschrift for writing such a nasty letter.[52] But also notable by its absence was a contribution from

Sam Lawrence. Lawrence had republished Kurt's backlist of novels and signed him to more when he had been down and out in Iowa City. He hadn't been invited to attend the party, either.[53]

IN THE course of her research for *How It Feels to Be Adopted*, Jill came across the Golden Cradle adoption agency in Philadelphia. Founded by Richard Elgart, a former auto parts supplier, Golden Cradle spent a quarter million dollars a year publicizing its services in bold black-and-yellow advertisements on buses, train trestles, park benches, and even Burger King tray liners asking, "Pregnant? Call in Confidence." Essentially a brokerage for unwed mothers and couples wanting to adopt privately, Golden Cradle was also listed in the Yellow Pages of 168 cities in twenty-one states, as well as forty-one college directories. In 1982, the fee for an adoption was about $10,000.[54]

Jill and Kurt brought home infant Lily to the town house on East Forty-Eighth on December 18, 1982. Three days later, Edie and a friend arrived to see the baby. Instead of her father acting the proud new dad, however, she could tell he was "very distraught." Once Jill was out of earshot, he took her aside. "Please don't congratulate me," he begged.[55]

To his old college friend Miller Harris, Vonnegut tried to be philosophical about revisiting, at his age, diaper changing, feeding times, finding a preschool, etc. Jill had wanted a baby, he said, and he didn't have the right to tell her no. Somehow, he would get through this.[56]

THE MONTH before Lily came into his life, a feature story appeared in *Philadelphia* magazine that further upset him. "Looking for Mr. Vonnegut," by David R. Slavitt, a writer friend on Cape Cod in the late 1960s, satirized the satirist himself, bearding the lion in his den. He began the piece by recalling Mark's wedding in the mid-1970s. It had been a sunny day, perfect weather for an outdoor ceremony in the yard of the big house in West Barnstable. There was a feeling of festiveness in the air except around Kurt, who was standing "in his own private rain. . . . Kurt is an unhappy man. It's part of his charm. (But Kurt isn't stupid, and he knows that.)" David, ambling over to the father of the groom, hailed him cheerily.

Kurt, apropos of nothing, said that he'd just been to the dentist and received a lecture about flossing. But flossing wasn't the issue, he said gloomily; the problem was that teeth were made to last a lifetime of perhaps thirty-five or forty years. "But now . . . people live too long."

"Cheer up, Kurt, it's only a wedding," Slavitt replied.[57]

Reading the article, Vonnegut could have tolerated the gibes about his moroseness. And to be fair, the places where Slavitt parodied his style—staccato sentences, graphics, lots of white space—were part of a pretty good send-up, too. But where Kurt really took offense was over the analysis of why he was popular. "The characters are silly and static," Slavitt said, of *Deadeye Dick*. "They don't develop. Nothing happens. Nothing means anything. There is a denial of all meaning, of all possibility of meaning, in his nihilistic ending. The defects don't matter, though. The book will do well, the critics won't be able to hurt his sales much—even though they'd like to. Kurt's readers will buy the book. He doesn't suppose they're very good readers anyway, which is why he writes the books as he does."[58]

It was a roundhouse swing at Vonnegut's motives, cuffing him not for writing pop lit but because he didn't care to try any harder, because he didn't respect his readers, who wouldn't know a good book from a bad one, anyway. Vonnegut's behavior and his writing were calculated with one end in mind, Slavitt contended: to get attention by acting dire, the way he had played the part of the baleful Ancient Mariner at Mark's wedding. "But you don't get a townhouse in the East 40s and a beach house in [Sagaponack] experimenting with tricks in art," Slavitt concluded. "Art is for kids. This is business."[59]

Kurt both called and wrote *Philadelphia* magazine to complain, in language that must have crackled because the editor answered that he was quite "distressed about your letter regarding David Slavitt." Slavitt, Vonnegut stormed to Miller Harris, had turned into a sideshow freak who would do anything to get attention.[60] He tried to get in touch with his "old friend" to have it out, but after volleys of answering machine messages back and forth, Slavitt finally responded in writing.

Kurt had no right to cry foul, he countered, because "you have willfully blurred the distinction most of us keep between our work and our lives, having put yourself into your work and having made yourself into a literary subject." After years of grafting his undisguised personal history onto his fiction, his life was as much a legitimate subject for criticism as the work itself. If Vonnegut wanted to be synonymous in readers' minds with Kilgore Trout, Eliot Rosewater, or Billy Pilgrim, "You have a right to do this—or anything else you want—but there are risks that go along with such practice."[61]

It was a rebuke, an accusation from someone who knew him well that his life seemed meretricious, inauthentic. The two men were never on friendly terms again.

THE SPRING of 1983 saw Vonnegut in no better frame of mind. Although he responded generously to requests for his autograph on posters and books for charity auctions, and he made attempts to get in touch with friends from college and high school as a way of lifting his spirits, feelings of having been wronged would erupt suddenly.

Flying to London in February on the Concorde, he sampled the caviar and the champagne onboard before being driven to Oxford University for a speech. At Oxford, he ranged over all kinds of afflictions assailing humankind—political, economic, ecological—riffing from one theme to another. (The editor of a Canadian literary magazine, hearing him not long before, marveled at his ability to seem "curiously at ease; in a chatty frame of mind even if he says little, or, literally, nothing; and chary of concluding.")[62] Winding down, Vonnegut indicated that he would take a few questions but not many. A young American from Iowa, Craig Canine, a graduate of Princeton studying English language and literature at Oxford, raised his hand. He prefaced his question by explaining that he was a writer just starting out. Did Mr. Vonnegut prefer any special "tools of the trade" on his desk—a favorite dictionary, maybe?

Kurt chuckled, apparently amused by such a jejune question—a favorite dictionary? The audience murmured and laughed in sympathy. Canine continued to stand, mortified, but waiting for an answer as Vonnegut turned him into a straight man while he extemporized about the craft of writing. No, he said finally, he had no "favorite dictionary," dismissing the notion by shaking his curly head, bemused. He pointed to another raised hand.

The next day, Canine wrote to Vonnegut a response he wished he'd had the presence of mind to say. "It is your prerogative to piss on everything till doomsday, Mr. Vonnegut: but why do it in public? And why do it pretending to be doing something else?" If the purpose of visiting

Oxford was to promote *Deadeye Dick*, why not just do that, "instead of half-seductively pretending to address people's serious interest in you and your work? . . . You have also proven that the 'layer of fat' insulating your intelligence (your words, not mine) is not so thick, or intransigent as to force you into assuming the dumb novelist pose, *vis-à-vis* academic criticism. You know what I mean—the trick of affecting an attitude of self-righteous philistinism." Thinking about Vonnegut making a fool of him, Canine said, he wished he would have given him the finger instead of a hand at the end of the evening.[63]

The next day, he brooded over sounding "incredibly priggish" instead of coldly condescending like Vonnegut had been, but it was too late to retrieve the letter.[64] He was surprised then, a few weeks later, to receive a response. It was a note from Vonnegut saying the enclosed check covered the cost of the ticket to his speech. The gesture was not done in the spirit of apology, however. The young man's reproach had angered him, and Vonnegut was glacially slow to forget.

Some years later, at the conclusion of a pleasant lunch with several people in NBC's exclusive Rainbow Room on the sixty-fifth floor of Rockefeller Center, a reporter for *Newsweek* took a moment before leaving to mention to Kurt that they had corresponded once. "Oh, when was that?" Kurt asked, interested.

Thinking they would laugh it off, Canine reminded him about the talk at Oxford and the refund check.

Vonnegut stiffened. "Oh. I remember. Funny, you don't *seem* like an asshole."[65]

HE WAS becoming noticeably flinty, defensive, and sarcastic about the "ghost" of him, as he called it, going around filling his shoes on stages in auditoriums. During a barnstorming tour of college campuses in April 1983, he spoke at Oakland University outside of Detroit. Unknown to him, in the audience was Dale Watson, one of the POWs who had ridden out of Dresden with him on a commandeered wooden cart at the end of the war.

As Vonnegut began to speak, Watson was a little bothered by Kurt's issuing the following caveat: "This is a speech I've given a hundred times but I do it to make money." Still, Watson expected his wife and a couple who had accompanied them would enjoy meeting Kurt on the strength of the old acquaintanceship. He sent a note backstage via an usher. After the speech ended, Watson and the others waited in the aisle, until they assumed Vonnegut hadn't received the message after all. They went home.

Then a few days later, a note arrived in the mail from Kurt acknowledging that Watson was the first of the American regiment in Dresden to "check in." Watson wasn't sure what to make of the words *check in.* They implied that some kind of recognition or even obeisance was finally being paid. Was Vonnegut being serious? He kept the note and wondered from time to time what his army buddy was insinuating.[66]

IN JUNE 1983, following months of chemotherapy, Jane announced that she had experienced "a remarkable healing experience." A CAT scan, she told friends, showed that there was no cancer anywhere. "The incredible relief of that being over, I can't tell you!" She was in such a good mood that she was going to reread all of her ex-husband's works again because they were "terrific."[67] Mark stuck to his diagnosis that any residual ovarian cancer was virulent.[68]

Then in November, exploratory surgery indicated that tumors had returned, requiring a new round of chemotherapy. The reappearance of cancer and the side effects of treatment—nausea, hair and weight loss, skin rash—struck Kurt as cruel, especially after Jane had been overjoyed about her inexplicable healing experience. "Never has anyone been less deserving of such agony. She always took such good care of her body."[69]

WINTER SETTLED in, a raw, rainy one in New York with freezing downpours in December 1983. Kurt attended a celebrity preview of the film *Scarface* starring Al Pacino, but after thirty minutes he walked out, muttering, "It's too gory for me."[70] Having seen men scream from being hit with pieces of red-hot shrapnel at the Battle of the Bulge, he knew "movies lie about deaths from gunshot" if they portray them as "instantaneous and free of gore, if they make them seem almost fun."[71]

He was in a black mood, particularly over how a tiny, late-in-life new family consisting of himself, Jill, and Lily had not been blossoming in some sentimental way like a flower in the autumn of his life, but closing on him like a flytrap.

Since their marriage, Jill had gradually become his self-appointed screener of calls, gatekeeper of the front door, and scheduler of his time. Some writers find this kind of partnership helpful because it gives them periods to work when someone else is deflecting requests to come to the phone and so on. How she played the role of the Sphinx at the entrance to Thebes was not unexpected for someone with a strong ego. But the way Jill conceived her relationship with her husband was hinted at in a phrase that struck novelist Anne Bernays as odd: "Jill said, 'I married *him.*'" As if marrying Vonnegut had been an accomplishment, a kind of career move.[72] Then, after Lily's adoption, the configuration of the Vonnegut family changed.

For example, his hope had been that somehow the most recent version of his will would be sufficiently clear to cover his nephews, his three children by Jane, and now Lily. But that was not to be. The precise sum of money left to all the children became the source of nagging discord—not only between him and Jill, but also between him and Jane. He confided to Edie that the pressure was awful. "Jill was haranguing him to put Lily on an equal basis to his other three children. She battered him relentlessly about it. And my mother was also being strong-willed, but not in such a howling way."[73]

The funeral meats for Kurt's memorial service weren't just cold: they hadn't even been served yet. It was as if he were floating above, a disembodied spirit listening to loved ones complain about what a rotten cheapskate he'd been.

Aggravating his home life still further were Jill's small gestures of disrespect toward his family. When Bernard came to visit his brother in the city, Jill would not permit him to stay in the guest room, so instead, Kurt asked Edie to take care of her uncle. Edie was single again after her divorce some years earlier from Geraldo Rivera. In the corner of her apartment on West Ninth Street she hung a bedsheet, and behind it her seventy-year-old uncle got undressed to sleep on the couch.[74]

AT THE end of December 1983, Vonnegut arranged to meet Loree for lunch during a convention of the Modern Language Association at the Hilton Hotel in Manhattan. She would be attending as a participant; he was slated to deliver a speech on censorship, similar in spirit to the one he gave earlier that year when he had accepted the Freedom to Read Award at the Chicago Public Library's Literary Arts Ball. In that speech he had said, "If I have been censored a lot, then teachers and librarians have had to defend my books a lot . . . even though I am, at my worst, no more dangerous than a banana split."[75]

Also at the lunch with Loree were Peter Reed, a Vonnegut scholar and friend, and Will Stone from Stanford University. Kurt was chatty, mentioning Lily's babyhood accomplishments at home, although he didn't say a word about Jill.[76] At the end of the meal, Kurt invited Loree to stop by the house to see his infant daughter.

The next day, she arrived and lifted dark-haired, one-year-old Lily from the arms of a nanny. As she fussed over the baby, Jill appeared and, according to Loree, behaved in a way that was "incomprehensible." Acknowledging their visitor with a lukewarm "Hi," she instructed Kurt to follow her downstairs to see something in her studio. Loree tagged behind, not knowing what else to do. The three of them stood staring at a new piece of equipment, wordlessly, until Kurt, growing agitated from the tension, broke the ice by saying that Loree had to go. He escorted her back upstairs, down the steep front steps of the brownstone, and hailed a cab at the curb.[77]

In her memoir, *Love as Always, Kurt*, Loree professed she was dumbfounded by Jill's "obvious indifference," adding, "I hoped my brief visit had not upset their relationship."[78] After all, it had been almost ten years since the secret hideaway weekend in Key West. When Loree arrived home, she wrote to Kurt rather disingenuously, "I count on you to tell me if my presence with Jill is not welcome. I like her a lot, but I don't want to be obtrusive."[79] In any case, when the door of the brownstone on East Forty-eighth Street closed behind Loree, Kurt's world became a little darker, a little more circumscribed.

When he was a boy, his mother did not like him to bring home his public school friends because they were déclassé. Now he was sixty-two years old and still required to seek permission or suffer punishment of some kind: a shouting match, the silent treatment, or a contest of who would be gone from the house the longest.

ONE MORNING the following March 1984, Don Farber called Kurt's private phone in his study several times with no answer. Vonnegut's writing regime hadn't changed for years—decades even. Up by dawn, hunched over the typewriter with a cup of coffee near at hand, and then typing and mumbling until lunch or so. It was midmorning when Don called back again with the same result, so he decided to ring the downstairs phone. Jill answered. She had no idea why Kurt wasn't up. (They didn't share a bedroom after Lily arrived.)[80] Don said he would be right over.

By the time Don arrived, Jill had discovered Kurt unconscious from a combination of alcohol, sleeping pills, and antidepressants.[81] Attending him at the bedside was his physician, Dr. Mortimer E. Bader. Don started to phone for an ambulance, but Jill insisted he was absolutely not to do that. It would create a scene—reporters would descend outside. They were going to call a private car, not an ambulance.

Farber, normally low-key, began shouting that her husband could be dying. Over Jill's protests, he called an ambulance anyway. She insisted Kurt be admitted to Payne Whitney Psychiatric Clinic on the Upper East Side, a small, turn-of-the-century facility where he wouldn't be gawked at. Don countered that he should go to St. Vincent's Hospital in Greenwich Village. Roused by the commotion, Kurt stirred and opened his eyes. Dazedly, he asked to go to St. Vincent's—he was familiar with it.[82]

Jill, furious, had to acquiesce.

KURT WAS at St. Vincent's for eighteen days in the care of Ralph A. O'Connell, Vonnegut's "Irish doctor," as he referred to him, who specialized in treating bipolar disorder. Mark, visiting his father, decided that he hadn't intended to kill himself because he hadn't tried hard enough.[83] His motives were typical of many people who attempt suicide, which is acting out a revenge fantasy against persecutors by making them feel guilty; shifting the burden of depression and anger onto them. By this logic, self-destruction becomes a triumph over someone else.[84]

At the end of his stay at St. Vincent's, Kurt didn't go home. He wanted out of Jill's orbit.[85] He wanted to be alone. Edie found him a small row house to sublet at 5 MacDougal Alley in Greenwich Village, a two-room studio with exposed brick and hardwood floors, located on a quiet, tree-lined street, half a block from Washington Square. Just as she had when her father went alone to Iowa City, then from West Barnstable to New York, she spent every day with him, walking the block and a half from her place to his, and painting at an easel in one room while he wrote in the other.

Loree assured him that she would remain steadfast, too. "I wish I were there right now to hug your wonderful, tousled head to my ample bosom and tell you something inane like: everything will be all right. And that my love for you is both unconditional and unaltered by all these years. And that I think of you every day, and doubtless will, until I have nothing left to think with."[86]

14: Dear Celebrity
1984–1991

MacDougal Alley in New York City was a haven that allowed Kurt to think, read, and write. Edie, his only regular visitor, sensed that he was drifting contentedly, out of earshot of "screaming, demanding people."[1] He had been underweight when he was admitted to St. Vincent's, bony and shoulder-stooped. But during his stay in the hospital, he ate "like a farmhand," he told Loree, and looked healthier.[2] He continued seeing Dr. O'Connell as an outpatient, and gradually his depression, the "gray drizzle of horror . . . a storm of murk," as his friend William Styron characterized his own periods of suffering, began to evaporate.

He was almost sixty-five, and following his suicide attempt Loree recommended that he consider retiring. "I mean, good citizens *do* retire, you know."[3] Twin enemies, age and illness, were extinguishing the lives of some of his contemporaries. One afternoon a few years earlier, after finishing lunch with Salman Rushdie in Sagaponack, Kurt had called his neighbor Nelson Algren to ask whether he could bring Rushdie over for cocktails. A police officer answered the phone instead. "This is his house, but Mr. Algren is dead."[4] Truman Capote, not quite sixty years old, had stopped over for a visit—he liked to swim in Kurt and Jill's pool—but then asked to lie down on their couch because he was in "great pain."[5] A week later, he died at the home of a friend in Los

Angeles. Irwin Shaw, whom Kurt had only recently come to know and consider a friend, died in Switzerland at age seventy-one. And Max Wilkinson, known for his orotund toasts, tailored suits, and calling everyone "my dear," was so despondent over the death of his wife, Mary, after a long illness, that he was unable to carry on and committed suicide.

In April 1984, a month after his release from the hospital, Kurt went alone to an international PEN conference in Tokyo, taking time to tour Japanese pottery shops in memory of his father, who loved making ceramics.[6] On his return, he contributed to the Mississippi Civil Liberties Union by donating two essays, "Fates Worse Than Death" and "The Worst Addiction of Them All," on nuclear disarmament and the arms race, respectively, for publication in a limited edition book that Nouveau Press released in December 1984 as *Nothing Is Lost Save Honor.*

He turned again to writing in MacDougal Alley, polishing a draft of a new novel, *Galápagos.* The latter half of 1984 was a year of puttering, of replenishment, and if he paused to consider, he had things to be grateful for. Three of his nephews resided in western Massachusetts near Nanny and her husband, Scott, who were starting a family. Jim Adams, once the scourge of West Barnstable, was a cabinetmaker and father to a baby daughter. All of the Adams brothers were married, in fact, all except Steve, who had inherited his uncle's gift for humor and was writing comedy in Los Angeles. Edie continued to paint and exhibit and was in love with a childhood friend from the Cape, John Squibb, whom both Kurt and Jane hoped she would marry.[7]

Yet he also had to accept now that Jane was not going to survive cancer. Kurt had never believed in her inexplicable healing experiences or her cobbled-together religion of positive thinking, meditation, and Christian worship. But privately he had held out hope that something wonderful might happen. He just wanted her suffering to end.[8] There was nothing to be done, though, and he began feeling intimations of grief for the girl he had bragged about marrying when he was only a harum-scarum fraternity brother at Cornell. Marrying her had been the beginning of his new life, an affirmation, following his mother's suicide and his exposure to death on a monstrous scale as a soldier.

In February 1985 he delivered *Galápagos,* completing his multiple book contract with Delacorte. For the first time in twenty years he wasn't under deadline to produce. As a reward for having completed a novel against the odds, he took a two-week trip at the end of March through Poland, East Germany, and Czechoslovakia. Riding tour buses and looking out the windows, he was just another American taking in the sights, although he also made a point of inquiring about the treatment of fellow writers in those discouraging places for artists and reporting back to PEN.[9]

After his trip to Europe, he returned to his home on East Forty-eighth Street and to Jill and Lily. It was Edie's impression that things were better. Lily, just entering the "terrible twos," had a nanny taking care of her. For Jill's forty-fifth birthday, Kurt threw her a party at the Tavern on the Green.

As a couple they presented themselves in a happier light now. One evening, James Lipton, host of *Inside the Actors Studio*, invited them to dinner at one of his favorite restaurants near his summer home outside New York, raving about the French pie he would order for them at the end. At last, he motioned the waiter over to request the pièce de résistance! But there was none to be had. Embarrassed, Lipton apologized to his guests. The following day, there was a knock on his door. Kurt and Jill were standing there, smiling, dressed in tennis outfits, and Jill was holding a flat box. They had driven out from the city, stopped at the restaurant, and picked up a whole pie for Lipton, which he laughingly accepted.[10]

Kurt was strong enough now to resume going on the speaking circuit, too. Most years during the 1980s, he went on two speaking tours at $8,000 to $10,000 per engagement, although the "compressed" itinerary tended to leave his "concentration on writing temporarily destroyed."[11] Unlike most writers, he was an extrovert, who enjoyed having people around, attending social events, and being interviewed. A solitary "scholar's day," as Cotton Mather called it, consisting only of writing, reading, and studying, was the equivalent to him of being kept after school. Coming home from abroad, he committed to a tour of ten campuses in two weeks, among them Miami Dade Community College, the University of Toledo, the University of Puget Sound, and the University of California/Berkeley, where students protesting a campus policy surrounded him as if he were a de facto leader.

Still not content to ride comfortably a little longer on his reputation as a man of letters despite having *Galápagos* slated for publication in the fall of 1985, or with busying himself as cochair of the program committee for the upcoming international PEN Congress in New York, he made adjustments to his publishing career.

To begin with, he did not automatically renew with his publisher, Delacorte. About ten years earlier, Dell/Delacorte had been sold to Doubleday. At that time, Vonnegut had expressed his concerns about the change. Dealing with a big house stacked with layers of management was not something he wanted to do.[12] Then in 1983 Doubleday dropped Sam Lawrence's imprint after his seventeen-year association with Dell/Delacorte.[13]

Lawrence had always been something of an anomaly in the publishing scene, surviving as an authors' impresario for more than twenty-five years and dodging the effects of mergers and consolidations. The year he began his independent imprint, 1965, he had only one book on his list, *The Ginger Man*, by J. P. Donleavy. Later he published Katherine Anne Porter's *Ship of Fools*, Richard Brautigan's *Trout Fishing in America*, Tim O'Brien's *Going After Cacciato*, and, of course, all of Vonnegut. So when Doubleday dropped him from its business model, Lawrence took his imprint to E. P. Dutton instead, relying on the loyalty of his author-clients to stay with him.

Consequently, he was astonished when he learned only through a friend, Helen Meyer, the former president of Dell, that Vonnegut was leaving him. Until that moment, he had assumed Kurt would follow him to Dutton—theirs was a partnership, after all. More shocking than hearing of Kurt's departure secondhand, however, was the revelation that Kurt had insinuated Lawrence swindled him. In the same manner that he had left Knox Burger breathless with hurt and anger, Kurt was abandoning Lawrence without a backward glance.

Lawrence wrote to Kurt: "You or Jill or Don Farber had the mistaken impression that I was paid out of your royalties with the implication that I was taking something away from you. It's the co-publisher who pays me for acquiring books, not the author." Nevertheless, Lawrence was willing to accept his decision to part company. "Kurt, we had a good run together. You owe me nothing and I owe you nothing. . . . I'm proud to have published your work at the time I did."[14] On a personal note, he wished he had been invited to contribute to Kurt's

Festschrift. Just as Knox had been omitted from the story of Vonnegut's success, Lawrence was crushed to think that he might be, too.

Vonnegut sent a copy of Lawrence's letter without comment to Don Farber for his files. Unable to find another publisher other than Doubleday that would meet his terms, Kurt accepted a quarter-of-a-million-dollar advance for his next novel, without the imprint of Seymour Lawrence.[15]

GALÁPAGOS, HIS eleventh novel, appeared in the fall of 1985 and treated themes of renewal, adaptation, and harmony—his hopes for his own life presented as a fantasy about evolution. It's distinctive among his work because it's the only novel-length predication he ever makes about the future of the human race, not just individuals, that's optimistic. Provided humanity doesn't exterminate itself, he considers the possibility that nature might reassert its governance one day.[16] If so, perhaps natural selection, the engine of randomness on Earth, will determine humankind's destiny, guided, although he doesn't say so directly, by the mystery of what we conceive of as God.[17]

The idea had occurred to him during a vacation trip with Jill to the Galápagos Islands three years earlier. This was his first visit to a South American country. The islands, an archipelago of volcanic cones straddling the equator about 850 miles west of Ecuador, have changed little since Charles Darwin went ashore there in 1835 and noted in his journal, "Nothing could be less inviting than the first appearance. A broken field of black basaltic lava is everywhere covered by a stunted brushwood, which shows little signs of life." All he could find at first were "wretched-looking little weeds."[18] As the young British botanist began exploring, he imagined that such a bleak place must resemble the "cultivated parts" of Hell.[19] But Darwin was seeing the landscape through the lens of the past, colored by nineteenth-century scientific opinion, and not what it might reveal about the future.[20]

Vonnegut's visit to the Galápagos Islands close to 150 years later, on the other hand, inspired him with thoughts of humankind starting over. What if this archipelago could become a kind of Petri dish where a small human gene pool evolves into a strange species of sea lions? Although he imagines them looking as strange as platypuses, they are happy and in a state of oneness with their surroundings.

This transmutation begins in *Galápagos* when a boatload of tourists is shipwrecked and marooned. Meanwhile, humanity catches a virus that prevents reproduction—the equivalent of the catastrophists' explanation for the disappearance of the dinosaurs. Over time, the brains of the humans on Galápagos, underused to begin with, diminish in size via genetic drift as well as natural selection, and their opposable thumbs, too—critical to the march of technology—recede. Finally, their sexual interests become as mild as sparrows, all of which brings the human species, now fur-covered amphibians, into balance with their ecosystem.

Reviewers tended to divide over the usefulness of this scenario. Some were unsettled by human degeneration similar to what H. G. Wells had described in *The Island of Doctor Moreau* where beasts are surgically crossed with men and women. Wells's purpose in his 1896 novel, however, was to attack vivisection. Reviewer Michiko Kakutani dubbed *Galápagos* a "well-crafted comic strip" with "admirable, if somewhat disorganized, inventiveness."[21] The reviewer for the *Times* of London saw *Galápagos* as bringing Vonnegut's "lifelong belief in the imperfectability of human nature to its logical conclusion."[22] In defense of Vonnegut's work in general, the science fiction author Thomas M. Disch, writing in the *Times Literary Supplement*, commended him as "still the same, droll, disingenuous, utterly middle-American, if now high middle-aged, Huck Finn." But because of his artlessness and accessibility, the literary establishment would continue to "comfortably dismiss Vonnegut as a naïf with a knack for low comedy, but not 'serious,' not an artist, not canonical."[23]

Reading the reviews, Kurt detected the same stigma associated with *Galápagos* that had been attached to his earliest work: critics, he continued to believe, couldn't tolerate science mixed with literature. They wanted *Silent Spring* on this shelf here and *Portnoy's Complaint* over there.[24] In fact, highbrows misunderstanding him, which he was convinced was true, added salt to a joke in a film in which he appeared about the time of *Galápagos*'s publication.

In October 1985, he accepted a cameo role in *Back to School*, starring Rodney Dangerfield, for $25,000. In the film, Dangerfield plays a millionaire undergraduate who hires Vonnegut to fudge a paper analyzing his own novels, figuring it will certainly receive an A. Kurt arrives at

Dangerfield's door, doffing his cap and ready to do Dangerfield's home-work for him. But Dangerfield's instructor returns the paper on Von-negut with a failing grade, accompanied by a superior smirk. "Whoever *did* write this doesn't know the first thing about Kurt Vonnegut!"

Aside from the jab at university professors, Dangerfield's response of disbelief and anger mirrored Vonnegut's frustration with some reviewers. The implication was that even Vonnegut wasn't sophisticated enough to critique his own fiction!

No DOUBT it was Vonnegut's sensitivity about being dismissed as friv-olous or, ironically, too serious and banned by a few school boards that increased his zeal for defending free speech, a conviction that came to define him in the later part of his life as much as his stand against war. Everything he believed about free speech as a fundamental right, Von-negut said, he learned in his public high school civics class in India-napolis.[25]

In 1983, for example, the Association of American Publishers applied for $50,000 from the National Endowment for Democracy, created dur-ing the Reagan administration, to help fund the work of selecting books for the 1985 Moscow Book Fair that would illustrate the diversity of publishing in America and "the strength of its democratic institu-tions."[26] Kurt, having served on a similar committee for the Moscow fair in 1979, agreed to serve this time as chairperson. Among his fellow committee members were the *Scientific American* editor Dennis Flana-gan, Toni Morrison, and the poet Rose Styron. At the end of their delib-erations, they created a master list of 313 books published in the previous five years that might be found in American households: the *Sears, Roe-buck Mail Order Catalog*, for instance; Allen Ginsberg's *Collected Poems 1947–1980*; *Elvis*, by Albert Goldman; *Jane Fonda's Workout Book*; *Iacocca: An Autobiography*; *The Butter Battle Book*, by Dr. Seuss; and the *Rand McNally Road Atlas*.

When the committee submitted its list, however, the president of the National Endowment for Democracy, Carl Gershman, raised concerns about the political balance of the members' choices, citing in particular Seymour Hersh's *The Price of Power*, Jonathan Kwitny's *Endless Ene-mies*, and Jonathan Schell's *The Fate of the Earth*. Too many titles repre-senting "one segment of the American political spectrum," Gershman said, were on the list, and he requested that the committee add a few more from a conservative perspective.[27] Responding in the leading conservative magazine, *National Review*, William F. Buckley Jr. expressed mock surprise that anyone should have expected a different outcome from a committee headed by Kurt Vonnegut, whose "name conjures up, of course, a writer highly talented, highly imaginative, and very much at odds with American foreign policy, in particular our policy of maintaining a nuclear deterrent force."[28]

Gershman's request didn't qualify as censorship, but Vonnegut was angered that his work on the committee, done in the spirit of good citizenship, was being impugned because of his opinions about contemporary issues—ecological, political, and otherwise. "It is nobody's business but mine and the committee's what books we select," he retorted, unwilling to bend.[29] But the committee had accepted $50,000 of tax money to do the work. The only way to be consistent now, since Vonnegut had made it clear that he and his colleagues would be beholden to no one, was to return the funds, which they did. Instead, the Association of American Publishers raised its own funds for the exhibition and for the book catalog listing the committee's original selections.

But when the catalog arrived at the Moscow Book Fair, Vonnegut's name no longer appeared as chairperson of the committee. He had insisted that it be removed in protest over the federal government trying to have a hand in choosing the titles of books for the fair.[30]

BUCKLEY, THE most prominent conservative intellectual of his day, wasn't through with Vonnegut yet, however. As the moderator of the highly regarded program *Firing Line* on public television, he was noted for his skill at forcing guests to defend their positions, while probing for logical inconsistencies in their arguments. His droll rebukes, usually coupled with merry winks and a grin like the Cheshire cat's, could be particularly devastating. As the date neared for the 1986 International PEN Congress in New York, Buckley invited the two cochairs of the program committee, Vonnegut and Norman Mailer, to appear on his program in December 1985, which was titled, significantly, "What Does PEN Have to Offer?"

A hint of trouble surfaced in the first moments of the program when Buckley introduced his guests by saying that PEN's upcoming "international conclave" in New York was for "the purpose of advancing ideals, the exact definition of which we aren't supposed to talk about, except that writers should be allowed to write." He let Mailer explain the work PEN does assisting writers imprisoned in countries where free speech is forbidden. Then, with PEN's mission clearly established for the audience, Buckley set up Vonnegut for a logical fall: "You said in a recent interview about PEN, 'We are apolitical, but we are also interested in the freedom of thought and speech.' When you said, 'but we are also,' did you imply to that extent you are political?"

Vonnegut agreed that was so. The freedom of thought and speech "isn't a widely held view around the world."

"Well, I am interested to hear you say that," replied Buckley, closing in, "because you were quoted as saying . . . 'What do I want my books to accomplish? Well, I hope eventually to destroy the American army as an effective fighting force.'" Buckley raised his eyebrows and laughed. "It seems to me that if you destroy the effective fighting force, there isn't much left there to intimidate those who would want to take away our freedom."

Before Vonnegut could answer, Mailer tried to redirect that conversation, but Buckley wouldn't hear of it. "No, because I am working my way into the position of PEN. PEN is an 'apolitical' body, but it really isn't." Clearly he meant to show that PEN had a political agenda, and if pacifists like Vonnegut were in charge, it wasn't representative of common American ideals.

Vonnegut, seeing the way things were going, and fearing apparently that he would embroil PEN in controversy on the eve of its international event, conceded, "My politics are grotesque, because I exaggerate."

"You're quite right," replied Buckley, laughing. "Yes."[31]

REGARDLESS, VONNEGUT was a dedicated believer in the importance of protecting free speech and would go to the barricades in defense of it. A few weeks after being filleted on Buckley's *Firing Line*, he joined the feminist Betty Friedan and the actress Colleen Dewhurst, who later became the head of the National Endowment for the Arts, at a press conference for the National Coalition Against Censorship. The office of the U.S. attorney general Edwin Meese hadn't yet released its final report— the Meese Report on Pornography, as it came to be known. Anticipating the headlines and editorials it would generate, the coalition through a press conference issued a report of its own, "The Meese Commission Exposed: Proceedings of a National Coalition Against Censorship." Vonnegut's sarcasm about the Meese Report combusted in the pages of the *Nation*, in which he speculated that some "pederastic Congressman" must have tacked the First Amendment onto a bill when no one was looking for the sake of protecting pornography.[32]

In February 1986 at the International PEN Congress, the theme of which was "The Writer's Imagination and the Imagination of the State," Vonnegut spoke about writers' involvement in politics, appearing on a panel with the journalist and Pulitzer Prize winner Frances FitzGerald, former presidential candidate George McGovern, the historian Arthur Schlesinger Jr., the Canadian prime minister Pierre Trudeau, and Mario Vargas Llosa. There again he warmed to the theme of defending free speech, especially writers' responsibility to do so. Many of the attendees judged it the best panel during the weeklong event.[33] In August, he spoke before a subcommittee of the Senate Foreign Relations Committee reviewing the McCarthy-era McCarran-Walter Act of 1952, part of which excluded certain aliens from immigrating to the United States on ideological grounds.[34] Representing the PEN American Center board as one of its executive board members, Vonnegut characterized the 1952 law as "embarrassing, foolish, mean-spirited and xenophobic. . . . The free exchange of ideas among nations and individuals does not endanger our security, but strengthens it, and the belief that, as citizens of the United States, all freedoms of expression are our rights."[35]

Following the hearings, Congress passed the Immigration Reform and Control Act of 1986 and, in 1990, stripped out altogether the ideological clauses of the McCarran-Walter Act.

PUBLICLY, Vonnegut's reputation as pundit and grouch was increasing, but personally he didn't feel that cranky. There was a lively rhythm to his life in the mid-1980s consisting of biannual college campus tours, constant requests for autographs, lectures, and reprint permissions, assuring him that he was current on the cultural scene and not yet a grand old man. He was drafting a new novel, *Bluebeard*; an art wholesaler expressed interest in three hundred of his lithographs and prints; and the comedian Dick Shawn paid him well for his film treatment based on characters in Shawn's play *The Second Greatest Entertainer in the Whole Wide World*.[36] It's not surprising that some letters to Vonnegut asking for a donation began "Dear Celebrity."

His courtesy could be quite touching too when he was in a good frame of mind. At Gonzaga University in Spokane, Washington, in 1986, he showed every consideration toward an embarrassed young writer.

Twenty-one-year-old Jess Walter was working in the sports department of a local newspaper, answering phones, and taking fiction writing workshops but not getting much of his own creative writing done. Then, hearing that his literary hero, Kurt Vonnegut, was coming to speak at Gonzaga, he concocted a plan that might get him an interview with his favorite author. He would attend Vonnegut's press conference pretending to be on assignment for *Esquire* and then sell the piece to the magazine.

On the day Vonnegut arrived at Gonzaga, Jess presented his phony press credentials, borrowed from the sports department, and was directed to the small room in the student union where Vonnegut's press conference would be held. He waited, completely alone. Suddenly, the door opened and Vonnegut strode in, accompanied by the event organizer. Well, said the organizer cheerily, glancing around—seeing that there was only one interviewer, why not make things easy and shove a pair of desks together?

Vonnegut sat down opposite his interviewer, sizing him up. Jess, looking down at the damp piece of paper in his hand, realized he was shaking. "So, if you were going to give advice to a young writer, someone who really admires you," his voice cracking, "what—what exactly would it be, huh?"

Vonnegut stared at him and exhaled smoke thoughtfully. "May I ask you a question first?"

"Sure!"

"How old are you?"

"Twenty-one."

"And you're working for *Esquire*?"

Jess's shoulders dropped. "Well, they haven't actually accepted the piece yet, but that's what I told the people here . . . that I was writing a piece for *Esquire*."

Vonnegut laughed. For twenty minutes they talked about selling to the fiction market, throughout which Jess took notes rapidly, until Vonnegut said, "But I might as well be telling you how to repair a Model A. The golden days of magazines are over. Do you mind if I get some rest? I'm really tired."

That night at the lecture, the young interviewer took a seat in the front row. Afterward, as fans were milling around, Vonnegut caught Jess's attention and motioned him over.

"Did you get everything you needed?"

The young, unpublished writer said he had indeed, knowing that it was obvious he would never get a salable story out of that misadventure.

"Good, I look forward to reading it."

"Me, too."

Twenty years later, Vonnegut returned to Gonzaga University, by which time Jess Walter had published two nonfiction books, his second novel was in bookstores, and he was finishing his third. This time, in anticipation of Vonnegut's visit, he wrote a feature for Spokane's alternative newspaper, describing how important it had been to him that his author-hero had been so understanding and generous. When he was growing up, no one in his household was college-educated; there had been no books to read, and no one read. Then, despite his lack of experience, Vonnegut had said of his dreadful attempt at an interview, "I look forward to reading it."

"Well, Mr. Vonnegut, here it is," Jess offered.

The following month, a package for him arrived. It smelled of Pall Malls. Inside was a leather-bound Franklin edition copy of *The Sirens of Titan*. And on the flyleaf: "To my fellow novelist, Jess Walter—This is the one book of mine that wrote itself, all the others refused. Kurt Vonnegut."[37]

JANE'S FRIEND on Scudder's Lane Betty Stanton (mother of Allison Mitchell, who appears in the introduction to *Slaughterhouse-Five*) received a call in 1986 from one of the Vonnegut children saying that now would be a good time to pay a visit to Jane. She was receiving hospice care in Washington, D.C. A nurse suggested Betty come for tea.

Jane was propped up on the couch, a bright scarf wrapped around her head, accentuating her pale skin. She and Adam had married in a quiet ceremony almost two years earlier. It was understood that their time as man and wife would be short, but they regarded marriage, even under such sad circumstances, as a life-affirming act.[38]

News of children and grandchildren occupied much of the two friends' visit during the late afternoon. They also shared memories of what Cape Cod had been like thirty years earlier when more of it was forested, a milkman delivered bottles with a layer of cream on top, and school was canceled when the New England snow was too deep. Then, as they reminisced, Betty noticed a manuscript lying on the coffee table. "I picked it up and I was looking at it and it was her book about the family. I said, 'Jane, this looks wonderful, you're a really good writer. Do you have a publisher?' And she said no."

Would she mind if a friend at Houghton Mifflin looked at it?

She would be pleased, she said.[39]

DURING THE last year of Jane's life, Kurt had been writing the words to a requiem. He never said it was for Jane, but considering the timing of it, and that it's unique among his works, it can be fairly assumed that he was thinking of the end of her life.

Describing the moment of inspiration, Kurt said he and his "second wife" were attending the premiere of Andrew Lloyd Webber's *Requiem Mass* featuring Placido Domingo and Sarah Brightman in February 1985 at St. Thomas Church in New York.[40] The music is a long lamentation, and Kurt, reading in the program the English translation of the Latin mass warning of judgment and perdition, bitterly noted that the singers "were behaving as though God were a wonderful person who had prepared all sorts of goodies which we could enjoy after we were dead," when the words, on their face, were "sadistic" and "masochistic."[41] He went home that night and worked late in his study writing new words to replace the "bellowing bullshit" of the mass, which he titled "Requiem: The Hocus Pocus Laundromat" to reflect his attempt at cleansing the original of its horror.[42] A classical scholar at New York University agreed to translate Vonnegut's English into Latin and, later, the composer Edgar David Grana wrote an original work to accompany the words.

Vonnegut's requiem asks that the departed be left in peace, now that their lives are over, since the Deity has not deemed us worthy of his attention, as evidenced by the amount of suffering that humanity constantly endures.

> My prayers are unheard,
> But Thy sublime indifference will ensure
> that I not burn in some everlasting fire.
> Give me a place among the sheep
> and the goats, separating none from none,
> leaving our mingled ashes where they fall.
> . . . O Time, O Elements
> Grant them rest. Amen.[43]

It's the prayer of a rationalist—if there can be such a thing—a meditation on the afterlife by a freethinker and secularist in the vein of his great-grandfather Clemens Vonnegut. It's also a gesture of fist-shaking scorn toward heaven by someone who has seen his former wife, his "dear Jane," racked by four years of purgatorial torment by one of the most painful cancers imaginable.[44]

"Requiem: The Hocus Pocus Laundromat" appeared in the *North American Review* in December 1986. On the sixteenth of that month, Jane awoke from semiconsciousness and asked Edie to call her father. "I dialed his number and put the phone on her ear. She was very, very weak. It was a sweet conversation. Like old childhood friends talking and she asked him how to leave the planet."[45]

"I told her on the telephone," Vonnegut wrote, "that a sunburned, raffish, bored but not unhappy ten-year-old boy, who we did not know, would be standing on the gravel slope of the boat-launching ramp at the foot of Scudder's Lane. He would gaze out at nothing in particular, birds, boats, or whatever, in the harbor of Barnstable, Cape Cod. . . . I told Jane that this boy, with nothing better to do, would pick up a stone, as boys will. He would arc it over the harbor. When the stone hit the water, she would die."[46]

Jane was unable to "let go," in Nanny's words, because with family members visiting she didn't want to miss anything, and she was reluctant to say goodbye. Three days later, the hospice nurse told her "she could go now," and she passed away in a coma at eight o'clock in the evening at her home in Washington, D.C., on December 19, 1986.

Kurt, Bernard, the six Vonnegut and Adams children and their spouses, three of Jane's five grandchildren, and many friends attended the memorial service. Afterward, Maria Donoso hugged Kurt. She told him that doubling the number of children in the family had been too much for both of them. He agreed that, as a couple, they had allowed themselves to be pushed to the margins, not being together enough, not listening.[47] As he looked back, what troubled him most was that when money and success finally came, and the children left to pursue their lives, Jane had seemed paralyzed for several years. It was pure happenstance, but it appeared that he had scooped up his winnings and left her alone with nothing. She hadn't wanted to complete her master's in social work or write book reviews, as he had once suggested. Not until the actual divorce and the last few years of her relationship with Adam did she come into her own. He consoled himself with thinking that finally they had learned to love each other all over again, but not as husband and wife. At the end, just in time, he thought, they had been able to say farewell affectionately.[48]

VONNEGUT WROTE a good deal of *Bluebeard* in Sagaponack in the potato barn converted by Frank Stella into a studio. Appropriately, the novel is about art and art theory. When it was released in spring 1987, many major publications, including *Newsweek*, the *New Yorker*, the *New York Review of Books* and the *Times Literary Supplement*, chose not to review it. As an extended debate on aesthetic theory and the role of an artist, it's convoluted and too allegorical. But when it's decoded, the novel is like a series of arguments between Kurt and Jill, which were occurring more frequently again.

Vonnegut, as if he expects he will be brought down by readers who are knowledgeable about twentieth-century art, includes an opening disclaimer that *Bluebeard* is a "hoax autobiography" and he isn't writing a "responsible history" of abstract expressionism or a roman à clef of an artist such as Jackson Pollock, Arshile Gorky, or Mark Rothko. This diffidence on Vonnegut's part is also the protagonist's problem: the painter Rabo Karabekian feels inadequate because he lacks authority.

Karabekian, an Armenian American artist, was a minor character in *Breakfast of Champions*, but here the story is all his own, narrated in the first person. He is in his early seventies, a few years older than the author, blind in one eye, and well aware that he has been a bad husband and father. He is divorced, then widowed, and his grown children will have nothing to do with him. A passive man, he is writing a combination diary and memoir in his splendid East Hampton home, which contains the world's largest private collection of abstract expressionist paintings. Critics have dismissed his work in that genre, however, as meaningless. Worse, from a technical standpoint, his paintings were executed with substandard paint, which begins disintegrating after a few months. The artist is decomposing, and so is his work.

Enter Circe Berman, aka Jill, as Kurt disclosed about the character's identity to his college friend Miller Harris.[49] Circe is the author of many popular novels for young adults—a parallel with Jill's *How It Feels* and *A Very Young* series of books about children. She also collects sentimental, Victorian photographs of "little girls on swings," matted on velvet with gilded frames. She thinks abstract art is ridiculous and mocks a masterpiece by Jackson Pollock, insisting that Karabekian paint a scene that would depict the Armenian massacre realistically.[50] (By this logic, *Slaughterhouse-Five* does a poor job of describing war because it isn't a literal description.) One day, without asking his permission, she removes Rabo's abstract art collection from his foyer and replaces it with photographs of nineteenth-century girls. This, she argues, puts innocence on display, making the viewer not want the children in the photographs harmed by disease or poverty.

Karabekian, finally roused out of his torpor, takes offense at her disregard for other people's privacy. The two get into a heated argument, she leaves, but then is accepted back.

To win his debate with Circe about realistic versus abstract art, Karabekian unlocks the old potato barn that once served him as a studio but has been nailed shut for years. Inside is his last will and testament: an enormous eight-paneled painting, eight feet wide and sixty-four feet long, depicting in ultrarealistic detail the scene Karabekian witnessed in a Czechoslovakian valley on V-E day. (It also happens to be the valley exactly as Vonnegut saw it when he was released as a POW.)[51] Circe is overwhelmed by the scope of the work, the implication being that Rabo/Kurt is capable of representational art, but he has moved beyond it (just as Vonnegut's first novel, *Player Piano*, was his most conventional). As artists, both men have taken greater and greater risks in their lifetimes, despite how the philistines attacked them.

Percolating on the side of the story is a romance between Karabekian and Marilee Kemp, a former Ziegfeld Follies showgirl who is as ambitious, intelligent, and perceptive as Circe but a victim of men. Unfortunately, most of the strains in the novel sympathetic to feminism are drowned out by the importance of women as seductive.

All in all, *Bluebeard* is an overlong, bumptious treatise on the value of Vonnegut's oeuvre as a writer, couched in an argument about aesthetic theory, at the center of which was Kurt's increasing friction with Jill.

HE HAD hoped that with Jane gone, and everything now settled about the will, he would enjoy a hard-earned peace in connection with it. He wanted it understood by his heirs of every degree and rank that he was not a mother lode of untapped treasure. He had already been more than generous, he told Nanny.[52]

On another front, he tried to prevent problems in the family that might result from Jane's posthumous book slated for publication in October 1987 by Houghton Mifflin as *Angels Without Wings*.

He knew she had been writing easily and rapidly during the year before her death, and he took for granted that a fictionalized memoir by her of the Adams boys coming to live in West Barnstable could be touching and wise.[53] But then the publisher requested permission to use his actual name—Jane referred to him in the manuscript as "Karl" for some reason—and asked whether he would contribute a foreword or afterword.

Kurt not only refused to allow his name to be used in his late wife's book, he also refused to sign a release permitting use of a pseudonym (the publisher used "Karl" anyway), nor would he contribute a foreword or introduction.[54] The risk of inciting more skirmishes because of what he did or didn't say was too great.

MARRIAGE IS made up of an infinite number of negotiations, ideally based on a sense of mutuality, but at some point Kurt realized that he was living in his home on his wife's sufferance. Perhaps it had started when he returned after living in MacDougal Alley. Reminders that he was constantly on probation took the form of having to clear small decisions with her and trying to keep a lid on things before trouble started. Somehow, he had been demoted from husband to companion.

When they traveled together, for example, Jill insisted they take a suite so that they would have separate bedrooms, just as they did at home. He wondered about the effect on Lily of never seeing her parents in the same bed—at home or anywhere else.[55] His much younger wife finding him sexually unattractive at sixty-five added to his sense of being tolerated.

Also, his time and emotional equanimity as the "house genius," as she referred to him, were worth very little.[56] He needed a reliable block every day of four to five hours to write. But if she needed to speak to him, it had to be right then; it couldn't wait until he took a lunch break. Shouts coming from downstairs were usually a storm warning that an argument, increasingly involving Lily as she got older, was about to burst into his study. His marriage made him rethink the meaning of the parable of Samson and Delilah, he told Edie. It "was not about cutting his hair off to rob him of his strength, it was about interrupting his concentration to rob him of his strength."[57] Many days he spent sitting in front of the typewriter feeling upset, glancing at the street below, burning down cigarettes to the tips of his fingers.

Friends of Kurt's noticed that how much they mattered to Jill tended to depend on their utility. Initially, an acquaintance would be idealized as someone who might be important to know. Then came time for the test. Once, for example, a physician friend of Kurt's, Robert Maslansky, dropped in to visit the couple. "What are these?" Jill asked, interrupting the conversation. She undressed completely, unasked, draping her clothes over a chair. On her stomach and hip were sprinklings of rashy blemishes, which she pointed to slowly. "Here, here, and here." Kurt said nothing.

"A reaction to penicillin it looks like," the doctor said. "Nothing to worry about."

"How did you know?" she asked.

"Dermatology 101."

Maslansky got the feeling that she wanted to bring him up short to demonstrate that another of Kurt's friends was subpar, in which case she would have dropped him.[58]

If other friends, family members, and couples hadn't appreciated her enough, or helped her, or acted considerately, in her opinion, she fired them, in a sense, gradually depriving Kurt of their company. To have conversations with people, he began using the excuse of needing to go to the post office to buy stamps and envelopes, despite Jill scolding him on his way out the door that he should have thought of that ahead of time, and anyway, he wasn't a poor man.[59]

He was rich, it was true, but the sense that the bottom could fall out any day had never left him from his days peddling articles and advertising copy in the 1950s. Low on energy, he went for the quick buck. Responding to an offer from *Time* magazine to write a series of one-page essays, for example, he delivered a two-page "concept statement" for $6,000 proposing to write six one-page pieces on how talking to one another preserves our humanity. *Time* accepted, and the fee was $150,000.[60]

He had to be careful about projects like these, however. Cozying up to corporations had gotten him into trouble once before. In 1984, the Center for Science in the Public Interest chastised him for appearing as a "coffee achiever" in a commercial sponsored by the National Coffee Association. Said the center's executive director in a letter to Vonnegut, in light of the health risks associated with drinking too much coffee, "if you are going to continue to appear in the ads, we suggest that you contribute your royalties from these commercials to appropriate charities of your choice."[61] As often as Vonnegut fulminated about the pernicious effects of big money and big corporations, he opened himself to charges of hypocrisy by getting into bed with them.

But the squabbles over his will, which continued even after Jane's death, adding to the choppiness of his marriage, indicated he had better look to his own devices for protecting himself financially as he neared seventy. His friend of thirty years Richard Gehman, for instance, the author of three thousand magazine articles, five novels, and twelve nonfiction books—once dubbed the "King of Freelance Writers"—had died at age fifty-one, bankrupt and ill, a twentieth-century Daniel Defoe hiding from his creditors.[62]

* * *

FOR THESE reasons—unhappiness, concerns about aging, and loneliness—Vonnegut's next novel, *Hocus Pocus*, published by G. P. Putnam in spring 1990, was his most depressive.

Continuing in the vein of realism that started with *Jailbird*, he draws a lifelike portrait of his narrator, Eugene Debs Hartke, and his surroundings, the details of which suggest that Vonnegut is nostalgic for his youth. Eugene Debs is the name of the Indiana socialist labor leader; Hartke is a nod to Senator Vance Hartke from Indiana, one of the first to vote against the Vietnam War; the narrator teaches at a prison, until recently Tarkington College, named for the Indiana author; and his father was a groundskeeper at Butler University in Indianapolis. There's also a Sam Wakefield (Vonnegut's novelist friend Dan, who graduated from Shortridge High School) and an Episcopalian priest named Alan Clewes (for Allen Clowes, who attended Orchard School with Alice and played the king to her queen in a school pageant).[63]

In addition to the parallels with real people and places, *Hocus Pocus* has a nonfiction, essayistic feel—a piece of rhetoric about the decline of the United States. Vonnegut is impatient with creating fantasy parables now and goes right to his complaint: that America isn't what it used to be.

The novel is set in 2001, and Eugene Debs Hartke isn't at home in the world any longer; too many good intentions have gone awry, too many opportunities have slipped by. He taught at a prison populated by poor black inmates, run for profit by the Japanese—in fact, all of the United States seems to be under absentee ownership—but when prison gang members launched a military operation to break out a drug dealer, all the inmates escaped. Because of the racist assumption that blacks could not possibly have planned the uprising without help, Hartke was arrested as the mastermind.

Now he is in prison, awaiting trial. Prison offers some consolation, though, Hartke says, because outside its high walls, America is "a thoroughly looted bankrupt nation whose assets had been sold off to foreigners, a nation swamped by unchecked plagues and superstition and illiteracy and hypnotic TV."[64] Meanwhile, he's writing his autobiography on scraps of paper the way Howard Campbell did in *Mother Night* and Walter Starbuck in *Jailbird*. Hartke's account of his life covers his early disappointment with his parents, his stint in Vietnam providing official disinformation during the war, his position as physics instructor at a college for dyslexics (he was dismissed for his pessimism), and finally his teaching at the prison, which eventually led to his downfall.

The villain in *Hocus Pocus* isn't a person, it's a problem: the cultural fragmentation, as Vonnegut sees it, besetting the country. National identity is impossible, he implies, when disenfranchised poor blacks, Hispanics, "Orientals," and foreigners—an "Army of Occupation in Business Suits"—have no reason to pledge allegiance to the United States. His tone is at various times wistful, then hectoring, then resigned like a teacher saddled with a class that never seems to catch on. The danger in this approach is that his voice as a writer of fiction will be diminished as he becomes less inventive, less imaginative, and more aggressively didactic. From *Hocus Pocus*, it's a straight, grouchy line to *A Man Without a Country* fifteen years later.

A remark by Jay McInerney in a review of *Hocus Pocus* yearns for a return of the old Vonnegut: "He is a satirist with a heart, a moralist with a whoopee cushion, a cynic who wants to believe."[65]

BERNARD O'HARE, Vonnegut's army sidekick and an eponymous character in a number of his novels, died in June 1990 of throat cancer and tuberculosis. Proud of being Irish and not bashful about how much he drank, he tried to josh a jury once into accepting that his client, arrested for driving while under the influence, was Irish too and that all Irishmen are born with a blood-alcohol level of point-one-zero. It didn't work, but even the judge admired his creative defense.[66]

Vonnegut attended the funeral in Hellertown, Pennsylvania. When it came his turn to throw a handful of dirt in the grave, he was prepared to toss in a pack of Pall Malls and a book of matches, but O'Hare's wife, Mary, said she had already slipped those into the pocket of her late husband's suit. Kurt was impressed.[67]

FRIENDS NOTICED another instance of Kurt's "own private rain," as David Slavitt described it, in the spring of 1991—only this time it was more like a thunderstorm. "I've never seen him so angry," Dan Wakefield reported to the Vonnegut scholar Jerome Klinkowitz.[68] His mood was unaccountable. *Hocus Pocus* had been a best seller, and he had another nonfiction anthology slated for publication, *Fates Worse Than Death: An Autobiographical Collage*, a quirky pastiche of commentary, memoir, and speeches—at least as entertaining as *Palm Sunday*. And Showtime, the television network, had adapted three of his short stories for airing in May: "All the King's Horses," "Next Door," and "The Euphio Question." His career was hardly entering twilight.

Perhaps, his friends speculated, Vonnegut's irritability was due to the Gulf War, Operation Desert Storm, which had started in mid-January, a full-out retaliation against Iraq for invading Kuwait, another conflict that incited his contempt for war. A year earlier he had visited Mozambique on a CARE-sponsored helicopter fly-in to report on the civil war there. The feature he wrote for *Parade* magazine was titled "My Visit to Hell."

But no, it was nothing as spectacularly grim and dispiriting as yet another war. In fact, what was upsetting him was so bourgeois, so vulgar, so *predictable* that he couldn't help but oscillate between resignation and rage.

Jill wanted a divorce. For months she had been carrying on an affair with Stephen M. DuBrul Jr., who stayed from time to time in the studio space she had rented across the street on East Forty-eighth Street.

DuBrul was an economist and investment banker and, until he founded DeBrul Associates, the president of the Export-Import Bank of the United States during the Carter administration. (His father, chief financial analyst for General Motors, had been one of the organizers of the National Recovery Administration under Roosevelt during the Great Depression.) At sixty-two, he was a man of medium height, sharp-featured, with thinning gray hair. His wife, the former Antonia Paepcke, whom he had met at Harvard in the mid-1950s, was from a Chicago family responsible for turning Aspen, a largely abandoned nineteenth-century mining town, into a winter resort. She was unaware that her husband of thirty years was dating a woman a few blocks away in Manhattan.[69]

To make it clear that Kurt was no longer wanted, Jill changed the locks on their home on East Forty-eighth Street and emptied the rooms and closets of his belongings. According to a statement he later supplied to his attorney, the breathlessness with which she announced to him that she and DuBrul were in love and talking marriage was almost as though Vonnegut were "her daddy rather than her husband. She also called several friends to tell them the wonderful news of the divorce and remarriage in prospect."[70] All the details came pouring out. Days she had supposedly gone on photo shoots she had been with DuBrul. Nights when she left to work in her gallery across the street were excuses for rendezvous.

The whole business struck Vonnegut as a "lugubrious, ill-natured, low comedy"—except for the maddening inconvenience of being banished from his own home.

In a way, though, Kurt wasn't surprised that his "unloving wife, wholly without domestic skills," who could barely stand to have him "touch her Rolodex," finally wanted out of the marriage. Nor was he all that amazed when she changed the locks on the brownstone he owned so he couldn't live there. What really took him aback were her final requests of him: make haste divorcing her, "remember her" in his will, and please leave her a parking space for her Cadillac in a nearby garage.[71]

Kurt Vonnegut, Arlene Donovan, Knox Burger,
jazz musician Eddie Condon, and Max Wilkinson
at Condon's Greenwich Village jazz club in the
early 1950s. *(Courtesy Knox Burger)*

The house on Scudder's Lane in West Barnstable, Cape Cod, Massachusetts. Kurt turned the annex, extending perpendicularly from the rear, into his study. *(Courtesy Edie Vonnegut)*

The crash of a commuter train into Newark Bay killed Kurt's brother-in-law. Thirty-six hours later, his sister, Alice, died. The Vonneguts took in the couple's four boys. *(Getty Images)*

Loree Rackstraw and Jane Vonnegut, spring 1966, while Kurt was teaching at the Iowa Writers' Workshop. *(Courtesy Rick Boyer)*

Mark Vonnegut, not long before he left for Vancouver, where his experiences contributed to a breakdown that he described in his book *The Eden Express. (Anne Bossi)*

Edie (foreground with camera) and
Nanny Vonnegut in 1968. *(Anne Bossi)*

Vonnegut in his study a few months before the publication of *Slaughterhouse-Five* in 1969. *(Getty Images)*

Kurt and Jane during one of his annual marsh tromps in West Barnstable. *(Anne Bossi)*

Photojournalist Jill Krementz and Vonnegut in 1980, a year after their marriage. *(Getty Images)*

Vonnegut during a visit to Prague in 1985 with his Czech translator Jaroslav Koran (left) and William P. Kiehl, U.S. embassy attaché for public affairs. *(Courtesy William P. Kiehl)*

Kurt and his daughter Lily outside their Manhattan home in 1989. *(Courtesy Margaret M. Berns)*

Vonnegut performs a rap version of Chaucer, backed by Special K and His Crew, while living apart from his wife, Jill, in Northampton, Massachusetts, in 2000. His grandson Max Prior is second from right. Jon Fishman, of the group Phish, huffed accompaniment on a vacuum cleaner tube. *(Courtesy Scott Prior)*

Vonnegut in Northampton. "Academia may not be the ideal place for a crotchety writer waiting to die," observed a writer for the *Boston Globe*. *(Courtesy Scott Prior)*

15: Waiting to Die

1992–2007

To escape from the dreadfulness of another divorce, Kurt retreated to Sagaponack for the summer of 1991. He could be alone and unmolested there, padding around in sneakers, shorts, and a T-shirt all day.[1]

The East Hampton house was refurbished now: a simple Yankee post-and-beam three story of weathered shake with a wood-shingled roof, no shutters, and no driveway, set back in a pocket of trees. Huge blue hydrangea bushes framed the front door, punctuated by a brass dolphin knocker. The swimming pool burbled quietly in back, and close friends knew they were welcome to drop by for a dip, even if his Honda wasn't out front. A pair of spare keys to the house was hidden inside a ball of tinfoil near the daylilies.[2]

Mornings after breakfast, he ambled up to the post office to pick up mail and send long letters; then he might stop in at the general store before returning home, noticing along the way how his neighbor's wild blueberries and peaches were coming into season with the warmer weather. His only companion, a white cat with one blue and one yellow eye, greeted him at home by rubbing sinuously around his ankles. On the mantelpiece was a Mark Twain coffee mug displaying a prominent mustache.

To liven things up before getting to work in the house, he might put some jazz on the stereo. Decorating his desk area were mementos: a key to the city of Indianapolis, a painting of Eugene Debs, a metal toy from the Indianapolis Children's Museum, which his father had helped found and design, and a miniature wooden Erie Canal boat, the kind he imagined Clemens Vonnegut had used during his journey from New York to Indiana.[3]

Feelings of despondency were hard to shake at times, though. Feeling blue, he wrote to Ian T. MacMillan, one of his students in Iowa, that the former workshop director Paul Engle had died a few months earlier; Nelson Algren was buried in Sag Harbor, not in Chicago where he belonged; Yates was impoverished and breathing oxygen while trying to finish a big book about writing speeches for Robert Kennedy; Bourjaily was married to a woman who treated him badly in front of his friends; and Donoso was seriously ill in Santiago, Chile.[4] As MacMillan read this roll call of how the mighty had fallen, he characterized it as a "mortality letter" from his old friend and teacher.[5]

The solitude was leavened a bit when male friends visited. It wasn't important that they go blue-fishing with him off Montauk, one of his pastimes. He could be content talking or watching television, particularly his favorite program, *Law & Order*. Robert Maslanksy, his doctor friend at Bellevue Hospital, cherished their long conversations about science and nature. The filmmaker Robert B. Weide, young enough to be Vonnegut's son, had an encyclopedic knowledge of the golden era of Hollywood comedy—the Marx Brothers, Laurel and Hardy, W. C. Fields, and Burns and Allen. For his delectation, Kurt would recite favorite one-liners and skits from seventy years ago as if he were amusing his sister, Alice, again by cracking wise. "We were just a couple of guys who didn't give a damn," Weide said later. "Kurt liked calm from his male friends so he could drink and hang out. There were no eggshells to walk on, we could just be buddies."[6]

Still, the isolation wasn't easy for him; he enjoyed socializing, and it was Jill who had penciled in all the invitations to dinners and galas on their calendar. By comparison, he had nothing to take him out of the house in Sagaponack except errands, long walks, and bicycle rides.

Even so, the news from Jill in mid-July hardly elated him. She wanted to call off the divorce. What happened, Kurt informed his attorney, was that "her potential groom," DuBrul, had "absquatulated for parts unknown," meaning that the relationship had ended without notice, so to speak.[7] (In fact, it was about this time that DuBrul met the artist Helen Frankenthaler, whom he later married.)[8] With the affair over, Jill could see no reason why she and Kurt shouldn't put aside their differences.

He didn't agree. She had mistreated him, "the half-dead goose which laid golden eggs for her for so many years," and he wanted a divorce on any grounds with as little fanfare as possible.[9] He would produce witnesses if he had to, and would insist on an accounting of her worth so financial arrangements could be made for nine-year-old Lily.

Jill waited until he was away from Sagaponack and then combed the house, or "woo pit," as Kurt derisively called it, looking for evidence that he had been unfaithful as well. She produced a phone bill with a long-distance call from Cedar Falls, Iowa, and a handful of cosmetics from the bathroom.[10]

Vonnegut's response through his attorney was that, yes, he liked Loree in Cedar Falls better than his wife and, second, the cosmetics would probably be of more use to a woman than a man, that was true. Other than that, he had no comment. When *Playboy* magazine interviewed him that fall and he was asked what he was working on, he replied, "On a divorce. Which is a full-time job."[11]

ACTUALLY, HE tried to devote as little attention to divorcing Jill as possible. For the next two years he lived on and off by himself in Sagaponack, going back to East Forty-eighth Street regularly to spend time with Lily or attend one of her school functions. Other than a deposition he provided his attorney explaining his reasons for wanting a divorce, the proceedings went nowhere.

His lack of action was typical of how he reacted to situations involving emotional pain—giving Knox the heave-ho as his agent, leaving his family in West Barnstable, separating from Jane, and dumping Sam Lawrence. Thinking about his behavior usually led to periods of depression, which in turn interfered with his work. When it came to human interaction not governed by civility or "common decency"—one of his favorite phrases—when people demanded his emotional involvement or called him to account, he was not a good fighter, or a good hugger, for that matter. Until he could write his way into a better frame of mind, personal problems would figuratively have to wait at the foot of the door to his study.

As AN author, however, he was entering a period of mellowness, crossing over into "grand old man of letters" territory. It was partially a function of his age, but also recognition that he had been an experimental, published author for forty years. In March 1992, he was inducted, along with Ann Beattie, Francine du Plessix Gray, and William Weaver (the preeminent English-language translator of Italian works) into the now combined American Academy and Institute of Arts and Letters.[12] Two months later, the American Humanist Association awarded him Humanist of the Year at its national conference in Portland, Oregon. "Humanists," he reminded the audience, "try to behave decently and honorably without any expectation of rewards or punishments in an afterlife. And, since the creator of the universe is to them unknowable so far, they serve as best they can the highest abstraction of which they have some understanding, which is their community."[13]

His name on a petition, such as the one in 1993 decrying the murder of journalists in Turkey, added gravitas beside signatures by other internationally recognized authors such as Antonia Fraser, Arthur Miller, Harold Pinter, Margaret Atwood, Mario Vargas Llosa, and Toni Morrison.[14] Two essays of his—"One Hell of a Country" and "America: Right and Wrong"—were widely reprinted, here and abroad.

Fellow writers respected his powers and reputation. George Plimpton approached him about writing a new libretto for Stravinsky's "L'Histoire du Soldat," which he did with brio. Out went the original Russian folktale, a mystical morality tale about evil, replaced by the story of the American infantryman Edward Donald "Eddie" Slovik, executed for desertion in 1945 and the only soldier ordered killed by a firing squad since the Civil War. In the program notes, Vonnegut explained that Stravinsky's fantasy "has less than nothing to do with the gruesome and humiliating life of any soldier in any war in any time," and he meant to correct the record. The piece's premiere a year later by the New York Philomusica Chamber Ensemble was not well received, but Kurt had been excited by the opportunity to extend his repertoire.[15]

His restoration as patriarch of his West Barnstable family happened gradually, too. He was now a grandfather several times over, and for his

seventieth birthday in November 1992 his children and nephews threw
a party. It was not in Boston or New York, but at a favorite restaurant of
theirs, the Dolphin restaurant in Barnstable, across from the county
courthouse. Jim Adams composed thirteen haiku for the occasion,
including this one.

> I've seen you reach out
> To say you love in your way.
> I've seen you. I thank you.[16]

Jim the hellion of yore was almost fifty and saw himself for what he
had been at fourteen when he landed in the Vonneguts' home: not only
troubled by his parents' sudden deaths but also the product of a troubled family.

Alice and James Adams at first glance had appeared wildly creative,
clever, and entertaining. Who else would have exotic birds flying free
everywhere—the walls and furniture of their home stenciled with
nature images—as if they lived in a playroom? But when the lights
came up on their theatrical lives, they were—as heavily madeup performers tend to be—a little grotesque. Alice's dyed blond bangs, waxy
red lips, and habit of cooing over animals betrayed a vein of immatu-
rity. Since childhood, when she would spin around crying "Soap opera!
Soap opera!" to fend off anything serious, not much had changed about
her. And Jim's pronouncements that the payoff of his latest scheme, his
ship, his big break was coming into view tended to be hamming it up
for his best audience, his family.

By the time of their deaths, the jig was pretty much up. Writing to
"Unky Kurt" later in 2002, Jim Adams Jr. said that as a boy he knew
that "Mom and Dad were getting into trouble well before they died.
Their peachy dream world was coming apart. Dad wasn't making any
money and they were up to their necks in debt. Mom was drinking a lot
and they were fighting on what seemed like a regular basis, screaming
about hatred and divorce." The boys' future looked bleak, and a college
education would have been out of the question. Then "you came swooping in and in the most gallant and unselfish way, took us home."

Jim was grateful, and sorry for "all the crap" he had given his uncle.
"And finally, I want to say that I love you. You're not my Dad, you're

Uncle K. You are who you are and, good Christ, you can be hard to get along with, but I love you just the same. So there."[17]

The seventieth birthday party had the effect of symbolically restoring Kurt to the head of the family table, as Dad, "Unky," and Grandpa. Jill, *la belle dame sans merci*, had released him into the embrace of his children. And they hoped it was part of a happy epilogue to his hexed marriage. It was no secret that he was seeing a woman in East Hampton, too—a former swimsuit model, blonde, about fifty, who took Outward Bound trips as respites from her job as an administrator at Columbia University. Vonnegut referred to this lover in the autumn of his life as another muse (his second one after Loree), who rekindled his enthusiasm for writing and painting.[18]

Having love and work in life—Freud's prescription for contentedness—made him stable. Romance offset the tedium of facing the pitiless blank page. The new book he was writing would be devoted entirely to Kilgore Trout or maybe the character "Kurt Vonnegut" because they were practically interchangeable. He was long overdue in finishing it, however. Physically, it was hard for a man his age to sit bent over a typewriter for hours, and by now he had a permanent stoop.

THUS, WITH everything well in hand it would seem, Kurt's announcement in early 1994 that he was reconciling with Jill naturally stunned his children and nephews. To Nanny, he offered the plaintive excuse that Jill was his "disease," to which she responded bitterly, "Oh, come on, Dad."[19] Regardless, he shelved the divorce, closed up the house in Sagaponack, and returned to live in Manhattan.

His deeper reason for reversing course and sailing toward Circe's cave again was out of concern for eleven-year-old Lily. She was no longer a tiny, photogenic girl, complementing her mother's work as a photographer of children. She was entering early adolescence, and the word *strong* defined her: she had a strong build like a gymnast and voiced her emotions strongly as well. She would not be ignored, and the split between her parents was precisely the opening she needed to get attention. Understandably, she was becoming an expert at playing one parent off the other. Another reason he was returning to his wife is implied in a letter he received from the novelist Herman Wouk, who had been married for fifty years: "Remote as we are from the literary scenes, we know of and regret your separation from Jill. The years are being kinder to us in that way, though we both ain't getting younger."[20]

Yes, he was getting old. He had been born four years after the end of World War I when there was still horse cavalry, when radio was a sensation, and when vast regions of the United States had no electricity. But the millennium was less than six years away now. He was a creature of the twentieth century, and the limit of his life was approaching. He had passed his three score and ten already, and if a person should live to be eighty, say the Psalms, "yet is their strength labor and sorrow; for it is soon cut off, and we fly away."

He was willing to make some concessions to the passage of time, and even technology, one of his favorite whipping boys. Arriving at the brownstone in Manhattan, he carried something new under his arm: a small word processor. Its mechanical predecessors—Underwoods and his favorite Smith Corona, which had clacked, whirled, and rang as they threaded words and sentences together—were forgotten. At first, Lily found she had trouble falling asleep without the sound of a typewriter carriage going back and forth like a loom in her father's third-floor study. He was home, though, signified by the odor of his Pall Mall cigarettes hanging in the air and the light under his door.[21]

THE PROBLEM with the book he was working on, which would become *Timequake*, was that it was episodic. No clear plot through-line yanked it together; he was hard-pressed to come up with a satisfactory "what-if" scenario, which is key to fiction. If he resorted to another autobiographical collage similar to *Palm Sunday* or *Fates Worse Than Death*, it would be his third book that was more journalistic than fictive. On the other hand, he had a book to deliver, and reflecting, writing about events that bridged the years, was mostly what interested him.

One haunting incident had occurred recently while he was speaking at the University of Rochester in New York. The lecture series coordinator drove him to the two-hundred-year-old Mt. Hope Cemetery, where Susan B. Anthony and Frederick Douglass, among dozens of other notable Americans, are interred. Then she guided him to the low, military-style headstone marking the grave of Edward "Joe" Crone, the model for Billy Pilgrim.

"But he's in Dresden," Vonnegut said, confused. "I saw him buried myself—in a paper suit—because there wasn't enough fabric to bury him in a suit of clothes."[22]

After the war, Crone's parents had spent five years searching for their son. His father, an insurance executive, wrote to men in Joe's regiment, two hundred in total, until one replied that he was certain Joe had died in Revier Hospital just outside Dresden and was buried in Görlitz. His parents traveled to East Germany and arranged for the remains to be reinterred in Mt. Hope Cemetery.[23]

Vonnegut had resisted identifying Crone as Billy Pilgrim until word reached him that Joe's parents had passed away. Now, in the quiet of the Victorian-era cemetery, he asked his host if she could let him have a few minutes to himself. From a distance, she saw him light a fresh cigarette, glance around at the enormous trees, and talk to the headstone, having a conversation across a gap of fifty years. He wept, but arriving back at the car a few moments later he seemed content. "Well, that closes the book on World War II for me."[24] To the Mt. Hope Cemetery, he later sent a check for placing flowers on Joe's grave every Memorial Day.[25]

Another small incident that put him in a philosophical mood stemmed from Bernard sending him spidery patterns on plates of glass. His scientist brother wanted to know whether they qualified as art.

How the patterns came about went all the way back to the 1950s when Bernard was analyzing lightning. One of his colleagues showed him the result when a high-voltage accelerator bombarded a sheet of plastic about one centimeter thick with high-energy electrons. It produced a beautiful permanent pattern that resembled frozen lightning. Bernard gave one of the sheets to a fellow scientist, Paul Matisse, who reported that his father-in-law, the French American Dadaist Marcel Duchamp, "was equally enchanted."[26]

Experimenting on his own, Bernard discovered an arts-and-craft method that eliminated the need for keeping a particle accelerator handy. Just by squeezing wet paint between glass panes and pulling them apart quickly, the crackle pattern became permanent when the paint dried. Now came the question he asked his brother, sending him several samples of his handiwork, "Is it art?"[27]

When they were children, Bernard had derided art as "ornamental," dismissing by implication their father's profession as an architect, their mother's hope to publish short stories in women's magazines, and Alice's untrained talent for drawing things that struck her fancy. Now he put the question to his younger sibling, the renowned novelist: Was art so simple to make, just a product of accident? Could his brother explain how art differed from a naturally occurring phenomenon? Bernard didn't bother to mention that identical patterns had already impressed Marcel Duchamp, however. Would his brother side with an acclaimed artist?

Kurt couldn't resist treating his scientist brother with a touch of condescension. Explaining art, he began, is like explaining where babies come from. An experimentalist in art, he continued, must display his work in a public place and stand by while people commented on it, thus issuing a mild challenge to Bernard to put himself in the arena of the arts and find out what it was like. Second, there is also the matter of the artist's relationship to the audience.[28] Art can't be too abstruse, it must involve the spectator or he or she will be discouraged and the piece will fail, an unconscious restatement of Duchamp's central belief, remarkably, that the spectator adds his contribution to the creative act by deciphering and interpreting it.

Finally, taking up Bernard's implied suggestion that art could be just a stroke of luck, like making pretty patterns on glass, Kurt answered that successful art required a degree of calculation and knowledge of the process; experience counted for a lot, too. But in addition there was always an element of mystery and the sublime.

Although he didn't say so, on this last point, the brothers overlapped in their desire to—as Bernard often said about his work—"find out what's going on."[29] They were very similar in that way, outside their laboratory and study. Both were seekers; both wanted to see into the heart of things; they wanted, in the scientific phrase, "reproducible results" that would explain how the universe operated. But they were also forced, as scientist and writer, to stand humbly before the countervailing, immutable power of sheer accident that could create art or destroy worlds.

TIMEQUAKE AT last yielded to Kurt's persistence at the end of the summer of 1996, although it was, in the end, only autobiographical fragments, musings, Kilgore Trout—another steamer trunk of items taken down from the attic of his memory. In the opening pages, he explains apologetically that *Timequake* is the detritus from a novel that had collapsed on itself. But there was nothing he could do. Like one of Melville's whalers who has told every joke, anecdote, and memory during long months at sea, he was falling into silence.[30] He needed a change— something to take him out of himself.

He flew to Denver in September 1996 for a showing of his pen-and-ink sketches at a gallery and for an event that combined books and beer. As a favor to the mayor, John Hickenlooper, the son of a fellow POW in Dresden, he designed a label for a special Denver microbrew, Kurt's Mile-High Malt, to celebrate the opening of the city's new library. Not only did he lend his name, the malt had the slight aroma of coffee too, the secret ingredient added to his great-grandfather Peter Lieber's Düsseldorfer dark lager.

While he was relaxing in Denver, Bernard may have informed him about the results of a doctor's appointment, but it's unlikely that he did, because Professor Vonnegut had decided to take the news about his health philosophically. A coughing fit had brought the coppery taste of blood in his mouth. Even though he had quit smoking thirty years earlier, a chest X-ray indicated lung cancer. His physician recommended starting a regime of chemotherapy immediately, but Bernard, having just passed his eighty-second birthday, declined because of his age. Also, he wanted to enjoy the time he had left by attending in December the annual conference in San Francisco of the American Geophysical Union, where many of his friends and colleagues would be.[31] One of the highlights was going to be a panel about fountains of electrified gases spewing from Earth into space. He wasn't going to miss that for anything.[32]

Meanwhile, Kurt attended a special screening in October for members of PEN of *Mother Night*, directed by Keith Gordon, from a screenplay by Robert B. Weide, with Nick Nolte in the role of the spy Howard Campbell. Thumbs-up was hoped for from this audience, because the official premiere of the film was only a few hours away.

Mother Night is a twitchy, on-the-edge novel to begin with, a mirthless satire involving Nazis, an American dupe, and betrayal. Saving it from becoming dreary is Vonnegut's deadpan, absurdist tone about awfulness. ("Andor is a sleepy, not very bright Estonian Jew.... He came this close to going up a smokestack of a crematorium.")[33] The novel and its plot, exaggerated to make a point, contain characters, like Adolf Hitler, who are comic impersonations of monsters.

But in the film, Vonnegut is not there to intervene the way he could in metafiction—there is no safe, ironic distance in the storytelling—so the film *Mother Night* unfolds pretty much as straight drama. The problem, Vonnegut later came to realize, was that filmed versions of his novels are one character short: himself.[34]

When the screening before the PEN audience ended, Vonnegut took his seat on a panel with director Gordon and screenwriter Weide at the front of the theater, and the floor was opened for questions. Immediately, the "discussion," as it was billed, became a debacle. Kurt had faced skeptical audiences but rarely a hostile one. The first person to speak up was an outraged Korean War veteran who, for some reason, defended his service as a radio operator and then made the claim that only two Jews had died while serving in the United States Armed Forces during World War II—why wasn't more made of this fact? The audience was dumbfounded.

Weide, whose father had been a signalman on the USS *John Muir* during the invasion of Okinawa, leaned over to his microphone: "You, sir, are full of crap."

"Oh, yeah? Well why don't you come down here and beat it out of me!"

Another member of the audience warned that the anti-Semitic slanders repeated by Campbell as a double agent would likely serve to recruit neo-Nazis.[35] Next, an African American woman said she was offended by the term *black humor*, to which Weide, who was losing his temper, replied, "I'm not bothered by 'white lies.'"[36] But the most upsetting remark to Vonnegut came from a woman who had survived the death camps. She said she was disgusted that someone would use the Holocaust for entertainment. Kurt, rather than mar the reception afterward by quite possibly getting into arguments, skipped it and went home.[37]

It was easier to ignore a negative book review in a newspaper than it was to dismiss being pilloried in front of an audience. What he couldn't get over was how an assembly of professionals in literature and publishing could be so uncomprehending about what he had meant. He attributed their reaction to not understanding that *Mother Night* was not about Nazis per se, or even about World War II: it was about moral ambiguity.[38] Film reviewers in general, however, recommended it.

* * *

WITHOUT TREATMENT and hospitalization, Bernard wasn't going to recover. In February 1997, Kurt began taking the train from New York City to the Rensselaer station, where one of his brother's sons, Kurt, would drive him the short distance to Albany. His brother was the color of pale buttermilk, underweight, and using suspenders to keep his pants up. The cold weather penetrated his bones, and he wore flannel shirts and a knit hat in the house, giving him the appearance of someone who was just about to go outside.

"I want to interview you," Kurt said during one of his first visits. He put a digital tape recorder on the kitchen table in front of Bernard.

"About what?"

"Well, you being a college professor, let's talk about all the co-eds you had fun with."[39]

That set the tone for their conversations, most of which consisted of reminiscing, particularly about Alice, guaranteed to provoke outbursts of wheezing laughter and coughing.

Bernard was known in the neighborhood as something of a character, a professor in a tweed jacket who drove down the street with pieces of scientific apparatus clamped to his 1949 Plymouth Special Deluxe Sedan (his father's car, still running). Most recently, he had attached his latest invention—a design for a new kind of anemometer—to the side-view mirror and observed its performance as he accelerated. No aspect or mystery involving weather was foreign to him.

To his colleagues, he was a noted atmospheric scientist, the recipient of twenty-eight patents, the author of 160 refereed articles in scientific journals, and professor emeritus of the University of Albany, a career that the American Meteorological Society recognized by giving him the Award for Outstanding Contribution to the Advancement of Applied Meteorology for his pioneering discoveries in weather modification. "One listened carefully when he spoke," said Kurt's physician friend Robert Maslansky.[40]

A few days before Bernard passed away, John Latham, climate scientist from the University of Manchester in England, called. The two men had been sparring in friendly exchanges in journals for twenty years. To Latham, it seemed as if he were hearing his friend speak through a waterfall. Bernard, barely conscious, said, "It's been lots of fun."[41] He died April 25, 1997.

His sons decided on a proper way to memorialize their father. On a clear day, Tiger Adams flew his cousins over Mount Greylock, the view from which gives out onto mountain swells. It was over Mount Greylock that cloud seeding was first tried while Bernard and his fellow scientists at General Electric observed the experiment, earthbound and watching the clouds. One of Bernard's sons opened a passenger door and allowed the wind to take his father's ashes into the blue void.

Kurt never fully reconciled with his brother, the "big bully" of his childhood, not to the extent that he might have. He never told him that he resented his interference in his life.[42] He couldn't, because doing that would have been a concession to his superiority. In writing about his relationship with him, he hid his feelings, too. "My longest experience with common decency, surely, has been with my older brother, my only brother, Bernard."[43]

WHEN *TIMEQUAKE* appeared in autumn 1997, Kurt declared it would be his last novel.[44] It was his fourteenth book, and he had struggled to finish it. Reviewers, sad to say, agreed he should have pulled it back entirely and not released it.

A timequake, as Vonnegut defined it, is a sneeze in the space-time continuum, and one occurs on February 13, 2001, jerking everybody instantaneously backward to February 17, 1991. Readers are supposed to imagine repeating their lives, knowing they will do exactly the same things: marry the wrong person again, bet on the wrong horse, or cause a serious accident, for instance. If we had foreknowledge of the consequences, we wouldn't do such destructive things, of course, but life in Vonnegut's view is grimly, implacably, depressingly deterministic. He tries to convey the heaviness of what inevitability feels like.

And then, as if to bid his readers farewell, he inserts himself into the text as he has many times before and attends a fantasy clambake in honor of Kilgore Trout. The guests include scholars, fellow writers, and family members. For their benefit, Trout shares a few characteristically bizarre insights, such as how World War II will always make great fodder for "show biz" because the Nazis wore sharp uniforms.[45] But he confesses to being old and sleepy now, the same thing Kurt, in his correspondence, had been mentioning to friends lately. Author and character are contemplating how far it is yet to "the undiscover'd country, from whose bourn / No traveler returns."[46]

ALTHOUGH TIRED, and in his midseventies, he still went on speaking tours because audiences thronged auditoriums to hear him. Some came who were admirers of his work; some out of curiosity; some to see a major figure in postwar American letters. He was in such demand as a commencement speaker that when the *Chicago Tribune* columnist Mary Schmich wrote a humorous address to college graduates in June 1997 headlined ADVICE, LIKE YOUTH, PROBABLY JUST WASTED ON THE YOUNG, it was misattributed to Vonnegut. As a result, the "Wear Sunscreen Speech," as it came to be known, supposedly delivered by Vonnegut at MIT, has been credited to him for years.

One of his most popular lectures was his chalk talk about the structure of stories, summarized from his University of Chicago thesis, "Fluctuations Between Good and Ill Fortune in Simple Tales," and honed at the Iowa Writers' Workshop.[47] Following a few self-deprecating introductory remarks, he would turn to a chalkboard and draw two lines: a vertical G-I axis (good fortune, ill fortune) and a horizontal B-E axis (beginning to end). The point where the lines met at the middle on the vertical axis marked, as Vonnegut explained, the start of an average day for a character. Then he would draw a slow arc upward toward good fortune, exclaiming, "Oh, boy! This is my lucky day." Slowly, the line would crest and begin to fall, to which he responded in a thoughtful voice, "Oh, *shit!*" getting a big laugh. The line continued sinking below the horizontal axis, creating a trough. This was the essence of the "man-in-the-hole" story, he said, and it was the author's business to get the character out of the hole, climbing toward betterment. Except in the case of Kafka, he added, who sends characters into the hole *and they stay there.* The audience roared.

He was also becoming endearing, as some elderly people are, and his remarks ridiculing politicians and failures in American society were increasingly met with sympathetic head-nodding and indulgent smiles. Much earlier in his career, he had been characterized as "bitter," "biting," "sardonic," and so on; more often now, he just seemed crotchety—

a grandfatherly figure for whom allowances must be made. During a speech in Madison, Wisconsin, in December 1997, while he was holding forth about the importance of extended family and stressing the need to be kind to each other, a woman entered at the rear of the auditorium holding a small child. The toddler let out a wail.

"Get that damn kid out of here!" Vonnegut barked.

It was the biggest laugh he got that night.[48]

Following his lectures, he simply left the stage—there was no longer a question-and-answer period. One night, Ollie Lyon's daughter, Mary, hurried to catch him as he was leaving a theater. Their families had been friends for forty years, and she wanted to give him a hug. Instead, as she came around to the front of the theater, she saw his curly head turning back and forth like an axle at the center of a moiling crowd of admirers. She tried to push closer but couldn't.

"Kurt!" she shouted. "Kurt!"

He looked back over his shoulder, surprised. "Mary!" He made some signs with his hand indicating where they could meet, not daring to say the name of the restaurant. Then he was borne away by the crush of people toward the idling car and disappeared into the night.[49]

His family bore with patience his remarks ex cathedra from the patriarchal throne, explaining that his financial successes—evidence to the contrary—had not been great but he had many heirs.[50] He spoke of what he would "bequeath" from his estate: one-third to Jill; two-thirds to be divided equally among his children, including Lily. After due consideration, he had decided that the Adams brothers had already inherited so much through the wills of relatives, and from proceeds of legal claims against the railroad that had killed their father, that he would not include them. "It used to trouble me that they had so much cash, and hence so many options, when my own children had so little."[51]

If only now he could be assured that he had crossed an imaginary finish line meaning his achievement was permanent. He was worried that the new millennium would find him puzzling, or culturally rootbound in the twentieth century.[52] Melville, for example, had died so long after publication of *Moby Dick* that obituary writers of metropolitan newspapers had to remind readers of who he was, or had been.

Perhaps it was possible to live too long. At a publication launch party in the Rainbow Room in the NBC building in New York City for Norman Mailer's *The Time of Our Time*—a thirteen-hundred-page anthology culled from fifty years of writing—the guests included many gray heads who had books on university syllabi all over the world. Vonnegut, looking around, commented to a reporter, "We all would like to have died as young as F. Scott Fitzgerald, but we didn't manage it."[53] Attending another party, this one for Lee Stringer's *Grand Central Winter: Stories from the Street,* Kurt waited down on the street, smoking cigarettes, his long legs poking from a recessed doorway, until it was time for him to introduce the young author.[54] He was there as a favor; literary bashes were no longer glamorous, just required—almost an act of noblesse oblige by someone who had seen it all and was asked to provide continuity in the flow of American literature.

He wanted assurance that his works would occupy a permanent, honorable place on bookshelves and in libraries. It galled him that his name wasn't a routine entry in American dictionaries, for instance, unlike many authors who were equally famous.[55] He wanted a summation, something durable because he was too tired to hole up in his study for years minting a book of fresh fiction. He was grateful that he would have to do practically nothing when plans were afoot to publish a collection of twenty-three of his stories from magazines called *Bagombo Snuff Box.*

One night, at a dinner party, he surprised his guests Clark Blaise and Bharati Mukherjee by pointing out that the Nobel Prize for Literature is announced in October. He wondered how many more Octobers he would be around.[56]

Adding to his weariness was his relationship with Jill. He lived day to day, grateful for the ones when no gut-wrenching argument erupted.[57] He had filed for divorce a second time in 1998 for unspecified reasons—making a total of three attempts at divorce between them—but withdrew the petition. Instead he continued to cohabit grimly on East Forty-eighth Street, spending most of the day in his study upstairs.

Something had to be done about his wife and daughter tearing at each other, however. Lily had gotten into trouble with some of her teachers, and Jill let it be known that she was making arrangements to place her in a residential school instead where she would be under supervision and not be permitted to leave. The classes were small, and there would be counseling available to help her straighten out.

But Kurt wouldn't stand for it. As the parent of six children, he knew the reasons for her misbehavior wouldn't evaporate by putting her in a "lock-down" situation, as he called it. On impulse, he loaded some luggage in the car and headed alone for Northampton, Massachusetts, where Nanny lived, checking into the Hotel Northampton.

It was early December 1999, cold and icy, but he hoped to reconnoiter the schools in the area, both public and private, thinking that, with luck, he could get Lily transferred in midyear. When he visited Northampton High School, sixty years old but renovated the year before, it reminded him in design and character of his alma mater, Shortridge High School. He was pleased with Northampton and moved it to the top of his list.

Then, returning to the hotel, he slipped and fell in the parking lot, hitting his face. The impact dazed him, and he got to his feet slowly, blood dripping from a gash. Later, Nanny knocked on the door of his room and found him "pretty banged up." They went to an emergency room, where the wound was closed with stitches, but a purplish bruise discolored one side of his face.[58]

In the meantime, Jill had come up with a compromise. The Beekman School, located on East Fiftieth Street, two blocks from their home, specialized in tutoring students through a college preparatory program. It was one of the oldest schools of its kind in the city, and Kurt was delighted by the idea. He drove home, believing that all had turned out well.

However, as a punishment for his bolting to Northampton, Jill informed him that he was no longer welcome to go on vacation with her and Lily to St. Barthélemy in the Caribbean during the winter holidays. The trip had been booked a year in advance, so Lily would be allowed to take a friend in his place. But if he dared object, she would cancel the trip altogether. They stopped speaking, and Kurt tended to his injury by himself.[59]

A MONTH later, for the Super Bowl game between the Tennessee Titans and the St. Louis Rams on January 30, 2000, he went to his study to watch the game alone and undisturbed.

His L-shaped study, about 180 square feet, was his sanctuary. There was a double bed in a corner beside one of three of deep-set, mullioned windows on the longest wall overlooking the street. On the walls, covered in pink and white wallpaper, hung framed originals of his lithographs—black line, sinuous shapes with primary colors in the style of his favorite period, abstract expressionism. The windows let light fall on a black leather Eames lounge chair at a coffee table on which his laptop sat, lid up. There was a television, and at the far end of the L, opposite the windows, was a desk, used primarily for recordkeeping. In small file cabinets he stored some letters and drafts of manuscripts, although as of September 1999 he had sold his papers to Indiana University and was sending, practically every week, anything he thought might be of interest to the university's Lilly Library.

As the pregame show got under way in the late afternoon, he installed himself into his chair, a pack of cigarettes at his elbow. Sometime after the kickoff at about a quarter after six, he moseyed downstairs to get something to eat on a tray.

While he was in the kitchen foraging, someone started pounding on the front door and shouting. It was his neighbor Hans von Stackelberg, acting head of the German Consulate, warning him that smoke was coming out of a window on the top floor. The two men hurried upstairs, toward a flickering glow illuminating the walls outside Vonnegut's study. A heaving cloud of smoke and heat met them at the top, the source of which was a wastebasket beside Kurt's chair, set afire by a burning cigarette. They kicked it over and stamped on the flames but red flakes of burning paper flew up around them. Von Stackelberg retreated to the landing, coughing, thinking Vonnegut was behind him.

"Mr. Vonnegut, you have to come out of there!"[60]

Kurt's hand emerged from the smoke and von Stackelberg grasped it. Supporting the older man, he led him down the stairs until Vonnegut was forced to sit down, breathless.

Outside the house, fourteen units of the Eighth Battalion from the East Fiftieth Street Fire Department arrived, blocking the street, their lights turning the buildings crimson as if the whole block were on fire. Jill stood on the sidewalk holding Flour, their white Maltese, wrapped in a towel, with Lily beside her. They watched a firefighter climb an extension ladder to the top floor, smash a window in the study, and use a long-handled pike to tear holes in the ceiling for ventilation.

The front door opened and a stretcher emerged carrying soot-covered Kurt down the steep steps. Lily sobbed, "I don't want to see him, I don't want to see him like this."[61]

Vonnegut's friend James Brady, a columnist for *Parade* magazine, invited Jill and Lily to wait with him in his home a few doors away. But Jill was "scared and angry both," he noticed. Vonnegut, catching sight of Brady, motioned him over to the rear door of the ambulance.

"OK, just don't preach," he said, taking Brady's hand. The fire was his fault. He asked his friend to ride with him to the hospital.[62]

According to Brady, the scene at New York–Presbyterian Hospital was a nightmare. Firefighters had brought the blaze under control within fifteen minutes, but Jill was incensed. Her rage seemed to fill the emergency room with an inflammable gas. Brady tried to calm her down, but she refused to be pacified.

When Don Farber entered the emergency room, the atmosphere combusted. "Get him away from me," she fairly screamed. "He's the real 'Mrs. Vonnegut,' not me! I won't talk to him. Keep him away!" She had never forgiven him for twice overriding her wishes when Kurt lay unconscious from pills and alcohol; moreover, one of his law partners had assisted Kurt with divorce proceedings against her.

Brady took Farber aside to talk confidentially, but the arrival of a young reporter from the *New York Daily News* set off another shouting match. Jill demanded the woman be arrested on the spot. Brady again intervened: "Jill, you're a journalist yourself, they won't arrest a reporter."[63]

Finally, by eleven o'clock Kurt was resting in a private room, having suffered serious smoke inhalation but no burns. Farber was seeing to hospital paperwork, leaving Jill to return home, where Lily and the fire marshals were waiting. Thinking back on what had happened, Kurt thought it would have been "so shapely" if he had died in the fire.[64] It was only by accident that he had been spared in the Dresden firestorm. Death returning for him in the same manner after fifty-six years, in another city and during another winter, would have closed the circle.

AFTER A few weeks of respiratory therapy in a private hospital, Kurt was scheduled for release, but he had no home to return to. Jill accused him of trying to burn down her house (although the brownstone belonged to him), and she changed the locks for the second time, Kurt told his daughters.[65] It would take months to repair the damage done by the fire; and for weeks afterward, a plywood board covered a broken window of his study like an eyepatch on the face of the building. She was going to teach him not to smoke at home, Brady wrote later.[66]

He had the option of living in Sagaponack, of course, but then the Adams brothers arrived at New York–Presbyterian, announcing they were taking him to Northampton, where, at least, he would be close to Nanny. Hours later, they deposited him at the Hotel Northampton, without apprising her of the plan ahead of time. To their way of thinking, he was too old to live alone in a seaside resort in midwinter, so there was no option.

Finding him ensconced at the Hotel Northampton as a fait accompli, Nanny took steps for him to live independently without involving herself too much in his problems. She was fed up with dealing with his "disease," as he called it—the melodrama of his marriage. A friend of hers, Kerry O'Keefe, had an upstairs apartment for rent in her turn-of-the-century home at 22 Philips Place. It had an outside entrance to recommend it too, for his privacy. Nanny paid for a month in advance, explaining the situation, and left a note at the hotel desk. "Dad, This is what I am here for: laundry; visits only when you ask. Here are keys to a place you can take or leave, a computer that you can take or leave, a cheap [physical] therapist you can take or leave."[67]

A few days later, at eight o'clock in the morning, O'Keefe was padding around her kitchen in her slippers and pouring herself a cup of coffee. Outside the window, a tall, stooped man appeared on her back porch, pausing at the foot of the stairs leading to the second-floor apartment. He looked around guardedly. "He was like an animal, like a wild animal prowling to see if it's safe."[68] Not wanting to scare him off, she moved quietly, getting ready for the inevitable meeting. A few moments later, from above, she could hear the floorboards creaking. She got dressed, thinking of a little speech she could make to welcome him as her guest.

She knocked gently. "Mr. Vonnegut? Mr. Vonnegut, are you in? I'm your new landlady. I just wanted to say hello."

She opened the door a few inches and peeked in. "Mr. Vonnegut?"

In the middle of the room was a plastic shopping bag with toiletries, the only sign that one of the most famous authors in the United States had arrived. The room was silent.

He was gone again.[69]

NANNY ARRANGED to pick up her father's laundry every day and "slip food under the door of the beast." She was afraid she might find him dead one day because, like Mark, she had grown up with a presentiment that he would kill himself someday if certain circumstances snapped into place.[70] His friends, hearing he was exiled from New York, took his side, paying a price when Jill found out about it. Vance Bourjaily sensed a "less than cordial feeling" from her because he and Kurt continued to call and correspond.[71] Robert B. Weide assured him there was no doubt he was better off in Northampton anyway: "Fuck New York."[72]

But he didn't like Northampton; he had just washed up there. Smith College attracts feminists to Northampton, as does Mount Holyoke College just five miles away. Vonnegut, coming across chalk graffiti— such as I FUCK WOMEN and I'M A VAGITARIAN—on campus sidewalks, complained to friends that he was living in the dyke capital of the world where a lipstick salesman would starve to death.[73] Admittedly, there were plenty of bookstores and cultural events on every hand to occupy him, but he belonged to an older, more conservative generation, and the ambience of the campus bothered him.

And then there was his unshakable companion, loneliness, to contend with, too. Kerry O'Keefe, his "Irish landlady," as he nicknamed her, cleaned the tenants' rooms once a week. Normally, he took his meals out, but on cleaning day he was always stubbornly in his room, ready for conversation. One morning, as she was waxing a table in the hallway, he came out from his apartment wearing nothing but boxer shorts. He looked at her; she paused and then went back to waxing. He returned inside and closed the door. "I don't think Kurt was a guy who disliked women," she said. "I feel like he was really wary of women." She found him "charming, cranky, immature, selfish."[74]

News that the author was residing in Northampton brought reporters to O'Keefe's doorstep. But her father had been a commissioner in the administration of John Francis "Honey Fitz" Fitzgerald in Boston, and journalists' importuning her for a story left her cold. "Forget it," she told them, feeling that she was protecting a "wounded, mean animal" from people who wanted to poke it.[75]

He couldn't hope for complete anonymity; he was too recognizable on the street for that. But he wanted to be with people on his own terms. He asked Nanny to invite Allison Mitchell, her childhood friend from West Barnstable, for a visit. They reminisced about the trip in the station wagon to the 1964 World's Fair; then Nanny asked Allison, a Reiki master, if she would try healing work on her father. She hesitated, knowing Kurt's almost obsessive need to wisecrack, but he lay down and said nothing—the giant who had come to the screen door when she was a child and frightened her to tears. "I was aware of how gentle and graceful he looked," she later recalled, "and his hands looked like a pianist's hands, really long, tapered. I was fascinated, I couldn't stop staring at his hands, they were so beautiful and very gentle."[76]

Meanwhile, on East Forty-eighth Street the plywood board stayed up on the window of Vonnegut's study as if hostile critics had finally defenestrated him.[77] Jill, hearing that Kurt was undertaking to divorce her a third time, stayed inside so she couldn't be served with papers. Somewhere on the street, a private detective bided his time, watching the address. What finally happened, as Nanny recounted it, was that one day when Jill was hurrying to an appointment, the detective came toward her in the opposite direction, posing as a dog walker, and slapped the divorce papers into her hand. She grabbed his sleeve and refused to let go, saying she would suffer irreparable damage from a divorce.[78] He pulled away and continued down the street.

KURT, PREPARING for a long siege, took a one-year lease on a two-bedroom, third-floor condominium in a renovated brick school building at 35 New South Street in Northampton. He wanted Lily to have a bedroom of her own on weekend visits. To Gail Godwin, his former student in Iowa, he provided a stoic update of his circumstances. He was in Northampton because he couldn't live in the same house with Lily and Jill, whose mutual hatred, though not unusual between teenage girls and their mothers, sickened him.[79]

The clothes in his closets were all new because he brought almost nothing from home. He was forced to accept, without having the chance to verify, that his archives and papers, although stored in metal file cabinets, had been destroyed in the fire.[80] To re-create how he liked to work, he positioned a low, blond wood end table in front of a plum-colored sofa in the living room, but the cushions made it hard to lean forward. He posted his grandchildren's drawings on the refrigerator door, tacked a few drawings of his own to the walls, and displayed in the kitchen a bumper sticker quoting him: YOUR PLANET'S IMMUNE SYSTEM/IS TRYING TO GET RID OF YOU.[81]

On her weekend visits, Lily was permitted to bring the family dog, Flour, along. One day, during a thunderstorm, someone saw Vonnegut taking the little Maltese for a walk. He followed behind, holding out an umbrella at arm's length to keep her dry as she skipped about his feet, while the rain poured down on him instead.[82]

KURT FELT less like a wayfarer when Smith College offered him a visiting fellowship for fall semester 2000, as writer-in-residence and distinguished senior lecturer in English, teaching two master classes in creative writing. Being an instructor on a college campus would be as comfortable as slipping into an old pair of shoes, and he decided he would cover everything: essays, speeches, poetry, plays, television/film scenarios, even librettos for opera.[83]

He was unaware that a few English professors wondered whether it was a good idea to invite him to teach.[84] He was seventy-eight, a World War II veteran, an American canonical author come to life, Pygmalion-like, addressing students young enough to be his children's children. Word reached the English Department that he had been scouting the Smith libraries and was upset that not one carried a complete collection of his works. Librarians were a little annoyed by a grizzled man who wanted to donate books but refused to fill out the paperwork, insisting, "I'm Kurt Vonnegut and this is a book by Kurt Vonnegut."[85] That was minor, of course, but indicative of a difference between the famous author and the atmosphere at Smith, which did not accommodate over-bearing males.

Trouble of a more serious sort surfaced almost as soon as the semester began. Guest lecturing in an anthropology class, Vonnegut reminded everyone expansively that beauty is everywhere, including "a young coed leaning over to grab a book." The professor looked down at the floor wondering, "Where's he going with this?"[86]

In October, he offered his popular man-in-the-hole lecture billed as "a performance with chalk on blackboard." He had the audience with him most of the way, mocking the National Rifle Association, for instance, and observing that writers are unlikely to be found in the English Department. But then he segued into one of his favorite anecdotes. There was a beautiful Indian woman who worked in the post office in his Manhattan neighborhood. He lusted for her and imagined her putting the jewel on her forehead in a glass of water before bed like dentures. There were audible gasps.

The next day, the Smith College newspaper, the *Sophia*, lit into the affair with the headline DEIFY CELEBS MUCH, SMITH? Why, asked an editorial, had the audience tolerated "Kurt Vonnegut saying such things, however the statements were intended, when they would have walked out on anyone else who uttered the same things?" Touching on the sensitive question of Vonnegut's relevance, the editorial asked, "How many of you read your first Vonnegut book in August?"[87]

But he was unbowed, defiant even: "I'll say whatever I want; that's the price of my freedom. If it hurts someone's feelings, too bad! That's the way it goes."

The *Boston Globe* picked up on the story later, observing unkindly, "Academia may not be the ideal place for a crotchety writer waiting to die."[88]

He waited in the rather dreary office the English Department had assigned him for appointments with students, but traffic was slow. As a gesture of penance he posted a red bumper sticker on his door: GOD IS COMING AND IS SHE PISSED. But come spring, he decided he had had enough; he would return to Manhattan and living with Jill. He couldn't stand the pressure, he told Nanny, of how she was like a fire alarm that wouldn't go off, month after month. By accepting blame for everything, all of it—whatever Jill wanted him to take the fall for—he could return home and eke out life with his books and friends around him.[89] Anyway, it was clear his work was not held in esteem at Smith, and the young women, in his opinion, were humorless.[90]

Nanny summoned reinforcements. Rather than allow her father to reenter a relationship that, by his own admission, was deleterious to his health, she beckoned Loree from Iowa. It seemed the logical thing to do. She was a retired English instructor at the University of Northern

Iowa and living alone. Their affair had led to a lifelong friendship, so perhaps he would listen to her. Flying in to Northampton, Loree met with the family for a briefing before seeing Kurt.

He had been miserable. In a rare letter to Knox (their friendship had never quite recovered), he described himself as an anchorite in the wilderness—celibate, lonely.[91] After Loree arrived, they were nowhere to be found for a week. Nanny suspected they were in the condominium, but no one answered the phone or the door. She was mortified, thinking how she was trying to effect some kind of dignified resolution to her nearly octogenarian father's marital problems, and here he was, ignoring everyone, cavorting with his gray-haired ladylove.

Then, unexpectedly, Loree reappeared to say goodbye. She had offered Kurt her home, she explained, and promised to take care of him. She was ready to tie her life to his immediately. But he had said no. His life was too crazy and too messed up.[92] She was leaving.

After she was gone, Kurt informed Nanny, not unkindly, that he wished to be left alone.[93] Warm weather was coming to Northampton, and Smith College was preparing for summer break. He would return to New York at his own speed.

VONNEGUT WAS not in a good frame of mind when he returned to East Forty-eighth Street. The way he had been received at Smith called up old feelings of inadequacy, so strange to experience at his age. The closure, the accolades he hoped for—an epilogue, in literary terms—was still not written, and he was too tired to expend any more energy trying to bring it about. In his unhappiest moments, he thought life wasn't worth living.[94]

Resentfully, he passed under Jill's yoke as one who has been defeated in arms. There were new conditions to his staying there: no smoking in the house; one drink per day (he made sure it was a belt of good scotch before dinner), and friends would be screened. Bourjaily, coming through New York from his home in California, was surprised when Jill said no, Kurt could not see him.[95] That friendship, from the days of drinking and skirt chasing in Iowa, was not on the list, so to speak. Instead, she was going to cultivate friendships she considered beneficial for her husband.

* * *

KURT DIDN'T enjoy attending parties. There were no familiar faces at them anymore. Their purpose was for celebrating an achievement, another year, but thoughts of loss preoccupied him: "I've lost my sister, my brother, my editor, my publisher. It's a whole generation gone by. Old war buddies of mine, my colleagues, my family."[96] He spent a lot of time sitting on his favorite bench in Dag Hammarskjöld Plaza a few blocks away with Flour beside him, doing nothing, just people watching. One day, Vonnegut's physician friend Robert Maslansky passed an hour or so conversing with him in his Bellevue Hospital office but felt troubled afterward. To his professional eye, his friend was exhausted and unwell. "Kurt is getting tired," Maslansky wrote to the novelist Arthur Phillips, "and he seems ready to call it a day."[97]

Late at night, unable to sleep, he began phoning people from his past. He had always enjoyed giving friends a ring unexpectedly, as much as he liked writing several letters a week, but now he found he had nothing to talk about. Instead, he told anecdotes from his books, or made provocative remarks calculated to get a rise out of the person—to prolong the conversation a little longer. Then, embarrassed or frustrated, he would say, "Well, you're a nice guy" or "Yeah" and hang up.[98]

The same entropy was affecting his correspondence—he had nothing to say. Instead of letters, he began using postcards to send his thoughts, as if hailing from a faraway place. His news from nowhere tended to be reflections on current affairs or regurgitations of one-liners from his writings.[99]

Likewise, in place of essays, he submitted squibs to major publications. On the first anniversary of the World Trade Center terrorist attacks, when thousands of flyers in search of lost loved ones were still visible in Manhattan, Vonnegut sent the *New York Times* a fax, pointing out that the United States was the only nation ever to pulverize human beings with atomic weapons, applying to sorrow a mystifying kind of moral calculus.[100] George W. Bush, he declared in an unpublished letter to *Rolling Stone*, was an evolutionary throwback. The White House, he fulminated in one of his occasional columns for the liberal magazine *In These Times*, had been "taken over by means of the sleaziest, low-comedy, Keystone Kops–style coup d'etat imaginable."[101] As Jacques Barzun pointed out in *The House of Intellect*, "the shortest way to popularity is to keep up a verbal war against the social order."[102]

There were those who took offense at his one-off pronouncements. A journalist for the *Australian*, hearing him describe terrorists as "very brave people," was too disgusted to continue the interview, explaining to readers, "He's old and he doesn't want to live any more.... And because he can't find anything worthwhile to keep him alive, he finds defending terrorists somehow amusing."[103]

Mark Vonnegut responded by defending his father in the *Boston Globe* as, essentially, a fond old man: "My father cares not a fig about the Middle East. He's never been there, doesn't think about their art or writing, may or may not be able to pick out some of their capitals and important rivers on a map. His true heroes are Abraham Lincoln and Mark Twain. He doesn't listen to me.... Like most people, my father can be wrong. I'll bet you can take most 83-year-olds out to lunch and they'll say one or two stupid things."[104]

REGARDLESS, KURT was still one of the most popular authors in the United States. During the first six months of 2005, his 1963 novel *Cat's Cradle* sold 34,000 copies and his 1969 *Slaughterhouse-Five* nearly 66,000 copies.[105] Billy Pilgrim was as familiar a name as Jay Gatsby, Humbert Humbert, or Sister Carrie. On lists compiled by Modern Library, *Time* magazine, and in anthologies of recommended reading, *Slaughterhouse-Five* ranked as one of the best books of the twentieth century.

For the independent publisher Seven Stories Press, a small house with an emphasis on free speech and human rights, Vonnegut being dropped by Putnam provided an opportunity. (After the inauspicious response to *Timequake*, Putnam declined to publish new work by him.) Seven Stories' Dan Simon stepped in, publishing in 1999 the seventy-nine-page *God Bless You, Dr. Kevorkian*, a series of interviews in the afterlife between Vonnegut and historical figures. Then in September 2005, Simon brought out *A Man Without a Country*, composed of essays and speeches written during the previous five years and illustrated with Kurt's drawings, including his man-in-the-hole chalk talk on story structure. The twelve "short riffs," as the *Jerusalem Post* characterized them, were well chosen—sharp, pugilistic, and unsubtle—a return of the juice that many of his readers, who spanned three generations now, expected from Vonnegut.[106] *A Man Without a Country* spent six weeks among the top fifteen nonfiction books on the *New York Times* best seller list. Asked in an interview why, despite saying he was finished with writing after *Timequake*, he was back with another book, Vonnegut replied, "Well, I had hoped to be dead."[107]

KURT HAD a novel he was working on, however, begun in Northampton, about a wisecracking lecturer who speaks to college audiences. The working title was *If God Were Alive Today* (never published), but he was stalled and sensed he wouldn't finish.[108] "Look, I'm old," he said irritably to a reporter. "Joe Namath isn't passing footballs into the crowds anymore. You ought to see what Mozart looks like by now. I'm old, for God's sake—I'm terribly tired."[109]

The winter of 2006–7 was hard on him. He caught a respiratory infection, and each breath had a faint whistle in it. Some days, he was too tired to rise from the sofa in the front room and rested with his arms turned palm-up at his sides, letting his head fall back. His ankles were so thin that someone with an average-sized hand could encircle them with a thumb and forefinger.[110] Responding to an invitation to speak at Cornell University, he said he wouldn't be able to attend. At eighty-four, he looked like an iguana, he said, hated to travel, and would be as interesting as the *Congressional Record*.[111]

One night, he called his "Irish landlady" in Northampton, Kerry O'Keefe, and sang her a vaudeville song he remembered from listening to the radio as a boy, crooning the lyrics almost in a whisper in his rumbling baritone. "Now," he said, when he had finished, "tomorrow night, you call me back at nine o'clock and sing me a song."

At nine the following evening his phone rang. O'Keefe, who had sung in clubs when she was young, treated him to a feeling rendition of "Come Rain or Come Shine."

When she had finished, he said, "Goodbye," furtively, as if someone were listening, and hung up.[112]

THE WINTER weather in New York City broke spectacularly on March 14, 2007. A day that seemed borrowed from May brought sun and warmth. Kurt had completed a speech to be delivered in a few weeks at Butler University because Indianapolis had declared 2007 "The Year of Vonnegut." After lunch, dressed in a baggy knit sweater and gray trousers—perforated in a few places by cigarette burns—Kurt put the leash on Flour to take her for a walk. A few hours earlier, he had been asked by a visitor, "Do you believe in God?"

"I don't know," he replied, "but who couldn't?"[113]

Outside the brownstone, as he and Flour reached the bottom steps, the little dog spun around to see if he was coming. He tripped over her leash, pitched forward full-length, and struck the right side of his face on the sidewalk, losing consciousness instantly.[114]

At Bellevue Hospital, Jill signed him in as "Kurt Krementz," and he was hurried into emergency surgery. X-rays showed a black puddle of what looked like spilled ink behind his forehead.[115] There was nothing to be done, the injury was too severe, and as days turned into weeks nurses came to check his chart and to see that he was comfortable.

One evening, as Mark was sitting by the bed, he saw his father's hand twitch. Then the index and middle fingers formed a V. Slowly, he brought his fingers to his lips. Drawing a breath, he paused, then exhaled in a long, drawn-out sigh and let his hand sink down to the bedclothes. He was still again.[116]

He died April 11, 2007.

Appendix:
Vonnegut-Lieber Family History

KURT VONNEGUT CALLED himself a "purebred kraut." He never thought of himself as being German in sympathy or outlook, however, but quintessentially American. "A lot of people think I speak English awfully good for somebody who was born in Germany. People frequently comment on how good my English is. Well, my great-grandfather was born in the United States and we're as patriotic as anybody, God damn it, we've been over here helping to build this country."[1]

The paterfamilias of the Vonnegut clan (during Kurt Jr.'s childhood there were close to thirty Vonneguts in the Indianapolis telephone directory) was a businessman from Germany named Clemens Vonnegut. In his frock coat and silk top hat, he tended the original garden that grew their fortunes. "The Vonnegut family," said Kurt Jr., "was built around what started as a general store on a mud street in Indianapolis."[2]

The son of a Roman Catholic tax collector for a duke in Westphalia, Clemens Vonnegut immigrated to the United States in about 1849. During the republican revolution of March 1848, he had joined demonstrations demanding that the Confederation of German States allow parliamentary elections, a constitution, and freedom of the press. But

[1]"Kurt Vonnegut at NYU," Pacifica Radio Archives, KPFT, November 6, 1970.
[2]*Kurt Vonnegut: American Made*, directed by Robert B. Weide, Whyaduck Productions, 1994.

the uprising failed, and the government ushered him out of Germany, along with tens of thousands of other troublemakers, agitators, failures, and paupers. His sources of inspiration were Benjamin Franklin, his "American Saint" of pragmatism and deism, and Voltaire, his hero of intellectual and religious skepticism.[3] He was frugal, hardworking, and adaptable because he was not hidebound by conventional ways of thinking. In other words, he was perfectly suited to succeed wherever there were opportunities and freedom. He arrived in New York at the age of twenty-four.

Fortunately, too, he was carrying a commission from a German silk and velvet ribbon firm to establish an agency in New York. But while examining these unfamiliar shores, he soon realized he appeared conspicuously Old World. First, his American counterparts in business were almost indistinguishable in appearance from their employees. He, on the other hand, arrived for appointments dressed as any Continental cosmopolitan might, wearing a top hat, cape, and wiggling a walking stick. Also, to his annoyance, his surname (*Fawn*-ne-goot) on the English tongue was mispronounced "Funny-gut," causing receptionists to smirk. He took to wearing plainer clothes. He also began introducing himself firmly as "*Vonne*gut."[4] Now he was ready for action as a new man.

After setting up the offices of the ribbon agency and completing his assignment, he resigned and applied for American citizenship. About the same time, a former classmate, Charles Vollmer, contacted him from Indianapolis about a business proposition. Vollmer needed a partner outfitting settlers going west. Clemens boarded a train in 1850 to Cincinnati, and then continued the rest of the way by stagecoach over rutted roads. Several times he had to get out and help free the wheels from the mud.[5] Such were the challenges of frontier entrepreneurship.

Indianapolis is almost precisely in the center of the state. If Clemens climbed to the roof of the four-story Asylum for the Blind, which provided the highest perspective of the town for sightseers, Indianapolis

[3]John G. Rauch, "An Account of the Ancestry of Kurt Vonnegut Jr. by an Ancient Friend of the Family," 1970, 21. Lilly Library, Indiana University, Bloomington.

[4]"Vonnegut" is a slight change from "Funnegut," which belonged to Clemens's Catholic forebears living near the little River Funne on a small estate, *ein gut*.

[5]"Seventy-Five Years of Vonnegut Hardware" (pamphlet), May 1927, Indiana Historical Society, Indianapolis.

appeared in the early 1850s as a cluster of one- and two-story homes with porches shaded by heavy-leafed maple trees, elms, oaks, and beeches and yards edged by whitewashed or iron fences. In the back-yards were chickens, sheds, and carriage houses. On Washington Street, where small businesses congregated—and Vollmer & Vonnegut opened its doors—there were narrow two- and three-story buildings with canopies providing dry places for pedestrians to stand out of the rain. The city had no brick- or gravel-paved streets and few sidewalks. A jumble of signs announced the wares for sale inside each establishment, mainly dry goods (fabric, thread, clothing), groceries, and hardware. Odors of beer, cheese making, tanning, cigar smoke, and horse droppings, of course, undulated on the hot summer air. After nightfall, the twinkling lanterns of the Bates and Little hotels were the only bright lights visible. This is where, over the next century, four generations of Vonneguts would live, and two architects in the family would invigorate the skyline with new structures to serve the needs of the capital as it grew from a population of 8,000—the year Clemens arrived—to 387,000 in 1940, when his great-grandson Kay left for Cornell University and never returned to the city to live.

If the aim of Vollmer & Vonnegut, purveyors of general merchandise, was to catch the settler trade headed for the Plains and beyond, it should have cast its line out a little farther—somewhere past the Mississippi at least; St. Louis would have been ideal. In any event, Charles Vollmer turned out to be a poor partner. He sold his interest in the store to Clemens after a few years and took off for the gold fields in California when news of big strikes echoed over the prairies like distant thunderclaps. After that, he disappeared completely; no word was ever heard from him again. No matter; Clemens was an excellent business-man on his own.

Across the street from Vonnegut Hardware was a German café where Clemens enjoyed having lunch. And there was a waitress he liked there, too: Katarina Blank. Her parents were German immigrants living on a wetlands farm west of Indianapolis. She was one of seven children and waiting tables to bring in money. They married in 1852, when he was twenty-eight and she twenty-four. Three of their sons were born above the hardware store: Clemens Jr., Bernard, and Franklin, named after Benjamin Franklin. The fourth and final child, George, was born in their unpretentious home on Market Street. Two of his sons diversified the hardware business over the years, two pursued other careers, but all remained in Indianapolis.

It's characteristic of Clemens that he couldn't wait to get involved in local civic affairs. The year the store opened, he joined friends in founding the Indianapolis Turngemeinde (gymnastic club) in a one-story wooden building on West Washington Street. Eventually, the Indianapolis Socialer Turnverein, as it was renamed, emerged in the mid-1800s as an organization promoting physical fitness, free thought, liberal politics, improved working conditions for laborers, the emancipation of women, and the abolition of slavery.[6] Clemens was one of the first presidents.

Refrains of Clemens's civic involvement and desire for social betterment can be heard in his great-grandson's novels such as *God Bless You, Mr. Rosewater*. But to really appreciate how Kurt's German American intellectual heritage influenced him, a small item appearing in the April 3, 1870, issue of the *Indianapolis Telegraph* provides an important clue. It announces the inaugural meeting, attended by a large number of people, of the freethinkers. The freethinkers were a religious rationalist group that attacked biblical infallibility and advocated the natural religion based on man's moral freedom. The movement was initiated during the era of the American Revolution. The stated purpose of the Indianapolis freethinkers was "the active spreading of free ideas of religious, political and social nature, and to awaken the feeling of togetherness of all like-minded people."[7] The turnout was large, and Clemens Vonnegut was chosen president. In 1900 he published, anonymously, *A Proposed Guide for Instruction in Morals from the Standpoint of a Freethinker for Adult Persons, Offered by a Dilettante.*

---

[6]Four years later, the Indianapolis Turn-Schwestern Verein—the Turn "sisters" for wives and daughters of the men's club—met for the first time. Initially it was intended to support the activities of the Turnverein, especially to promote and oversee the girls' athletic classes and to supervise the Turnverein library. Soon the members' discussions included undertaking charity work in the city such as running a soup kitchen and offering sewing classes for poor children. They were more than do-gooders, though; as minutes from their meetings indicate, they saw themselves as having "the same spiritual interests" as the freethinkers. A discussion devoted to the "rights of women" appears on one of their agendas. (Athenaeum Damenverein & Women's Auxiliary Records, 1876–1999, Mss 039, Special Collections and Archives, IUPUI University Library, Indiana University and Purdue University, Indianapolis.)

[7]Giles R. Hoyt, Claudia Grossman, Sabine Jessner, eds., "Minutes of the Freethinker Society of Indianapolis, 1870–1890," translated by Charles Spencer and Kaethe Schwarz, Indiana Historical Society, Indianapolis, 1988.

* * *

CLEMENS'S SECOND son was Bernard Vonnegut, Kurt's grandfather, who was born August 8, 1855, and died in August 1908. After working for just a year at Vonnegut Hardware, he was close to a nervous breakdown. Kurt said of him, "The family legend is that Bernard Vonnegut when a boy was working with his brothers in the family hardware store, and he began to weep. He was asked what the trouble was, and he said that he didn't want to work in a store. He said he wanted to be an artist instead."[8] To restore his health and spirit, it was arranged that he work in the fresh air as a carver with mallet and chisel in the Ittenbach Contracting Company's stone yard.[9] He was a gifted stonecutter, the owner pronounced, and the family sent him to Europe to study design.

Returning for graduate studies at MIT, he went next to New York and associated with artists, architects, and set designers. He was happy, but his family insisted he come home and settle down. On September 19, 1883, Bernard married Nannette Schnull, who was born and raised in Indianapolis, and whose father, Henry, had long been a prominent wholesale merchant. In 1888, Bernard entered into partnership with Arthur Bohn, under the firm name Vonnegut & Bohn. His business card alone indicated his superlative work. At the turn of the twentieth century, his offices were located in the richly carved, V-shaped Vance Building on a downtown corner. And printed on his business card was a single word that spoke eloquently of his standing in a city where the interurban cars were still pulled by mules: the word *elevator.*

Bernard and Nannette had three children: Irma, Alex, and Kurt, the father of Kurt Vonnegut Jr.

KURT JR.'s mother, Edith, was lovely, with auburn hair close to red, a complexion like porcelain, and blue-green eyes.[10] Her family's wealth originated with her grandfather Peter Lieber, a limping Civil War veteran and former private secretary to Indiana governor Oliver P. Morton. In 1868, Peter and his brother Herman purchased a brewery

[8]Kurt Vonnegut, *Palm Sunday* (1981; reprint, New York: Delta, 1999), 39.
[9]*Indiana and Indianans: A History of Aboriginal and Territorial Indiana and the Century of Statehood* (Chicago: American Historical Society, 1919), 2173–75.
[10]Rauch, "Ancestry of Kurt Vonnegut," 65.

in Indianapolis. They dubbed their venture City Brewery, P. Lieber & Company.

Since they knew practically nothing about brewing beer, they hired an expert brewmaster. Herman's father-in-law, Jacob Metzger, a German immigrant, provided the bottling factory. (Some sources say he also bottled Budweiser, Bass Ale, and Guinness Extra Stout.) The secret family recipe for Lieber Lager Beer, later Gold Medal, was adding a pinch of coffee grounds to the hops. At that time, beer cost about a dollar a barrel to manufacture and sold for eight. Profits were enormous.

In 1889, an offer from an English syndicate to combine three Indianapolis breweries into one was accepted, and Peter became the first president of Indianapolis Brewing Company; his son Albert, Edith's father, was the first managing director.

Smart businessman that he was, Peter had always watched the political winds for signs of changes that might affect his balance sheet. Since the Civil War, he had been a Republican, which was typical of former Union soldiers. But in 1880, when the Grand Old Party, at the insistence of the Methodist Church, adopted a plank recommending a restraint upon the beer and liquor trade, he was outraged. He promptly changed his politics and was thereafter a Democrat, and an aggressive, active one. He contributed heavily to Grover Cleveland's reelection campaign in 1892, for which he was rewarded with an appointment as consul general to Düsseldorf. He retired to live in Germany, the place of his birth, and left the Indianapolis Brewing Company in Albert's hands.

With the old man out of the way, Albert began to milk the company. He enjoyed a cozy relationship with the British representative of the syndicate, a Colonel Thompson, and the two agreed to create a special account for off-the-books expenditures. They disguised the money they skimmed off for personal use as enormous purchases of ice. Ice paid to create Vellamada, Albert's four-hundred-acre summer residence with hunting grounds. He commissioned his cooper smiths at the brewery to build German-style outbuildings everywhere on the property. There were servants, an English butler, horses, a liveried footman, carriages, and motorcars.

In town, he was a playboy, the head of a rich men's club with a singular initiation rite. Newcomers were blindfolded and submitted to having their butts sprayed with beer. Then they were official members of the "W-A" or "Wet-Ass" club and presented with a gold pin. One of them owned the English Hotel and Opera House on Monument Circle, where he could take his fellow W-As to meet actresses and especially chorus girls from musical comedies after the show.[11]

Somehow, this nonsense seemed not to have affected the Indianapolis Brewing Company at all. In 1899, Albert announced that he was considering selling out to the American Malting Company for one lump sum. "I should say it will require at least a billion dollars to do the work," he commented airily, when a workingman was glad to get a dollar a day. "The consumer will not lose," he added.[12]

In 1885, he had married Alice Barus, an accomplished musician and daughter of the nationally known choir and symphony conductor Carl Barus. But she died of pneumonia when Edith was nine and her brothers were seven and five. A billion-dollar deal, hundreds of employees, Albert could handle; three grieving children, he could not, Edith discovered. Too hastily for his children's good, Albert reappeared on the social scene as a widower in London-tailored clothes. He caught the attention of a strange and beautiful woman, Ora D. Lane from Zanesville, Ohio, who went by the nickname "O.D."

Despite his relatives' misgivings, Albert married O.D. anyway, and it wasn't long before the new Mrs. Lieber became known behind her back as "Odious." The root of her eccentric nature had a malignant twist.

She told her husband that his wretched children were tormenting her—they were conspiring to harm her. When she went to bed at night, she slipped a loaded pistol under her pillow. She flung her miseries in his face in public. Edith watched in misery as her father, once kindly and gentle, began beating her brothers.[13] He finally divorced his second wife, but the settlement lopped off a big piece of his fortune. He married a third time, a widow named Meda Langtry, who was plain looking and uninteresting, except that she was only slightly older than Edith. They had been in school together. By the end of this three-act tragicomedy,

---

[11]Rauch, "Ancestry of Kurt Vonnegut," 57.
[12]"New Billion Dollar Trust: Gigantic Project to Combine the Breweries in This Country—Eastern Capitalists Interested," *New York Times*, June 11, 1899.
[13]Edie Vonnegut, interview, September 20, 2007.

Edith felt deep insecurities about her place in the world, made worse by periods of depression.

Prohibition and the Great Depression finally ruined Albert Lieber. "When I got to know him," said his grandson Kurt Jr., "there wasn't much to know. He was in bed all the time with a flabby heart. He might as well have been a Martian. What do I remember about him? His mouth was slackly open. It was very pink inside."[14]

[14]Vonnegut, *Palm Sunday*, 33.

Notes

Unless otherwise attributed, all interviews are by the author; all e-mails are addressed to the author.

Abbreviations

CC	Crowell-Collier Publishing Company records, 1931–55, New York Public Library, New York, NY
CSS	Charles Scribner's Sons archives, Princeton University Library, Princeton, NJ
EV	Edith Vonnegut
JDP	José Donoso Papers, Princeton University Library, Princeton, NJ
JDP1	José Donoso Papers, University of Iowa, Iowa City, IA
JV	Jane Vonnegut
KB	Knox Burger
KV	Kurt Vonnegut
LL	Lilly Library, Indiana University, Bloomington, IN
NV	Nanny Vonnegut
SLPF	Seymour Lawrence Publishing Files, Special Collections, University of Delaware Library, Newark, DE

Prologue: Out of Print and Scared to Death

1. KV to Sarah Crawford, September 18, 1965, private collection.
2. KV to Sarah Crawford, September 28, 1965, private collection.
3. KV to KB, August 7, 1965, private collection.
4. Miller Harris to KV, August 16, 1965, private collection.
5. KV to John C. Gerber, July 11, 1965, faculty/staff files, University of Iowa, Iowa City.
6. KV to Steve Wilbers, September 16, 1976, private collection.
7. KV to KB, August 7, 1965, private collection.
8. KV to Stephen Wilbers, September 16, 1976, private collection.
9. T. George Harris, "University of Iowa's Paul Engle, Poet-Grower to the World," *Look*, June 1, 1965.

10. KV, "New World Symphony," in *A Community of Writers: Paul Engle and the Iowa Writers' Workshop*, ed. Robert Dana (Iowa City: University of Iowa Press, 1999), 115.

11. Saul Maloff, "The Time, the Space, the Quiet," *New York Times*, November 29, 1981.

12. KV, "To Be a Native Middle-Westerner," *Nuvo Newsweekly*, May 20, 1999; and KV to JV, September 17, 1965, private collection.

1: You Were an Accident

1. Charlotte Cathcart, *Indianapolis from Our Old Corner* (Indianapolis: Indiana Historical Society, 1965), 27.

2. John G. Rauch, "An Account of the Ancestry of Kurt Vonnegut Jr. by an Ancient Friend of the Family," 1970, 68, LL.

3. Ibid., 70.

4. "Kurt Vonnegut at NYU," Pacifica Radio Archives, KPFT, November 6, 1970.

5. Rauch, "Ancestry of Kurt Vonnegut," 68.

6. Ibid., 26.

7. Neal Auction Company, New Orleans, LA, "Winter Estates Auction," February 7–8, 2004: "Still Life: The Remains of the Portfolio Club Supper."

8. KV, "To Be a Native Middle-Westerner."

9. According to census documents, the Vonneguts had a German American servant (Cannie Hattenbach, fifty-one) living with them in 1930.

10. *Kurt Vonnegut: American Made*, directed by Robert B. Weide, Whyaduck Productions, 1994.

11. KV, interview, March 13, 2007.

12. Ibid.

13. Ibid.

14. Irma Vonnegut Lindener in "Happy Birthday, Kurt Vonnegut: A Festschrift for Kurt Vonnegut on his Sixtieth Birthday," ed. Jill Krementz (New York: Delacorte, 1982), 13.

15. KV, "To Be a Native Middle-Westerner."

16. Evans Woollen, interview, February 16, 2008. Woollen, a prominent Indianapolis architect, lived in the Vonnegut home for twenty-five years.

17. Ibid.

18. Jacob Piatt Dunn, *Greater Indianapolis: The History, the Industries, the Institutions, and the People of a City of Homes* (Chicago: Lewis, 1910), 964–66. These buildings are still used for their original purposes.

19. Ibid.

20. Ibid.

21. *Kurt Vonnegut: American Made*, Weide.

22. KV to Ben Hitz, November 22, 1997, private collection.

23. KV, interview, March 13, 2007. As a compensation, he liked to think that there had been some "very deep bonding there which was painful to them in later years," meaning his aunt and uncle became attached to him, loved him while his parents were away.

24. "Cape Cod Author Sees Some Flaws in Age of Electronics," *Cape Cod Standard-Times*, December 14, 1952.

25. Rauch, "Ancestry of Kurt Vonnegut," 71.

26. Caterina Cregor, *The Path Well Chosen: History of the Orchard School, 1922–1984* (Indianapolis: Orchard School Foundation, 1984), 67.

27. KV, interview, March 13, 2007.

28. KV, "The Last Word," *New York Times*, October 30, 1966.

29. KV, interview, December 13, 2006.

30. Rauch, "Ancestry of Kurt Vonnegut," 29.

31. KV, *Palm Sunday*, 53.

32. KV, interview, December 13, 2006.

33. Ben Hitz, interview, November 11, 2006. Hitz was a lifelong friend after the two met at the Orchard School. His namesake, "Dr. Benjamin Hitz," appears in Vonnegut's short story "2BO2B." *Jailbird* is dedicated to him.

34. KV interview, March 13, 2007.

35. *Kurt Vonnegut: American Made*, Weide.

36. KV, interview, March 13, 2007.

37. Ibid.

38. Hank Nuwer, "A Skull Session with Kurt Vonnegut," in *Conversations with Kurt Vonnegut*, ed. William Rodney Allen (Jackson: University of Mississippi Press, 1988), 245.

39. Nolan Young, interview, June 21, 2008. Nolan and Owen Young Jr. are Mrs. Young's grandchildren.

40. Owen Young Jr., interview, June 19, 2008. Mrs. Young was strict with her children and grandchildren, assigning them daily chores.

41. KV, interview, March 13, 2007.

42. Ibid.

43. Owen Young Jr., interview, June 19, 2008.

44. Ibid. Young became bishop of Bethel Tabernacle Church in Indianapolis.

45. KV, *Wampeters, Foma & Granfalloons* (New York: Delta, 1999), xxiii.

46. KV, interview, March 13, 2007.

47. Kurt Jr.'s great-uncle Theodore Franklin Vonnegut was a friend of Riley's. Apparently, this Vonnegut had a literary bent, too. His master of arts thesis at Indiana University, later published as a booklet in 1926, was "Indianapolis Booksellers and Their Literary Background, 1820–1860: A Glimpse of the Old Book Trade of Indianapolis."

48. KV, interview, March 13, 2007.

49. KV, *Wampeters, Foma & Granfalloons*, xxiii.

50. KV, "Bernard Vonnegut: The Rainmaker," *New York Times*, January 4, 1998. This uncle on his mother's side was Carl Barus, Hazard Professor of Physics at Brown University in the 1920s, and cofounder and fourth president of the American Physical Society.

51. KV, interview, December 13, 2006.

52. Ibid.

53. In home movies, whenever Kurt Jr. realizes the camera is rolling, he whirls on Bernard and tries to hit him.

54. KV, interview, December 13, 2006.

55. *Kurt Vonnegut: American Made*, Weide.

56. Patricia Bosworth, "To Vonnegut, the Hero Is the Man Who Refuses to Kill," *New York Times*, October 25, 1970.

57. *Kurt Vonnegut: American Made*, Weide.

58. KV, interview, March 13, 2007.

59. Freud believed the sexual curiosity of youngsters is the true source of scientific inquisitiveness. Peter Gay, *Freud: A Life for Our Time* (New York: Norton, 1988), 25.

60. KV, interview, December 13, 2006.

61. "Friends" of the family, the Reinhardts, persuaded the Vonneguts to invest in a deal involving coal, oil, and mining concerns. It was a sure thing, they said; that's how they were holding out against the downturn in the economy. Actually, they were cat's-paws for crooks who were preying on panicky people eager to make money fast. The Reinhardts got their cut from whomever they were fronting for. The Vonneguts lost their investment. KV, interview, March 3, 2007.

62. Rauch, "Ancestry of Kurt Vonnegut," 71.

63. KV, *Palm Sunday*, 52.

64. "Moving Ma Bell, Vonnegut Style," *Indianapolis Magazine*, October 1976.

65. Henry James Cargas, "Kurt Vonnegut" (interview), *Christian Century*, November 24, 1976.

66. KV, *Fates Worse Than Death: An Autobiographical Collage* (New York: Berkley, 1992), 23.

67. Owen Young Jr., interview, July 2, 2008.

68. "Kurt Vonnegut," *Authors and Artists for Young Adults*, vols. 6, 24, Gale, 1992–99 (Farmington Hills, MI: Thomson Gale, 2006).

69. KV, interview, March 14, 2007.

70. KV, *Timequake* (1997; repr., New York: Berkley, 1998), 32.

71. Evans Woollen, the architect who later owned the home, removed the living room ceiling, which was the floor of the master bedroom, to create a cathedral effect. He said Kurt Jr. told the next owners, the Hickmans, "I never minded the removal of the master bedroom, because I had such bad memories of my mother and father fighting verbally in that room and being able to hear it from the living room below." Evans Woollen, interview, February 16, 2008.

72. KV, *Fates Worse Than Death*, 28.

73. *Kurt Vonnegut: American Made*, Weide.

74. Ibid.

75. KV, *Fates Worse Than Death*, 34.

76. Ibid., 36.

77. Charlie Reilly, "Two Conversations with Kurt Vonnegut," *College Literature* 7 (1980): 1–29.

78. Catherine Alford Zaring, "Time Traveling Through Indianapolis with Kurt Vonnegut Jr.," *Indianapolis Home and Garden*, November 1978.

79. *Kurt Vonnegut: American Made*, Weide.

80. KV, interview, March 13, 2007.

81. KV to Catherine Glossbrenner Rasmussen, December 1977, private collection.

82. Jerome Klinkowitz, interview, October 21, 2007.

83. Walter A. Vonnegut, journal, August 12, 1938, private collection. Walter was Kurt's second cousin and three weeks younger.

84. KV, "The Lake," *Architectural Digest*, June 1988, 30.

85. Walter A. Vonnegut, interview, April 7, 2007.

86. KV, interview, March 13, 2007.

87. KV, "The Lake," 30.

88. KV, interview, March 13, 2007.

89. KV, *Palm Sunday*, 20.

90. According to George Latham, a classmate of Bernard's at the Park School and an Indianapolis historian, anger at the German community intensified when it came to light that certain Das Deutsche Haus board members owned "Kaiser bonds." This was an understandable mistake, albeit a real blunder, since German Americans

owned or ran most of the major banks in the city. Charles Latham, interview, August 6, 2010.

91. KV, "Speech at the Athenaeum, Indianapolis," October 10, 1996.
92. Irma Vonnegut Lindener, interview by James A. Glass, OH #20 (Indiana Historical Society, 1978), 14.
93. United States Selective Service System, World War I Selective Service System Draft Registration Cards, 1917–18, National Archives and Records Administration, Washington, DC.
94. Ancestry.com, New York Passenger Lists, 1820–1957 (database online) (Provo, UT: Generations Network, 2006). Records of the U.S. Customs Service, Record Group 36, National Archives, Washington, DC.
95. KV, "Speech at the Athenaeum, Indianapolis."
96. Studs Terkel, "Kurt Vonnegut," in *Will the Circle Be Unbroken? Reflections on Death, Rebirth, and Hunger for a Faith* (New York: New Press, 2001), 222.
97. Kathryn Hume, "Vonnegut's Melancholy," *Philological Quarterly* 77, no. 2 (Spring 1998): 221.
98. KV, *Palm Sunday*, 53.
99. KV to NV, January 26, 1973, private collection.
100. Emily Glossbrenner Diamond, interview, February 7, 2008.
101. Walter A. Vonnegut, interview, April 7, 2007.
102. Alex Vonnegut to Morris Fishbein, January 16, 1955, Morris Fishbein Papers, University of Chicago, Chicago, IL.
103. Emily Louise Diamond, interview, February 7, 2008.
104. "Kurt Vonnegut, SHS Alum, Achieves Fame as a Novelist," Shortridge High School *Echo*, September–October, 1962.
105. Frank McLaughlin, "An Interview with Kurt Vonnegut," *Media & Methods*, May 1973, 38–41, 45–46.
106. *Kurt Vonnegut: American Made*, Weide.
107. KV, interview, March 13, 2007.
108. Scott Vonnegut, "A Remembrance of Kurt Vonnegut" (memorial service, New York, April 2007).
109. KV, interview, March 13, 2007.
110. *Kurt Vonnegut: American Made*, Weide.
111. JV Yarmolinsky, *Angels Without Wings: How Tragedy Created a Remarkable Family* (Boston: Houghton Mifflin, 1987), 27.
112. The three main characters in *Cat's Cradle* are the Hoenikker siblings: Frank, Angela, and Newt; *The Sirens of Titan* features Malachi Constant, Beatrice Rumfoord, and their son, Chrono; and in *God Bless You, Mr. Rosewater*, Eliot Rosewater, his ex-wife, and his father are at odds.
113. *Kurt Vonnegut: American Made*, Weide.
114. Laura Sheerin Gaus, *Shortridge High School, 1864–1981 in Retrospect* (Indianapolis: Indiana Historical Society, 1985), 162.
115. KV, interview, March 13, 2007.
116. Gaus, *Shortridge High School*, 151.
117. KV, interview, March 14, 2007.
118. Ibid.
119. KV to Frank Cruger, February 4, 1977, private collection.
120. Ibid.
121. KV, *Palm Sunday*, 54.

122. KV, interview, March 14, 2007.

123. Marge (Mary Jo) Schmoll to KV, March 5, 1987, Vonnegut mss., LL.

124. Evans Woollen, interview, February 16, 2008. Vonnegut mentioned his window-gazing during an unexpected visit to his childhood home, where Woollen then lived, in 1965.

125. Hume, "Vonnegut's Melancholy," 221.

126. *Kurt Vonnegut: American Made*, Weide.

127. Walter A. Vonnegut, diary entry, January 13, 1939, private collection. He was Kurt's second cousin; his father was Walter A. Vonnegut, a stage actor; his mother, Marjorie, later married the journalist Don Marquis, the creator of *archy and mehitabel*, the life and times of a cat who believes she is Cleopatra reincarnated and her friend, a cockroach who can't hit the shift key on a typewriter. As a child, Walter starred in 1933 with his parents in Eugene O'Neill's *Ah, Wilderness!* on Broadway. The cast included George M. Cohan opposite Walter's mother and, in his very first role, the expressionless, baby-faced killer in the *Maltese Falcon*, Elisha Cook Jr.

128. KV to NV, December 29, 1979, Vonnegut mss., LL.

129. Kilgore Trout became Vonnegut's alter ego in his novels.

130. George Jeffrey, interview, January 5, 2007.

131. Zaring, "Time Traveling Through Indianapolis with Kurt Vonnegut Jr."

132. KV, interview, December 13, 2006.

133. United States Patent Office, K. Vonnegut, Tobacco Pipe, #2,395,596, filed October 30, 1944. He withdrew the first patent in 1938 and improved the design.

134. KV, interview, March 13, 2007.

135. Ben Hitz, interview, November 15, 2007. Hitz was Vonnegut's coeditor for the Tuesday edition. The *Echo* later drew on the talents of future senator Richard G. Lugar, Republican from Indiana, and Dan Wakefield, best known for his novel *Going All the Way*. Wakefield's novel, according to 106-year-old Miss Jeanette Grubb, the last surviving faculty member of Shortridge in the 1930s, did not go over well with his female classmates, some of whom recognized themselves.

136. KV, *Wampeters, Foma & Granfalloons*, 256.

137. Reilly, "Two Conversations with Kurt Vonnegut," 1–29.

138. *Shortridge Daily Echo*, September 15, 1938.

139. Ibid., September 22, 1938.

140. Trish Mumford, "Everybody Loved Vonnegut's Tricks," *Cape Cod Times*, July 30, 2008.

141. *Shortridge Daily Echo*, September 21, 1939.

142. McLaughlin, "An Interview with Kurt Vonnegut," 38–41, 45–46.

143. KV, interview, March 13, 2007.

144. Ibid.

145. Ibid.

146. Ibid.

147. KV, interview, December 13, 2006.

2: One of the Biggest Fools on the Hill

1. Rauch, "Ancestry of Kurt Vonnegut," 54.

2. Rodney S. Gould to Fred Harwood, April 24, 2007, private collection.

3. KV, interview, March 13, 2007.

4. David Young, "Telling It Like It Was," in "Happy Birthday, Kurt Vonnegut," 21–23.

5. Ibid.

6. Rodney S. Gould, letter to his children, December 21, 2005, private collection.

7. Young, "Telling It Like It Was," 21–23.

8. KV, "Everything's Okely Dokely with Moakley," Speaking of Sports, *Cornell Daily Sun*, December 4, 1941.

9. Miller Harris, interview, January 1, 2007.

10. Reilly, "Two Conversations with Kurt Vonnegut."

11. Robert Scholes, "A Talk With Kurt Vonnegut," in *Conversations with Kurt Vonnegut*, 114.

12. KV, "In Defense of the Golden West," Well All Right, *Cornell Daily Sun*, March 4, 1942.

13. KV, "Albino for a Day, or in the Pink," Well All Right, *Cornell Daily Sun*, March 24, 1942.

14. KB, interview, June 18, 2007.

15. Ibid.

16. Ibid.

17. Emily Louise Diamond, interview, February 7, 2008. Jane Cox, whom Kurt later married, was from the same social stratum. "My parents were very conservative, reactionary, Indiana types who would never dream not only of voting for a Democrat, but of practically speaking to anyone who did." JV, interview by Marge Schiller, December 1969, interview 639, transcript, McCarthy Historical Project, Eugene J. McCarthy Papers, Elmer L. Andersen Library, University of Minnesota, Minneapolis, Minnesota.

18. Emily Louise Diamond, interview, February 7, 2008.

19. *Essential Vonnegut: Interviews Conducted by Walter Miller*, CD-ROM (New York: HarperCollins, 2006).

20. Wilfrid Sheed, "The Now Generation Knew Him When," *Life*, September 12, 1969, 66.

21. KV, "Finding the News in the News," Well All Right, *Cornell Daily Sun*, May 22, 1941.

22. KV, "Bayonet Drill at the Rate of Seven in 20 Seconds, or, Oh for a Couple of Nazis," Well All Right, *Cornell Daily Sun*, April 22, 1941.

23. KV, interview, March 13, 2007.

24. KV, *Palm Sunday*, 60.

25. Butler University has a policy of not releasing transcripts, but Vonnegut didn't take "courses in bacteriology and qualitative analysis in the summer school of Butler University," as he claimed in *Timequake*, according to a reference librarian in Special Collections, Rare Books, and University Archives, Irwin Library, Butler University. Throughout his life he felt the need to embellish his education and remind people, as he did a PBS interviewer: "Look, I don't mean to intimidate you, but I have a master's degree in anthropology." "Kurt Vonnegut," *NOW*, PBS, October 7, 2005.

26. KV, "Mr. Anthony, What I Want to Know," Berry Patch, *Cornell Daily Sun*, October 24, 1942.

27. KV, interview, March 13, 2007.

28. Ben Hitz, interview, December 15, 2006.

29. S. A. Leonard and R. F. Cox, *General Language: A Series of Lessons in Grammar, Word Study, and History of the English Language* (Chicago: Rand McNally, 1925).

30. EV, interview, September 20, 2007.

31. Mark Vonnegut, "Personal Reflections on Diagnosis," *Journal of Mental Health* 19, no. 4 (August 2010): 373–75.

32. At one point she was semicomatose for about a year in a state hospital and spent

another year there until she was permitted to leave. Riah Fagan Cox, "I Remember Jones," family memoir, circa 1940s, private collection.

33. Ben Hitz, interview, November 15, 2007.

34. Kendall Landis, interview, June 12, 2008.

35. Victor Jose, interview, January 5, 2007. Jose was a friend from Shortridge High School who ran into Vonnegut at City News while Jose was there interviewing for a job.

36. Isabella Horton Grant, interview, January 26, 2008.

37. The book is in EV's possession.

38. KV, "Ramblings of One Who Is Weak in the Exchequer, and in the Mind," Well All Right, *Cornell Daily Sun*, October 8, 1941.

39. Robert Scholes, "Chasing a Lone Eagle: Vonnegut's College Writing," in *The Vonnegut Statement*, ed. Jerome Klinkowitz and John Somer (New York: Seymour Lawrence, 1973), 47.

40. KV, "We Chase a Lone Eagle and End up on the Wrong Side of the Fence," Well All Right, *Cornell Daily Sun*, October 13, 1941.

41. Ibid.

42. *A Century at Cornell: Published to Commemorate the Hundredth Anniversary of the Cornell Daily Sun*, ed. Daniel Margulis (Ithaca, NY: Cornell Daily Sun, 1980).

43. George Lowery, "Kurt Vonnegut Jr., Novelist, Counterculture Icon and Cornellian, Dies at 84," Chronicle Online, posted on April 12, 2007.

44. "Fifth Column," Beer and Skittles, *Cornell Daily Sun*, May 25, 1942.

45. KV, "The Lost Battalion Undergoes a Severe Shelling," Well All Right, *Cornell Daily Sun*, May 4, 1942.

46. KV, "We Impress *Life* Magazine with Our Efficient Role in National Defense," Well All Right, *Cornell Daily Sun*, May 23, 1941.

47. Ibid.

48. KV, "The Lost Battalion Undergoes a Severe Shelling."

49. "Fifth Column," *Cornell Daily Sun*.

50. Emily Louise Diamond, interview, February 7, 2008. This was "bad Uncle Dan," whom Vonnegut often referred to. "When I got home from World War II, my Uncle Dan clapped me on the back, and he said, 'You're a man now.' So I killed him. Not really, but I certainly felt like doing it." Kurt Vonnegut, Syracuse University commencement speech, May 8, 1994.

51. Lieutenant Walter A. Vonnegut, B-17 navigator with the 381st Bombardment Group, was forced to bail out over Holland and was a prisoner of war for eighteen months. Colonel Franklin F. Vonnegut flew during World War II, Korea, and Vietnam.

52. KV, "How're You Going to Keep 'Em Down on the Farm, After They've Seen Lockheed?" Well All Right, *Cornell Daily Sun*, October 22, 1942.

53. Bernard Vonnegut to Robert H. Avery, February 20, 1985, M. E. Grenander Department of Special Collections and Archives, State University of New York at Albany.

54. KV, "In Which Mr. Willkie and We Raise Stinks on Opposite Sides of the Fence," Well All Right, *Cornell Daily Sun*, September 29, 1942.

55. Kendall Landis, interview, June 12, 2008.

56. Landis asserted that there was an affair, and remarks on Jane's health questionnaire for the Office of Strategic Services indicate she was sexually active. Office of Strategic Services, see "Jane M. Cox, 1944–45," open file (declassified), Modern Military Records, National Archives and Records Administration, College Park, MD.

57. Miller Harris, interview, January 1, 2007. Harris became a managing editor of the *Cornell Daily Sun*.

58. KV, interview, March 13, 2007.

59. Ibid.

60. Rauch, "Ancestry of Kurt Vonnegut," 73.

61. KV, *Palm Sunday*, 65.

3: To War in the Bridal Suite

1. KV, interview by Christopher Bigsby, *Kaleidoscope,* BBC, September 20, 1984.

2. KV, interview, March 13, 2007.

3. Ibid.

4. KV to Robert Maslansky, September 7, 1983, private collection.

5. KV, interview, March 14, 2007. "Whenever we were told to fire it, we had to build it first. We practically had to invent it. . . . If you study the 240-millimeter howitzer, you don't even have time left over for a venereal-disease film." David Hayman, David Michaelis, George Plimpton, and Richard Rhodes, "Kurt Vonnegut: The Art of Fiction LXIV," *Paris Review,* Spring 1977.

6. Thomas F. Marvin, *Kurt Vonnegut: A Critical Companion* (Westport, CT: Greenwood, 2002), 5.

7. An indication of how the war shaped an entire generation and influenced American culture for decades is that among the soldiers who participated in the ASTP were Robert J. Dole, Edward I. Koch, Heywood Hale Broun, Henry A. Kissinger, Gore Vidal, and Andy Rooney. See Louis E. Keefer, *Scholars in Foxholes* (Reston, VA: Cotu, 1998).

8. KV, *Palm Sunday*, 65.

9. Guy Reel, "Kurt Vonnegut's Letters Recount His Days at UT," University of Tennessee *Daily Beacon,* November 29, 1978.

10. KV to Robert Maslansky, September 7, 1983, private collection. Richard Gehman later became a chronicler of Hollywood celebrities and married the actress Estelle Parsons. Vonnegut had a knack for meeting interesting people.

11. KV, interview, March 14, 2007.

12. Kendall Landis, interview, June 12, 2008.

13. Many years later, Boyle's son, wounded in Vietnam and recuperating in Walter Reed Hospital, was surprised to receive from his father a copy of *Slaughterhouse-Five* autographed by Vonnegut. "To Bruce Boyle who was the wise commander of me and Bernard V. O'Hare in World War II. Peace." When the younger Boyle was preparing to leave the *Philadelphia Bulletin* because the newspaper had folded, Vonnegut called and asked whether there was anything he could do to help. Bruce Boyle, "Remembering Kurt Vonnegut," Books, Inq. Blog, posted April 12, 2007.

14. Dale Watson, interview, February 9, 2008. Watson was in Vonnegut's regiment and later a POW with him in Dresden.

15. Donna Lewis, interview, July 27, 2008.

16. KV to Jerry Klinkowitz, December 11, 1976, private collection.

17. "Questionnaire for Architects' Roster and/or Register of Architects Qualified for Federal Public Works," June 13, 1946, American Institute of Architects, Washington, DC.

18. Rauch, "Ancestry of Kurt Vonnegut," 73.

19. KV to Jerry Klinkowitz, December 11, 1976, private collection.

20. Ibid.

21. Ibid.

22. Robert Hipkiss, *The American Absurd: Pynchon, Vonnegut, and Barth* (Fort Washington, NY: Associated Faculty Press, 1984), 58.

23. KV to Jerry Klinkowitz, December 11, 1976, private collection.

24. KV, *Jailbird* (New York: Delacorte, 1979), xiii.

25. Ibid.

26. Donald M. Fiene, "Getting Through Life: The Autobiography of Donald M. Fiene" (unpublished manuscript), University of Louisville Special Collections.

27. James Alexander Thom, "The Man Without a Country," *Spokesman*, Bertrand Russell Foundation, October 2007.

28. KV, *God Bless You, Mr. Rosewater; or, Pearls Before Swine* (1965; repr., New York: Delta, 1998), 196.

29. KV, *Breakfast of Champions* (1973; repr., New York: Delta, 1999), 186.

30. KV, interview, December 13, 2006.

31. NV, interview, September 20, 2007.

32. Dale Watson, interview, February 9, 2008.

33. "The 106th: The Story of the 106th Infantry Division," Stories of the Ground, Air, and Service Forces in the European Theater, *Stars & Stripes* in Paris, 1944–45.

34. KV, interview, March 14, 2007.

35. John P. Kline, "The Service Diary of German War Prisoner #315136," Camp Atterbury Blog, n.d.

36. Robert Kelton, interview, February 15, 2008.

37. KV, interview, March 14, 2007.

38. Hayman et al., "Kurt Vonnegut," 166.

39. Bernard V. O'Hare III, "Battle of the Bulge: Language Error May Have Saved Lives," Lehigh Valley Ramblings.com, December 14, 2007.

40. Robert Kelton, interview, February 15, 2008.

41. KV, "Dear people" letter, mid-May 1945, Vonnegut mss., LL.

42. Ibid.

43. Gifford Doxsee, "World War II Letter," January 10, 1981, Mahn Center for Archives and Special Collections, Athens, OH.

44. Ibid.

45. Clifford Stumpf, "A Day in May: A Story of a Prisoner of War" (unpublished memoir), as quoted in Heidi M. Szpek, "Religious Expression Among the Men of Slaughterhouse Five," *International Journal of the Humanities* 2, no. 2 (2006): 1437. Professor Szpek's father was in Dresden with Vonnegut.

46. James Mills, interview, March 15, 2007.

47. Geoff Taylor, *Piece of Cake* (London: Peter Davies, 1956), 179–80.

48. Doxsee, "World War II Letter."

49. Alice Vonnegut to Mrs. Kelton, April 14, 1945, private collection.

50. Tom Jones in *Shadows of Slaughterhouse Five: Recollections and Reflections of the American Ex-POWs of Schlachthof Fünf*, ed. Heidi M. Szpek (Bloomington, IN: iUniverse, 2008), 176.

51. Alex Vonnegut to Helen Vonnegut, January 11, 1945, private collection.

52. Dale Watson, interview, February 9, 2008.

53. "Over the previous few months there had been a scattering of daylight raids by American formations on the suburban industrial areas and on the marshaling yards just outside the city center. . . . But most citizens put these incidents down to mischance or poor navigation, and still consider[ed] the city inviolable." Frederick Taylor, *Dresden: Tuesday, February 13, 1945* (New York: Harper Perennial, 2005), 5.

54. Ibid., 199. The commissioner took the precaution, however, of commandeering

engineers to design and build underground, reinforced concrete bunkers beneath his office and in his backyard at home.

55. Hitler created organizations for boys and girls fourteen and older, the Hitler Youth and the Society of German Maidens. They were indoctrinated with Nazi beliefs; participation was mandatory.

56. Hayman et al., "Kurt Vonnegut," 169.

57. *Shadows of Slaughterhouse Five.* Raymond T. Makowske recalled "someone [possibly Vonnegut] keeping a log with the intent of writing a book." *SS* is short for *Schutzstaffel,* German for "Protective Squadron." It was an elite force committed to Nazi ideology that coordinated the arrest of Reich enemies and the Holocaust.

58. James M. Slagle, "Lexington Man Meets Author Who Shared Prison Camp," in *American Ex-Prisoners of War: Non Solum Armis,* ed. Gardner N. Hatch, W. Curtis Musten, and John S. Edwards (Nashville: Turner, 1995), 63–64.

59. *Shadows of Slaughterhouse Five,* 225–38.

60. Doxsee, "World War II Letter."

61. Robert Kelton, interview, February 15, 2008.

62. Ervin Szpek, "My Service Memoirs: A POW in Dresden," in *American Ex-Prisoners of War,* 64–65. Also, Lou Curto to KV, March 28, 1983, Vonnegut mss., LL.

63. James Mills, interview, March 15, 2007.

64. "Slaughterhouse Guards and Men of Confidence," in *Shadows of Slaughterhouse Five,* 225–38.

65. James Mills, interview, March 15, 2007.

66. Ibid. The POWs' failure to respect their betters could be infuriating. A German officer passed a work crew one morning and hailed them with *"Guten Tag!"* They waved back. "Fuck you!" they said cheerily. The following morning the officer greeted them again with *"Guten Tag!"* and received the same hearty "Fuck you!" in reply. The third morning he glared at them as he passed. *"Schweine!"*

67. Doxsee, "World War II Letter."

68. Frank Voytek in *Shadows of Slaughterhouse Five,* 220.

69. Alex Vonnegut to Ella Vonnegut Stewart, July 4, 1945, private collection.

70. KV, interview, March 13, 2007.

71. Thomas C. Ballowe in *Shadows of Slaughterhouse Five,* 225.

72. Lou Curto to KV, March 28, 1983, Vonnegut mss., LL.

73. Catherine Williams, "Dresden Bombing," *The Pulteney St. Survey,* Hobart and William Smith Colleges, Spring 2001.

74. KV, *Fates Worse Than Death,* 106.

75. "Dresden Bombing," *The Pulteney St. Survey.*

76. Doxsee, "World War II Letter."

77. Raymond T. Makowske, "During the Battle of the Bulge and POW (*Kriegsgefangen*) in Dresden (Slaughterhouse 5)," Indianamilitary.org; also, KV to William Amos, May 12, 1985, Vonnegut mss., LL.

78. KV to William Amos, May 12, 1985, Vonnegut mss., LL.

79. Floyd Harding in *Shadows of Slaughterhouse Five,* 232.

80. Duane Fox in ibid., 230.

81. Harding in ibid., 232.

82. Alex Vonnegut to Ella Vonnegut Stewart, July 4, 1945, private collection.

83. Doxsee, "World War II Letter."

84. Ibid.

85. Tom Jones in *Shadows of Slaughterhouse Five,* 234.

86. Taylor, *Dresden*, 3. Shrove Tuesday is equivalent to Mardi Gras in the United States.

87. Ibid., 5.

88. "Smashing Blows at Dresden," *New York Times*, February 15, 1945.

89. Andrei Cherny, *The Candy Bombers: The Untold Story of the Berlin Airlift and America's Finest Hour* (New York: Putnam, 1998), 96.

90. Alexander McKee, *Dresden, 1945: The Devil's Tinderbox* (1982; repr., New York: Barnes and Noble, 2000), 130.

91. KV, *Armageddon in Retrospect* (New York: Putnam, 2008), 37.

92. McKee, *The Devil's Tinderbox*, 137.

93. Robert Kelton, interview, February 15, 2008.

94. James Mills, interview, March 15, 2007.

95. My thoughts on the importance of these hours in Vonnegut's life were influenced by the following: R. Gordon, "Death and Creativity: A Jungian Approach," *Journal of Analytical Psychology* 22, no. 2 (1977): 106–24; Leon F. Seltzer, "Dresden and Vonnegut's Creative Testament of Guilt," *Journal of American Culture* 4, no. 4 (Winter 1981): 55–69; and Christina Grof and Stanislav Grof, MD, *The Stormy Search for the Self* (Los Angeles: Jeremy P. Tarcher, 1990).

96. Dale Watson, interview, February 9, 2008.

97. Szpek, "My Service Memoirs," 65.

98. In this wave was Rodney S. Gould, Vonnegut's fraternity brother from Cornell, flight navigator with crew 7973 of the 305th "Can Do" bomb group.

99. James Mills, interview, March 15, 2007.

100. Szpek, "My Service Memoirs," 65.

101. Ibid.

102. Doxsee, "World War II Letter."

103. James Mills, interview, March 15, 2007.

104. Hayman et al., "Kurt Vonnegut," 70.

105. Ibid.

106. Makowske, "During the Battle of the Bulge."

107. KV, *Armageddon in Retrospect*, 40.

108. In *Slaughterhouse-Five*, Vonnegut writes, "[A] rabid little American I call Paul Lazzaro in this book had about a quart of diamonds and emeralds and rubies and so on. He had taken these from dead people in the cellars of Dresden." The model for Lazzaro might have been a POW named Lou Curto. "He was dangerous and opportunistic, having no problem to prey on weaker POWs. The jewelry was known to few. Curto got the jewelry, so the story goes, by cutting off the fingers of bodies." Ervin Szpek Jr., e-mail, August 30, 2007. One of the former POWs, Raymond Makowske, saw Curto in Atlantic City after the war "and could only nod a greeting." Years after the publication of *Slaughterhouse-Five*, Curto wrote Vonnegut a wheedling letter, the motive for which sounded suspiciously litigious: "Could you send me a photo of yourself, I'm trying to remember it's been so long. I hope you don't feel like I'm imposing. . . . You must know me because you mentioned the jewelry and only few close prisoners would know that." Lou Curto to KV, March 28, 1983, Vonnegut mss., LL.

109. Doxsee, "World War II Letter."

110. James Mills, interview, March 15, 2007.

111. Alex Vonnegut relating the story in a letter to Ella Vonnegut Stewart, July 4, 1945, private collection.

112. The witnesses had been selected because they knew Palaia well. Doxsee, "World War

II Letter." Vonnegut chose the title *Palm Sunday* for his 1981 collection of short stories, speeches, essays, letters, and other previously unpublished pieces.

113. U.S. War Department, Judge Advocate General's Office, War Crimes Office, File No. 2080, interview with PFC Harry E. J. Kingston, September 23, 1946, in Heidi M. Szpek, "Religious Expression Among the Men of Slaughterhouse Five." Gifford Doxsee said Palaia's mother was home on the day of the executions when the front door blew open, and her son's framed picture fell from a side table, shattering on the floor. "Michael's dead!" she screamed. Doxsee, interview, February 6, 2008.

114. Alex Vonnegut to Ella Vonnegut, July 4, 1945, private collection.

115. Makowske, "During the Battle of the Bulge."

116. James Mills, interview, March 15, 2007.

117. Lee Roloff, "Kurt Vonnegut on Stage at the Steppenwolf Theatre, Chicago," *TriQuarterly*, Fall 1998, 17.

118. James Mills, interview, March 15, 2007.

119. Roloff, "Kurt Vonnegut."

120. "Dresden Bombing," *The Pulteney St. Survey*.

121. KV to George Strong, April 23, 1989, private collection.

122. Bernard V. O'Hare's diary, May 21, 1945, private O'Hare family collection.

123. Ibid.

124. Terkel, *Will the Circle Be Unbroken?*, 223.

125. KV, *Timequake*, 82.

4: Folk Society and the House of Magic

1. Bob Thompson, "So He Goes, Not Quietly," *Washington Post*, April 13, 2007.

2. EV, interview, September 20, 2007.

3. Jane Cox to Isabella Horton Grant, July 1, 1945, private collection.

4. Marcia Gauger, interview, September 6, 2008. Gauger was Jane's roommate in Washington during the war.

5. Jane Cox to Isabella Horton Grant, July 1, 1945, private collection.

6. Ibid.

7. Kendall Landis, interview, June 12, 2008.

8. Marcia Gauger, interview, September 6, 2008. "Lochinvar" is a poem by Sir Walter Scott. Young Lochinvar is a knight who rides tirelessly to prevent his love from marrying the wrong man. "But ere he alighted at Netherby gate / The bride had consented, the gallant came late: / For a laggard in love, and a dastard in war, / Was to wed the fair Ellen of brave Lochinvar." He wins her anyway, and they gallop off on his steed. Did Jane detect the allusion?

9. Marcia Gauger, interview, September 6, 2008.

10. Alex Vonnegut to Ella Vonnegut Stewart, July 4, 1945, private collection.

11. Rick Callahan, "Vonnegut Memorial Library to Open in Indianapolis," Associated Press, August 18, 2010.

12. Alex Vonnegut to Ella Vonnegut Stewart, July 4, 1945.

13. KV, *Wampeters, Foma & Granfallons*, 160.

14. Norma Jean Seiler Baldwin to Isabella Horton Grant, July 30, 1945.

15. "Jane M. Cox, 1944–45," open file (declassified), Office of Strategic Services.

16. Ben Hitz, interview, November 11, 2007.

17. Vonnegut maintained throughout his life that his father was permanently ruined by the Depression and never recovered his spirit or standing as an architect. In fact, in 1946, Kurt Sr. became a principal in the firm of Vonnegut, Wright and Yeager

with two offices: one in Indianapolis and another in Terre Haute. That year, the firm completed a questionnaire and estimated its annual income at 4 million dollars based on projects completed or on the board, which would be 43 million dollars in today's dollars. "Questionnaire for Architects' Roster and/or Register of Architects Qualified for Federal Public Works," June 13, 1946, American Institute of Architects, Washington, DC.

18. KV, "The Lake," 35.
19. KV, interview, March 14, 2007.
20. JV to Scammon Lockwood, November 7, 1945, private collection.
21. Donald M. Fiene, "Elements of Dostoevsky in the Novels of Kurt Vonnegut," *Dostoevsky Studies* 2 (1981): 132.
22. KV, *Kaleidoscope*, BBC Radio 4, September 20, 1984.
23. Thompson, "So He Goes, Not Quietly."
24. JV to Scammon Lockwood, November 7, 1945, private collection.
25. Scammon Lockwood to JV, November 10, 1945, private collection.
26. Ibid.
27. JV to Scammon Lockwood, November 7, 1945, private collection.
28. Hayman et al., "Kurt Vonnegut," 182.
29. KV, "To Be a Native Middle-Westerner."
30. KV, *Wampeters, Foma & Granfalloons*, 174.
31. KV, *Palm Sunday*, 90 and 222. Schools of anthropology differ in their outlook and methods.
32. KV, "A Very Fringe Character," in *An Unsentimental Education*, ed. Molly McQuade (Chicago: University of Chicago Press, 1995), 236.
33. Marvin, *Kurt Vonnegut: A Critical Companion*, 7.
34. KV, "A Very Fringe Character," 237.
35. KV mss., LL.
36. KV to KB, n.d. 1959, private collection. His work shirt idea was twenty years too early.
37. Walter A. Vonnegut, interview, April 7, 2007.
38. KV, "A Very Fringe Character," 237–38.
39. Ibid.
40. *Essential Vonnegut: Interviews Conducted by Walter Miller.*
41. Milton Singer and James Redfield, "Robert Redfield," in *American National Biography Online,* February 2000.
42. Robert Redfield, *The Little Community and Peasant Society and Culture* (Chicago: University of Chicago Press, 1956).
43. Redfield, "The Folk Society," *American Journal of Society* 52, no. 4 (January 1947): 297.
44. KV, "The Lake," 27.
45. KV to Charles Angoff, August 21, 1947, Vonnegut mss., LL. "Brighten Up!" was later included in *Armageddon in Retrospect* (New York: Putnam, 2008).
46. KV, interview, March 14.
47. *Kurt Vonnegut: American Made*, Weide.
48. James Sydney Slotkin, *Social Anthropology: The Science of Human Society and Culture* (New York: Macmillan, 1950).
49. George Stocking, e-mail, July 9, 2007. James Slotkin taught at the university from 1946 until his death by suicide in the 1960s.
50. KV to Miller Harris, February 11, 1951, private collection. One of Professor Slotkin's primary interests was Native American peyote cults.

51. Ibid.
52. Ibid.
53. KV, *Bagombo Snuff Box: Uncollected Short Fiction* (1999; repr., New York: Berkley, 2000), 7. The 1946 thesis proposal was not, as has been often stated, "On the Fluctuations between Good and Evil in Simple Tales."
54. KV to Miller Harris, February 11, 1951, private collection.
55. KV, "A Very Fringe Character," 237.
56. Summer 1947, Vonnegut mss., LL.
57. Fred Eggan to KV, July 25, 1947, Vonnegut mss., LL.
58. Sol Tax to KV, July 24, 1947, Vonnegut mss., LL.
59. Summer 1947, Vonnegut mss., LL.
60. Jerry Klinkowitz, letter to author, October 29, 2007.
61. Walter A. Vonnegut, interview, April 7, 2007.
62. Victor Jose, interview, January 5, 2007.
63. Ibid.
64. "—30—A City News Bureau Farewell" (Chicago, February 26, 1999), booklet, private collection.
65. Victor Jose, interview, January 5, 2007.
66. KV, "A Very Fringe Character," 239.
67. KV and JV to Walter A. and Helen Vonnegut, September 1, 1947, private collection.
68. "Schenectady Works Welcomes You!" Schenectady Public Library (General Electric booklet, 1949).
69. B. S. Havens et al., *Early History of Cloud Seeding* (New Mexico Institute of Mining and Technology, State University of New York at Albany, and General Electric, 1979).
70. Ibid.
71. Joan Cook, "Lemuel Ricketts Boulware, 95; Headed Labor Relations for G.E.," *New York Times*, November 8, 1990.
72. Kurt and JV to Walter A. and Helen Vonnegut, September 1, 1945, private collection.
73. KV, letter, October 19, 2006.
74. KV, "A Very Fringe Character," 240.
75. Nelson Lichtenstein, *American Capitalism: Social Thought and Political Economy in the Twentieth Century* (Philadelphia: University of Pennsylvania Press, 2006), 15.
76. JV to Walter A. and Helen Vonnegut, November 6, 1947, private collection.
77. Gloria and Jack Ericson, interview, September 8, 2007. The Ericsons purchased the house from the Vonneguts.
78. JV to Gloria and Jack Ericson, August 3, 1951, private collection.
79. Ibid.
80. Ibid.
81. *Kurt Vonnegut: American Made*, Weide.
82. Ibid.
83. John Dinsmore, "Kurt & Ollie," *Firsts*, October 1992, 15.
84. Ibid.
85. *Kurt Vonnegut: American Made*, Weide.
86. JV to Walter A. and Helen Vonnegut, November 6, 1947, private collection.
87. Dinsmore, "Kurt & Ollie," 15.
88. Ollie M. Lyon Jr. in "Happy Birthday, Kurt Vonnegut," 32.
89. Bob Pace in ibid., 34–35.
90. Charles Proteus Steinmetz joined General Electric in 1894, two years after the company was founded, and ranked in the popular imagination with Tesla, Marconi,

and Edison, developing two hundred patents during his thirty years at the Schenectady Works.

91. KV to Alex Vonnegut, November 28, 1947, Vonnegut mss., LL.

92. KV to Jerome Klinkowitz, April 13, 2007, private collection.

93. Jonathan R. Eller, "Kurt Vonnegut: A Publisher's Dream," in *Mustard Gas and Roses: The Life & Works of KV* (LL, 2007), 7.

94. KV to KB, February 23, 1955, private collection.

95. Dinsmore, "Kurt & Ollie," 15.

96. Handwritten note, n.d., Vonnegut mss., LL.

97. KV to KB, June 24, 1949, CC, referring to a previous rejection from Burger.

98. KV to KB, July 21, 1952, private collection.

99. David Standish, "Kurt Vonnegut: The *Playboy* Interview," *Playboy*, July 20, 1973.

100. Ibid.

101. Ibid.

5: Stop Being Such a Hardheaded Realist

1. Frank Houston, "The Salon Interview: Kurt Vonnegut," Salon.com, October 8, 1999.

2. KV, *Bagombo Snuff Box,* 39.

3. KB, interview, August 6, 2007.

4. Donald L. Miller, *D-Days in the Pacific* (New York: Simon and Schuster, 2005), 229.

5. Richard Gehman, "Nobody Quite Like Him," *Chicago Tribune*, April 2, 1967.

6. Robert Byrne in "Knox Burger, 1922–2010: 'Honest Prose and Nerves of Steel'" (memorial booklet, New York, February 2010).

7. KB, interview, August 6, 2007.

8. KV to KB, June 24, 1949, CC.

9. KB to KV, June 27, 1949, CC.

10. KV to Miller Harris, February 6, 1951, private collection.

11. KB to Joseph Carroll, n.d., CC.

12. KB, interview, August 6, 2007.

13. KV to Miller Harris, February 6, 1951, private collection.

14. KV to KB, July 2, 1949, CC.

15. KB to KV, July 8, 1949, CC.

16. KB to KV, July 13, 1949, CC.

17. KB to KV, July 26, 1949, CC.

18. KB to KV, July 19, 1949, CC.

19. William Price Fox, interview, July 12, 2008.

20. George Greenfield, *A Smattering of Monsters: A Kind of Memoir* (Rochester, NY: Camden House, 1995), 179–80.

21. Kurt Vonnegut, "He Comes to Us One by One and Asks Us What the Rules Are," *Chicago Tribune*, July 15, 1973.

22. KB to KV, September 27, 1949, CC.

23. KB to Kenneth Littauer, October 13, 1949, CC.

24. KV, *Fates Worse Than Death*, 26.

25. Ibid. A small article appeared in the *Schenectady Gazette* headlined "GE Writer Has Story Accepted."

26. Gloria and Jack Ericson, interview, September 8, 2007.

27. Dinsmore, "Kurt & Ollie," 14–17.

28. Ibid.

29. Gloria and Jack Ericson, interview, September 8, 2007.

30. Ibid.

31. Ibid.

32. Jack Ericson, interview, September 8, 2007.

33. KV to Miller Harris, October 25, 1950, private collection.

34. KV, review of *The Boss* by Goffredo Parise, *New York Times*, October 2, 1966.

35. "Class Notes," *Cornell Alumni Magazine*, January–February 2006.

36. Dinsmore, "Kurt & Ollie," 15.

37. Gloria and Jack Ericson, interview, September 8, 2007.

38. Vance Bourjaily, interview, March 17, 2008. Vonnegut later talked to his friend and fellow novelist Bourjaily about his "lonely days" at General Electric.

39. KV to Miller Harris, February 16, 1950, private collection.

40. JV to Fred S. Rosenau, April 13, 1950, private collection.

41. KV to Miller Harris, February 28, 1950, private collection.

42. KV to Miller Harris, May 19, 1950, private collection.

43. JV to Fred S. Rosenau, "March something," 1950, private collection.

44. KV to NV, July 7, 1978, private collection.

45. KV Sr. to KV Jr., November 9, 1950, private collection.

46. KV to Frank Ernest Hill, Columbia University, October 6, 1950, Archives and Collections, Schenectady Museum and Suits-Bueche Planetarium, Schenectady, NY.

47. C. G. Suits and J. M. Lafferty, *Albert Wallace Hull: A Biographical Memoir* (Washington, DC: National Academy of Sciences, 1970), 216–18.

48. KV to Neil B. Reynolds, Advertising and Publicity Department, General Electric, October 23, 1950, Archives and Collections, Schenectady Museum and Suits-Bueche Planetarium, Schenectady, NY.

49. Suits and Lafferty, *Albert Wallace Hull*, 218.

50. *Kurt Vonnegut: American Made*, Weide.

51. Neil B. Reynolds to Frank Ernest Hill, Columbia University, January 26, 1951, Archives and Collections, Schenectady Museum and Suits-Bueche Planetarium, Schenectady, NY.

52. D. Anne Estes to Donald C. Farber, August 23, 1977, Vonnegut mss., LL. Estes, president of Estes Lund & Co., related the anecdote while requesting an autographed copy of *Player Piano* for her client Al Berry.

53. KB, interview, August 6, 2007.

54. Vic Jose, interview, January 5, 2007.

55. James Cheney, e-mail, September 30, 2007.

56. Gloria and Jack Ericson, interview, September 8, 2007.

57. James Cheney, e-mail, September 30, 2007.

58. Ibid.

59. KV to Miller Harris, February 6, 1951, private collection.

60. KV to Miller Harris, October 25, 1950, private collection.

61. JV to Gloria and Jack Ericson, August 3, 1951, private collection.

62. KV, *Bagombo Snuff Box*, 9.

63. EV, interview, September 20, 2007.

64. KV, interview, December 13, 2006.

65. Gloria Ericson, interview, September 8, 2007.

66. Jack Ericson, interview, September 8, 2007.

6: The Dead Engineer

1. JV to Walter A. and Helen Vonnegut, January 10, 1952, private collection.

2. Ibid.

3. EV, interview, September 20, 2007.

4. JV to Walter A. and Helen Vonnegut, January 10, 1952, private collection.

5. Ibid.

6. Harry Brague to Kenneth Littauer, July 6, 1951, CSS. Maxwell Perkins hired Brague in 1946. He became Hemingway's editor in the late 1950s. A colorful description of New York publishing as an old boys' club appears in an essay by Charles Scribner Jr., "I, Who Knew Nothing, Was in Charge," *New York Times*, December 9, 1990.

7. Kenneth Littauer to Harry Brague, September 5, 1951, CSS.

8. JV to Walter A. and Helen Vonnegut, January 10, 1952, private collection.

9. KV to Harry Brague, November 30, 1951, CSS.

10. Kenneth Littauer to Harry Brague, July 26, 1951, CSS. "I told him that he'd better hurry."

11. KV to Harry Brague, November 30, 1951, CSS.

12. KV to Harry Brague, December 24, 1951, CSS.

13. KV, *Player Piano* (1952; repr., New York: Delta, 1999), 320.

14. Ray Bradbury, by comparison, placed stories about rockets and Martians in major magazines, but they were generally romances, flights of fancy, not science fiction. Vonnegut later wrote to Bradbury asking for advice and received a friendly reply. KV to KB, fall 1959, private collection.

15. Arthur Schlesinger Jr., *The Vital Center: The Politics of Freedom* (Boston: Houghton Mifflin, 1949). The phrase "age of anxiety" is Schlesinger's.

16. KV to KB, April 12, 1952, private collection.

17. KV to KB, May 29, 1952, private collection.

18. KV to KB, n.d., private collection.

19. Joe David Bellamy, "Kurt Vonnegut for President: The Making of a Literary Reputation," in *Literary Luxuries: American Writing at the End of the Millennium* (Columbia: University of Missouri Press, 1995), 143.

20. KV, *Timequake*, 162.

21. KV to KB, July 21, 1952, private collection.

22. KV to KB, n.d., private collection.

23. KB, interview, August 6, 2007.

24. KV to Harry Brague, April 16, 1952, CSS.

25. Flo Conway and Jim Siegelman, *Dark Hero of the Information Age: In Search of Norbert Wiener, the Father of Cybernetics* (New York: Basic Books, 2005), 288. Siegelman was later a creative writing student of Vonnegut's at Harvard.

26. Ibid.

27. KV to Harry Brague, July 31, 1952, CSS.

28. Alex Vonnegut to relatives, August 30, 1952, private collection.

29. Greg Rickman, *To the High Castle: Philip K. Dick, A Life* (Long Beach, CA: Fragments West/Valentine Press, 1989).

30. KV, *Player Piano*, 72.

31. An insightful discussion of women depending on men in *Player Piano* appears in Margaret J. Daniels and Heather E. Bowen, "Feminist Implications of Anti-Leisure in Dystopian Fiction." *Journal of Leisure Research* 35, no. 4 (Fall 2003): 423. Worth pointing out too is that sexual relations, at least between Paul and Anita, are imbalanced and dissatisfactory. But here Vonnegut seems to be saying unapologetically as a man, not an author, that having raunchy sex isn't something ladies do. Proteus catches Anita in flagrante with a more powerful man but intellectualizes the situation. "Don't you think an explanation is in order?" he asks. Hours later, he stumbles into the arms of a prostitute and spends the night with her, though "once during the

remainder of the night with her, [he] awoke from a dream in which he saw his father glowering at him from the foot of the bed." Apparently, nice people shouldn't concern themselves with sex at all. Vonnegut's bourgeois attitudes about sex will be a pattern in his personal and creative life until they are reconciled around the time of writing *Slaughterhouse-Five.*

32. KV, *Player Piano*, 146.
33. Hume, "Vonnegut's Melancholy," 221.
34. Frederick R. Karl, *American Fictions: 1940/1980* (New York: Harper, 1983), 246.
35. Leonard Feinberg, *The Secret of Humor* (New York: Rodopi, 1978), 153.
36. Sukhbir Singh, *The Survivor in Contemporary American Fiction: Saul Bellow, Bernard Malamud, John Updike, Kurt Vonnegut, Jr.* (Delhi: B. R. Publishing, 1991), 172.
37. Karl, *American Fictions*, 344.
38. KV, interview, March 13, 2007.
39. KV to KB, May 29, 1952, private collection.
40. Harry Brague to KV, August 21, 1952, CSS.
41. Joe David Bellamy and John Casey, "Kurt Vonnegut Jr.," in *Conversations with Kurt Vonnegut*, ed. William Rodney Allen (Jackson: University of Mississippi Press, 1988), 157.
42. KV to Miller Harris, February 28, 1950, private collection.
43. Norman Snow to Harry Brague, September 4, 1952, CSS.
44. KV to Harry Brague, March 8, 1953, CSS.
45. KV to KB, February 9, 1953, private collection.
46. KV to KB, February 20, 1953, private collection.
47. Ibid.
48. KV to KB, February 20, 1953, private collection.
49. Ibid.
50. Ibid.
51. KV to KB, March 13, 1953, private collection.
52. KV to KB, May 11, 1954, private collection.
53. Ibid.
54. Kathi Scrizzi Driscoll, "Kurt Vonnegut Receives Tribute from Comedy Club," *Cape Cod Times*, August 20, 2007.
55. The Vonneguts' participation in the Barnstable Comedy Club can be traced over the years in the *Barnstable Patriot*, 1953–64.
56. KV to Harry Brague, February 7, 1954, CSS.
57. Ibid.
58. KV to KB, May 11, 1954, private collection.
59. KV, *Timequake*, 15.
60. KV to KB, May 11, 1954, private collection.
61. KV to KB, May 27, 1954, private collection. Burger agreed to revise the play *Emory Beck* as a favor, but it was useless.
62. Rhonda Ruthman, e-mail, March 14, 2009.
63. Ibid.
64. KV to Harry Brague, March 11, 1954, CSS.
65. KV to Harry Brague, February 7, 1954, CSS.
66. Harry Brague to KV, August 12, 1953, CSS.
67. KV to Harry Brague, May 7, 1954, CSS.
68. KV to KB, May 27, 1954, private collection. A common denominator in Kurt's dislike of other men is that they had been former officers. Brague had enlisted as a

private, same as Vonnegut, but rose to captain. He participated in the Normandy invasion and was awarded the Combat Infantry Badge, the Purple Heart, the Bronze Star, and the Certificate of Merit. "L. Harry Brague Jr. is Dead; Editor at Scribner's was 55," *New York Times*, March 23, 1968. Said Vonnegut in an interview with *Playboy*, "I hate officers. . . . They're all shits. Every officer I ever knew was a shit." David Standish, "*Playboy* Interview," in *Conversations with Kurt Vonnegut*, 96.

69. KV to KB, May 7, 1954, private collection.
70. Kenneth Littauer to Harry Brague, May 5, 1954, CSS.
71. KV to Fred S. Rosenau, March 31, 1954, private collection.
72. KV to KB, February 1, 1960, private collection.
73. KV to KB, October 25, 1955, private collection.
74. Carolyn Blakemore, interview, June 16, 2008.
75. Michael MacCambridge, *The Franchise: A History of Sports Illustrated Magazine* (New York: Hyperion Books, 1998).
76. KV to KB, October 26, 1954, private collection.
77. Harry Brague to Kenneth Littauer, February 24, 1954, CSS.
78. KV to Fred S. Rosenau, March 10, 1953, private collection.
79. KV to Fred S. Rosenau, March 31, 1954, private collection.
80. NV, interview, September 20, 2007.
81. EV, interview, September 20, 2007.
82. Allison Mitchell, interview, February 7, 2008. Mitchell is Nanny Vonnegut's best friend in the first chapter of *Slaughterhouse-Five*, as she indeed was when they were children.
83. KV to KB, October 26, 1954, private collection.
84. KV to KB, October 24, 1954, private collection.
85. KV to KB, February 1, 1955, private collection.
86. KV to KB, March 1, 1955, private collection.
87. JV, journal, n.d., private collection. Jane emptied her mind of thoughts and recorded memorable moments on random pieces of paper that her daughters later kept.
88. Rauch, "Ancestry of Kurt Vonnegut," 75.
89. Ibid., 74.
90. KV to Ben Hitz, April 18, 1984, private collection.
91. EV, interview, September 9, 2007.
92. KV, interview, March 13, 2007.
93. Leslie A. Fiedler, *Love and Death in the American Novel* (New York: Meridian Books, 1962), 94.
94. KV to Harry Brague, November 30, 1954, CSS.
95. KV Sr. to KV Jr. and JV, January 8, 1955, private collection.
96. Vonnegut couldn't have anticipated it, but novels by other important yet little-known authors at the time were brushing against his in bus terminals: William S. Burroughs, Robert Bloch, Ray Bradbury, Harlan Ellison, and P. G. Wodehouse, for example.
97. KV to KB, February 23, 1955, private collection.
98. KV to KB, February 1, 1955, private collection.
99. Ibid.
100. KV to KB, March 1, 1955, and April 16, 1955, private collection.
101. NV, interview, September 20, 2007.
102. KV to KB, April 16, 1955, private collection.
103. Ibid.
104. Ibid.

105. JV Yarmolinsky, *Angels Without Wings*, 7.
106. EV, interview, September 20, 2007.
107. Ibid.
108. Ollie M. Lyon Jr., 1955, private collection.
109. KV to Fred S. Rosenau, Spring 1955, private collection.
110. KV to Fred S. Rosenau, May 1955, private collection.
111. Ellen Rosenau, interview, December 30, 2009.
112. KV to KB, September 1, 1955, private collection.
113. KV to KB, October 25, 1955, private collection.
114. KV, interview, March 13, 2007.
115. KV to KB, Summer 1955, private collection.
116. Ibid. "Something Borrowed" premiered in mid-July 1957 ("Play by Barnstable Man to Premiere Tuesday at Orleans," *Barnstable Patriot*, July 18, 1957). In its next iteration, it became *Penelope* and finally *Happy Birthday, Wanda June*.
117. KV to Harry Brague, November 30, 1954, CSS.
118. Ruth Grismer to KV, October 15, 1957, Vonnegut mss., LL.
119. KV to KB, October 25, 1955, private collection.
120. EV, interview, September 20, 2007.
121. KV to Jerome Klinkowitz, January 11, 2002, private collection.
122. Caleb Warren, interview, September 19, 2007: "I remember Steve mentioning it. There were always birds flying around his house uncaged. His father liked that: parrots and bird shit all over the kitchen and just landing on his shoulders." Kurt Adams will be referred to in the text by his nickname, Tiger.
123. Kurt Adams, interview, September 20, 2007.
124. Ibid.
125. Rauch, "Ancestry of Kurt Vonnegut," 76.
126. EV and NV, e-mails, May 4, 2010.
127. KV, interview, March 14, 2007.
128. KV, "The Latest Word," *New York Times*, October 30, 1966.
129. Mark S. Bourbeau, interview, June 19, 2008.
130. JV to Walter A. and Helen Vonnegut, January 5, 1958, private collection.
131. *Kurt Vonnegut: American Made*, Weide.
132. Filomena Gould, "Cape Cod Popular Haven for Hoosiers," *Indianapolis News*, June 29, 1957.
133. JV to Walter A. and Helen Vonnegut, January 5, 1958, private collection.
134. JV, journal, July 10–13, 1957, private collection.
135. Gould, "Cape Cod Popular Haven for Hoosiers."
136. JV, journal, July 10–13, 1957, private collection.
137. Ibid.
138. KV, "Have I Got a Car for You!" *In These Times*, November 24, 2004.
139. JV to Walter A. and Helen Vonnegut, January 5, 1958, private collection.
140. Houston, "The Salon Interview: Kurt Vonnegut"; also, Mark S. Bourbeau, interview, June 19, 2008.
141. JV to Walter A. and Helen Vonnegut, January 5, 1958, private collection.
142. *Cape Cod Standard-Times*, January n.d., 1958.
143. JV, journal, Winter 1958, private collection.
144. JV to Alex Vonnegut, rough draft of a letter, Winter 1958, private collection. NV, interview, September 23, 2007.
145. JV Yarmolinsky, *Angels Without Wings*, 7.
146. Ibid., 16.

147. KV, *Slapstick; or, Lonesome No More!* (1976; repr., New York: Dial, 2006), 16–17.

148. Martin Amis, *The Moronic Inferno* (New York: Penguin, 1991), 135.

149. KV, interview, March 13, 2007.

150. KV, *Slapstick*, 13.

151. "Father Missing in Rail Wreck, Mother of Four Dies of Cancer," *New York Times*, September 18, 1958.

152. Judy Peet, "A Day Bayonne Can't Forget," *Star-Ledger*, September 18, 2008.

153. "Find Engineer in Crash Had Heart Ailment," *Chicago Tribune*, September 17, 1958.

154. Peet, "A Day Bayonne Can't Forget."

155. "Father Missing in Rail Wreck."

156. Gael Greene, "I'm Not Saying the News Killed Her . . ." *New York Post*, September 18, 1958.

157. NV, interview, September 20, 2007; also, Scott Vonnegut, e-mail, March 2, 2009.

158. Greene, "I'm Not Saying the News Killed Her."

159. KV, *Slapstick*, 13.

7: Cooped Up with All These Kids

1. JV to Alex and Raye Vonnegut, September 25, 1958, private collection.

2. JV Yarmolinsky, *Angels Without Wings*, 61.

3. Donna Lewis (pseudonym), interview, July 27, 2008.

4. Ibid.

5. JV Yarmolinsky, *Angels Without Wings*, 115.

6. Peter Adams Nice, interview, June 8, 2009.

7. JV Yarmolinsky, *Angels Without Wings*, 68.

8. Ibid., 67.

9. Ibid., 66.

10. NV, interview, September 20, 2007.

11. Greene, "I'm Not Saying the News Killed Her."

12. JV Yarmolinsky, *Angels Without Wings*, 39.

13. Mark Vonnegut, *The Eden Express: A Personal Account of Schizophrenia* (New York: Praeger, 1975), 58.

14. JV Yarmolinsky, *Angels Without Wings*, 44.

15. Ibid., 70.

16. EV, interview, September 20, 2007.

17. Caleb Warren, interview, September 19, 2007.

18. JV Yarmolinsky, *Angels Without Wings*, 145.

19. Nan Robertson, "The Vonneguts: Dialogue on a Son's Insanity," *New York Times*, October 23, 1975.

20. Donna Lewis, interview, July 27, 2008.

21. JV Yarmolinsky, *Angels Without Wings*, 109; also, Kurt Adams, interview, September 20, 2007. "It was just a place to be," he said.

22. Kurt Adams, interview, September 20, 2007.

23. JV Yarmolinsky, *Angels Without Wings*, 90.

24. Ibid., 104; also, Caleb Warren, interview, September 19, 2007.

25. James C. Adams Jr., e-mail, April 12, 2009.

26. JV Yarmolinsky, *Angels Without Wings*, 81.

27. Caleb Warren, interview, September 19, 2007.

28. James C. Adams Jr., e-mail, April 10, 2009.

29. Kurt Adams, interview, September 20, 2007.

30. JV Yarmolinsky, *Angels Without Wings*, 82.

31. Ibid., 87.

32. Betty Stanton, interview, February 9, 2008.

33. Harry Brague to KV, November 12, 1954, CSS.

34. Harry Brague to KV, June 19, 1956, CSS.

35. KV to Harry Brague, October 26, 1957, CSS.

36. Harry Brague to KV, November 8, 1957, CSS.

37. KV to Harry Brague, November 13, 1957, CSS.

38. JV to Kenneth Littauer, November 21, 1957, private collection.

39. Kurt Adams, interview, September 20, 2007; also, Betty Stanton, interview, February 9, 2008; also, Emily Louise Diamond, interview, February 7, 2008.

40. JV, journal, n.d., private collection.

41. KV, *Palm Sunday*, 66.

42. Ray Bradbury, foreword to *The Ultimate Egoist: The Complete Stories of Theodore Sturgeon*, vol. 1, ed. Paul Williams (Berkeley, CA: North Atlantic Books, 1999), ix.

43. Kurt Vonnegut, foreword to *A Saucer of Loneliness: The Complete Stories of Theodore Sturgeon*, vol. 7, ed. Paul Williams (Berkeley, CA: North Atlantic Books, 2002).

44. Klinkowitz and Lawler, *Vonnegut in America*, 20–21.

45. KV to KB, Spring 1959, private collection.

46. A number of titles in the line provided material for movies and television such as Jack Finney's *The Body Snatchers*; Roy Huggins's *77 Sunset Strip*; Henry Kane's *Peter Gunn*; Albert Conroy's *Mr. Lucky*; and Donald Hamilton's *The Big Country*, which became one of director William Wyler's best Westerns.

47. KB to Jerome Klinkowitz, September 24, 1971, private collection.

48. Klinkowitz and Lawler, *Vonnegut in America*, 19.

49. EV, interview, September 9, 2007.

50. KV to KB, Spring 1959, private collection.

51. KV, *Timequake*, 234.

52. KV to "Gentlemen," April 15, 1959, CSS.

53. Brague died in 1968 in his fifties from an undiagnosed illness.

54. KB, interview, August 6, 2007.

55. *Kurt Vonnegut: American Made*, Weide.

56. Ibid.

57. Richard Giannone, *Vonnegut: A Preface to His Novels* (Port Washington, NY: Kennikat, 1977), 27.

58. KV, *The Sirens of Titan: A Novel* (1959; repr., New York: Dial, 1998), 2.

59. Ibid., 232.

60. James Baird, "Jeffers, Vonnegut, and Pynchon: Their Philosophies and Fates," *Jeffers Studies* 4, no. 1 (Winter 2000): 17–28.

61. Alan Vaughn, *Patterns of Prophecy* (New York: Hawthorn Books, 1973), 28. Vonnegut was mistaken about a detail: Jim Adams commuted regularly to New York.

62. JV Yarmolinsky, *Angels Without Wings*, 32.

63. Jerome Klinkowitz, *Vonnegut in Fact: The Personal Spokesmanship of Personal Fiction* (Columbia: University of South Carolina Press, 1998), 112.

64. Edward James and Farah Mendlesohn, eds., *The Cambridge Companion to Science Fiction* (Cambridge: Cambridge University Press, 2003), 45.

65. Herbert G. Klein, "Kurt Vonnegut's *The Sirens of Titan* and the Question of Genre," May 1999, *Erfurt Electronic Studies in English*. October 16, 2008, http://www.uni-erfurt.de/eestudies/eese/artic99/klein2/5_99.html.

66. William Wolf, "Thru Time and Space with Kurt Vonnegut, Jr.," *Chicago Tribune*, March 12, 1972.

67. KB to Jerome Klinkowitz, September 24, 1971, private collection.
68. KV to KB, Summer 1959, private collection.
69. JV Yarmolinsky, *Angels Without Wings*, 121.
70. KB, interview, August 6, 2007.
71. W. Edward Harris, *Miracle in Birmingham: A Civil Rights Memoir, 1954–1965* (Indianapolis: Stone Work Press, 2004). Nice was later appointed judge of the Circuit Court in 1974 and was again publicly denounced, this time for commuting four death penalty cases to life in prison without parole. Transferred to Family Court of Alabama, where it was assumed he would be innocuous, he refused to send juveniles to adult court. "No youth," he said, "should be given the death penalty." He was defeated for reelection in 1998. Representative Earl F. Hilliard of Alabama, "One Man Stood Alone Against Hate," speaking to the United States House of Representatives, 107th Congress, January 29, 2002.
72. Peter Adams Nice, interview, June 8, 2009.
73. JV Yarmolinsky, *Angels Without Wings*, 131.
74. Ibid.
75. Caleb Warren, interview, September 19, 2007.
76. Allison Mitchell, interview, July 7, 2008. Allison is the other little girl, in addition to Nanny, who appears in the opening pages of *Slaughterhouse-Five*.
77. Kurt Adams, interview, September 20, 2007; also, EV, interview, September 20, 2007.
78. KV to KB, December 7, 1959, private collection.
79. Ibid.
80. Kurt Adams, interview, September 20, 2007.
81. Allison Mitchell, interview, July 7, 2008.
82. Caleb Warren, interview, September 19, 2007.
83. Ibid.
84. Ibid.
85. Allison Mitchell, interview, July 7, 2008.
86. KB to KV, April 15, 1960, private collection.
87. KV to KB, May 12, 1960, private collection.
88. EV, e-mail, May 24, 2010.
89. KV, "In-the-Bone Reading" (excerpt from "For the Love of Books), *Biblio* 4, no. 3 (March 1999): 18.
90. C. M. Newman to Kenneth Littauer, May 20, 1960, "Vonnegut, Kurt," *The New Yorker* Records, New York Public Library.
91. Sam Stewart to KB, August 8, 1960, private collection.
92. Eve Marie Dane, "Kurt Vonnegut's Play Premiered at Orleans," *Cape Cod Standard-Times*, September 8, 1960.
93. KB to KV, June 29, 1960, private collection.
94. KV to KB, September 29, 1960, private collection.
95. KV to KB, January 29, 1960, private collection.
96. KV to KB, February 6, 1961, private collection.
97. KB to KV, March 13, 1961, private collection.
98. KV to KB, October 12, 1961, private collection; also, "The Barnstable Comedy Club Will Present Theater Workshop Productions, March 4," *Barnstable Patriot*, February 23, 1961.
99. "Kurt Vonnegut Named President of Comedy Club," *Barnstable Patriot*, June 15, 1961.
100. KV to KB, July 10, 1961, private collection.
101. KV to KB, June–July 1961, private collection.

102. John D. Garr to Kenneth Littauer, August 3, 1961, Vonnegut mss., LL.

103. KV to KB, July 1961, private collection.

104. Eleven of the twelve appear in the later collection *Welcome to the Monkey House*. The story that was not included was "Hal Irwin's Magic Lamp."

105. KV to KB, September 16, 1961, private collection.

106. KV, "Harrison Bergeron," in *Welcome to the Monkey House* (1968; repr., New York: Delta, 1998), 7.

107. Vonnegut offered this explanation about the story's origin. In high school, he envied classmates who were smarter and more popular. Later, he suspected that rebels and assassins—Lee Harvey Oswald or John Wilkes Booth—never overcame their jealousies of others and became "Handicapper Generals" through violence. Darryl Hattenhauer, "The Politics of Kurt Vonnegut's 'Harrison Bergeron,'" *Studies in Short Fiction* 35, no. 4 (1998): 387+.

108. KV to KB, July 16, 1961, private collection.

109. KV to KB, September 16, 1961, private collection.

110. KV to William Amos, May 12, 1985, Vonnegut mss., LL.

111. Ibid.

112. KV, *Mother Night* (1961; repr., New York: Delta, 1999), xiii.

113. Ibid., v.

114. Howard Zinn, interview, November 19, 2007.

115. Karl, *American Fictions*, 345.

116. Brian W. Aldiss, *Billion Year Spree: The True History of Science Fiction* (New York: Doubleday, 1973), 314.

117. KV to KB, Spring 1962, private collection.

118. KV to KB, March 1962, private collection.

119. KV to KB, Spring 1962, private collection.

120. Carolyn Blakemore, interview, June 16, 2008.

121. Suzanne McConnell, interview, January 18, 2007. Jane told her at Iowa.

122. Caleb Warren, interview, September 19, 2007.

123. Ibid.; also, Allison Mitchell, interview, July 7, 2008.

124. NV, interview, September 20, 2007.

125. EV, interview, September 20, 2007.

126. Ray Mungo, interview, January 22, 2007.

127. EV, interview, September 20, 2007.

128. Betty Stanton, interview, February 2, 2008. Stanton, Allison Mitchell's mother, was the Vonneguts' neighbor. She knew of an opening at Hopefield Riverview school and encouraged Kurt to apply.

129. KV, "Speaking of Books: Science Fiction," *New York Times*, September 5, 1965.

130. Betty Stanton, interview, February 2, 2008. According to Ms. Stanton, Kurt mentioned he might write a story about the authoritarian headmaster and his stupefied charges.

131. KV to KB, September 29, 1962, private collection.

132. Allison Mitchell, interview, February 7, 2008.

133. Kurt Adams, September 20, 2007.

134. Standish, "*Playboy* Interview."

135. *Kurt Vonnegut: American Made*, Weide.

136. "Cape Cod Author Sees Some Flaws in Age of Electronics," *Cape Cod Standard-Times*, December 14, 1952.

137. Donald A. Moffitt, "Weather Makers: New Theories, Tools Tested in Search for Control of Atmosphere," *Wall Street Journal*, n.d., 1962.

138. "His brush with science, tangential though it was, instilled in him a profound dislike of technology as panacea; it is possible that his brother's profession influenced him also in this respect." David H. Goldsmith, *Kurt Vonnegut: Fantasist of Fire and Ice* (Bowling Green, OH: Bowling Green University Popular Press, 1972), ix.

139. KV, *Cat's Cradle* (1963; repr., New York: Delta, 1998), 6.

140. Ibid., 21.

141. Ibid., 43.

142. Lauren Mazow, "Kurt Vonnegut: On Religion" (interview), January 18, 1988, Vonnegut mss., LL. Religion, said Vonnegut in this interview, is "what you give people when you have nothing else to give them." "Karass" was the name of one of Vonnegut's Cape Cod neighbors. "All I know about him," said Vonnegut, "is his mailbox." C. D. B. Bryan, "Kurt Vonnegut, Head Bokononist," *New York Times*, April 6, 1969.

143. KV, *Cat's Cradle*, 266.

144. Ibid., 287.

145. Morris Dickstein, *Gates of Eden: American Culture in the Sixties* (New York: Basic Books, 1977), 97.

146. Gillian Pye, "Comedy Theory and the Postmodern," *Humor: International Journal of Humor Research* 19, no. 1 (2006): 53–70.

147. KV, *Cat's Cradle*, 162.

148. Jerome Klinkowitz, *Vonnegut in Fact*, 10.

149. Terry Southern, "After the Bomb, Dad Came Up with Ice" (review), *New York Times*, June 3, 1963.

150. KV to KB, October 1963, private collection.

151. Standish, "*Playboy* Interview," July 20, 1973.

152. KV, "Teaching the Unteachable," *New York Times*, August 6, 1967.

153. James Brady, "Kurt Vonnegut Meet Jon Stewart," Forbes.com, January 1, 2006.

154. Mark Vonnegut, introduction to *Armageddon in Retrospect*, 1.

155. Caleb Warren, interview, September 19, 2007.

156. James C. Adams Jr., e-mail, May 12, 2009.

157. Allison Mitchell, interview, July 7, 2008.

158. Jeff Moravec and Dan Rank, "The Iowan Interview: Kurt Vonnegut, Jr.," *Northern Iowan*, April 5, 1977.

159. Ibid.

160. Ibid.

161. Goldsmith, *Kurt Vonnegut*, 5.

162. Dale Peck, "Kurt's Conundrum," in *Hatchet Jobs: Writings on Contemporary Fiction* (New York: New Press, 2005), 193.

163. KV, *God Bless You, Mr. Rosewater*, 275.

164. Ibid., 266.

165. Jerome Klinkowitz, *Kurt Vonnegut* (London and New York: Methuen, 1982), 29–30.

166. Mazow, "Kurt Vonnegut: On Religion" (interview).

167. Ibid.

168. KV to L. Rust Hills, September 18, 1964, Hills mss., LL.

169. KV to Sarah Crawford, September 18, 1965, private collection.

170. KV to Sarah Crawford, n.d., private collection.

171. Glendy Culligan, "Scratch a Satirist and Find Sentiment Ready to Explode" (review), *Washington Post*, April 10, 1965.

172. Martin Levin, "Do Human Beings Matter?" (review), *New York Times*, April 25, 1965.

173. "Hoosier Women Honored by Theta Sigma Phi," *Indianapolis Star*, April 3, 1965.

174. KV to L. Rust Hills, March 24, 1965, Vonnegut mss., LL.

175. Allison Mitchell, interview, February 7, 2008.

176. NV, interview, September 20, 2007.

177. KV, *Slaughterhouse-Five; or, The Children's Crusade, a Duty-Dance with Death* (1969; repr., New York: Dial, 2005), 18.

178. Ibid., 19. It seems more likely that Vonnegut appropriated the phrase "children's crusade" from the 1968 presidential election, which drew millions of young people in support of candidate Eugene McCarthy. The press dubbed their participation "the children's crusade."

179. KV to Miller Harris, June 25, 1965, private collection.

180. KV to John C. Gerber, July 11, 1965, University of Iowa, University Archives, Iowa City.

181. KV to KB, August 7, 1965, private collection.

182. KV, "Speaking of Books: Science Fiction," *New York Times*, September 5, 1965.

183. Frederik Pohl, interview, September 13, 2007.

8: A Community of Writers

1. KB, interview, November 20, 2007.

2. KV to NV, June 1, 1971, private collection.

3. KV to NV, March 17, 1974, Vonnegut mss., LL.

4. KV to JV, September 21, 1965, private collection.

5. KV to JV, September 17, 1965, private collection. He included a floor plan of the apartment, with marginalia, in a letter to Jane on September 21.

6. KV to Max Wilkinson, September 18, 1965, Vonnegut mss., LL.

7. KV to JV, September 17, 1965, private collection.

8. Ibid.

9. KV to JV, September 18, 1965, private collection.

10. Ibid.

11. KV to Sarah Crawford, September 18, 1965, private collection.

12. KV to JV, September 18, 1965, private collection.

13. KV to JV, September 17, 1965, private collection.

14. KV to JV, September 23, 1965, private collection.

15. KV to Sarah Crawford, September 25, 1965, private collection.

16. Stephen Wilbers, *The Iowa Writers' Workshop* (Iowa City: University of Iowa Press, 1980), 86.

17. Paul Engle, "The Writer and the Place," in *A Community of Writers: Paul Engle and the Iowa Writers' Workshop*, ed. by Robert Dana (Iowa City: University of Iowa Press, 1999), 3.

18. KV to Ian T. MacMillan, July 17, 1999, private collection.

19. KV, *Palm Sunday*, 93.

20. KV to KB, November 1, 1965, private collection.

21. KV, unpublished thesis, "Fluctuations Between Good and Ill Fortune in Simple Tales," Vonnegut mss., LL.

22. Ibid.

23. Ibid.

24. KV to KB, November 1, 1965, private collection.

25. KV to KB, September 28, 1965, private collection.

26. George W. Stocking Jr., Distinguished Service Professor Emeritus, University of Chicago, e-mail, July 9, 2007.

27. KV, *Palm Sunday*, 288. Still, when he was later in a financial position to do so, he made regular donations to the university (KV to JV, July 28, 1971, private collection).
28. KB to KV, October 1, 1965, private collection.
29. John Casey, interview, December 1, 2006.
30. Suzanne McConnell, interview, January 18, 2007.
31. Philip Damon, interview, January 29, 2007.
32. John Irving, e-mail, January 28, 2007.
33. KV to KB, September 28, 1965, private collection.
34. Philip Damon, interview, January 29, 2007.
35. Ian T. MacMillan, interview, February 1, 2007.
36. KV, "A New Scheme for Real Writers," *New York Times*, July 14, 1974.
37. KV to JV, September 28, 1965, private collection.
38. KV to KB, September 28, 1965, private collection.
39. Anonymous, e-mail, February 8, 2008.
40. Ibid.
41. KV to JV, September 28, 1965, private collection.
42. KV to NV, September 30, 1965, private collection.
43. KV to JV, September 28, 1965, private collection.
44. KV to Sarah Crawford, September 28, 1965, private collection.
45. Sarah Crawford Fox, interview, June 19, 2008.
46. KV to NV, September 30, 1965, private collection.
47. Robert A. Lehrman, e-mail, January 10, 2007. Many of these writers practiced in other genres besides the ones mentioned.
48. Ibid.
49. KV, "Teaching the Unteachable."
50. KV to L. Rust Hills, September 29, 1965, Vonnegut mss., LL.
51. Ian T. MacMillan, e-mail, February 1, 2007.
52. Suzanne McConnell, e-mail, January 12, 2007.
53. John Casey, interview, December 1, 2006.
54. Barry Kaplan, interview, September 21, 2007.
55. KV, *A Man Without a Country*, ed. Daniel Simon (New York: Seven Stories Press, 2005), 25.
56. Robert A. Lehrman, interview, January 23, 2007.
57. John Casey, interview, December 1, 2006.
58. Suzanne McConnell to KV, July 12, 1997, private collection.
59. Ibid.
60. John Casey, interview, December 1, 2006.
61. Philip Damon, interview, January 29, 2007.
62. KV to JV, September 28, 1965, private collection.
63. Suzanne McConnell, interview, January 18, 2007.
64. Philip Damon, interview, January 29, 2007.
65. Ibid.
66. Ibid.
67. Ibid.
68. Robert A. Lehrman, interview, January 23, 2007.
69. KV to JV, September 24, 1965, private collection.
70. Suzanne McConnell to Vance Bourjaily, December 1980, private collection.
71. Ibid.
72. Ian T. MacMillan, e-mail, February 1, 2007.

73. KV to JV, September 28, 1965, private collection.
74. KB to KV, October 1, 1965, private collection.
75. KV to JV, September 28, 1965, private collection.
76. KV to KB, September 28, 1965, private collection.
77. KV to JV, October 2, 1965, private collection.
78. Ibid.
79. Ibid.
80. KV to JV, October 9, 1965, private collection.
81. Rick Boyer, e-mail, August 27, 2007.
82. Vance Bourjaily, interview, March 17, 2008.
83. Loree Rackstraw, *Love as Always, Kurt: Vonnegut as I Knew Him* (Cambridge, MA: Da Capo Press, 2009), 56.
84. Loree Rackstraw, e-mail, April 17, 2008.
85. KV to KB, November 1965, private collection.
86. Blake Bailey, *A Tragic Honesty: The Life and Work of Richard Yates* (New York: Picador, 2004), 322.
87. EV, interview, September 20, 2007.
88. EV, e-mail, December 13, 2008.
89. EV, interview, September 20, 2007.
90. EV, e-mail, December 13, 2008.
91. EV, interview, September 20, 2007.
92. KV, *Player Piano*, 249.
93. KV, *Cat's Cradle*, 266.
94. Marvin, *Kurt Vonnegut*, 63.
95. Loree Rackstraw, *Love as Always, Kurt*, 10.
96. KV to JV, October 2, 1965, private collection.
97. KV to Miller and Mary Louise Harris, April 28, 2000, private collection.
98. Ian T. MacMillan, e-mail, February 1, 2007.
99. KV to KB, November 1, 1965
100. KV to Paul Engle, December 3, 1965, Paul Engle Papers, University of Iowa, Iowa City.
101. Philip Damon, interview, January 29, 2007.
102. Marvin Bell, "Remembering Kurt Vonnegut," at "The Writing University" website, University of Iowa, April 15, 2007.
103. Suzanne McConnell, interview, September 21, 2007; also, Barry Jay Kaplan, interview, September 21, 2007.
104. Philip Damon, interview, January, 29, 2007.
105. Ian T. MacMillan, e-mail, February 1, 2007.
106. KV, "Form of Fiction Term Paper Assignment," November 30, 1965, private collection.
107. Ibid.
108. KV, "Teaching the Unteachable."
109. Gail Godwin, letter to author, March 7, 2007.
110. Alvin P. Sanoff, "Creating Literature on the Plains of Iowa (50th Anniversary of Iowa Writers' Workshop)," *U.S. News & World Report*, June 2, 1986.
111. KV to José Donoso, October 29, 1982, JDP.
112. Barry Jay Kaplan in "Happy Birthday, Kurt Vonnegut," 47.
113. Robley Wilson, e-mail, July 30, 2008.
114. Robert A. Lehrman, interview, January 23, 2007; also, Sarah Crawford Fox, interview, June 21, 2008.
115. Bell, "Remembering Kurt Vonnegut."
116. Ian T. MacMillan, e-mail, February 1, 2007.

117. KV to Paul Engle, November 12, 1965, Paul Engle Papers, Coe College, Cedar Rapids, Iowa.

118. KV to KB, January 20, 1966, private collection.

119. JV to Emily Louise Diamond, Christmas 1965, private collection.

120. Ibid.

121. Rackstraw, *Love as Always, Kurt*, 8.

122. Ibid., 11.

123. EV, interview, September 20, 2007.

124. NV, interview, May 3, 2008.

125. KV to KB, January 20, 1966, private collection.

126. KV to KB, March 5, 1966, private collection.

127. Rackstraw, *Love as Always, Kurt*, 16.

128. Ibid., 17.

129. Ian T. MacMillan, e-mail, February 1, 2007.

130. Rackstraw, *Love as Always, Kurt*, 17.

131. KV to NV, November 8, 1989, Vonnegut mss., LL.

132. KV to KB, June 20, 1966, private collection.

133. Robert A. Lehrman, interview, January 23, 2007.

134. John Casey, interview, December 1, 2006.

135. Saul Madoff, "The Time, the Space, the Quiet," *New York Times*, November 29, 1981.

136. KV to KB, April 3, 1966, private collection.

137. Nancy Bulger, interview, June 13, 2010. Bulger, a former member of Edie's circle of teenage girlfriends, the Herd, was home from college when she attended the parties.

138. JV to Maria Pilar Donoso, July 2, 1966, JDP1.

139. Kurt Adams, interview, September 20, 2007.

140. JV to Maria Pilar Donoso, July 2, 1966, JDP1.

141. KV to KB, January 20, 1966, private collection; also, Mark Vonnegut, e-mail, April 27, 2009.

142. James C. Adams Jr., e-mail, May 2, 2009.

143. KV to KB, October 28, 1966, private collection.

144. Richard Wilson to KV, August 5, 1966, Richard Wilson Papers, Syracuse University Library, Syracuse, NY.

145. KV to Richard Wilson, August 9, 1966. Richard Wilson Papers, Syracuse University Library, Syracuse, NY. Vonnegut had met Wilson at the Milford Science Fiction convention, which is where Eliot Rosewater blurts out his affection for science fiction writers in *God Bless You, Mr. Rosewater*: "I love you sons of bitches. I really do. You're all I read any more. You're the only ones crazy enough to really care about the future."

146. KV to KB, October 28, 1966, private collection.

147. "Mrs. Rackstraw Reads from 'Incomplete Puritan,'" *Northern Iowan*, April 30, 1968.

148. John Casey, interview, December 1, 2006.

149. Ibid.

150. KV to KB, March 6, 2001, private collection.

151. Elizabeth Venant, "A Fresh Twist in the Road for Novelist Richard Yates, a Specialist in Grim Irony, Late Fame's a Wicked Return," *Los Angeles Times*, July 9, 1989.

152. Stephen Amidon, "A Heavy Price" (book review), *New Statesman*, November 22, 2004.

153. Suzanne McConnell to Vance Bourjaily, December 1980, private collection.

154. Jerome Klinkowitz, interview, October 26, 2007.

155. KV to William Price Fox, October 14, 1966, Thomas Cooper Library, University of South Carolina.

156. KV to KB, October 3, 1966, private collection.
157. KV, "The Last Word," *New York Times*, October 30, 1966.
158. Ibid.
159. C. D. B. Bryan, "Kurt Vonnegut on Target," *New Republic*, October 1966, 21–22+.
160. Dan Wakefield, interview, January 25, 2007.
161. Ibid.
162. J. P. Donleavy, contributor, "Seymour Lawrence: An Independent Imprint Dedicated to Excellence" (booklet printed by Houghton Mifflin, New York, November 1, 1990).
163. Jayne Anne Phillips, "The Wizard" (speech read at Seymour Lawrence's memorial service), 1994.
164. Dan Wakefield, interview, January 25, 2007.
165. KV, *Bagombo Snuff Box*, 2.
166. KV to Carolyn Blakemore, Thomas Cooper Library, William Price Fox Papers, University of South Carolina.
167. Frank Dunlap, "God and Kurt Vonnegut at Iowa City," *Chicago Tribune*, May 7, 1967.
168. Robert A. Lehrman, interview, January 23, 2007.
169. Dunlap, "God and Kurt Vonnegut at Iowa City."
170. Maria Pilar Donoso, "Beer Party in Iowa," in *The World Comes to Iowa: The Iowa International Anthology*, ed. Paul Engle, Rowena Torrevillas, and Hualing Nieh Engle (Ames: Iowa State University Press, 1987).
171. John Casey, interview, December 1, 2006.
172. Some would argue that Laurence Sterne's *Tristram Shandy*, Chaucer's *Canterbury Tales*, and Cervantes's *Don Quixote* were forerunners of this approach.
173. William Kittredge in *Seems Like Old Times*, ed. Ed Dinger (Iowa City: Iowa Writers' Workshop, 1986), 66.
174. Gail Godwin, letter to author, March 7, 2007.
175. KV, interview, March 14, 2007.
176. Rackstraw, *Love as Always, Kurt*, 29.
177. KV to Richard Gehman, August 10, 1967, private collection.
178. Suzanne McConnell in *Seems Like Old Times*, 40.
179. Robert A. Lehrman, interview, January 23, 2007.
180. NV, interview, May 3, 2008.
181. NV, interview, September 20, 2007.
182. NV, interview, September 23, 2007.
183. KV to Seymour Lawrence, June 22, 1967, SLPF.
184. KV to Seymour Lawrence, September 19, 1967, SLPF.
185. KV to Knox Burger, October 7, 1967, private collection.

9: The Big Ka-BOOM

1. Kurt Vonnegut to José Donoso, October 22, 1967, JDP.
2. Ibid.
3. Ibid.
4. Leningrad, scene of the nine-hundred-day siege by the Germans, was renamed St. Petersburg in 1991.
5. Fiene, "Getting Through Life," book 8, "Out of Darkness into the Light (1970–1974)," part 2.
6. Bernard O'Hare III, e-mail, May 18, 2009.
7. KV to Seymour Lawrence, October 29, 1967, SLPF.
8. It took fifteen years to get one. The Trabant accelerated (if *accelerated* is the right word) from zero to sixty in twenty-one seconds.

9. McKee, *The Devil's Tinderbox*, 312.

10. Gerhard Müller to Kurt Vonnegut, April 4, 1988, private collection. The residents of Coventry, England, whose town had been destroyed by the Luftwaffe, raised three-quarters of a million euros to rebuild the church, which resumed services in 2005.

11. McKee, *The Devil's Tinderbox*, illustration 54.

12. KV, *Slaughterhouse-Five*, 1.

13. Bell, "Remembering Kurt Vonnegut."

14. Donoso left the workshop the same year as Kurt. "At the end of two years I realized that for me teaching and writing fiction did not work together—as it did for Kurt Vonnegut, who taught at the same college at the same time I did, and wrote one of his best novels there—and no matter how cozy the fastness of an American university, I had to get out." José Donoso, "A Small Biography of the Obscene Bird of Night," *Review of Contemporary Fiction* 19, no. 3 (1999): 123.

15. Ibid.

16. José Donoso to Kurt Vonnegut, October 16, 1967, Vonnegut mss. LL.

17. Kurt Vonnegut to José Donoso, October 22, 1967, JDP. Over the next eighteen months, Vonnegut kept peppering Donoso with encouragement, including successfully recommending him for a Guggenheim Fellowship. When *The Obscene Bird* was finally published in 1970, after forty drafts, it was hailed as Donoso's masterpiece. Sahron Magnarelli, *Understanding José Donoso* (Columbia: University of South Carolina Press, 1992), 93.

18. Hipkiss, *The American Absurd*, 52.

19. Ibid.

20. Kurt Vonnegut, *Kaleidoscope*, BBC 4.

21. KV, "In-the-Bone Reading."

22. Jim Knipfel, "Reading Louis-Ferdinand Céline," *Context: A Forum for Literary Arts and Culture* 8 (November 2001), October 18, 2008, www.dalkeyarchive.com.

23. Ibid.

24. KV, *Slaughterhouse-Five*, 27.

25. Louis-Ferdinand Céline, *Journey to the End of the Night*, trans. Ralph Manheim (1934; repr., New York: New Directions, 2006), 173.

26. KV to Seymour Lawrence, October 29, 1967, SLPF.

27. KV to Seymour Lawrence, n.d., SLPF.

28. KV to Seymour Lawrence, January 21, 1968, SLPF.

29. KV to Seymour Lawrence, November 15, 1967, SLPF.

30. KV to Gail Godwin, November 25, 1967, Gail Godwin Papers, University of North Carolina, Chapel Hill. Gail Godwin, "Waltzing with the Black Crayon" [studying with Kurt Vonnegut at Iowa], *Yale Review*, January 1999.

31. Robert E. Scholes, *The Fabulators* (New York: Oxford University Press, 1967), 12.

32. Ibid., 48.

33. Bryan, "Kurt Vonnegut on Target."

34. Jody "Joe" Clark played bass guitar at one time for the J. Geils Band.

35. L. B. Shriver, e-mail, April 25, 2009.

36. KV, *Wampeters, Foma & Granfalloons*, 34.

37. Ibid.

38. KV, *Fates Worse Than Death*, 188.

39. KV, *Palm Sunday*, 175.

40. Christianity is not a fad, but the Broadway production of the rock opera *Jesus Christ Superstar* (1971) testifies to how the Gospel suddenly took on shades of *Hair: The American Tribal Love-Rock Musical* (1968).

41. "Carol Troy Interviews Kurt Vonnegut," *Rags*, March 1971, 24–26.
42. KV, *Palm Sunday*, 177.
43. Gerald Clarke, *Capote: A Biography*, 2nd paperback ed. (Cambridge, MA: Da Capo Press, 2005), 249.
44. KV to Seymour Lawrence, April 30, 1968, SLPF.
45. Carol Mallory, "The Kurt & Joe Show," *Playboy*, May 1992.
46. Standish, "*Playboy* Interview."
47. Ibid.
48. Cargas, "Kurt Vonnegut," 1048–150.
49. Michael Wood, "Dancing in the Dark," *New York Review of Books*, May 31, 1973.
50. Mallory, "The Kurt & Joe Show."
51. Granville Hicks, "Literary Horizons," *Saturday Review*, March 29, 1969.
52. KV to Seymour Lawrence, June 11, 1968, SLPF.
53. JV, interview by Marge Schiller, December 1969, interview 639, transcript, McCarthy Historical Project, Eugene J. McCarthy Papers, Elmer L. Andersen Library, University of Minnesota, Minneapolis.
54. Ibid.
55. Gordon Keith Mantler, "Black, Brown and Poor: Martin Luther King Jr., The Poor People's Campaign and Its Legacies" (PhD thesis, Duke University, 2008).
56. Arnold Bossi, interview, May 14, 2009.
57. "Village Roundup," *Barnstable Patriot*, June 27, 1969.
58. JV, interview, McCarthy Historical Project.
59. EV, interview, September 20, 2007.
60. NV, interview, September 23, 2007.
61. JV interview, McCarthy Historical Project.
62. Ibid.
63. KV to KB, July 18, 1968, private collection.
64. JV, interview, McCarthy Historical Project.
65. Ibid.
66. Arnold Bossi, interview, May 14, 2009.
67. JV, interview, McCarthy Historical Project.
68. Ibid.
69. Ibid.
70. Rackstraw, *Love as Always, Kurt*, 33.
71. Ibid.
72. Eve Guarnuccio, interview, February 8, 2008.
73. Ibid.
74. Ibid.
75. Anonymous, interview, February 9, 2008. Before Jimmy's mental condition deteriorated to the point where she became paranoid and reclusive in the late 1970s, she published two novels, *The Big Win* (1969) and *Some Parts in the Single Life* (1971). Vonnegut wrote an enthusiastic blurb for the first novel, which apparently was too late for the hardcover edition but was used for the Bantam paperback edition. His remarks were reprinted on the sleeve of her second novel.
76. Suzanne McConnell, interview, January 8, 2007.
77. Ibid.
78. Ibid.
79. Suzanne McConnell, letter to author, April 8, 2008.
80. Ibid.
81. Sarah J. Griffith, "The Moral Egotist: Evolution of Style in Kurt Vonnegut's Satire"

(bachelor's thesis, University of Michigan, 2008), 13. The quote is from Griffith's research; my additional research indicates Vonnegut quit by the end of January.

82. Suzanne McConnell, letter to author, April 8, 2008.

83. Ibid.

84. Vonnegut mss., LL.

85. Ibid.

86. Ibid.

87. KV to Bernard O'Hare, September 14, 1968, private collection.

88. Bernard O'Hare Jr., e-mail, August 19, 2010.

89. KV to Seymour Lawrence, October 21, 1968, SLPF.

90. Larry L. King, "Old Soup" (review), *New York Times*, September 1, 1968.

91. Richard Rhodes, "Vonnegut Springs the Mousetrap," *Chicago Tribune*, August 18, 1968.

92. Israel Shenker, "Kurt Vonnegut, Jr. Lights Comic Paths of Despair," *New York Times*, March 21, 1969.

93. "46 and Trusted," *Newsweek*, March 3, 1969.

94. Garry Trudeau in "Happy Birthday, Kurt Vonnegut," 119.

95. Bob Baird, "Witnessing History During 40 Years in a Newsroom," *Journal News* (New York), June 3, 2008.

96. KV, *Wampeters, Foma & Granfalloons*, 97.

97. Philactos and Stanker, "Gregory Appeals for Students to Change American Society," *Statesman*, Stony Brook University, September 27, 1968. The two young journalists attended the conference at Valparaiso University.

98. KV, *Wampeters, Foma & Granfalloons*, 97.

99. Ibid., 90.

100. KV to KB, November 23, 1963, private collection. Vonnegut doesn't discuss the book at length, but the letter indicates he read Mailer's book.

101. "46 and Trusted."

102. Ibid.

103. KV, *Wampeters, Foma & Granfalloons*, 93.

104. Walter Sullivan, "Strike to Protest 'Misuse' of Science," *New York Times*, February 6, 1969.

105. Max Wilkinson to Warren Hinckle, August 25, 1968, McFarlin Library, University of Oklahoma, Tulsa.

106. Pam Black, "Ramparts," *Folio: The Magazine for Magazine Management*, April 1, 2004.

107. Rita Lang Kleinfelder, *When We Were Young: A Baby-Boomer Yearbook* (New York: Prentice Hall, 1993), 501.

108. Robert B. Weide, interview, May 23, 2010.

109. KV, *A Man Without a Country*, 20.

110. Griffith, "The Moral Egotist," 45.

111. KV, *Slaughterhouse-Five*, 4.

112. Ibid., 29.

113. Peter J. Reed, "Kurt Vonnegut," *Dictionary of Literary Biography*, Documentary Series, vol. 3 (Detroit: Bruccoli Clark/Gale Research, 1983), 321–76.

114. Clark Mayo, *Kurt Vonnegut: The Gospel from Outer Space* (San Bernardino, CA: Borgo Press, 1977), 4.

115. KV, *Slaughterhouse-Five*, 34.

116. During the seventeenth and eighteenth centuries, leaders in the arts took a great interest in science: Keats, Coleridge, Dr. Johnson, and Mary Shelley, to name a few. (See Richard Holmes, *The Age of Wonder: How the Romantic Generation Discovered*

the *Beauty and Terror of Science* [New York: Pantheon Books, 2008].) But there seems to be a presumption today, echoing Vonnegut's earliest complaints, that literary people generally don't "do" science.

117. Richard Morris, *Time's Arrows: Scientific Attitudes Toward Time* (New York: Simon and Schuster, 1985), 19.

118. Ibid., 144–45 and 158.

119. Greg Mitchell, "Meeting My Maker: A Visit with Kurt Vonnegut, Jr., by Kilgore Trout," *Crawdaddy*, April 1, 1974, 51.

120. Gregory N. Derry, *What Science Is and How It Works* (Princeton, NJ: Princeton University Press, 1999), 236.

121. KV, *Slaughterhouse-Five*, 93.

122. Ibid., 75. Interesting to think about is that Vonnegut's father was superintendent of matériels control at Fall Creek Ordnance Plant near his home in Indianapolis during the war.

123. Ibid., 109.

124. Ibid.

125. Morris, *Time's Arrows*, 58–59.

126. J. D. Bernal, *A History of Classical Physics: From Antiquity to Quantum* (1972; repr., New York: Barnes and Noble Books, 1997), 238.

127. KV, *Slaughterhouse-Five*, 86.

128. KV, "Knowing What's Nice," *In These Times*, November 6, 2003.

129. Paul Juhasz, "No Matter What the Actual Hour May Be: Time Manipulation in the Works of Ambrose Bierce," *Ambrose Bierce Project Journal* 4, no. 1 (Fall 2008), November 22, 2009, www.ambrosebierce.org/journal4juhaszl.html.

130. KV, *Slaughterhouse-Five*, 26.

131. Roy Morris Jr., *Ambrose Bierce: Alone in Bad Company* (New York: Oxford University Press, 1999), 52.

132. Gordon, "Death and Creativity," 106–24.

133. KV, *Slaughterhouse-Five*, 29.

134. Wildhack was the surname of a brother and sister at the Orchard School in Indianapolis. "I didn't know them very well. It was such a wonderful name." KV, interview, March 13, 2007.

135. KV, *Slaughterhouse-Five*, 170.

136. KV, *Wampeters, Foma & Granfalloons*, 279.

137. "Kurt Vonnegut," Granville Hicks Collection, McFarlin Library, University of Tulsa, Tulsa, OK.

138. J. M. Crichton, "Sci-Fi and Vonnegut," *New Republic*, April 26, 1969.

139. Leslie A. Fiedler, "The Divine Stupidity of Kurt Vonnegut: Portrait of the Novelist as Bridge over Troubled Water," *Esquire* 74, September 1970, 195–97.

140. Elaine Woo, "His Popular Novels Blended Social Criticism, Dark Humor," *Los Angeles Times*, April 12, 2007.

141. Arch Whitehouse, "Dresden Under Fire" (letter), *New York Times*, May 18, 1969.

142. "Vonnegut Book Widely Reviewed," *Barnstable Patriot*, April 10, 1969.

143. *Essential Vonnegut: Interviews Conducted by Walter Miller.*

144. KV, *Slaughterhouse-Five*, 86 and 160.

145. *Essential Vonnegut: Interviews Conducted by Walter Miller.*

10: Goodbye and Goodbye and Goodbye

1. Kurt Adams, interview, September 20, 2007.

2. EV, interview, September 20, 2007.

3. Dan Wakefield, "Kurt Vonnegut," in *Indiana History: A Book of Readings*, ed. Ralph D. Gray (Bloomington: Indiana University Press, 1994), 283–84.

4. Kurt Adams, interview, September 20, 2007.

5. Wakefield, "Kurt Vonnegut."

6. Standish, "*Playboy* Interview."

7. Ibid.

8. Bryan, "Kurt Vonnegut, Head Bokononist."

9. Donald M. Fiene to KV, December 4, 1976, Fiene mss. 1975–76, LL.

10. Richard Todd, "The Masks of Kurt Vonnegut, Jr.," *New York Times Magazine*, January 24, 1971.

11. Hume, "Vonnegut's Melancholy," 221.

12. Joe Alino to KV, June 3, 1974, Vonnegut mss., LL.

13. Kevin Maledy to KV, November 1974, Vonnegut mss., LL.

14. KV, *The Sirens of Titan*, 189.

15. KV to JV, March 12, 1974, private collection.

16. Mark Vonnegut, "Happy Birthday, Kurt Vonnegut," 155.

17. EV, "Happy Birthday, Kurt Vonnegut," 156–57.

18. Barry Jay Kaplan, interview, September 21, 2007.

19. EV, e-mail, May 1, 2008; KV to Seymour Lawrence, June 16, 1969, SLPF.

20. Dana Cook, "Deadeye Kurt," Salon.com, posted April 12, 2007.

21. NV, interview, September 20, 2007.

22. Jail, incarceration, and miscarriages of justice are ubiquitous in Vonnegut's works. In the short story "Ed Luby's Key Club," a naive young couple is jailed for a murder they didn't commit. The police chief, the mayor, and all the leading citizens of Ilium—all authority figures—conspire against them. KV, *Look at the Birdie* (New York: Delacorte, 2009).

23. Chris Warnick, "Student Writing, Politics, and Style, 1962–1979" (PhD diss., University of Pittsburgh, 2006).

24. "Young Writers Say They Don't Read," *New York Times*, May 23, 1969.

25. KB to KV, June 12, 1970, private collection.

26. John F. Birmingham, interview, October 22, 2009; also, Birmingham, *The Vancouver Split* (New York: Simon and Schuster, 1973).

27. Al Brodax to Donald L. Farber, August 6, 1976, Vonnegut mss., LL.

28. Bellamy, *Literary Luxuries*, 144–45.

29. Clarence Petersen, "Hang a Medal on Him," *Chicago Tribune*, October 27, 1968.

30. KB to KV, November 12, 1969, private collection.

31. KV to KB, July 11, 1969, private collection.

32. Robert L. Short, *Something to Believe In: Is Kurt Vonnegut the Exorcist of Jesus Christ Superstar?* (New York: Harper and Row, 1978), 283–84.

33. KV, "Excelsior! We're Going to the Moon. Excelsior!" *New York Times*, July 13, 1969.

34. *Essential Vonnegut: Interviews Conducted by Walter Miller.*

35. Dana Hornig, "Kurt Vonnegut, Campus Hero," *Barnstable Patriot*, September 4, 1969.

36. Walter Cronkite, interviewed for "Washington Goes to the Moon," part 1 (transcript), Public Radio Exchange, Cambridge, MA.

37. *Essential Vonnegut: Interviews Conducted by Walter Miller.*

38. Cronkite, interviewed for "Washington Goes to the Moon."

39. Hornig, "Kurt Vonnegut, Campus Hero."

40. KV to Seymour Lawrence, October 21, 1968, SLPF.

41. Wakefield, "Kurt Vonnegut," 281.
42. KV, *Kaleidoscope*, BBC 4.
43. KB to KV, November 12, 1969, private collection.
44. Ibid.
45. Mark Vonnegut, *The Eden Express*, 57.
46. KV to Seymour Lawrence, October 17, 1969, SLPF.
47. KV to José Donoso, March 28, 1968, JDP.
48. NV, interview, September 23, 2007.
49. JV to KV, May 27, 1971, private collection.
50. Mark Vonnegut, *The Eden Express*, 57.
51. Vance Bourjaily, interview, March 17, 2008.
52. KV, "Tribute to Allen Ginsberg," speech at the Wadsworth Theater, Los Angeles, May 30, 1997.
53. Vance Bourjaily, interview, March 17, 2008.
54. KV, "Biafra: A People Betrayed," *McCall's*, April 1970, 68–69, 134–38.
55. Vance Bourjaily, "What Vonnegut Is and Isn't," *New York Times*, August 13, 1972.
56. Ibid.
57. Ibid.
58. Dan Jacobs, *The Brutality of Nations* (New York: Paragon House, 1988).
59. KV, "Biafra."
60. KV to KB, February 28, 1970, private collection.
61. KB, "Notes on Kurt Vonnegut's Present Involvements," February 5, 1970, private collection.
62. The sign KNOX BURGER ASSOCIATES, LTD. can be seen on a wrought-iron fence in Woody Allen's film *Annie Hall*.
63. KV to KB, April 14, 1970, private collection.
64. KB to KV, April 18, 1970, private collection.
65. KV to KB, April 24, 1970, private collection.
66. KB to KV, July 10, 1970, private collection; also, KB to KV, July 14, 1970, private collection.
67. "Production Firm Formed by Lester M. Goldsmith," *Box Office*, May 11, 1970.
68. Bosworth, "To Vonnegut, the Hero Is the Man Who Refuses to Kill."
69. KV to KB, July 16, 1970, Vonnegut mss., LL.
70. KV to Donald C. Farber, May 15, 1970, Vonnegut mss., LL.
71. Kevin McCarthy, in "Happy Birthday, Kurt Vonnegut," 69.
72. Robert Fulton to Donald C. Farber, August 13, 1970, Vonnegut mss., LL.
73. Ibid.
74. KB to KV, August 14, 1970, private collection.
75. Tom Jones and Harvey Schmidt, *The Fantasticks: The Complete Illustrated Text*, 30th ed. (Montclair, NJ: Applause Books, 2000), 15. One of Vonnegut's favorite television actors, Jerry Orbach, was in the original cast.
76. KB, interview, August 6, 2007.
77. Barry Jay Kaplan, interview, September 21, 2007.
78. KV, introduction to *Happy Birthday, Wanda June* (New York: Dell, 1971), vii.
79. Mark Vonnegut, e-mail, April 27, 2009.
80. Mark Vonnegut, *The Eden Express*, 7.
81. Ibid., 25.
82. KV to Mark Vonnegut, October 31, 1974, private collection.
83. EV, e-mail, August 16, 2009.
84. NV, interview, September 23, 2007.

85. KV, *Palm Sunday*, 172.
86. Ibid.
87. JV to José and Maria Pilar Donoso, May 7, 1970, JDP.
88. Ibid.
89. KV, interview, December 13, 2006.
90. Ibid.
91. KV to Bernard Vonnegut, September 16, 1977, private collection.
92. George Stocking, e-mail, July 12, 2007.
93. Raymond T. Smith to George Stocking, e-mail, July 12, 2007.
94. Robert Reinhold, "Vonnegut Has 15 Nuggets of Talent in Harvard Class," *New York Times*, November 18, 1970.
95. Kurt Vonnegut to José Donoso, December 2, 1970, JDP.
96. Jim Siegelman in "Happy Birthday, Kurt Vonnegut," 72. Siegelman was in the class.
97. Reinhold, "Vonnegut Has 15 Nuggets of Talent in Harvard Class."
98. Jerry Hiatt, interview, October 18, 2009. Hiatt was in the class.
99. Todd, "The Masks of Kurt Vonnegut Jr."
100. Reinhold, "Vonnegut Has 15 Nuggets of Talent in Harvard Class."
101. Jerry M. Hiatt, interview, October 18, 2009.
102. Ibid.
103. Reinhold, "Vonnegut Has 15 Nuggets of Talent in Harvard Class."
104. KV to Seymour Lawrence, February 26, 1971, SLPF.
105. Dianne Wiest, interview, October 20, 2009.
106. KV to José Donoso, December 2, 1970, JDP.
107. Bosworth, "To Vonnegut, the Hero Is the Man Who Refuses to Kill."
108. Jill Krementz, interview by Brian Lamb, "The Writer's Desk," *Booknotes*, C-SPAN, June 1, 1997.
109. Dianne Wiest, interview, October 20, 2009.
110. Lynn Meyer, interview, August 22, 2008.
111. EV, interview, September 20, 2007.
112. Gay Talmey, interview, February 19, 2008.
113. Ibid.
114. Tony Kent, interview, November 27, 2007. Kent changed his name from Krementz. At one time, he was a fashion photographer in Paris.
115. "Jill Krementz," Contemporary Authors Online, Gale, 2007. From Literature Resource Center (Farmington Hills, MI: Thomson Gale, 2007).
116. Krementz, interview by Brian Lamb, "The Writer's Desk."
117. "Jill Krementz," Contemporary Authors Online.
118. Vance Bourjaily, interview, March 17, 2008.
119. Bernard Gotfryd, interview, November 23, 2007.
120. "Jill Krementz," Contemporary Authors Online.
121. "Lunch with Jill Krementz," David Patrick Columbia and Jeffrey Hirsch, New York Social Diary.com, posted January 13, 2005.
122. "Jill Krementz," Contemporary Authors Online.
123. Dianne Wiest, interview, October 20, 2009.
124. Vance Bourjaily, interview, March 17, 2008.
125. Bosworth, "To Vonnegut, the Hero Is the Man Who Refuses to Kill."
126. Ibid.
127. Todd, "The Masks of Kurt Vonnegut Jr."
128. William Wolf, "Thru Time and Space with Kurt Vonnegut, Jr.," *Chicago Tribune*, May 12, 1972.

129. KV to José Donoso, December 2, 1970, JDP.
130. EV, interview, September 20, 2007.
131. Carolyn Blakemore, interview, June 16, 2008; also Lynn Meyer, interview, August 22, 2008.
132. Marcia Gauger, interview, September 6, 2008.
133. NV, interview, September 20, 2007.
134. KV to KB, December 30, 1970, private collection.
135. KV to NV, September 30, 1972, private collection.
136. Barry Kaplan, interview, September 21, 2007.
137. Ibid.
138. Vance Bourjaily, interview, March 17, 2008.
139. Ibid.
140. EV, interview, September 20, 2007.
141. Robertson, "The Vonneguts: Dialogue on a Son's Insanity."
142. Jeffrey Lott, "The Good Hippie," *Swarthmore College Bulletin*, March 1, 2003.
143. Mark Vonnegut, *The Eden Express*, 120.
144. Ibid., 47.
145. Ibid., 43.
146. EV, interview, September 20, 2007.
147. EV, e-mail, December 13, 2008.
148. NV, interview, May 3, 2008.
149. NV, interview, September 20, 2007.
150. KV to Seymour Lawrence, July 15, 1970, SLPF.
151. Todd, "The Masks of Kurt Vonnegut Jr."
152. KV to Seymour Lawrence, February 26, 1971, SLPF.
153. KV to José Donoso, March 2, 1971, JDP.
154. JV to Don Farber, January 23, 1971, private collection. The note is on personal stationery headed "Mrs. Kurt Vonnegut, Jr.," suggesting how much her identity was still tied to his while the "second wave," activist phase of the feminist movement was at its height.
155. JV to Jerome Klinkowitz, January 17, 1971, private collection.
156. Caleb Warren, interview, September 19, 2007.

11: Cultural Bureaucrat

1. Mark Vonnegut, *The Eden Express*, 146.
2. Ibid., 123–24.
3. Robertson, "The Vonneguts: Dialogue on a Son's Insanity."
4. KV, "Surviving Niagara," *Guardian*, January 25, 2003.
5. Hollywood Hospital was a mansion that provided services as a detox center for Vancouver's more affluent drunks. It was also a walk-in LSD boutique, offering a guided twelve-hour LSD trip for six hundred dollars. Patients would check in, get a physical examination, fill out a psychological profile, and disclose in writing their personal histories, complete with "hang ups." After taking LSD, they retired to a therapy suite, where plush sofas, a high-end sound system, and fanciful artwork encouraged a restful experience. Cary Grant was a patient. (Jake MacDonald, "Peaking on the Prairies," *The Walrus*, June 2007.) Mark didn't participate in the guided acid trips.
6. KV, "Surviving Niagara."
7. KV to Vance Bourjaily, n.d., Vance Bourjaily Papers, Bowdoin College, Brunswick, ME.

8. Walter A. and Christopher Vonnegut interview, April 7, 2007. Some months before, Mark had knocked on Walter's door at 2:00 A.M. He and his girlfriend were on their way to Vancouver but had missed the ferry and needed a place to sleep. The next morning, Christopher Vonnegut, who is Mark's age, had just arrived home from a hitch in the army. "I was there in the living room unpacking all this stuff," recalled Christopher, "and Mark was reading a book and I tried to engage him, but he clearly didn't want to talk, he wanted to read."

9. Mark Vonnegut, *The Eden Express*, 129 and 136.

10. Standish, "*Playboy* Interview."

11. Mark Vonnegut, *The Eden Express*, 174.

12. "Happy Birthday, Kurt Vonnegut," 81. Kurt was a self-conscious actor. Justin Kaplan, whose *Mr. Clemens and Mark Twain* (1967) won both the Pulitzer Prize and the National Book Award, enlisted Vonnegut for a part in a documentary about Mark Twain. The director placed him on the banks of the Mississippi. "Kurt just wasn't right for it," Kaplan said. Justin Kaplan, interview, December 10, 2009.

13. Donald C. Farber to Phyllis West, November 3, 1976, Vonnegut mss., LL.

14. Mark Vonnegut, *The Eden Express*, 155.

15. Caleb Warren, interview, September 19, 2007.

16. "In Vonnegut's View, Life Is Absurd But Not Worth Leaving," *Chicago Tribune*, June 14, 1976.

17. Lynn Meyer, interview, August 22, 2007.

18. KV to JV, March 1, 1971.

19. Geraldo Rivera, *Exposing Myself*, written with Daniel Paisner (New York: Bantam Books, 1991), 120.

20. EV, interview, September 20, 2007.

21. KV to JV, May 11, 1971, private collection.

22. KV to JV, March 7, 1971, private collection.

23. KV to JV, March 1, 1971, private collection.

24. KV to JV, May 11, 1971, private collection.

25. Betty Stanton, interview, February 2, 2008.

26. Kurt Vonnegut (KV's nephew), interview, September 19, 2007.

27. NV, interview, September 23, 2007.

28. KV, "Bernard Vonnegut: The Rainmaker," *New York Times*, January 4, 1998.

29. *Kurt Vonnegut: American Made*, Weide.

30. Geraldine Meany, *(Un)Like Subjects: Women, Theory, Fiction* (London: Routledge, 1993), 186.

31. KV, *Wampeters, Foma & Granfalloons*, xv.

32. JV to KV, May 27, 1971, private collection.

33. KV, *Slaughterhouse-Five*, 254.

34. JV to KV, May 27, 1971, private collection.

35. Ibid.

36. Ibid.

37. JV to KV, May 28, 1971, private collection.

38. Ibid. Jane is quoting Kurt's remark back at him.

39. KV, "Torture and Blubber," *New York Times*, June 30, 1971.

40. L. B. Shriver, e-mail, April 25, 2009.

41. JV to KB, July 12, 1971, private collection.

42. KV to JV, July 19, 1971, private collection.

43. JV to KV, July 23, 1971, private collection.

44. KV to JV, July 28, 1971, private collection.

45. JV to José and Maria Pilar Donoso, August 25, 1971, JDP.

46. As an example of Kurt's affection for traditions, one Christmas, shortly after the Adams boys arrived, he tossed an odd-looking piece of turned wood into the fireplace. Horrified, Jim Adams said it was a present he had made in shop class. Kurt fished it out and proclaimed it the "Christmas banana," which must be charred every year after the presents were opened. Edie still has it, although the "banana" is looking much reduced after fifty years of ritual burning.

47. Geraldo Rivera, "And So It Goes," Geraldo.com, posted April 20, 2007.

48. Anonymous, interview, December 4, 2009.

49. KV to NV, June 1, 1971, private collection.

50. Ibid.

51. KV to NV, October 2, 1971, private collection.

52. KV to José Donoso, October 24, 1971, JDP.

53. KV to Vance Bourjaily, Late Spring 1971, Vance Bourjaily Papers, Bowdoin College, Brunswick, ME.

54. Lynn Meyer, interview, August 22, 2007.

55. EV, e-mail, May 4, 2008.

56. "Miss Jill Krementz" is listed as a guest on the program for a speech given by Vonnegut at the Amerika Haus, Frankfurt, October 16, 1971, SLPF.

57. John Rauch to JV, November 12, 1971, private collection. Rauch was referred to as "Uncle" in deference to his age. A Harvard graduate like Alex Vonnegut, he was a prominent Indianapolis lawyer. During his long civic career, he served as president of the board of trustees for the Art Association of Indianapolis (1962–76); chairman of the board of the Indiana Historical Society (1957–76); an organizer of the Park School Foundation; and as director of both the Indianapolis Symphony and the Children's Museum.

58. KV to JV, November 15, 1971, private collection. This letter refers to Jane's nightmares about drowning.

59. Standish, "*Playboy* Interview."

60. Mark Vonnegut, introduction to *Armageddon in Retrospect*, 4.

61. KV, *Breakfast of Champions*, 275.

62. Eric Levin, "The Slipperiest Rung on the Ladder of Success May Be Your Own Fear of Winning," *People*, November 10, 1980.

63. EV, interview, September 20, 2007.

64. Justin Kaplan, interview, December 10, 2009.

65. KV to JV, January 4, 1972.

66. Donald C. Farber to KV, January 5, 1972, and March 13, 1973, Vonnegut mss., LL.

67. Kurt shared tips with Knox in the mid-1950s about hot developments in technology, via his friends at General Electric. One product was the zinc alloy Zncube. (See Clifford B. Hicks, "Tailor-Made Metals for Tomorrow," *Popular Mechanics*, May 1957, 94.) Vonnegut recommended he and Knox invest in Illinois Zinc, but they didn't.

68. KV, *Breakfast of Champions*, 129.

69. KV to JV, November 16, 1972, private collection.

70. Charles K. Hyde, *Copper for America: The United States Copper Industry from Colonial Times to the 1990s* (Tucson: University of Arizona Press, 1998).

71. Gerald L. Lopez to the partners of Texas International Drilling Fund, July 9, 1975; Charles A. Perlitz III, Mitchell Hutchins, Inc., to KV, January 5, 1977; M. Martin Rom to the investors in Multivest, March 7, 1975, Vonnegut mss., LL.

72. "Kurt Vonnegut," episode 316, *Real Time with Bill Maher*, HBO, September 9, 2005.

73. KV, *God Bless You, Mr. Rosewater*, 189.

74. Ibid., 30–31.

75. Marvin, *Kurt Vonnegut: A Critical Companion*, 111.

76. KV, *God Bless You, Mr. Rosewater*, 23.

77. "Rubin Relents," *Time*, August 11, 1980.

78. Wolf, "Thru Time and Space with Kurt Vonnegut, Jr."

79. *Essential Vonnegut: Interviews Conducted by Walter Miller.*

80. Sally Quinn, "Sad Song for McGovern," *Washington Post*, June 24, 1972.

81. "Carol Troy Interviews Kurt Vonnegut," *Rags.*

82. A young woman sent a photo of herself in front of a movie poster for a pornographic movie, preparing to eat a banana split heaped with whipped cream.

83. Illegible signature, July 7, 1975, Vonnegut mss., LL.

84. *Essential Vonnegut: Interviews Conducted by Walter Miller.*

85. Mayo, *Kurt Vonnegut: The Gospel from Outer Space*, 45.

86. *Essential Vonnegut: Interviews Conducted by Walter Miller.*

87. KV, "Introduction," in *Our Time Is Now: Notes from the High School Underground*, ed. John Birmingham (New York: Bantam, 1970), x.

88. KV, *Welcome to the Monkey House*, xv.

89. The author attended an appearance by Hunter Thompson in the early 1970s. "Duke," carrying a bottle of liquor, seemed to be enjoying the nonsense of his onstage character as much as the college students trying to provoke him.

90. Rodney S. Gould, e-mail, January 4, 2010.

91. Hilary Masters, e-mail, January 10, 2010.

92. KV, *Wampeters, Foma & Granfalloons*, xiii–ix.

93. Kurt Adams, interview, September 20, 2007.

94. Todd, "The Masks of Kurt Vonnegut, Jr."

95. KV to JV, May 1, 1972, private collection. Jill wasn't living with Kurt; according to a personal note to Bernard Malamud dated August 1, 1972, her address was 971 First Avenue. Oregon State University, Special Collections, Bernard Malamud Papers, 1949–2007.

96. KV to JV, May 1, 1972, private collection.

97. KV, *Wampeters, Foma & Granfalloons*, 202.

98. Scott Horton, "November 1972: Vonnegut vs. the Republicans," *Harper's*, April 2007.

99. KV, *Wampeters, Foma & Granfalloons*, 189.

100. Ibid., 195.

101. KV to NV, September 10, 1972, private collection.

102. Fiene, "Getting Through Life," part 2.

103. The reception of *Slaughterhouse-Five* was the first indication that Vonnegut's novels don't translate easily to the screen, not thus far, at least. His explanation was that they lacked a character—himself as the narrator. Another difficulty is that his characters tend to be personified ideas, which was his intention.

104. Donald M. Fiene to KV, May 12, 1972, Fiene mss., LL.

105. KV to Donald M. Fiene, October 12, 1972, Fiene mss., LL.

106. Fiene, "Getting Through Life," book 8, part 2.

107. Donald M. Fiene, "Kurt Vonnegut's Popularity in the Soviet Union and His Affinities with Russian Literature," *Russian Literature Triquarterly* 14 (1976): 166–84.

108. Fiene, "Elements of Dostoevsky in the Novels of Kurt Vonnegut."

109. Ibid.

110. Fiene, "Getting Through Life," book 8, part 2.

111. Ibid.

112. KV, "Invite Rita Rait to America!" *New York Times Book Review*, January 28, 1973.

113. KV to JV, October 19, 1972, private collection.

114. Dag Hammarskjöld, *Markings* (New York: Knopf, 1964), 10.

115. KV to JV, November 26, 1972, private collection.

116. Ibid.

117. KV, *Breakfast of Champions*, 4.

118. Ray Mungo, interview, January 22, 2007.

119. Ibid.

120. KV to JV, December 27, 1972, private collection.

121. JV to KV, January 4, 1973, private collection.

122. JV to Donald Farber, May 14, 1972, Vonnegut mss., LL.

123. Lynn Meyer, interview, August 22, 2007.

124. JV to KV, March 12, 1973, private collection.

125. C. Gerald Fraser, "Protesters Hold Vigils and Walks," *New York Times*, January 21, 1973.

126. KV, "Physicist, Purge Thyself," *Chicago Tribune*, June 22, 1969.

127. KV to Jerome Klinkowitz, November 29, 1972, private collection.

128. Donald C. Farber to KV, February 18, 1975, Vonnegut mss., LL.

129. KV to NV, September 10, 1972, private collection.

130. KV, *Sirens of Titan*, 1.

131. KV, *Breakfast of Champions*, 215.

132. Griffith, "The Moral Egotist," 50.

133. William Rodney Allen, *Understanding Kurt Vonnegut* (Columbia: University of South Carolina Press, 1991), 105.

134. KV, *Breakfast of Champions*, 215.

135. Woo, "His Popular Novels Blended Social Criticism, Dark Humor."

136. Standish, *"Playboy* Interview."

137. KV, *Breakfast of Champions*, 301.

138. Ibid., 302.

139. *Essential Vonnegut: Interviews Conducted by Walter Miller.* Martin Amis took heart from the "largeness of vision" and "irreverence for language" found in Joseph Heller, Saul Bellow, and Kurt Vonnegut. "I think it makes American writers more ambitious and that's a healthy thing because they tackle bigger subjects. There's a fatal sort of quiet about the English novel: you get these finely tuned little novels about middle-life crises." Michiko Kakutani, "What Motivates Writers?" *New York Times*, August 20, 1981.

140. Standish, *"Playboy* Interview."

141. Ben Yarmolinsky, interview, February 20, 2008.

142. Neil A. Lewis, "Adam Yarmolinsky Dies at 77; Led Revamping of Government," *New York Times*, January 7, 2000.

143. Robert Sargent Shriver Jr., speech, memorial for Adam Yarmolinsky, Albin O. Kuhn Library, University of Maryland, Baltimore, May 4, 2000.

144. Lewis, "Adam Yarmolinsky Dies at 77."

145. Caleb Warren, September 19, 2007.

146. David R. Slavitt, interview, August 5, 2007.

147. EV, interview, September 20, 2007.

148. David R. Slavitt, interview, August 5, 2007.

149. Caleb Warren, interview, September 19, 2007.

150. KV to Vance Bourjaily, October 26, 1973, Vance Bourjaily Papers, Bowdoin College, Brunswick, ME.

151. KV to NV, October 21, 1973, private collection.

152. KV, "A New Scheme for Real Writers."

153. KV to Josephine Harris, April 13, 1970, Special Collections, University of Delaware.

154. Standish, "*Playboy* Interview."

155. KV quoted in Paul Engle, "A Point that Must Be Raised: The Equalization of Fiction," *Chicago Tribune*, June 10, 1973.

156. Peter Reed, *The Short Fiction of Kurt Vonnegut*, vol. 1 of Contributions to the Study of American Literature (Westport, CT: Greenwood Press, 1997), 22.

157. KV to JV, December 5, 1973, private collection.

158. Glenys G. Unruh and William M. Alexander, *Innovations in Secondary Education* (New York: Holt, Rinehart and Winston, 1974), 63–64.

159. KV, letter to members of the American Civil Liberties Union, n.d., Department of Special Collection, Stanford University Libraries. The ACLU filed suit on behalf of the teacher, and on June 9, 1970, she was reinstated.

160. "Court Throws Book at School Board Censors," *Chicago Tribune*, August 31, 1976.

161. "Good Citizenship," *Coshocton Tribune*, July 11, 1974.

162. William K. Stevens, "Dakota Town Dumbfounded at Criticism of Book Burning by Order of the School Board," *New York Times*, November 16, 1973.

163. "Novel Is Burned by School Board," *New York Times*, November 11, 1973.

164. KV to Charles McCarthy, November 16, 1973, SLPF.

165. "The Growing Battle of the Books," *Time*, January 19, 1981. Although the teacher lost his job, he won an out-of-court settlement in a suit filed on his behalf by the American Civil Liberties Union. *Slaughterhouse-Five* is one of the one hundred most often banned or challenged books in the United States, according to the American Library Association.

166. Robley Wilson, e-mail, November 27, 2007.

167. KV, interview by Loree Rackstraw, August 1973, Rod Library Special Collections and University Archives, University of Northern Iowa, Cedar Falls.

168. NV, interview, September 20, 2007.

169. Edward Grossman, "Vonnegut & His Audience," *Commentary*, July, 1974, 40.

170. Tom W. Smith, "Liberal and Conservative Trends in the United States Since World War II," *Public Opinion Quarterly* 54 (1990): 479–507.

171. KV, "Address to Graduating Class at Bennington College, 1970," first published in *Vogue* as "Up Is Better Than Down," Kurt Vonnegut Papers, McFarlin Library, University of Tulsa, Tulsa, OK.

172. Sheldon Frank, review of *Wampeters, Foma & Granfallons*, by Kurt Vonnegut Jr., *Chicago Tribune*, May 12, 1974.

173. Benjamin DeMott, "Vonnegut's Otherworldly Laughter," *Saturday Review*, May 1, 1971, 38.

174. KV to JV, October 30, 1974, private collection.

12: Ripped Off

1. Loree Rackstraw, e-mail, June 28, 2010.

2. KV, *Hocus Pocus* (1990; repr., New York: Berkley, 1997), 113.

3. Rackstraw, *Love as Always, Kurt*, 54.

4. Ibid., 56.

5. Philip José Farmer, interview, February 2, 2008.

6. Rackstraw, *Love as Always, Kurt*, 58.

7. Donald C. Fiene to Loree Rackstraw, April 6, 1977, Loree Lee Rackstraw Papers, Rod Library Special Collections, University of Northern Iowa, Cedar Rapids.

8. Philip José Farmer, interview, February 2, 2008.

9. KV, letter to the editor, *Science Fiction Review*, November 15, 1975.

10. Philip José Farmer, interview, February 2, 2008.

11. Mark Royden Winchell, *Too Good to Be True: The Life and Work of Leslie Fiedler* (Columbia: University of Missouri Press, 2002), 284. The timing of Fiedler's remarks on television in April 1975 indicating that he had read the novel, and Loree's recollection that Kurt had received a call from Farmer seeking permission only in February, can be explained this way: an installment of *Venus on the Half-Shell* had already appeared in the December 1974 issue of the *Magazine of Fantasy and Science Fiction*. Apparently, Farmer's publisher, Dell, wanted Vonnegut's permission at the last minute to use "Kilgore Trout" as the author of the complete novel.

12. Susan Read to KV, July 28, 1975, Vonnegut mss., LL.

13. Per Lippert to KV, January 26, 1976, Vonnegut mss., LL.

14. Donald M. Fiene to KV, June 27, 1975, Fiene mss., LL.

15. Philip José Farmer, Peoria, Illinois, February 25, 1999. The Official Philip José Farmer Home Page, www.pjfarmer.com.

16. KV, letter, September 2, 1975, *Science Fiction Review*, November 1975, 10.

17. KV to Vance Bourjaily, June 19, 1975, Vance Bourjaily Papers, Bowdoin College Library, Brunswick, ME.

18. Frederik Pohl, interview, September 13, 2007.

19. Ibid. These deliberations eventually led to the Copyright Act of 1976, which remains the primary basis of copyright law in the United States.

20. KV to Seymour Lawrence, May 6, 1976, SLPF.

21. KV to Seymour Lawrence, July 15, 1976, SLPF.

22. Dan L. Fendel to KV, June 19, 1975, Vonnegut mss., LL.

23. KV to Donald C. Farber, June 27, 1975, Vonnegut mss., LL.

24. KV to Dan L. Fendel, June 27, 1975, Vonnegut mss., LL.

25. KV to Donald C. Farber, June 28, 1975, Vonnegut mss., LL.

26. Dan L. Fendel to KV, n.d., Vonnegut mss., LL.

27. Donald C. Farber to L. Glenn Hardie, August 1, 1975, Vonnegut mss., LL.

28. KV, *Slapstick*, 9.

29. Ibid., 11.

30. Ibid., 12.

31. "Kurt Vonnegut at NYU," Pacifica Radio Archives.

32. Vonnegut often mentioned birthdays, anniversaries, and holidays in his letters. "Today would have been my sister's fifty-ninth birthday. Think of that." KV to Seymour Lawrence, November 18, 1966, SLPF. He wrote to Gail Sheehy, author of *Passages*, expressing his admiration for her interpretation of stages in life.

33. KV, "The Noodle Factory" (speech, Connecticut College, New London, CT, October 1, 1976).

34. KV to NV, March 17, 1974, private collection.

35. Standish, "*Playboy* Interview."

36. "In Vonnegut's View Life Is Absurd, But Not Worth Leaving," *Chicago Tribune*.

37. KV to NV, April 29, 1977, private collection.

38. KV to NV, August 25, 1975, private collection.

39. NV, interview, September 23, 2007.

40. NV to KV, February 14, 2002, private collection.

41. Nancy J. Andreasen, a professor of psychiatry at the University of Iowa with a PhD in English, conducted a fifteen-year study of thirty creative writers on the faculty of the Iowa Writers' Workshop. Thirty percent of the writers were alcoholics, compared with 7 percent in a group of nonwriters. Eighty percent of the writers had had an episode of affective disorders, i.e., a major bout of depression including manic-depressive illness, compared with 30 percent in the control group. Two thirds of the ill writers had received psychiatric treatment for their disorders. Two of the thirty writers committed suicide before the study ended. The study appears in the October 1987 issue of the *American Journal of Psychiatry*. Ann Waldron, "Writers and Alcohol," *Washington Post*, March 14, 1989.

42. KV to Irina Grivnina, April 10, 1979, Fiene mss., LL. KV to KB, February 20, 1953, private collection.

43. KV to Miller Harris, August 10, 1988, private collection.

44. KV, *Bluebeard: A Novel* (1987; repr., New York: Delacorte, 1998), 14–15.

45. Dan Wakefield, interview, April 29, 2010.

46. Annie G. Rogers, "Marguerite Sechehaye and Renee: A Feminist Reading of Two Accounts of a Treatment," *International Journal of Qualitative Studies in Education* 5, no. 3 (July 1992): 245–51.

47. Short, *Something to Believe In*, 292.

48. Ibid.

49. Jed Horne, "Mark Vonnegut Traces His Harrowing Journey Through Wildest Schizophrenia," *People*, November 3, 1975.

50. Moravec and Rank, "The Iowan Interview: Kurt Vonnegut, Jr.," *Northern Iowan*, April 5, 1977.

51. John Leonard, "Why Is Kurt Vonnegut Smiling?" *New York Times*, March 25, 1976.

52. KV, *Palm Sunday*, 186.

53. KV to Donald C. Fiene, May 19, 1976, Fiene mss., LL.

54. EV, e-mail, January 11, 2010.

55. KV, *Slapstick*, 36.

56. Karl, *American Fictions*, 501.

57. Ira Berkow, "He's Fighting to Stay on Top," Associated Press, December 10, 1976.

58. KV to Osborn Elliot (*Newsweek* editor), December 20, 1975, Vonnegut mss., LL.

59. Berkow, "He's Fighting to Stay on Top." In his review of *Breakfast of Champions*, Prescott had called the novel "manure, of course. Pretentious, hypocritical manure."

60. Roger H. Sale, "Kurt Vonnegut: Writing with Interchangeable Parts," *New York Times*, October 3, 1976.

61. Seymour Epstein, "Hi Ho, or Vonnegut Isn't Quite so Funny as He Used to Be," *Chicago Tribune*, October 10, 1976.

62. Arlene Donovan, interview, June 17, 2008.

63. Marvin, *Kurt Vonnegut*, 11.

64. Berkow, "He's Fighting to Stay on Top."

65. KV, *Breakfast of Champions*, 4.

66. Seltzer, "Dresden and Vonnegut's Creative Testament of Guilt," 55–69.

67. KV, *Slapstick*, 13.

68. Ibid., 21.

69. Donald C. Fiene to Loree Rackstraw, May 9, 1977. Lora Lee Rackstraw Papers, Rod Library Special Collections, University of Northern Iowa, Cedar Rapids, Iowa.

70. Berkow, "He's Fighting to Stay on Top."

71. "In Vonnegut's View, Life Is Absurd But Not Worth Leaving," *Chicago Tribune*.

72. Short, *Something to Believe In*, 300.

73. Vance Bourjaily, interview, March 17, 2008.

74. "Jill Krementz," Contemporary Authors Online.

75. KV to NV, March 15, 1977, private collection.

76. Bellamy, *Literary Luxuries*, 114.

77. Jerome Klinkowitz, *Keeping Literary Company: Working with Writers since the Sixties* (Albany: State University of New York, 1998), 195.

78. Moravec and Rank, "The Iowan Interview: Kurt Vonnegut, Jr."

79. Ibid.

80. KV to Donald C. Fiene, November 11, 1977, Fiene mss., LL.

81. KV to Donald L. Farber, November 12, 1977, Vonnegut mss., LL.

82. Lewis, "Adam Yarmolinsky Dies at 77."

83. EV, interview, September 20, 2007.

84. NV, interview, May 3, 2008.

85. JV to KV, September 23, 1978, private collection.

86. KV to NV, April 29, 1977, private collection.

87. Ibid.

88. KV to Bernard Malamud, February 9, 1979, Bernard Malamud Papers, Harry Ransom Humanities Research Center, University of Texas, Austin.

89. KV to Donald C. Fiene, February 10, 1979, Fiene mss., LL.

90. KV to Vance Bourjaily, January 19, 1978, Vance Bourjaily Papers, Bowdoin College, Brunswick, ME.

91. Donald C. Fiene to KV, April 18, 1979, Fiene mss., LL.

92. KV to Donald C. Fiene, May 14, 1979, Fiene mss., LL.

93. Seymour Lawrence to KV, February 11, 1979, Vonnegut mss., LL.

94. KV, "Speech at the Anti-Nuclear Rally," Washington, DC, May 6, 1979, SLPF.

95. KV to Donald C. Fiene, February 10, 1979, Fiene mss., LL.

96. Lynn Meyer, interview, August 22, 2008.

97. KV to KB, n.d. 1953, private collection.

98. KV to NV, July 10, 1979, private collection.

99. Jill Krementz to Emma Vonnegut, August 10, 1979, private collection.

100. KV to KB, September 15, 1979, private collection.

101. KV to Gail Godwin, September 14, 1979, Gail Godwin Papers, Wilson Library, University of North Carolina.

102. Stephen Singular, "The Sound and Fury Over Fiction: John Gardner Rails Against Fellow Novelists," *New York Times*, July 8, 1979.

103. KV to Donald C. Fiene, February 10, 1979, Fiene mss., LL.

104. In addition to the shelter sixty feet belowground in *Slaughterhouse-Five*, Paul Proteus is kidnapped by the Ghost Shirt Society in *Player Piano* and held in an air-raid shelter, Howard Campbell in *Mother Night* writes his memoirs from a basement cell in Old Jerusalem, and Eliot Rosewater's relative Fred finds the Rosewater family history in his basement.

105. Walter Shear, "Kurt Vonnegut: The Comic Fate of the Sensibility," in vol. 31 of *The Feeling of Being: Sensibility in Postwar American Fiction* (New York: Peter Lang, 2002), 215–39.

106. KV, *Player Piano*, 320.

107. KV to NV, September 8, 1979, private collection.

108. Ibid.

109. Ibid.

110. Ibid.

111. Kendall Landis, interview, June 12, 2008.

13: Looking for Mr. Vonnegut

1. KV to José Donoso, January 28, 1981, JDP.
2. EV, e-mail, June 23, 2008.
3. NV, interview, September 20, 2007.
4. KV to José Donoso, January 28, 1981, JDP.
5. KV to Donald M. Fiene, December 20, 1980, Fiene mss., LL.
6. KV to José Donoso, January 28, 1981, JDP.
7. Seymour Lawrence to KV, February 2, 1981, Vonnegut mss., LL.
8. KV to José Donoso, January 28, 1981, JDP.
9. KV to Donald M. Fiene, September 20, 1980, Fiene mss., LL.
10. *Essential Vonnegut: Interviews Conducted by Walter Miller.*
11. Suzanne McConnell, interview, January 18, 2007.
12. JV, journal, n.d.
13. KV, *Palm Sunday*, 227.
14. Ibid., 229.
15. JV to José Donoso and Maria Pilar Donoso, January 30, 1982, JDP.
16. JV, notes, March 3, 1981, private collection.
17. JV to José Donoso and Maria Pilar Donoso, January 30, 1982, JDP.
18. Ibid.
19. JV Yarmolinsky, *Angels Without Wings,* 131.
20. KV to José Donoso, January 28, 1981, JDP.
21. John Irving, e-mail, January 28, 2007.
22. KV to Jerry Klinkowitz, January 16, 1981.
23. John Leonard, review of *Jailbird*, by Kurt Vonnegut Jr., *New York Times*, September 7, 1979.
24. KV, *Palm Sunday*, 291.
25. Ibid.
26. Malcolm Cowley and Alfred Kazin, quoted in "Behind the Cover: How Five Critics Saw the Decade," *Chicago Tribune*, December 16, 1979.
27. Anatole Broyard, "Reputations Die Slow," *New York Times*, April 19, 1981.
28. KV to Anatole Broyard, April 19, 1981, Christopher Lehmann-Haupt Collection, Howard Gotlieb Archival Research Center, Boston University.
29. Curt Suplee, "Vonnegut's High-Voltage Visions," *Washington Post*, May 15, 1981.
30. Donald C. Farber to Daniel M. Pepper, May 21, 1981, Vonnegut mss., LL.
31. Donald M. Fiene to Kurt Vonnegut, July 9, 1982, Fiene mss., LL. Fiene had received a letter from Vonnegut on June 28 outlining the details.
32. Suplee, "Vonnegut's High-Voltage Visions."
33. KB to KV, July 20, 1982, private collection.
34. Ibid.
35. KV to KB, July 25, 1982, private collection.
36. KB to KV, September 7, 1982, private collection.
37. KV to José and Maria Pilar Donoso, October 29, 1982, JDP.
38. Ibid.
39. KV to NV, September 16, 1982, private collection.
40. Paul A. Camp, "A Birthday Bash for Claiborne—And It's a Potluck Feast," *Chicago Tribune*, September 16, 1982.
41. John Thiel, e-mail, December 17, 2008. Thiel was taking notes for the magazine *Ionisphere: The Journal of the National Fantasy Fan Federation* and said Vonnegut extemporized from his prepared speech.

42. KV, "Eugene V. Debs Award" (speech), Holiday Inn, Terre Haute, IN, November 7, 1981, Fiene mss., LL.

43. KV, *Deadeye Dick: A Novel* (1982; repr., New York: Dial, 1999), 235.

44. KV, "Avoiding the Big Bang," *New York Times*, June 13, 1982.

45. KV, *Deadeye Dick*, 104.

46. Ibid., 127.

47. KV, *Slapstick*, 2.

48. KV, *Deadeye Dick*, 1.

49. Amis, *The Moronic Inferno*, 133.

50. Loree Rackstraw to KV, January 7, 1984, Vonnegut mss., LL.

51. Judy Klemesrud, "Jill Krementz Carves a Niche," *New York Times*, November 14, 1982.

52. KV to KB, November 18, 1982, private collection.

53. "Happy Birthday, Kurt Vonnegut" (guest list), Gail Godwin Papers, Wilson Library, University of North Carolina, Chapel Hill.

54. Elizabeth C. Hirschman, "Babies for Sale: Market Ethics and the New Reproductive Technologies," *Journal of Consumer Affairs* 25, no. 2 (1991): 358+.

55. EV, e-mail, June 23, 2008.

56. KV to Miller Harris, December 20, 1982, private collection.

57. David R. Slavitt, "Looking for Mr. Vonnegut," *Philadelphia*, November 1982, 79+.

58. Ibid.

59. Ibid.

60. KV to Miller Harris, December 20, 1982, private collection.

61. David R. Slavitt to KV, January 17, 1983, Vonnegut mss., LL.

62. Roger Langen to Donald L. Farber, March 9, 1983, Vonnegut mss., LL. Langen was editor of the *Literary Review of Canada* and arranging for an interview with Vonnegut through Farber.

63. Craig Canine to KV, February 19, 1983, Vonnegut mss., LL.

64. Craig Canine, e-mail, January 5, 2010.

65. Ibid.

66. Dale Watson, interview, February 9, 2008.

67. JV to Maria Pilar Donoso, October 21, 1983, JDP.

68. KV to José and Maria Pilar Donoso, August 30, 1984, JDP.

69. Rackstraw, *Love as Always, Kurt*, 104.

70. Kristin McMurran, David Hutchings, and Pamela Lansden, "The Famous Turn Out For (and Some Are Turned Off by) the Bicoastal Previews of Al Pacino's Bloody 'Scarface,'" *People*, December 19, 1983, 55.

71. Bill McCloud, "What Should We Tell Our Children about Vietnam?" *American Heritage*, May–June 1988.

72. Anne Bernays, interview, December 4, 2009.

73. EV, e-mail, January 9, 2010.

74. Scott Vonnegut, e-mail, September 27, 2010.

75. KV, "No More Dangerous Than a Banana Split," *American Libraries*, February 1983.

76. Rackstraw, *Love as Always, Kurt*, 106.

77. Ibid., 107.

78. Ibid., 107–8.

79. Loree Rackstraw to KV, January 7, 1984, Vonnegut mss., LL.

80. KV to Lester J. Tanner (attorney), July 1991, private collection.

81. NV, interview, September 20, 2007.

82. EV, e-mail, January 9, 2010.

83. NV, interview, September 20, 2007.

84. León Grinberg, *Guilt and Depression*, trans. Christine Trollope (London: Karnac Books, 1992), 107.

85. EV, e-mail, January 9, 2010.

86. Loree Rackstraw to KV, March 18, 1984, Vonnegut mss., LL.

14: Dear Celebrity

1. EV, e-mail, December 18, 2008.

2. Loree Rackstraw to KV, March 18, 1984, Vonnegut mss., LL.

3. Ibid.

4. KV, "Algren as I Knew Him," in Nelson Algren, *The Man with the Golden Arm* (New York: Seven Stories Press, 1999), 368.

5. KV, interview, March 12, 2007.

6. KV to Ben Hitz, April 18, 1984, private collection.

7. Kurt Adams played matchmaker for both Nanny and Edie. His roommate at college, Scott Prior, became Nanny's husband, and John Squibb, a friend from Barnstable, married Edie in September 1985.

8. KV to José and Maria Pilar Donoso, February 16, 1985, JDP.

9. KV to NV, March 11, 1985, private collection.

10. James Lipton, interview, July 30, 2009.

11. KV to Paul Engle, June 27, 1985, Paul Engle Papers, Stewart Memorial Library, Coe College, Cedar Rapids, Iowa.

12. KV to Helen Meyer, March 12, 1976, SLPF.

13. Ibid.

14. Seymour Lawrence to KV, May 14, 1985, Vonnegut mss., LL.

15. Vonnegut mss., LL.

16. Patrick J. Deneen, "Folk Tales," *Claremont Review of Books*, Winter 2007.

17. Gilbert McInnis, "Evolutionary Mythology in the Writings of Kurt Vonnegut, Jr," *Critique: Studies in Contemporary Fiction* 46, no. 4 (Summer 2005): 383–96.

18. Charles Darwin, *Journal of Researches into the Geology and Natural History of the Various Countries Visited by H.M.S. Beagle* (London: Henry Colburn, 1839), 454.

19. Richard Darwin Keynes, ed., *Charles Darwin's Beagle Diary* (Cambridge: Cambridge University Press, 1988), 352.

20. Edward J. Larson, *God and Science on the Galapagos Islands* (New York: Basic Books, 2001), 61.

21. Michiko Kakutani, "Books of the Times," *New York Times*, September 25, 1985.

22. "Kurt Vonnegut," in Contemporary Authors Online.

23. Thomas M. Disch, "Jokes Across the Generation Gap," in *On Science Fiction* (Ann Arbor: University of Michigan Press, 2005), 67–74.

24. KV to Donald L. Fiene, November 15, 1985, Fiene mss, LL.

25. Standish, "*Playboy* Interview."

26. William F. Buckley, "Care Package to Moscow," *National Review*, June 28, 1985.

27. "Hitting the Books," *Time*, May 27, 1985.

28. Buckley, "Care Package to Moscow."

29. "Hitting the Books," *Time*, May 27, 1985.

30. Herbert Mitgang, "Soviet Bars Three from Book Fair," *New York Times*, September 4, 1985.

31. "What Does PEN Have to Offer?" episode 673, *Firing Line*, December 2, 1985. Southern Educational Communications Association.

32. KV, "He Leadeth Us from Porn; God Bless You Edwin Meese," *Nation*, January 25, 1986, 65+.

33. Rhoda Koenig, "At Play in the Fields of the Word," *New York Magazine*, February 3, 1986, 40–47.

34. President Truman vetoed the McCarran-Walter Act bill because he regarded it as "un-American." The veto was overridden in both the House and the Senate, 2–1.

35. Robert Pear, "U.S. May Back Some Changes in Aliens Law," *New York Times*, August 12, 1986. Also "Testimony of Kurt Vonnegut before the International Economic Policy Subcommittee of the Senate Foreign Relations Committee," PEN American Center, August 11, 1986.

36. Donald C. Farber to Bruce Campbell, December 27, 1985, Vonnegut mss., LL. Unfortunately, Mr. Shawn died suddenly.

37. Jess Walter, interview, November 23, 2007.

38. EV, e-mail, March 2, 2010.

39. Betty Stanton, interview, February 9, 2008.

40. KV, *Fates Worse Than Death*, 70.

41. Ibid., 71.

42. KV, "Requiem: The Hocus Pocus Laundromat," *North American Review*, December 1986, 31.

43. Ibid., 29–35.

44. KV to NV, June 21, 1988, private collection.

45. EV, e-mail, April 6, 2010.

46. KV, *Timequake*, 135.

47. KV to NV, November 8, 1989, private collection.

48. Ibid.

49. KV to Miller Harris, August 10, 1988, private collection.

50. KV, *Bluebeard*, 137.

51. KV to George Strong, April 23, 1989, private collection. Strong was one of the soldiers on the wooden cart used by Vonnegut and other ex-prisoners to return to Dresden.

52. KV to NV, May 5, 1987, private collection.

53. KV to José Donoso, January 28, 1981, JDP.

54. KV to Larry Kessenich, March 7, 1987, Vonnegut mss., LL.

55. KV to Lester J. Tanner (attorney), July 1991, private collection.

56. A novelist who wishes to remain anonymous recalls the "house genius" nickname for Kurt.

57. EV, e-mail, December 13, 2008.

58. Robert Maslansky, MD, interview, November 20, 2007.

59. KV interviewed by David Brancaccio, NOW (PBS), October 7, 2005.

60. Barbara Isard to Donald C. Farber, December 9, 1987, Vonnegut mss., LL.

61. Michael F. Jacobson, executive director, Center for Science in the Public Interest, to KV, January 23, 1984, Vonnegut mss., LL.

62. Richard Gehman Papers, Helen A. Ganser Library, Millersville University, Millersville, PA.

63. Susan S. Neville, "Kurt Vonnegut," in *Sailing the Inland Sea: On Writing, Literature, and Land* (Bloomington: Indiana University Press, 2007).

64. KV, *Hocus Pocus*, 87.

65. Jay McInerney, "Still Asking the Embarrassing Questions," *New York Times*, September 9, 1990.

66. The Honorable Arnold Rappaport, Court of Common Pleas, Lehigh County, Allentown, PA, Bar Memorials, February 4, 2008.
67. KV to NV, June 13, 1990, private collection.
68. Jerome Klinkowitz, *Vonnegut's America* (Columbia: University of South Carolina Press, 2009), 124.
69. Anonymous, interview, March 25, 2010.
70. KV deposition to Lester Tanner (attorney), July 1991, private collection.
71. Ibid.

15: Waiting to Die

1. KV to Lester Tanner (attorney), July 1991, private collection.
2. Robert Maslansky, MD, interview, November 20, 2007.
3. Neville, *Sailing the Inland Sea*, 39.
4. KV to Ian T. MacMillan, July 17, 1991, private collection. Vonnegut, along with Woody Allen, contributed to a "rescue fund" for Yates. Kurt Vonnegut to Loree Rackstraw, February 15, 1991, private collection. Kurt also organized a fund to pay the medical bills of Andre Dubus, his former student at Iowa who was struck by an automobile in 1986 and wheelchair-bound for the rest of his life.
5. Ian T. MacMillan, e-mail, August 30, 2007.
6. Robert B. Weide, interview, May 24, 2008.
7. KV to Lester Tanner (attorney), July 1991, private collection.
8. Stephen M. DuBrul to Peter Drucker, September 22, 1992, Claremont Colleges Digital Library.
9. KV to Lester Tanner (attorney), July 1991, private collection.
10. Ibid.
11. Mallory, "The Kurt and Joe Show."
12. Under the old rules, a member of the academy had to pass away before a member of the institute was eligible for the academy.
13. KV to Jerome Klinkowitz, November 15, 1993, private collection.
14. "Murder in Turkey" (letter), *New York Review of Books*, May 13, 1993.
15. Allan Kozinn, review of "Kurt Vonnegut's Reinterpretation of 'L'Histoire du Soldat,'" *New York Times*, May 8, 1993. Vonnegut missed the larger theme of social inequity he might have written about. Slovik grew up poor in Detroit. His first of a series of juvenile arrests was for stealing bread. On the last day of his life, he wrote to his wife, "They are not shooting me for deserting the United States Army— thousands of guys have done that. They're shooting me for bread I stole when I was 12 years old."
16. James C. Adams Jr., "Thirteen Haiku," Vonnegut mss., LL. Vonnegut sent the letter to a few close friends.
17. James C. Adams Jr. to KV, November 11, 2002, Vonnegut mss., LL.
18. KV to Miller and Mary Louise Harris, April 28, 2000, private collection.
19. NV, interview, September 20, 2007.
20. Herman Wouk to KV, August 12, 1993, Vonnegut mss., LL.
21. Robert B. Weide, interview, May 24, 2008.
22. Reverend Rosemary Lloyd, "A Dream of Peace" (sermon, First Church in Boston, Boston, MA, April 15, 2007). Crone's headstone is in range 4, lot 116. Lloyd was a lecture series coordinator at the time who guided Vonnegut to Mt. Hope.
23. "Pvt. Edward Crone, Jr. Believed to Have Died in German Prison Camp," *New York Post*, July 19, 1945.
24. Lloyd, "A Dream of Peace."

25. Williams, "Dresden Bombing," *The Pulteney St. Survey*.
26. Bernard Vonnegut, "Adventures in Fluid Flow: Generating Interesting Dendritic Patterns," *Leonardo* 31, no. 3 (1998): 205.
27. Bernard Vonnegut to KV, n.d., Vonnegut mss., LL.
28. KV to Bernard Vonnegut, October 11, 1995, private collection.
29. Michel Lopez, "Talk Soup," *Albany Times Union*, April 13, 1997.
30. KV to Ollie M. Lyon Jr., June 18, 1996, private collection.
31. Kurt Vonnegut (KV's nephew), interview, March 26, 2010.
32. Ibid.
33. KV, *Mother Night*, 7.
34. Jerome Klinkowitz, "Robert Weide's *Mother Night*: A Review," *North American Review*, September–October 1997, 44–48. Klinkowitz argues that Vonnegut's voice is more evident in *Mother Night* than in his other films, but the "one character short" problem is typical, to some degree, of all films made from Vonnegut's novels.
35. Robert B. Weide, "The Morning After Mother Night," *Realist*, Autumn 1997.
36. Robert B. Weide, interview, May 24, 2008.
37. KV to KB, October 24, 1996, private collection.
38. KV to Emily Louise Diamond, November 13, 1996, private collection.
39. KV, interview, September 19, 2007.
40. Robert Maslansky to KV, April 28, 1997, private collection.
41. John Latham, e-mail, February 28, 2010.
42. KV, interview, December 13, 2006.
43. KV, *Slapstick*, 3.
44. KV to Jerome Klinkowitz, January 19, 1997, private collection.
45. KV, *Timequake*, 23.
46. *Hamlet*, act 3, scene 1.
47. It appears in *A Man Without a Country*.
48. Victor Schultz, e-mail, November 25, 2006.
49. Mary Robinson, interview, June 7, 2007.
50. KV to NV, January 20, 1996, private collection.
51. Ibid.
52. Jerome Klinkowitz, *Vonnegut's America*, 124.
53. Matthew Flamm and Alexandra Jacobs, "Mailer Time," *Entertainment Weekly*, May 22, 1998, 63.
54. Lee Stringer, interview, November 27, 2007.
55. KV, interview, March 14, 2007.
56. Anonymous, interview, December 19, 2007.
57. KV to NV, December 3, 1999, private collection.
58. Ibid.
59. KV to NV, December 14, 1999, private collection.
60. "Vonnegut in Critical Condition Following Fire," CNN, February 1, 2000.
61. James Brady, "Taps for Kurt," Forbes.com, posted on April 12, 2007.
62. Ibid.
63. Ibid.
64. KV, interview by Leonard Lopate, *The Leonard Lopate Show*, September 27, 2005.
65. NV, e-mail, July 9, 2010.
66. Brady, "Taps for Kurt."
67. NV to KV, January 2000, private collection.
68. Kerry O'Keefe, interview, September 20, 2007.
69. Ibid.

70. NV, interview, September 20, 2007.

71. Vance Bourjaily, interview, March 17, 2008.

72. Robert B. Weide to KV, March 5, 2000, private collection.

73. Tracy Kidder, *Home Town* (New York: Random House, 1999), 214; also, KV to KB, March 6, 2001, private collection.

74. Kerry O'Keefe, interview, September 20, 2007.

75. Ibid.

76. Allison Mitchell, interview, February 7, 2008.

77. KV to KB, March 25, 2000, private collection.

78. NV, e-mail, May 16, 2008.

79. KV to Gail Godwin, July 1, 2000, Gail Godwin Papers, Wilson Library, University of North Carolina, Chapel Hill.

80. Doug Blackburn, "New York State of Mind," *Times Union*, December 17, 2000.

81. Ibid.

82. Ben Bush, review of *A Man Without a Country*, *San Francisco Chronicle*, October 9, 2005.

83. Laurie Fenlason, "Acclaimed Satirist and Best-Selling Novelist to Give Public 'Performance' at Smith," Smith College press release, September 26, 2000.

84. David Abel, "So It Goes for Vonnegut," *Boston Globe*, May 5, 2001.

85. Ibid.

86. Ibid.

87. Ibid.

88. Ibid.

89. NV, interview, September 20, 2007.

90. KV to Richard Hiscock, June 26, 2005, private collection.

91. KV to KB, March 6, 2001, private collection.

92. NV, interview, May 3, 2008.

93. NV to KV, May 7, 2001, private collection. In this letter, Nanny acknowledges her father's request.

94. NV to KV, May 7, 2001, private collection. "I accept that you find life not worth living."

95. Vance Bourjaily, interview, March 17, 2008. Bourjaily's wife, Yasmin Mogul, said in Jill's defense that "it becomes very difficult on the younger woman when the older person keeps resorting to alcohol and is not able to function in a way that is safe. With drinking buddies there is a definite consequence later on. And the consequence is not then, when the friends are gone, but later when you are there, and you have to take care of things."

96. J. Rentilly, "The Best Jokes Are Dangerous, an Interview with Kurt Vonnegut," *McSweeney's*, September 2002.

97. Robert Maslansky to Arthur Phillips, November 23, 2003, private collection.

98. Walter A. Vonnegut, interview, April 7, 2007.

99. KV to Jerome Klinkowitz, June 24, 2004, private collection. KV to Benjamin DeMott, September 24, 2004, private collection.

100. KV to the editors of the *New York Times*, September 12, 2002, private collection.

101. Matt Tyrnauer, "America's Writing Forces (Gore Vidal, Norman Mailer, Kurt Vonnegut)," *Vanity Fair*, July 2003, 126.

102. Jacques Barzun, *The House of Intellect* (New York: Harper, 1959), 7.

103. David Nason, "Darkness Visible," *Australian*, November 19, 2005.

104. Mark Vonnegut, "Twisting Vonnegut's Views on Terrorism," *Boston Globe*, December 27, 2005.

105. "Six Sleepers for Fall," *Publishers Weekly*, August 29, 2005, 27.
106. John Freeman, "Laughing Back at Life," *Jerusalem Post*, October 21, 2005.
107. KV, interview by Leonard Lopate, WNYC, September 27, 2005.
108. Douglas Brinkley, "Vonnegut's Apocalypse," *Rolling Stone*, August 24, 2006.
109. Rick Callahan, "Year of Vonnegut," Associated Press, January 11, 2007.
110. KV, interview, March 14, 2007.
111. KV to Alice Fulton, February 8, 2007, private collection.
112. Kerry O'Keefe, interview, September 20, 2007.
113. KV, interview, March 14, 2007.
114. This is a summary of interviews with Lily Vonnegut, Edie Vonnegut, and Knox Burger.
115. Robert Maslansky, MD, interview, November 12, 2007.
116. Robert B. Weide, interview, April 20, 2010.

Bibliography

Vonnegut Bibliography

Works Appearing in Magazines and Newspapers

(ar) = article
(cl) = column
(es) = essay
(ex) = excerpt
(pl) = play
(rv) = review
(ss) = short story

"Report on the Barnhouse Effect," (ss) *Collier's*, February 11, 1950; "Thanasphere," (ss) *Collier's*, September 2, 1950; "EPICAC," (ss) *Collier's*, November 25, 1950; "All the King's Horses," (ss) *Collier's*, February 10, 1951; "Mnemonics," (ss) *Collier's*, April 28, 1951; "The Euphio Question," (ss) *Collier's*, May 12, 1951; "The Foster Portfolio," (ss) *Collier's*, September 8, 1951; "Any Reasonable Offer," (ss) *Collier's*, January 19, 1952; "The Package," (ss) *Collier's*, July 26, 1952; "The No-Talent Kid," (ss) *Saturday Evening Post*, October 25, 1952; "Souvenir," (ss) *Argosy*, December 1952; "Tom Edison's Shaggy Dog," (ss) *Collier's*, March 14, 1953; "Custom-Made Bride," (ss) *Saturday Evening Post*, March 27, 1954; "Ambitious Sophomore," (ss) *Saturday Evening Post*, May 1, 1954; "Deer in the Works," (ss) *Esquire*, April 1955; "The Kid Nobody Could Handle," (ss) *Saturday Evening Post*, September 24, 1955; "The Boy Who Hated Girls," (ss) *Saturday Evening Post*, March 31, 1956; "Miss Temptation," (ss) *Saturday Evening Post*, April 21, 1956; "This Son of Mine," (ss) *Saturday Evening Post*, August 18, 1956; "A Night for Love," (ss) *Saturday Evening Post*, November 23, 1957; "Long Walk to Forever," (ss) *Ladies' Home Journal*, August 1960; "Harrison Bergeron," (ss) *Fantasy & Science Fiction*, October 1961; "The Runaways," (ss) *Saturday Evening Post*, April 15, 1961; "My Name Is Everyone," (ss) *Saturday Evening*

Post, December 16, 1961: also as "Who Am I This Time?"; "The Lie," (ss) *Saturday Evening Post*, February 24, 1962; "Go Back to Your Precious Wife and Son," (ss) *Ladies' Home Journal*, July 1962; "Lovers Anonymous," (ss) *Redbook*, October 1963; *The Boss* by Goffredo Parise, (rv) *New York Times*, October 2, 1966; "The Last Word," (rv) *New York Times*, October 30, 1966; "Teaching the Unteachable," (es) *New York Times*, August 6, 1967; "Welcome to the Monkey House," (ss) *Playboy*, January 1968; "Fortitude," (pl) *Playboy*, September 1968; "Physicist, Purge Thyself," (es) *Chicago Tribune*, June 22, 1969; "Excelsior! We're Going to the Moon, Excelsior!" (es) *New York Times*, July 13, 1969; "Biafra: A People Betrayed," (ar) *McCall's*, April 1970; "Invite Rita Rait to America!" (es) *New York Times Book Review*, January 28, 1973; "A New Scheme for Real Writers," (es) *New York Times*, July 14, 1974; "Un-American Nonsense," (es) *New York Times*, March 24, 1976; "Slapstick; or, Lonesome No More!" (ex) *Playboy*, September 1976; "Books into Ashes," (es) *New York Times*, February 7, 1982; "Avoiding the Big Bang," (es) *New York Times*, June 13, 1982; "Fates Worse Than Death," (es) *North American Review*, December 1982 (transcript of lecture, St. John the Divine, New York, May 23, 1982); "The Worst Addiction of Them All," (es) *Nation*, December 31, 1983; "The Idea Killers," (ar) *Playboy*, January 1984; "A Dream of the Future (Not Excluding Lobsters)," (ss) *Esquire*, August 1985; "He Leadeth Us from Porn; God Bless You, Edwin Meese!" (ar) *Nation*, January 25, 1986; "Can't We Even Leave Jazz Alone?" (es) *New York Times*, December 14, 1986; "Requiem: The Hocus Pocus Laundromat," (es) *North American Review*, December 1986; "Skyscraper National Park & Musings on New York," (ar) *Architectural Digest*, November 1987; "The Lake," (ar) *Architectural Digest*, June 1988; "My Fellow Americans: What I'd Say If They Asked Me," (es) *Nation*, July 1988; "The Courage of Ivan Martin Jirous," (es) *Washington Post*, March 31, 1989; "Slaughter in Mozambique," (ar) *New York Times*, November 14, 1989; "My Visit to Hell," (ar) *Parade Magazine*, January 7, 1990; "Notes from My Bed of Gloom; Or, Why the Joking Had to Stop," (es) *New York Times Book Review*, April 22, 1990; "Hocus Pocus," (ex) *Penthouse*, September 1990; "Heinlein Gets the Last Word," (es) *New York Times Book Review*, December 9, 1990; "Something's Rotten," (es) *New York Times*, April 11, 1991; "Why My Dog Is Not a Humanist," (es) *Humanist*, November 1992; "Timequake," (ex) *Playboy*, December 1997; "Bernard Vonnegut: The Rainmaker," (cl) *New York Times*, January 4, 1998; "Last Words for a Century," (ar) *Playboy*, January 1999; "To Be a Native Middle-Westerner," (es) *Nuvo Newsweekly*, May 20, 1999; "Surviving Niagara," (cl) *Guardian*, January 25, 2003; "Dear Mr. Vonnegut (with Divers Hands)," (cl) *In These Times*, May 26, 2003; "Knowing What's Nice," (cl) *In These Times*, November 6, 2003; "Cold Turkey," (es) *In These Times*, May 31, 2004; "I Love You, Madame Librarian," (es) *In These Times*, August 6, 2004; "Wailing Shall Be in All Streets," (ex) *Playboy*, April 2008.

Novels

Player Piano (1952)
The Sirens of Titan (1959)
Mother Night (1962)
Cat's Cradle (1963)
God Bless You, Mr. Rosewater; or, Pearls Before Swine (1965)
Slaughterhouse-Five; or, The Children's Crusade, a Duty-Dance with Death (1969)
Breakfast of Champions; or, Goodbye Blue Monday! (1973)
Slapstick; or, Lonesome No More! (1976)
Jailbird: A Novel (1979)
Deadeye Dick (1982)
Galápagos: A Novel (1985)
Bluebeard: A Novel (1987)

Hocus Pocus (1990)
Timequake (1997)

Collections
Canary in a Cat House (1961)
Welcome to the Monkey House: A Collection of Short Works (1968)
Bagombo Snuff Box: Uncollected Short Fiction (1999)
God Bless You, Dr. Kevorkian (1999)
A Man Without a Country (2005)
Armageddon in Retrospect; and Other New and Unpublished Writings on War and Peace (2008)
Look at the Birdie: Unpublished Short Fiction (2009)
While Mortals Sleep: Unpublished Short Fiction (2011)

Nonfiction
Wampeters, Foma & Granfalloons (1974)
Palm Sunday: An Autobiographical Collage (1981)
Nothing Is Lost Save Honor (1984)
Fates Worse Than Death: An Autobiographical Collage of the 1980s (1991)

Plays, Works for Television, Adaptations
"D.P." (1958, produced as "Auf Wiedersehen"; 1985, produced as "Displaced Persons")
Penelope (1960); later revised as *Happy Birthday, Wanda June* (1970)
Between Time and Timbuktu; or, Prometheus-5, a Space Fantasy (1972)
"EPICAC" (1974, 1992)
The Chemistry Professor [based on *Dr. Jekyll and Mr. Hyde*] (1978)
"Who Am I This Time?" (1982)
"All the King's Horses" (1991)
"The Euphio Question" (1991)
"Next Door" (1991)
"Fortitude" (1992)
"The Foster Portfolio" (1992)
"More Stately Mansions" (1992)
L'Histoire du Soldat (libretto) (1993, 1997)
"Harrison Bergeron" (1995)

Children's Book
Sun, Moon, Star (1980)

Works Cited

Books
Aldiss, Brian W. *Billion Year Spree: The True History of Science Fiction.* New York: Doubleday, 1973.
Allen, William Rodney, ed. *Conversations with Kurt Vonnegut.* Jackson: University of Mississippi Press, 1988.
———. *Understanding Kurt Vonnegut.* Columbia: University of South Carolina Press, 1991.
Amis, Martin. *The Moronic Inferno.* 1986; repr., New York: Penguin, 1991.
Bailey, Blake. *A Tragic Honesty: The Life and Work of Richard Yates.* New York: Picador, 2004.

Bellamy, Joe David. "Kurt Vonnegut for President: The Making of a Literary Reputation." In *Literary Luxuries: American Writing at the End of the Millennium*, 137–52. Columbia: University of Missouri Press, 1995.

Bernal, J. D. *A History of Classical Physics: From Antiquity to Quantum*. 1972; repr., New York: Barnes and Noble Books, 1997.

Bradbury, Ray. Foreword to *The Ultimate Egoist: The Complete Stories of Theodore Sturgeon*, vol. 1. Edited by Paul Williams. Berkeley, CA: North Atlantic Books, 1999.

Céline, Louis-Ferdinand. *Journey to the End of the Night*. Translated by Ralph Manheim. 1934; repr., New York: New Directions, 2006.

Charles Darwin's Beagle Diary. Edited by Richard Darwin Keynes. Cambridge: Cambridge University Press, 1988.

Cherny, Andrei. *The Candy Bombers: The Untold Story of the Berlin Airlift and America's Finest Hour*. New York: Putnam, 1998.

Clarke, Gerald *Capote: A Biography*. 2nd paperback ed., New York: Da Capo Press, 2005.

Conway, Flo, and Jim Siegelman. *Dark Hero of the Information Age: In Search of Norbert Wiener, the Father of Cybernetics*. New York: Basic Books, 2005.

Cregor, Caterina. *The Path Well Chosen: History of the Orchard School, 1922–1984*. Indianapolis: Orchard School Foundation, 1984.

Darwin, Charles. *Journal of Researches into the Geology and Natural History of the Various Countries Visited by H.M.S. Beagle*. London: Henry Colburn, 1839.

Derry, Gregory N. *What Science Is and How It Works*. Princeton, NJ: Princeton University Press, 1999.

Dickstein, Morris. *Gates of Eden: American Culture in the Sixties*. New York: Basic Books, 1977.

Dinger, Ed, ed. *Seems Like Old Times*. Iowa City: Iowa Writers' Workshop, 1986.

Disch, Thomas M. "Jokes Across the Generation Gap." In *On Science Fiction*, 67–71. Ann Arbor: University of Michigan Press, 2005.

Donoso, Maria Pilar. "Beer Party in Iowa." In *The World Comes to Iowa: The Iowa International Anthology*, edited by Paul Engle and Hualing Nieh Engle, 33–38. Ames: Iowa State University Press, 1987.

Dunn, Jacob Piatt. *Greater Indianapolis: The History, the Industries, the Institutions, and the People of a City of Homes*. Chicago: Lewis, 1910.

Engle, Paul. "The Writer and the Place." In *A Community of Writers: Paul Engle and the Iowa Writers' Workshop*, edited by Robert Dana, 1–10. Iowa City: University of Iowa Press, 1999.

Feinberg, Leonard. *The Secret of Humor*. New York: Rodopi, 1978.

Fiedler, Leslie A. *Love and Death in the American Novel*. New York: Meridian Books, 1962.

Fonda, Peter. *Don't Tell Dad*. New York: Hyperion, 1998.

Gaus, Laura Sheerin. *Shortridge High School, 1864–1981 in Retrospect*. Indianapolis: Indiana Historical Society, 1985.

Gay, Peter. *Freud: A Life for Our Time*. New York: Norton, 1988.

Giannone, Richard. *Vonnegut: A Preface to His Novels*. Port Washington, NY: Kennikat, 1977.

Goldsmith, David H. *Kurt Vonnegut: Fantasist of Fire and Ice*. Bowling Green, OH: Bowling Green University Popular Press, 1972.

Greenfield, George. *A Smattering of Monsters: A Kind of Memoir*. Rochester, NY: Camden House, 1995.

Grinberg, León. *Guilt and Depression*. Translated by Christine Trollope. London: Karnac Books, 1992.

Grivetti, Louis G. In *We Were Each Other's Prisoners: An Oral History of World War II American and German Prisoners of War*, edited by Lewis H. Carlson, 116–99. New York: Basic Books.

Grof, Christina, and Stanislav Grof, MD. *The Stormy Search for the Self*. Los Angeles: Jeremy P. Tarcher, 1990.

Hammarskjöld, Dag. *Markings*. New York: Knopf, 1964.

Harris, W. Edward. *Miracle in Birmingham: A Civil Rights Memoir, 1954–1965*. Indianapolis: Stone Work Press, 2004.

Hatch, Gardner N., W. Curtis Musten, and John S. Edwards, eds. *American Ex-Prisoners of War: Non Solum Armis*. Nashville, TN: Turner, 1995.

Havens, B. S., et al. *Early History of Cloud Seeding*. New Mexico Institute of Mining and Technology, State University of New York at Albany, and General Electric, 1979.

Hipkiss, Robert. *The American Absurd: Pynchon, Vonnegut, and Barth*. National University Publications. Fort Washington, NY: Associated Faculty Press, 1989.

Hyde, Charles K. *Copper for America: The United States Copper Industry from Colonial Times to the 1990s*. Tucson: University of Arizona Press, 1998.

Jacobs, Dan. *The Brutality of Nations*. New York: Paragon House, 1988.

James, Edward, and Farah Mendlesohn, eds. *The Cambridge Companion to Science Fiction*. Cambridge: Cambridge University Press, 2003.

Jones, Kaylie. *Lies My Mother Never Told Me: A Memoir*. New York: William Morrow, 2009.

Karl, Frederick R. *American Fictions: 1940/1980*. New York: Harper, 1983.

Kidder, Tracy. *Home Town*. New York: Random House, 1999.

Kitchin, William Copeman. *A Wonderland of the East*. Boston: Page, 1920.

Kleinfelder, Rita Lang. *When We Were Young: A Baby-Boomer Yearbook*. New York: Prentice Hall, 1993.

Klinkowitz, Jerome. *Keeping Literary Company: Working with Writers since the Sixties*. Albany: State University of New York, 1998.

———. *Kurt Vonnegut*. London and New York: Methuen, 1982.

———. *The Vonnegut Effect*. Columbia: University of South Carolina Press, 2004.

———. *Vonnegut in Fact: The Personal Spokesmanship of Personal Fiction*. Columbia: University of South Carolina Press, 1998.

———. *Vonnegut's America*. Columbia: University of South Carolina Press, 2009.

Klinkowitz, Jerome, and Donald L. Lawler, eds. *Vonnegut in America: An Introduction to the Life and Work of Kurt Vonnegut*. New York: Delacorte, 1977.

Larson, Edward J. *God and Science on the Galapagos Islands*. New York: Basic Books, 2001.

Leonard, S. A., and R. F. Cox. *General Language: A Series of Lessons in Grammar, Word Study, and History of the English Language*. Chicago: Rand McNally, 1925.

MacCambridge, Michael. *The Franchise: A History of Sports Illustrated Magazine*. New York: Hyperion Books, 1998.

Magnarelli, Sahron. *Understanding* José Donoso. Columbia: University of South Carolina Press, 1992.

Marvin, Thomas F. *Kurt Vonnegut: A Critical Companion*. Westport, CT: Greenwood, 2002.

Mayo, Clark. *Kurt Vonnegut: The Gospel from Outer Space*. San Bernardino, CA: Borgo Press, 1977.

McKee, Alexander. *Dresden, 1945: The Devil's Tinderbox*. 1982; repr., New York: Barnes and Noble, 2000.

Meany, Geraldine. *(Un)Like Subjects: Women, Theory, Fiction*. London: Routledge, 1993.

Miller, Donald L. *D-Days in the Pacific.* New York: Simon and Schuster, 2005.

Morris, Richard. *Time's Arrows: Scientific Attitudes Toward Time.* New York: Simon and Schuster, 1985.

Morris Jr., Roy. *Ambrose Bierce: Alone in Bad Company.* New York: Oxford University Press, 1999.

Peck, Dale. "Kurt's Conundrum." In *Hatchet Jobs: Writings on Contemporary Fiction,* 190–200. New York: New Press, 2005.

Rackstraw, Loree. *Love as Always, Kurt: Vonnegut as I Knew Him.* Cambridge, MA: Da Capo Press, 2009.

Redfield, Robert. *The Little Community and Peasant Society and Culture.* Chicago: University of Chicago, 1956.

Reed, Peter J. "Kurt Vonnegut." In *Dictionary of Literary Biography.* Vol. 3 of Documentary Series. Detroit: Bruccoli Clark/Gale Research, 1983.

———. *The Short Fiction of Kurt Vonnegut.* Vol. 1 of Contributions to the Study of American Literature. Westport, CT: Greenwood Press, 1997.

Rickman, Greg. *To the High Castle: Philip K. Dick, A Life.* Long Beach, CA: Fragments West/Valentine Press, 1989.

Rivera, Geraldo. *Exposing Myself.* Written with Daniel Paisner. New York: Bantam Books, 1991.

Schlesinger Jr., Arthur. *The Vital Center: The Politics of Freedom.* Boston: Houghton Mifflin, 1949.

Scholes, Robert. "Chasing a Lone Eagle: Vonnegut's College Writing." In *The Vonnegut Statement,* edited by Jerome Klinkowitz and John Somer, 45–54. New York: Seymour Lawrence, 1973.

———. *The Fabulators.* New York: Oxford University Press, 1967.

———. "A Talk With Kurt Vonnegut." In *Conversations with Kurt Vonnegut,* edited by William Rodney Allen, 111–32. Jackson: University of Mississippi Press, 1988.

Shear, Walter. "Kurt Vonnegut: The Comic Fate of the Sensibility." In vol. 31 of *The Feeling of Being: Sensibility in Postwar American Fiction,* 215–39. New York: Peter Lang, 2002.

Short, Robert L. *Something to Believe In: Is Kurt Vonnegut the Exorcist of Jesus Christ Superstar?* New York: Harper and Row, 1978.

Singh, Sukhbir. *The Survivor in Contemporary American Fiction: Saul Bellow, Bernard Malamud, John Updike, Kurt Vonnegut, Jr.* Delhi: B.R. Publishing, 1991.

Slotkin, James Sydney. *Social Anthropology: The Science of Human Society and Culture.* New York: Macmillan, 1950.

Suits, C. G., and J. M. Lafferty. *Albert Wallace Hull: A Biographical Memoir.* Washington, DC: National Academy of Sciences, 1970.

Szpek Jr., Ervin E., and Frank J. Idzikowski. *Shadows of Slaughterhouse Five: Recollections and Reflections of the American Ex-POWs of Schlachthof Fünf.* Edited by Heidi M. Szpek. Bloomington, IN: iUniverse, 2008.

Taylor, Frederick. *Dresden: Tuesday 13 February 1945.* New York: Harper Perennial, 2005.

Taylor, Geoff. *Piece of Cake.* London: Peter Davies, 1956.

Terkel, Studs. "Kurt Vonnegut." In *Will the Circle Be Unbroken? Reflections on Death, Rebirth, and Hunger for a Faith,* 221–27. New York: New Press, 2001.

Theodore Probst, George. *The Germans in Indianapolis, 1840–1918.* German-American Center: Indianapolis, 1989.

Unruh, Glenys G., and William M. Alexander. *Innovations in Secondary Education.* New York: Holt, Rinehart and Winston, 1974.

Vaknin, Sam. *Malignant Self-Love: Narcissism Revisited*. Prague: Narcissus, 2001.

Vaughn, Alan. *Patterns of Prophecy*. New York: Hawthorn Books, 1973.

"Vonnegut, Kurt." In *Authors and Artists for Young Adults*. Vols. 6, 24: Gale, 1992–99. Farmington Hills, MI: Thomson Gale, 2006.

Vonnegut, Kurt. "Algren as I Knew Him." In Nelson Algren, *The Man with the Golden Arm*, 367–69. New York: Seven Stories Press, 1999.

——. *Armageddon in Retrospect*. New York: Berkley, 2008.

——. *Bagombo Snuff Box: Uncollected Short Fiction*. 1999; repr., New York: Berkley, 2000.

——. *Between Time and Timbuktu; or, Prometheus-5, a Space Fantasy*. New York: Dell, 1972.

——. *Bluebeard*. New York: Delacorte, 1987.

——. *Breakfast of Champions; or, Goodbye Blue Monday!*. 1973; repr., New York: Dell, 1999.

——. *Canary in a Cat House*. New York: Fawcett, 1961.

——. *Cat's Cradle*. 1963; repr., New York: Delta, 1998.

——. *Deadeye Dick*. 1982; repr., New York: Dial, 2006.

——. *Fates Worse Than Death*. 1991; repr., New York: Berkley, 1992.

——. Foreword to *A Saucer of Loneliness: The Complete Stories of Theodore Sturgeon*, vol. 7, edited by Paul Williams. Berkeley, CA: North Atlantic Books, 2002.

——. *Galápagos*. New York: Delta, 1985.

——. *God Bless You, Dr. Kevorkian*. 1999; repr., New York: Washington Square Books, 2001.

——. *God Bless You, Mr. Rosewater; or, Pearls Before Swine*. 1965; repr., New York: Delta, 1998.

——. *Hocus Pocus*. New York: Berkley, 1997.

——. *Jailbird*. New York: Delacorte, 1979.

——. *Look at the Birdie*. New York: Delacorte, 2009.

——. *A Man Without a Country*. Edited by Daniel Simon. New York: Seven Stories Press, 2005.

——. *Mother Night*. 1961; repr., New York: Delta, 1999.

——. "New World Symphony." In *A Community of Writers: Paul Engle and the Iowa Writers' Workshop*, edited by Robert Dana, 113–15. Iowa City: University of Iowa Press, 1999.

——. *Nothing Is Lost Save Honor*. Jackson, MS: Nouveau Press, 1984.

——. *Palm Sunday: An Autobiographical Collage*. New York: Delacorte, 1981.

——. *Player Piano*. 1952; repr., New York: Delta, 1999.

——. *The Sirens of Titan*. 1959; repr., New York: Dial, 1998.

——. *Slapstick; or, Lonesome No More!*. 1976; repr., New York: Dial, 2006.

——. *Slaughterhouse-Five; or, The Children's Crusade, a Duty-Dance with Death*. 1969; repr., New York: Dial, 2005.

——. *Timequake*. New York: Putnam, 1997.

——. *Utopia 14*. New York: Bantam, 1954.

——. "A Very Fringe Character." In *An Unsentimental Education*, edited by Molly McQuade, 236–42. Chicago: University of Chicago Press, 1995.

——. *Wampeters, Foma & Grandfallons*. 1974; repr., New York: Delta, 1999.

——. *Welcome to the Monkey House: A Collection of Short Works*. 1968; repr., New York: Delta, 1998.

——. *While Mortals Sleep: Unpublished Short Fiction*. New York: Delacorte, 2011.

Vonnegut, Mark. *The Eden Express: A Personal Account of Schizophrenia*. New York: Praeger, 1975.

Wakefield, Dan. "Kurt Vonnegut." In *Indiana History: A Book of Readings*, edited by Ralph D. Gray, 276–84. Bloomington: Indiana University Press, 1994.

Wilbers, Stephen. *The Iowa Writers' Workshop*. Iowa City: University of Iowa Press, 1980.

Winchell, Mark Royden. *Too Good to Be True: The Life and Work of Leslie Fiedler*. Columbia: University of Missouri Press, 2002.

Yarmolinsky, Jane Vonnegut. *Angels Without Wings: How Tragedy Created a Remarkable Family*. Boston: Houghton Mifflin, 1987.

Journal Articles

Baird, James. "Jeffers, Vonnegut, and Pynchon: Their Philosophies and Fates." *Jeffers Studies* 4, no. 1 (Winter 2000): 17–28.

Daniels, Margaret J., and Heather E. Bowen. "Feminist Implications of Anti-Leisure in Dystopian Fiction." *Journal of Leisure Research* 35 no. 4 (Fall 2003): 423+.

Donoso, José. "A Small Biography of the Obscene Bird of Night." *Review of Contemporary Fiction* 19, no. 3 (1999): 123.

Fiene, Donald M. "Elements of Dostoevsky in the Novels of Kurt Vonnegut." *Dostoevsky Studies*, 2 (1981): 129–41.

———. "Kurt Vonnegut's Popularity in the Soviet Union and His Affinities with Russian Literature." Russian Literature *Triquarterly* 14 (1976): 166–84.

Gordon, R. "Death and Creativity: A Jungian Approach." *Journal of Analytical Psychology* 22, no. 2 (1977): 106–24.

Hattenhauer, Darryl. "The Politics of Kurt Vonnegut's 'Harrison Bergeron.'" *Studies in Short Fiction* 35, no. 4 (1998): 387+.

Hirschman, Elizabeth C. "Babies for Sale: Market Ethics and the New Reproductive Technologies." *Journal of Consumer Affairs* 25, no. 2 (1991): 358+.

Hume, Kathryn. "Vonnegut's Melancholy." *Philological Quarterly* 77 no. 2 (Spring 1998): 221.

Klein, Herbert G. "Kurt Vonnegut's *The Sirens of Titan* and the Question of Genre." *Erfurt Electronic Studies in English* 5 (1998): n.p. Web.

Knipfel, Jim. "Reading Louis-Ferdinand Céline." *Context: A Forum for Literary Arts and Culture* 8 (November 2001): n.p. Web.

McInnis, Gilber. "Evolutionary Mythology in the Writings of Kurt Vonnegut Jr." *Critique: Studies in Contemporary Fiction* 46, no. 4 (Summer 2005): 383.

Pye, Gillian. "Comedy Theory and the Postmodern." *Humor: International Journal of Humor Research* 19, no.1 (2006): 53–70.

Redfield, Robert. "The Folk Society." *American Journal of Society* 52, no. 4 (January 1947): 293–308.

Reilly, Charlie. "Two Conversations with Kurt Vonnegut." *College Literature* 7 (1980): 1–29.

Rogers, Annie G. "Marguerite Sechehaye and Renee: A Feminist Reading of Two Accounts of a Treatment." *International Journal of Qualitative Studies in Education* 5, no. 3 (July 1992): 245–51.

Seltzer, Leon F. "Dresden and Vonnegut's Creative Testament of Guilt." *Journal of American Culture* 4, no.4 (Winter 1981): 55–69.

Smith, Tom W. "Liberal and Conservative Trends in the United States Since World War II." *Public Opinion Quarterly* 54 (1990): 479+.

Stumpf, Clifford. "A Day in May: A Story of a Prisoner of War" (unpublished memoir). In Heidi M. Szpek, "Religious Expression Among the Men of Slaughterhouse Five," *International Journal of the Humanities* 2, no. 2 (2006): 1437.

Vonnegut, Bernard. "Adventures in Fluid Flow: Generating Interesting Dendritic Patterns." *Leonardo* 31, no. 3 (1998): 205–7.

Magazines
Amidon, Stephen. "A Heavy Price" (book review). *New Statesman*, November 22, 2004.
Black, Pam. "Ramparts." *Folio: The Magazine for Magazine Management*, April 1, 2004.
Brinkley, Douglas. "Vonnegut's Apocalypse." *Rolling Stone*, August 24, 2006.
Bryan, C. D. B. "Kurt Vonnegut on Target." *New Republic*, October 8, 1966.
Buckley, William F. "Care Package to Moscow." *National Review*, June 28, 1985.
Cargas, Henry James. "Kurt Vonnegut" (interview). *Christian Century*, November 24, 1976.
"Class Notes." *Cornell Alumni Magazine*, January–February 2006.
Crichton, J. M. "Sci-Fi and Vonnegut." *New Republic*, April 26, 1969.
DeMott, Benjamin. "Vonnegut's Otherworldly Laughter." *Saturday Review*, May 1, 1971.
Deneen, Patrick J. "Folk Tales." *Claremont Review of Books*, Winter 2007.
Dinsmore, John. "Kurt & Ollie." *Firsts*, October 1992.
Fiedler, Leslie A. "The Divine Stupidity of Kurt Vonnegut: Portrait of a Novelist as a Bridge Over Troubled Water." *Esquire*, September 1970.
Flamm, Matthew, and Alexandra Jacobs. "Mailer Time." *Entertainment Weekly*, May 22, 1998.
Fleming, James R. "The Climate Engineers." *Wilson Quarterly*, Spring 2007.
"46 and Trusted." *Newsweek*, March 3, 1969.
Freedman, David, and Sarah Schafer. "Vonnegut and Clancy on Technology." *Inc.*, December 15, 1995.
Grossman, Edward. "Vonnegut & His Audience." *Commentary*, July 1974.
"The Growing Battle of the Books." *Time*, January 19, 1981.
Harris, T. George. "University of Iowa's Paul Engle, Poet-Grower to the World." *Look*, June 1, 1965.
Hayman, David, David Michaelis, George Plimpton, and Richard Rhodes. "Kurt Vonnegut: The Art of Fiction LXIV." *Paris Review*, Spring 1977.
Hicks, Clifford B. "Tailor-Made Metals for Tomorrow." *Popular Mechanics*, May 1957.
Hicks, Granville. "Literary Horizons." *Saturday Review*, March 29, 1969.
Horne, Jed. "Mark Vonnegut Traces His Harrowing Journey Through Wildest Schizophrenia." *People*, November 3, 1975.
Horton, Scott. "November 1972: Vonnegut vs. the Republicans." *Harper's*, April 2007.
Klinkowitz, Jerome. "Robert Weide's *Mother Night*: A Review." *North American Review*, September–October 1997.
Koenig, Rhoda. "At Play in the Fields of the Word." *New York Magazine*, February 3, 1986.
Levin, Eric. "The Slipperiest Rung on the Ladder of Success May Be Your Own Fear of Winning." *People*, November 10, 1980.
Lott, Jeffrey. "The Good Hippie." *Swarthmore College Bulletin*, March 1, 2003.
MacDonald, Jake. "Peaking on the Prairies." *Walrus*, June 2007.
Mallory, Carol. "The Kurt & Joe Show." *Playboy*, May 1992.
McCloud, Bill. "What Should We Tell Our Children about Vietnam?" *American Heritage*, May–June 1988.
McLaughlin, Frank. "An Interview with Kurt Vonnegut." *Media & Methods*, May 1973.
McMurran, Kristin, et al. "The Famous Turn Out for (and Some Are Turned Off by) the Bicoastal Previews of Al Pacino's Bloody 'Scarface.'" *People*, December 19, 1983.

Mitchell, Greg. "Meeting My Maker: A Visit with Kurt Vonnegut, Jr., by Kilgore Trout." *Crawdaddy*, April 1, 1974.

"Moving Ma Bell, Vonnegut Style." *Indianapolis Magazine*, October 1976.

Rentilly, J. "The Best Jokes Are Dangerous, an Interview with Kurt Vonnegut." *McSweeney's*, September 2002.

Roloff, Lee. "Kurt Vonnegut on Stage at the Steppenwolf Theater, Chicago." *TriQuarterly*, Fall 1998.

Sanoff, Alvin P. "Creating Literature on the Plains of Iowa (50th Anniversary of Iowa Writers' Workshop)." *U.S. News & World Report*, June 2, 1986.

Sheed, Wilfrid. "The Now Generation Knew Him When." *Life*, September 12, 1969.

"Six Sleepers for Fall." *Publishers Weekly*, August 29, 2005.

Slavitt, David R. "Looking for Mr. Vonnegut." *Philadelphia*, November 1982.

Standish, David. "Kurt Vonnegut: The *Playboy* Interview." *Playboy*, July 20, 1973.

Thom, James Alexander. "The Man Without a Country." *Spokesman*, Bertrand Russell Foundation, October 2007.

Tyrnauer, Matt. "America's Writing Forces (Gore Vidal, Norman Mailer, Kurt Vonnegut)," *Vanity Fair*, July 2006.

Vonnegut, Kurt. "Biafra: A People Betrayed." *McCall's*, April 1970.

———. "He Leadeth Us from Porn; God Bless You Edwin Meese." *Nation*, January 25, 1986.

———. "In-the-Bone Reading" (excerpt from "For the Love of Books"). *Biblio*, March 1999.

———. "The Lake." *Architectural Digest*, June 1988.

———. Letter to the editor, *Science Fiction Review*, November 15, 1975.

———. "No More Dangerous Than a Banana Split." *American Libraries*, February 1983.

———. "Requiem: The Hocus Pocus Laundromat." *North American Review*, December 1986.

———. "Surviving Niagara." *Guardian*, January 25, 2003.

———. "To Be a Native Middle-Westerner." *Nuvo Newsweekly*, May 20, 1999.

"Weather or Not," *Time*, August 28, 1950.

Weide, Robert B. "The Morning After *Mother Night*," *Realist*, Autumn 1997.

Williams, Catherine. "Dresden Bombing." *Pulteney St. Survey*, Hobart and William Smith Colleges, Spring 2001.

Zaring, Catherine Alford. "Time Traveling Through Indianapolis with Kurt Vonnegut Jr." *Indianapolis Home and Garden*, November 1978.

CD-ROM

Essential Vonnegut: Interviews Conducted by Walter Miller, CD-ROM. New York: HarperCollins, 2006.

Online Sources

Brady, James. "Kurt Vonnegut Meet Jon Stewart." Forbes.com, January 1, 2006.

———. "Taps for Kurt." Forbes.com, April 12, 2007.

Columbia, David Patrick, and Jeffrey Hirsch. "Lunch with Jill Krementz." New York Social Diary.com, January 13, 2005.

Houston, Frank. "The Salon Interview: Kurt Vonnegut." Salon.com, October 8, 1999.

Juhasz, Paul. "No Matter What the Actual Hour May Be: Time Manipulation in the Works of Ambrose Bierce." *Ambrose Bierce Project Journal* 4, no. 1 (Fall 2008), www.ambrosebierce.org/journal4juhaszl.html, November 22, 2009.

"Krementz, Jill." In *Contemporary Authors Online*, Gale, 2007. Reproduced in *Literature Resource Center*. Farmington Hills, MI: Thomson Gale, 2006.

Singer, Milton, and James Redfield. "Robert Redfield." In *American National Biography Online*, February 2000.

Stewart, Gaither. "Kurt Vonnegut: Anarchist and Social Critic." Countercurrent.org, April 15, 2008.

Unpublished Sources and Booklets

Byrne, Robert. In "Knox Burger, 1922–2010: 'Honest Prose and Nerves of Steel'" (memorial booklet). New York, February 2010.

Cronkite, Walter. Interviewed for "Washington Goes to the Moon," part 1 (transcript). Public Radio Exchange, Cambridge, MA.

Donleavy, J. P., contributor. "Seymour Lawrence: An Independent Imprint Dedicated to Excellence" (booklet). New York: Houghton Mifflin, 1990.

Fiene, Donald M. "Getting Through Life: The Autobiography of Donald M. Fiene" (unpublished manuscript). University of Louisville Special Collections, 1961– .

Griffith, Sarah J. "The Moral Egotist: Evolution of Style in Kurt Vonnegut's Satire." Bachelor's thesis, University of Michigan, 2008.

"Happy Birthday, Kurt Vonnegut: A Festschrift for Kurt Vonnegut on his Sixtieth Birthday." Edited by Jill Krementz. New York: Delacorte, 1982.

Lloyd, Reverend Rosemary. "A Dream of Peace" (sermon). First Church in Boston, Boston, MA, April 15, 2007.

Mantler, Gordon Keith. "Black, Brown and Poor: Martin Luther King Jr., the Poor People's Campaign and Its Legacies." PhD thesis, Duke University, 2008.

Mazow, Lauren. "Kurt Vonnegut: On Religion" (interview), January 18, 1988. Vonnegut mss., Lilly Library, Indiana University, Bloomington.

Rauch, John G. "An Account of the Ancestry of Kurt Vonnegut Jr. by an Ancient Friend of the Family," 1970. Lilly Library, Indiana University, Bloomington.

Vonnegut, Jane. Interview by Marge Schiller, December 1969, interview 639 (transcript). McCarthy Historical Project, Eugene J. McCarthy Papers, Elmer L. Andersen Library, University of Minnesota, Minneapolis.

Warnick, Chris. "Student Writing, Politics, and Style 1962–1979." PhD diss., University of Pittsburgh, 2006.

Recordings, Broadcasts, and Films

Krementz, Jill. Interview by Brian Lamb. "The Writer's Desk," *Booknotes*, C-SPAN, June 1, 1997.

"Kurt Vonnegut." Episode 316, *Real Time with Bill Maher*, HBO, September 9, 2005.

Kurt Vonnegut: American Made. Robert B. Weide, director. Whyaduck Productions, 1994.

Kurt Vonnegut: A Self-Portrait. Harold Mantell, producer. Films for the Humanities, 1975.

"Kurt Vonnegut at NYU." Pacifica Radio Archives, KPFT, November 6, 1970.

Lowery, George. "Kurt Vonnegut Jr., Novelist, Counterculture Icon and Cornellian, Dies at 84." Chronicle Online, April 12, 2007.

Vonnegut, Kurt. Interview by Christopher Bigsby. *Kaleidoscope*, BBC, September 20, 1984.

Vonnegut, Mark. Interview by Neal Conan. "Armageddon Reveals Unpublished Vonnegut Work," National Public Radio, April 1, 2008.

"What Does PEN Have to Offer?" Episode 673, *Firing Line*, December 2, 1985. Southern Educational Communications Association.

Lectures and Speeches

Shriver Jr., Robert Sargent (speech). Memorial for Adam Yarmolinsky. Albin O. Kuhn Library, University of Maryland, Baltimore, May 4, 2000.

Spolarich, Aaron. "The Vonnegut Families of Lake Maxinkuckee" (lecture). Antiquarian & Historical Society of Culver, Culver, IN, June 23, 2007.

Vonnegut, Kurt. "Eugene V. Debs Award" (speech). Holiday Inn, Terre Haute, IN, November 7, 1981.

———. "The Noodle Factory" (speech). Connecticut College, New London, CT, October 1, 1976.

———. "Speech at the Athenaeum, Indianapolis." October 10, 1996.

———. "Speech at the First Parish Church" (Unitarian). Cambridge, MA, January 27, 1980.

———. Syracuse University Commencement (speech). Syracuse University, May 8, 1994.

———. "Tribute to Allen Ginsberg" (speech). Wadsworth Theater, Los Angeles, May 30, 1997.

Acknowledgments

I am indebted to these generous people for sharing memories and, in some instances, correspondence with Kurt Vonnegut: James Alexander Thom, Stephen J. Gertz, Daniel L. Fendel, Richard C. Hiscock, James Rosenau, Ellen Rosenau, Lucy W. Rosenau, Arnold Bossi, Anne Bossi, Dianne Wiest, John Birmingham, Jerry Hiatt, Greg Hansen, Rob and T. J. MacGregor, Mark Bourbeau, Robert A. Lehrman, Marc Pachter, Bernard Gotfryd, Ben L. Ross, William Price Fox, Marcia Gauger, Sarah Crawford Fox, Arlene D. Donovan, Kendall Landis, Steve Weissman, MD, Alan T. Nolan, Owen Quentin Young Jr., Nolan N. Young, Al Brodax, James McGrath Morris, Clifford Hayes, Katherine Burger, Rodney C. Gould, Richard Reisem, Pat McNees, Carolyn Blakemore, John Updike, Cathy Parrish, Kaylie A. Jones, Gay Talmey, Elsa Lauber, Betty Stanton, Jonathan Mitchell, Eve Guarnuccio, Clark Blaise, Bette Farmer, Allison Mitchell, Lillian A. Ruffen, Paul Albright, Ray Mungo, Lee Stringer, John Thiel, Connie Winters, Andros Sturgeon, Kerry O'Keefe, James Mills, Ervin Szpek Jr., John Dinsmore, Joe Petro III, Robert Nedelkoff, Jim Siegelman, Benjamin Hitz, Miller Harris, John Casey, Caleb T. Warren, John Irving, Victor Jose, Michael Tarabulski, George Jeffrey, Bryant "Bud" Gillespie, Valerie Heller, Ben Blickle, Judith E. Burns, Gail Godwin, Dan Wakefield, Philip Damon, Joan Uda, Ian T. Macmillan, Suzanne McConnell, Barry Jay Kaplan, David Markson,

Mary Robinson, Tom Fuller, Dan Simon, Gloria and Jack Ericson, Jim Cheney, Nancy Bulger, Kirk and Mary Herrick, Cliff Hayes, Lynn Meyer, Bernard V. O'Hare, David Breithaupt, Gary Giddins, Jess Walter, Hilary Masters, Jayne Anne Phillips, Patrick Hinely, Jim Tushinski, Robley Wilson, Sarah Griffith, Levi Asher, Rhonda Ruthman, Margaret Bern, Rick Archer, L. B. Shriver, Lewis Brague, Charlie Donahue, Tom Kirkendall, Craig Canine, Justin Kaplan, Dave Mangan, Margot Sheehan, Anne Bernays, L. Rust Hills, Victoria Bay, Joan Mellen, Cindy Lee Berryhill, Miles Chapin, Paul Williams, Frederik Pohl, Evans N. Woollen, Majie Alford Failey, Jesse Kornbluth, Calvin Branche, Rick Boyer, Rick Krementz, Jules Fisher, Robert Maslansky, MD, Lee Stringer, Kimberly Marlowe Hartnett, the Reverend Daniel E. Budd, Mary V. Wilkinson, Muffin MacGuffin, Seymour Gers, MD, Tony Kent, Judith and Donald C. Fiene, Vance Bourjaily, Byron Burford, Stephen Wilbers, the Honorable Isabella Horton Grant; men of the 106th Division, 423rd Regiment at the Battle of the Bulge: Robert Kelton, Donald Betlach, Dale Watson, Gifford Doxsee, Raymond Hinkle, William F. Shipley, Michael Croteau, Alexander H. Marsh, James Mills, Harley W. Slaback; and former members of the Office of Special Services (OSS).

Among the journalists who took time to find articles and photographs related to Vonnegut and his family are the following: George Patrick Lowery, the *Cornell Chronicle*; Jeffrey Lott, the *Swarthmore Bulletin*; Brittany McLeod, *Philadelphia Magazine*; David Hoppe, *Nuvo Newsweekly*; Megan Fernandez, *Indianapolis Monthly Home*; and David Still II, *Barnstable Patriot*.

Librarians, curators, and institutions were eager to help me to the point that I cannot adequately express my gratitude, beginning with the Lilly Library at Indiana University, Bloomington, which granted me an Everett Helm Visiting Fellowship to begin my research into Vonnegut's papers. All of the following professionals deserve my deepest thanks: Chris Hunter, Schenectady Museum and Suits-Bueche Planetarium; Evan Fay Earle and Elaine Engst, Carl A. Kroch Library, Cornell University; Sally Childs-Helton, PhD, Irwin Library, Butler University; Anthony L. Onstott, Park Tudor School, Indianapolis; Tony Williams, CARE USA; Lucy Loomis and Hannah Van Petten, researcher, Sturgis Library, Barnstable, Massachusetts; Richard W. Clement, Kenneth Spencer Research Library, University of Kansas; Greg Wysk, State Historical Society of

North Dakota; Sharon Butsch Freeland, Broad Ripple Village Association, Indianapolis; Janet LeBrun, Speakers Worldwide, Inc.; Susan Sutton and Paul Brockman, Indiana Historical Society, Indianapolis; John McDonald, HFCC Federation of Teachers, Detroit; Maddie Thompson and Breon Mitchell, Lilly Library, Indiana University; Gerald Peterson, Rod Library, University of Northern Iowa; Julia Gardner, University of Chicago Library; Susan P. Waide and Dr. Isaac Gewirtz, New York Public Library; Meg Sherry Rich, John Delaney, Ben Primer, AnnaLee Pauls, and Charles E. Greene, Princeton University Library; Grant Holcomb, University of Rochester; Lisa Browar, Linda Hall Library of Science, Engineering and Technology, Kansas City; Tim Johnson and Kris Kiesling, Special Collections and Rare Books, Peggy Johnson, Technical Services, and Jennifer Reckner and Wendy Pradt Lougee, all at the University of Minnesota; Ellen Alers and Christine De Groot, Smithsonian Institution Archives; Elizabeth B. Dunn, Rare Book, Manuscript, and Special Collections Library, and Kelly Wooten, Sallie Bingham Center for Women's History and Culture, both at Duke University; Dennis Sears, Rare Book and Manuscript Library, University of Illinois, Urbana-Champaign; Margaret N. Burri, Milton S. Eisenhower Library, Johns Hopkins University; Aidan J. Smith, the University Library, University of North Carolina at Chapel Hill; Shelter Island Historical Society, New York; Roy Speckhardt, American Humanist Association; Kathy Kienholz, American Academy of Arts and Letters; Richard P. Gulla, Massachusetts Medical Society; Brian Keough, Science Library, University at Albany, SUNY; Gerald L. Peterson, University of Northern Iowa; T. K. Nenninger, National Archives and Records Administration; Leroy Cole Atkins II and Simon D. Levy, Washington and Lee University; B. J. Gooch, Transylvania University Library, Lexington, Kentucky; Ann E. Butler, Fales Library and Special Collections, New York University; Richard Doyle and Hongbo Xie, Stewart Memorial Library, Coe College; L. Rebecca Johnson Melvin, University of Delaware Library; Jeffrey Makala, Thomas Cooper Library, University of South Carolina; and Jonathan Jackson, Special Collections Research Center, Syracuse University Library.

My thinking about Vonnegut, his life and work, was enriched, amplified, and in some cases challenged by scholars who welcomed me into their intellectual community: Hank Nuwer, associate professor, Franklin College; Dr. Robert T. Tally Jr., assistant professor of English,

Texas State University; Bruce Dobler, associate professor emeritus, University of Pittsburgh; Dr. John Latham, emeritus professor of physics, University of Manchester, UK, and senior research scientist, National Center for Atmospheric Research, Colorado; Heidi M. Szpek, PhD, associate professor of religious studies and philosophy, Central Washington University; Eric S. Rabkin, Arthur F. Thurnau Professor of English, University of Michigan; Kathryn Hume, professor of English, Penn State University; Thomas F. Marvin, associate professor of English, Indiana University–Purdue University, Indianapolis; Charles Wright, emeritus professor of English, University of Virginia; David Coleman, associate professor, University of Virginia; Loree Rackstraw, emeritus professor of English, University of Northern Iowa; Alan Wald, H. Chandler Davis Collegiate Professor of English and American Culture, University of Michigan; Noël Sturgeon, trustee of the Theodore Sturgeon Literary Trust; and Susan Farrell, professor of English, College of Charleston.

The Vonnegut extended family is distinctive for their courtesy and generosity, traits that can be found in the eldest members to the youngest: Walter A. Vonnegut, Kurt J. Adams, James C. Adams Jr., Kit Vonnegut, Ben Yarmolinsky, Arthur E. and Anna P. Lindener, Kurt Vonnegut (Kurt Vonnegut Jr.'s nephew), Scott Vonnegut, Emily M. Diamond, Scott Prior, Richard C. Vonnegut Jr., Alfred Keller Glossbrenner, John Squibb, Catharine G. Rasmussen, Richard C. Vonnegut Sr., and Walter G. Vonnegut.

Nanny Vonnegut Prior and Edith Vonnegut Squibb, in particular, are exemplars of the sort of kindness that their father spoke and wrote about so often. In addition, Mark Vonnegut, MD, and Donald C. Farber, coexecutors of the Vonnegut estate, worked patiently and professionally with me.

Also, the story of Vonnegut's life could not have been complete without the exceptional generosity of Robert B. Weide, who donated his time, advice, and professional and personal materials from his thirty-year friendship with the author. I am deeply grateful to him for reading an early draft of the manuscript and improving it.

My agent, Jeff Kleinman of Folio Literary Management, and editor, Helen Atsma of Henry Holt and Co., guided me through difficult territory, always looking back to see that I was following (and not falling behind).

I've saved the best and most important for last. My wife, Guadalupe, never tired of offering support and encouragement as I researched and wrote this biography. She was my honest critic, editor of early drafts, devil's advocate, amanuensis, and in-house librarian over the course of four years. Ours is a partnership of love and respect. Thank you, Guadalupe.

Index